Atlas
Architectures of the 21st Century
Asia and Pacific

Luis Fernández-Galiano (Ed.)

Atlas
Architectures of the 21st Century
Asia and Pacific

Fundación **BBVA**

The BBVA Foundation's decision to publish this book does not imply any responsibility for its content, or for the inclusion therein of any supplementary documents or information facilitated by the authors.

No part of this publication, including the cover design, may be reproduced, stored in a retrieval system or transmitted in any form or by any means, electronic, mechanical, photocopying, recording or otherwise, without the prior written permission of the copyright holder.

First edition: January 2010

© Of the texts: their authors, 2010
© Of the photographs: their authors, 2010

Published by:
© Fundación BBVA, 2010
Plaza de San Nicolás, 4. 48005 Bilbao

Edition and Production:
Arquitectura Viva S.L.
Magda Anglès, Gina Cariño, Beatriz G. Casares, María Cifuentes, Luis Fernández-Galiano, Cuca Flores, Laura González, Luis Játiva, Beatriz Lazo, Covadonga Lorenzo, Laura Mulas, Jesús Pascual, José Jaime S. Yuste

Translations:
Gina Cariño, Myung-Seok Hyun, Laura Mulas, Akinobu Yoshikawa

Printed by: Artes Gráficas Palermo
Bound by: De la Fuente
ISBN: 978-84-923846-5-5
Legal Deposit: M-270-2010

Printed in Spain

This book is printed on totally chlorine-free paper in conformity with the environmental standards required by current legislation.

Atlas
Architectures of the 21st Century
Asia and Pacific

9 Luis Fernández-Galiano
Eastern Dawns. An Architectural Journey from Central Asia to the Pacific

1. Central Asia
14 Takashi Tsubokura
The Next Metropolis of Central Asia. Astana, a Geopolitical Node in the Steppes
22 Norman Foster, **Palace of Peace and Reconciliation,** Astana, Kazakhstan
26 BIG, **National Library,** Astana, Kazakhstan
28 OMA/Rem Koolhaas, **Almaty Science Campus,** Talgar, Kazakhstan

2. Pakistan
32 Hammad Husain
Coexisting Contrasts. Pakistan, Islamic Tradition and Recent Tribulations
40 Ahed, **Aga Khan Higher Secondary School,** Gilgit
42 Arcop, **Al-Azhar Garden Housing,** Karachi
44 Aedas, **KPT Tower,** Karachi

3. Indian Subcontinent
48 Rahul Mehrotra
Between Computers and Geomancy. India, Global Flows and Local Assertions
58 Arup, **Druk White Lotus School,** Shey, Ladakh, India
62 Morphogenesis, **Pearl Academy of Fashion,** Jaipur, Rajasthan, India
64 Studio Mumbai, **Palmyra House,** Mumbai, India
66 RMA, **TISS University Campus,** Tuljapur, Maharashtra, India
70 Anna Heringer, **DESI Building,** Rudrapur, Dinajpur, Bangladesh
72 Richard Murphy, **British High Commission,** Colombo, Sri Lanka
76 Williams & Tsien, **Banyan Park,** Mumbai, India

4. China
80 Jianfei Zhu
A Third Path between State and Market. China, Critical Exchanges with the West
94 Norman Foster, **International Airport,** Beijing
102 Herzog & de Meuron, **National Olympic Stadium,** Beijing
110 PTW, **National Swimming Center,** Beijing
116 Paul Andreu, **National Grand Theater,** Beijing
122 OMA/Rem Koolhaas & Ole Scheeren, **CCTV Headquarters,** Beijing
128 Steven Holl, **Linked Hybrid Residential Complex,** Beijing
132 Atelier FCJZ/Yung Ho Chang, **UF Soft R&D Center,** Beijing
136 In+of Architecture/Wang Lu, **Hope Primary School,** Leiyang, Hunan
140 Amateur Studio/Wang Shu & Lu Wenyu, **History Museum,** Ningbo, Zhejiang
144 Zhang Lei, **Two Brick Houses,** Gaochun, Jiangsu
146 Zaha Hadid, **Opera House,** Guangzhou
150 Studio Pei Zhu, **Yue Minjun Museum,** Qingcheng, Sichuan
152 Ai Weiwei, **Ordos 100,** Ordos, Inner Mongolia

5. Korea
156 Mann-Young Chung
Experiment and Experience. South Korea, the Vertigo of Urban Hyperdensity
166 Mass Studies, **S-Trenue Tower,** Seoul
168 UnSangDong, **Gallery Yeh,** Seoul
172 Dominique Perrault, **Ewha Women's University,** Seoul
178 FOA, **Dulnyouk Publishers,** Paju Book City, Gyeonggi
182 Álvaro Siza, **Multifunctional Hall,** Anyang, Gyeonggi
186 MVRDV, **Power Center,** Gwang Gyo, Gyeonggi

6. Japan
- 190 Taro Igarashi
  After the Earthquake and the Bubble. Japan, a Refined and Technological Mannerism
- 198 Toyo Ito, **Tama Art University Library,** Tokyo
- 202 Jun Aoki, **SIA Aoyama Building,** Tokyo
- 206 Ryue Nishizawa, **House in Moriyama,** Tokyo
- 210 Kazuyo Sejima, **Apartments in Okurayama,** Yokohama, Kanagawa
- 214 Junya Ishigami, **KAIT Workshop,** Atsuki, Kanagawa
- 220 Takaharu & Yui Tezuka, **Fuji Kindergarten,** Tachikawa, Tokyo
- 224 Kengo Kuma, **Town Hall,** Yusuhara, Kochi
- 226 Sou Fujimoto, **Musashino Art University Library,** Kodaira, Tokyo

7. Taiwan
- 230 Ching-Yueh Roan
  A Weary Tiger. Taiwan, the Search for a Post-Industrial Identity
- 236 Linli Su, **Wood Sculpture Museum,** Sanyi
- 240 Toyo Ito, **Stadium for World Games,** Kaohsiung
- 244 UNStudio, **Star Place Shopping Center,** Kaohsiung
- 248 MAD, **Convention Center,** Taichung

8. Southeast Asia
- 252 Evan J.S. Lin & C.J. Anderson-Wu
  Cultures at the Crossroads. Southeast Asia, an Inorganic Urbanization
- 260 Kerry Hill, **The Chedi Hotel,** Chiang Mai, Thailand
- 262 Vo Trong Nghia, **Wind and Water Café,** Ho Chi Minh City, Vietnam
- 264 Norman Foster, **Petronas University,** Bandar Seri Iskandar, Malaysia
- 268 OMA/Rem Koolhaas & Ole Scheeren, **Mahanakhon Tower,** Bangkok, Thailand
- 270 Kazuhiro Kojima, **New HUA Campus,** Ho Chi Minh City, Vietnam

9. Singapore
- 274 Peter G. Rowe
  Tropical Excellence. Singapore, towards a Vibrating and Livable City
- 286 WOHA, **Moulmein Rise Tower,** Novena
- 290 Grant, **Gardens by the Bay Park,** Marina South
- 292 Daniel Libeskind, **Reflections Residential Complex,** Keppel Bay

10. Australia and Pacific
- 296 Haig Beck & Jackie Cooper
  An Insular Continent? Australia and New Zealand, Propositive Regionalism
- 306 John Wardle, **Nigel Peck Center,** Melbourne, Victoria
- 308 Phooey, **Children's Activity Center,** Port Phillip, Victoria
- 310 Glenn Murcutt, **Walsh House,** Kangaroo Valley, New South Wales
- 314 m3architecture, **University Laboratory,** Gatton, Queensland
- 316 Denton Corker Marshall, **Broadway Building,** Sydney, New South Wales

- 319 Photographic credits
- 320 Contributors

Atlas
Architectures of the 21st Century
Asia and Pacific

THIS ATLAS is the first volume of a series of four which update and substantially develop the work published in 2007 by the BBVA Foundation, *Atlas. Global Architecture circa 2000*. The initial project dealt in a single volume with the architecture of the planet at the threshold of the millennium, and aimed to take stock of the most important works completed after the Fall of the Berlin Wall in 1989, an event that marked the end of the Cold War and also the end of the 'short 20th century' that began in 1914 with World War I. With the perhaps unreasonable purpose of reflecting at the same time the 'state of the world' and the 'state of the art', the book combined what Franco Moretti calls 'distant reading', through ten long essays by experts on the different regions of the globe, with the 'close reading' provided by the detailed documentation on the most noteworthy buildings of the period, grouped into the same geographical areas. Inspired by the conceptual history of Reinhart Koselleck, this collective project tried to offer a broad panoramic account of the recent past through something like a convergence of stories, tightly interwoven to create a tapestry where all the main currents that shape our time are combined with the distinctive features of the regions and the singularity of events, so that the smooth continuity of patterns becomes the weft that ties together the changes, innovations and events that alter the course of history.

The positive reception of the first project encouraged the BBVA Foundation to take on an even more ambitious endeavor: documenting with four volumes, published in consecutive years, the latest architecture of the different continents. With the same intellectual coordinates and publishing characteristics as the previous edition, this project has several new features, beyond the very obvious one of multiplying the extension by four and the less evident one of increasing the works published per volume to almost double the initial number. In the first place, it only covers works completed very recently, transforming the broad historical balance of the first book into an attempt to register the temperature of the present; with a similar purpose, it includes unbuilt projects, extending its reach to an immediate future; lastly, it eliminates the restrictions of the first *Atlas,* which only featured three works per region and one building per office (compelled by the synthetic nature of the account), so allowing the most significant countries and the architects with greater international presence to assert their dimension and influence. The result, as can be seen in this first volume, are publications less stringently modulated than the initial *Atlas:* while maintaining the division of each book into ten geographical chapters, the extension of the essays and the number of featured works and projects are commensurate with the relevance of the region in question.

Dividing the planet into four areas necessarily called for a continental criterion, though somehow modified to make the volumes even in extension. The insufficient demographic size of Oceania was solved, as is customary, by adding the Pacific to the Asian continent; the smaller economic scale of Africa was made up for with the inclusion of the Middle East, as is also frequent; the Americas are dealt with in a single volume, avoiding a perhaps unnecessary fragmentation; and, inevitably, Europe includes the Russian territories in Asia. The most complex decisions had to with the allocation of Turkey, finally included in the Middle East due to convenience rather than to conviction, and the western delimitation of Asia, which was finally established in the deserts of Central Asia, adding to the African volume the areas stretching from Iran. Hence, this first volume, *Asia and Pacific,* commences in the territory of 'The Great Game' and travels through the continent all the way to the ocean; the second of the series, *America,* will explore it from the Arctic to the Southern Cone; the third, *Africa and Middle East,* will go from South Africa to the Bosphorous; and the fourth, *Europe,* will start the itinerary in Russia to conclude it at the *finis terrae* of the Iberian Peninsula. This volume covers the first stage of the journey, and it seems only appropriate that it should be precisely the one covering the continent destined to leave its mark on the current century.

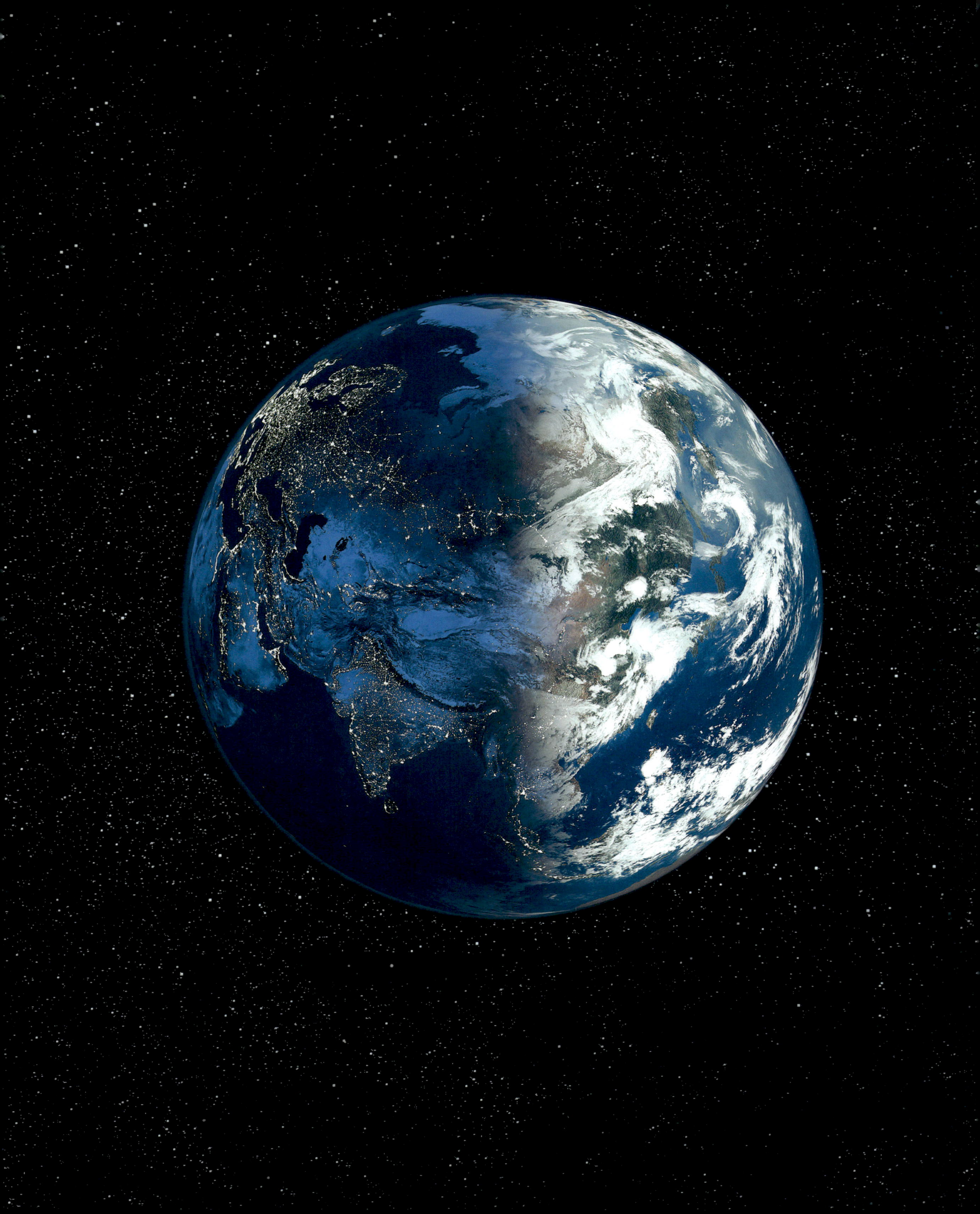

Luis Fernández-Galiano
Eastern Dawns
An Architectural Journey from Central Asia to the Pacific

In Asia, the most unstable areas of the world coexist with the most dynamic, giving rise to an urban landscape of sharp social and economic contrasts.

ASIA'S CENTURY had its inaugural feast in Beijing. The 2008 Olympic Games staged China's emerging strength for the world to see, and the event left in its wake the footprint of emblematic architectures, presided by the huge tangle of steel of the National Stadium. As on other occasions, historical changes raise or raze constructions that reveal the nature of political, economic or social changes: the 20th century was closed with the fall of the Berlin Wall, and the collapse of New York City's Twin Towers opened a new period for the American superpower and for the world. Today, a tour of the latest architectures of a continent on the rise throws light on the convulsions of a delivery that is giving birth to this century of Asia, where the turbulences and tribulations that accompany structural transitions coexist with the formidable energy that has brought about the greatest creation of urban mass in the history of humanity: this built landscape does not herald a near or distant future; it is already the present of the planet.

Europeans have jubilantly celebrated the 20th anniversary of the fall of the Wall, perhaps the last time for the history of the world to be acted out on a continent now reduced to irrelevance, as Timothy Garton Ash has remarked. But this popular and institutional euphoria conceals a collective disappointment with the frustration of the hopes raised by that event. The end of the Cold War did not bring with it a generous distribution of the dividends of peace under the fair governance of a single power, but a chain of armed conflicts on the edges of the tectonic plates of civilizations, an economic deregulation that increased the instability of the system, and an accelerated dismantling of traditional social and ideological fabrics, and all in the context of a growing awareness of the risks of climate change.

During this period, the transit from the liberal democratic nation-state to what Philip Bobbitt calls the 'market-state', where the consumer has replaced the citizen, in turn led to an intellectual and emotional disarmament of the West that is evident in the ambiguous nature of the contemporary confrontation between our 'states of consent' and the 'states of terror' that have arisen in the cracks of the system: a struggle that tragically came to the fore in the 9/11 attacks, to persist through wars waged in scorched lands whose fiasco highlights the American imperial power's impotence in governing the globe single-handedly. But the same continent that is the scene of these military crises is witnessing the appearance of new geopolitical actors whose rise heralds a multilateral world, and in particular the emergence of a Chinese giant with values and organizational methods of its own that presents itself as the opposite pole of planetary reference: Asia's century is still the G-2 century, but could well end up being China's century.

The contemporary interaction between East and West is eloquently manifested through the articles and projects compiled here, which seek to document the presence in Asia of European and American architects while reflecting the impact on the continent of the historical landmarks that sprinkle that relationship. The journey or narration appropriately begins in Astana, a new city that aspires to be the metropolis of Central Asia, built – as Takashi Tsubokura explains – on the site of a fortress of czarist Russia, and designated as capital of Kazakhstan, an oil-rich land of steppes that became independent as a result of the fragmentation of the Soviet Union that was triggered by the fall of the Berlin Wall. In those virgin lands, until recently furrowed by caravans so plagued by dangers that the route was called the blood road, the Japanese Kisho Kurokaza outlined an urb – in the tradition of new capitals like Brasilia or Chandigarh – whose symbolic heart is a pyramid raised by the British Norman Foster, where the synchretic will of a paternalistic and authoritarian regime seeks to unite the ethnicities and religions that

The political, social and economic dawn of Asia is paradoxically expressed through the oneiric night images of its sleepless metropolises, where a few signature skyscrapers coexist with many strictly commercial buildings. These 'neon tigers' stand out in the skylines of Tokyo (below), Hong Kong (next page, top) or Shanghai (next page, below), showing the extraordinary strength of a continent called upon to lead the 20th century.

inhabit the boundless territory that Kipling had imagined as the scene of the 'Great Game' of western powers.

If current Kazakhstan is a consequence of Berlin's 11/9, today's Pakistan can only be explained in terms of New York's 9/11. As Hammad Husain abrasively points out, the country's history since independence in 1947 has been marked by wars, military coups and the arms race with India, but its present troubled situation has been provoked by the destruction of the Twin Towers and the subsequent war in Afghanistan, which has spilled into Pakistan and destabilized its institutions. Determined to reconcile its Islamic-Mongolian heritage with modernity, the country built a new capital, Islamabad, designed by the Greek planner Constantinos Doxiadis as a futuristic city that defers as much to the cosmopolitanism of Karachi as to the traditionalism of Lahore, and numerous western architects, from Jacobsen to Kahn, were summoned to design a young nation's institutional buildings. Although not all the projects materialized – Kahn, for example, would end up raising in Dhaka the National Assembly of the eventually independent Bangladesh –, the influence of the modern masters is still felt today, in tune with vernacular traditions and in competition with the recent impact of what is called the 'Dubai effect': a hypermodernity that wastes energy, ignores climate and flaunts luxury, what seems to be a distinctive sign of the most trivial globalization.

In a more extreme manner, India – tackled in meticulous detail by Rahul Mehrotra –, is torn between the modernizing impact of the capital and information flows that thickly cover the planet and the resistant tenacity of the local habits and memories, as vividly illustrated by the contrast between the ubiquitous IT (information technology) parks, proof of the country's incorporation into the global market, and the likewise proliferating temples and mosques, signs of identity and manifestations of defense in the face of the uniform culture of cosmopolitan internationalization; an anti-modern reaction emphasized by the unexpected popularity of Vasti, an archaic sacred building code based, like the Chinese Feng Shui, on geomancy. At this difficult crossroads, and in the wake of masters like Balkrishna Doshi, Charles Correa or Raj Rewal, a new generation of architects tries to reconcile its global outlook and its local roots to shape a kaleidoscopic and pluralist panorama, as is only fitting in a country whose democratic system allows the expression of a variety of identities that cannot be manifested with the same freedom in more autocratic regimes.

China may be one of those regimes, but as Jianfei Zhu persuasively argues, in the increasingly 'symmetrical' exchange with the West the Middle Kingdom puts forward its own ideological model, which is as much an autonomous political, economic and social model as it is a uniquely different way of relating architecture and city to the market. This third road between capitalism and socialism, which knows how to use the talent of foreign architects like those who built the symbolic works of Olympic Beijing – from Norman Foster to Herzog & de Meuron –, and import western ideas like the critical nature of the discipline of architecture, now also exports a pragmatic conception of construction that has influenced personalities like Rem Koolhaas, minting a post-critical instrumentality that sets aside notions like resistance or transgression to defend the quantitative and integrative: an architecture of magnitude that can offer more habitable space to the people of the world, as China itself has done through a huge effort of urbanization; and a more ethical and organic architecture, in the Confucian spirit of interrelation and interdependence, and in the framework of a strong state which guides both market and society.

The rift between capitalism and socialism that the Chinese try to repair is clearly seen in the 38th parallel, which separates an archaic, paleocommunist North Korea ruled by a dynasty incapable of providing welfare to its people, from a dynamic South Korea, where indiscriminate internationalization has brought both strong economic development and the social and professional tensions that Mann-Young Chung explores through four oppositions of terms that inform current Korean architecture, and that range from the contrast between contextual urbanity and nostalgic rurality to the split between solid experience and radical experiment. Highly globalized, and accustomed to operating in hyperdense environments like Seoul, this cosmopolitan architecture has had periods of depression like the Asian financial crisis of 1997 and the trauma of the subsequent IMF intervention, and moments of exaltation like the simultaneous celebration in Korea and Japan of the 2002 Football World Cup. But beyond this roller coaster of collective emotions, it practices a realistic negotiation with the gales of the markets, even though its resistant economy and solid institutions have sometimes suffered its strain.

Japan, as Taro Igarashi suggests, also saw the financial convulsions reflected in its architecture, in this case with the additional impact of a natural calamity: the 1995 Kobe earthquake put an end to its flirtations with

10 Atlas: Asia and Pacific

deconstructivist fractures and demolitions, and the bursting of the colossal real estate bubble in turn punctured the full balloon of postmodern architecture. The emergence of a minimalism influenced by the immaterial nature of information technology, and of organic currents evoking a yearned return to nature, coexists with the internationalization of architects – who are building everywhere, from veterans like Tadao Ando or Toyo Ito to the younger Kengo Kuma, Shigeru Ban or Kazuyo Sejima and Ryue Nishizawa – and with the notorious presence of architectures devoted to fashion, which have raised the planet's most visible flagship stores in two Tokyo neighborhoods, Omotesando and Ginza. At the heart of global exchanges, but with a refined building culture that handles the products of globalization with elegant mannerism, Japan – including its latest generation, with young figures like Fujimoto or Ishigami – still has lessons for those who will listen to its subdued music.

The financial and physical tremors also hit the architecture of Taiwan, which Ching-Yueh Roan describes as still affected by the impact of the Asian crisis of 1997 and the earthquake that devastated the center of the island in 1999. The complex history of the country, whose independence has never been acknowledged by China, has caused an isolation with respect to other nations of East Asia that has left it with no other options but dialogue with the West or self-withdrawn monologue, giving rise to a series of phases where cosmopolitan modernization has alternated with the recuperation of roots: the liberalization of the 90s brought on a period of accelerated globalization, but after the earthquake, a new social and political climate engendered an architecture more concerned with identity and more infused with social conscience and local attachment, of which a good example is the cooperative activism of architects like Ying-Chun Hsieh, who confront the weak economy of the post-bubble generation with rare realism.

It is difficult to sum up the features common to the countries of Southeast Asia (Vietnam, Laos, Myanmar, Cambodia, Thailand, Malaysia, Singapore, Indonesia, and the Philippines), but Evan J.S. Lin and C.J. Anderson-Wu identify the influence of the main religions – Buddhism, Islam and Catholicism – and the tropical climate as the factors that shaped vernacular architectures in this crossroads of cultures, now deeply transformed by the successive impacts of decolonization after the World War II, modernization in the context of the struggle between blocs, and current globalization, which has produced inorganic urbanization, with Export Processing Zones and industrial parks juxtaposed with booming metropolises like Bangkok, Kuala Lumpur, Jakarta or Manila. This acceleration of growth has not been free of tensions, and a new generation of architects – inspired by figures like Ken Yeang – now looks back to cultural heritage and urban sustainability, exploring a path that reconciles identity with integration in the world's flows.

Few areas are as integrated into these flows as Singapore, a city-state located at the crossroads of the planet's sea routes whose uniqueness deserves a study separate from the rest of Southeast Asia, here carried out comprehensively by Peter Rowe. His text describes the transition from an industrial economy to one based on knowledge, and spells out the successes of a model based on a strong state that promotes meritocracy, self-sufficiency and hard work; features recalling China, to whose race the majority of the inhabitants of this enclave in Islamic Malaysia belong. Both urban planning and architecture are oriented towards excellence and competition, although nowadays, as in other prosperous zones of the world, material consumerism and entertainment present a panorama in conflict with the determination to guarantee the economic and ecological sustainability of its peculiar political system, which combines bureaucratic state control and social cohesion.

Our itinerary comes to an end in Australia, which Haig Beck and Jackie Cooper present in a broad historical context the tenacious clash between the architectural expression of isolation and the forces that drive cultural globalization. In the wake of the critical regionalism defended by Kenneth Frampton, the authors of the article successively touch on the Mediterranean climate of Sydney, which has so influenced Glenn Murcutt's architecture, the continental climate of Melbourne, where Peter Corrigan's populist talent flowered, and the subtropical climate of Brisbane, whose remoteness from the two great cities fostered peculiar, experimental and light constructions; and in the same spirit of looking to the physical environment as a source of architectural form, they end their expedition in the fresh humid climate of New Zealand, where, as in Australia, the cultural insecurity of provinces and an acritical acceptance of universal patterns are resisted with an architecture that is tectonic, light and integrated into the landscape, one that could serve as inspiration for many other regions of the world. There can perhaps be no better purpose for the body of works brought together in this at once modest and ambitious Atlas of Asia and the Pacific.

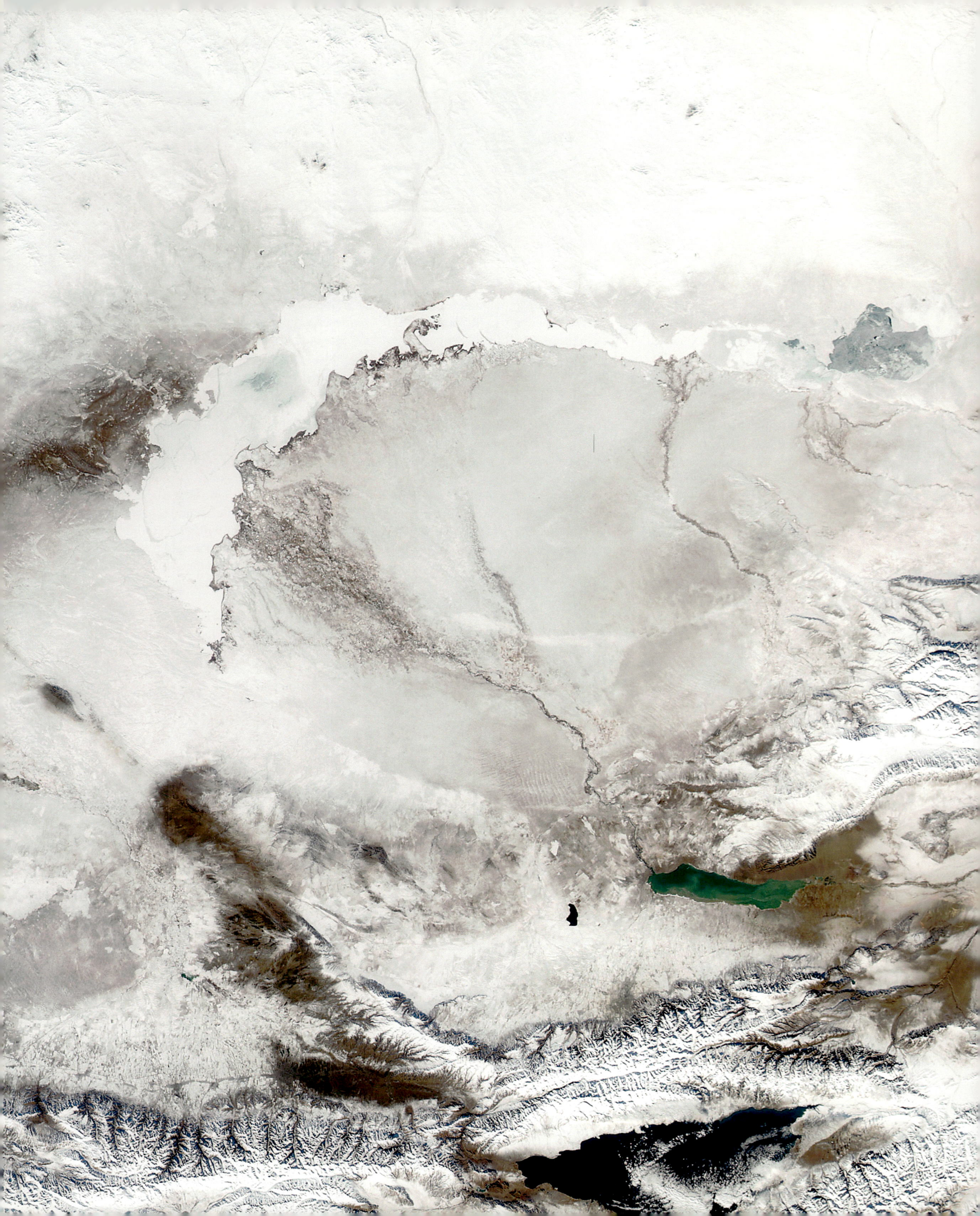

Central Asia

Surrounded by giants like China and Russia, the old Soviet republics of Central Asia are outlined as essential pieces in the geopolitical map, and more in particular Kazakhstan, which has managed to establish its position as a strategic territory thanks to the discovery of oil and gas reserves. With a charismatic leader, Nursultan Nazarbayev, in power since 1991, the country has moved its capital from the old Almaty to the current Astana, a city better connected with the rest of the republic, and that reinvents itself today at a fast pace with works by local and foreign architects: the Japanese Kisho Kurokawa designed the master plan of the city, and the British Norman Foster took the baton with the construction of icons like the pyramid of the Palace of Peace, which help to shape the new Kazakh identity, within the frame of an effervescent panorama that has allowed other offices, like the Danish BIG or the Dutch UNStudio, to enter into the territory of 'The Great Game'.

Takashi Tsubokura
The Next Metropolis of Central Asia
Astana, a Geopolitical Node in the Steppes

Monumental axis, Astana

The new capital of Kazakhstan was an outpost of the Tsarist Russia, and today the symbolic center of a prosperious oil republic.

President Nazarbajev changed the capital of the country from Almaty to Astana; the new urban center began to grow on the left bank of the Ishim River, with symbolic buildings some of which are still under construction.

IN DECEMBER 1997, the Government of the Republic of Kazakhstan officially announced that the new capital of the Republic was to be Astana City (former Akmolinsk). The new capital has been rapidly developing with an enormous foreign investment attracted by vast oil reserves of the country. It suddenly became a focal point in the whole Central Asia. This city, as other main cities in Kazakhstan, originated from one of fortresses of Tsarist Russia. As early as the 18th century, the Russian Government was making a plan to colonize the Kazakh steppes, through which to exert trade and political influence on Central Asia. Colonization was realized with the help of military detachments, that penetrated into the territory of the present Republic of Kazakhstan to construct military settlements. During the first half of the 19th century, one of such settlements was constructed on the right bank of the Ishim River, not far from the hill Akmola, the top of which retained traces of ancient burials. Akmola literally means 'White Grave'. Russian officers and Cossack guards lived there and caravan merchants stayed for rest.

A student of local lore, A. F. Dubitsky writes as follows: "It is worth remembering that an ancient caravan road called 'Blood Road' ran through Kara-Utkel (literally 'Black Ford') which connected Russia with Central Asia. Caravan merchants did not like this place; robbers used to make ambushes in the thick growths of honeysuckle, buckthorn and willow on the left bank of the Ishim. This could be an explanation of why in June 1830 lieutenant colonel F. Shubin decided to locate his guarding Cossack troop at the very place Kara-Utkel, which was the origin of Akmolinsk". At first it consisted of only several flagstones and adobe barracks. However, the constant attacks from local population forced the Tsarist government to take fortification measures for Akmolinsk. A rather low protection embankment and a moat were constructed on three sides of the fortress, then the central north bastion was crowned with a stocky tower. Its upper part was built of pine logs and had small loopholes for gunfire, while the lower part of adobe walls had a big embrasure for cannons.

Akmolinsk had played an important role in trade since the middle of the 19th century. Tatar merchants came from all over, attracted by encouraging privileges and the cancellation of customs duties. Russian goods were transported here to meet a big demand in Central Asia. Losing its defensive

New urban center of Astana

After the collapse of the Soviet Union, Kazakhstan became an independent republic and Astana changed its name (from Tselinograd to Akmolinsk, until acquiring its current name in 1997), and also changed its appearance: at Lenin Square, previously presided by a statue, 16 meters tall, of the communist leader, all the socialist symbols were removed, and the Soviet architecture was concealed under different kinds of claddings.

Old Lenin Square

significance, with the growth of trade and handicraft industry, Akmolinsk began to develop as an administrative, commercial and industrial town of the Ishim steppe.

The settlements, which had been formed outside of the fortress since then, were based on the nationalities or classes of their inhabitants, as you see from their names, such as Cossack village, Soldiers' settlement or Tatar and Jatack (Kazakh) settlements. Street names of those days also show the cultural and religious diversity of the town: Dumskaya (Council Street), Krepostnaya (Fortress Street), Gostinodvorskaya (Hotel Court Street), Mechetnaya (Mosque Street), Karavannaya (Caravan Street), Bolnichnaya (Hospital Street), Bolshaya Bazarnaya (Big Bazaar Street), Tserkovnaya (Church Street), Torgovaya (Trade Street), Stepnaya (Steppe Street), Meshanskaya (Petit Bourgeois Street), and so on.

The Construction of a Socialist City
In the post-revolution period at the beginning of the 20th century, Akmolinsk stagnated due to the ravages of the Civil War between the Red Army and the White Army. During World War II, Germans, Chechens, Ingushes, Koreans, Polish and other ethnic groups living in Soviet territory were deported to Kazakhstan. Factories together with their workers were evacuated here from the regions occupied by the Germany Army.

In 1954, the Soviet leader Nikita Khrushchev launched the Virgin Lands campaign aimed at boosting wheat production in the Kazakhstan steppes. Trains carried in volunteers from various parts of USSR. Akmolinsk rapidly grew especially from the time when it was designated as the center of the Virgin Lands in 1960, and was renamed Tselinograd (literally 'Virgin Land City') in 1961.

The housing development of the Tselinograd era was based on the construction method with large-size pre-cast concrete panels called 'Typical Project' and a neighborhood unit system called 'Mikroraion' (micro district). In these years 5-storied pre-cast concrete apartment buildings were built along the main streets instead of the former so-called 'Stalin houses', with high ceilings, bay windows and stucco moldings on their facades. That characteristic cityscape of Soviet cities, endless ranks of concrete rectangular parallelepipeds, appeared in this small steppe city.

The Master Plan of 1962, by the Leningrad Gorstroiproject (Leningrad Institute of Urban Planning) portrays a model lifestyle corresponding to three linear zones: an industrial zone on the north side of the railway, a residential zone in the middle and the southernmost recreational zone along the Ishim River. This is a quite famous scheme as 'linear city', which city planners had discussed since 1930s. Parallel arrangement of industrial, residential and park zone provides inhabitants with the shortest transverse access to and from work, and recreation at every point of the city. This advantage can be preserved in the future, since these three zones should grow in parallel with each other.

Ethnic groups and classes which formed each settlement in the 19th century were totally gone and the city became a homogeneous collection of residential districts. Religious facilities as important public centers in former Akmolinsk were excluded from urban planning consideration in this master plan. Race and religion became taboo subjects, since all inhabitants were officially unified into the Soviet proletariat.

The central square of the city had already formed outside the moat of the fortress since the end of the 19th century. Originally it accommodated trade rows and the Alexandro-Nevsky Cathedral, but in the Tselinograd period it was gradually

Presidential Palace, Astana

reconstructed as the Soviet administrative center called Lenin Square.

This square was really a good sample of Soviet socialist iconography. A bronze statue of Lenin, 16 meters high, used to dominate the whole square, standing with his back against the tallest building (the Giproselhoz design institute). On the facade of the massive building visible to the left (The House of Soviets) were Lenin's and Karl Marx's portraits painted in red. All the buildings of this period had a white or gray tonality. Repetition of the same section and regularly arranged windows reflected industrial aesthetics characteristic of this period.

The main point of the central square of the Tselinograd days was a combination of representational figures of socialist heroes and anonymous architecture for the background. It was nothing else but a visual representation of "an orderly society led by socialism".

Astana, the New Capital

As the result of the collapse of the Soviet Union and the independence of the Republic of Kazakhstan in 1991, the former Tselinograd was renamed Akmola at that time (1992), then the new name Astana was adopted in 1998, subsequently to the transfer of the capital. The aforesaid central square in the existing urban area was temporarily occupied by government bodies moved from the former capital Almaty. Socialist symbols such as a statue of Lenin and a Karl Marx portrait were removed and all the buildings of the Tselinograd period were reconstructed.

Now the facade of the Parliament (former Giproselhoz) and of the President's Administration (former House of Soviets) have the silhouette of a ziggurat or a pyramid. They are formed with aluminum cladding and colored glazing at the center of each facade. The inverted trapezoid element at the top of each building's facade is suggestive of a keystone of classical arch. A large National Emblem of the Republic is hung on each of them. Simple solids of the Tselinograd period were thoroughly covered with this kind of superficial graphics, which changed these buildings out of all recognition.

Why were these buildings of the Tselinograd period mainly refurbished this time? For one thing it was because these utilitarian buildings of the 1960s and 1970s generally had flat, ornament-free and colorless surfaces. It was easy and effective to apply this kind of cosmetic architecture. However, there was a political idea underlying this urban renewal. It was a change of city image from a provincial utilitarian town reflecting the well-being and status of a basically industrial society into a high-status urban capital city. Something must have been substituted for that Pan-Soviet architecture as a product of Soviet monopoly.

The caravan route and colonial rule which formed Akmolinsk-Tselinograd are also the two underlying motives of present-day Astana. Since independence from the Soviet Union, Kazakhstan has been pushing on autonomous policy on domestic and foreign affairs. One of the reasons why president Nazarbayev transferred the capital from Almaty to Astana is its good access to all the major cities of the Republic by rail and road. Another reason, though not officially announced, is to 'Kazakhize' the northern part of present Kazakhstan territory, where Russian inhabitants have held majority. The latter is the important strategy of preventing a territorial dispute with the Russian Federation. The influx of Kazakh population mainly from the southern regions is rapidly changing Astana's racial proportion again. The new capital is, as it were, the modern version of the fortress, but this time constructed on the Kazakh side.

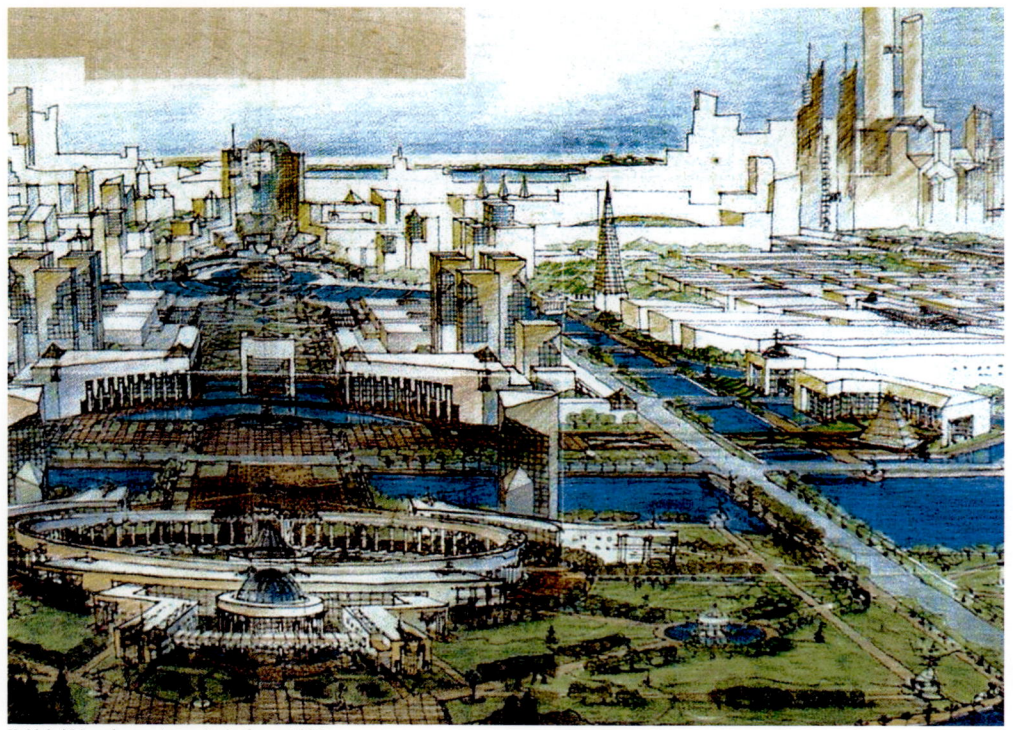

Kaldybai Montahayev, Astana in the future, 1996

Two years before the change of capital, a national competition was called for the design of Astana's urban plan. The results, however, did not satisfy president Nazarbajev, who called an international competition. Kurokawa's project won, but it underwent several changes and the final Plan was not approved until 2001. The design by the local architect Kaldybai Montahayev, of 1996, anticipated the current profile of the city.

The Master Plan by Kurokawa

Back in 1996, a local design competition for the new capital was conducted by the Ministry of Construction and Architects Union of Kazakhstan. As a result, the proposal prepared by a design company, Ak Orda, was selected for the first prize. In this master plan, the linear zoning principle of the city established in the 1960s was completely overthrown, and the city was to be expanded to the south across the Ishim River. They proposed to accommodate a large part of the administrative and business functions on the left bank, which became the starting point of the subsequent capital development in all respects. The ongoing construction of the new city center is undoubtedly originated with this proposal in which an architect from Almaty, Kaldybai Montahayev, played a leading role.

However, president Nazarbayev seems to have not been satisfied with this proposal by local architects. As reflected in the report *The Study on the Master Plan for the Development of the City of Astana in the Republic of Kazakhstan,* of the Japan International Copperation Agency: "The Government of the Republic of Kazakhstan decided to conduct an 'International Tender for the Draft of the Master Plan of Development of the New Center of Astana', which was announced publicly by foreign mass media in April 1998. Terms and the program of the tender were sent to the 40 applicants from 19 different nations around the world, of which 27 tender proposals were submitted. On 6 October 1998, the President of the Republic of Kazakhstan considered presented materials and awarded the first prize to Kisho Kurokawa Architect & Associates, Japan. His basic concepts in his proposal focus around the three key words drawn from the cosmology of Kurokawa's architectural thoughts; 'symbiosis', 'metabolic city' and 'abstract symbolism.'

The word 'symbiosis', one of Kurokawa's

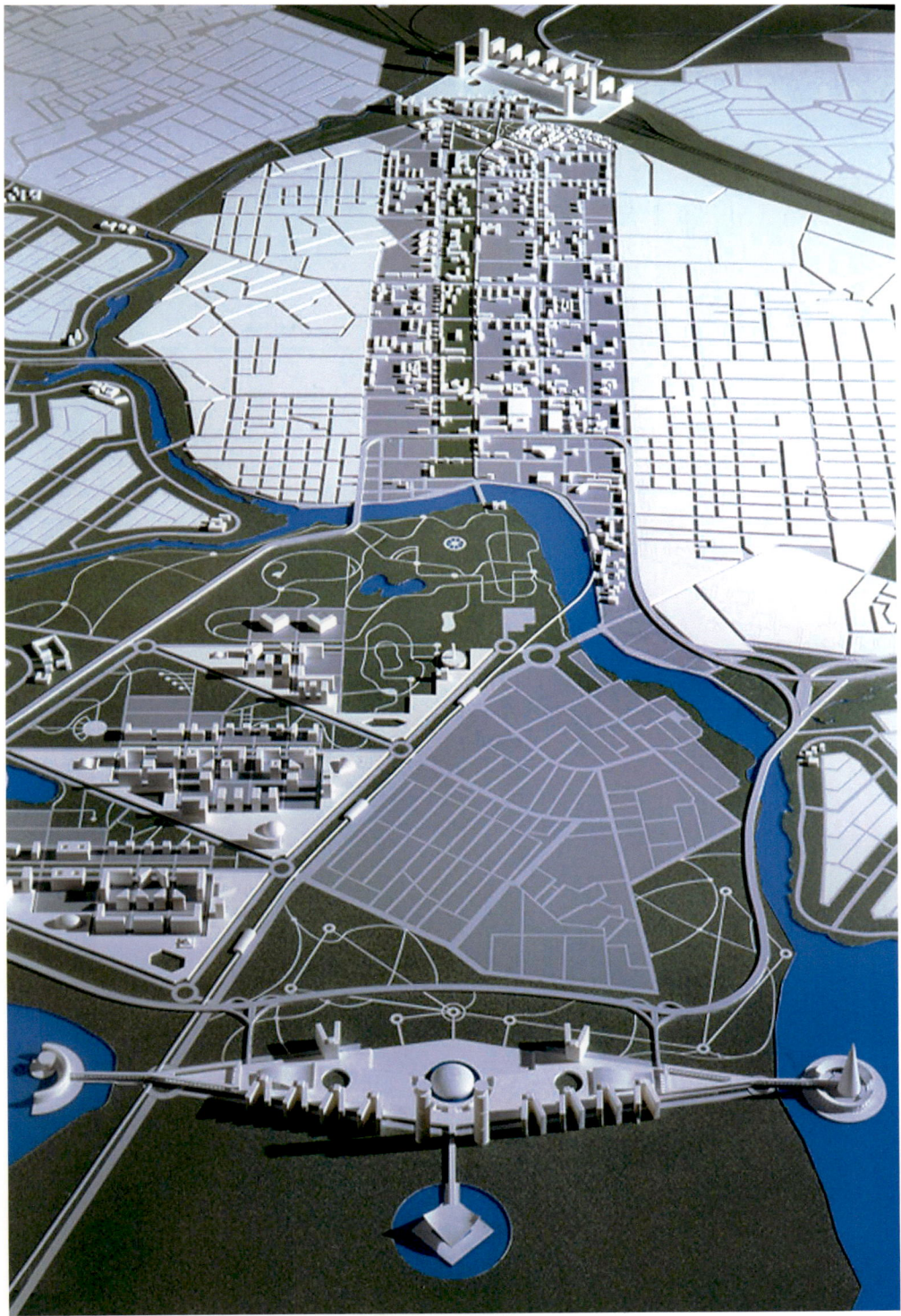

Kisho Kurokawa, Astana Master Plan

Atlas: Asia and Pacific 17

Kisho Kurokawa, Astana International Airport (2005)

favorite incantations, refers to a "new, creative relationship born from competition and tension", a "positive relationship in which the participants necessarily attempt to understand each other, despite opposition". On an urban scale it may mean symbiosis of new and old city areas, symbiosis of eastern and western culture, and so on. In this proposal Kurokawa had an idea of preserving old buildings, bridges, water towers and even big trees in the existing town in order to make a contrast with newly developed city areas. A new riverside residential area is also intended as the embodiment of symbiosis of nature and man-made environment.

'Metabolic city' is, so to speak, an enlarged reproduction of the linear zoning brought up in the Soviet Master Plan of 1962. The former simple three zones were subdivided into seven. They comprise a northern green buffer zone (as necessary to protect the capital against sandstorms); a regenerated industrial zone; an intermediate green zone (for environmental protection); existing urban areas; a new residential zone; a new city-center zone and a southern eco-park zone. Kurokawa, one of the originators of the Metabolist movement in the 1960s, had a high opinion of the linear structure of former Tselinograd, which, in his opinion, should enable the new capital to adjust its future development maintaining balance and order.

Of course, Kurokawa was convinced of the realization of his own proposal, since he won the international tender. However, the following unexpected problem awaited the highly motivated Japanese delegation: "In December 1999, a Master Plan for Astana, Capital City of Kazakhstan, prepared by a Saudi Binladin Group, was submitted to the Municipality of Astana. On 10 February 2000, this master plan was approved with an obligation that some of the areas not fully covered in the Master Plan be additionally filled in by the Government."

This is how it happened: after the local competition in 1996, the Astana municipality had been developing the above-mentioned Ak Orda's proposal and finally completed a master plan with Arab funds. Meanwhile president Nazarbayev, unsatisfied with the local proposal, conducted the international competition and invited Kurokawa and Japanese money. The President was so eager to turn Astana into a high status capital city second to no others, that he did not mind the municipality's actions at all.

I remember the irritated face of Kurokawa, who had just come back from the first mission to Astana. He had the Saudi plan printed out on a scale of 1:20,000 and spread out on the big table of a conference room in his Tokyo office. Several sets of felt-tip color pens were prepared. Having rolled his sleeves up, Kurokawa fixedly stared at the Saudi plan which was about one and a half meters in diameter. Then he began to single-mindedly draw his own master plan on a sheet of large-sized tracing paper laid on it.

Thus Kurokawa's Astana Master Plan came into existence. He pushed his aforesaid concepts into the Saudi plan's skeleton this time, which you see easily comparing these three plans. Ironically enough, Kurokawa was forced to accept symbiosis with the post-Soviet politics in Kazakhstan, which he never dreamed of. In August 2001 the Government of the Republic officially approved the Japanese master plan and canceled the Saudi master plan.

By the way, one of the aforesaid concepts of Kurokawa, that of 'abstract symbolism', was applied to his design of the new passenger terminal building of Astana international airport, which was completed

Baiterek Tower, Astana

In the airport of Astana Kurokawa resorted to his 'abstract symbolism', with geometric patterns and forms characteristic of traditional Kazakh culture. For their part, the buildings raised on the left bank of the River Ishim follow monumental axes flanked by iconic buildings and high-rise commercial developments. Meanwhile, the Soviet legacy has been concealed under a postmodern skin in order to express the new identity of the country.

The House of Soviets and the Design Institute in Astana

The same buildings after their remodelation

in 2005. As he mentions in *The Philosophy of Symbiosis:* "Abstract symbolism utilizes the common geometric features that everyone can understand, and express the traditional cultural aspects of Kazakhstan in the abstract. A triangle as seen in decoration of nomad people, a cone as seen in nomad hats or trees, a circle or a semi-circle which is the shape of the moon and symbolizes the universe are the examples of such geometric features. By applying abstract symbolism, the capital that reflects the tradition and culture shall breed the affection by the nation, and construct the landscape fit for an international city."

A spherical dome, planned in the middle of the symmetrical terminal building, accommodates landside concourses on its first and second floor. Both the VIP lounge, the airport offices and an observation platform hang from its inner surface. The dome has a round glazed opening at its top, while its front part was cut along a curved approach road and functions as the glazed main entrance. On the airside, a common gate lounge stretches from one end to the other end of the building. This partition-less curved gallery was realized by a line of special-feature columns with four arms which Kurokawa called 'spider columns'.

Kurokawa tried to adopt local traditional dome architecture by manipulating pure geometrical forms, which must have preserved his honor as a contemporary architect. However, the spherical dome does not seem to be so 'abstract', since he covered it with blue aluminum cladding and put a Kazakh ornament in a belt, considering feelings of Kazakhstan side. And furthermore, the cutting of the dome's front led to a serious drawback. Visitors always reach the central point of the dome just as they go through the entrance, which does not allow them to enjoy it to the full. Kurokawa surely applied a dome, but was indifferent to its role as the main part of a spacious sequence.

Norman Foster and the New Center
No matter what master plan was approved, new buildings designed by local architects were completed one after another and the new city center gradually emerged on the left bank of the Ishim River. It extends east and west for about 4 kilometers and contains not only governmental facilities such as the Presidential Palace, the Parliament, the Supreme Court and ministries, but also all kinds of buildings, for example, an opera theater, hotels, embassies, a mosque, office buildings of private enterprises and high-rise apartment buildings.

Judging from the appearances formed up to now, the new city center is indeed a three-dimensional version of the aforesaid supergraphics of the reconstructed existing central square. It well shows the taste and the methods of local architects and city planners. Applying postmodernism vaguely, they mix west and east, as well as classics and modernism. Ironically, the result has become close to the Socialist Realism of the 1950s in spite of their intension to establish a newborn Kazakhstan identity. Quite a few people seem to have had a sense of crisis under such circumstances. They started to hold more international competitions or to designate famous foreign architects for some important projects. At this point Norman Foster came into the game in the place of Kurokawa.

In 2006, Foster's pyramid, the Palace of Peace and Reconciliation, was erected at the eastern end of the new city center's main axis, directly opposite the Presidential Palace across the Ishim River. It was none other than president Nazarbayev that conceived the idea of this building. Back in September 2003, he invited representatives of eighteen religions for two days of

Hotel towers in the new center of Astana

Atlas: Asia and Pacific

Astana's new symbolic center has two landmark buildings by Norman Foster, located at the ends of the city's monumental axis: the Palace of Peace and Reconciliation and the Kahn Shatyry Entertainment Center.

Other foreign firms are also working in the country: the Danish BIG have designed the National Library in Astana, and the Dutch OMA/Rem Koolhaas a science campus near Almaty, the old capital.

discussion in his new capital. This First Congress of World and Traditional Religions issued a declaration of a shared commitment to values of peace and religious tolerance, then voted to convene further gatherings in Astana, to be held once every three years. At that very moment, the image of the permanent palace to house the congress flashed across the President's mind: "A pyramid would do..."

The completed pyramid is 62 meters in height and is exactly as wide and long as it is tall. Visitors enter the building from below, through a promenade cut into the raised ground as the base. Then they go up to the ground floor, where Foster's most important concept, that of 'single space', manifested itself in the form of the central atrium around whose edge five floors of accommodations were distributed. The triangulated steel frame, which registers on the facades as a net of stainless steel lines, appeared again and we understand this pyramid is rather a geometric crystal than a just platonic solid. A slight mound in the center of the floor is the glazed oculus of the 1,500-seat opera house buried below. And there is nothing else in this atrium.

A blue and yellow light permeates from up high, through stained glass designed by Brian Clarke. However, the atrium is not just dark, but dull and somehow monotonous. Unlike the Pantheon in Rome, this atrium has a vertical section in the shape of a gourd, which does not allow the glazed top to throw any light on its internal surface. The building section well shows this uncomfortable relation between the skylight and the inclination of the atrium's glass wall. The ring-shaped congress chamber at the top of the pyramid blocked the last rays of the sun and turned the atrium into a cave. There are no chances of the colored light's playing on a white ceramic frit applied to the full-height glazing around the atrium.

Foster's second building in Astana, the Khan Shatyry Entertainment Center, is now under construction at the other end of the new city center's axis. This shows how highly his buildings are regarded in the city planning scale. While Kurokawa was entangled in the political dispute and retreated, Foster seems to have established his unchallenged position in present Astana.

The Post-Soviet Government
Denial of the Soviet era and longing for national symbol; these are the two sides of the same coin. This phenomenon, common to state leaders and mere architects, is characteristic of young post-Soviet nations in Central Asia. In Astana, the former can be observed in the aforesaid reconstruction of the existing central square, while the latter reveals itself in the design which local architects show off in the new city center. Both Kurokawa and Foster were shocked by these strong desires at their meetings with the President, and tried to live up to his

Norman Foster, Palace of Peace and Reconciliation, Astana (2006)

BIG, National Library, Astana

OMA/Rem Koolhaas, Almaty Science Campus, Talgar

expectations in their own way better than that of local architects. They had an enough strong will and authority to hold fast to their special-feature concept in their approaches to whatever new national symbols.

At this point we come to realize a special property of this profession which we often want to regard as no longer related to contemporary architecture. Contemporary architecture is connected not only with the present age, but also with old power which dates back to ancient times. In Kazakhstan, both local and invited architects go back to their primary role of thousands of years, that is, a court architect serving powerful persons. "Leaders of developing countries often prefer strong forms and images. Such plans as small buildings scattered in the woods are not effective." Kurokawa thus inspired his staff, making his proposal for the aforesaid international tender for the master plan. He was not only a man of philosophy and concepts, but also a veteran with rich practice in competitions. The architect could become fully pragmatic as the need arose. In that proposal he concentrated his attention on president Nazarbayev from the beginning and designed the new capital as if it were a building whose client was the President. Kurokawa exactly got to the point. And Foster could embody it more admirably.

However, there was a problem, too. The Palace of Peace as well as the passenger terminal building of the airport was far from the Pantheon in Rome or the pyramids in Giza. They were not shrines but modern public institutions with complicated programs. Though it would have been easier to accommodate most of the required functions in the other parts of the buildings, these architects planned an excessive number of rooms and elaborate structures facing the main atrium. Perhaps they felt diffident of the primitiveness of those given geometrical forms and tried to make their buildings worthy of contemporary architecture.

In advanced countries, even such established architects as Kurokawa and Foster had collaborated with the decentralized power designing museums, hotels, office buildings, and so on. Sometimes it was a mayor, sometimes it was an entrepreneur. These architects were used to adopting more exquisite forms and more sophisticated compositions that represented such limited authority in democratic societies. And it seems to be the very reason why they betrayed their 'inexperience', when more primitive and 'strong' forms were required in Kazakhstan at the initial stage of authoritarian power.

Following Kurokawa and Foster, several foreign architects and design companies have made their debut in Kazakhstan: Manfredi and Luca Nicoletti with an Opera House in Astana, and SOM with new business centers like Esentai Park or the Almaty Financial District. The Dutch team OMA has designed the Naukograd Technopolis (a university science campus in Talgar), the Danish studio BIG has planned the new National Library of Kazakhstan, and Arata Isozaki's office has been involved in the master plan for the Tekeli Campus of University of Central Asia.

That Akmolinsk of the 19th century rises again in my mind: the fortress, Russian Orthodox churches coexistent with mosques, trade rows of caravan merchants next to Cossack soldiers' barracks. I also think about the rise and fall of Tselinograd in the 20th century. All these disappeared or were abandoned as detestable memories. This steppe city, located where a blood road crossed a black ford near by a white grave, was always a temporary residence of the then ruler and his peddlers. A sandstorm blew away their architecture, like a drift of leaves, in each end of the times. I wonder if this city will preserve anything which commemorates this post-Soviet dynasty in the 21st century.

Norman Foster, Khan Shatyry Entertainment Center, Astana (2006)

Norman Foster
Palace of Peace and Reconciliation
Astana (Kazakhstan)

Client
Sembol Construction
Architects
Foster & Partners,
Tabanlioglu Architecture
Collaborators
Brian Clarke (artist)
Consultants
Buro Happold, Arce (structures); GN Engineering & HB Technik, DS Mimarlik, Studio Dinnebier, Karina (fire consultants), Sound Space Design (acoustics)
Photos
Nigel Young

In September 2003, a Congress of Leaders of World and Traditional Religions was held in Astana, the capital of Kazakhstan. In the wake of its success, president Nursultan Nazarbayev decided to make it a triennial event and build a permanent venue for it that would in interim years be a seat of global ecumenical understanding and unity, equality and non-violence. The Palace of Peace and Reconciliation thus houses a center for research on different denominations, offices for their representatives, and a library of spiritual religious literature. In addition, it endeavors to express the country's diverse but harmonious spirit by serving as a cultural and educational center for the ethnic and geographical groups that coexist in what is the largest of the former Soviet republics, housing a national history museum and a university of civilization. In addition, the 25,000 square meter premises include an auditorium and a range of exhibition and conference rooms.

The programmatic diversity is unified within the pure form of a pyramid rising 62 meters on a 62x62 meter square base. Raised to a total of 77 meters by a podium covered with earth berm and containing a 1,500 seat opera house, the pyramid is made of a diamond-pattern latticework of tubular steel clad in pale silver-gray stone, with glazed inserts that allude to the varying internal functions.

Spatially, the pyramid is organized around an atrium animated by shifting colored light patterns. A glass lens on the atrium floor casts light into the auditorium below and creates a sense of vertical continuity from the very bottom to the very peak. Elevators take one up to a reception area of 'hanging gardens', where ramps wind up to the circular congress chamber at the very top. Inspired by the United Nations Security Council meeting room, the chamber is held up by four leaning pillars representing the hands of peace. There, every three years, delegates of the world's main faiths can admire the stained glass apex that artist Brian Clarke has rendered in gold and blue, the colors of the Kazakh flag, and with a flock of doves, universal symbols of peace, flying towards the sun.

The building had to be designed to withstand the expansion and contraction caused by the Astanian climate, with temperatures ranging from 40°C in summer to -40°C in winter, and the construction schedule was tight, the building needing to be ready for the second congress in 2006. The structural answer to such demands was to use prefabricated components.

The Palace came about on the initiative of President Nursultan Nazarbayev and takes the form of a pyramid rising 62 meters on a 62x62 meter base, with a cladding of a triangular order rendered in glass and stone.

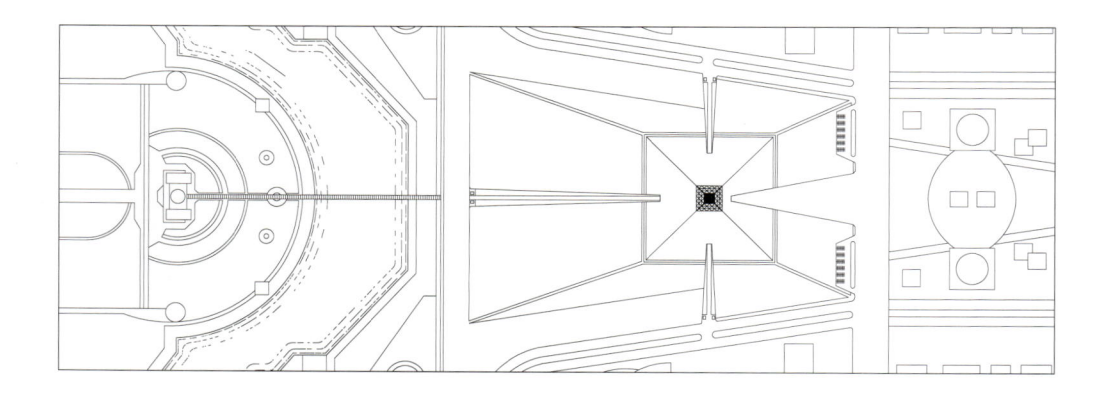

The Palace of Peace is intended to be a point of encounter for all of the world's confessions. The mound serving as its podium contains an opera house seating 1,500. The oculus crowning this underground auditorium becomes the floor of the building's ground-level foyer. At the top, under the blue and gold stained glass windows decorated with doves in flight, is the chamber that will take in the triennial Congress of World Religions.

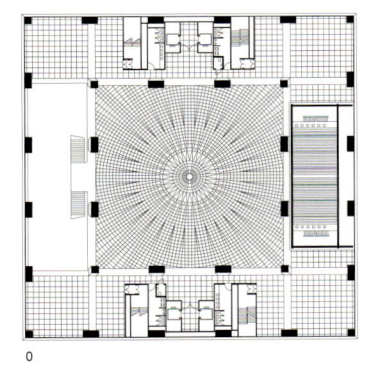

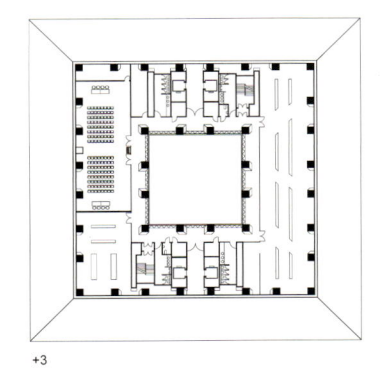

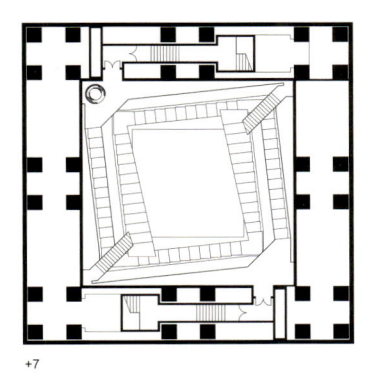

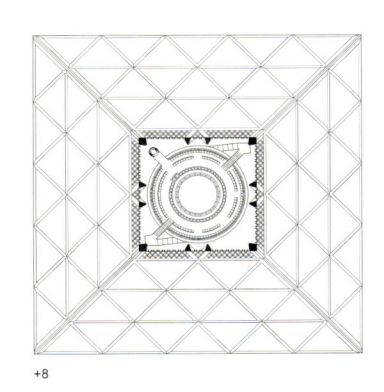

Atlas: Asia and Pacific 23

24 Atlas: Asia and Pacific

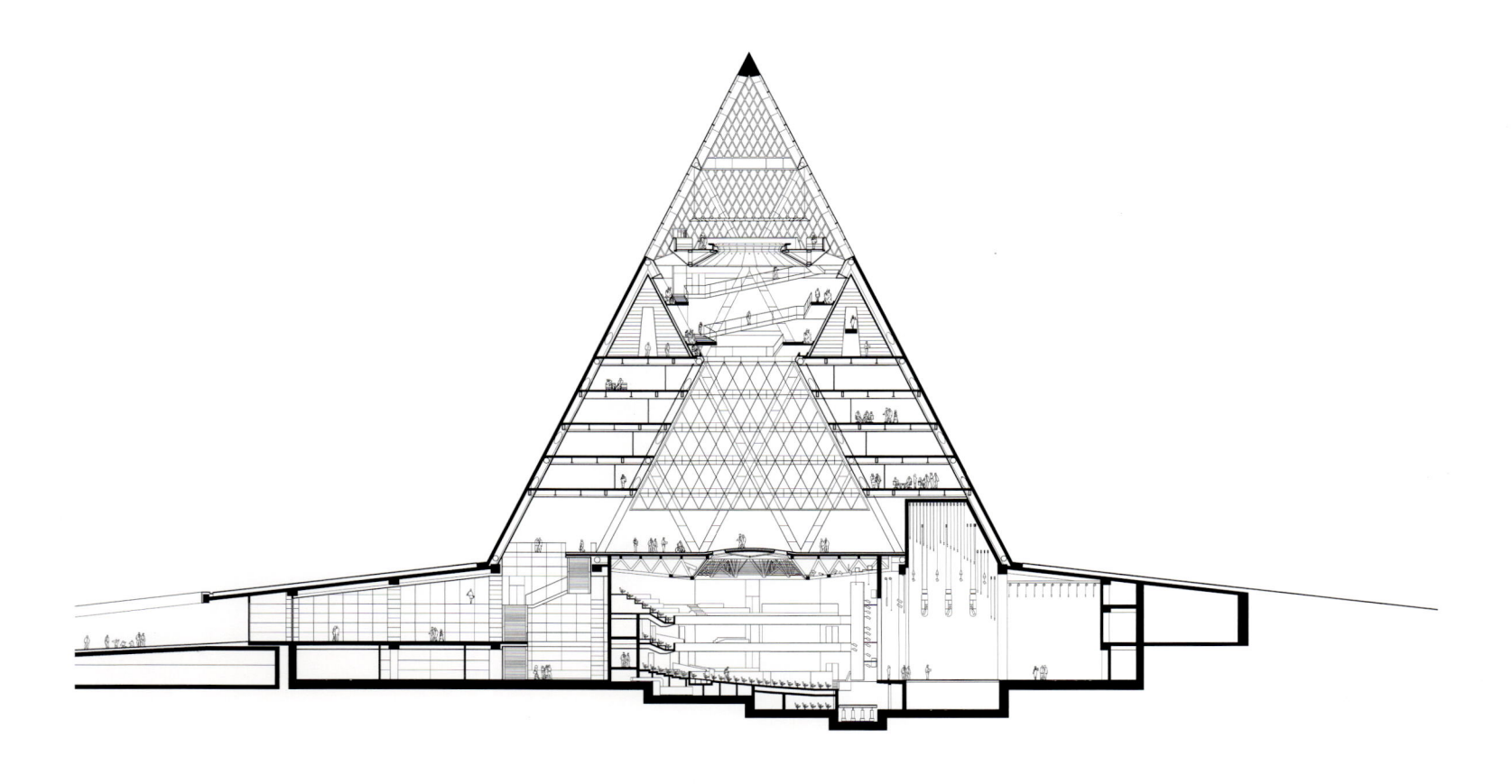

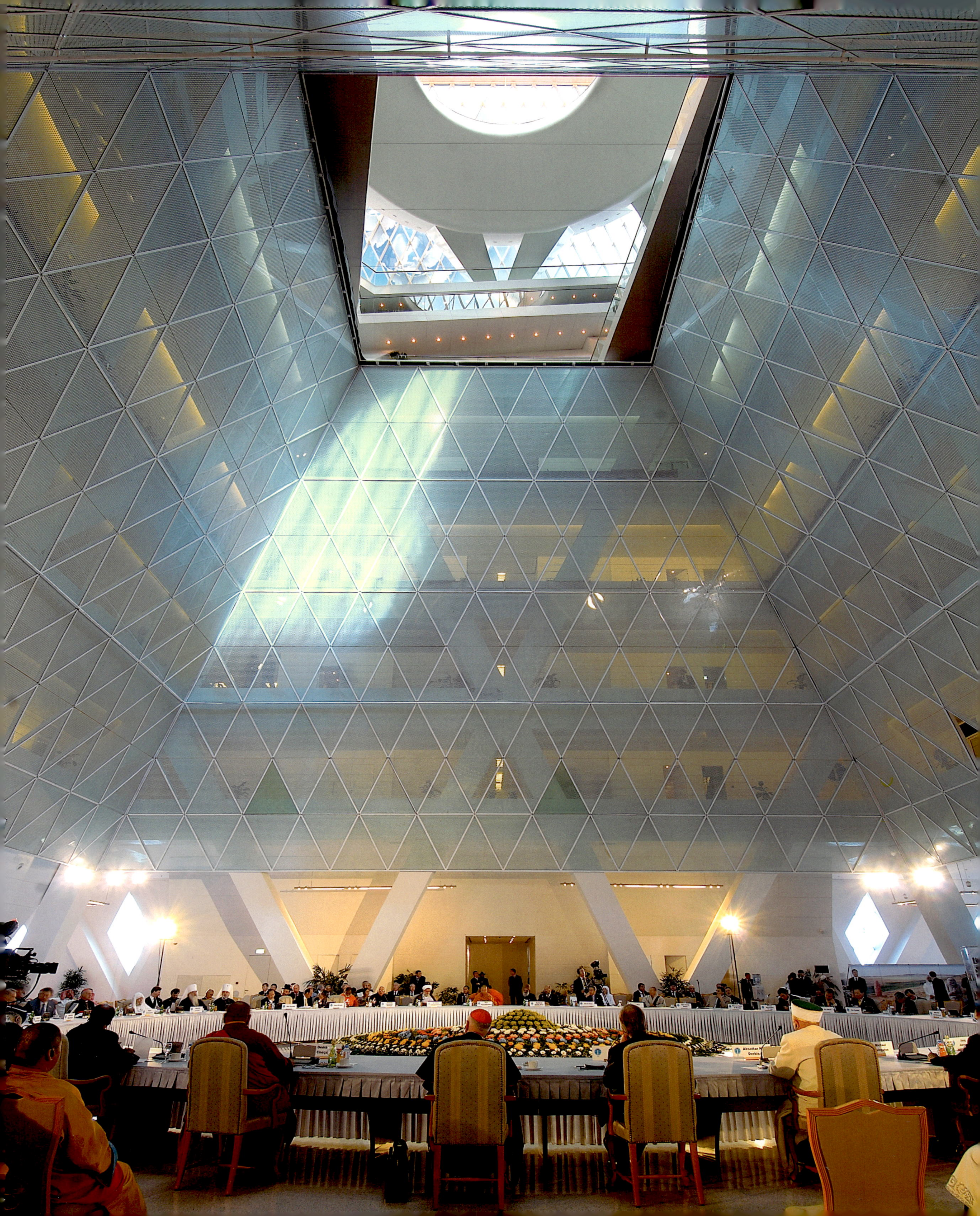

BIG
National Library
Astana (Kazakhstan)

Client
Kazakhstan Presidential Office
Architects
BIG: Bjarke Ingels
Collaborators
Thomas Christoffersen (project leader); Amy Campbell, Jakob Henke, Johan Cool, Jonas Barre, Daniel Sundlin

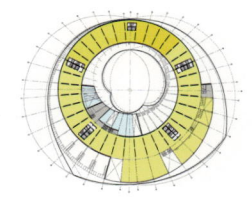

The National Library will stand as a symbol of the Kazakh nation. Its curved volume rises on a park that is a recreation of the country's diverse landscapes, with plant species and rocks brought in from all the provinces.

The Nursultan Nazarbayev National Library, named after the first president of the Republic of Kazahkstan, will rise in the center of Astana and command views of the entire city from its circle of vantage points. Encompassing not just books, it is intended to serve as an archive for historical records and as a multifunctional cultural and civic center for the nation's capital. All segments of the community will be served by the library, which will provide venues for meetings and events. It will also be a showcase of the country's nature. Like Astana itself, located at the heart of the Kazakh mainland, the new national library will stand at the very heart of a recreated Kazakh landscape, with the park around the building designed as a living library of trees, plants, minerals, and rocks taken from all over the country, allowing visitors to experience a true cross section of Kazakhstan's natural scenery.

In addition, the building endeavors to embody a new national symbol in the fusion, across time and space, of four universal archetypes: the circle, the rotunda, the arch, and the yurt (the circular domed tent originally used by nomads in central Asia). It was explicitly stated that the clarity of the circle, the courtyard of the rotunda, the gateway of the arch, and the soft silhouette of the yurt would together create a new national monument that would be at once local and universal, contemporary and timeless, unique and archetypal.

More exactly, a circle spirals around a vertical core, producing a building that goes about transforming from a horizontal layout where library and support functions are placed next to each other, to a vertical order where they are stacked on top of one another, through a diagonal organization that combines vertical hierarchy, horizontal connectivity, and diagonal view lines. One might also think of it as the clarity of a linear arrangement, ideal for archives and libraries, being mixed with the conveniences that can be offered by an infinite loop. Wrapping the transforming composition of spaces with a continuous skin then yields a Möbius strip volume where facades move from inside to out and back again, and walls become roof and back again.

Geometrically patterned openings on the skin create beautifully daylit spaces that are perfect for reading. Because of the warping and twisting of the exterior, some spaces receive more sunlight than others. To minimize cooling loads on the library, high-tech computer modeling was used to calculate thermal exposure on the building envelope and regulate solar impact.

The starting point of the national library's spatial organization is a spiral with several centers that twirls around a vertical void. An envelope that looks like a woven yurt gives the library its definitive volume.

In this way, the most is made of the advantages of the horizontal, vertical, and diagonal orders: functional contiguity, clear-cut hierarchy, and views mutually generated between the different parts of the complex.

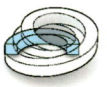

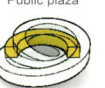

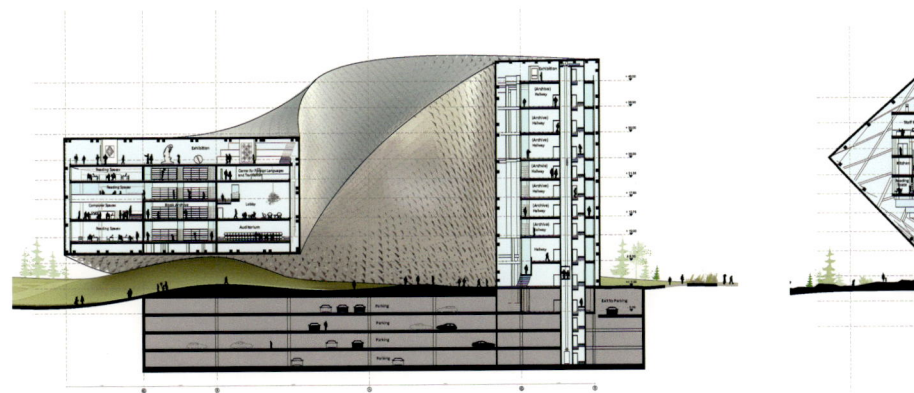

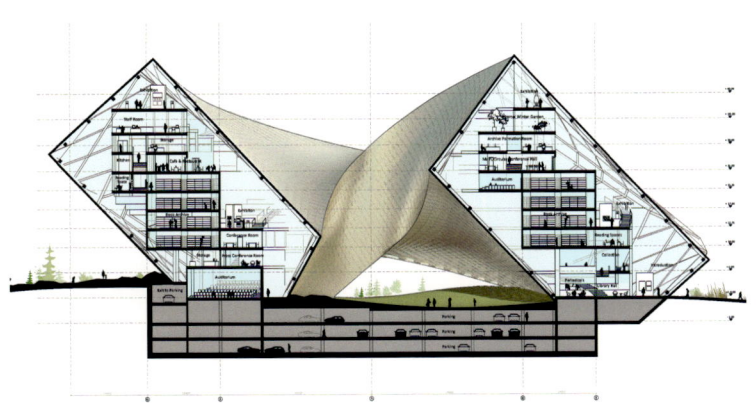

Public Functions | Public plaza | Exhibition hall | Reading rooms
Open bookshelves | Archive | Scientific research room | Administration

Atlas: Asia and Pacific 27

OMA/Rem Koolhaas
Almaty Science Campus
Talgar (Kazakhstan)

Client
Kazakh Institute of Oil and Gas
Architects
OMA: Rem Koolhaas
Collaborators
Rem Koolhaas, Reinier de Graaf,
Richard Hollington, Behnaz Assadi,
Ludwig Godefroy, Arie Gruijters,
Olaf Härtel, Bin Kim, Mirai Morita,
Max Rink, Ian Robertson,
Laurant Troost, Edward Solodukhin

ONE MAJOR MISSION of architecture and urbanism is to shape communities, and often in the past century they have done so from scratch. Here is a case where architecture is called upon to instantly deliver the social and cultural environment that cities normally develop organically through time. Maybe because of its limited size, the pretext of a brand new university campus in the middle of nowhere makes a particularly good starting point for creating urban life in a single stroke.

A green field in the province of Almaty, capital of the country until 1996 and located more than an hour's drive from the nearest city, is the chosen site for the new campus of the prestigious Kazakh-British Technical University (KBTU), and campus design here serves to generate an entire 'naukograd' technopolis that will be home as well to a new engineering headquarters for the Kazakh Institute of Oil and Gas (KING), but also to a residential community and a public zone with shops and entertainment serving that community and attracting visitors. Its isolated location presents the challenge of creating a masterplan that simultaneously capitalizes on the idyllic surroundings and overcomes its remoteness. It has to be both scenic and urban, and not fall into the trap of low-density settlement with a spattering of stand-alone objects separated by a gentle pedestrian network.

Hence, instead of confining each program to its own building, the campus follows a scheme that maximizes interaction and flexibility. An internal circulation system of bridge-blocks suspended in mid-air between buildings produces synergy between disciplines and departments, especially during the harsh Kazakh winter. In summer, it is the green fields underneath and between the buildings that act as the carriers of campus/urban life.

There is indeed a lot of overlap between the four principal programs addressed: academic, work, residential, public. Dormitories slip between residential and academic, the public area serves the other three, and so on. Taking into account the individual characteristics of each program and the specific relations between them, the complex has been arranged in three different forms: bars, loops, and blocks. The result, which is seemingly influenced by Escher's paradoxical forms, incorporates a wide range of envelopes and modules. The modular system creates an elevated city that reconciles its rational organization with the site's natural topography, which is kept intact. Above, roof terraces connecting the bars create a second horizontal landscape.

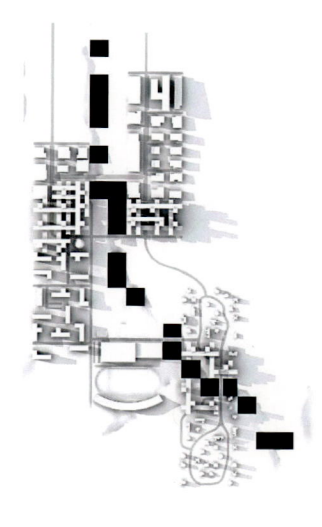

Taking up nearly 200,000 square meters, the project program is organized in zones. Between the offices section and the university departments, the main public space works like a mixed-use precinct for students and employees, creating an enclave of urban activity, while the residential area, which is less dense and somewhat isolated from the rest, capitalizes on the spectacular surroundings by offering views of the landscape and mountains.

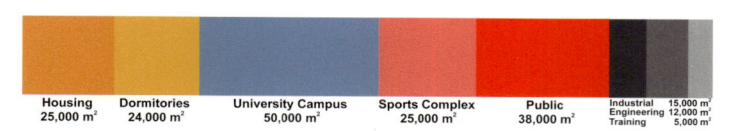

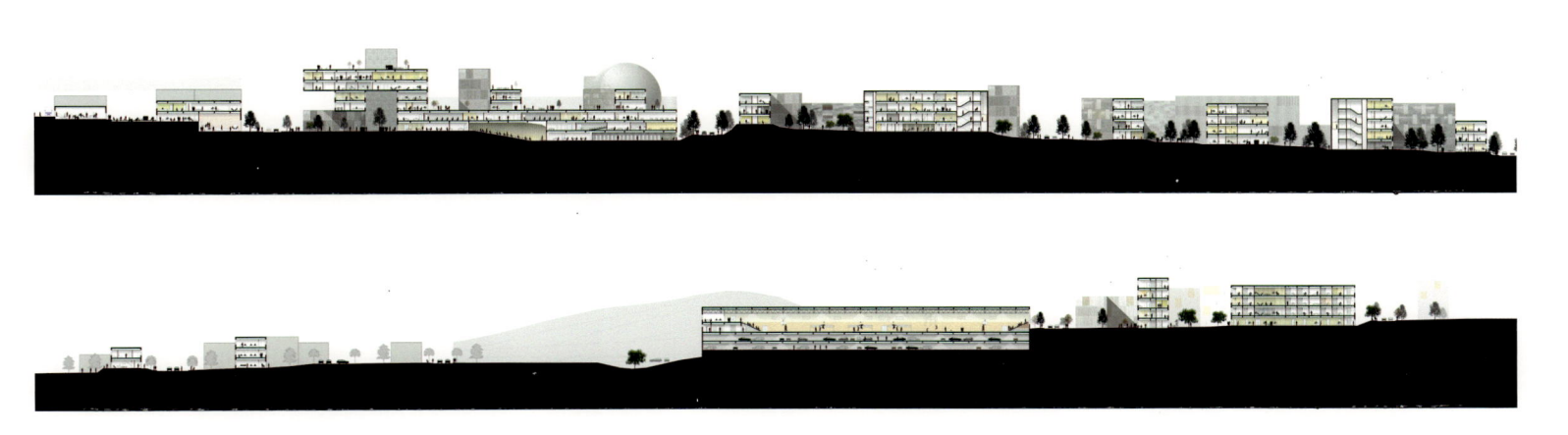

| Housing 25,000 m² | Dormitories 24,000 m² | University Campus 50,000 m² | Sports Complex 25,000 m² | Public 38,000 m² | Industrial Engineering Training | 15,000 m² 12,000 m² 5,000 m² |

Atlas: Asia and Pacific

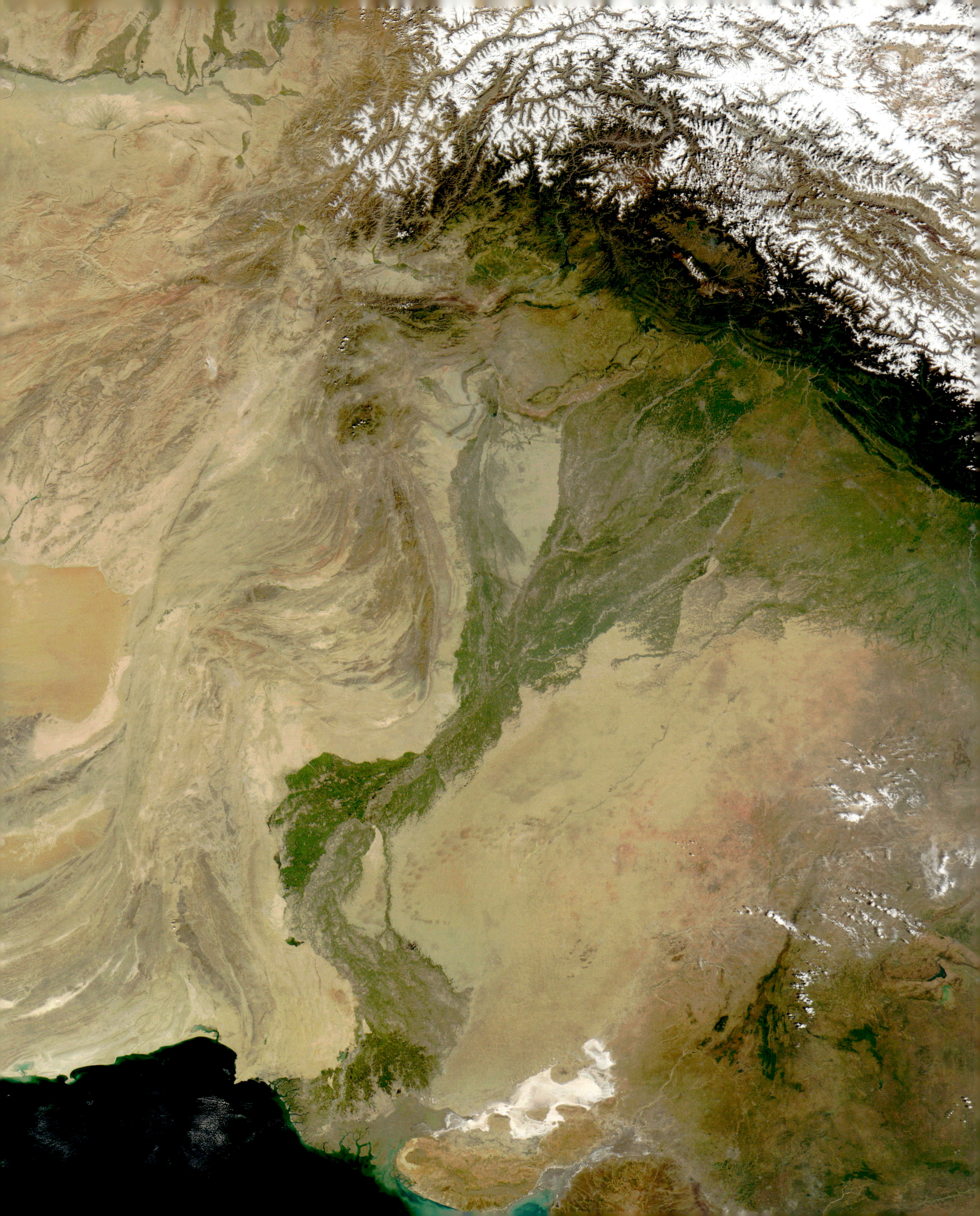

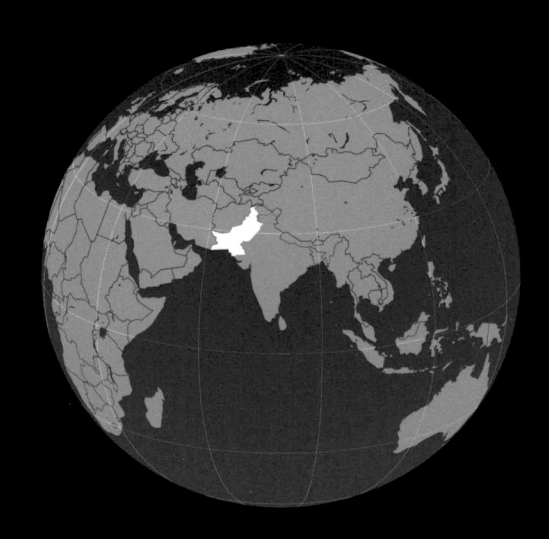

Pakistan

This young Muslim country has struggled through a turbulent history, with several coup d'états and internal wars; and it has also been the victim of a difficult geographic location, between Afghanistan and the territories of Kashmir, disputed with India. Both circumstances together have turned sustainable progress into a challenge for the country. Pakistan changed its capital from Karachi to Islamabad, and set out to build a new city with the help of foreign architects. However, the old capital continues to be the most important financial and commercial center, as the size of the projects selected here clearly shows: the KPT Tower wishes to revitalize the seafront of Karachi, and the Al-Azhar Garden residential complex, to offer a permanent settlement for a community of Muslim refugees. The Higher Secondary School in Gilgit, for its part, located close to the Himalaya, tries to reduce the inequalities between the rural and the urban worlds through education.

Hammad Husain
Coexisting Contrasts
Pakistan, Islamic Tradition and Recent Tribulations

Nayyar Ali Dada, Alhamra Arts Council, Lahore (1979)

Held together by the common cause of religion, the young country's eventful history determines its prospects for stability today and in the future.

WHEN THE HIJACKED planes rammed into the Twin Towers of the World Trade Center on September 11, 2001, few in Pakistan knew their country was about to change forever. Within a few months there was a full-fledged war being waged right next to Pakistan's western borders. An influx of refugees from Afghanistan made the situation worse. Along with these came a horde of Taliban and Al Qaeda militants, fleeing the American war machine. Eight years later, Pakistan is battling this militant monster which continues to draw its oxygen from neighboring Afghanistan. Some say it's an existential war; others call it a counter-Jihad. What is certain is that Pakistan – bruised, battered but resilient – is braced for turbulent years ahead.

Pakistan's sixty-two years of history have been very eventful. Three military coups, four wars and an arms race with India, a proxy war against the Soviets and a full scale conflict against the Taliban and numerous domestic socio-political issues have kept the country from gaining the stability needed for sustained growth.

When Pakistan came into being in August 1947, there were only a handful of qualified local architects. Foreign architects were commissioned for all important projects whereas the locals had to be content with apprentice-standard small-scale work. The new government did not have confidence in the local architects and till the 1960s, almost twenty years after independence, major projects continued to be awarded to foreign architects. Louis Kahn, Gio Ponti, Arne Jacobsen, Edward Durrell Stone, Michel Ecochard and Marcel Breuer were some of the well known international architects who were invited by the Government of Pakistan to design the major public buildings of the country. Not all succeeded in getting commissions.

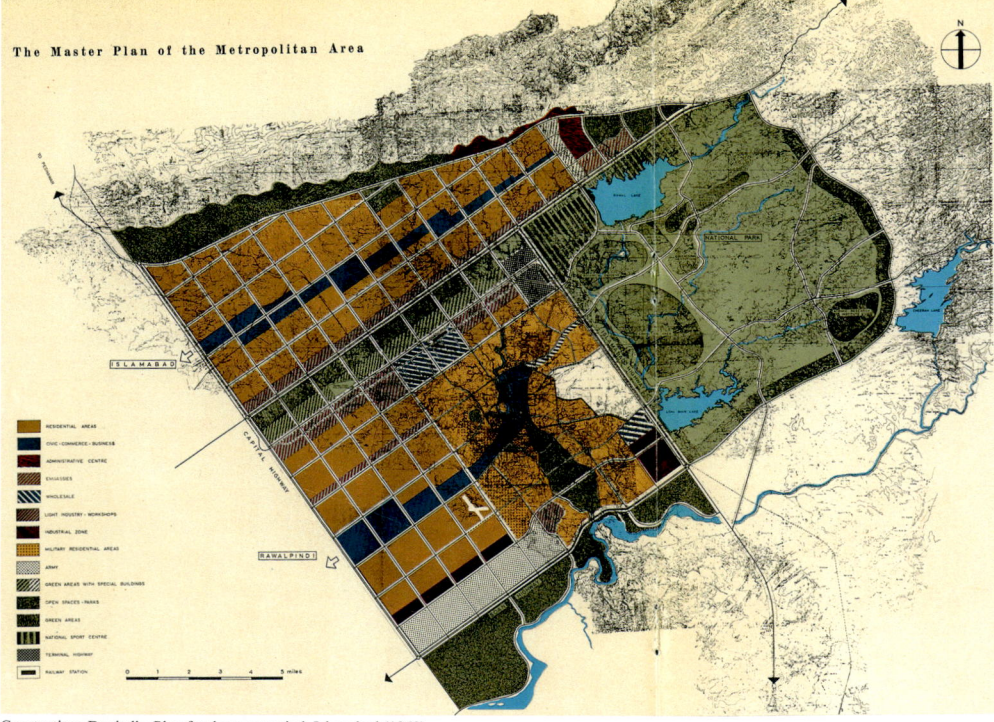

The influence of the Modern Movement in the configuration of the image of Pakistan is perceived in the work of some local architects, followers of the vernacular philosophy of Le Corbusier or Kahn.

Constantinos Doxiadis, Plan for the new capital, Islamabad (1960)

32 Atlas: Asia and Pacific

Located to the north of Pakistan, far from possible attacks by sea and close to the disputed frontier of Kashmir, Islamabad finally became the capital of the country in the sixties, after Karachi and Rawalpindi.

The Greek urban planner and architect Constantinos Doxiadis set forth his Master Plan for the city, whose central axis was Jinnah Avenue, with tree-lined roads, green belts, residential developments and zoning of uses.

View of Jinnah Avenue, main axis of Islamabad

The profession of architecture kept struggling for recognition in the first three decades after independence till the formation of the Pakistan Council of Architects and Town Planners (PCATP) in 1983, after which architecture gained considerable legitimacy as a profession.

The post-1983 era saw maturity, growth and acceptance for the profession. New architecture schools opened up and architects started getting jobs in government departments, where, till then, design posts were occupied by engineers. Private practices expanded and architects came to be accepted as professionals with a permanent place in the construction industry, distinct from civil engineers.

Master Builders
The first generation of architects of Pakistan, including Mehdi Ali Mirza, Khawaja Zaheeruddin and Mohammad Abdul Ahed, was mostly trained abroad and was deeply influenced by the Modern Movement and by modernist masters like Mies van der Rohe and Frank Lloyd Wright. Most buildings designed during the 1950s and 1960s were purely functional and modernist. Le Corbusier's presence in neighboring India had its effect across borders; his influence and style permeated into Pakistani architectural offices. Several buildings were designed in strict Corbusian functional mannerism, notably the Grindlay Bank, Islamabad (1984), by Anwar Said, and the Burmah Shell Building, Karachi (1978), by Habib Fida Ali. However, the modernist master who left an indelible mark on the region was Louis Kahn, who came to this region to design the Parliament building in Dhaka, Bangladesh (formerly part of Pakistan). Lahore-based Nayyar Ali Dada's initial work – the Alhamra Arts Council, Lahore (1979) – is inspired by Kahn's philosophy, but later Dada started incorporating local vocabulary in his functionalist designs. Others from the second generation of architects, apart from Dada, who successfully interpreted modernism in local context, include Arshad Shahid Abdulla and Ejaz Ahed with, among their other works, two high-rise buildings in Islamabad: the NIC building (1993) and the Habib Bank Tower (1999) respectively.

Having had successful architects and Pakistani masters as teachers, the third generation of architects has come of age, and diversity has become the hallmark of Pakistani architecture. On the one hand, architects are exploring the design typologies and construction technologies of the region's glorious architectural past, using brick and lime mortar with the help of master craftsmen, whereas on the other, fiercely bold experimentations are being conducted in postmodernist and deconstructivist philosophy in urban centers.

One interesting aspect, however, that has come out of these layered phases, is that whereas most post-war architects in developed societies have progressed towards specialization and have been groomed in the corporate culture, the Pakistani architect, because of less-than-desired industrial support and emphasis on individuality, has continued to work as a master builder in the Vitruvian definition, and as propagated by revolutionaries like Andrea Palladio and Walter Gropius. The philosophy of the Bauhaus, where the craftsman was promoted over industrial support, is still the strength of the 21st-century Pakistani architect. The demanding market, which most architects venture into with the aim of earning a living, more than to make a stylistic statement, expects the architects to understand and control every aspect of their buildings and have 'craftsman skills' like Mies and Wright had acquired from their 'working class' background and in their experiences before their architectural careers. The Pakistani architect is trained to multi-task, to

Aerial photograph of Islamabad showing the layout of the Plan by Doxiadis

The profession of architect was not recognized in Pakistan until 1983. Hence, after independence all the buildings needed to house the institutions of the young country were commissioned to foreign figures. However, projects by modern masters like Jacobsen or Kahn were rejected on account of not reflecting Islamic tradition. Durrell Stone would in the end undertake the construction of the main buildings in a Wrightian style.

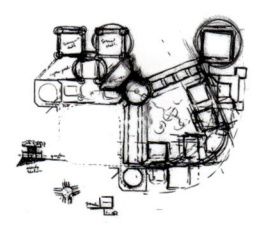

L. Kahn, Presidential House

coordinate the office-client-site triangle and to remain deeply involved in the complete building process as a team leader.

The Ups and Downs of Economy
There have been intermittent periods of growth in the last few decades. The economy saw an unprecedented growth from 2002 till 2007. During this prosperous period, the profession of architecture kept pace with the country's economy and grew in leaps and bounds. With the surge in the construction industry, all architectural offices were flooded with work. A lot of investment flowed into housing schemes, public and private sector commercial buildings, high-rise towers, corporate interiors, and residences and farmhouses. Architectural offices that had been used to working at a leisurely pace found themselves with heavy workloads. Classified sections of newspapers started getting advertisements seeking architects, engineers, draftsmen and other technical people.

Before long, reality dawned upon the construction sector; the service industry was not prepared to cater to the exponential increase in development projects and demand of professionals. There were not enough architects, engineers and skilled people. Gradually, the demand for work exceeded the supply of architects. This vacuum was filled by large foreign architecture and construction companies, which moved in to grab the unclaimed pie of the market. The Pakistani construction and service industries missed the opportunity to cash in on the booming sector as they were not equipped to handle so much workload.

Contrasting Cultures
The historical city of Lahore, the second-largest in Pakistan after Karachi, has over the past many centuries been the heart of many empires, which have left their marks on the flavor of the city. While the city itself may have grown in proportions beyond any limits imagined, it has managed to maintain that elusive element that makes it stand out among other cities; the intangible quality that marks its streets that weave a labyrinthine web around its historic roots. Juxtaposed with this inorganic, informal pattern is the seemingly more ordered, controlled logic of new

Edward Durrell Stone, Presidential Palace, Islamabad (1966)

Kenzo Tange, Supreme Court, Islamabad (1993)

The last important building on Constitution Avenue, where the Parliament is located, is the Supreme Court by the Japanese Kenzo Tange, a monument of bold geometric forms decorated with Islamic symbols. The Great Mosque of Islamabad is a work by a Turkish architect; though initially it did not find popular support because of its departure from tradition, in the end it has obtained general acceptance.

developments. So Lahore is a city of anachronisms but still echoes down length of its eight-lane boulevards, declaring its presence to all those who are drawn to its many wonders, and those who have claimed it as their identity.

Karachi tried asserting its cosmopolitan and international identity over Lahore, but it is a scuffle of just contrasts. Karachi, a metropolitan city with a population of over 16 million, stands out for its amalgamation of influences, that come together to constitute deeper, more nuanced meanings. Lahore, in contrast, causes the visitor to stop in his tracks, and behold what lies around him, each constituent of its existence ringing true to the quintessential flavor that emanates from its bold identity. Islamabad, with its relatively recent beginnings, lacks what can be thought of a distinct flavor. Attempts at instilling that mystical flavor into the veins of the city have taken many forms, among them an attempt at importing it from the city of Lahore. However, the rigid, orderly, grid-iron plan of Islamabad with axial roads and strictly controlled development sets it apart from Lahore. It is the city that projects the modern face of Pakistan. At least this is what its Greek planner Constantinos Doxiadis planned.

The Capital Project
Pakistan's new capital city of Islamabad was called the 'City of the Future' by Doxiadis, his idea of 'dynapolis' – a city expanding in a linear fanshape from an initial point – was to cope with the explosive urbanization and growth of the 1960s in a developing country like Pakistan.

A blend of loosely-knit ethnic groups, Pakistan was held together by religion and the Capital project was an attempt to modernize Pakistan by weaving a diverse population into a unified entity and to lay the foundation for a modern and progressive Pakistan. The aim was to transform a rural agrarian society into an urban and cosmopolitan culture through the Capital project. Conceived in 1959 by the military ruler General Ayub Khan, the project was intended to be a modern, planned city that would be an ideal seat of government tucked away in the foothills of the Margallah range. Doxiadis Associates prepared the Master Plan and it was approved in 1960. It was a planned city with wide tree-lined roads, green belts, planned residential sectors, earmarked commercial areas, proper zoning and large-scale structures to be designed by foreign architects.

The initial development of Islamabad was undertaken by renowned foreign architects who created buildings which projected an image of modernity. For a people who prided themselves on their rich history and architectural traditions, modernist public buildings designed by western architects were received with lukewarm enthusiasm. Kamil Khan Mumtaz, in his book *Architecture in Pakistan* writes: "When the Parliament building was first mooted in 1962, it was suggested that the Parliament house will have to be carefully designed to reflect our past culture, at the same time utilizing modern methods of construction." The government decided to entrust the design of major public buildings to world-famous architects and Arne Jacobsen was invited to design the Parliament building. However, his proposal was criticized for his uncompromising 'modern' design and was replaced by Louis Kahn, who in turn, was

Vedat Dalokay, Great Mosque of Islamabad or Faisal Mosque (1976-1986)

Atlas: Asia and Pacific **35**

During the last decade, and in spite of the current difficulties, the country has experienced a strong urban growth due to the improved economic situation and to the arrival of global investors, mainly Asian and from the Persian Gulf. As a result, more local architects are called to design and build important institutional buildings, which incorporate external influences without losing their regional identity.

Aedas, KPT Tower, Karachi

also relieved of his project. According to the government spokesman: "The reason for the rejection of Professor Kahn's design was his inability to modify the design so as to reflect Pakistan's desire to introduce Islamic architecture in Islamabad's public buildings."

The services of Edward Durrell Stone were next solicited. Senior bureaucrats, who "admired his love for Mughal buildings and the spirit of grandeur the Mughal buildings emanate", recommended him. This was the single most important factor in the minds of the decision-makers when they proposed later that Stone should undertake all the major public buildings of the central square, including the President's house, the Parliament, the Supreme Court and the Foreign Office. The chairman of the Capital Development Authority, according to their official records, told Stone: "There is a grave dissatisfaction in the Government and among our people regarding the architecture of the public buildings put up so far in Islamabad. We are proud of our long and beautiful architectural heritage and we see no reason why the buildings of Islamabad should not reflect it."

Stone finally designed the President's house, the Parliament, the Cabinet building and the Quaid-i-Azam University in Islamabad, ironically in a Wright-inspired, straight horizontal line language, devoid of any Islamic or traditional vocabulary. Louis Kahn's rejected proposal was far superior in design and spatial quality and he went on to produce one of his greatest masterpieces in Dhaka, Bangladesh. The last important building on the Constitution Avenue, the Supreme Court, designed by Kenzo Tange with Shin Toki in the 1980s, is an imposing formalist building derived out of triangular forms, with an unsuccessful attempt to 'Islamize' it with stick-on symbols.

Turkish architect Vedat Dalokay's modern design of the Grand Mosque of Islamabad, built in late 1970s, received severe criticism from bureaucrats and the general public alike for being a clear departure from the traditional mosque form and devoid of influence of Islamic architecture.

This gradual change in the way architecture has been perceived over the years has had several effects on the society. The most prominent is the realization that East and West, tradition and modernity, are not poles apart. In fact, they are very capable of fusion. There are no clear cut divisions of black or white, but several shades of grey. Having a rich tradition and a glorious architectural history does not mean being a slave to that custom. It is evident that typologies and styles lose importance in the wake of functionality and diversity. The Faisal Mosque in Islamabad has been a merger of all the perceived contrasts and it has braved the test of time against all pre-conceived biases of a partisan society. It has cast a lasting influence in changing the mindset of a society that has generally been averse to influences outside the confines of their own traditions and culture.

The Emerging Cityscape

The amount of construction done in the last decade is probably more than the last few decades combined. There are several reasons for this: the high economic growth experienced by the country in this period; substantial foreign investment in the construction sector; and increased interest in the Pakistani market of multinational architecture firms like Atkins (United Kingdom), TAK (Malaysia) and Meinhardt (Singapore), and real estate firms such as Emaar, Damac & Al-Ghurair from the Gulf countries. Local architects also produced significant works both in quality and

Arif Masood, Pakistan National Monument, Islamabad (2006)

Ejaz Ahed, Aga Khan Higher Secondary School, Gilgit (2002)

quantity. Arshad Shahid Abdulla's MCB Tower, Karachi (2005), the tallest building of Pakistan, with its simple form and clean modernist lines; Ejaz Ahed's Higher Secondary School, Gilgit (2002), an inspiring vernacular functionalist building in a barren mountainous landscape; Arif Masood's Pakistan National Monument, Islamabad (2006), a high-profile esoteric national unity concept scaled up to a monument; and Nayyar Ali Dada's Serena Hotel (2002), Islamabad, with a modern rendering of traditional *jharokas* and rooftop concrete arches inspired from the Great Mosque of Córdoba in Spain, which add an 'Islamic' touch to an otherwise modern building.

Glitzy corporate buildings have been a phenomenon of the last decade and a number of insurance companies, multinational firms, local and foreign banks have built custom-designed buildings: the Faysal Bank, Islamabad (2005) by Nasir Iqbal, a steel and glass building with subdued light-colored glossy tiles on the facade; the MCB building, Islamabad (1998) by Arshad-Shahid Abdulla, a formalist building with Louis Kahn monumentality and square punctures of varying sizes in a monolithic, solid form; and the Habib Bank provincial headquarters in Lahore (1997), by Nayyar Ali Dada, a symmetric, red-brick building with windows designed as modern glass *jharokas*. Dada's rendition of facades by adding local vocabulary on a functional plan (as in the Serena Hotel, Islamabad) has produced interesting results but in some instances he has resorted to superficially applying a layer of tradition over an inherently modern building with the intention of fusing modernity with tradition.

An Artist's Canvas
The bulk of construction in Pakistan caters to the residential sector. According to government figures, there is a shortfall of seven million houses in the country. Successive governments have attempted to address this issue but, with a high population growth rate, as many as half a million houses are required each year to keep the shortfall figure static. One such effort was the Prime Minister's Housing Scheme (PMHS), launched in 1999, which envisaged building half a million low-cost houses on unused government land all over the country. The scheme also promised to jump-start the ailing construction support industry. Forty-two different industries were short-listed, such as cement, steel, electrical cables, ceiling fans, paint etc. Manufacturers were asked to provide their annual production capacity to cater to the PMHS. Most architecture and engineering firms were also invited to participate. It was a promising scheme, but was cut short by the October 1999 military takeover by General Pervez Musharraf, and was eventually scrapped.

However, private investment in housing increased after the military takeover and small and medium scale housing schemes started springing up with easy installment plans in collaboration with banks. Although these individual efforts did contribute towards reducing the housing problem in cities, the shortage of housing remained an issue in smaller towns and rural areas. In 2002, the government started a policy of bringing in foreign investment and one of the sectors that were prioritized was the housing sector.

Large foreign real estate multinationals like Emaar and Damac of Dubai came up with Dubai-style housing developments in the major cities of Pakistan. The positive aspect of the presence of such experienced real estate development firms in the country was to increase the housing units

Naeem Pasha & Suhail Abbasi, National Art Gallery, Islamabad (1996-2007)

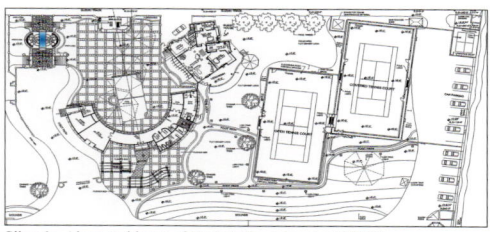

Sikander Ajam, residence of Nasir Jaffer, Islamabad (2003)

With a population close to 170 million inhabitants, Pakistan has a seven million shortfall in housing, which the high birth rate contributes to increasing. The attempts of successive governments to provide a solution to this issue have failed. Paradoxically, there is more and more demand of luxury houses, and this building type has become one of the main sources of work for architects, who in some cases are also the owners.

Yasmeen Lari, Angoori Bagh residential complex, Lahore (1975)

in the country and bring in foreign investment, however, the houses offered were not only targeted at the affluent strata of the society, they were offered on installments without much foreign investment by these conglomerates. The policy of the government to woo these multinationals and their willingness to relax rules and bend over backwards to accommodate investors resulted in less-than-desired results.

Private houses and villas constitute one of the largest and the most consistent markets for architects. Some of the good specimens of these in the last decade across the country include Nasir Jaffer's farmhouse, Islamabad (2003) by Sikander Ajam, an unorthodox crescent-shaped house built around a swimming pool with trellised walkways and manicured lawns; Shahid Kareem's residence, Lahore (2003) by Kamil Khan Mumtaz, conceived on traditional design principles and built around a central atrium lounge with a vaulted brick roof incorporating cut brick and stucco plaster details; Dr. Nasir Raza's residence, Islamabad (2005) by Salman Mansur, designed in a bold postmodernist vocabulary with contrasting colors; and former Pakistani president Pervez Musharraf's high-profile farmhouse in Islamabad (2009) by Hammad Husain, a functionalist, Moroccan-style design with subtle curves in the plan and rolling landscape merged with the house. Interestingly, but not surprisingly, some of the good houses built in the last two decades include self-designed houses of architects: Najeeb Omar's residence in Karachi (2000), a modern house built on a traditional plan around an internal courtyard and fused with landscaping and vegetation; Shakeel Qureshi's residence in Lahore (2001), a multi-terraced, energy-efficient house that utilizes circulating water for cooling; Suhail Abbasi's residence in Islamabad (1999), a split-level house with local craftsmen detailing in brick and a plan reminiscent of traditional rural plans with small spaces flowing into other spaces; and Naeem Pasha's residence in Islamabad (1994), designed on modern principles with skillful use of brick in facade rendering, window brackets and skylights.

In stark contrast to these rich suburbs are the lower-income neighborhoods, known as *mohallas* in almost all cities of Pakistan which form the bulk of the city. Most of these *mohallas* are either shoddily planned or not planned at all. Built on small plots, these houses, in many instances, in the absence of enforced laws, go up to as high as four storeys. The roof is an important part of the living and it is used for a multitude of activities including sleeping in hot summer days, kite flying and family gatherings in winters. Because of narrow streets and attached houses with common walls, there is very little ventilation in these compact houses. This fact makes the roof more useful. Some examples of successful architect-designed low-cost mass housing schemes have been Arcop's Al-Azhar Garden, Karachi (2007), and Yasmeen Lari's Angoori Bagh housing in Lahore (1975).

Apartment living is relatively new to Pakistan; hence, apartment blocks can only be seen in major cities. These mid-rises, rarely going higher than five storeys, have been the preferred choice of the working middle-class. However, with property prices sky-rocketing, apartment living is slowly creeping into the lifestyles of the upper income group also. As is the case with most of the residential buildings, including houses, architects are only employed by this group. As a result, high-end apartments are well-designed, functional and aesthetically pleasing while the middle-class apartment buildings, more often than not are cramped and poorly designed. Some of the prominent high-end apartment buildings designed lately are Al-Ghurair Giga, Rawalpindi (2009) by Tariq Hasan, and Khudadad Heights, Islamabad (2009), by Nasir Iqbal.

Architects who have started practicing in the last decade are more exposed to international influences and at the same time more aware of the quest for reviving the traditional concepts that had been swept away by the onslaught of the

K. Khan Mumtaz, residence of Shahid Karim, Lahore (2003)

Modern Movement. From amongst the international masters, Geoffrey Bawa and Charles Correa's regionally sensitive work is influencing young inquisitive minds as much as Zaha Hadid and Rem Koolhaas's avant-garde designs. Significant creative work has been produced by Shahid Khan, Fawad Suhail, Azar Raza, Designer's East and Hanif Daud. The market for custom-designed houses is ever expanding and architects are increasingly being given a 'blank canvas' by clients in search of excellence.

Energy Crisis and Sustainability
Pakistan has been hit badly by the global energy crisis and the rising international oil prices. The energy shortage and increasing utility prices have necessitated a move towards energy-efficient buildings. The traditional Pakistani house, built with lime mortar and lime plaster, had a central courtyard, verandahs, two-foot-thick walls, clay roof insulation and double-height ceilings with ventilators at the top to allow accumulated heat to escape. Even British architects, during the 200 years of colonial rule, adopted this climate-derived, vernacular style in their buildings. However, when air-conditioning permeated the urban Pakistan homes, these traditional concepts were slowly discarded in favor of mechanized thermal control-dictated designs. With temperatures in summer soaring up to 46 degrees Celsius and frequent power outages, living inside a poorly ventilated and badly insulated house becomes very uncomfortable. Recently, the focus has gradually started reverting towards the traditional vernacular concepts, not necessary in style, but in terms of thermal comfort. Lately, the 'Dubai-effect', as it is called in Pakistan – mindlessly high- energy consuming glass-clad buildings in extreme hot climates – has started influencing designers and builders in Pakistan. The under-construction Centaurus, a much-hyped 7-star hotel in Islamabad, designed by the British firm Atkins of Burj-al Arab, Dubai fame, is one such example. However, with the recent crash of the Dubai glamour bubble and the simultaneous energy crisis in Pakistan, the race for going higher and glassier has abruptly slowed down. Architects and decision makers in the construction industry are now gradually shifting their focus towards energy-efficient techniques and green technologies for a sustainable future. Ejaz Ahed's competition-winning, climatically sensitive design for the Islamabad City Hall (due to be completed in 2011) aptly represents this shift in focus.

One may say that the ever elusive silver lining may soon become a reality in Pakistan.

The onslaught of foreign investment, the discovery of new talent and the generally more educated and informed clientele has broadened the horizons for architects, and provided them new avenues for the execution of these design philosophies. There is now a better opportunity for the architect to influence the life of the common man, if not directly then by implication. This must be understood in the face of the constraints the architect has to overcome at every step of the process; from the planning phase to the execution. Although Pakistani architecture is looking for a definitive and clear direction, the constant search for appropriate and applicable architecture has begun to show results – in a bruised, battered but resilient Pakistan.

Arcop Associates, Al-Azhar Garden Housing, Karachi (2004)

Ahed
Aga Khan Higher Secondary School
Gilgit (Pakistan)

Client
Aga Khan Education Services
Architects
Ahed Associates: Ejaz Ahed,
Iftikhar Azam
Collaborators
Zahida Khanum, Arshad Kamal,
Zunaira Mufti, Syed Muhammad Ovais
Consultants
Mienhardt, Technia & A.S.

A walkway defined by a trellis with plants welcomes students arriving at the school, the windows of which are painted a bright ocher color that strikes a contrast with the green of the triangular roofs.

THE AGA KHAN Higher Secondary School and the Professional Development Center in Gilgit are part of the literacy campaign that is being undertaken in the Northern Areas of Pakistan, close to the Afghanistan border, with the financial support of Prince Karim Aga Khan. Nestled in the slopes of the snow-covered Karakoram mountain range, the school and the development center together spread over a five-hectare site along both sides of Konodas Road and set new standards for building in this remote region.

The architectural expressions of the two complexes are compatible and unifying. Nevertheless, there are inherent and marked differences. Whereas the PDC school is a composition of fragmented blocks organized in accordance with a site-planning strategy, the HSS is a single building that twists and turns as it hugs the contours of the terrain in response to the changing landscape.

Over 600 students, many boarding at the Shah Karim Hostel next door, use the HSS daily. The school building sits approximately four meters below noisy Konodas Road and has views of the hills to the north and the fast-rushing Gilgit River to the south. Students enter the building through a semi-covered trellis along an assembly and play court. The natural slope of the terrain is carved to provide steps for the casual spectator to stop and sit on and enjoy the view. On the south is a large field for team sports like cricket and football.

The school's central knuckle is the media resource center, which affords exceptional views from the reading hall. The geometry creates a natural entry from the north courtyard and a covered court that can be used in severe weather. The classrooms are arranged on the north for a comfortable amount of natural light, while the south side of the central spine is lined with laboratories and seminar rooms. Interiors are punctuated with skylight wells and interest is maintained through overlooking double-height spaces. The simple internal concrete walls are accentuated with splashes of bright ocher and green that enliven the atmosphere. The furniture is light and flexible to facilitate the rearrangements required to adapt to different functions and group activities. Administrative offices and staff rooms are clustered togeher on the east side, where a formal entrance is crowned with a stylized open book element. A block of classrooms and related facilities will be added in the next expansion phase.

Situated close to the Afghanistan border, nestled in the slopes of the Karakoram range, the school is part of a literacy campaign that is being undertaken in the rural areas of north Pakistan. The complex adapts to the rugged terrain through two principal volumes which are connected by a raised central core, the media resource center, whose large windows make light pour in and lead directly out to the courtyard.

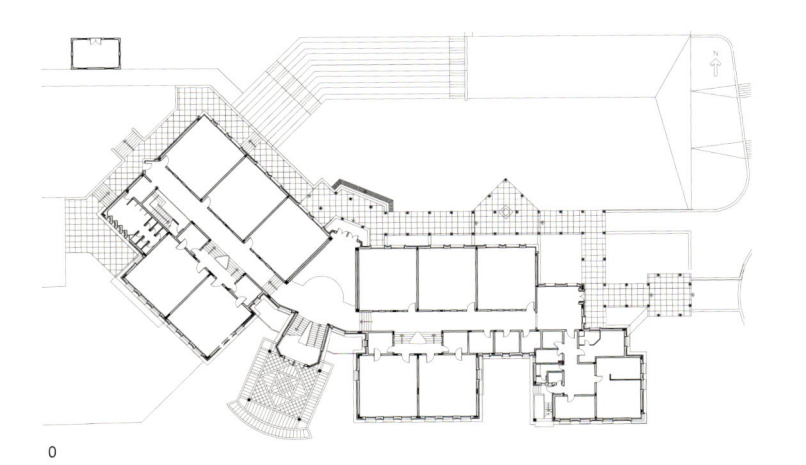

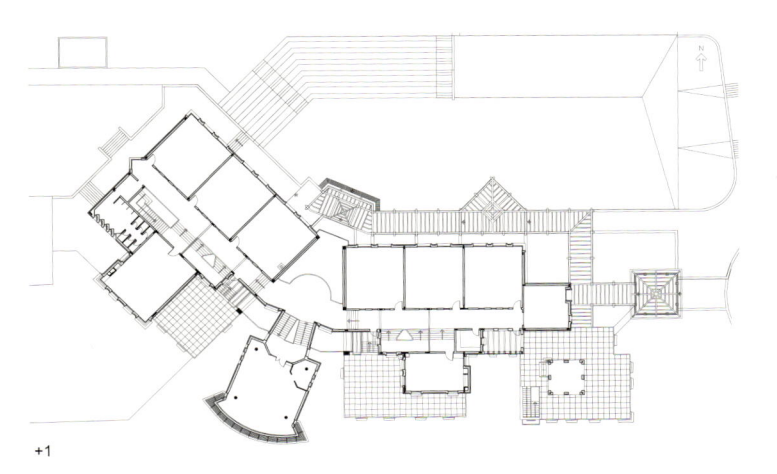

Arcop
Al-Azhar Garden Housing
Karachi (Pakistan)

Client
Pioneer Multipurpose Cooperative Society
Architects
Arcop Associates: Yawar Jilani, Mahbood Khan
Consultants
Aga Khan Planning and Building Services Pakistan (technical); A. Saadat (plumbing); M. Ayub & Assoc. (electrical); Mienhardt (structure); Matrix (infrastructure)
Photos
Amean J. /Aga Khan Trust for Culture

Built to bring together the Momins, a Muslim community scattered in Pakistan after its expulsion from India, this residential complex is a rectangular village organized with streets, squares, and courtyards.

THE MAIN PURPOSE of the Al-Azhar Garden development in Karachi, Pakistan's second most important city, was to offer affordable housing to the 'Momins', a Muslim community that migrated there from the northern Indian state of Gujarat in 1947, after both India and Pakistan obtained independence from the British Raj. After sixty years of uprootedness, the Momins finally have a place where they can develop a sense of belonging, a home for a community that is quite homogeneous, with more or less uniform incomes and a fundamental element of cohesion: religion.

In contrast to Karachi's tattered urbanity, the estate is divided into distinct clusters that are neatly organized around plazas, gardens, and courtyards linked by ceremonial pathways converging in a central node containing the mosque, a vocational school, a clinic, and convenience stores. The development works like a cooperative and has all the services of a small town or urban development, including security systems. The 1,090 dwellings - whose floor areas range from 200 to 80 square meters - are connected by internal transport, and residents have a civic center for weddings and other events. There is also an office complex and twenty-two parks named after the Gujarat villages the Momins came from.

All this was decided in consultation with community spokespersons, who actively took part in design and all throughout construction by calling for more greenery and a layered sequence of spaces separating public from private. Hence the numerous *chowks* and *maidans* (squares and plazas) taken from traditional architecture. To unite a group amid the anonymous sprawl of Karachi, a chaotic city that has undergone a process of degradation, but also to address desires for individuality within the community, each block has its own facade ornaments and color palette.

Various mechanisms were devised to create shadows, natural ventilation, and water recycling systems besides using vernacular architectural features and a low-cost building system, post-and-beam with brick infill, to reduce construction and maintenance costs and keep within the budget of 100 euros per square meter.

Standard dwelling A

Standard dwelling B

Each of the blocks, built with low-cost materials, is organized around an inner square or *maidan*, bringing light and natural ventilation into all the rooms. The facades feature decorative elements with nature motifs and use a color palette that ranges from ocher tones to pink hues, helping to individualize the different pieces within the estate. Spokespersons of the Momin community took active part in the overall design process.

Atlas: Asia and Pacific 43

Aedas
KPT Tower
Karachi (Pakistan)

Client
Karachi Port Trust
Architects
Aedas; MM Pakistan (local architects)
Collaborators
D. Kingdom (project director),
D. Barnes (design director), J. Kimpian (sustainability/advanced modelling),
A. Naqvi (director, Pakistan)
Consultants
Mott MacDonald UK (structural/civil and façade engineer); Mott MacDonald Dubai (building services); Franklin & Andrews (quantity surveyors); Gina Barney (vertical transportation); Control Risks (security consultants); Colliers (commercial letting agent)

Rising 78 stories and a total of 352 meters to the crown, the KPT Tower will on completion be the tallest building in the country. The project adapts the glazed skin of the shaft to a unique helicoidal geometry.

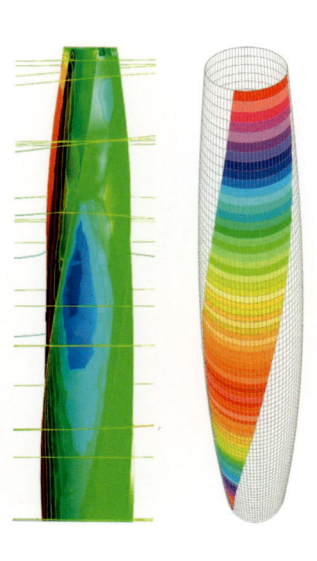

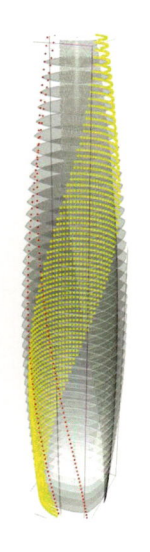

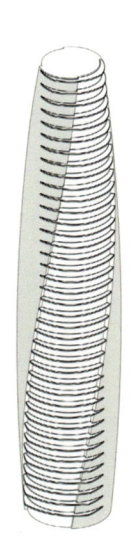

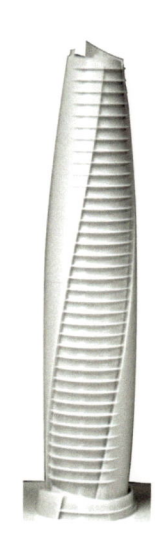

CAPITAL OF INDEPENDENT Pakistan until the building of Islamabad, Karachi remains the country's largest city both population-wise and activity-wise, and is one of the fastest growing metropolitan areas in the world. Its bustling dynamism owes much to its proximity to major shipping routes and its seaport, Pakistan's biggest and busiest. The operations of the Port of Karachi is overseen by a federal government agency called the Karachi Port Trust (KPT), which has now taken it upon itself to contribute to the current mushrooming of high-rises in what is dubbed the "City of Lights," and to do so by building some in the new business district situated in the harbor zone, on a large swath of reclaimed land that is a promising area for prime development. Intended to act as a catalyst for the total regeneration of the waterfront, the KPT Tower complex incorporates a carefully considered mix of transport, residential, civic, corporate, and retail programs.

At the center of the operation is a helical skyscraper with glazed outer skin, soaring 332 meters to the top floor and 352 to the crown, and containing 78 stories above ground and two below. Four lower monoliths arranged around a lake, with heights ranging between 84 and 134 meters, echo the main structure. The towers will provide a high-end selection of condominiums and office and retail units, and a 250-bed five-star hotel including luxury-serviced apartments and a swimming pool, all looking out to immaculate views of the Arabian Sea below and the Indian Ocean beyond. The premises will also feature a 1,200-seat convention center, an exhibition hall, and a huge underground car park.

The design takes into account that at peak time, the start of the work day, the building will have to cope with the arrival of 9,000 workers. This determined such matters as the number and position of entrances, security bays, and elevators. There are two floors of lobby, as well as double-stacked lanes for guards to check cars.

Repetition and efficiency will be instrumental in keeping the costs down, and sustainability targets will be achieved through a combination of strategies. The shading system used in the towers and their glazed surfaces and orientation are calculated to reduce energy use by up to 80 percent at peak times. The cladding design incorporates good thermal insulation and G values. And the twisting curved form of the towers deflects down-winds away from pedestrian areas at ground level.

44 Atlas: Asia and Pacific

The complex that the KPT skyscraper presides over at the seafront of a new development area in the Port of Karachi includes four lower monoliths meant for residential, commercial, and office use, besides a luxury hotel with privileged views of the Arabian Sea below and the Indian Ocean beyond. Other programs present in the project are a convention center, an exhibitions hall, and an underground car park.

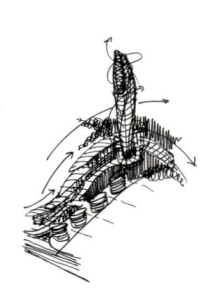

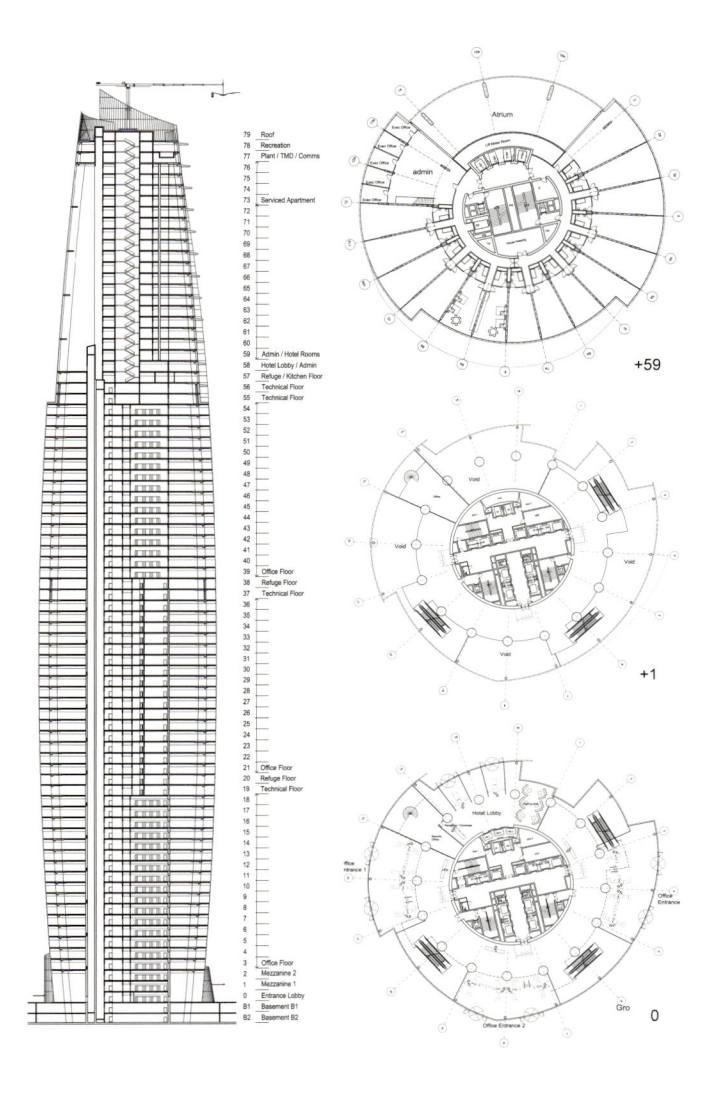

Atlas: Asia and Pacific 45

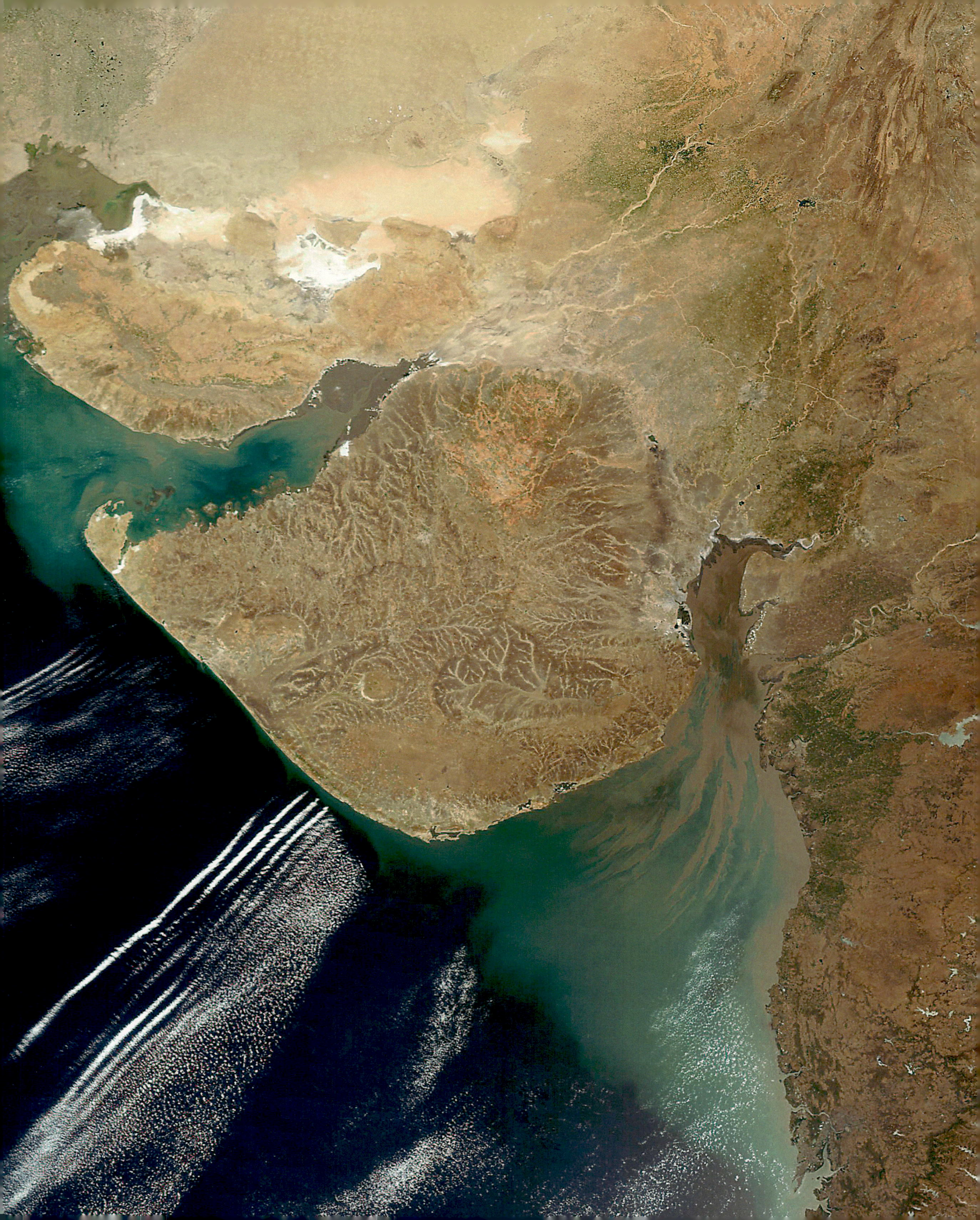

Indian Subcontinent

After the disappearance of the British Raj, the region was divided into several states, and each one of them has developed following different paths through which to face the challenges of globalization. India moves forward at a great speed without turning its back to traditional buildings methods and passive climate control systems, as can be seen in the Academy of Fashion in Jaipur by Morphogenesis, the summer house on the outskirts of Bombay by Studio Mumbai, the school in Shey by Arup or the university campus in Tuljapur by RMA. These last two illustrate the situation of the rural areas of the country, while the project for a technological park by Williams & Tsien in Bombay refers to a more urban context. The rest of the Subcontinent also pays attention to sustainability: in Bangladesh, Anna Heringer designs self-construction projects and in Sri Lanka, Richard Murphy uses vernacular ventilation methods in the new diplomatic residence of the old colonial power.

Rahul Mehrotra
Between Computers and Geomancy
India, Global Flows and Local Assertions

In its architecture, the world's second most populated country endeavors to reconcile the new global trends with its rich traditions.

With the independence of India, political priorities shifted to social issues and regional balance. The 1990s witnessed the economic liberalization of the country, and the built environment ceased to be in the government's hands.

Until 1990, the influences of western modernism and the first generation of Indian modernist architects loomed large on the architectural scene in India. However, the last twenty years have seen interesting developments, with local practitioners dominating the scene during fuzzy economic and political transitions. Starting in 1990, a particularly fascinating chapter opened in the history of architecture in India, neatly overlapping with the "on-the-ground" liberalization of the Indian economy and substantial transformations in the built landscape characterizing this process. India's economic liberalization brought out many contradictions inherent in the rapid economic mobility engulfing the country, taking a complex shape in which varying forms of architecture and built paraphernalia coexist in close proximity, creating some bizarre visual adjacencies. As the economy has opened up to the globalization process, the last four or five years have witnessed new and emerging influences as a new generation of global architectural firms are asserting their presence and influence on India's architectural scene. These firms are harbingers of new trends and shifts, growing from the confidence of global capital to be situated in India.

However, the emerging landscape is not a neat expression of this new condition, but rather a messy negotiation of multiple realities and modernities comprising the Indian landscape. In fact, this diversity has persisted in India despite dramatic transitions experienced over the centuries, particularly during the last century, when the new Indian nation transitioned out of colonial rule and embraced modernism as the vehicle to construct a national identity – to encounter modernity as well as strive toward it. This phenomenon's dual aspect not only generated a multiplicity of 'alternative modernities' in architectural expression, but also blurred the boundary between the modern and contemporary. Thus, India's emerging architectural and urban landscape is one where global flows transform the local while simultaneously being transformed by them. Local assertions adopt multiple forms, resulting in a construct of disparate and startling forms of coexistence that characterize the built environment.

Interestingly, this process of economic liberalization was preceded in previous decades by an emphasis on social resolution. Regionalism in the political landscape resulted from a series of negotiations throughout the country on issues of class, caste, and social mobility. Once the political system settled these concerns, emphasis within the political system shifted to economic integration. Indeed, addressing social integration issues was crucial to establishing the foundation for liberalizing India's economy and opening it up to embrace the forces of globalization. A crucial instrument facilitating this aspiration of wielding the Indian market as a whole was infrastructure – both physical and social. For this reason, since 2000 India has seen significant investment in infrastructure and a frenzied acceleration of physical development, although architecture has emerged as a visible manifestation of this process in only the last few years.

Ironically, although the emphasis had been to wield the nation both socially and economically, as well as through infrastructure, the 1990s saw the rapidly disappearing role of the state in the creation or influencing of the built environment and a quickly fading emphasis on a pan-Indian identity. Thus, the most significant shift in the 1990s was that of the assertion of regional identities facilitated by the fragmentation of the centralized political power structure in the country to that of a coalition of multiple regional parties. This political decentralization has impacted both on the official and privately driven production of architecture; a kind of stylistic decentralization (or regionalism) has

The development of infrastructures since the year 2000 has helped to articulate India's interior market, coinciding with political decentralization. Previously, all large-scale projects were designed for the central government, so local practitioners lacked the resources to manage these works with the competence and speed needed. This resulted in the outsourcing of this type of commission to global firms in Asia, America and Europe.

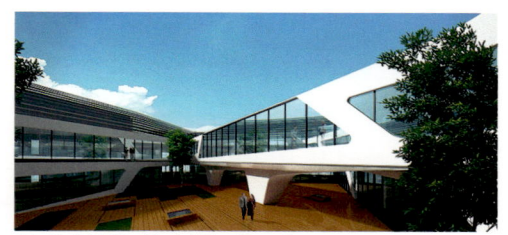

Zaha Hadid, ILPL office building, Chennai

facilitated the expression of multiple modernities that have taken on strikingly different forms. These multiple modernities have emerged due to this fundamental political and economic transformation; the form they have taken has ranged from global architectural influences to the resurrection of the faith-based practice of the ancients. The massive transformations that have occurred in the political and economic landscape have necessitated the constructions of new meanings. Thus, the new and varied form of contemporary architecture in India cannot be easily discerned when viewed using the earlier narratives of a neat and linear progression of modernism and its adaptations to the locale. This is further complicated in a democracy where local assertions are not easy resolutions, but often result in hybrids taking on unexpected forms that sometimes evoke ancient imagery and practices.

Although pluralistic responses to this transformative condition emerged, in the last few years, architectural projects that capture the imagination of both the profession and society are those resulting from the global flows as well as resisting the globalization process. Such resistance ranges from attempts to sensitize and localize global architecture with a renewed emphasis on people-centric sustainable building practices to the faith-based production of religious buildings.

Global Flows

In India today, hyper-consumption – fuelled by a rapidly growing economically mobile middle class – is resulting in the construction of a new landscape of global derivates or the images of globalization. The quantum of such architecture is increasing as globalization "hits the ground", and its tremendous impact on the profession as well society's perception of architecture is perpetuated through the media. However, architecture's limitations in these global flows are only too evident: a predictability and detachment of the built form from its ambient environment, a divorce from place and community, and an indifference to the imperatives of tectonic innovation and material resources. Such architectural production stems from the need to respond to large-scale infrastructure projects (e.g., housing, hospitals, schools, colleges, and commercial developments) resulting from the liberalization of India's economy and allowing private participation in otherwise largely government-controlled sectors. Most importantly, this form of global architecture and the practices involved in its production thrive on the competence to provide predictable and stable services for (often impatient) capital searching for a host terrain in which to invest. Consequently, design services are often outsourced to western firms perceived to be competent and well experienced in configuring global buildings – namely, those well versed in the use of new materials and technologies that meet international standards as well as facilitate the predictable value of the building's performance. This notion of design by remote and often detachment to the locale furthers – not diminishes – the value of this form of global architecture.

Historically – more accurately, since independence in 1947 – most architectural practices in India have been artesian-like practices: small-scale studio-based practices. The few large firms engaged in architectural design were deemed commercial and not seen as ideologically committed to the socialist state's nation-building agendas. Furthermore, the country's only large-scale architectural or infrastructure projects were managed by the state and run through government departments. Thus, private enterprise never engaged with large-scale architecture; the market for this did not exist until the 1990s, when the economy was liberalized and the government devolved

SOM, Chhatrapati Shivaji International Airport, Bombay (completion scheduled for 2010)

Martand Khosla, cafeteria of JMI University, Delhi (2005)

itself of the responsibility for managing and delivering projects. Consequently, large-scale firms' culture did not develop in India and the profession was ill prepared for the global corporate practice now patronized in the new global economy. The Indian practitioner's inability to respond to large-scale infrastructure with the same competency and speed of a global firm resulted in outsourcing to global firms from Singapore, America, and some parts of Europe that now command the largest share of infrastructure and large-scale building projects in India.

Weapons of Mass Construction
The nature of these projects ranges from developer-initiated housing schemes for the upper and middle classes to high-end luxury hotels, shopping malls, and master planning for large-scale township and special economic zones. However, recently, the most representative and visible projects are the information technology (IT) parks set up outside growing IT cities: Cyber-Abad in Hyderabad, Electronic City in Bangalore, and Tech Park in Chennai are good examples of these developments. Zaha Hadid's ILPL Project in Chennai, Fox & Fowle's Tech Park in Noida and Pei Cobb Freed & Partners' Wave Rock in Hyderabad are poignant examples of global flows landing on the ground as alien objects sans a reality check on the locale. Designed, crafted, and engineered in the West, they represent the impotency of global architecture (if it can be called a style) to inspire or respond to the locale. Their inefficient response to basics such as climate, light, and air, and their dogmatic use of glass make them uneconomical and unstainable propositions. However, their power lies in their ability to potently represent the power of capital and its universalizing symbolism. Thus, they serve as iconic beacons for investment in new terrains, reassuring other capital that it is safe to land there. Interestingly, developers who have a larger stake in the special economic zones or IT parks in which they are located usually underwrite these iconic buildings. In short, it is a particular nature of patronage supporting these global follies. Recent work by Indian architect Hafeez Contractor on the Infoysis campus in Mysore and the numerous Singapore-style shopping malls under construction in Bangalore, Hyderabad, Gurgaon, and Mumbai testify to this blatant and aggressive onslaught on India's terrain by these weapons of (global) mass construction.

Interestingly, other infrastructure-related projects (e.g., new airports, housing estates) are subject to greater reality checks from the locale and thus tend to become somewhat more culturally specific. Social norms, densities of occupation, and many other related aspects must be negotiated in these projects, unlike the autonomous nature of IT parks and office buildings. Airports

Morphogenesis, Pearl Academy of Fashion, Jaipur (2008)

In their works, the architects of the first generation of the global India try to reconcile their new alliances with the local background, using at the same time a more universal language. Often educated in western countries, they are well-trained in production dynamics, but their strong connection to context endows their works with a deep understanding of India's culture and traditional building processes.

Gurjit Matharoo, Prathama Blood Bank, Ahmedabad (2007)

throughout India must accommodate spatial innovation to respond to teeming crowds in departure lounges or arrival ceremonies that are still a social norm in India. These projects deal with such resistances while negotiating the fact that they are often extensions to or renewals of existing airports, intended to accommodate a functioning transition between the old and new. Adaptations evolve naturally, and these global formulae are quickly adapted and localized. Examples include the Mumbai airport (designed by SOM New York) and the Chennai, Raipur and Vadodara airports (designed by Gensler in collaboration with New York-based Fredrick Schwartz Architects). These projects, in addition to integrating responses to social conditions, appear more sensitive to their orientation, siting, and addressing of sustainable design parameters.

Other civic buildings, such as the proposed Center of Modern Art in Kolkata by Herzog & de Meuron and the International Convention Center by RMJM, encode distinct global strains while nevertheless holding to the promise to be localized in responses-albeit through material and texture. The most potent example of this negotiation of the locale is Mumbai's Banyan Park project, by Williams & Tsien. Designed as the headquarters for Tata Consulting Services, the project extends the Indian tradition of buildings located around courtyards and weaves a narrative of circulation to wield together complexly diverse programs in a wooded site. The engagement with local crafts, textures, materials, and ornaments somehow localizes these buildings while addressing a global IT program and allied services. Recognizing the labor-intensive processes of building in India, this project's buildings are being built through a prototyping process integral to the construction sequence. Naturally, this feedback loop, which potentially results in trial and error, is possible when the project is afforded the luxury of time.

In the global projects and practices described thus far, adaptation to the locale varies in direct relation to the level of impatience of the capital driving these projects. The IT parks are manifestations of the most impatient, while institutional projects, like that of the Tata Consulting Services, are the most patient and able to respond more authentically to the locale's contingencies. Such practices challenge construction norms and tradition. These buildings are built with prescriptive instructions and often in partnership with vendors who develop the palate of material via a series of negotiations involving costs, schedules, and predictability of delivery. Such projects are often on difficult ground, involving displacement and contested conversions of land uses. Their big, bold, powerfully represented plans

Kiran Ventakesh, Indian Institute of Journalism and New Media, Bangalore, Tamil Nadu (2000)

and images, together with the incisive objectivity of professionals detached from the locale, become instrumental in cutting through the thick layer of local resistance- often successfully.

Local Assertions
In a mutinous democracy like India, global flows do not effortlessly erase and remake landscapes; rather, they continually negotiate their space with the locale and are often (at least spatially) forced to occupy local fissures or contested terrains within cities or on the periphery of urban centers. Furthermore, although the most obvious terrain of global flows is preempted by the western or foreign architect, an entire landscape of architecture inspired by the spontaneous local resistance is emerging in India driven by Indian practitioners. These practitioners, while limited by their operational scale, are grappling with questions of global flows' relevance to India's social, cultural, and economic milieu.

Thus, what results from this local resistance (to the otherwise all unifying global flows of capital, building, and cultural seduction) is unique and takes on many forms, ranging from versions of a sensitized global architecture to the resurrection of faith-based reactions and the resurfacing of ancient practices and forms. Mediating these polar ends is a vital, potent in-between ground of practitioners committed to sustainability ideals – practitioners who are inspired by the locale and are highly cynical of the universalizing trends perpetuated by the ensuing forms of global flows. The single unifying factor in these disparate responses is that they are all essentially reactions to people's displacement and dislocation from the center of the architectural and development debate.

The first of these groups are practitioners who bring locale sensibilities when dealing with global architecture; they seek to resist global flows on their terms. These are usually local Indian practitioners equipped with western training but insightful about the locale. They are the inheritors of the rich tradition of modernism in India and recognize that modernism demands respect for the inherent qualities of building materials, expressiveness of structure, functional justification for form, and the subtle integration of icons and textures from the larger landscape in which it is set. They clearly see nationalism as distinct from regional concerns, which is their context. Their endeavor is to create a distinctive identity without resulting in cliques or literal nemeses. Most importantly, they aim to make globalization relevant for India in terms of the physical form it takes.

The chief patrons of this approach are public cultural institutions and private institutions (e.g., schools, resort hotels, private homes). During the 1980s and 1990s,

Bimal Patel, extension of the Indian Institute of Management, Ahmedabad, Gujarat (1987)

52 Atlas: Asia and Pacific

While the many business parks and commercial complexes 'land' on the ground without attempting to relate to it, the new institutional buildings accommodate innovative programs and offer an architectural expression of their own, heir to the rich modern tradition of India, with materials and spatial configurations taken from the local repertoire. This dialoguing approach to design challenges the global aesthetic.

Balkrishna Doshi, Charles Correa, and Raj Rewal were the forerunners of this mode. More recently, since India's economic liberalization, a new generation of architects has emerged, one who has chosen to negotiate this complex landscape of reconciliation between the local and global in new ways. Sanjay Mohe, Mathew & Gosh, Prem Chandravarkar, and Kiran Venkatesh in Bangalore, along with Bimal Patel and Gurjit Matharoo in Ahmadabad, Jacob George in Kochi, Bijoy Jain and Kapil Gupta in Mumbai, and Morphogenesis and Martand Khosla in Delhi, all belong to the first generation of architects in India's economic global era. These architects seek to reconcile their alliances to the locale while speaking a more universal language of the globalizing world. Their training (often western) equips them to understand the dynamics of production using new technologies and materials, while their rootedness in the context layers their work with a deep understanding of the culture of the place and the processes of building in India. They bring a western rigor to their buildings while demonstrating an adept negotiation of labor-intensive modes of production.

Among these architects, some push the boundaries of imagery further while others articulate more finely lessons from tradition. Sanjay Mohe's HLL Research Center, an addition to the Indian Institute of Management at Bangalore, demonstrates a deftness with which global programs can find alternate expressions using local materials, traditional space configurations, and construction processes. Similarly, Jacob George's houses in Cochin create fresh, new expressions for the hot and humid climate using steel, glass, and an array of new materials. Kapil Gupta, with his London-based partner Chris Lee, are creating an entire generation of buildings in Mumbai using cutting-edge technologies of digital fabrication while inventing new forms and programs for the city. Their work

Sanjay Mohe (Mindspace), HLL Research Center, Bangalore, Tamil Nadu (1998)

A new trend in the works built recently in India for private clients is the adoption of a language of neomodern abstraction, combining materials of industrial origin with other materials handmade by craftsmen, paying special attention to the adaptation to the climate conditions. In this way, though visually these works are in tune with the global aesthetic, their final form is the result of a careful dialogue with the place.

Prem Chandavarkar, Flower Auction Hall, Bangalore (2006)

ranges from boutiques to restaurants and office buildings. Similarly, Morphogenesis and Martand Khosala in Delhi are exploring the innovation of program and building as an intrinsically linked process. for example, in his JMI Canteen building, Khosala reconfigured the ordinary program of a cafeteria using an open Miesian-like pavilion made from industrial materials, but with an extraordinary sophistication. These architects explore the limits of standard technologies by applying them in new visions of appropriate forms. Bimal Patel's extension to the Louis Kahn Indian Institute of Management in Ahmedabad and Gurjit Mathroo's various works around Gujarat extend the modernist tradition in India of exposed reinforced concrete as well as its application to new programs. Mathroo's explorations of this material and its plastic expression for programs as varied as a crematorium to a blood bank have been refreshingly startling. Bijoy Jain's highly stylized articulation of traditional forms, rigorously using materials, expresses a struggle to find an aesthetic minimalism relevant for India. Prem Chandravarkar's flower auction hall and Kiran Ventakesh's Indian Institute of Journalism and New Media all drive to find new expression for programs emerging in the new India. These projects and practitioners all challenge global trends in that they are sensible climatic responses that use local materials and techniques, recognizing the imperatives of the local economy as it transitions to its new avatar. In short, these deeply rigorous and committed struggles resist the juggernaut of global expression.

The Return of the Sacred
At the other end of the spectrum is an emerging phenomenon perpetuating the resurfacing of ancient practices in numerous temples and an entire range of institutional buildings being built across India. In addition to being clear strains of resistance to modern identity, these trends are symbolic of the collision course religious chauvinism has with the integrative mechanisms of globalization. Communities are concerned about the threat to their identities as well as their autonomy and freedom to dissent as this phenomenon questions the basic foundations of the nation-state and its time-tested capacity to absorb influences from the world in constructing, enriching, and perpetuating its own identity.

This approach to architectural production manifests itself in two clear ways. The first is religious buildings employing ancient imagery as a natural expression of the growing fundamentalism coinciding with the globalization process. These temples are built by master craftsmen (often a hereditary position). The Global Vipassana pagoda in Mumbai (completed in 2008) and the Oneness temple (completed in 2008), the Iskcon Sai Radha Krishna temple in Bangalore (completed in 2006), and thousands of smaller temples and mosques across urban and rural India are examples of the fervor with which this counter-modernity is asserting itself on the landscape. The second manifestation of this counter-modernity is the amazing resurrection of the belief in Vastu (i.e., the sacred rules of building). Much like Feng Shui, Vastu probably had its roots in geomancy, subsequently being codified in religion. Today, specialized practitioners hold the power of interpretation and have turned it into a full-blown practice that brings a new conservatism to architecture and the innovations of form without necessarily challenging the emerging vocabulary and imagery of global identities, but rather

Jacob George, house in Cochin, Kerala (2005)

setting some rather stringent rules for its operation and thereby attempting to localize its spirit. Its representation is embedded within the imagery of global forms, making its presence subtle, yet powerful. Although Vastu's use and application are folded into or camouflaged by seemingly global forms and imagery, the icons of the ancients are visible resistance to the purity of the landscapes of global flows. Temples appear adjacent to new high-rise towers or embedded in the lobbies of shopping malls, creating an emerging hybridity particular to India.

Emerging Activisms
Located in the space between the ancient resurrections and the adaptation of global forms is an entire range of projects and practitioners that are perhaps emerging as the most potent force in the last few years. This space holds the potential to negotiate the multiple modernities that have emerged and shape a sustainable direction for new architecture in India in the coming decades. This approach reenergized itself with new vigor in the 1990s with the onslaught of globalization and the ensuing marginalization and displacement. This mode now encompasses architect activists and practitioners who have consciously chosen to be more reflective, considering the consequences of their actions and how to effectively counter global flows marginalizing both tradition and people. These practitioners enter into a potentially more fulfilling relationship with the site, with its history with the community of users whose needs they address, and with the members of the collaborating workforce.

Mainstream practitioners (both global as well as local) view this stream suspiciously because they challenge the more orthodox patterns of professional practice. These are in fact experiments in and subversions carried on at the margins of conventional practice. By choosing to operate at the boundaries of the dominant structure of capital, these practitioners made explicit moral choices in the face of globalization. They innovate in both technology and patronage; their projects are often supported or commissioned by the state, the corporate sector (trusts, foundations, and so on), or – more likely – NGOs, charitable trusts, and similar patrons. Sometimes these projects are self-generated and propositional in nature. In the same spirit, these practitioners reject certain sources of patronage, such as developers and real estate speculators, and treat with suspicion technologies of mass production (e.g., reinforced cement concrete and steel) that represent centralized capital's control of construction. These practitioners' buildings are characterized by the vigorous use of local material. The most recurring theme in this model of practice is the exploration of alternative technologies and building methods. Whether the early and seminal works of Laurie Baker in Kerala or more recent endeavors by Chitra Vishawanathan in Bangalore, Ashok Lal and Revathi Kamath in Delhi, Anupama Kundoo in Auroville, or Gerard Da Cunha in Goa, all are united to make an architecture that grows from the soil.

Yet their architecture, although robust and vigorous in its moral and ideological stance, suffers from the awkwardness of architecture in formation. Disparate elements often clumsily collide to create new hybrid forms. Not overwhelmed by issues of architectural and aesthetic concerns, these buildings are often arranged and conceived with a looseness that allows for flexibility in terms of materials and the building process. Thus, although this mode of practice seemingly extends traditions and attempts to express an economy of means, its literal visual translation often subverts rather than extends vernacular traditions and lacks the aesthetic robustness that makes the vernacular idiom timeless. In fact, their approach is not self-conscious, but rather based on community participation and the resituating of architecture from formal production processes squarely into the fabric of users' lived experiences.

The implicit thrust of this body of emerging work involves constructing new

Bijoy Jain (Studio Mumbai), Palmyra House, Nandgaon, Maharashtra (2007)

A reaction to globalizing tensions in India is the return to ancient practices like Vastu, a sacred building method (right) which has its roots, like Chinese Feng Shui, in geomancy. There has also been an increase in the number of Hindu – and also Buddhist – temples built with traditional techniques: an emphasis on materials, programs and timeless forms that can also be observed in school projects that reflect a contemporary calling.

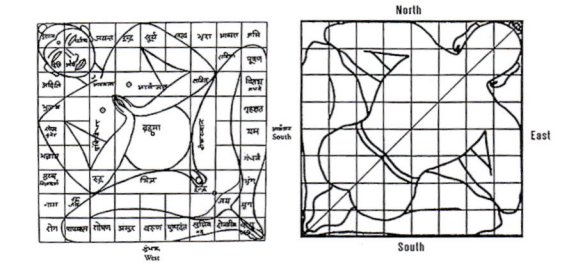

meaning around the question of sustainable design. The absence of the 'social' in discussions about sustainability in the globalizing West makes the processes triggered by this alternative mode relevant for future architectural imaginations in India. The western rating approach is an example of how the broader ecology of a building, which includes the social, is ignored in the quest to focus on the material. The LEED rating, in particular, tends to (perhaps unwittingly) create hegemony among western codes. These ratings do not lead to more ecological solutions, but provide a chemical or mechanical fix to any design problem (to meet the rating requirements). An entire green industry is developing around this in both the west and India. Discussions about sustainability in the globalizing world have also been preempted by high technology; consequently, craft – or the new craft of architecture (especially in the west) – builds on the idea of the complete disappearance of traditional crafts. However, in India's context, craft is a continuous and living tradition. These practices pointedly address this issue of craft, which is in fact celebrated in their approach.

The most potent examples of this approach are the numerous houses built by Chitra Vishanwathan across southern India using local materials, a band of trained craftsmen, and sustainable design configurations. Her success lies in the manner in which she has managed to upscale her production and replicate this approach in more than one hundred houses built in the last five years. Meanwhile, Ashok Lal in Delhi bridges the gap between the various practices emerging from this landscape of resistances. In building the Development Alternatives World Headquarters in New Delhi, he innovates technologies to create a sustainable and energy-efficient building without mechanical fixes that characterize global green architecture. Passive cooling, recycled

Chandubhai Sompura, Global Vipassana Pagoda, Bombay (2008)

Gerard Da Cunha, Nrityagram Dance Village, Bangalore (1990)

material, and shading devices are all seamlessly orchestrated in this project. In another vein, Parul and Nimsh Patel in Gujarat and Rajasthan have demonstrated the potency and continuity of India's craft tradition. Their work ranges from historic preservation to new buildings and employs craftspeople and traditional materials with an explicit view to reestablish the relevance of traditional decision-making processes in the contemporary context. The traditional craftsman becomes the central figure in the process, with the architect operating simply as a collaborator.

Thus, these practices emphasize the intimacy of the scale, a direct involvement in building, and an activist preoccupation with political and civic issues that impinge on architecture. These practitioners are an argument for architectural diversity and an acknowledgement of the differences critical to the evolution of relevant architecture. Moreover, recognizing human creativity acquires special meaning in the age of atomizing privatism. This access to a broader base of skills and concerns is particularly important in the face of globalization, which has reduced the character of the built form to a thin veneer of glamour.

Architecture of Resistance
As the world – and India, in particular – become increasingly global, we must be cautious about accepting things becoming increasingly similar as they begin to look more alike, as a superficial and formal overview of India's emerging landscape might suggest. With the influx of foreign capital and the many architectural firms that have followed, most readings of the contemporary Indian architectural scene have unfortunately locked their gaze on this narrow spectrum. However, a deeper excavation of the site, including mapping disparate forms and modes of practice, results in another view. In fact, the pluralism in the emerging landscape becomes more striking than before when differences would presumably be erased by the globalization process.

India's architecture has clearly developed its own resistances to the globalization phenomenon, creating a kaleidoscopic representation of the multiple modernities coexisting in the Indian landscape. Thus, any reading of this highly pluralistic condition in India (and perhaps all of Southeast Asia) requires a continual negotiation and mapping of differences to present a clear picture of the emerging landscape. Within India's democratic political framework, multiple aspirations express themselves in completely different ways architecturally, rather than allowing one entity to prevail and remake the landscape in its image. This intrinsic resistance to any singular force (whether global flows or political ambitions) reforming the other is what could and perhaps already does distinguish India's architecture from say China or the Middle East, where it grows from more autocratic regimes. Such architecture of resistance is born from the inherent pluralism existing in democracy, making India's contemporary architecture unique in the emerging global landscape.

Arup, Druk White Lotus School, Shey, Ladakh (2005)

Arup
Druk White Lotus School
Shey, Ladakh (India)

Client
Drukpa Trust
Architects
Arup
Collaborators
S. Macintosh, R. Reinardy, C. Sohie, J. Rose, I. Hazard, J. Fleming, M. Minami, M. Self, D. Rooney, O. Diallo, R. McGowan, F. Galeazzi, D. Richter, M. Monczakowski, I. Grace, L. Dep, J. Siddhu, N. Marlow, V. Coy.
Photos
Christian Richters

THE ANCIENT KINGDOM of Ladakh, bordered by Pakistan and Tibet, now belongs to India. Situated in the northwestern part of the country, delimited by the Indus River and the Karakoram and Himalaya mountains, the town of Shey spreads out at an altitude of 3,500 meters and is home to one of few communities that still go by traditional Buddhist beliefs. Known as 'Little Tibet', Ladakh is remote (its roads are blocked up by snow in winter), sparsely populated, and highly vulnerable to earthquakes. Extreme temperatures (very cold winters and very hot summers), intense and prolonged exposure to solar rays, and severe lack of rain paint a harsh mountain desert landscape. Through Drukpa, a British foundation, the idea of building a modern learning center for children of very remote villages, one that also catered to the specific needs of the region, materialized in this school complex for 850 pupils between the ages of four and eighteen.

Ladakh's complex geographical and cultural situation is reflected in the project design, which looks simple but addresses the needs of children who, for one, have to learn as many as four languages and alphabets (Tibetan, Hindi, Urdu, and English), in a pedagogical program following the

Situated in the midst of desert land at a high altitude, in a region known as 'Little Tibet', the school takes in almost 900 pupils in horizontal granite volumes and diaphanous classrooms rendered in wood.

The school's remote location and the reduced budget avaialble for its construction limited the range of materials to be used as well as the hiring of labor, so granite was extracted from a nearby quarry and local people, children and grown-ups alike, were called in to work. Inspired by Buddhist mandalas, the design involves a path linking the dormitories to the heart of the complex, where the classrooms and the crèche are.

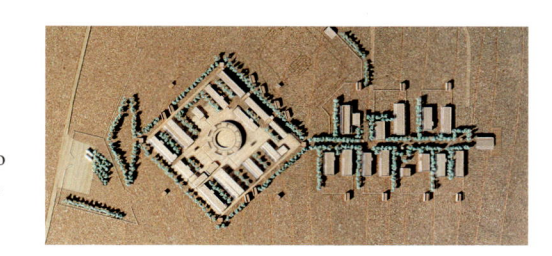

Montessori method for the early years. The design of the school is based on Buddhist mandalas, with a main zone for classrooms and flexible multi-purpose spaces. Six dormitories were added to ensure school attendance, laid out perpendicularly to a pedestrian path that connects them to the central facilities. Surrounded by a garden irrigated with recycled water, each one has a dining room, bathrooms, and several rooms that can take in eight students.

Poor accessibility and intentions to minimize impact on the environment led to the use of local materials, such as the solid blocks of granite taken from a nearby quarry for the outer walls, the adobe bricks prepared close to the site, or the wood from poplar and willow trees that is used for the joists and the roof frame, respectively. The beams and pillars made of firwood as well as the glass elements were transported to the spot from neighboring Kashmir. Elements of local building techniques were resorted to as well, such as the wooden eaves in the roof, earth-clad to insulate it from the cold and improve its overall thermal functioning. Wood is also used in the interior, both for the floors and for the large windows that abundantly give the classrooms the benefits of direct sunshine and warmth.

Among the strategies applied to capitalize on passive solar gain are the building's radiation-maximizing orientation, the functioning of the south facades as Trombe walls, and the use of solar thermal panels, which take care of heating and hot water without depending on fossil fuels. Water, a scarce resource, is saved through dry latrines with forced ventilation (by solar chimneys). The setting up of photovoltaic panels has recently been completed. Because the place is at such a high altitude and the skies here are so clear and bright, these panels suffice to generate all the electricity needed for the entire school to function.

This school, the project for which has been in process since 1997, presents several tactics for capitalizing on passive solar inputs and thereby minimizing dependence on fuels for heating classrooms. In winter the south-facing Trombe walls reinforce the solar gains obtained through the large windows situated on the same sides. In summer, the interior spaces are shielded from the sun by mobile protective devices.

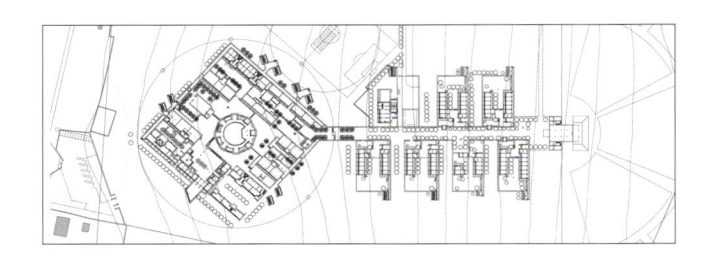

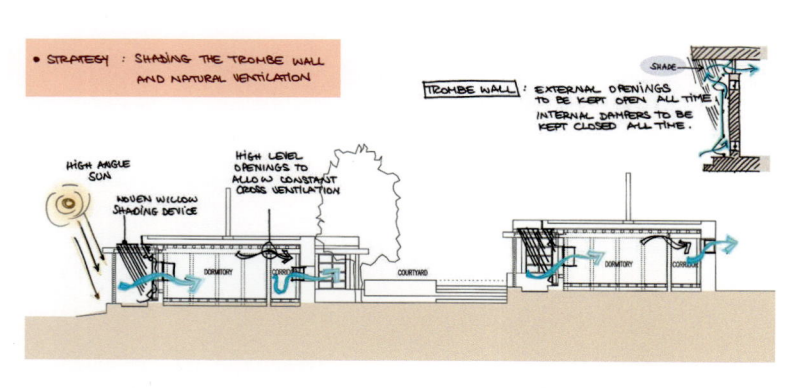

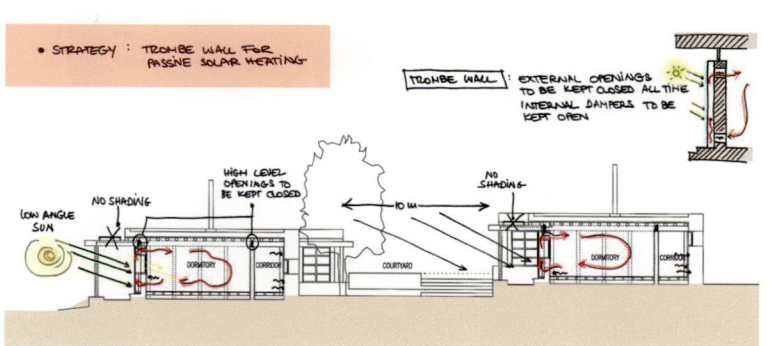

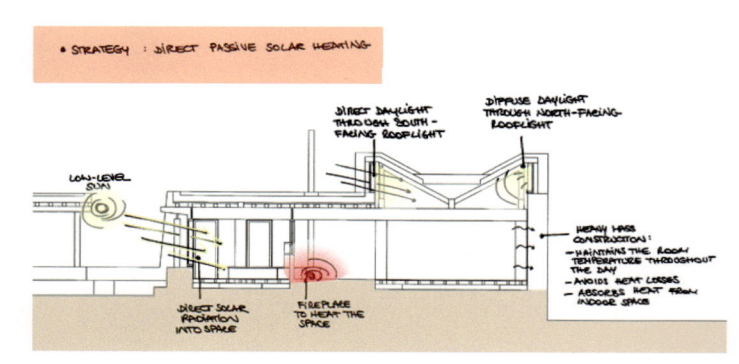

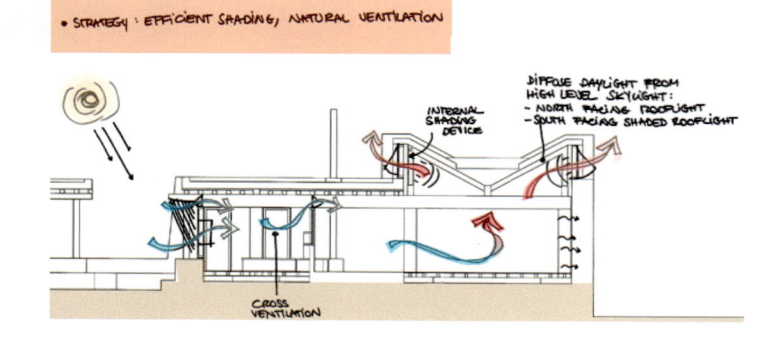

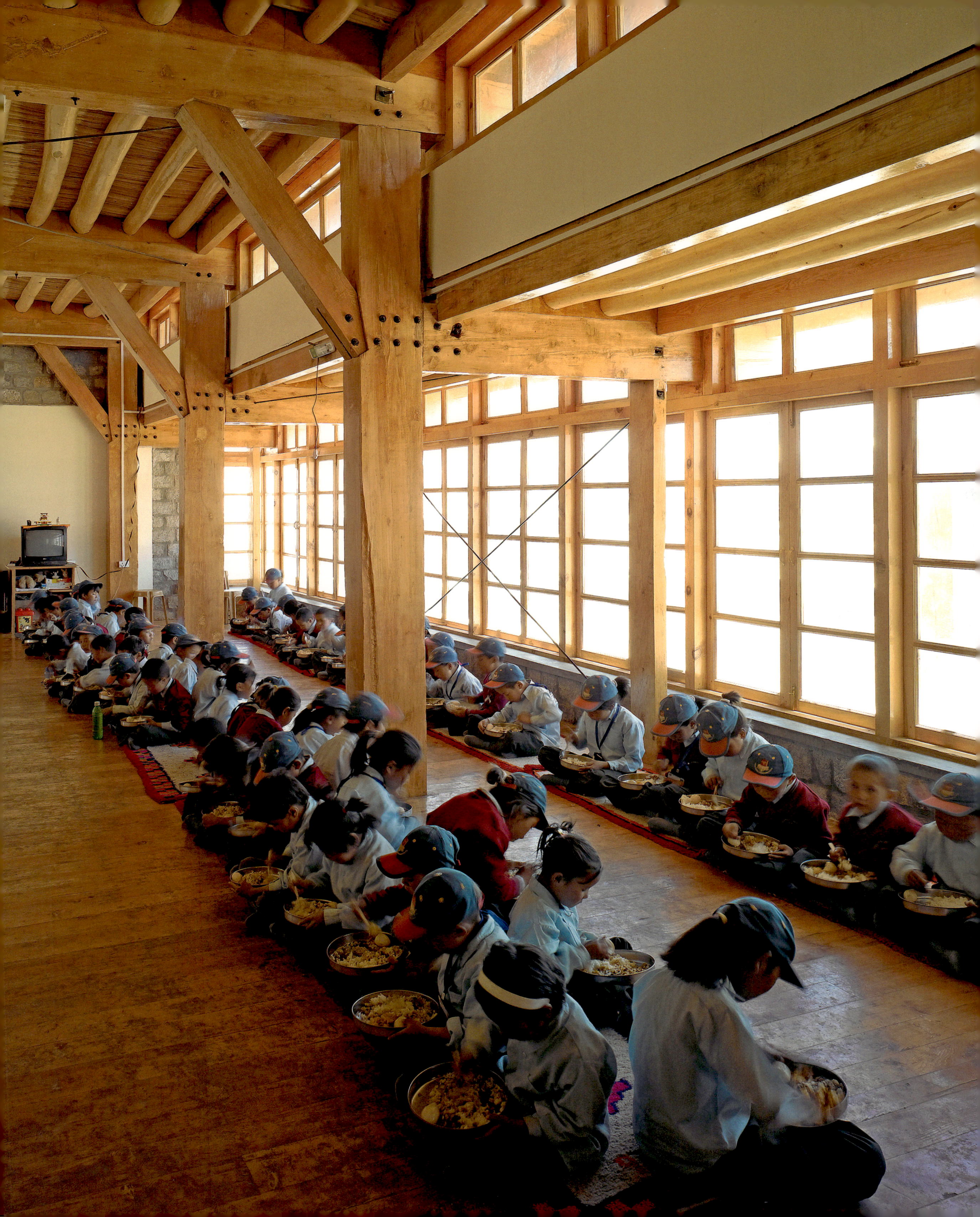

Morphogenesis
Pearl Academy of Fashion
Jaipur, Rajasthan (India)

Client
Pearl Academy of Fashion
Architects
Morphogenesis: Sonali Rastogi, Rudrajit Sabhaney, Anna Kristiana Bergbom, Shruti Dimri, John Alok Decruz
Consultants
N M Roof Designers (structure); Integral Designs (electrical); Tech Consultancy (plumbing); Design Centre (HVAC); Oracles (landscaping)
Contractor
R.G. Colonizers
Photos
Edmund Sumner/View/Album

A recreational place for students to gather in, the sinuous courtyard features a sheet of recycled water that helps to mitigate extreme temperatures, eliminating the need to resort to electrical systems.

DESIGNED TO BE a low-cost and environmentally sensitive campus, the Pearl Academy of Fashion is located in an industrial setting on the outskirts of Jaipur, the capital of Rajasthan, in a territory that is characterized by a desert climate and extreme temperatures. These severely adverse conditions presented the opportunity to incorporate passive climate control systems that would also reduce dependence on electrical devices, and so it was that the architects went on to reinterpret methods of thermal adaption used in the region, such as the *haveli,* the traditional inward-looking block with rooms along corridors that look onto inner courtyards, or the *jaali,* the stone latticework that works to reduce the impact of solar heating on the building and lets breezes flow freely.

To create the right microclimate inside the school, a double skin acts as a climate barrier. On the outside, in the manner of the *brise-soleil,* is a perforated stone screen borrowed from the local *jaali* but updated through the latest technology: the density of the perforations and the positioning of the panels were calculated through a computer program that analyzed the orientations of the facades and the shadows that would be created. Separated 1.2 meters from this outer skin, a second envelope painted an orangey ocher incorporated an inner drainpipe that through an evaporation system would keep heat from increasing excessively in the classrooms and halls.

The traditional courtyard takes on amorphous shapes within the framework of a cloister, giving rise to shaded zones that contribute to temperature control in the interior spaces and terraced wells while allowing natural lighting in the studios and workshops. The two-story volume rises over a pilotis system that generates a large half-buried space one can enter from all four sides of the building's perimeter. Serving as an exhibition and recreation venue, this space features a sheet of recycled residual water that reinforces the building's natural, evaporation-based climate control scheme. Through all these systems, the temperature inside stays steady at 27 degrees, even when it is 47 degrees outside.

The combination of local materials like stone with steel, glass, or cement has helped to reconcile climatic needs with the limited initial budget, calculated for the built 11,745 square meters at 1,400 rupees (about 20 euros) per square meter. The final product is a representative building for a school of fashion where advanced technology and a minimalist aesthetic come together, without forgetting the cultural context of its location.

The fashion school, situated in the outskirts of the Rajasthan capital, is set over the ground by means of a pilotis system, creating a half-buried space through which one can get to the inner courtyards directly. Enveloped with a perforated stone screen that acts as a climate barrier, the two-level volume of the academy is conceived as a model of sustainability adjusted to an institution with a limited budget.

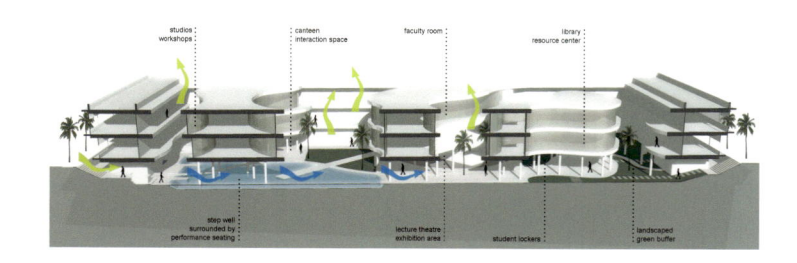

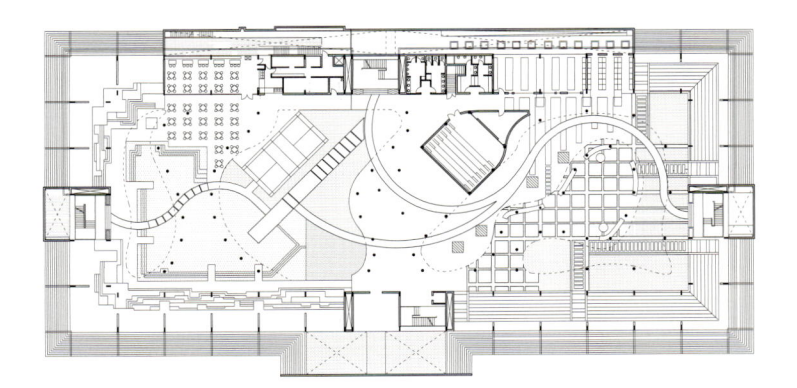

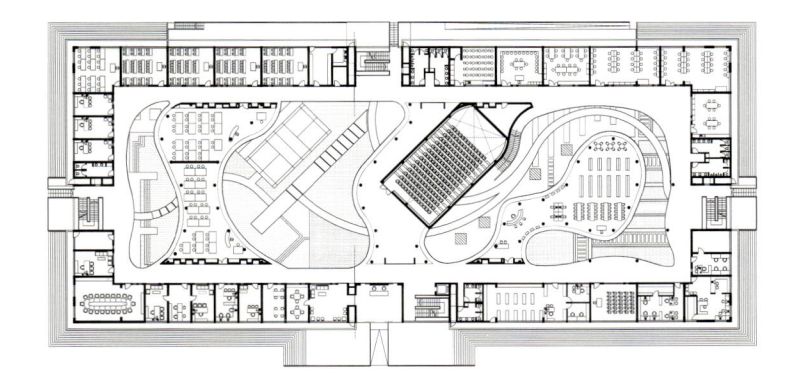

Studio Mumbai
Palmyra House
Mumbai (India)

Client
Bijoy Jain
Architects
Studio Mumbai: Bijoy Jain
Collaborators
Mangesh Mhatre, Jeevaram Suthar, Roy Katz, Samuel Barclay (project); Faheem Khan, Mohammed Nizam, Punaram Suthar, Jean Marc Moreno, Pandurang Malekar (construction)
Consultant
Faheem Khan (electricity)
Photos
Samuel Barclay;
Hélène Binet (p. 64 bottom)

In the construction of this sedate vacation house situated on the banks of the Arabian Sea, certain building systems that had long fallen into disuse in India were brought back and updated with the latest technology.

LOCATED AN HOUR away from Mumbai (formerly Bombay), the world's second most populous city with its 20 million inhabitants, the house stands on the banks of the Arabian Sea like a refuge from the hustle and bustle of the metropolis. Nestled in a dense coconut grove are two long prismatic volumes, each measuring 23 meters long and 4 meters wide, rising two floors, and stretching slightly obliquely with respect to the other. At the bissectrice of the angle they form, an 18x3.5 meter swimming pool has been laid on a platform of basalt stone, the same material used for the foundations. The structures overlook a network of wells and aqueducts, weaving this complex landscape into an inhabitable whole. With a pump and an irrigation channel, one of the wells supplies the house with water.

In a hot humid tropical climate, it is very important to trap breezes and induce air to move indoors. So the Palmyra House was clad with wooden slats and the ceilings rise as high as 5.75 meters. The living room, study, and main bedroom, along with a large bathroom and an outdoor shower, are found in the building situated more to the north, on the upper level, while the prism on the south part of the site contains the kitchen, dining room, and guest rooms. Set in the plaza between the two buildings, the pool provides a domestic channel for swimming while giving endless vistas of palm trees and the sea to the west.

The structural scheme consists of a slab of reinforced concrete resting on stone foundations, over which rises a frame of supports and beams. This skeleton is hand-prepared with traditional technology using *ain* wood, a local material resembling teakwood in color and hardness. The slats, which strike a contrast with the vertical figures of the posts, were handcrafted with the bark of trunks of palmyra, a local palm tree species. The exterior skins - miradors, cornices, and gutters - are coated with handworked copper sheets.

The interior surfaces are clad with teakwood and given a continuous finish known as Indian Patent Stone that is used in floors and walls. IPS is obtained by preparing a 30 millimeter layer of cement, sand, and gravel mixed together (proportion 1:2:4), covering it with a 10 millimeter paste of cement and sand (proportion 1:3), adding pigments, and finally polishing the result, a stucco-like surface that is decorative and resistant. The walls of the irrigation channel and the patios of the pool are built with basalt brought in from local quarries.

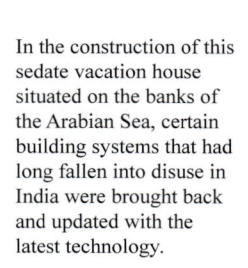

The two volumes making up this vacation house for a client who wanted a 'refuge' from the hustle and bustle of the city are laid out to dodge the many coconut trees that grow on the beach. The wooden slats that seal them allow breezes to blow through. Between them is an elongated swimming pool that gets its water from a nearby well. The three elements 'touch' ground through a platform of roughly worked basalt stone.

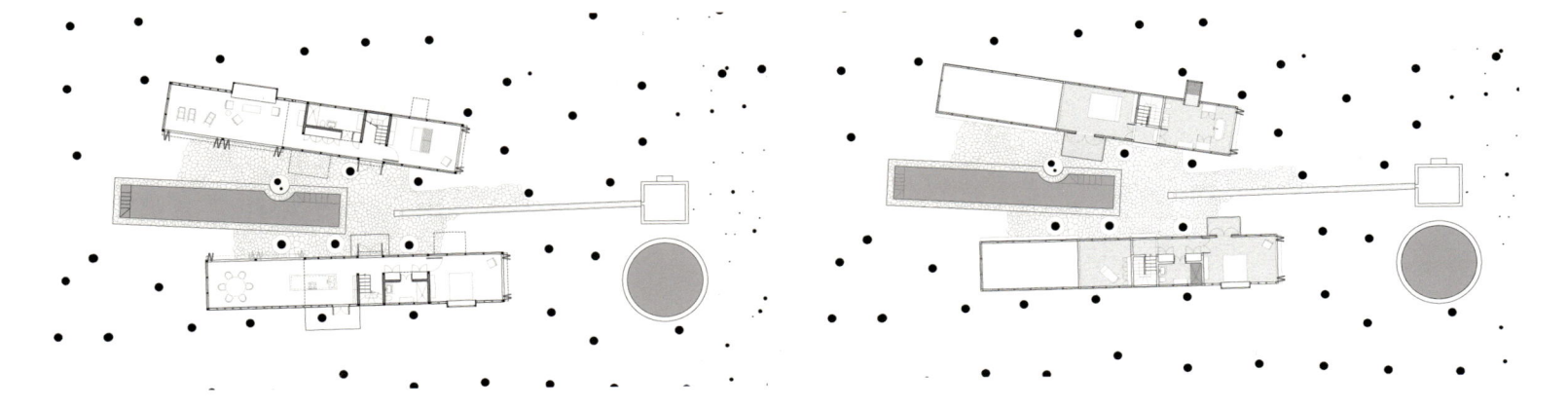

Atlas: Asia and Pacific 65

RMA
TISS University Campus
Tuljapur, Maharashtra (India)

THE TATA EMPIRE of companies, high on *noblesse oblige*, operates on its conviction that the true purpose of industry is not so much to create wealth, but to build society by generating an equitable allocation of wealth, and that this can be achieved through the education and training of young adults. Thus the Tata Institute of Social Sciences, an outgrowth of the Sir Dorabji Tata Graduate School of Social Work, founded in 1936.

Based in Mumbai, the TISS covers an extensive field of action ranging from reforestation to health and infrastructure. In line with the Tata Group's commitment to improve communities in areas where its companies are active, it decided to open a campus in a grassroots rural context. The chosen site was Tuljapur, a town situated in the dry and depressed hinterland of the Indian state of Maharashtra. Responding to the agenda and needs of the institute and to the conditions of the place, its climate included, as well as to patterns traditionally used in the region, the design of the campus masterplan focuses on creating clusters of buildings around courtyards and terraces, generating a whole interplay of open and covered spaces intended to multiply uses as well as encourage social interaction.

Client
Tata Institute of Social Sciences
Architects
RMA Architects: Rahul Mehrotra
Collaborators
Ajay Mirajgaokar; Romil Sheth; Nilesh Borker
Consultants
Scheme Consultants; N.B. Dharmadhikari; D.R. Bellare; Sunil Services; John Mechel Technologies; Structwel Engineers.
Contractors:
Khamitkar & Associates; Kruti Constructions
Photos
Rahul Mehrotra

The Tata Group's Institute of Social Sciences campus, located in a remote Indian town, is integrated into the environment through local building materials and techniques and passive cooling systems.

The so-called 'wind towers' are a simple mechanism for cooling interior spaces in hot dry climates. Of probable Persian origin, it consists of a raised tube that traps hot air from outdoors and cools it by means of a body of water situated at the top of the 'tower'; air moves down as its temperature drops, generating a breeze that contributes to a fresh feeling. The effect is then reinforced by the presence of courtyards.

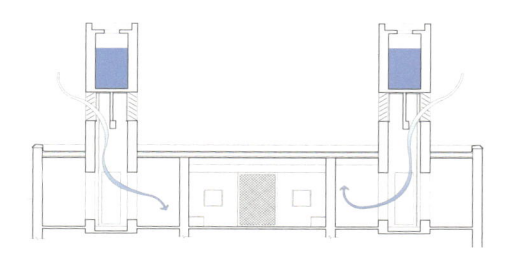

The first cluster to go up consisted of two student dormitories facing one other, for men and for women, each a prismatic volume with a square floor plan and its own inner courtyard; and on the other hand a volume containing a dining room and serving to close up the west side to help delimit a larger court with the other two buildings. The three pieces are unified externally by a wall stressing the project's overall horizontal note. Countering this image are small blocks emerging on top here and there, the 'wind towers' designed for the passive cooling of interiors.

Subsequently construction work began on the program's other elements: the actual pedagogical building containing classrooms, a book and media library, and administration; a cluster of residences, in rows, for teachers and office personnel; lodgings for guests; another housing compound for service staff; and facilities like a clinic, a daycare center, and sport installations. First to be finished were the teachers' accommodations, which present the same plinth of black basalt stone with staggered forms that marks the entrance into the campus, and the classrooms in the pedagogical building.

To make the complex blend into the environment while facilitating the building process and also reducing costs, the architects chose to resort to local materials that could be easily obtained, such as the black basalt stone used to build the load-bearing walls. For the roof, they opted for an innovative and inexpensive system revolving around vaults constructed with Ferro cement (concrete screens with steel wire meshes distributed uniformly in the transversal section), that have the capacity to support very heavy loads while saving on material. The vaults were molded and cast on site through simple techniques that could be easily performed and learned by the local youth, in the hope that similar technologies would thereafter be replicated throughout the region.

68 Atlas: Asia and Pacific

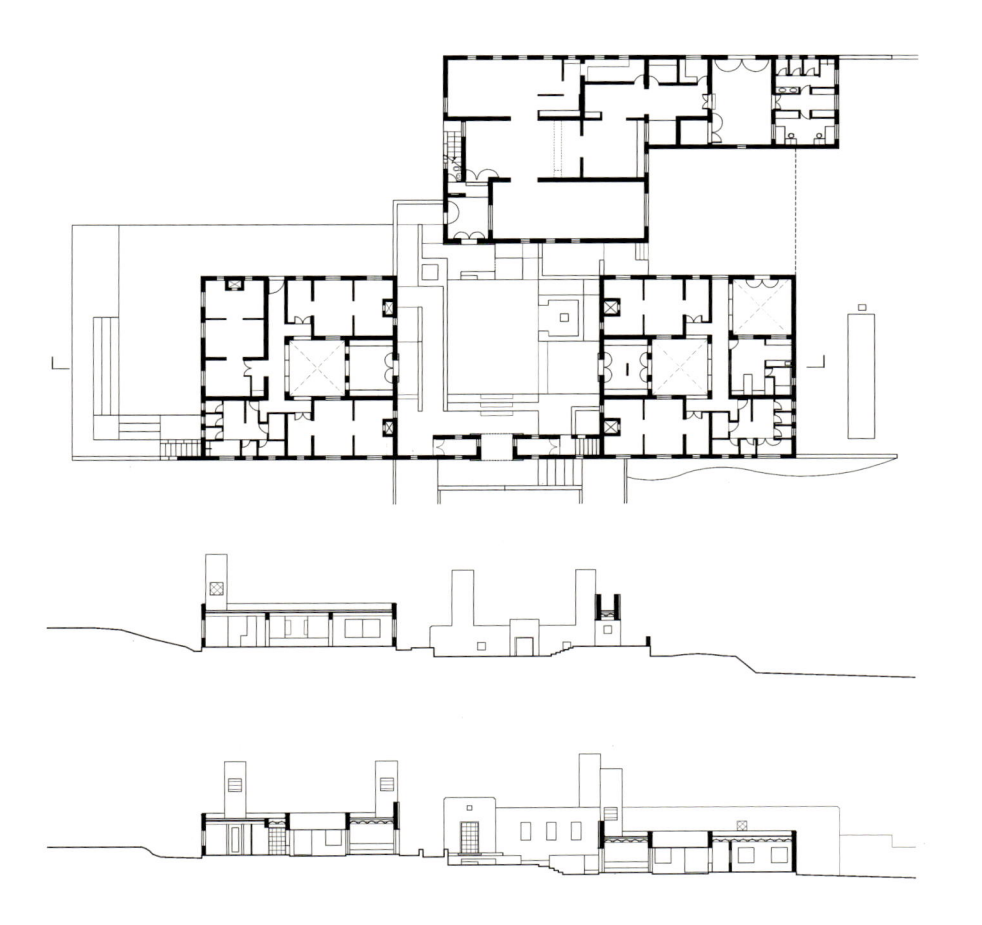

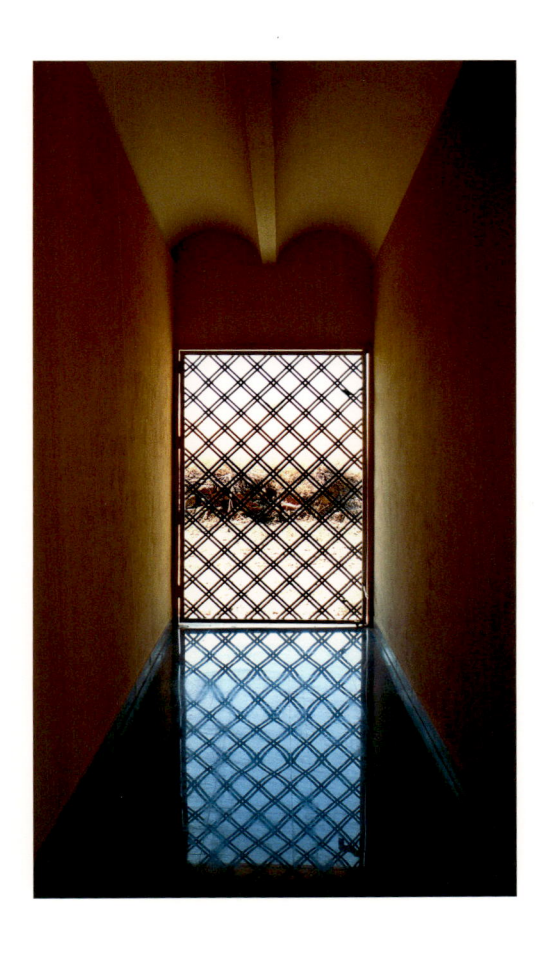

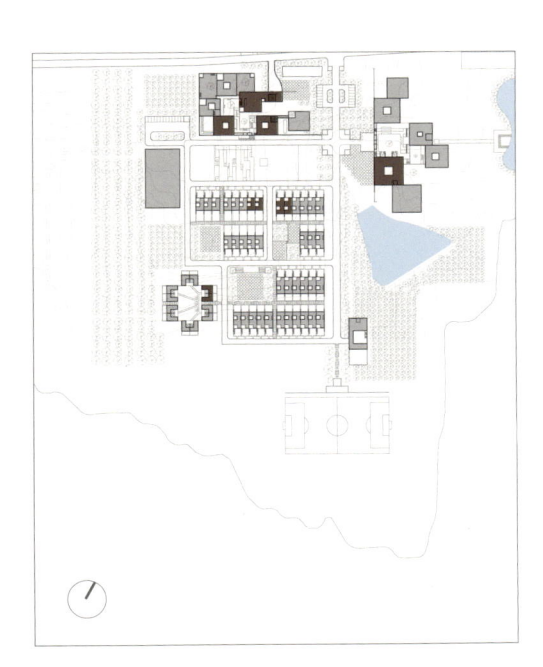

In the overall layout of the school complex, the courtyards appear as central elements in all the buildings, and also as outdoor spaces that serve to organize the way the interiors relate to one another while providing places for vegetation to grow in. The first cluster of buildings to be carried out was the one that grouped together the student accommodations and a dining room; the teachers' dwellings were next.

Atlas: Asia and Pacific **69**

Anna Heringer
DESI Building
Rudrapur, Dinajpur (Bangladesh)

Client
Dipshikha for DESI (Dipshikha Electrical Skill Improvement)
Architect
Anna Heringer with BASEhabitat, BRAC University and Dipshikha
Collaborators
Stefan Neumann, Montu Ram Saw, Shoeb Al Rahe, Khondaker Hasibul Kabir, Azit Ray
Consultants
Martin Rauch (earthbuilding); Oskar Pankraz (energy); Jakoub Schaub (solar panels)
Photos
Alexandra Grill (p. 70 above); Kurt Hoerbst (p. 70 bottom); B.K.S. Inan (p. 71)

In Bangladesh, 75% of the population lives in rural areas where dwellings are made of earth and bamboo. This project gives a village in Rudrapur two educational centers and homes for several families.

Bangladesh is a densely populated country, counting close to 176 million people, majority of whom - a good 75% - live in rural areas, in villages of houses of bamboo and earth. Although these local materials are cheap, abundant, and durable, the growing demand for housing comes with an increased demand for brick, cement, and corrugated iron sheets, which do more harm on the environment and are less in tune with the resources, conditions, and traditions of the place. To effect a sustainable development over time, five concepts were put down: save land through vertical instead of horizontal expansion; use of vernacular building materials (earth and bamboo) in techniques combining advanced techniques and traditional resources with the aim of maximizing autonomy; strengthen the local economy through the use of low-cost local materials and labor; raise comfort; reinforce local identity.

The DESI building is an innovative intepretation of the traditional Bangladeshi house. Normally, in rural areas, all domestic activities - cooking, sleeping, ablution - are assigned to separate constructions around a central courtyard. Here all functions go under one same roof, including spaces for work and teaching. The project addresses a use that is unrelated to agriculture, but nevertheless maintains a strong connection with the rural context and culture.

The building contains classrooms, two offices, and two dwellings for teachers. It has a separate block for bathrooms, and this provides two showers and two toilets for teaching staff and another restroom for students at ground level. Photovoltaic panels cover 100% of the complex's energy needs, besides feeding an engine that pumps water from a well to a deposit. A system of thermal solar panels takes care of hot water needs. The toilets operate with a two-chamber septic tank, the first time for such a plumbing system to be used in earthen constructions in Bangladesh: proof that traditional local materials and building systems are not imcompatible with the requirements of modern life.

The building show a perfect balance between high-tech and low-tech, with the most basic constructional methods combining with innovative systems of producing energy out of renewable sources. The passive heating and cooling systems utilized and the optimization of natural light and ventilation are such that the modest system of solar panels suffices to make the building self-reliant energy-wise. The project has served to train seventy craftsmen in techniques of building with earth.

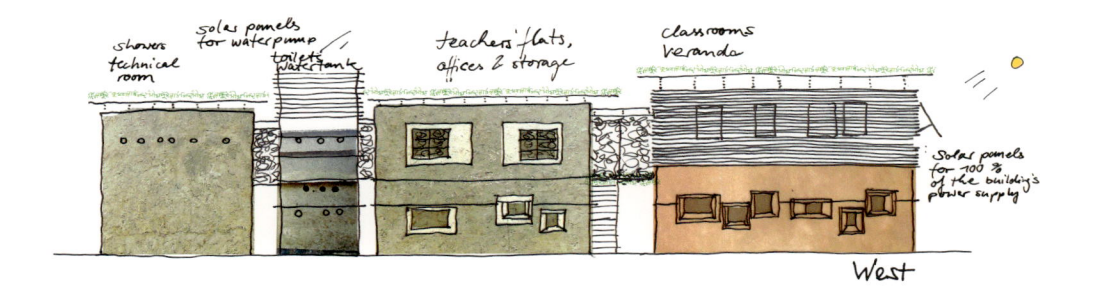

Sponsored by an NGO working for development in rural areas, the training school has two floor levels. The ground story contains a classroom with a gallery for practical classes, two offices, the students' restrooms, and the building installations. Upstairs are a second classroom and two teachers' apartments with their respective bathrooms. The novelty is the juxtaposition of traditional and modern technologies.

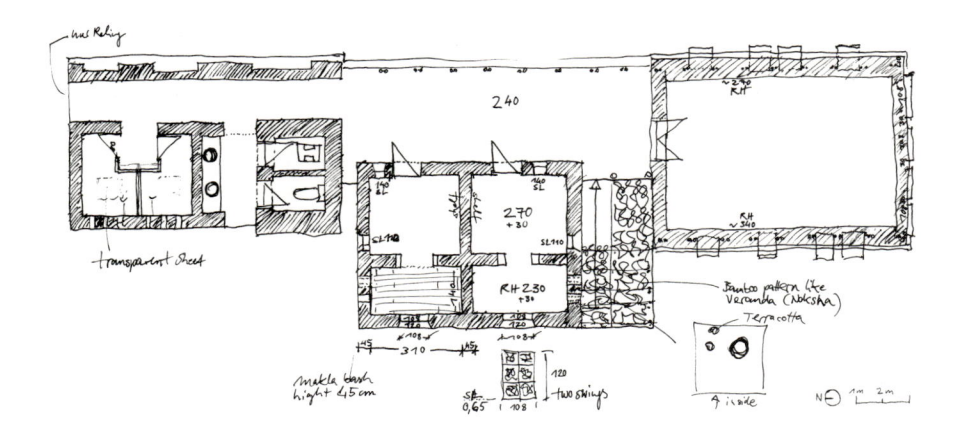

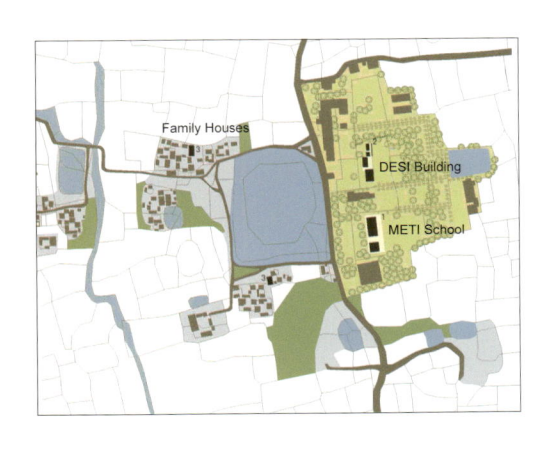

Atlas: Asia and Pacific   71

Richard Murphy
British High Commission
Colombo (Sri Lanka)

Client
British Foreign & Commonwealth Office
Architects
Richard Murphy Architects; Milroy Perera Associates (local partners)
Collaborators
Matt Bremner (project architect); Edmond Shipway (project manager and quantity surveyor);
Consultants
SKM Anthony Hunts (structure); Fulcrum (services); Speirs & Major (lighting); Gross.Max (landscaping); Summers Inman (planning supervisor)
Photos
David Morris, Matthew Bremner (p. 72 above)

The design of the embassy aims to offer pleasant and flexible work spaces within a modest architectural framework inspired by Sri Lankan culture and local materials like *kalugal* stone or coconut timber.

In the year 2001, a limited competition was held to obtain a design for the new British High Commission building in Colombo, the capital of Sri Lanka. The site was a 0.8 hectare piece of land located right next door to the High Commissioner's Residence. A High Commission today is much reduced from the popular 19th-century image. The design here is deliberately self-effacing, as befits the embassy of a former colonial power. It focuses on creating a pleasant working environment and allowing for future flexibility and rearrangement of departments. The security brief was of top concern and the building is designed against bomb threats and terrorist attacks.

There are two main entrances situated on opposite sides: a vehicular and pedestrian one leading to an inner court and *porte-cochère,* and a consular entry. Unusually for an embassy, the design is one-story. The building is arranged around several small courtyards, encouraging office workers to switch off the air conditioning, open their windows towards the courtyards, and induce a breeze through their offices by means of a thermal chimney operating down the middle of each 'leg' of the design. The glass chimney also lets in daylight, which reflects upward to the polished underside of the concrete vaulted roof structure.

The offices are laid out along an open 'spine', with departments placed in individual legs of cellular offices off the central axis. This fosters inter-staff contact and communication. The only public areas are a conference room opening onto a social functions courtyard, and the trade section with its own entrance from the foyer courtyard. A staff 'club' with a swimming pool, tennis court, garden, and crèche is found along one boundary.

The pools, fountains, and weirs are taken from traditional Sri Lankan architecture. Every courtyard has moving water in it, and the objective is to create not only a variety of landscape experiences, but also a different sound of water in each court. At night the pools are illuminated in diverse ways and the glass chimneys glow like giant lanterns along the boundary wall.

Local materials were used wherever possible, such as terracotta tiles in the roofs, coconut timber panels in the interior walls, and *kalugal* stone in the boundary walls. Splashes of color occur on inner boundary walls, a homage to Sri Lankan life in general as well as to the Mexican architect Ricardo Legorreta. The heavy roof vaults of in-situ concrete span large distances, thereby minimizing columns and maximizing flexibility in future re-partitionings.

Among the most significant elements of the project are the large thermal chimneys that were designed to induce natural breezes and thus reduce the need for air conditioning in the building. These glass chimneys also serve as skylights that allow and regulate the entrance of daylight, which is made to slide vertically up the walls of the chimneys to the polished underside of the concrete vaulted roof structure.

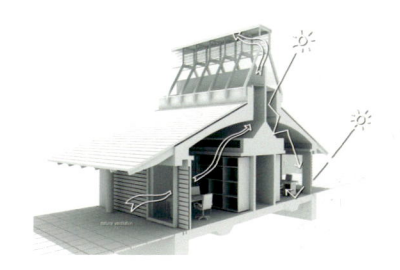

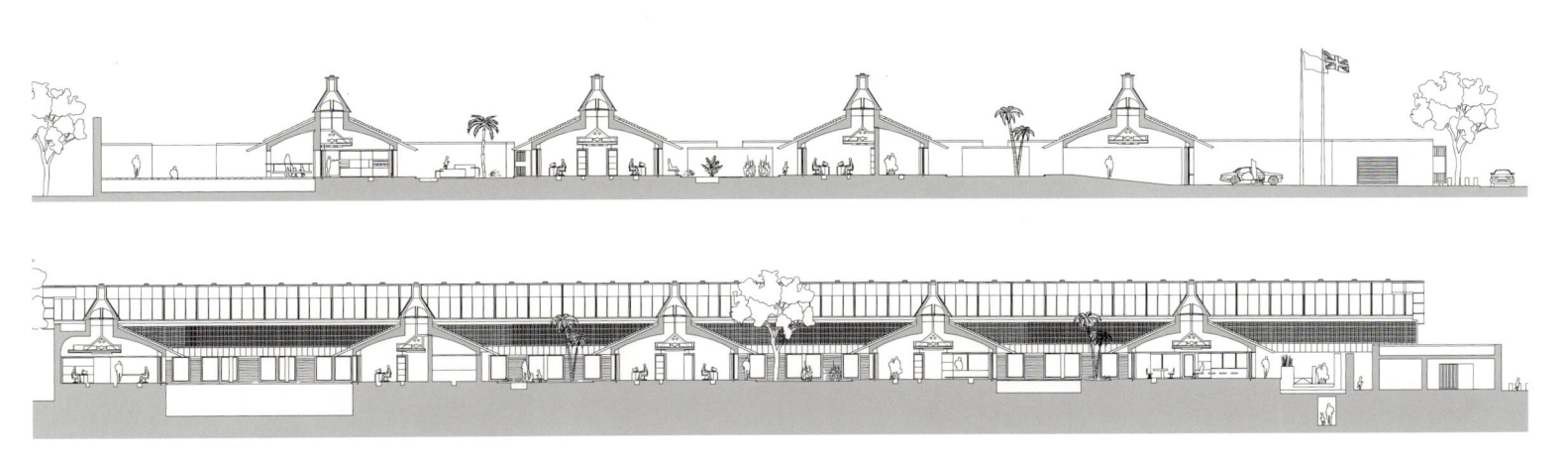

Atlas: Asia and Pacific 73

74 Atlas: Asia and Pacific

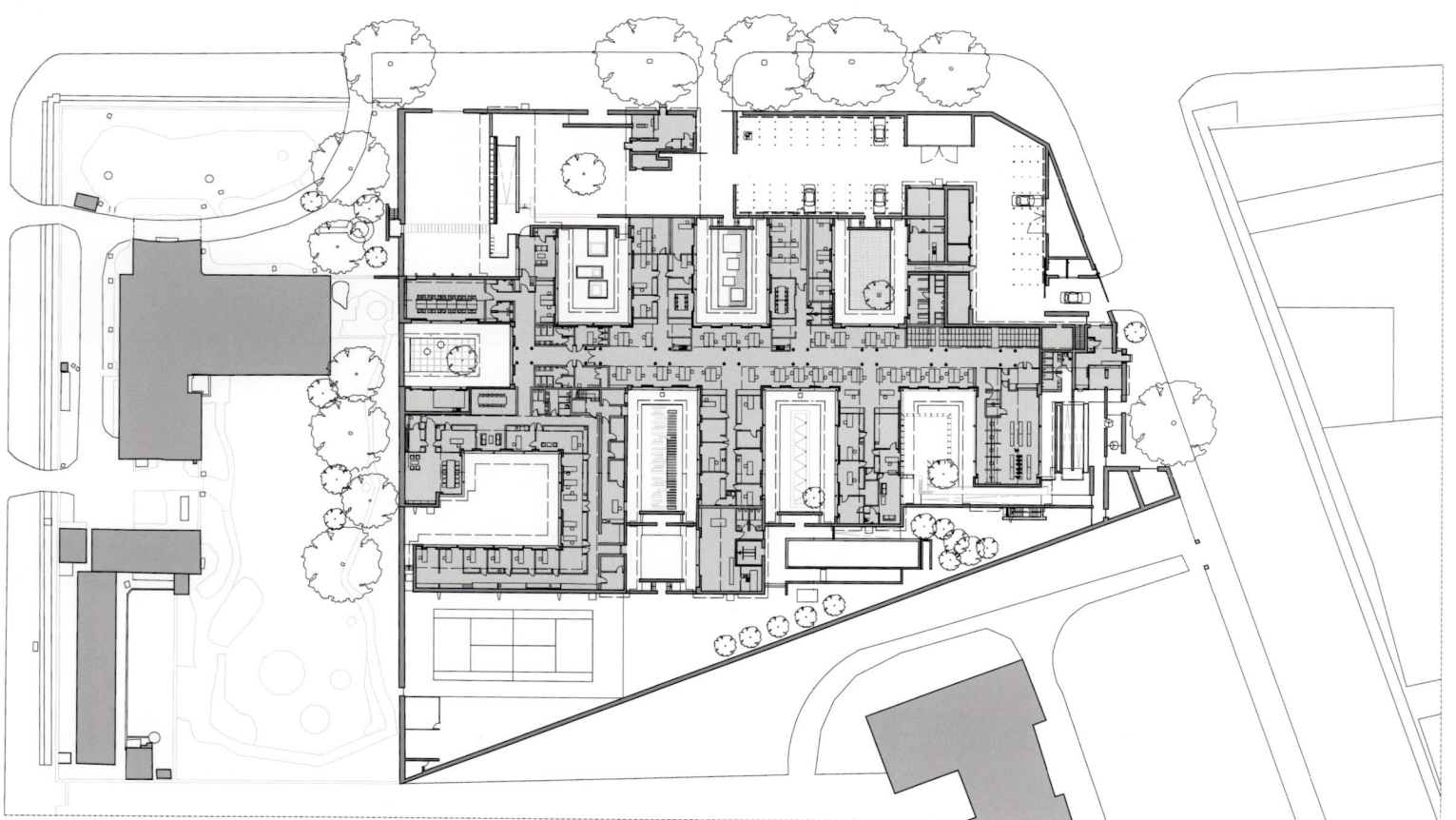

The office spaces of the embassy and consulate are distributed along a spinal axis from which 'legs' of cellular offices stick out. In between these pieces are open-air courtyards that, besides contributing to the building's ventilation and thermal conditioning, feature water elements taken from traditional Sri Lankan architecture - fountains, pools, and weirs -, giving rise to a rich variety of visual and sound experiences.

Williams & Tsien
Banyan Park
Mumbai (India)

Client
Tata Consultancy Services
Architects
Tod Williams, Billie Tsien
Collaborators
P. Schulhof, S. Chauhan (project managers); M. Bendel, A. Kim, D. Later, E. Testa (project architects); A. Andersen, B. Buck, J. Pelle, D. Lee, A. Mehta, A. Paradiso, P. Warren (project staff); Somaya & Kalappa (associate architects): B. Somaya; S. Roy Choudjury, S. (senior project architects)

THE TATA GROUP, founded in the year 1868 by the industrialist Jamsetji Tata, is India's largest private conglomerate, with interests in areas including tea, hotels, steel, automobiles, energy, communications, and information technology. Part of this empire is Tata Consultancy Services (TCS), the country's largest provider of software and business process outsourcing services.

Under construction for completion in 2012, TCS headquarters are located on a wooded site close to Mumbai International Airport, in a 'campus' that, besides offices for 2,000 people, boasts a training center, a library, a conference center, an auditorium, a recreation center, a cafeteria, and other facilities. Known as Banyan Park, with its over nine hectares it is Mumbai's largest protected parkland, home to a hundred bird and butterfly species as well as to numerous botanical specimens including the banyan, a fig that is India's national tree.

In deference to this special setting, the components of the corporate campus are kept low. Twelve buildings are connected by raised, shaded passageways that provide refuge from the region's intense heat and seasonal monsoons. Spaces are configured around exterior courtyards. Elliptical occuli in the roofs filter daylight and air down into these courtyards besides diffusing natural light into the workspaces. 'Breakout' areas situated off the hallways allow employees to engage with each other while viewing the surrounding verdant landscape.

All materials used are indigenous or manufactured in India. Concrete and local stone give a sense of permanence and mass. Other materials demonstrate India's great capacity for handiwork and crafts. A bridge at the campus entrance is clad with *jaali*, a manually perforated stone latticework screen frequent in Islamic and Indian architecture, often with patterns inspired by calligraphy and geometry. The roofs and occuli are covered in China tile mosaics. Women Weave, a non-profit organization with the double mission of empowering Indian women and keeping an Indian handloom craft alive, is making tapestries for the interiors in the tie-dye *ikat* tradition. Modern reinterpretations of these ancient techniques add character and beauty to the campus and exalt a sense of place particular to India.

The TCS corporate campus is in a park that is rich in indigenous species, and besides offices for 2,000, it will have a range of company facilities including a training center, a library, and a cafeteria.

All materials used for the construction of the corporate campus are local or manufactured in India, and in many cases the craft methods utilized are indigenous too, such as the latticework screens cladding the pedestrian bridge.- of stone sculpted in the *jaali* technique; which is then repeeated in the prefabricated concrete panels of the facades -, the tile mosaics of the occuli and roofs, or the traditional *ikat* tapestries woven for the interiors.

Atlas: Asia and Pacific 77

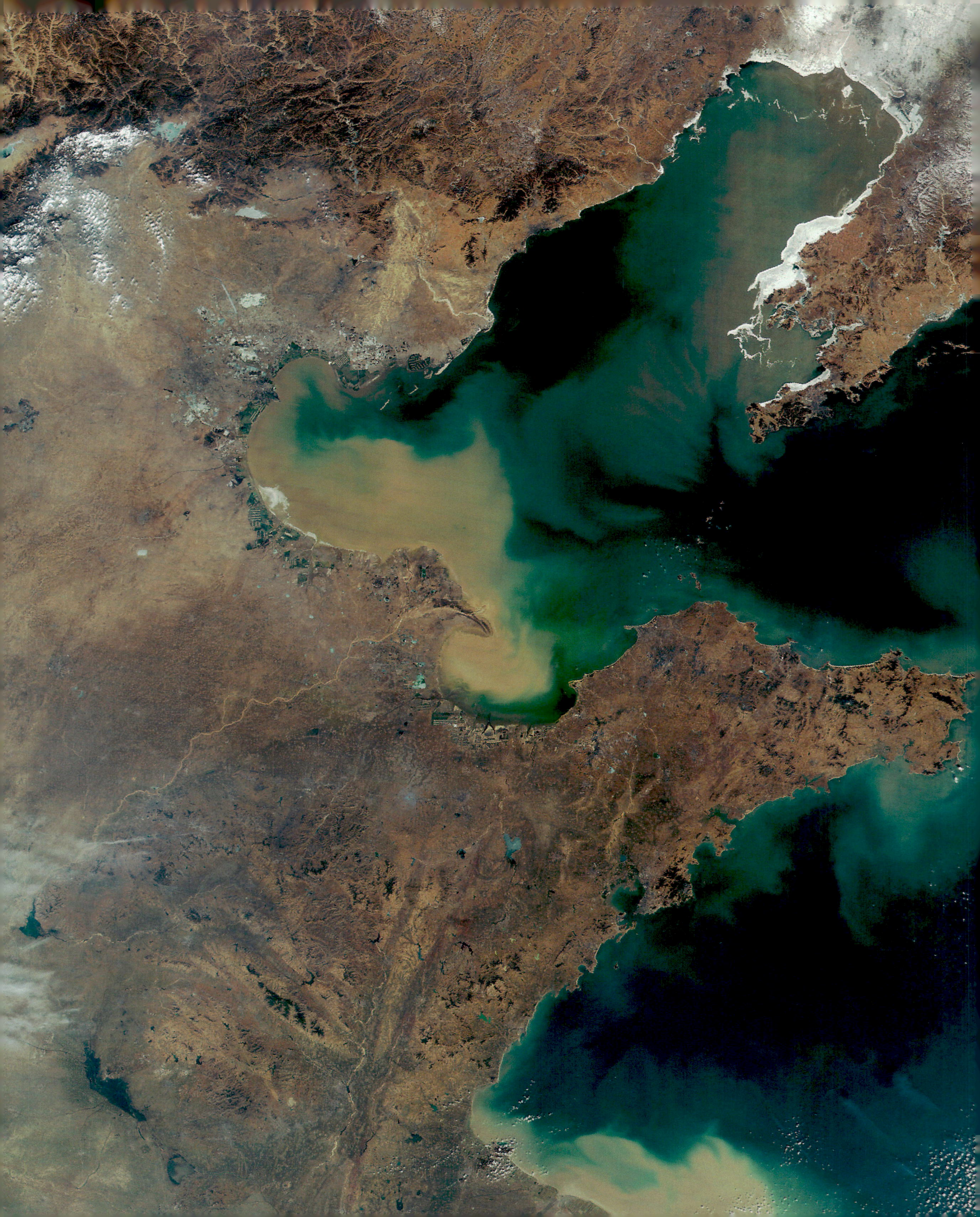

China

As the main emerging world power, China has attempted to represent its economic, political and cultural model through architecture. As soon as Beijing became the designated venue for the Olympic Games of 2008, the nation launched a colossal program of construction works. The sports event demanded new infrastructures like the Airport by Foster; facilities like the Stadium by Herzog & de Meuron or the Swimming Center by PTW; and also representative icons like the CCTV by OMA or the Grand Theater by Andreu. All this coincided with the surfacing of a generation of architects that established a dialogue both with western tradition and with their own, as can be seen in the works of Chang, Shu, Lu or Lei. The urban explosion has triggered new residential forms like the Linked Hybrid by Holl or the Ordos 100 complex by Ai Weiwei; and projects still in progress like the Opera House of Zaha Hadid or the Museum by Pei Zhu, two examples of cultural promotion.

Jianfei Zhu
A Third Path between State and Market
China, Critical Exchanges with the West

Both local and foreign architects benefit from the opportunity offered by China as laboratory of architectural and urban experimentation.

OMA/Rem Koolhaas & Ole Scheeren, CCTV Headquarters, Beijing (2009)

The artist and architect Ai Weiwei collaborated in the initial design of the National Stadium; in his works he reflects upon China's fast-paced modernization and its impact on the country's ancestral traditions.

As CHINA becomes one of the largest construction sites in the world today, three issues are arising. One concerns a 'symmetrical' exchange between China and the West. It is important to develop this observation, to capture a large picture of design practice in China and a growing international discourse on China. Both historical and geopolitical perspectives have to be employed for such an observation. The second issue concerns the position of 'critical architecture' for China and elsewhere. China and parts of Asia may have provided cases for an instrumentalist viewpoint that can lend its support to a post-critical argument as Koolhaas's studies have already attested. Yet this 'China' and 'Asia' refer to a pragmatic practice in these countries, not to the new critical 'avant-garde' I have also identified elsewhere. There are both critical and instrumental practices overlapping here in China. A crucial question therefore remains. Do we need critical architecture in China and elsewhere, in the face of a generic contemporary instrumentalism in these countries, and in the world at large with a neoliberal ideology of globalization? If the answer is yes, and if the post-critical thinking is also persuasive in transcending a negative criticality in the West, then what kind of new critical architecture should we adopt? Are there signs we can identify in China today which are relevant for the search of a different criticality?

The third issue concerns China's current politico-economic development and its likely position in the capitalist world or 'the capitalist world-system' in Immanuel Wallerstein's terms. Current observations have identified a trajectory in China that is neither 'communist' nor 'capitalist', but a third path in which the state plays a synthetic leadership which doesn't subject itself to market capitalism much promoted by the neoliberal voices, especially in the United

Herzog & de Meuron, National Stadium, Beijing (2008)

Only a few weeks after the designation of Beijing in 2001 as venue for the 2008 Olympic Games, the Chinese administration launched an ambitious plan of construction works. These included the extension of the airport, which became the world's largest building with a project in which up to 50,000 construction workers participated simultaneously; the new headquarters of China Central Television; and numerous sports facilities.

Norman Foster, Beijing Airport (2008)

States (at least before the current financial crisis). From different perspectives, Tu Wei-ming, Peter Nolan, David Harvey and Satoshi Ikeda have identified signs of a new development towards a post-capitalist world-system in which China plays an important role. What does that mean for architecture? If that implies a new ethics and cultural aspiration, what is its implication for 'critical architecture'? Can 'criticality' be recomposed to absorb not only western ideas but also those that do not postulate notions of autonomy, negation and transgression?

A Global Historical Background
According to Immanuel Wallerstein, a capitalist world-system emerged around 1450-1500 when Europe acquired the Americas as its colonies, where Europe and the Americas each assumed the position of 'core' and 'periphery' in production, economy and political domination. By the end of the 19th century, this system had expanded to cover almost the entire world with vast areas of colonies as periphery and the advanced nations as its core, in which there existed a global division of labour and a hierarchy of importance in production, finance and politico-military power. Using this theory, China around 1900 was at the periphery after many defeats, a loss of land and resources, and after being transformed into semi-colonies since 1840. In an ambivalent relation with the West or the core states, China was the victim of this aggressive capitalist modernity, yet the Chinese still looked to the West for ideas and knowledge for self-strengthening, modernization and social progress. While western architects were practicing in China, Chinese students went to study architecture in the advanced nations including Japan, the United States and countries in western Europe. What they learned was predominantly a Beaux-Arts system of design well developed in Europe before and in full swing in North America in the 1920s and 1930s. A flow of ideas and disciplinary knowledge from the West into China can be clearly identified.

Today, China appears to be moving into a core position in the world, or converging with the core States in many aspects in the world-system. The Beaux-Arts system is no longer the dominating design paradigm; design and construction are now a much internationalized enterprise. The speed and scale of urbanization in China are generating an astonishing landscape of ongoing building sites and a strange new urbanity of immense quantities.

The commitment to international practice and the need to raise profiles in the world have also attracted almost all influential architects to design in China, giving rise to an international discourse on China while some overseas architects and theorists are speculating on the implications of the development of China and Asia. With such a landscape unfolding in and around China, there appears to be a flow of images and impacts from China to the West and the world at large. Yet the flow of influence in the old direction, from the West into China, remains active in new conditions: while western and overseas architects are active in China, the Chinese students continue to flock to the classical core states, the advanced countries, to study architecture as before. What is really happening here in contemporary China? An accurate description of a crucial 'moment' is necessary, a moment I described as that of symmetry in between China and the core states, in a fluid, ongoing history that has never witnessed this moment before or after. In my argument, a moment of symmetry occurred around 2000. The interrelation between China and the West or the core states has perhaps moved on beyond this moment since new developments

Atlas: Asia and Pacific

Norman Foster, Beijing Airport (2008)

have already emerged. Yet this moment has to be grasped and recorded.

Contemporary Chinese Architecture
In the 1990s and 2000s, a major breakthrough in a local historical perspective was the arrival of a new generation of Chinese architects on the national and international stage. Educated in the post-Mao era at the universities from 1977 onwards, with teaching programs open to western and international influence, and in some cases having studied abroad in the advanced countries, and having already experimented ideas and designs before in diverse settings, these architects emerged 'suddenly' around 1996-2000, with a purist and experimental modernism based on individual research as never seen before in China. The key characteristic of these architects is their individual authorship in design, and their experiment with internal disciplinary knowledge and methods on the issues of tectonics, space and experience. In so far as their focus is upon these internal or autonomous ideas of architecture, and their intention is to challenge mainstream decorative practice in the Beaux-Arts modern tradition, its variations in the post-Mao 1980s, and its current popular and commercial tendencies, these designs are 'critical' in this historical context. The emergence of these architects is part and parcel of a social, political and economic liberalization in China in the 1980s and 1990s, the emergence of a civil society and a middle class (in relation to but increasingly distanced from a capitalist bourgeois class), and the opening of private design practice (with a registration system installed in 1994-1995). The most representative of these architects are Yung Ho Chang (Book-Bike Store, 1996), Liu Jiakun (Hedouling Studio, 1997), Wang Shu (Chenmo Studio, 1998, 'A Room with

PTW Architects, National Swimming Center; Herzog & de Meuron, National Stadium, Beijing (2008)

82 Atlas: Asia and Pacific

The night of Beijing now lights up with a number of symbolic architectures designed by foreign firms, like the emblematic Olympic Stadium, nicknamed 'the bird's nest', which rises close to the gleaming bubbles of the Swimming Center, or new large-scale icons like the dragon-shaped Airport, the ovoid dome of the National Theater or the loop-shaped skyscraper that will become the headquarters of China Central Television.

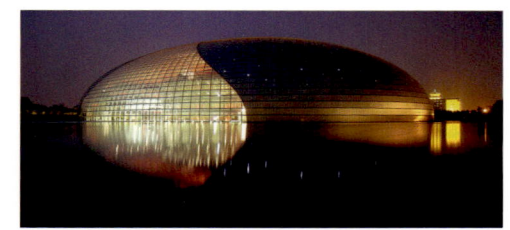

Paul Andreu, National Grand Theater of China, Beijing (2008)

a View', 2000, and Suzhou University Library, 2000), Cui Kai (Extension to Foreign Languages Press, 1999, and Convention Center of Foreign Language Press, 2004), and Qingyun Ma (Father's House, 2003, and Winding Garden of Qingpu, 2004).

Another crucial development of the 1990s and now is a 'flooding' of international participation in China or, more precisely, an emergence of a sea of interflows in design practice between Chinese and overseas architects for projects in the country. This situation turns China into a 'global' construction site in many ways: the scale of urbanization, the quantity of construction and the size of foreign direct investment (FDI) are among the largest in the world in comparison; since 1994, the FDI has increased dramatically to cover more areas of China beyond the former Special Economic Zones (SEZ). China joined the World Trade Organization and won the bid to host the 2008 Olympic Games in 2001, and the architects for the design of the major projects were selected through international competitions. These processes attracted more architects from around the world to participate in China, and also 'star' architects mostly from Europe to design prominent buildings of national significance.

Building on Three Scales

The last development identified above, the 'flooding' or the interflow of overseas and Chinese architects working alongside or together in China today, is in fact a summary description of the entire scene in the country now. To observe design thinking and practice in contemporary China, it is important to examine this sea of interflows. On the one hand there is a 'generic city' everywhere in China: a hybrid landscape of high-rises and super-blocks, of commercial

OMA/Rem Koolhaas & Ole Scheeren, CCTV Headquarters, Beijing (2009)

Atlas: Asia and Pacific

Construction in China has an intermediate scale consisting of experimental housing developments, like that of the Japanese Riken Yamamoto or of the American Steven Holl, which incorporate circulation systems between the blocks. There are also cultural centers in this same category: like the free-flowing spaces of the building in Shenzhen by Arata Isozaki, or the courtyards of the solid museum by David Chipperfield.

Arata Isozaki, Shenzhen Cultural Center (2006)

functions and large housing complexes, designed by Chinese and overseas architects. On the other hand there are buildings from earlier decades, of all qualities and with fragments of still earlier historical fabrics, coexisting in a most heterogeneous landscape at lower altitudes across the urban ground. Against this background there are three groups of influential or controversial designs, which may be clustered as large, medium and small in scale.

The first are the 'mega-buildings', those large landmark projects of municipal and national significance, such as cultural facilities in large cities and those for, or associated with, the 2008 Olympic Games in Beijing (and the World Expo in Shanghai of 2010). The clients are public, mainly city or state government or their subordinate organizations. The architects are predominantly Europeans (from the United Kingdom, France, Germany, the Netherlands and Switzerland among others). And the prominent examples include Rem Koolhaas's CCTV building, Herzog & de Meuron's National Olympic Stadium and Norman Foster's extension to Beijing Airport, with the structural engineers of Arup behind all three.

The second are the 'medium buildings', most notably cultural facilities and substantial housing developments. The clients are mixed; they can be public or private, that is, government agents or property developers. The most prominent architects come from a variety of western countries but the most noted among them are arguably the Japanese, as in the case of Riken Yamamoto's Jianwai SOHO housing towers (2003) and Arata Isozaki's Cultural Center in Shenzhen (2006).

The third are the 'small buildings', small in terms of scale and function, not impact and significance. They include offices, studios, houses and villas. The clients here are typically private. The eminent architects for these designs are Chinese and international. Among the overseas architects, the national origins are global, yet the Japanese architects (besides Korean and other Asian architects) are again amongst the influential. Kengo Kuma's designs, such as the Bamboo Wall House, which is part of the series of model villas designed for the Commune by the Great Wall, outside Beijing (2002), or his recent Z58 office in Shanghai (2006), are among the most distinctive. Another crucial example is Office dA (Mónica Ponce de León and Nader Tehrani) from Boston, with its design for a 200 square meter gatehouse in Tongzhou, outside Beijing (2004), a small project that displays rich interlays of skin and structure, material and space. The Chinese architects here are the 'breakthrough generation' identified above, and increasingly some younger architects such as Tong Ming. While the main

Riken Yamamoto, Jianwai Soho residential towers, Beijing (2003)

84 Atlas: Asia and Pacific

David Chipperfield, Liangzhu Culture Museum, Hangzhou (2007)

agendas for these Chinese architects are to express material texture, tectonics, details, space, light and experience in relation to a personal, vernacular or traditional life-world resisting modern traditions and mindless designs, the agendas of the overseas architects at this end, though operating on another level inside a western trajectory of 'deconstruction' and 'neomodernism', share the same critical interest in materiality, tectonics, space and experience. In fact, western and Japanese architects operating on larger scales, in these 'edgy' or reflective cases like Isozaki, Yamamoto, Herzog & de Meuron, and Koolhaas, remain tectonic or post-tectonic in a more radicalized form of new modernism. The common theme here is identifiable, and should be further emphasized. Another phenomena which should be noted here is that of 'group design', where architects from China, Asia and around the world are each invited to design, for example, a villa for a property developer to showcase new ideas in design and lifestyle. This is the case of the aforementioned Commune by the Great Wall for the developer SOHO China, and of the ongoing CIPEA (China International Practice Exhibition of Architecture) in Nanjing promoted by another developer. These are crucial venues for the convergence of common yet different ways of thinking amongst the Chinese and overseas architects, opening up a window for learning and observation.

These three prominent groups of designs are in fact productions of 'symbolic capital', marks of distinction in the local, national and international market. They are collaborations between the architect and the powerful client, private or public, to mark a sign of distinction or symbolic supremacy for a commercial body, a municipality, or the nation, in a competitive market and a fluid mass culture of images at different levels. At these levels, a formal capital in design is employed for the cultural, social and commercial visibility that the developers or the municipal and national bodies need. The resources offered by architects, especially their reputation and knowledge, along with the resources of the political and commercial authorities, form a joint venture that enhances the effective power of both systems. That the world's most prestigious architectural honour, the Pritzker Prize, was given to Norman Foster, to Rem Koolhaas and to Herzog & de Meuron in 1999, 2000 and 2001, who were soon the designers of China's largest national landmarks of 2008 (the airport extension, the CCTV, the National Stadium), clearly reveals this collaboration at the highest international level.

New Possibilities
This situation, however, should not prevent us from appreciating these moments of

Steven Holl, Linked Hybrid Residential Complex, Beijing (2009)

Office dA, Gatehouse, Tongxian (2003)

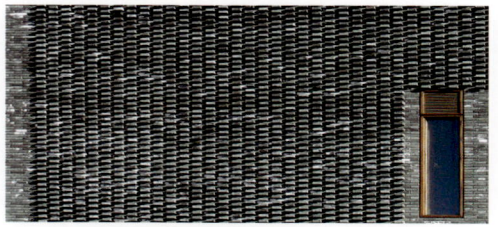

The third group of constructions in China are smaller scale buildings like houses or offices. Again, there are several foreign teams working in this category, like the Boston-based Office dA, whose work plays with texture. Moreover, collective projects like the Commune by the Great Wall or Jinhua Park bring together architects from different parts of the world to provide a stimulating variety of results.

participation and these openings of possibilities. Firstly, not all commercial and political authorities are always suppressive: they can be progressive or suppressive in a humanistic judgment, depending on the specific historical case. Against a colonized past and a highly regimented Maoist period, the post-Mao political and economic reform – in principle and in this particular history – is progressive and liberating for the Chinese nation (despite the increasing problems like the social and environmental cost, that must be dealt with as well). Secondly, there is a dialectic relationship between power and design that we cannot deny. While design serves political and commercial powers, powerful support also allows design knowledge to develop and to be materialized.

In this aspect, there is a lot of design thinking and experimentation happening in China, with architects and their ideas crossing the national borders in this sea of exchange, thanks to this politico-economic opening or support. Here we can identify primarily two currents moving in opposite directions: a flow of impact from China to the West and the world; and a flow of impact from the world and the West into China. In the first flow of influence, it seems that China as a whole asserts a certain impression upon the world and the western professional circles. Here a pragmatic attitude for efficient design and building to serve a large society in active modernization offers a window or scenario to rethink some of the established ideas in the West (after so much criticism of 'instrumental modernity'). In the opposite direction, it seems that primarily the quality design with reflexivity and radical architectural ideas of western and some Asian architects, especially the Europeans and Japanese, have had the most effect upon China. Here tectonics, purism, critical design and concerns for the public (with its social democratic values) are among the most distinctive in terms of western influence on the Chinese scene. Let me now examine the two flows of impact more closely.

From China to the West
Since *AA Files* (no. 36, 1996) and *2G* (no. 10, 1999) devoted monographs to China, there has been a stream of special issues in *A+U* (2003), *Architectural Record* (2004), *AV Monographs* (2004) and *Volume* (2006). Special exhibitions on the subject have also been staged, mostly in Europe, such as that at the Aedes of Berlin (2001), the Centre Pompidou in Paris (2003), the Netherlands Architecture Institute in Rotterdam (2006), and recently the 15th Vienna Architecture Congress at the Architekturzentrum Wien (2007). Impressive catalogues were published with these events. Forums and lectures such as that at Royal Academy of Arts in London (2006) or the previously mentioned congress in Vienna, with the show 'China Production', added unique opportunities to introduce the Chinese scene. This public discourse on China in the West and the rest of the world imparts a central impression which may be best summarized in the covers of the relevant issues of *2G,* 'Instant China', and *Architectural*

Kengo Kuma, Bamboo House, Commune by the Great Wall, Beijing (2002)

Herzog & de Meuron, Jinhua Pavilion, Jinhua (2006)

Fernando Romero, Bridge-Pavilion, Jinhua (2006)

Record, "China (…) builds with superhuman speed, reinventing its cities from the ground up", behind which were magical skylines of soaring towers. This imparts an imagination of China and also, if and when taken seriously, a window onto another reality of an instrumentalist architecture for active modernization.

The focused reflection on China by architect-theorists so far may be best exemplified by Rem Koolhaas. We can identify a sequence of statements that overlaps with observations on China and Asia in Koolhaas's writings. Here we are encountering possibly the most serious theoretical reflections in the West today on a real or effective architecture for active modernization, using China and parts of Asia as its primary archive and laboratory. In the 1995 book *S, M, L, XL,* four articles, on 'urbanism', 'bigness', 'Singapore' and 'the generic city', are particularly relevant. In 'What Ever Happened to Urbanism?', Koolhaas says that we must be dare to be 'uncritical', to accept the inevitable urbanization across the world, and to explore an inevitable design thinking that facilitates this new material condition. In the second article, Koolhaas argues that an architecture of 'bigness', with its maximum quantities, can disassociate itself from the exhausted artistic and ideological movements in western architecture, and 'regain its instrumentality as vehicle of modernization'. In the third article, Koolhaas uses Singapore as a convincing reality outside the West, to explore 'the operational' and 'city-making' in architecture, ideas that had, according to him, been long forgotten since the 1960s in the West, and that may bring us in the West back to a heroic and functioning modernism with enough magnitude and capacity for urban and socioeconomic transformation. In 'The Generic City', Koolhaas challenges the ideas of identity and regionalism in full swing in the 1980s and 1990s, and encourages a recognition of a universal modern city found everywhere, one which has been much criticized in the West, yet positively embraced in Asia ('the Generic City is largely Asian').

In *Mutations* (2000), Koolhaas publishes the speech 'Pearl River Delta', which summarizes some of the ideas behind the forthcoming book *Great Leap Forward* (2001). Koolhaas apparently provides a rationalization for a focus on Asia to possibly a western audience to which the speech was given. Koolhaas observes that modernization has its peaks of intensity in different locations, and that while it was first in Europe and then the United States, 'today, it is clear that modernization is at its most intense in Asia, in a city like Singapore or in the Pearl River Delta'. These Asian cities can teach us about what is happening now. 'To renew the architectural profession and to maintain a critical spirit, it is important to (…) observe these emergent conditions and to theorize them'. In *Great Leap Forward,* Koolhaas describes that Asia is now in a relentless process of building, on a scale unseen before, in a maelstrom of modernization that destroys existing conditions and creates a new urban substance. A new

Antonio Ochoa, Cantilever House, Commune by the Great Wall, Beijing (2002)

Atlas: Asia and Pacific **87**

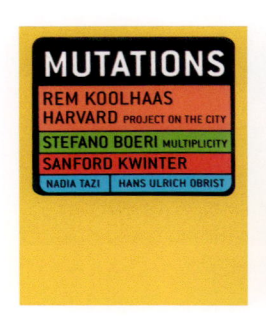

Aside from designing the loop-shaped headquarters for the National television, Rem Koolhaas centered a good part of his theoretical studies on the cities and architecture of China, gathered in several publications.

The building boom in the Asian country was followed closely by western publications, with enthusiastic covers and praise devoted to the fast execution of the works, which have changed the urban profiles day by day.

theory of urbanism and architecture is needed, and the seventy terms identified at the end of the book to describe the Pearl River Delta of China may serve as a beginning of this new theory.

This focused observation on China by the architect-theorist published in the West is then related to the third channel of influence: the actual participation of western and overseas architects in projects in China, and that are instantly reported in the West. Koolhaas of course won the competition for the new China Central Television Headquarters (CCTV) in 2002, which was completed in 2008. The commissions to western and overseas architects for stadiums, gymnasiums, grand theatres, airports, museums, expo buildings, and the less famous but more pervasive large-scale housing developments, are part of this impact upon the West that, at least implicitly, suggests an instrumentalist architecture of scale and bigness for active urbanization and modernization. Perhaps in the end the CCTV building and the National Olympic Stadium will remain as the lasting beacons for this alternative architecture of quantities engaged in social and material progress.

This trend, as best reflected in Koolhaas, has been picked up in another debate on 'post-critical' pragmatism, as argued for by Robert Somol, Sarah Whiting and Michael Speaks, and as observed by George Baird in the past few years, in a discussion that has relayed between the United States and parts of Europe (especially in the Netherlands). They have identified a discontent with the critical tradition that has controlled and exhausted the profession in the West by now, a trend towards pragmatism, of 'diagrams' and 'effects', a trend already exemplified in Koolhaas according to Somol, Whiting and Speaks. Although they have identified Koolhaas, they haven't acknowledged a geographical site or laboratory that is Asia and China in Koolhaas's thinking, or any site in terms of a real world-historical development in modernization. There are however more important issues to be raised. That these post-critical theorists haven't picked up a geographical site itself is perhaps less a problem when we confront another issue: the possibility of a new criticality emerging from this crossing onto new sites. For at a theoretical level, a central issue remains as to the composition of a new criticality to be proposed, one that may absorb post-critical arguments yet remain socially committed and progressive. If China is indeed in the grip of a most intense instrumentalism in architecture, and yet if there are indeed public and socialist ideals to safeguard and a disciplinary criticality to maintain and develop, then will there be new patterns of criticality emerging here? Are there clues and possibilities we can pick up in China as a site of theoretical reflection for the formulation of a new criticality? I will provide a preliminary discussion at the end.

From the West to China
In the opposite direction, there is also a flow of influence from the West and the world into China. Here we can identify two agents with which this impact has been realized. The first were the western and some Asian architects providing quality designs in China; the second was the Chinese 'breakthrough generation' educated in the post-Mao era, represented by Chang, Liu, Cui, Ma, Wang, among others, and that has emerged since 1996. While the first have brought western ideas into China, the second have also been agents for the transmission of western ideas as they studied in the post-Mao education system, open to international influence, and some leading members have also studied in the West.

Overseas architects here have provided 'large', 'medium' and 'small' projects such as the CCTV Headquarters by the Dutch Rem Koolhaas and Ole Scheeren, the Beijing National Stadium by the Swiss Herzog & de Meuron, the Jianwai SOHO

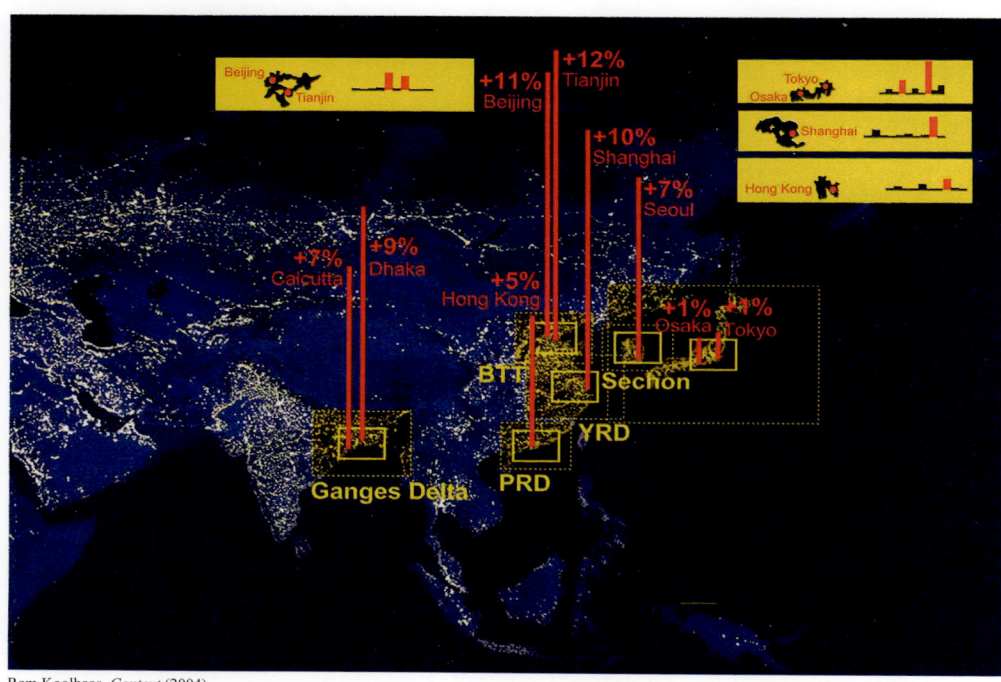

Rem Koolhaas, *Content* (2004)

88 Atlas: Asia and Pacific

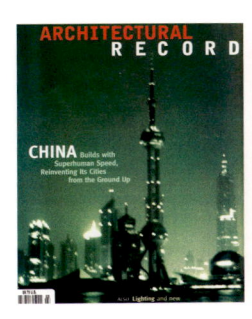

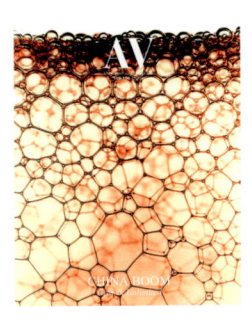

housing development by the Japanese Riken Yamamoto, the Linked Hybrid housing by the American Steven Holl, the Z58 building by Kengo Kuma, the Shenzhen Cultural Center by Arata Isozaki and the Tongzhou Gatehouse by Office dA. In the western architectural context, these architects come from a time of 'new modernism' and 'deconstruction' that attempted to transcend historicist postmodernism in the 1980s and 1990s. Their own interest in purism and tectonics, though in a more radicalized shape, coincided with the local Chinese agenda to transcend Beaux-Arts historicism and the mindless popular commercialism. The well-established critical approach with form, autonomy, authorship and reflexivity in the West has certainly been much appreciated in China by those interested in transcending the local mainstream traditions.

The second agent, the Chinese, in fact have all sorts of relations with these overseas architects, perhaps most tangibly through their works for the Commune by the Great Wall, the CIPEA, the book *Great Leap Forward* and various other collaborations. Having studied in an open education system after 1977-1978 and having studied abroad in some cases, they have made critical transgressions in China by emphasizing autonomy, tectonics and reflexive authorship. The earliest crucial examples include those emerging after 1996: Yung Ho Chang's Book-Bike-Store (1996), Morningside Mathematics Center (1998), Shizilin Villa (2004) and Jishou University (2008); Liu Jiakun's Hedouling Studio (1997) and Buddhist Sculpture Museum (2002); Cui Kai's Extension to the Main Office (1999) and Convention Center for the Foreign Language Press (2004) or his recent Desheng Up-town Office Complex (2005); Wang Shu and Lu Wengyu's Chenmo Studio (1998), the Wenzhen College Library of Suzhou University (2000), 'A Room with a View' (2000), the Xiangshan College of the China Academy of Art in Hangzhou (2005) or the Ningbo Historic Museum (2008); and Qingyun Ma's Central Commercial District of Ningbo (2002), Zhejiang University Library in Ningbo (2002), Father's House in Xian (2003), Shopping Maze of Wuxi (2003) and the Winding Garden of Qingpu (2004). New architects such as Tong Ming (Dong's House and Restaurant, Suzhou, 2004) are also emerging in recent years.

All of these architects write clearly to explain their design approach: while Chang and Ma have a stronger theoretical basis (having studied in the United States), Liu and Wang explore their ideas with a stronger reference to Chinese traditions interlaced with western concepts; lastly, Cui's writings reveal directly his working strategies in a Chinese reality of design in institutes for large clients. As for the more reflective of western methods, both Ma and Chang have a strong thematic focus for each project, although Ma seems to have a stronger urban emphasis and Chang explores more for a cultural theme in specific cases.

Chang's writings were the earliest in mounting a clear challenge to the Chinese modern traditions by using autonomy as his primary critical category. He thus represents a critical thrust of this generation at this moment. In 1998, in his article 'A Basic Architecture', Chang defends a non-discursive architecture based on a pure tectonic logic of building and its intrinsic poetic (of the steps, the columns, the walls, the openings, the skylight, the courtyard, and so on), for which he cites the works of Mies van der Rohe and Giuseppe Terragni as exemplars. In the article 'Learning from Industrial Architecture' (2002), he claims that, once meaning is removed, architecture is an entity in itself, pure and autonomous. Chang here argues for a basic architecture that is not dependent on another reality, such as a representation of a social ideology imposed from outside, but an intrinsic system on its own, one which may have the capacities to transcend the Beaux-Arts

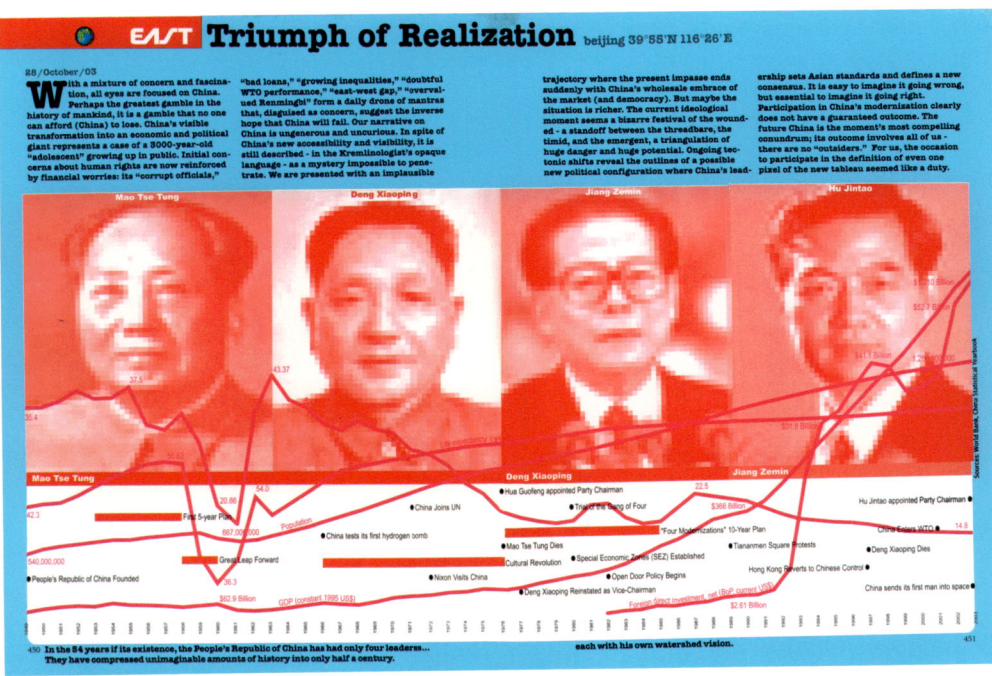

Rem Koolhaas, *Mutations* (2001)

Yung Ho Chang, Jishou University, Jishou (2008)

Cui Kai, Desheng Complex, Beijing (2005)

modern tradition in China of 'fine arts' and 'decorations' and its recent postmodern and other variations. Chang recommends the Bauhaus system as an alternative to the decorative and the 'fine arts' traditions. In his more recent writings of 2004, his 'bourgeois' and 'rightist' position for an autonomous architecture against decorative expressions of ideology in the Maoist Beaux-Arts tradition has shifted to a leftist viewpoint opposing 'bourgeois' capitalism. In 'The Third Attitude' he advocates a position that is neither a pure critical research nor a commercial practice, but a 'critical participation', and that it is important to emphasize autonomy as a means to oppose and criticize a rising capitalism. In 'The Next Decade' (2004), Chang reveals that he would combine research and service to society, focus more on urban strategies, with concerns for the public domain. Although there is a shift in the object of critique from the Beaux-Arts tradition to a new capitalist aggression in China, the emphasis on autonomy (in a critical participation) remains a central method for a reflective and critical agenda. The important development here is not so much a mature critical architecture, well-developed in China through these architects, but the emergence of a self-conscious critical intention, clearly written and well demonstrated in the works built between 1996 and 2000 and afterwards in the history of modern Chinese architecture.

A Moment of Symmetry

If we combine the two aforementioned observations, that is, if the flow of impact from China to the West, and that from the West into China, are related together as simultaneous developments occurring around 2000 in the opposite direction, a symmetrical exchange is clearly in sight. While China is absorbing a 'criticality' from the West, the West is absorbing a 'post-criticality' (or instrumentalism) from China. While the first may be best represented in the Chinese architects of Chang's generation and his writings, the second is best represented in Koolhaas and his writings. While in the first what has been absorbed in China was in surplus in the West, that is, notions of rigor, discipline, internal disciplinary knowledge, autonomy, reflexivity and critical authorship; in the second what has been acknowledged in the West was in surplus in China, that is, examples of instrumentalist architecture, built with efficacy, offering quantities and capacities, for a large society in active urbanization and modernization.

What makes this symmetrical exchange occur is a stark difference of the two worlds when they opened to each other, or when they opened to each other to such a point that an interflow between them started to occur, in the late 1990s. The stark contrast of the two made a natural exchange of energies between them, in which what is in surplus on the one side is naturally exported to the other. When the two gradually merged into a larger and hybrid whole, with new confluences and barriers emerging, the relationship is being replaced by new patterns of interaction.

It is important to note that instrumentalism in architecture, although at its most intensive now in Asia, has also occurred before in the United States and in Europe at the high time of capitalism and industrialization in the 19th and 20th century. Even at the present, post-critical thinking arises in the West due to a neoliberalism of free market economy and technological revolution occurring in these countries (but also everywhere else including Asia and China). On the other hand, criticality, though well-developed in the European tradition and more so in architecture since the 1960s in the post-modern critique of instrumental modernity, can also be found in Asia and China in the past and in its modern history (though more in the intellectual and political, rather than architectural, discourse). And even within this generation, in Chang, Ma and Cui, and particularly in Liu and Wang, Chinese intellectual sources are also actively used so that their criticality is not entirely western either. Furthermore, in terms of

Liu Jiakun, Luyeyuan Stone Sculpture Museum, Xinmin (2002)

The texture, the materials, the poetic of space and the reflection upon the vernacular styles are concerns present in the works of the latest generation of Chinese architects, who build in different scales for public and private clients: large university campuses carried out in concrete, bold museum volumes built in stone or brick, and also small and detailed single-family houses with bamboo-lined interiors.

Qingyun Ma, Father's House, Lantian

direction of impact carried out by certain 'agents', there are also new developments. While Koolhaas and the Chinese architects have been talking to the western and Chinese audience respectively, they have shifted to new audiences as well: Koolhaas engaging with the Chinese audience concerning Beijing while Ma and Chang, now teaching in the United States, are initiating new programs with 'Chinese' influences.

In the fluid history unfolding today, new trends are emerging that are surely to confuse and replace this symmetry. One of these new trends in China is an increasing interest in the indigenous Chinese intellectual and cultural traditions, and a use of this long historical resource to mount a critical architecture. This poses a new problem worth investigating: in the ongoing debate concerning the critical and the post-critical now moving across the Pacific to Asia and China, are there non-western intellectual resources to be employed for this search of a new criticality? Are there signs in China and in the discourse on China that can be identified and studied for a new formulation of criticality?

A New Critical Discourse
According to Wallerstein, the capitalist world-system has core nations, which have been shifting in membership and geographical location. This system, according to Wallerstein, though having evolved since 1450-1500 with a repeatable pattern of cycle and movement, may not survive and may go through structural change in the new environment today, given the ecological limitations of the planet. If we adopt this theory, many questions can be asked. If China is moving closer to the status of a core state, how will it relate to classical core states such as the United States? Will China bring about significant change to the world-system? And since this system may mutate significantly, in which direction will this occur and what is the likely impact China will bring about for this mutation?

David Harvey has observed that Chinese state authority, with a long-term communist commitment to social equity, has displayed determination to lead and supervise, and not subject itself to, the capitalist class in China and the flow of commerce and finance into the country from the international market dominated by the United States economy.

Peter Nolan has also identified tendencies in China to develop its own 'third way' (which is neither bourgeois-capitalist nor proletarian-communist), so that it may resolve social and ecological crises, maintain stability and relative fairness, while resisting a totally free market economy and its global practice much promoted by the United States. Nolan indicates that by making it work in China out of necessity for survival and development, China is also likely to offer a solution to capitalism at large, which always had its own contradictions long identified by Adam Smith. What China can offer is not only a few rules but a whole moral philosophy developed in its tradition. According to Nolan, China has a long tradition of a social, ethical and comprehensive 'third way', which included a pervasive yet non-ideological state, a method of enabling and controlling the market, and a moral philosophy of duty, relationship and interdependence which allows the state to supervise the market in an organic social environment.

Amateur Studio, Ningbo History Museum (2008)

Collective initiatives like the residential complex Ordos, located in the Mongolian steppes, or the Shanghai World Expo 2010, of greater dimensions and in an urban context, gather local and foreign architects and serve as a good examples of the current architectural trends and the areas of convergence a among them. Other proposals, such as that of the young studio Pei Zhu, assert their presence with voices of their own.

Pei Zhu, Art Museum of Yue Minjun, Qingcheng

Satoshi Ikeda, with his observations on China's tradition, its current performance in 'market socialism', and the world-system dominated by the US-led neoliberalism, has also made a similar observation to Nolan's. According to Ikeda, with a long tradition and with its current behavior, the Chinese state today is neither bourgeois nor proletarian; it doesn't subject itself to the command of the capital, yet is able to attract global capital and sustain growth. In this way, China may break away from the fate of other smaller Asian countries, and attain a core status outside of, or at the least not being a subordinate to, the US-led market economy. With this, there may emerge a China-led post-capitalist world-system, one which doesn't uphold neoliberalism and bourgeois ideology of free market and endless accumulation as absolute rules, one which employs a neutral and pervasive state to balance concerns of development, society and ecology, one which can secure better 'bargains' for the populations of the periphery or the 'third world' in the global politico-economic order.

The key issue here is a pervasive and non-ideological state in a Chinese tradition of organic interrelationships in social and ecological ethics, a notion that escapes western categories in social theory as developed in the past few centuries within the western world. When state, market and society are related in ways different from that found in the modern western world, then all other western categories including notions of the critical, such as 'resistance', 'transgression', 'autonomy', 'avant-garde', may not be applicable in China either if without significant modifications. Today we can identify indications of a pervasive and non-ideological state emerging in China that is neither capitalist nor communist in the classical sense. Almost all policies implemented in post-Mao China explore this new path that moves in between the apparent contradictions. If the state is pervasive and organically embedded in society, and if market economy is also organically situated in society in a subordinate relation to the state, and if cultural and critical practice is also socially embedded, then the entire composition of a critical architecture will also have to be relational, organic or embedded, rather than confrontational or oppositional. The contemporary Chinese political system is surely to evolve with more market democracy, political participation, and the effective jurisdictions introduced, yet the Chinese tradition of relational ethics, already providing a middle path through western categories and oppositions in the post-Mao era, is likely to remain and to bring about a new social system. In such a context, criticality has to be defined as a relational practice.

Glimpses of these developments can already be discerned. Amongst the Chinese architects, there has been a use of indigenous ideas for a critical architecture in this generation. Liu Jiakun and Wang Shu are exemplary in this. Wang's recent theorization of a critical project, 'thinking by hand', 'to reconstruct life-world amidst collapsing modern cities in China', employs more indigenous ideas in the intellectual tradition and patterns of a rural-urban environment from China's past. These increasing appropriations of Chinese ideas may introduce a holistic and organic viewpoint into their critical reflections.

Regarding the mode of critical practice, another three aspects must be noted. Firstly, these architects have always been working in a local Chinese manner in which a critical social positioning cannot be entirely autonomous and confrontational. The autonomy I identified above was a relative and relational autonomy. They were gaining relatively more autonomy comparing to the situations in the past, and the autonomy achieved today remain embedded and relational. A confrontational and negative criticality in the western tradition cannot be applied here in this organic social setting with its long tradition. Secondly, in both Ma and Chang's writings, one can identify a distancing from a certain western practice of a critical design opposing commercial practice. Both have said in different occasions that there was a separation between 'theory' and 'practice' in the United States, a situation the Chinese architects cannot and should not follow. What the architects should do, according to them, was a critical practice embedded in reality. Liu Jiakun has also theorized his ideas of involving with the client in planning at the earliest stage, so as to protect autonomous concerns for form and public space. Wang Shu and Cui Kai's work also displays an

MOS, residence in Ordos

92 Atlas: Asia and Pacific

Mass Studies, Pavilion of South Korea, Shanghai Expo 2010

BIG, Pavilion of Denmark, Shanghai Expo 2010

active dialogue with the client for their new or critical ideas. Thirdly, Chang in 2004 has particularly framed this as 'the Third Attitude', one which didn't separate research and practice, critique and participation, one which integrated the two in what he termed as a 'critical participation'.

If we observe conceptualizations of relevant categories in western social theory and in architecture, we do find a model of thinking based on 'confrontation' between concepts and between social positions or categories (which in turn is related to an Aristotelian tradition of confrontational dualism). For example, in Jürgen Habermas's theory of 'civil society', the concept is defined in a clear, distinctive and oppositional confrontation with 'state authority' and 'market capitalism'. For him, in order to restore a life-world of social communities and a democratic civil society, we need to establish a 'dam' to prevent the flooding or aggressive invasions of state and capital, or rational bureaucracy and market capitalism. To actually move on to promote and protect civil society (which inevitably employs aspects of capital and authority one way or another), one then has to 'corrupt' the theory somewhat, as the theory doesn't allow a more organic and relational perspective for such a compromise. In another example, Peter Eisenman's theory of the critical and the transgressive is also clear, confrontational and uncompromising: "…the critical as it concerns the possibility of knowledge was always against any accommodation with the status quo". Again this theorization itself doesn't allow a relational perspective to emerge, even though a relational 'compromise' or 'corruption' always happens when a 'critical' building, when constructed, allies with power, resources and capital one way or another. If this moment of being uncritical is internalized in a new critical project, then we have to look for a new formulation. For this, a non-western philosophical tradition may offer useful insights. According to many studies, for example in Tu Wei-ming's writings, China and East Asia are providing alternative approaches to modernity and capitalism, bringing with them organic and relational ethics found in traditional moral practice such as in Confucianism. This, in turn, is related to a general Chinese philosophy of duality represented by forces of yin and yang which are mutually related and transformative rather than exclusive and confrontational. A political consequence of this is a relational civil society in between state and society which escapes a dualist, confrontational conception of the 'public sphere' in Habermas according to a recent debate. In this tradition, state, society and market had worked in a network of social relations with formal and informal settings. More importantly, this networked and relational practice had been theorized and culturally and morally internalized in a long tradition. In such a tradition, a pervasive, benevolent, moralistic but politically non-ideological state coordinates market and society, in which a transformative thrust, a 'critique', unfolds in relation to others or other forces.

Given all these considerations, we may identify two contributions China is likely to bring about to the world. As China attains more influence, it may, as identified above in the symmetry, export an instrumentalist architecture of quantities and capacities that loosens or disentangles the rigor and restrictions of 'critical architecture' disseminated from the classical core states of the western world. This pragmatic and 'junk' architecture of magnitude may be more useful for the populations of the periphery or even the middle class and 'working people' everywhere else. Another possible contribution is a reform of the idea of the critical by bringing in a 'relational' perspective, so that the agenda is no longer critique as confrontation or negation of the opposed other, but critique as participation with and possible reform of the related other, including agents of power, capital and natural resource, in an ethical and organic universe.

EMBT, Spanish Pavilion for the Shanghai Expo 2010

Atlas: Asia and Pacific

Norman Foster
International Airport
Beijing (China)

Client
Beijing Capital International Airport
Architect
Norman Foster
Collaborators
Mouzhan Majidi; B. Timmoney; L. Law, S. Chiu, J. Parr, M. Gentz, L. Fox, R. Hawkins; M. Atkinson, J. Ball, C. Bamford, A. Chan, Y. Wei-Yang Chiu, R. Davolio, M. de Andres, R. de Castro Pereira, G. Dittrich, W. Duerrich, A. Etspueler, T. Fan, C. Foster, K. Fox, M. Gamini, G. Ho, D. Holder, D. Chun Lin, J. Luo, A. Mc Mullen, J. Nicholls, D. Picazo, S. Roche, R. Sibbe, D. Sze, P. Tang, W. Walshe, J. Wang, I. Wong, S. Woon, Z. Yu, J. W. Zhu
Consultants
BIAD (local architect); NACO (airport consultant); Arup (structural and mechanical engineers); Michel Desvigne (landscape architect); Speirs and Major (lighting); Davis Langdon (quantity surveyor); BNP (bagging handling); Logplan (APM and airport engineers); Reef (facade maintenance); Schumann Smith (technical specifications); Design Solutions (retail)
Photos
Nigel Young; Tim Griffith/Arcaid (p. 96); Iwan Baan (pp. 100-101)

JUST FOUR YEARS after the commission was formalized, the world's largest building, Terminal 3 at Beijing Capital International Airport, opened its doors. The 1.3 million square meters estimated to be used by 50 million passengers per annum were designed and completed at a frenetic pace, in just over four years, bringing together 50,000 workers at one point. Besides its incomparable size and technology, the complex also sought to be the latest in operational efficiency, passenger comfort, and sustainability.

Its function as a welcoming space, specially thought out with the athletes participating in the Beijing Olympics in mind, led the architects to address concepts like user-friendliness and upliftment. They designed a soaring aerodynamic roof and a dragon-like form that celebrate the thrill and poetry of flight. The sinuous golden roof resonates with the Forbidden City, and the interior palette of red through orange to yellow evokes the traditional colors of China while establishing a clear-cut zoning system and contributing to easy wayfinding in such an enormous airport.

Three long volumes are arranged in a line that fans out at either end to accommodate the usual arrival and departure halls. The

With its 1.3 million square meters, Terminal 3 of Beijing's airport is the world's largest building. The construction process, from the time the design was presented to its inauguration shortly before the opening of the Olympic Games of 2008, took just over four years. Such a feat came to require 50,000 workers in three daily shifts. The elongated form and the skylights on the roof that look like scales recall a Chinese dragon.

south volume embraces an oval garden, at the center of which is a fourth, hazelnut-shaped volume. This is the so-called GTC (Ground Transportation Center), the train station that connects the airport to the city center. Although the terminal's length from north to south is over three kilometers, the visual links between the three elements are maintained. Along the central axis lies a courtyard flanked by a sequence of red pillars that continues along the external edges of the building, in evocation of traditional Chinese temples.

In a single, sweeping welcome gesture, the terminal's curved cantilever embraces people arriving by road or from the GTC. The welcome concept continues inside with the arrivals area placed on the upper level, allowing newly-landed visitors to experience the space from the best vantage point. The roof is a steel space frame with colored metal decking and triangular perforations. It curves, raising at its midpoint to create a cathedral-like space, and tapering towards the edges of the building.

The terminal incorporates a range of passive energy-saving concepts like south-east orientated skylights and an integrated environmental-control system that minimizes energy consumption and carbon emissions.

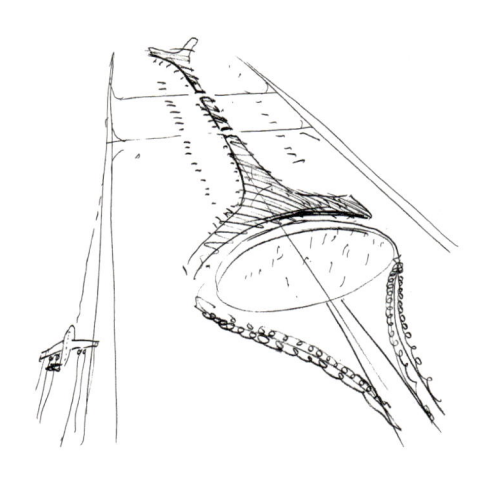

Atlas: Asia and Pacific 95

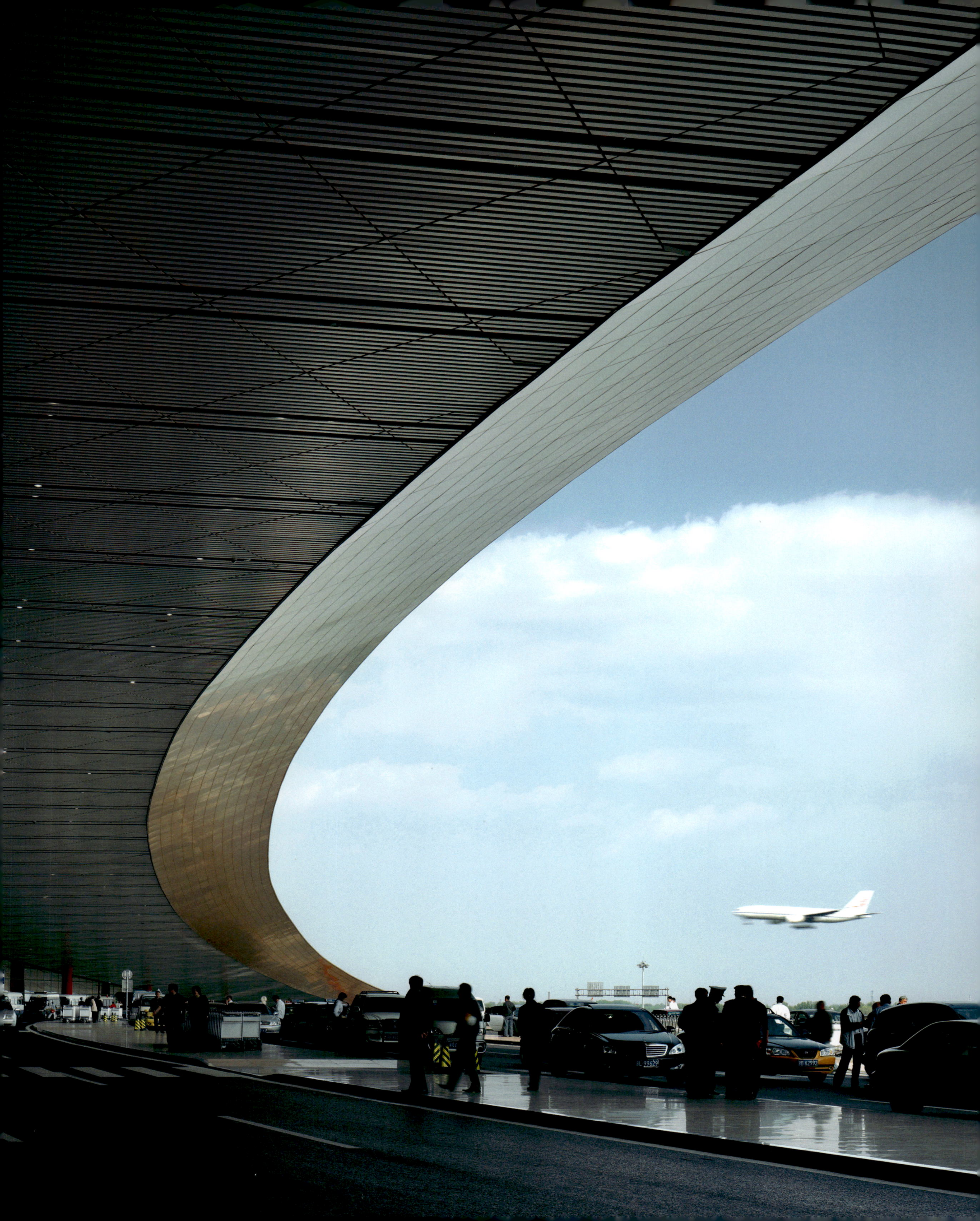

+3

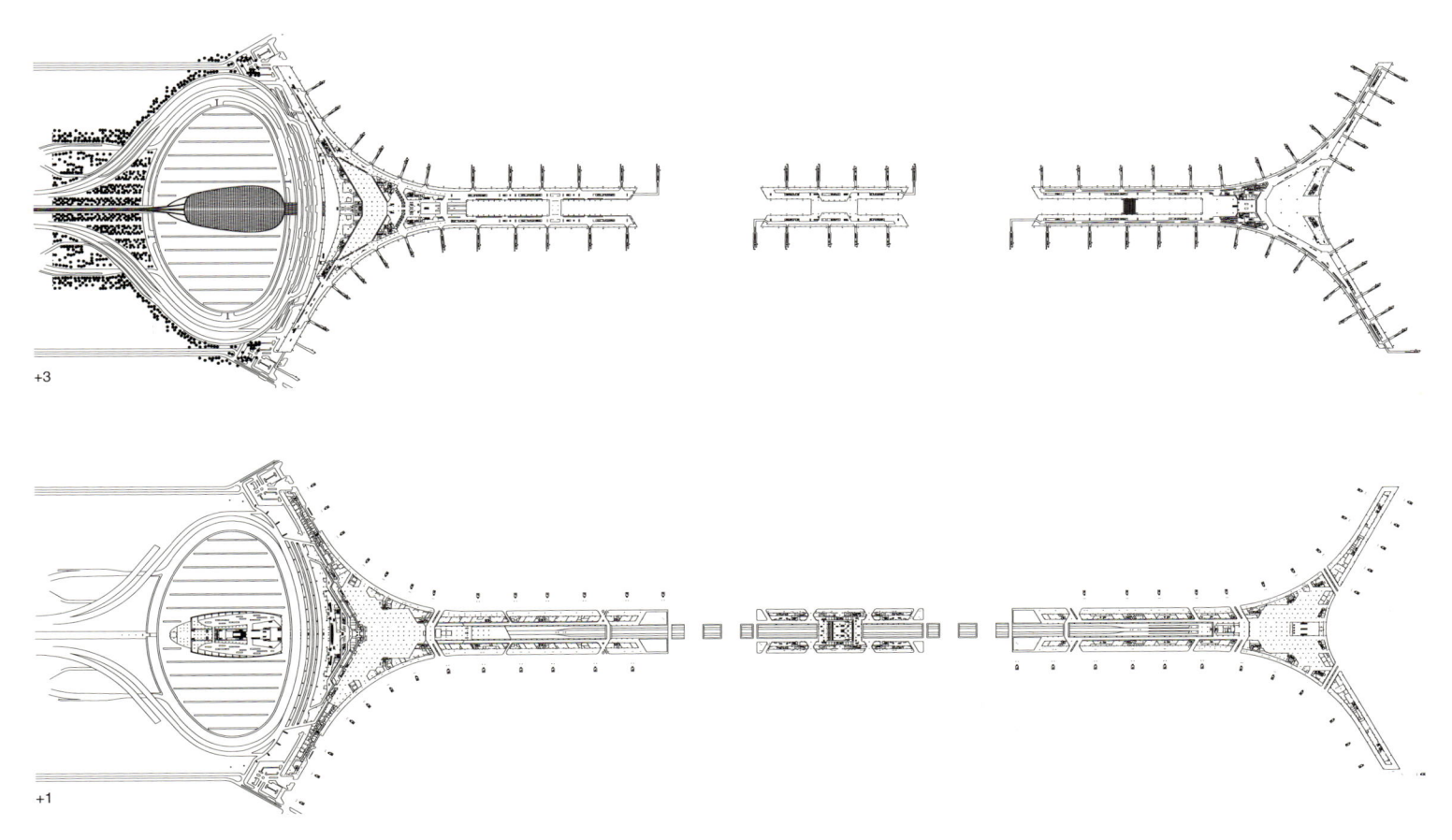

+1

Atlas: Asia and Pacific

The building consists of three elongated volumes that together form an axis stretching over three kilometers, along which as many as 58 docking bays are situated. The far ends of the terminal open up like a fan to accommodate the arrival and deparure halls, which receive natural light in abundance thanks to the east-facing triangulated skylights. Transport systems for movement within the terminal flow along the central axis.

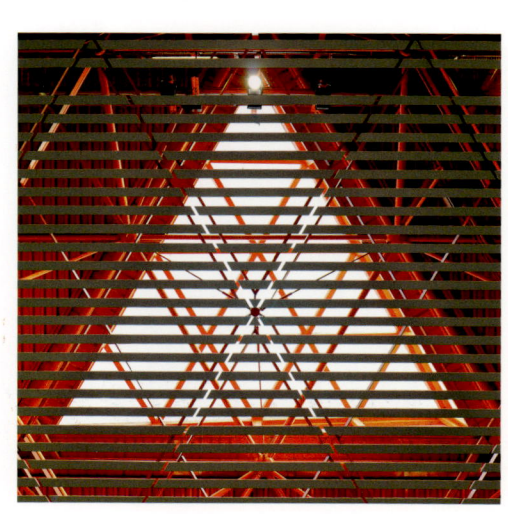

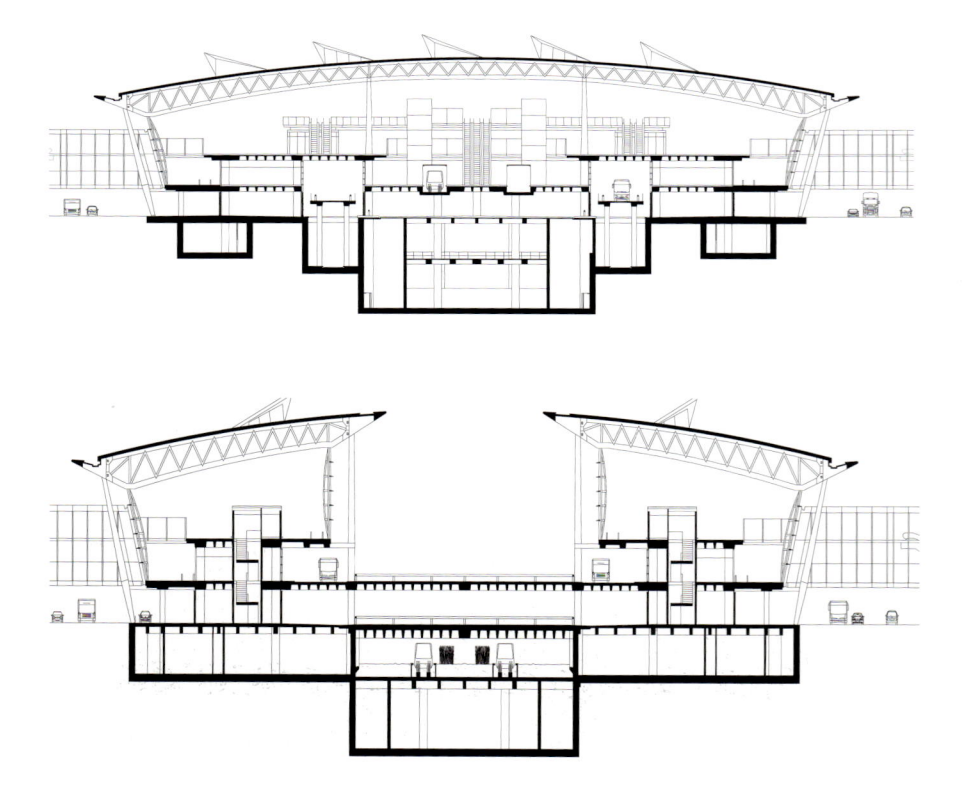

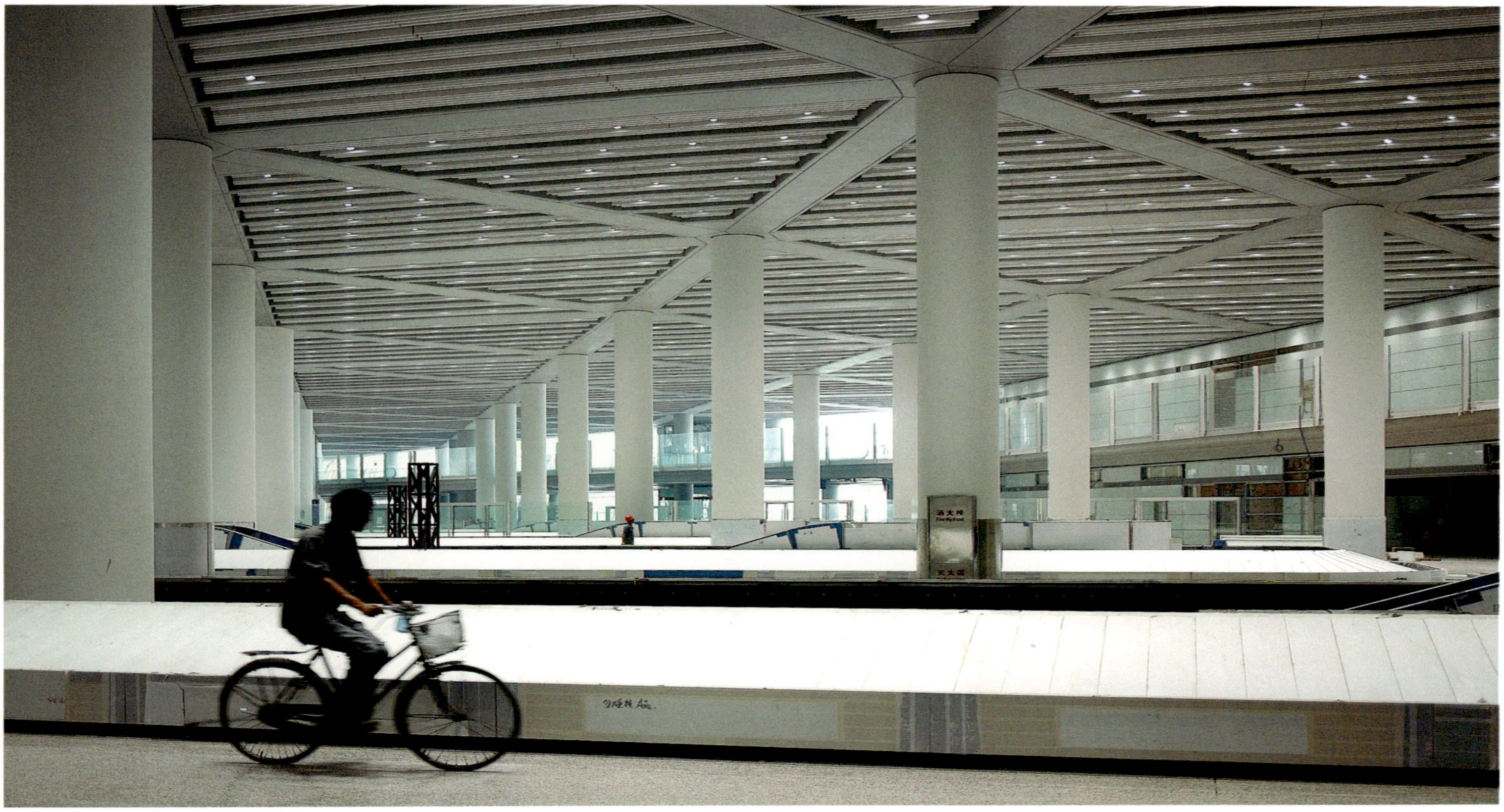

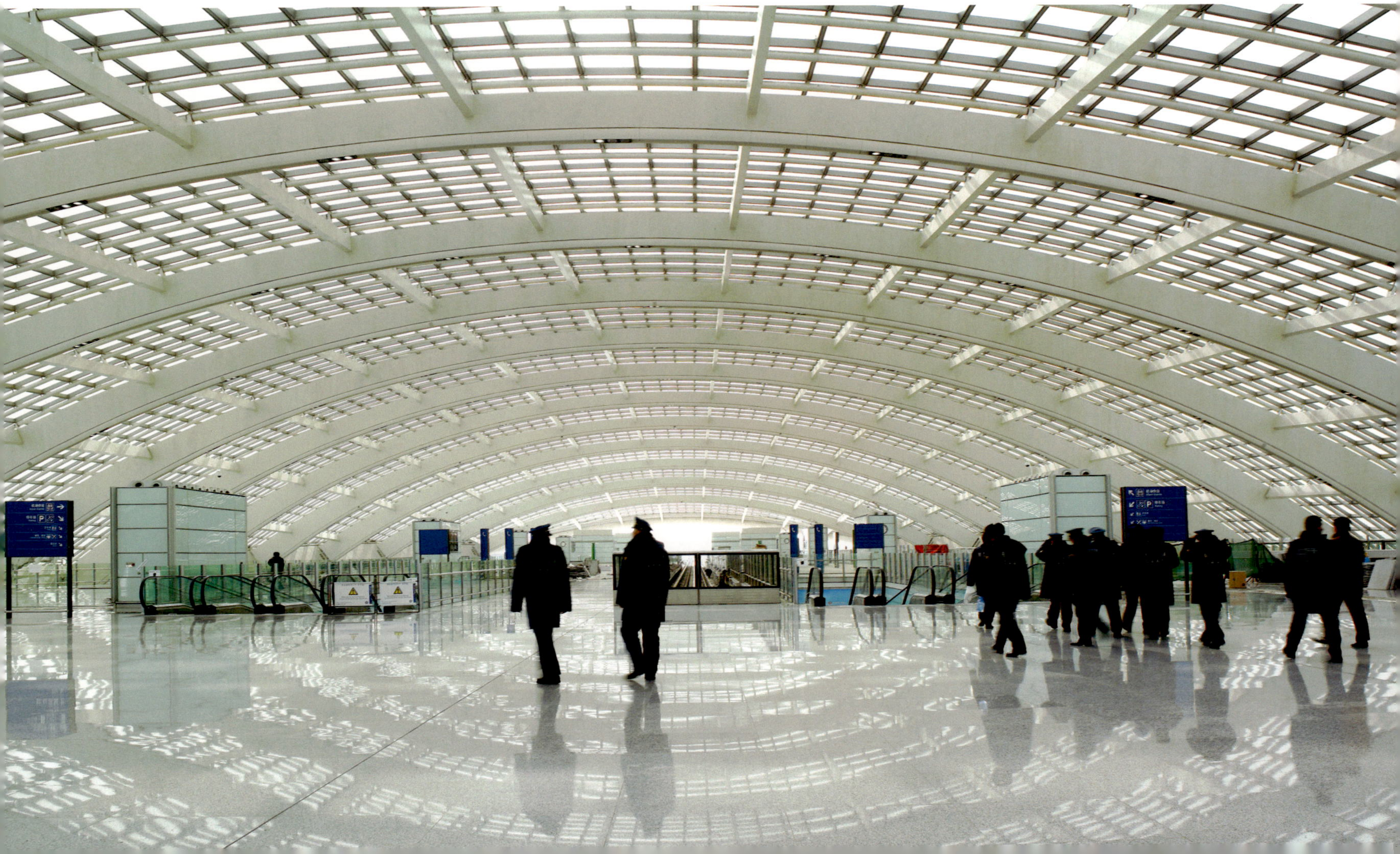

The construction statistics are staggering: over ten million cubic meters of earthworks, close to 20,000 foundation piles, some 200,000 tons of steel reinforcements tucked into 800,000 cubic meters of concrete, and a 360,000 square meter roof built with almost 20,000 tons of steel for the structure and over 25,000 tons for the columns. Only Chinese-owned companies were contracted to undertake the building works.

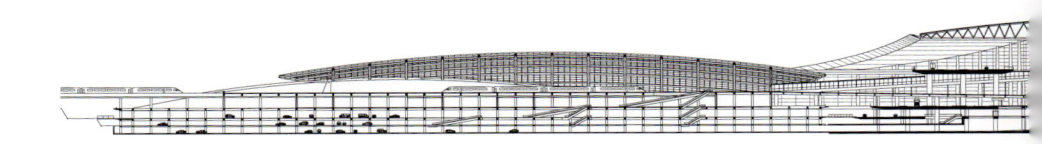

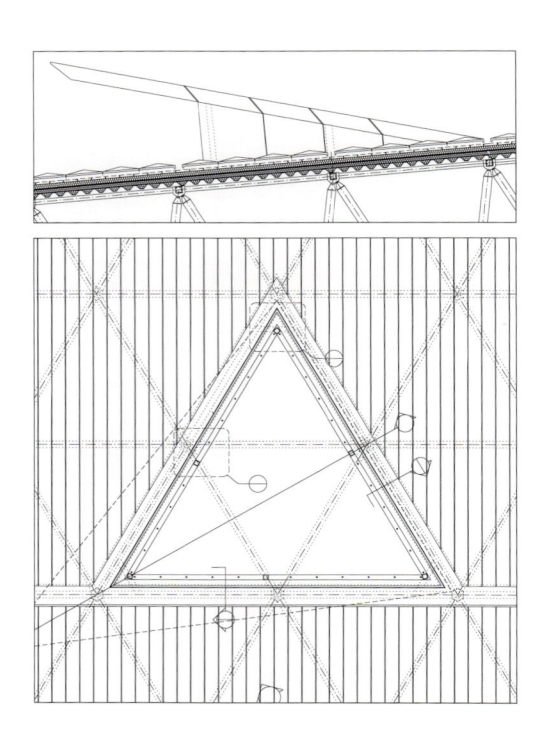

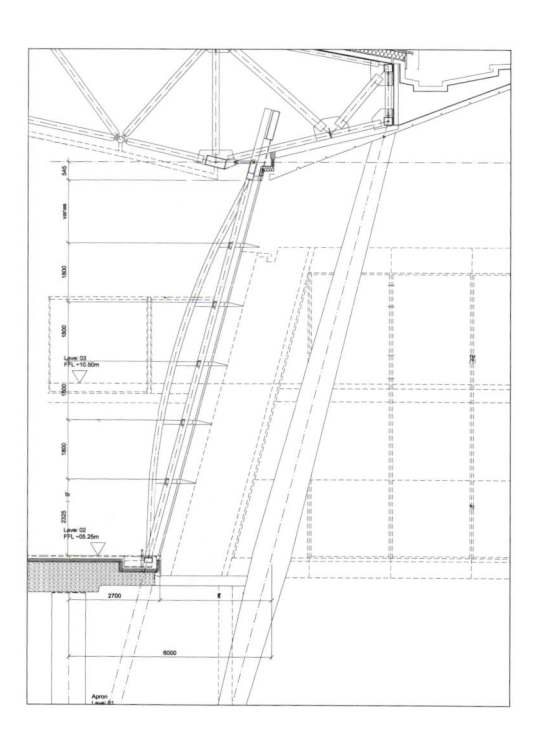

100 Atlas: Asia and Pacific

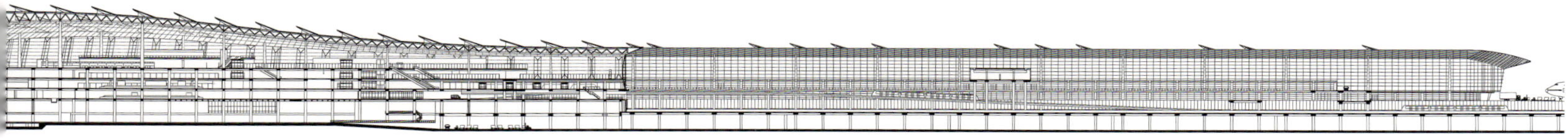

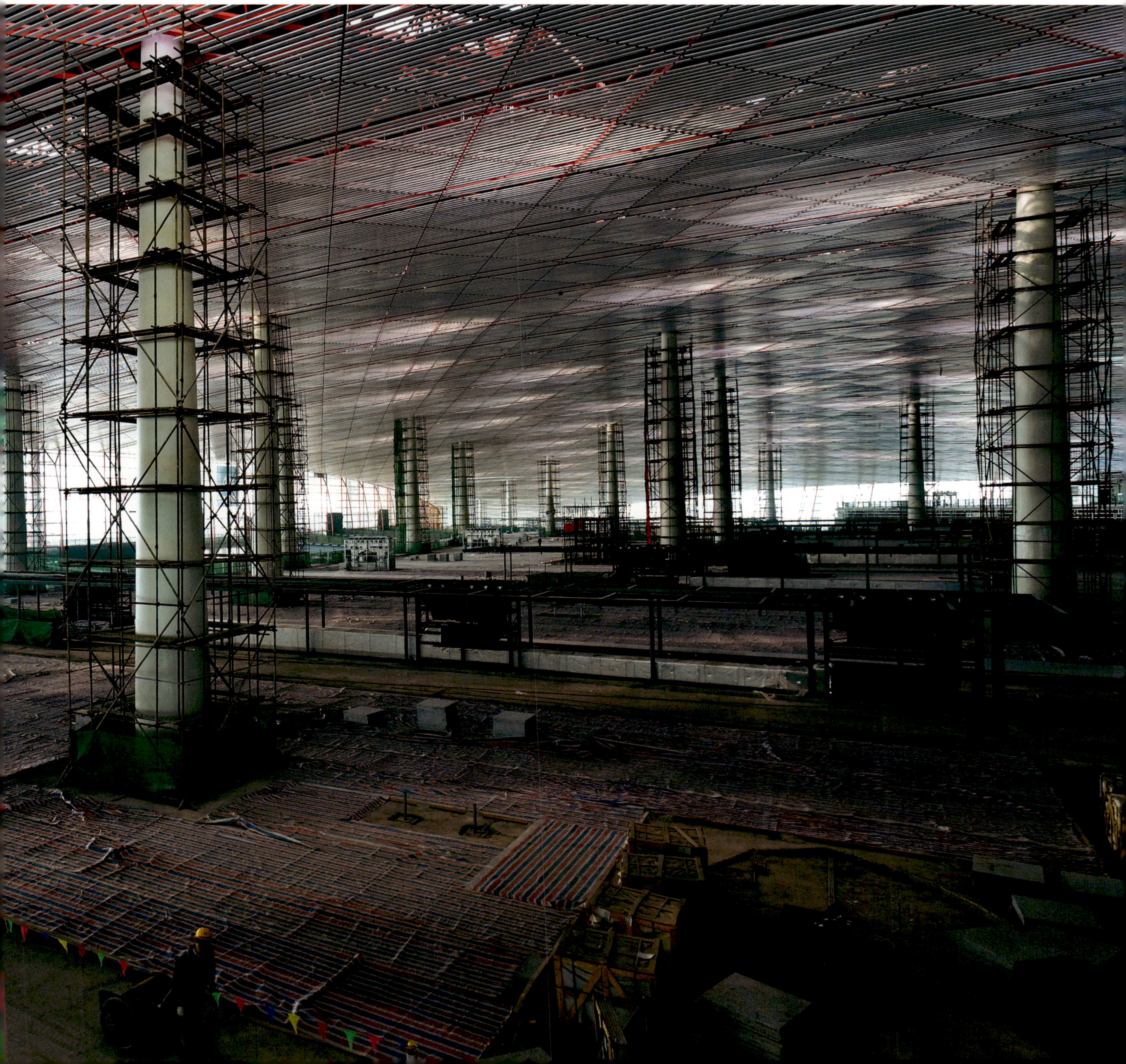

Herzog & de Meuron
National Olympic Stadium
Beijing (China)

NORTH OF BEIJING, on a gentle rise located at the center of the Olympic Park, stands the new National Stadium of China. From the very beginning, the idea was to create a type of urban enclave that would work to attract and generate a broad range of public activities, and in so doing infuse new life into that section of the city in the wake of the Games. Not in vain, the Chinese people themselves nicknamed the stadium 'bird's nest' very early on, fondly making it their own even when it was still on the drawing board.

From afar, the stadium looks like a giant collective bin, or a huge bowl whose undulating edge echoes the rising and falling movement of the circulation ramps inside. From a distance one can distinguish not only the rounded form of the building, but also the scheme of the loadbearing structure, which encircles the premises while seeming to push into it as well. But this compact geometric form that one discerns from afar blurs as it is approached, to later split into separate parts and appear as a tangle of pillars, beams, and stairs. The result is that the actual stadium is surrounded by a 12 meter wide concourse ring that is facade, structure, decoration, and public space all at once. People gather in this Piranesian space

Client
National Stadium
Architects
Jaques Herzog, Pierre de Meuron, Stephan Marbach (partners); Linxi Dong, Mia Hägg, Tobias Winkelmann, Thomas Polster (architects in charge); P. Becher, B. Berec, A. Berger, F. Beyreuther, A. Branco, M. Carreno, X. Chen, S. Chessex, M. Corradi, G. Espinoza, H. Focketyn, A. Fries, Y. He, V. Helm, C. von Hessert, Y. Huang, P. Heuberger, K. Jackowska, U. Kamps, H. Kikuchi, M. Krapp, H. Lai, E. Liang, K. Liu, D. Mak, C. Mojto, C. Pannett, D. Pokora, C. Röttinger, R. Rossmaier, L. Rotoli, M. Safa, P. Schaerer, R. Sokalski, H. Song, A. Verschuere, A. Voigt, C. Weber, T. Wolfensberger, P. van Wylick, C. Zanardini, X. Zhang
Consultants
Ai Weiwei (artistic consultant); China Architectural Design & Research Group, Ove Arup (sport engineering and architecture); R&R Fuchs (cladding)
Photos
Iwan Baan; Julia Jungfer/arturimages (p. 104); David Sundberg/Esto (p. 107)

The idea of a continuous enclave of curved forms where the loadbearing structure coincides with the facade was inspired at the outset by traditional Chinese vessels with flat profiles. As the object lost opacity and matter, the concept steadily evolved towards that of a 'bird's nest', and the picture gelled so well in the imagination of the Chinese that this became the name by which the National Stadium is popularly known.

to patronize its restaurants, bars, hotels, and shops, or simply to stroll on the platforms and the walkways that criss-cross diagonally and vertically. The concourse acts as the link between the city and the sport arena, but it is simultaneously an autonomous urban enclave. It is here that the project's true potential lies.

The geometries of the plinth and the stadium converge in a single element, like a tree and its roots. Pedestrian access to the arena is chanelled in a grid of terse slate paths that are designed like prolongations of the stadium's structural grid. The gaps between paths are filled with recreational facilities for visitors. The entrance to the stadium is slightly raised, in such a way that from it one has a panoramic view of the entire Olympic ring.

The stadium has an image that is pure structure: facade and structure are one and the same. The loadbearing elements support each other and converge in a kind of spatial tangle that leans at a 13-degree angle from the vertical and contains facades, stairs, and the bowl and roof within it. So that the latter also protects the premises from inclement weather, the spaces of this structural framework are filled with the soft materials that birds use to seal the gaps between the interwoven twigs of their nests. The lower part of the roof is clad with PTFE (polytetrafluoroethylene), an acoustic membrane that reflects sound to maintain the stadium's cheery atmosphere while concealing the structure so that it does not draw the audience's attention away from the sport spectacle.

Because all the installations in the building - restaurants, halls, shops, and restrooms -, form autonomous units, building them does not prerequire a facade. This allows the natural ventilation of the premises, an important contribution to the sustainability of the building.

Situated on a gentle rise of the terrain, the stadium has a capacity for 80,000 spectators, who enter the premises from all four sides into a ring that encircles the grandstands. This concourse space acts as a covered urban enclave, complete with restaurants, bars, hotels, and shops. The tiers have been designed without interruptions, evoking the image of a bowl and concentrating views and attention on what is happening on the field.

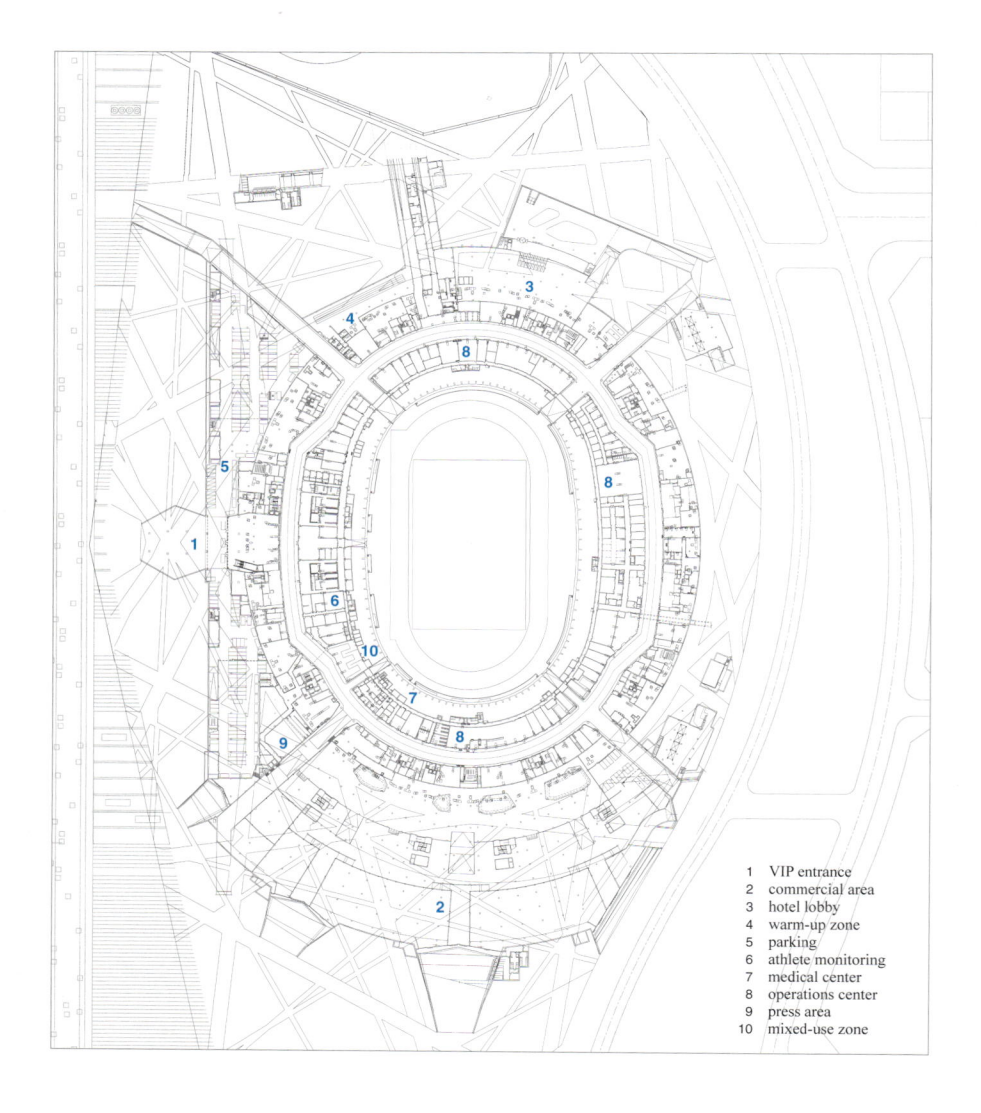

1. VIP entrance
2. commercial area
3. hotel lobby
4. warm-up zone
5. parking
6. athlete monitoring
7. medical center
8. operations center
9. press area
10. mixed-use zone

104 Atlas: Asia and Pacific

Second floor   Third floor   Roof

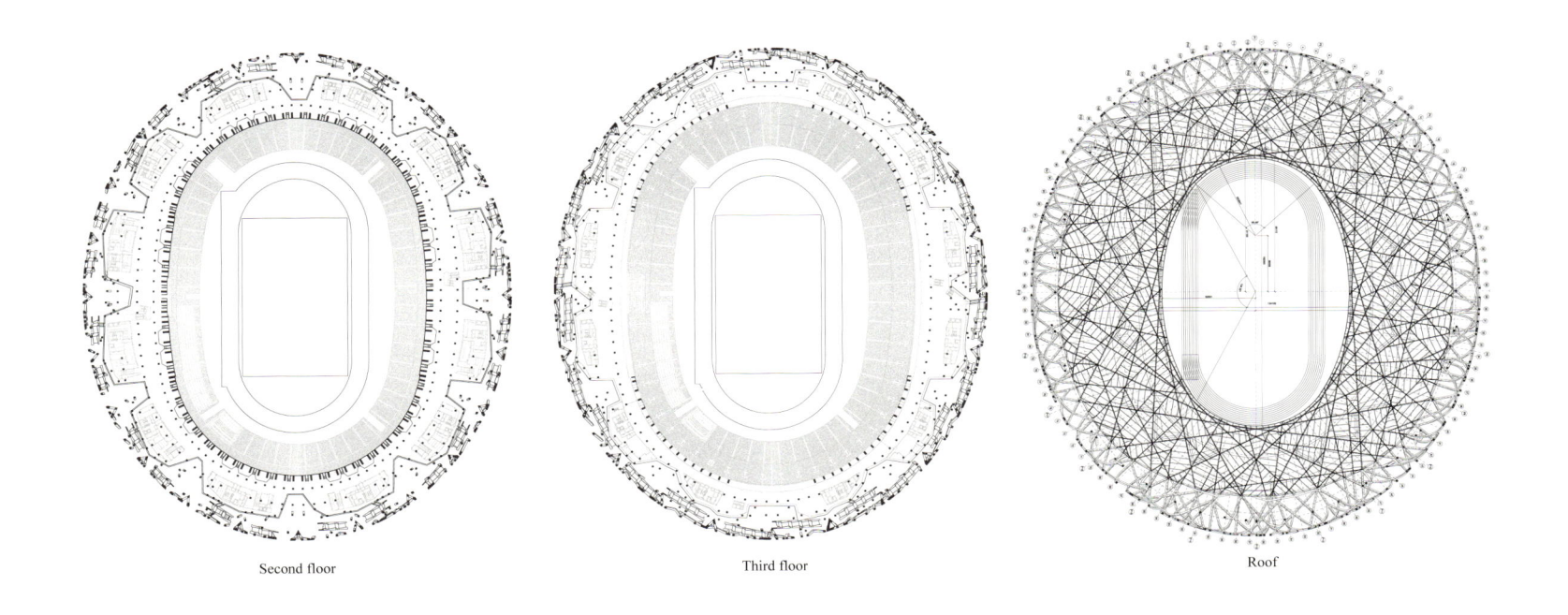

106 Atlas: Asia and Pacific

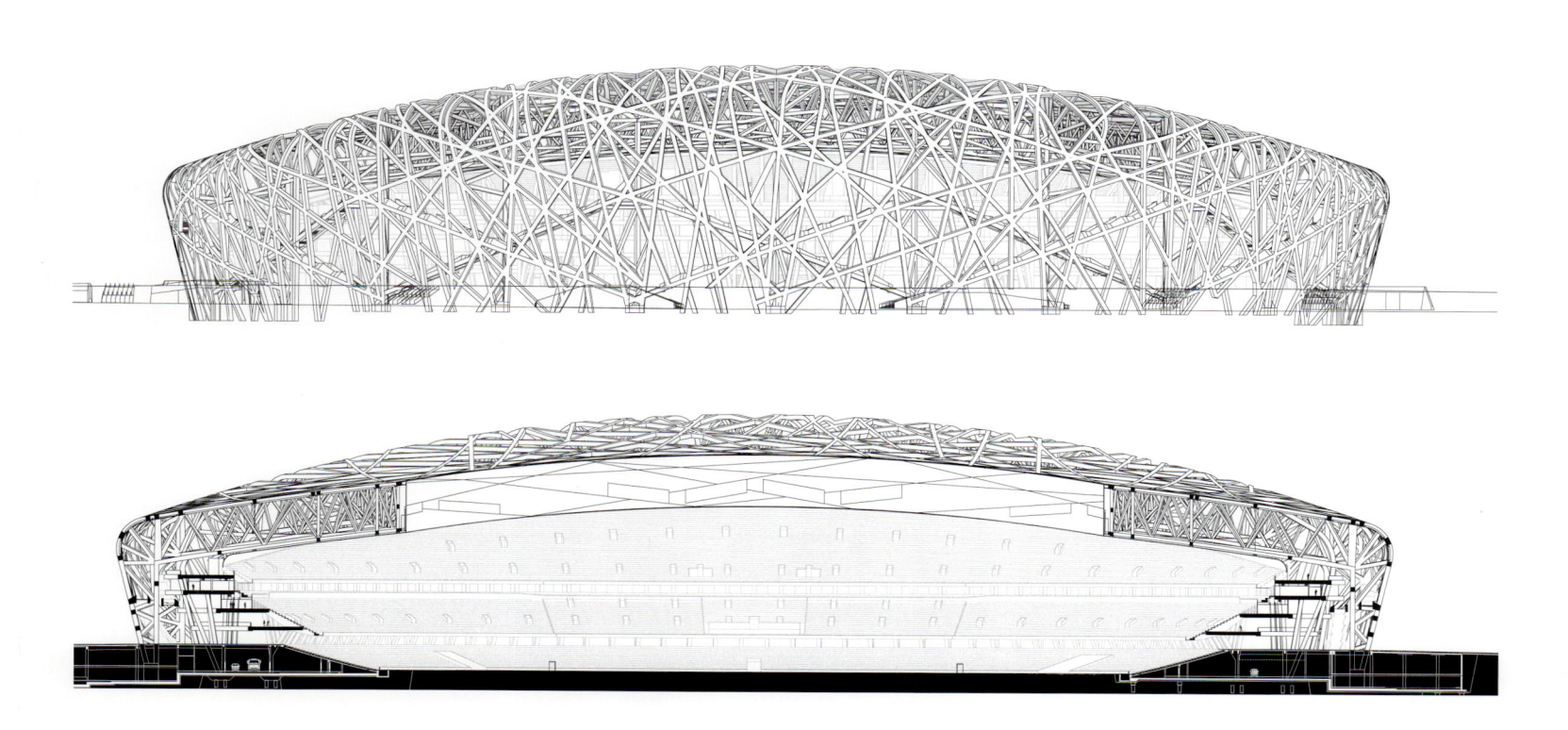

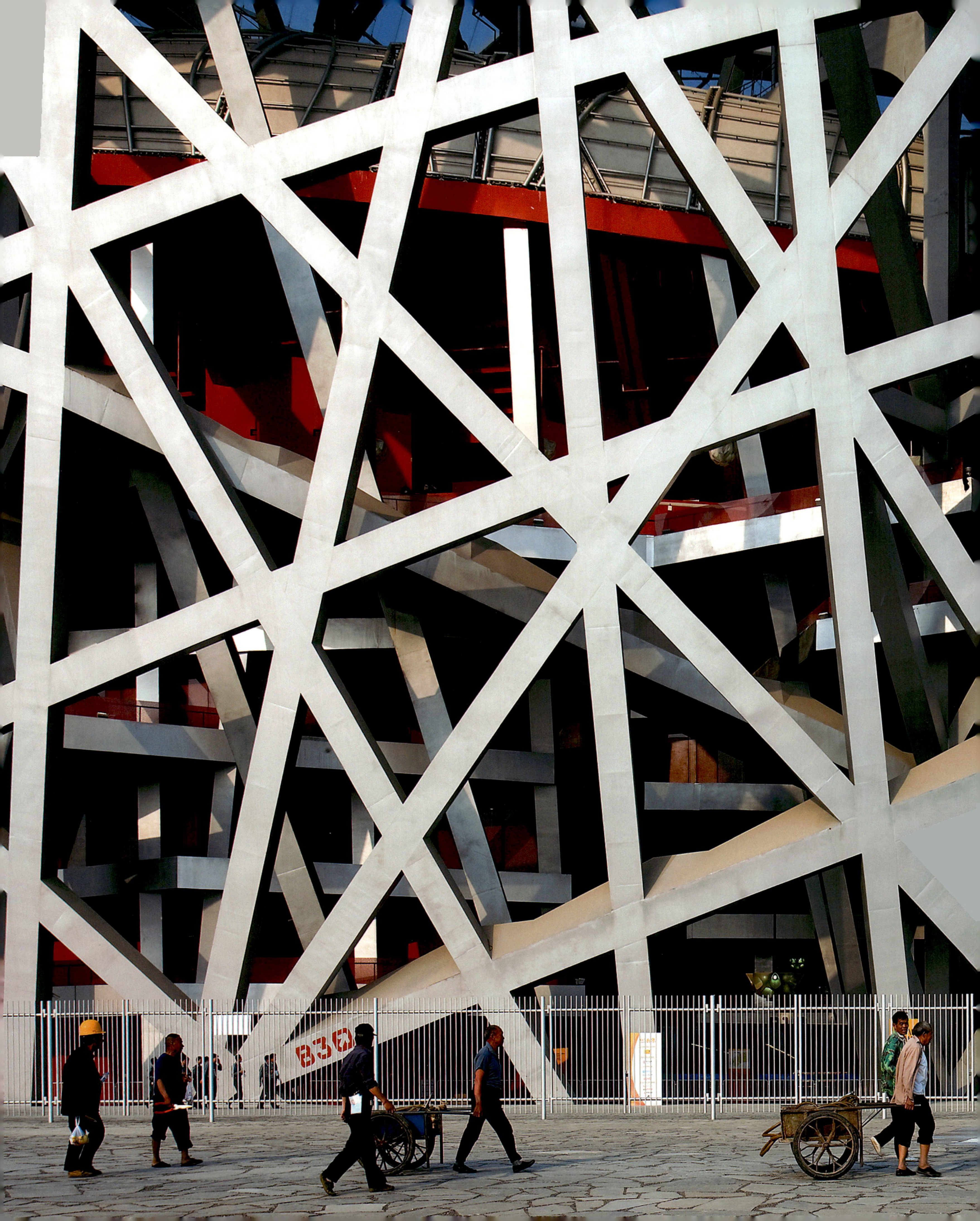

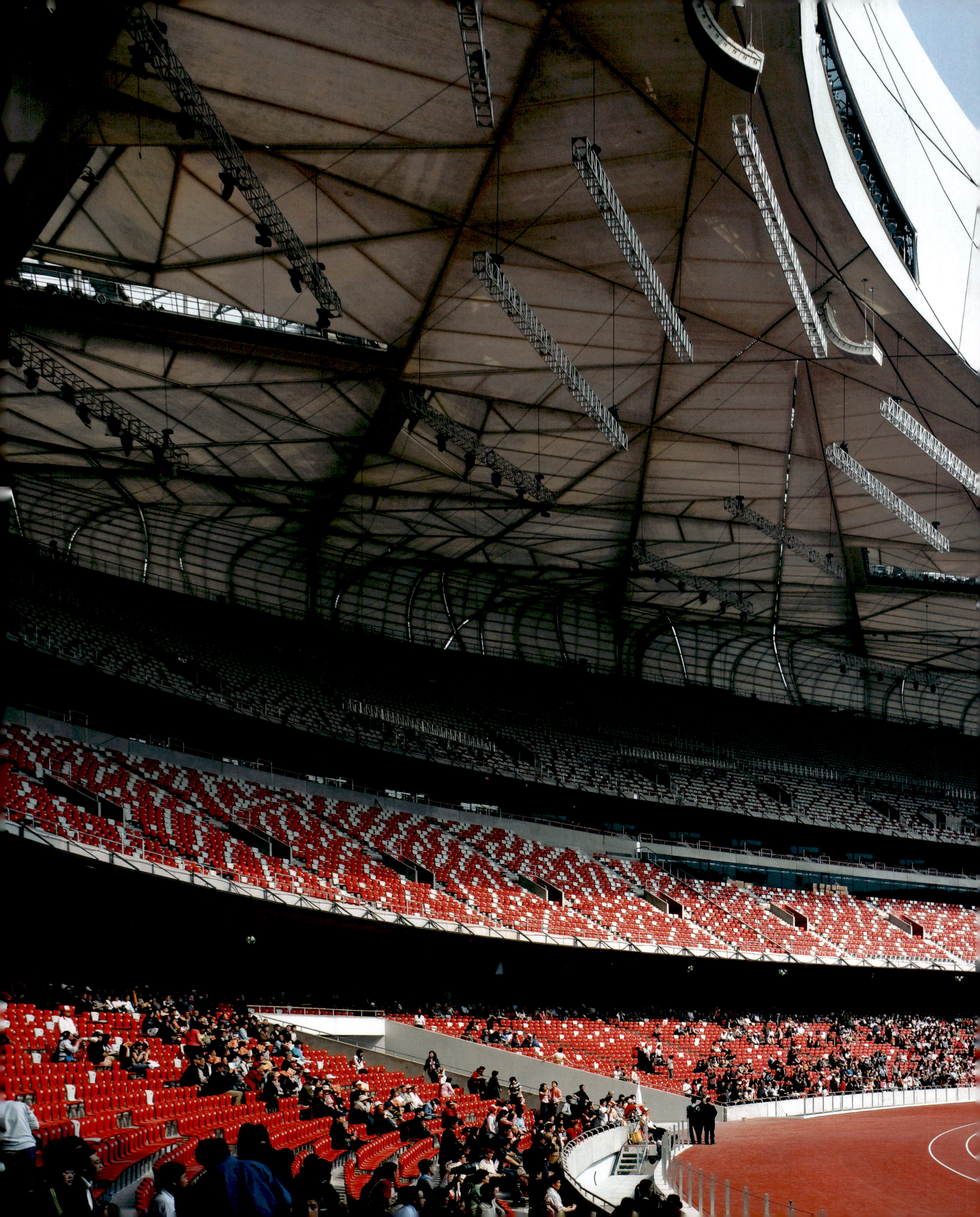

Despite the porous and random-like image of its loadbearing envelope, the Olympic Stadium is the world's largest steel-structured building. The skin that separates the facade of the grandstand is a layer of PTFE that serves to improve the acoustics of the stadium's interior. After being the symbol of the Olympic Games of 2008, the construction is now a landmark of the Chinese capital and a venue for other uses and events.

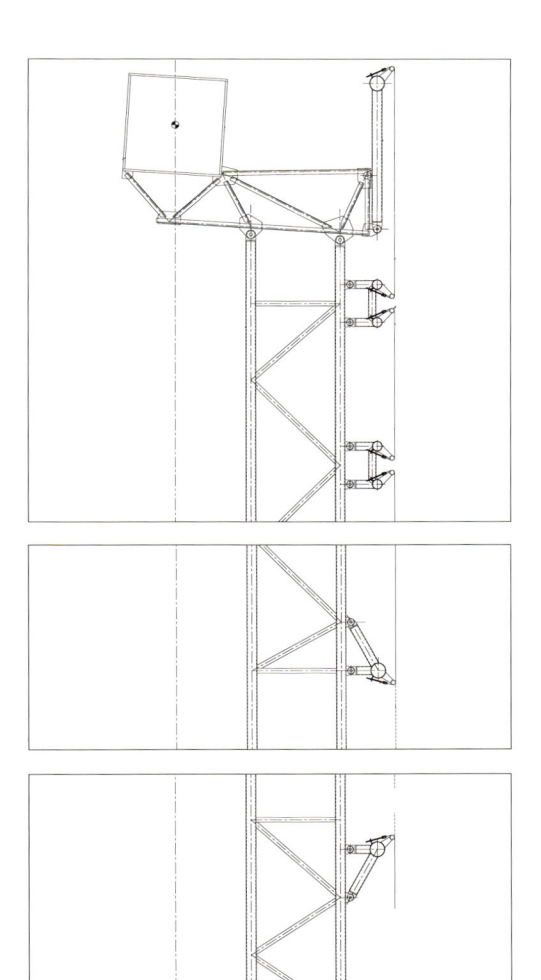

Detail of PTFE skin

Atlas: Asia and Pacific 109

PTW
National Swimming Center
Beijing (China)

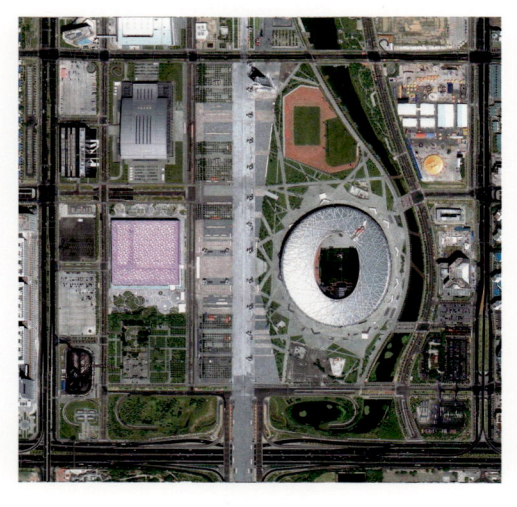

Client
Municipal Government of Beijing
Architects
PTW, CSCEC and Arup
Collaborators
PTW: John Bilmon (director), Mark Butler, Chris Bosse; CSCEC+ design: Zhao Xiaojun, Wang Min, Shang Hong
Consultants
Arup: T. Carfrae (director), P. Macdonald (structure), K. Ma (installations), H. Schepers (air conditioning), M. Lewis (telecommunications)
Photos
Marcel Lam/Arcaid (p. 111);
Tim Griffith / Arcaid (p. 112);
Iwan Baan (pp. 114 bottom, 115);
ChinaFotoPress/Getty Images (p. 114 top)

The National Swimming Center has a square-shaped floor plan and is next to the Olympic Stadium. The latter is known as the 'bird's nest' while the former, inspired by bubbles, is referred to as the 'watercube'.

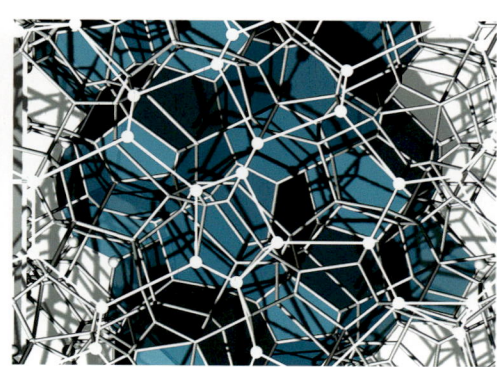

THE NATIONAL SWIMMING CENTER rises next to the Olympic Stadium and is conceived as its partner in a yin-yang relationship where one is fire, the other water; one is material, the other volatile; one is curved, the other polyhedric. Referred to as the 'watercube', it associates water with the square, the basic shape of the traditional Chinese house.

The structure of the volume is inspired by the phenomenon of water bubbles, evoking the state of aggregation of foam. Behind the seemingly random arrangement of bubbles is a geometric pattern found in nature, as in crystals. The structure's design was arrived at through the model discovered by the scientists Weaire and Phelan, which ruled that the most efficient way to divide space into cells of equal volumes was by making 75% of them have fourteen sides and the remaining 25%, twelve. Hence this volume of tetrakaidecahedrons and dodecahedrons which was twisted and sectioned to obtain the desired random image.

Unlike in stadiums with huge beams, pillars, cables, and struts, here architecture, structure, and envelope are confused. On the mass of 'soap suds', a box is sculpted, and the interior spaces are excavated, illustrating the metaphor of a natural state becoming a cultural state. The 'foamy walls', 3.6 meters thick, mark a 177x177 meter perimeter and rise 31 meters. Closing the prism is a roof with a 7.2 meter edge.

Inside the building we find a recreational swimming pool on the south side, a waterpolo pool on the east side, and the Olympic pool at the center. The structure is built with 22,000 steel beams, each one as small and light as possible to minimize the overall weight. The builders also conceived compact sections that would behave like plastic during an earthquake.

The National Swimming Center is clad with cushions made of ETFE membranes, which besides having excellent insulation properties, work to generate a greenhouse effect. In this way, the solar energy that penetrates the building gets trapped inside the structure, with the help of the double skin. The preheated air is used to warm up the different interior spaces as well as the swimming pools.

This air chamber acts like a coat in winter, whereas in summertime it is opened to allow air to circulate freely and cool the enclosure. The transparent skin minimizes the building's need for artificial lighting during the day and makes it a lantern at night, a beautifully colored one thanks to the more than 440,000 LED lamps that have been installed inside the bulding's envelope.

The volume, a 177x177 meter square rising 31 meters, is clad with a blanket formed by 4,000 ETFE cushions that serve as thermal insulation. LED lamps have been placed inside these membranes in order to prolong the cube's enigmatically weightless and changing image way into the night, when the building becomes a lantern of cold colors striking a contrast with the red glow of the Olympic Stadium.

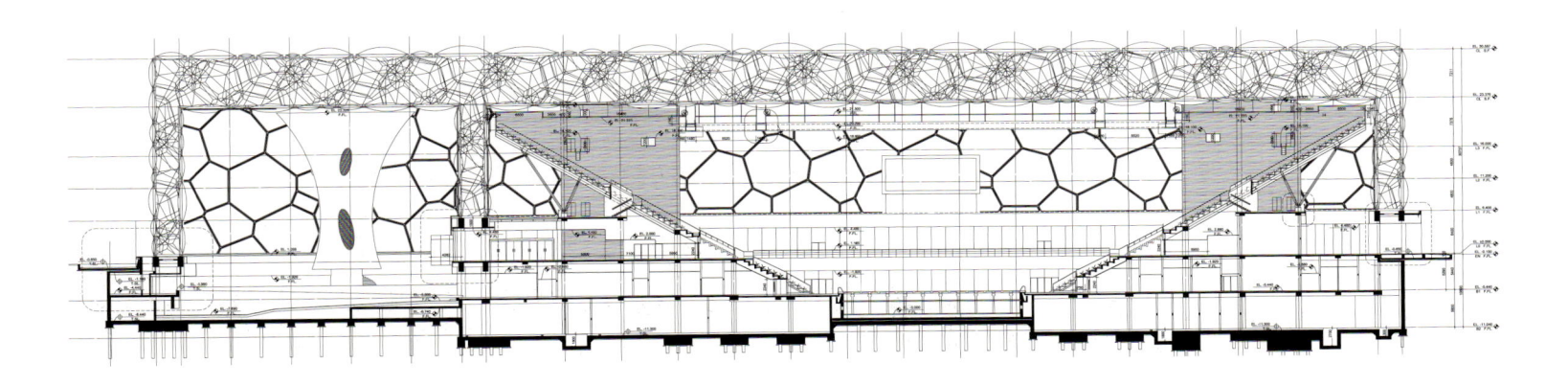

Atlas: Asia and Pacific

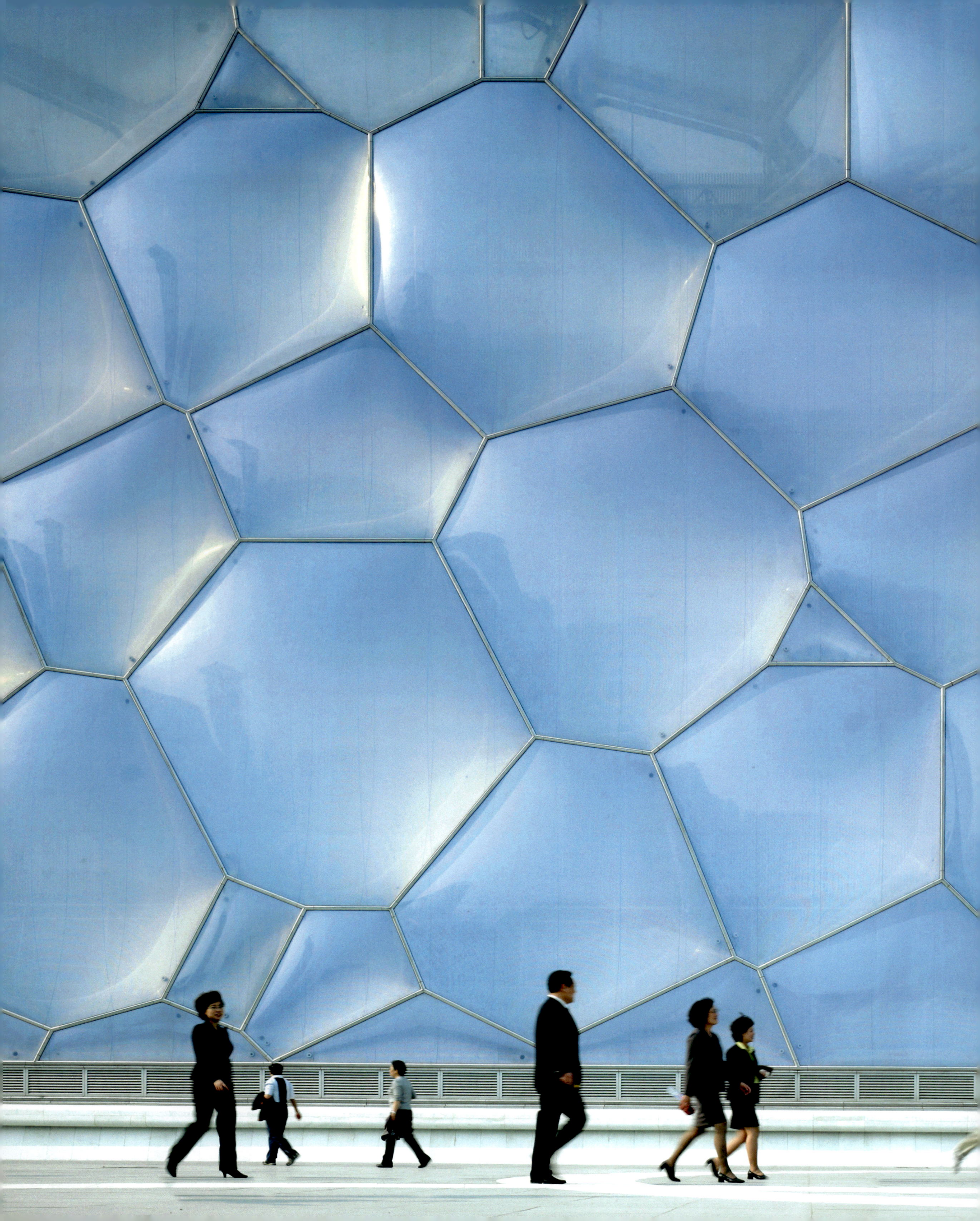

The skin formed by ETFE cushions has an automatic open/close system that makes it possible for air to circulate as desired. This also helps to cool the facade in summertime, while during the cold winter months it works like a greenhouse. In moderate seasons, heat is used to warm up the swimming pools and the interior spaces. The cushions have varying degrees of transparency, depending on where in the facade they are.

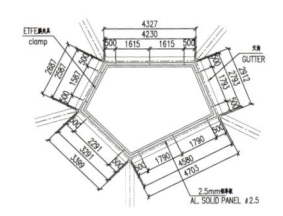

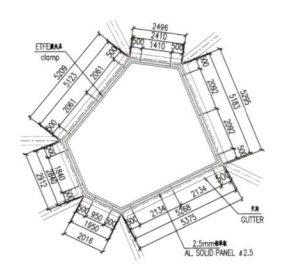

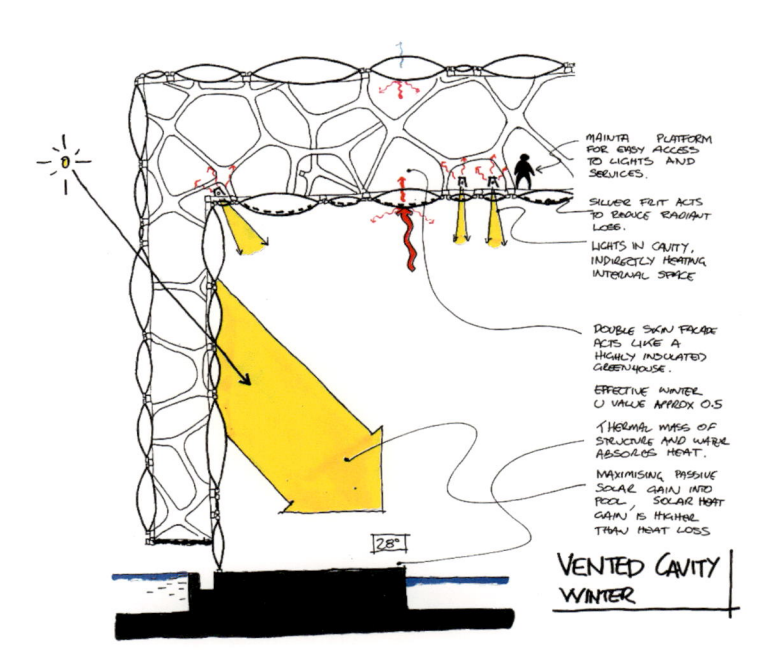

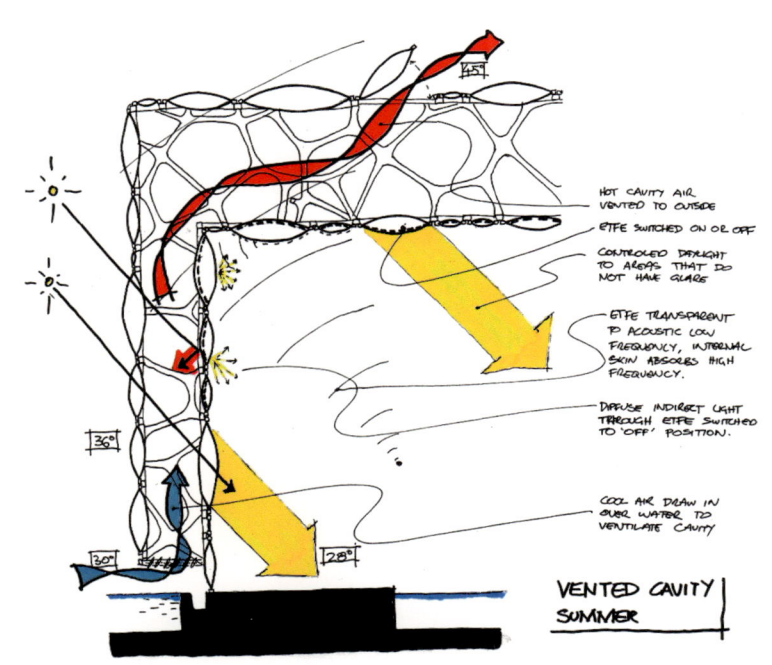

VENTED CAVITY WINTER

VENTED CAVITY SUMMER

During the Olympic Games of 2008, the so-called 'watercube' was the scene of competitions in lap and synchronized swimming as well as diving, yielding a total of 25 world records beaten. Seating capacity reached 17,000 in the course of the event, but is currently down to 6,000. The building is being used as a recreational center that includes a gym, a skating rink, and a movie theater besides the actual swimming pool facilities.

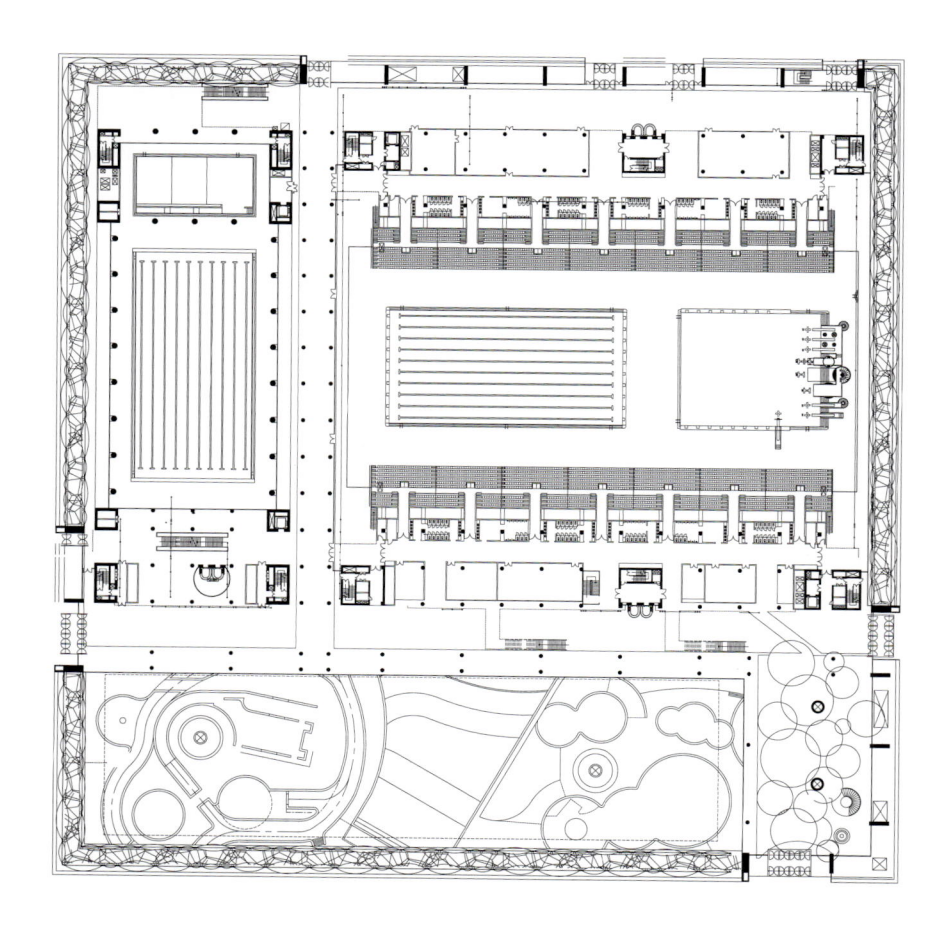

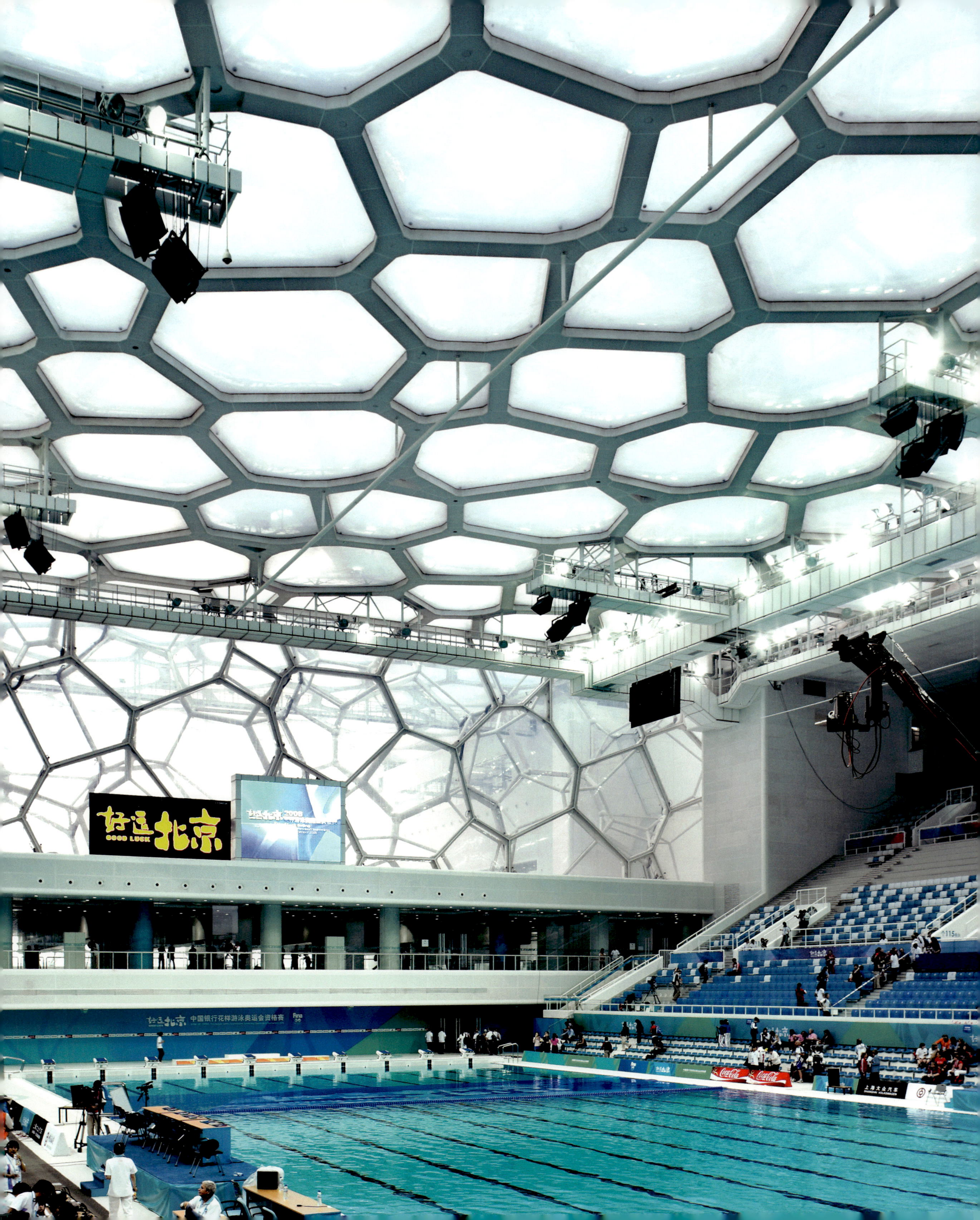

好运北京
GOOD LUCK

Paul Andreu
National Grand Theater
Beijing (China)

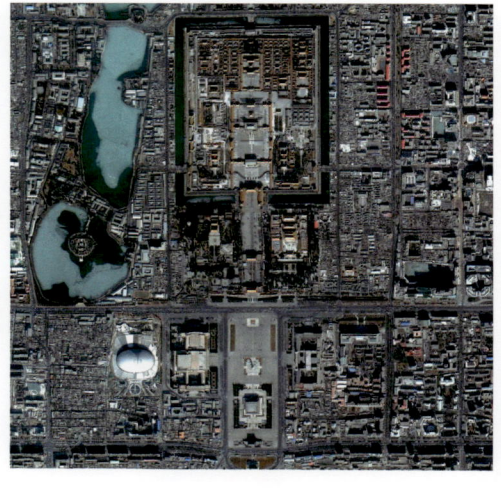

Just 500 meters from Tiananmen Square and the Forbidden City in Beijing, on a man-made lake right by the People's Palace, rises the new National Grand Theater of China, a half-spheroid wrapped in a titanium shell. This shiny opaque skin is divided into two parts by a glass surface that gives the building natural light at daytime and turns it by night into a glowing lantern that shows the interior space to onlookers.

In its enigmatic character, the theater has no entrance that can be discerned from outside. Entry is through a transparent underwater catwalk that stretches around the volume. This serves to emphasize the image of the object while creating the metaphor of a bridge that connects everyday life to the world of the stage.

With its 149,500 square meters of usable floor space, the building contains three different auditoriums as well as a series of exhibition spaces. At the center of the interior, where the ceiling is highest, is the grand opera house that seats 2,416. To the right of this is the concert hall for 2,017, and to the left is a theater for 1,040. The interior is conceived more as an open people's forum than as an elitist cultural institution. It is planned like an urban district, complete with streets, squares, shops, restaurants, and

Client
National Grand Theater of China
Architects
Paul Andreu & ADPi
Collaborators
François Tamisier /ADPi, Hervé Langlais; Alain Le Pajolec /ADPi (international department)
Consultants
Felipe Starling /ADPi (chief project engineer), Setec (structures and installations); M. Vian (acoustics); M. Rioualec (stage); Ruling Zhang Blein (artistic adviser)
Photos
Guang Niu/Getty Images (pp. 116-117); Christian Richters (pp. 118-119); Andy Ryan (pp. 120, 121 bottom); Paul Maurer (p. 121 top)

Like an enormous pearl emerging from the water, China's National Grand Theater is conceived as an island of culture afloat in a man-made lake. Its titanium skin gives it an image that changes with the light and time of day.

In contrast with the geometry of the buildings around (the prismatic forms of government headquarters and the pitched tiled roofs of the Forbidden City), the theater's half-spheroid cuts an enigmatic abstract figure, but conveys a clearly populist message. Its interior is laid out like a public space, with streets, squares, shops, and restaurants set amid the three auditoriums: an opera house, a theater, and a concert hall.

resting and waiting areas. All three auditoriums open on to this public space, and the doors are strategically located to ensure that the public is distributed evenly within the premises, avoiding bottlenecks. In a complex laid out with efficiency and economy in mind, the underwater level accommodates all of the theater's ancillary and secondary spaces. Upstairs, below the roof, is a rest area that offers a new perspective of the city beyond.

While the theater is dressed with bands of silk in red, violet, and mandarin orange, the white concert hall has a curving ceiling that amounts to a work of abstract art. The opera house is surrounded along its outer edge by a golden metal mesh that conceals the view of vertical circulation elements moving around the hall. This ring represents the symbolic distance one has to cross before entering the performance space. In a way, the entire project can be defined as a play of envelopes, passages and crossings, lights and transparencies.

Since this is a national building, the components of the marble flooring were brought in from the country's twenty-two provinces. The only imported element was the Brazilian mahogany that clads the building's titanium skin on the inside.

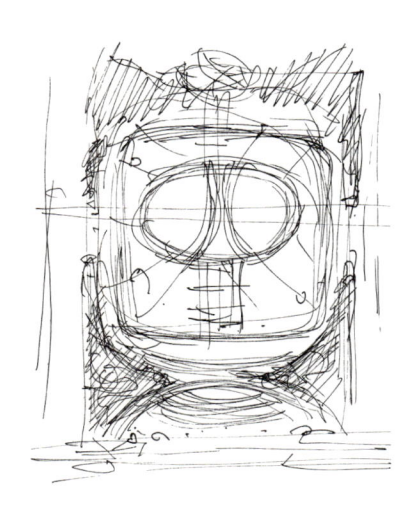

Atlas: Asia and Pacific 117

At night, the huge patch of glass that divides the titanium shell into two parts reveals the three volumes that the building contains within. At the center is the grand opera house with seating for 2,416 people, and flanking it are the theater and the concert hall for 1,040 and 2,017, respectively. Access is through a passage that stretches under the artificial lake. In this way, the half-spheroid's surface is uninterrupted.

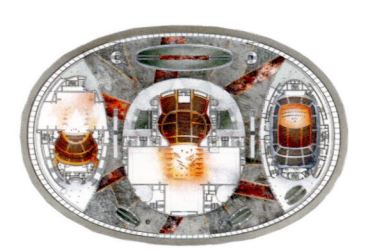

A good part of the building's nearly 150,000 square meters of usable floor space is situated underneath the three auditoriums, in several levels of basement. This is where the installations and ancillary spaces are assigned to, organized in accordance with a set of efficiency criteria not too different from those applied in industrial production. Commercial and recreational areas are arranged in a north-south axis behind the theaters.

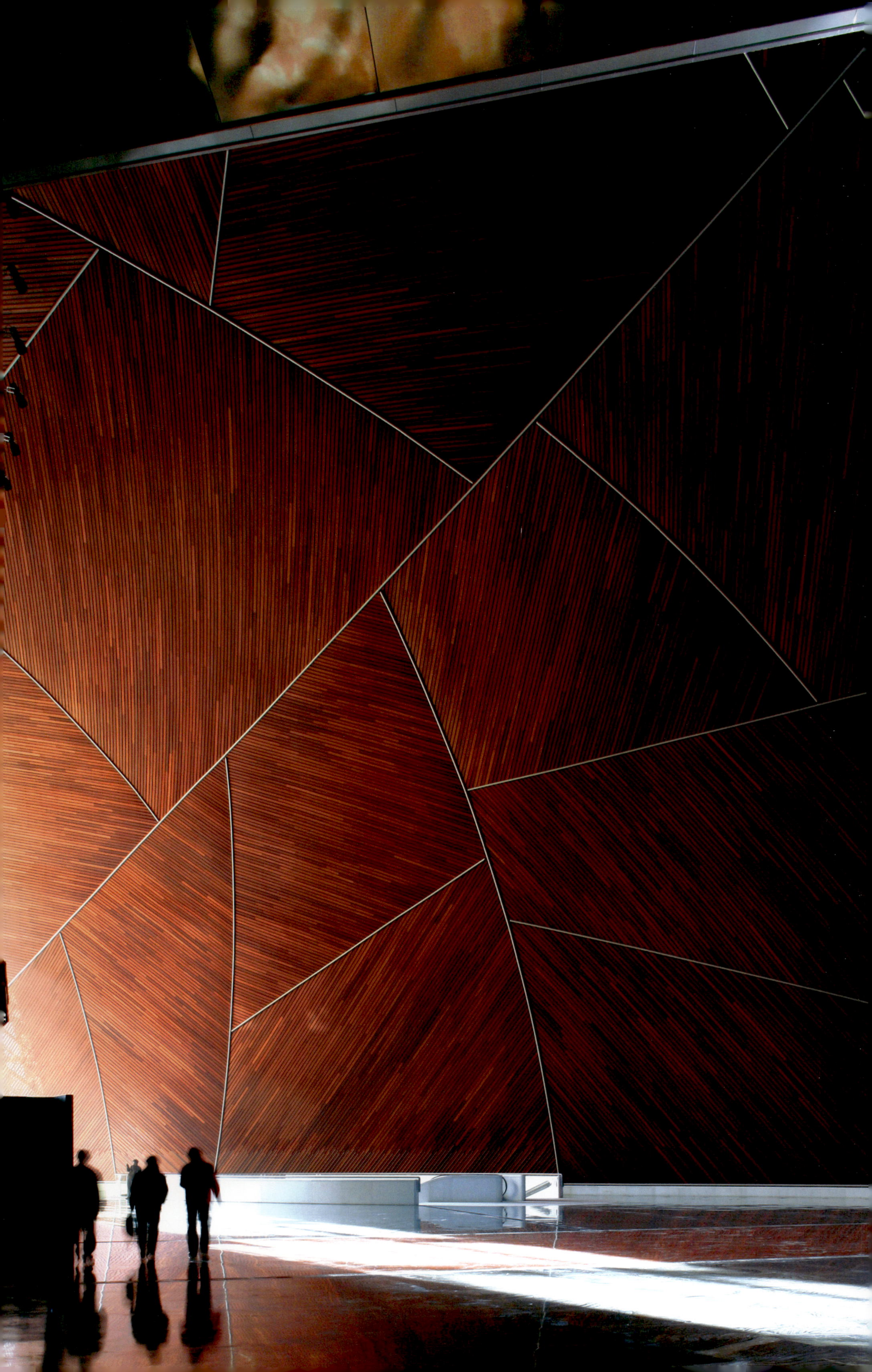

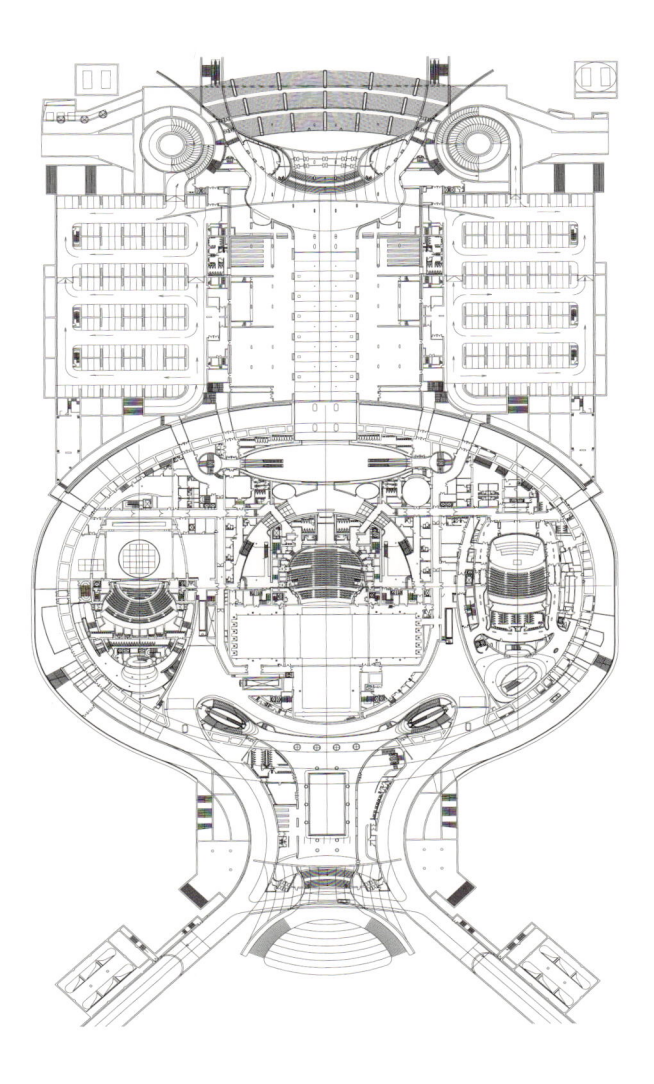

The construction of the colossal shell, which is 213 meters long, 144 meters wide, and 46 meters high, is based on Vierendeel-type ribs set 2.43 meters apart and joined together by horizontal connectors with 20 centimeter diameters. The three auditoriums are mixed structures consisting of metal pillars and floor slabs of reinforced concrete. Under the dome that soars over the foyer, one can discern the golden metal mesh that wraps the opera house like a veil concealing the vertical communication elements situated around the hall. All materials are local, except the Brazilian mahogany cladding the intrados.

OMA/Rem Koolhaas & Ole Scheeren
CCTV Headquarters
Beijing (China)

THE SCULPTURAL figure of the new headquarters of CCTV, China Central Television, rises along Beijing's third beltway, on a 10 hectare site in the city's new business district, an area expected to accommodate over 300 skyscrapers. The 450,000 square meter complex contains the space necessary for the company to carry out the entire process of television-making and control the operations of its over 250 channels, proof of the vigorous expansion of a state network that until recently only had 16. Completing the complex is the TVCC, Television Cultural Center, which will include a Mandarin Hotel and the so-called Media Park, conceived to be a continuation of the new business district's green zone, open to the general public for the celebration of events and equipped to be a set for outdoor film shooting.

Soaring 234 meters, this new addition to the Beijing skyline is divided into five sections: administrative, commercial, news, broadcasting, and production, all fitted in a single loop of interconnected activity. From a shared production platform containing seven floors above ground and three under, two structures shoot up at a six-degree slant. One is for broadcasting, the other for services, research, and education. They

Client
China Central Television
Architects
OMA: Rem Koolhaas & Ole Scheeren
Collaborators
Dongmei Yao (project manager); Charles Berman, David Chacon, Chris van Duijn, Erez Ella, Adrianna Fisher, Anu Leinonen, Andre Schmidt, Shohei Shigematsu, Hiromasa Shirai, Steven Smit (project architects); G. Bojalil, J. Bravo Da Costa, C. Canas, H. Chacon, D. Cheong, S. Derveaux, K. Engelman, G. Estourgie, T. Fang, P. Feng, S. Gibson, C. James, A. Kapade, M. van der Kar, P. Kroese, P. Lee, X. Liu, S. Maddox, J. Monteleone, C. Murphy, S. Ogata, R. Otero, D. Ooievaar, T. Schroeder, W. Shi, K. Tai, F. Tsai, J. Tsoi, X. Wang, L. Willis, V. Willocks, Y. Wu, T.T. Xu, D. Zschunke
Consultants
ECADI (local architects and engineers); Arup (structure and installations); Front (curtain wall); ECADI, Sandy Brown (broadcast); LPA (lighting); Dorser Blesgraaf, DHV (acoustics); dUCKS Scéno (theater scenography); Lerch Bates (vertical transportation); DMJMH+N (high-rise consultant); Inside Outside (landscape); S. Scanlon (buildability); Qingyun Ma (strategy)
Photos
Iwan Baan;
Goh Chai Hin/Getty images (p. 125)

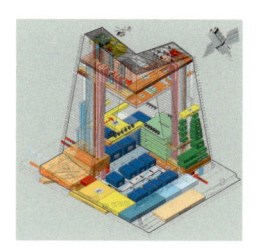

The Chinese capital's new business district features the loop-like headquarters of the country's state television network, CCTV, composed of two structures shooting up at a six-degree slant and joining high up to form a huge cantilevered penthouse for management offices. Rather than competing in the race for the height record, this unique skyscraper rising 230 meters and 54 floors was a structural challenge.

merge on the thirty-sixth floor to form a huge cantilevered management penthouse in nine to thirteen levels.

The tragedy of skyscrapers is that they are marked out to be emblems and have the potential to be incubators of new programs and cultures, and yet most of them accommodate merely routine activities that are subject to predictable patterns within a container of little imagination: as verticality soars, creativity crashes. The CCTV chose not to compete in the hopeless race for the height record, which is ephemeral, opting instead to be an icon of a high-rise that inserts itself into the urban space in a three-dimensional experience. Consolidating the entire television program in one single building has the effect of making employees permanently aware of the work performed by their colleagues, thereby materializing a chain of interdependence that fosters solidarity and collaboration rather than isolation and opposition. Without jeopardizing the security of the people working in the building and the technology installed within, public visitors are admitted into the loop for a tour through the whole volume that connects all the elements of the program while affording spectacular views of Beijing and the Forbidden City.

The structure was a challenge for the project's engineers, who had to ensure its stability at all stages of construction. The solution was a loadbearing facade, an exoskeleton, formed by a triangular mesh of diagonal, horizontal, and vertical elements. The positions of the columns and diagonal tubes on the facades reflect the distribution of loads on the building envelope, and the system is completed inside by a scheme of pillars. Through a special seismic simulation program, the engineers of Arup worked closely with the Beijing Geotechnical Institute to guarantee that the CCTV would withstand strong earthquakes.

Besides administration, contained within the cantilevered volume above, the CCTV loop accommodates four other aspects of television networking: commercial, newsrooms, broadcasting, and production. The latter is situated over the recording studios, which are buried under the plaza, protected by the construction. The programmatic complexity is not reflected in the facade, which shows the structural tensions.

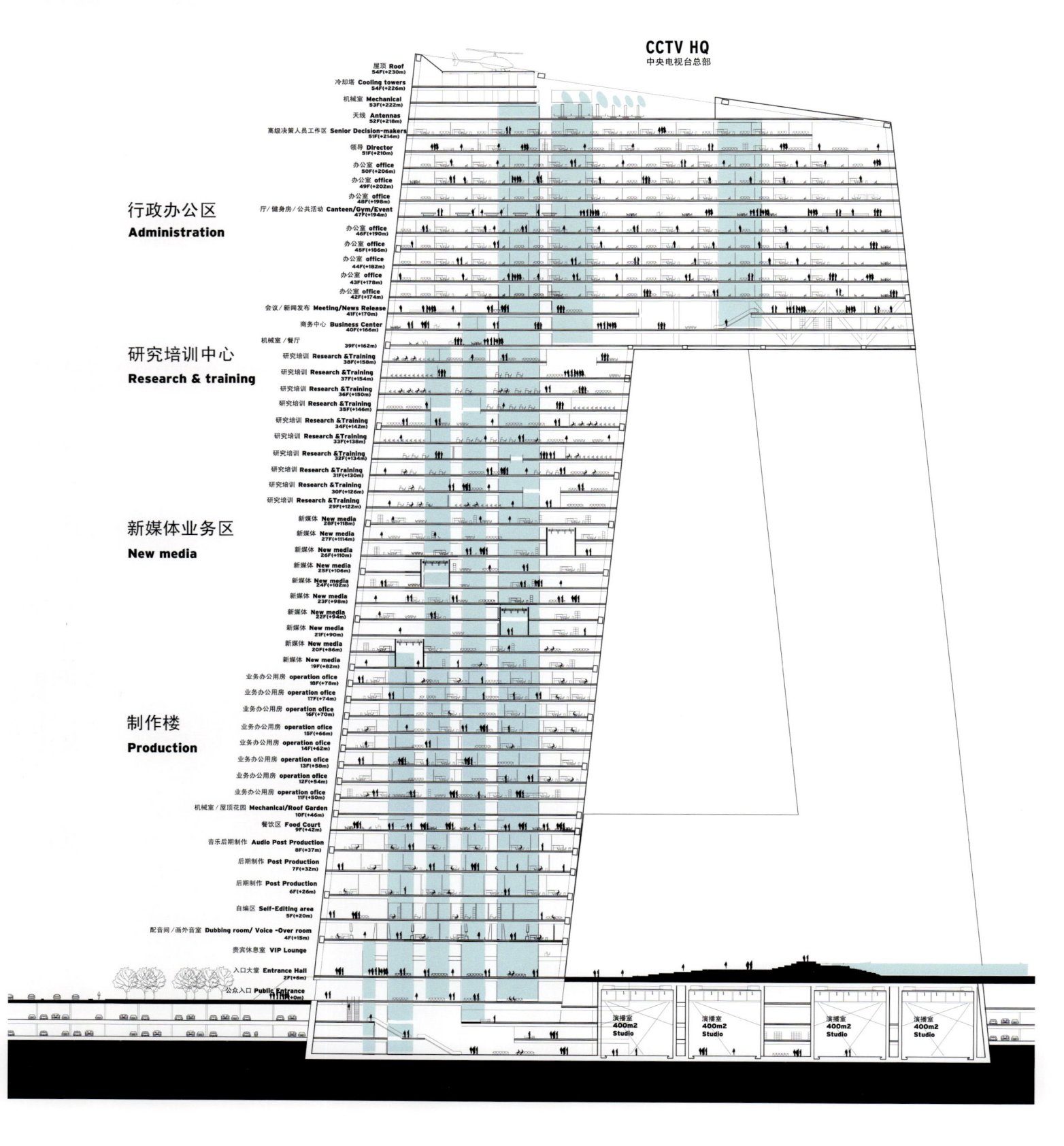

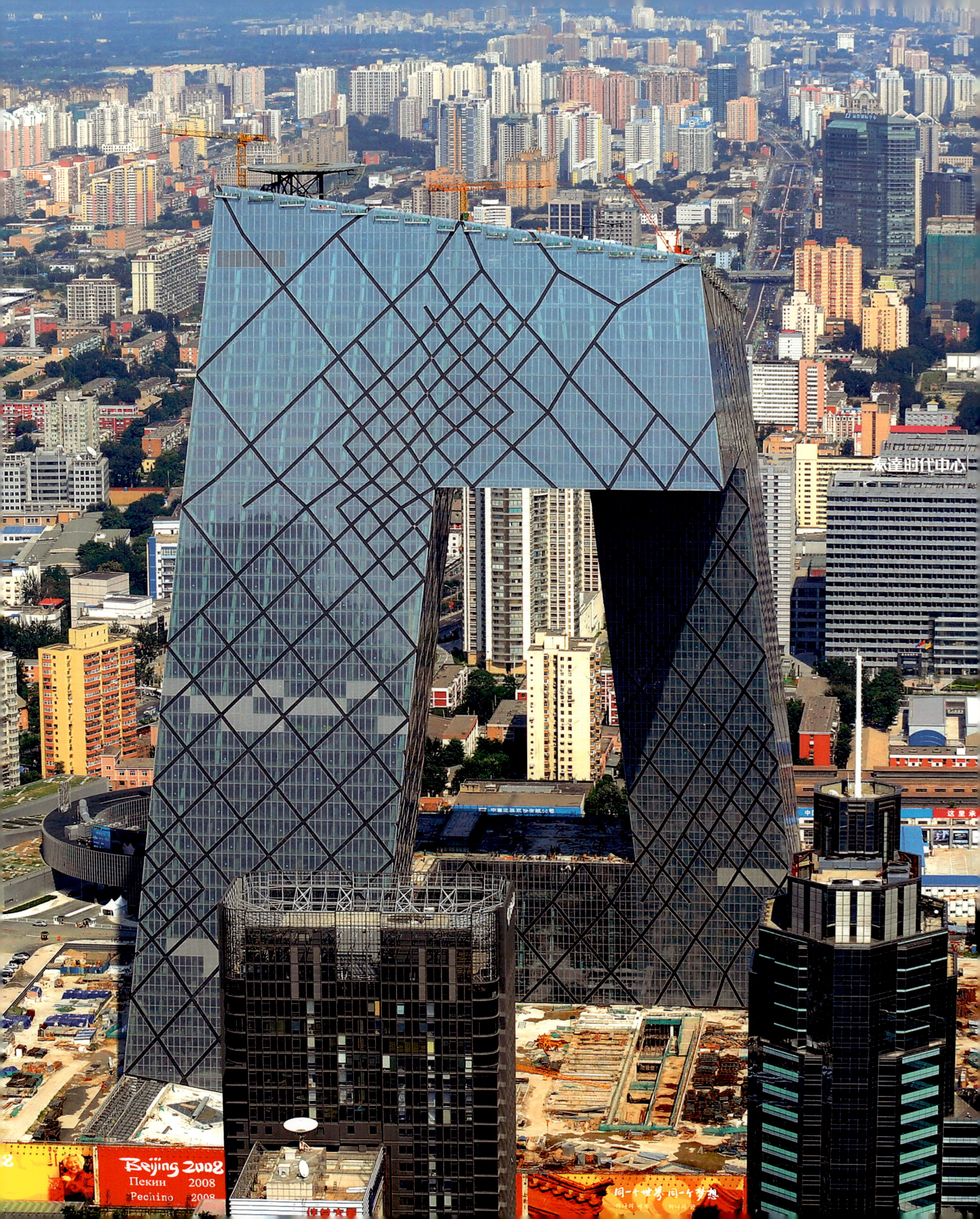
Beijing 2008
Пекин 2008
Pechino 2008

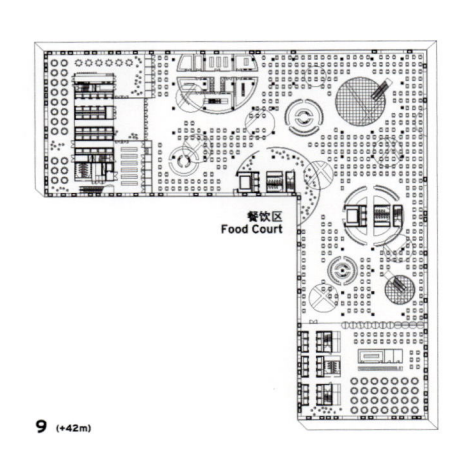

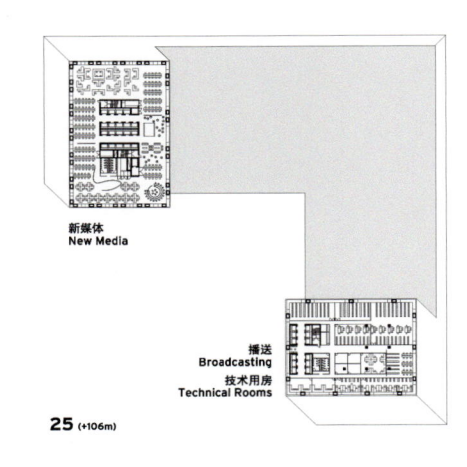

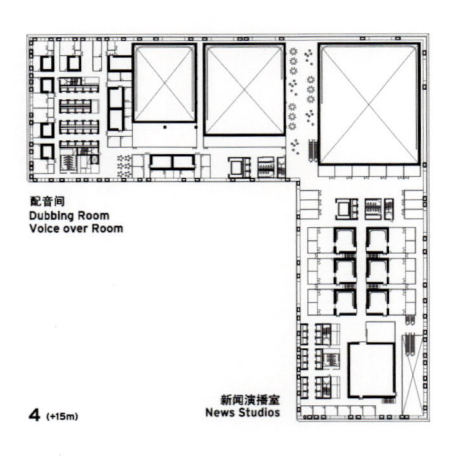

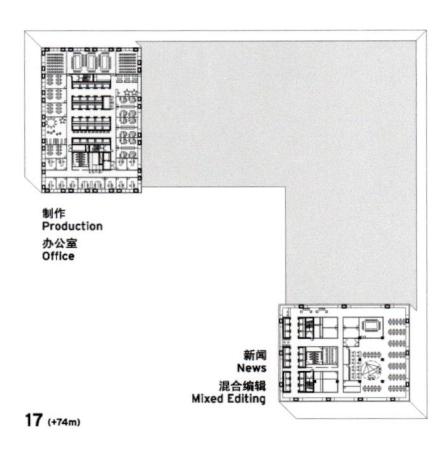

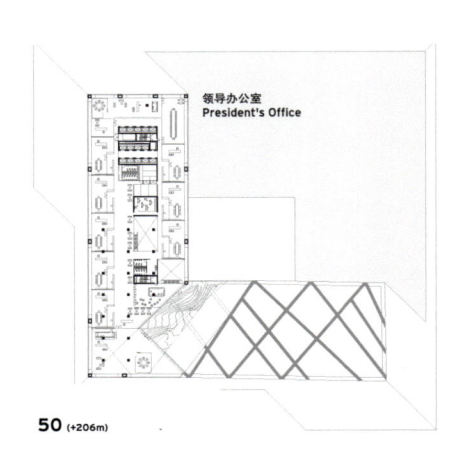

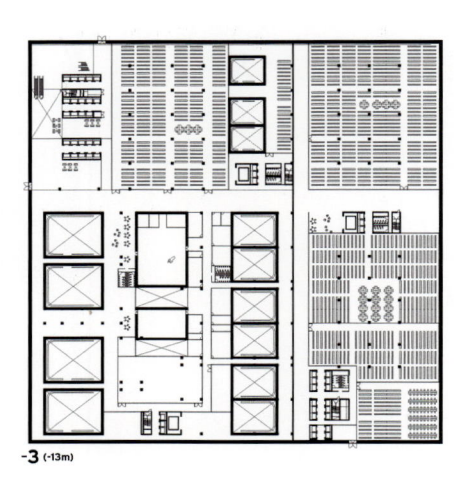

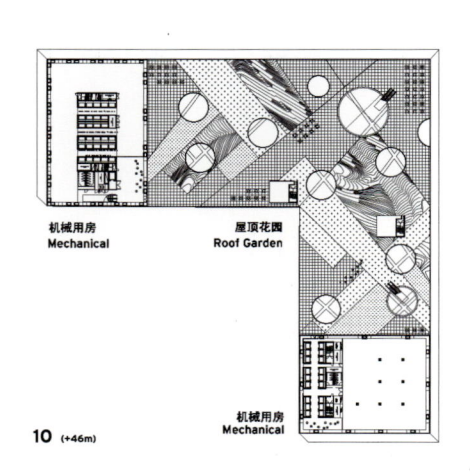

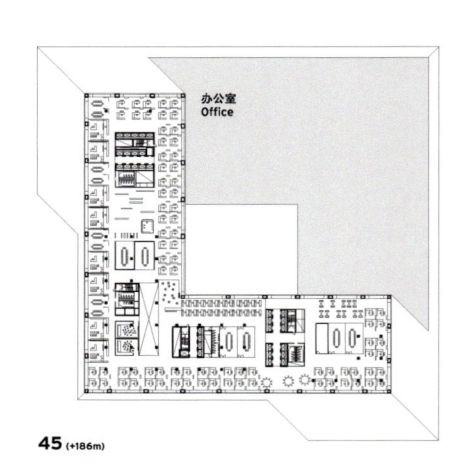

9 (+42m) 餐饮区 Food Court	25 (+106m) 新媒体 New Media / 播送 Broadcasting 技术用房 Technical Rooms	56 (+230m) 屋顶 Roof 直升机停机坪 Helipad
4 (+15m) 配音间 Dubbing Room / Voice over Room / 新闻演播室 News Studios	17 (+74m) 制作 Production 办公室 Office / 新闻 News 混合编辑 Mixed Editing	50 (+206m) 领导办公室 President's Office
-3 (-13m)	10 (+46m) 机械用房 Mechanical / 屋顶花园 Roof Garden / 机械用房 Mechanical	45 (+186m) 办公室 Office

126 Atlas: Asia and Pacific

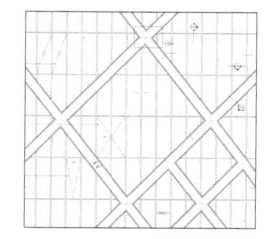

Structurally, the facade is an exoskeleton built in accordance with a standard 'diagrid' (diagonal grid) pattern. In this way, the resulting 'tube' is capable of withstanding vertical and lateral loads as well as seismic pressures of intensity 8, as calculated by simulation programs developed by Arup. The positions of the columns and diagonals of the facade reflect the distribution of forces on the skin of the building.

Steven Holl
Linked Hybrid Residential Complex
Beijing (China)

Cliente
Modern Group
Architect
Steven Holl
Collaborators
Li Hu (design architect); Hideki Hirahara (project architect); Y.Chen; C. McVoy, T. Bade; G. Ambrose, Y. Chan, R. Dias, G. Dong, P. Englaender, G. Guscianna, Y. Jang, E. Lalonde, J.Lee, R. Liu, J. MacGillivray, M. Uselman; J. Anderson, L. Bao, C. Beerli, J. Brazier,C. Caggiula, K. Cai, G. Cao, S. Chow, S. Holm Christensen, F.O. Cottier, C. Deptolla, M. Fung, M. Emran Hossain, G. Kwon, E. Li, T. Lin, C. Manning, M. Matsubayashi, G. Mitroulias, D. Nakayama, O. Schmidt, J. Tse, L. Wang, A. Wiegner, L. Wu, N. Yaffe, L. Zhao; Beijing Capital Engineering Architecture Design (local architects)
Consultants
Guy Nordenson and Associates, China Academy of Building Research (structural engineering); Transsolar, Beijing Capital Engineering Architecture Design, Cosentini (mechanical engineering); L'Observatoire International (lighting); Front, Xi'an Aircraft Industry Decoration Engineering, Shenyang Yuanda Aluminium Industry Engineering, Beijing Jianghe Curtain Wall (facade); EDAW, Beijing Top-Sense Landscape Design (landscaping); China National Decoration (interior design)
Photos
Shu He; Iwan Baan (p. 131)

ASPIRING TO EXEMPLIFY the modern residential complex of the 21st century, this ambitious 220,000 square meter project is located adjacent to the former perimeter of Beijing, and is conceived as a city within a city where 644 apartments are equipped with the services and establishments deemed necessary for the everyday life of 2,500 inhabitants, including moviehouses, daycare centers, cafés, and laundries. The premises also include a 60-room hotel. In contrast to the free-standing objects and blocks that have proliferated in the Chinese capital in the past decades, this development focuses on creating a public space that fosters interpersonal relations.

The complex is a three-dimensional urban space where the buildings, whether at, below, or above ground level, are interlinked. The ground floor is an exercise in micro-urbanism, featuring passages for residents and visitors alike to walk through, while in the semi-public central park area are five mounds made with earth excavated during pre-construction site preparation, each one a special recreation center for a particular age group. The rooftops of the lower structures are turned into tranquil green spaces that also serve as tapestries to look at from higher stories. From the 12th to the 18th floors, the eight towers are connected by a huge loop of bridges that contain facilities like a swimming pool, a fitness gym, and a café. These mid-air structures are built with two beams in parallel lattices, with diagonals at different angles that make it possible for bars to have the same tension and dimensions. At the connection to the towers, base isolators allow independent movement of 40 centimeters during earthquakes.

For sustainable development, the project resorts to recycling graywater for irrigating the green roofs and refilling cisterns. To shoulder the complex's heating and cooling load, it plants 655 geothermal wells shooting down a hundred meters underground. Solar gain and heat control systems are installed in the windows, and heating and cooling mechanisms are integrated into the slabs.

The polychromy of traditional Chinese architecture is echoed in the bright colors used to paint the window jambs and the undersides of the skybridges.

In contrast to the urban development model characterized by isolated buildings, the system that Beijing has followed in the past decades, this 220,000 square meter complex is conceived as a microcosm of a city, a three-dimensional urban enclave containing high-quality communal spaces, efficient infrastructures that are energy-saving, and the facilities and services that are deemed necessary for the everyday life of 2,500 residents.

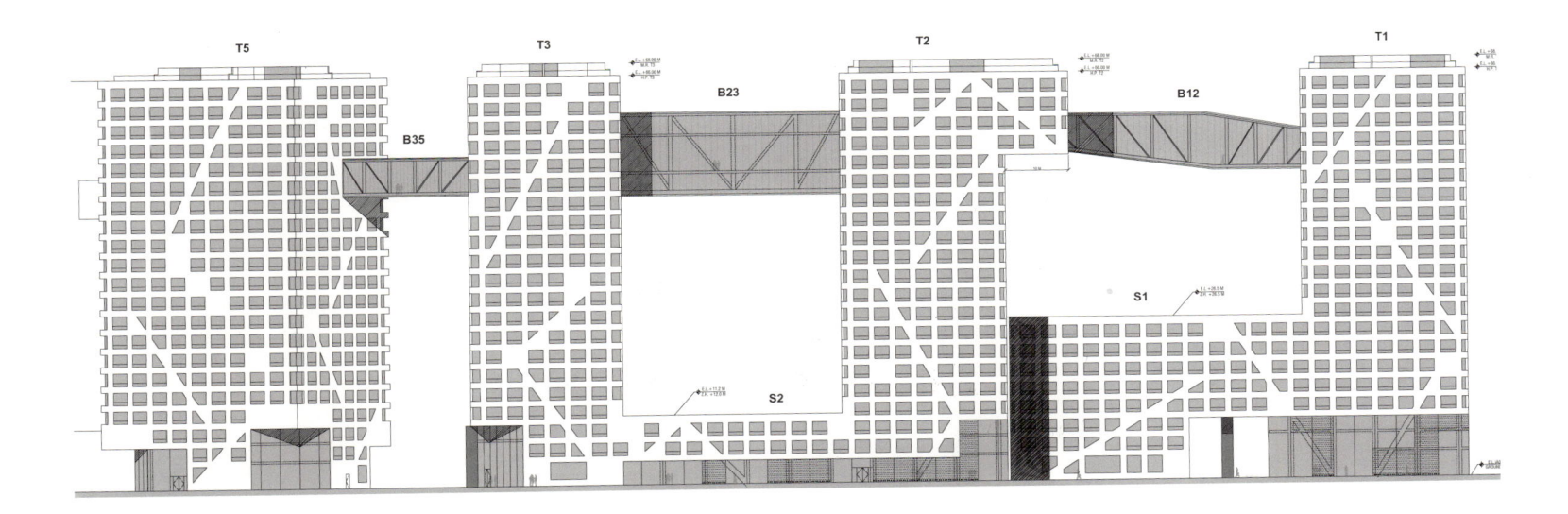

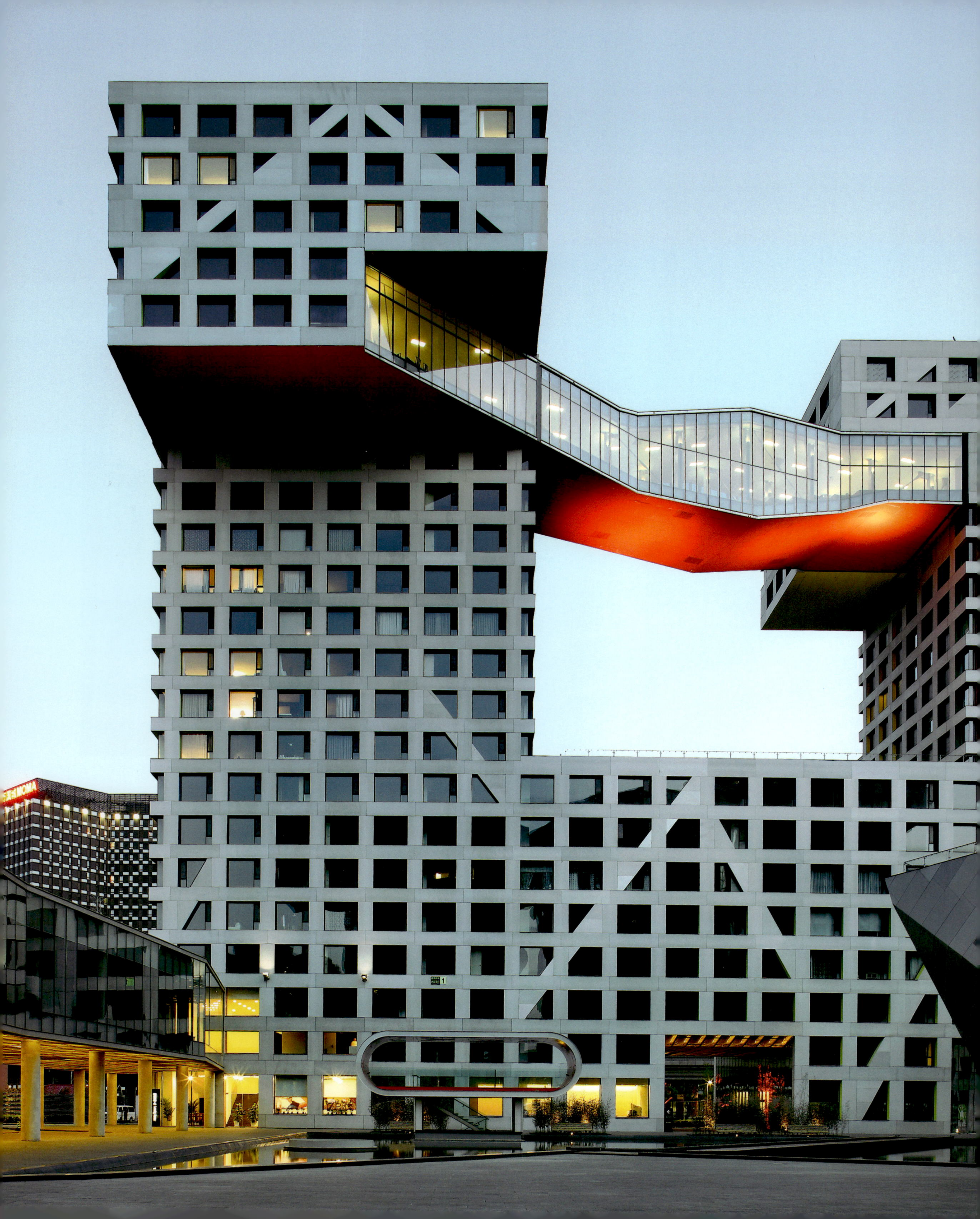

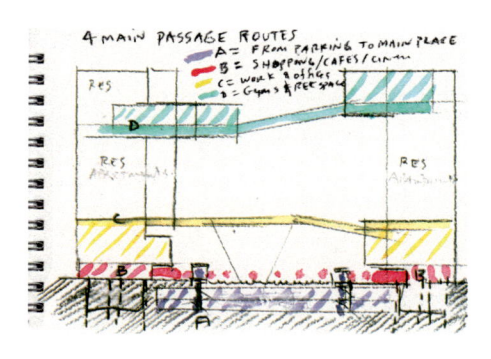

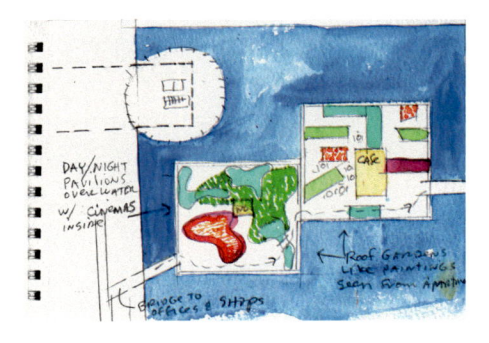

The complex offers different dwelling types, the number of bedrooms ranging from one to five, and all the apartments have openings facing two directions, following Feng Shui principles. The loop that connects the buildings at the high floor levels provides the community with sport, commercial, and recreational facilities. At ground level is an artificial landscape formed by five thematic mounds.

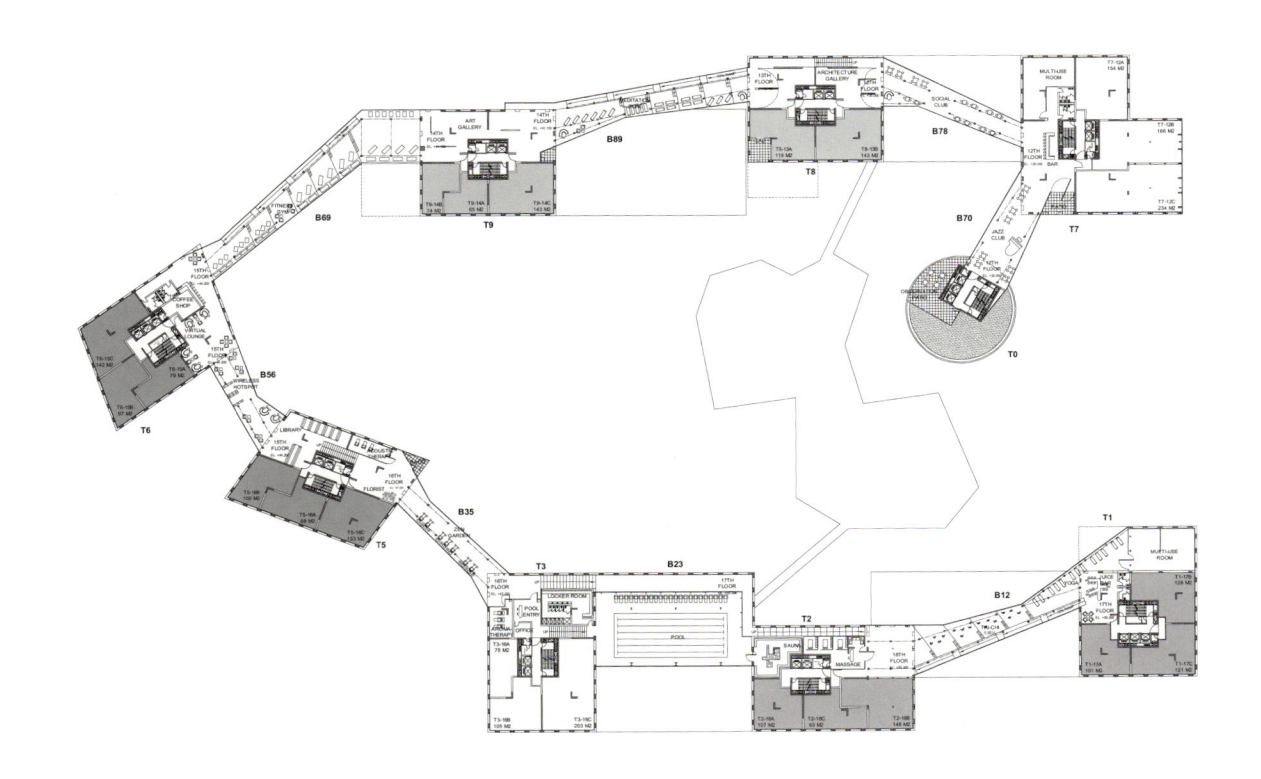

Atlas: Asia and Pacific 131

Atelier FCJZ/Yung Ho Chang
UF Soft R&D Center
Beijing (China)

Client
UF SOFT
Architects
Atelier FCJZ:Yung Ho Chang
Collaborators
Jia Iianna, Chen Long, Liu Yang, Bai Chen, Hao Shuang, Zang Feng, Yang Jing
Consultants
Beijing AS Architectural Design & Consultation Company
Photos
Shu He

THE LEADING PROVIDER of management software solutions and services in Asia entrusted its research and development center in Beijing to the studio named 'Feichang Jianzhu', which means 'unusual architecture', and indeed, the complex is worthy of that name.

This project revolved around a holistic concept of the office as a workplace with built-in facilities for rest and interpersonal relations. A widespread feature of traditional and conventional office building design is the corridor, which requires users to commute before communication, whether formal or non-formal and whether planned or spontaneous, takes place. In this case, the structure of the building is designed in such a way that communication and commutation can happen simultaneously.

The corporate center basically comprises three long parallel volumes. These are interconnected here and there by minor volumes and bridges crossing over transversally at different levels, with open-air terraces and courtyards of varying sizes arising in between where co-workers can meet and mingle and that give the complex a touch of nature through patches of lawn.

There are three main prototypes for architectural space organization, each of

Like a paradoxical fortress of concrete dotted with a multitude of holes, this center for scientific research and development presents a bold and closed exterior image, whereas the interior is decidedly open, varied, and flexible.

The technological park of UF Soft, a Chinese company that supplies software solutions and services all over Asia, was designed around a holistic concept of the office as a workplace with built-in spaces for users to rest and relate with one another in. Three teamwork models (central, linear, gridded) generate different ways of organizing work and communication spaces, which are then all reflected in the facades.

them corresponding to a particular teamwork model: central, linear, and gridded. These three models generate three different communication space systems, as well as three different relationships between work space and communication space. Each prototype layout structure is designed to allow for maximum use flexibility as well as independence of teams. Furthermore, each pattern occupies a separate floor in a volume, always in a distinct way.

Different elevation patterns are deployed to reflect these varying layout structures. The materials used for the building's skin as well as the number, types, and sizes of facade openings all tell us something about the organizational dynamics going on inside. Three main skin textures are used: glazing with wooden blinds, concrete segments measuring 190x390 milimeters and accompanied by square-shaped windows, and concrete segments sized 90x390 milimeters with band windows.

This science park has a total built area of 46,121 square meters and includes desks for as many as 3,000 research engineers. The complex was designed to maximize per capita work space; that is, the space per table length, which in turn supports either individual or group work, as needed.

Atlas: Asia and Pacific 133

The floor plan is based on three elongated prisms laid out parallel to one another and connected at various points of the premises, and at different levels, by a series of outdoor 'bridges' and terraces. Each type of working space organization corresponds to a facade pattern that arises from a particular combination of a few set elements: windows and glazed openings, wooden blinds, prefabricated pieces of concrete, and small glass block elements.

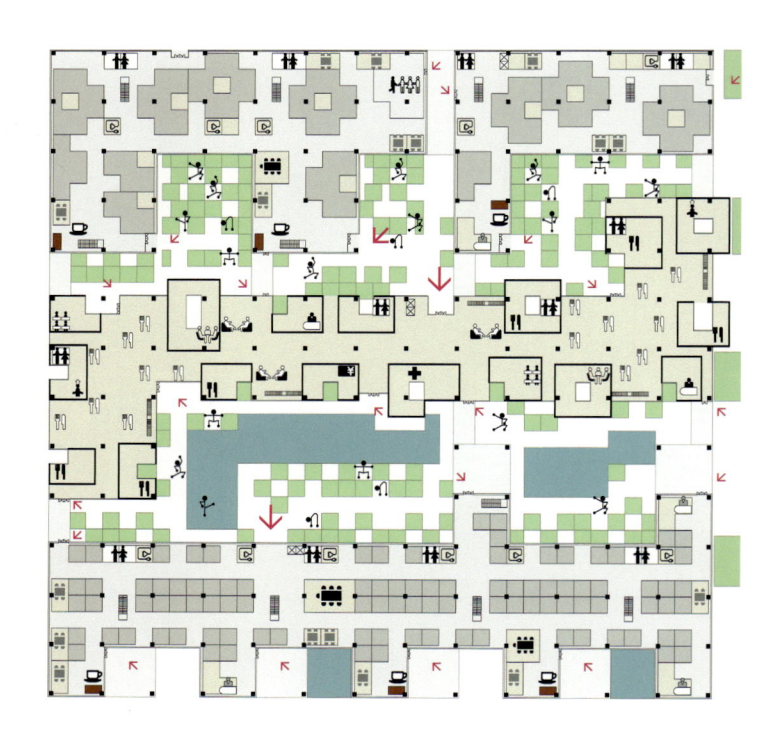

134 Atlas: Asia and Pacific

Atlas: Asia and Pacific **135**

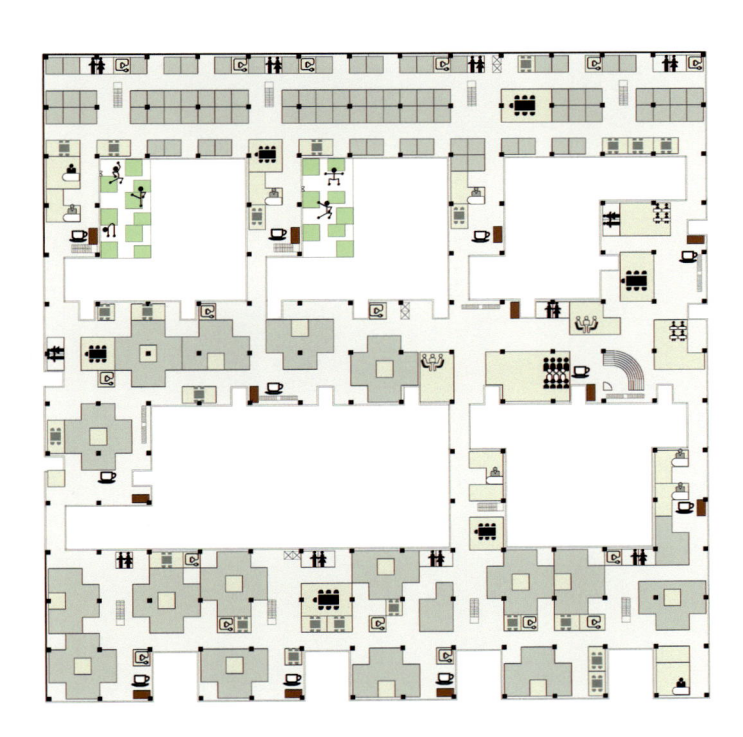

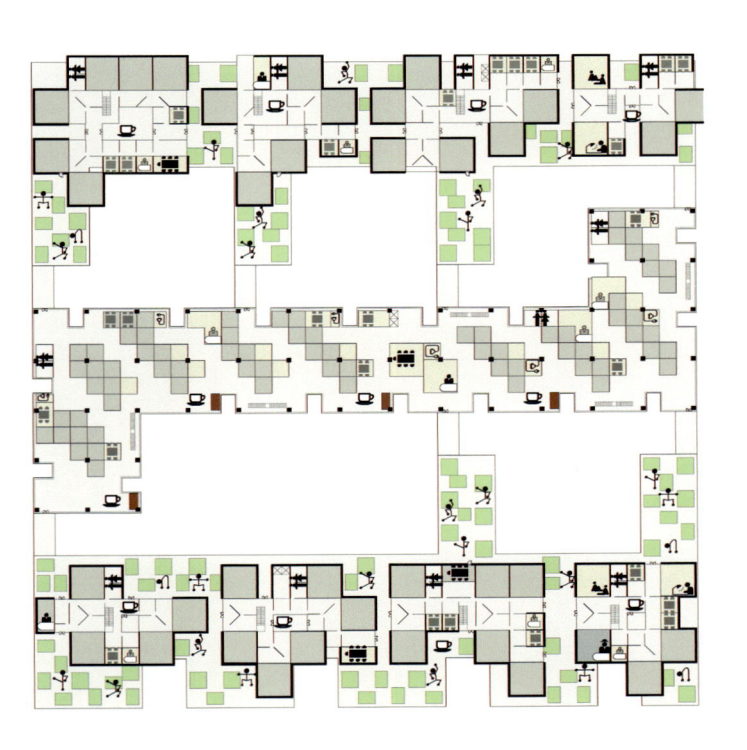

In+of Architecture / Wang Lu
Hope Primary School
Leiyang, Hunan (China)

Client
Zhejiang Association of Commerce in Hunan
Architects
in+of Architecture: Wang Lu; Tsinghua University
Collaborators
Lu Jiangsong, Huan Huaihai, Zheng Xiaodong
Contractor
Farmers of Maoping Village
Photos
Christian Richters

On July 19, 2006, rainstorms and mountain floods caused by Typhoon Bilis destroyed the original buildings of a primary school in Maoping Village, a small community 30 kilometers south of Leiyang, in Hunan Province. The Zhejiang Association of Commerce (ZS) urgently raised 500,000 RMB (50,000 euros) to build the new ZS Hope Primary School besides provide for new classroom desks, blackboards, and uniforms. The floor area of the school is 1,168 square meters and the construction cost, including interior plaster rendering, was 300,000 RMB, amounting to only 300 RMB (30 euros) per square meter.

Wang Lu's studio started site analysis on August 5, barely a month after the storms and floods, and with the villagers' help, finished construction on December 8, 2007, just sixteen months later.

Design work involved learning from the experiences of the townsfolk and making an in-depth analysis of their particular way of life. Charged with a modern sensibility, the team of architects sought to invoke the local spirit and keep alive both the memory of the past and the good tradition of structures well-suited to local conditions, all the while also seeking to expand the values of local culture by giving the building a true spirit

The school is the result of efforts made in solidarity with rural Maoping Village, whose original primary school was destroyed by a typhoon in 2006. It was replaced through funds raised and manual help from locals.

The team of architects traveled to the place to learn the building traditions and way of life of the townsfolk. Both in size and in volume, with its pitched roof, the new school blends with the surrounding houses. It also uses the same materials: baked brick for the pillars and loadbearing walls, and wood for the roof structure, the window frames, and the finishes. The construction sits on terraced ground.

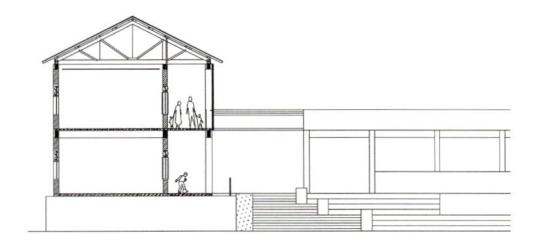

of the times besides making it represent its humanistic, educational function.

Maoping Village and its houses follow the contours of the hills. The two-story schoolhouse stands on terraced ground embedded into a slope. The configuration, cross-section, materials, and colors of the building are isomorphic to the surrounding houses, and the scale of its gables is commensurate with them. The breaking-up of the structure by sky-wells corresponding to teachers' offices and staircases makes the building resemble a cluster of local houses and blend with the environment.

To minimize costs and adapt to local techniques, bricks were the main material used: red for the building, gray for the pavements. The north facade has some brick latticeworks to echo local tradition, reduce loads, and ensure ventilation. Latticework of this kind, on its north wall, becomes the only decor in the lobby, from where one has a digitalized view of the landscape outside. The south facade, with its wooden framework screen as its integral part, similarly borrowed from the language of local architecture, and in this case took on symbolic significance. Evoking an unfolded role of bamboo slips for writing, the facade gives the schoolhouse an air of scholarship.

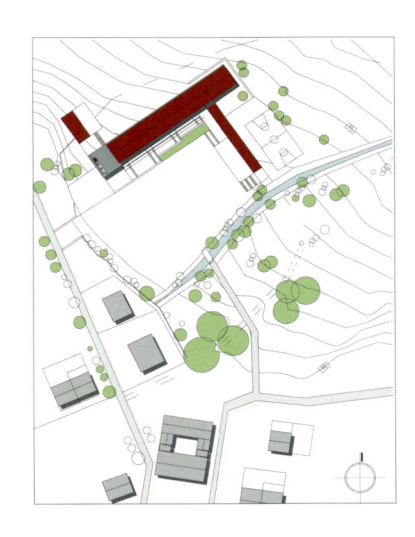

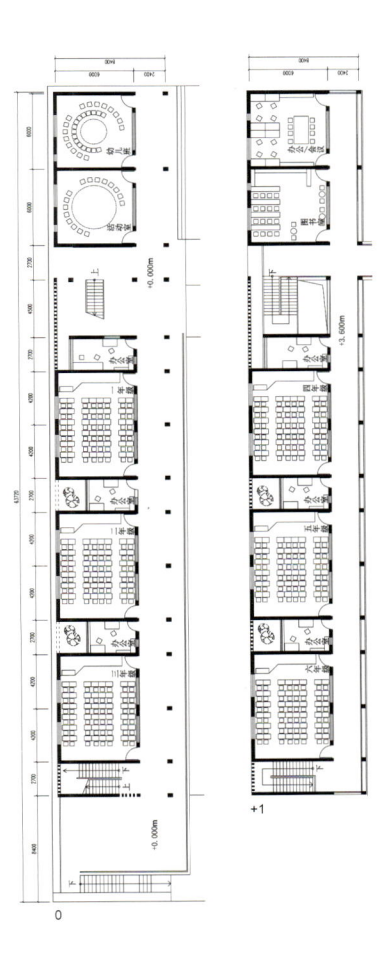

Atlas: Asia and Pacific **137**

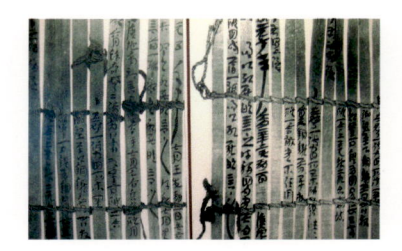

Because of the scarcity of financial resources available for the raising of the school, materials were made the most of. The brick latticeworks on the north facade are usual in the area. They spare the non-loadbearing walls of extra weight, help in ventilation, allow views, and become decorative motifs that have the effect of integrating the building into its environment. The wooden poles evoke roles of bamboo slips for Chinese writing.

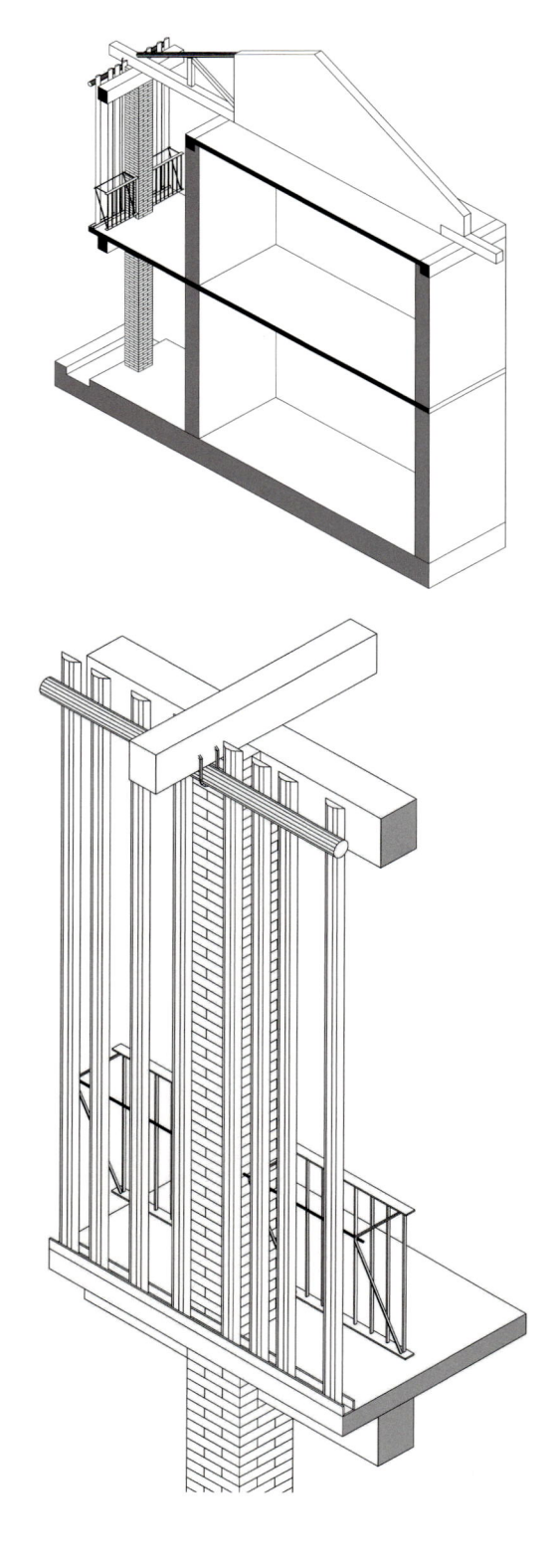

138   Atlas: Asia and Pacific

Building techniques traditionally used in the area were applied in the construction of this school, in this case by local volunteers. Simple wooden trusses rest on loadbearing walls of brick and pillars of the same material, forming a covered gallery on the top floor, protected from the sun. The gaps between supports are modest - 6 meters between walls, 4.2 between pillars - but enough to obtain diaphanous classrooms.

Amateur Studio/Wang Shu & Lu Wenyu
History Museum
Ningbo, Zhejiang (China)

Clients
Ningbo Museum, City Government of Ningbo
Architects
Amateur Architecture Studio:
Wang Shu & Lu Wenyu
Collaborators
Song Shuhua, Jiang Weihua, Chen Lichao (design); Architectural Construction Research Institute Architecture, China Academy of Art (design and construction design); Wu Qingbing (construction manager); Hu Jun (construction supervisor); Lin Mi (management supervisor)
Consultants
Shentu Tuanbing, Chen Yongbing (structural design); Ningbo Yinzhou Urban Investment & Construction (construction supervision)
Contractor
Zhejiang Second Construction Group; Ni Liangfu (foreman)
Photos
Iwan Baan

The museum rises from the ground like a stone block amid a landscaped plaza in the outskirts of Ningbo. The exterior finish uses a huge amount of materials salvaged from remains of old dwellings in the region.

THE MUSEUM IS a three-story block on the northwestern edge of an empty plaza in Yinzhou, a blooming district in the outskirts of the booming southern Chinese city of Ningbo. It rises on rice fields that over the years have turned fallow as a result of urbanization. Because of the way in which the 24 meter high walls of the bamboo-cast concrete facade are treated, the form of the building strikes the approaching visitor as strange. Where a line is supposed to be straight, for instance, it curves a bit, resulting in something that looks more like a living creature than like a solid construction. Or, perfectly blending into its surroundings, the building gives the impression that it has been there for centuries or even forever, left to the elements by natural forces. It is a museum of archaeology that is fittingly designed and built as if by archaeological time.

On coming closer, visitors find themselves intrigued by the surfaces of the facades, inconsistently rendered as they are with seemingly ill-fitting pieces. The technique is borrowed from what is known in the area as *wapan* tiling, a tradition of emergency wall building in the wake of a typhoon. In a nod to local building practices as well as to the archaeological finds that the museum contains and displays, the walls are coated with more than twenty varieties of gray- and red-colored bricks and roof tiles that were salvaged from destruction sites in the region, particularly the remains of farmers' homes.

Wang Shu of Amateur Architecture Studio in Beijing guided hired craftsmen and builders in mock-up experiments with the recycled pieces, and the imperfection and randomness of the facade is due to the fact that the workers had no means of controlling the portions of the different materials. The deliberately haphazard positioning of the small rectangular windows, which give no information whatsoever about the building's interior spaces and contents, further contributes to the erratic irregular effect of the object as a whole.

Both the carved geological form of the building and the petrous nature of its skin are a salute to the mountains, as is the composition of the 30,000 square meter museum space. Three staircases create three valleys, one of them outside. Four caves define the entrance, the lobby, and the cliffs of the exterior valley. A mountainous topography is superimposed. Paths stretch from the ground into a maze of pathways.

The north wing rests on a pond whose banks are covered with reeds. The water flows over a dam at the middle entry and onto a large field of cobblestones.

Designed to evoke the mountains, on plan the building shows three 'valleys' - two inside and one outside - taken up by staircases. Bamboo stems were used to build the formwork of the concrete walls, a rarely applied technique. The main court of the museum cuts through the entire volume, reaching all the way to the passable roof. Its finish, based on pieces of u-glass, strikes a strong contrast with the other surfaces of the building.

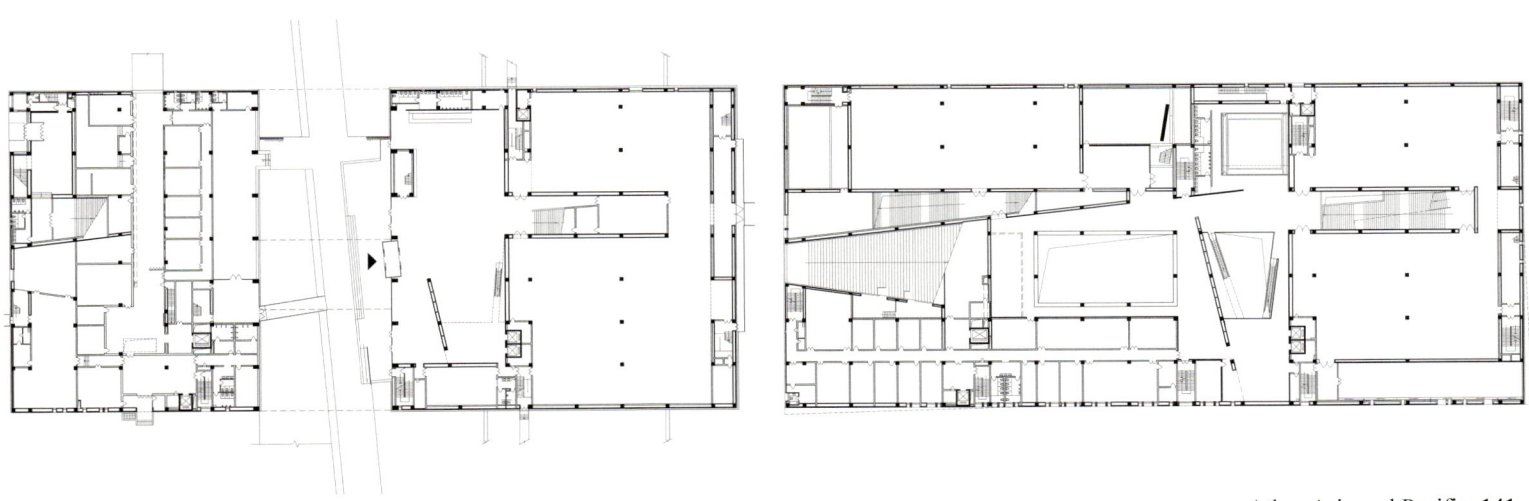

Atlas: Asia and Pacific 141

142 Atlas: Asia and Pacific

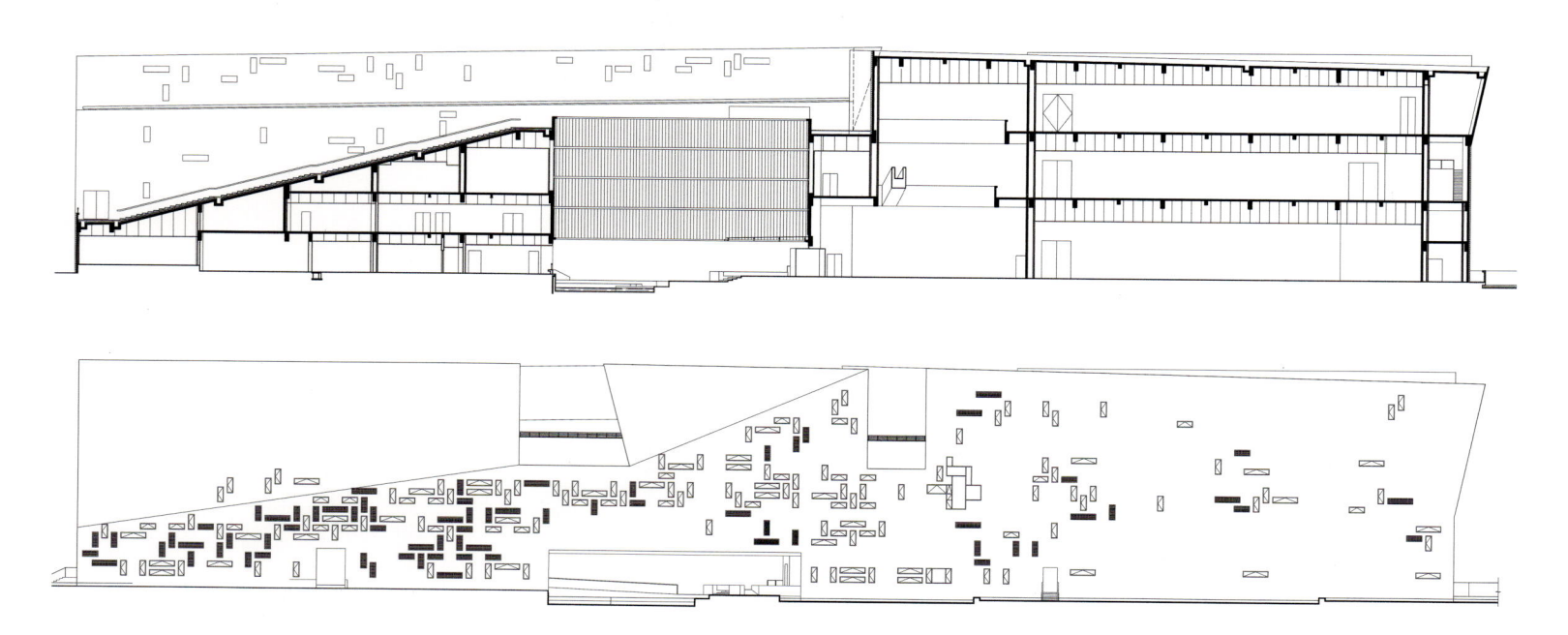

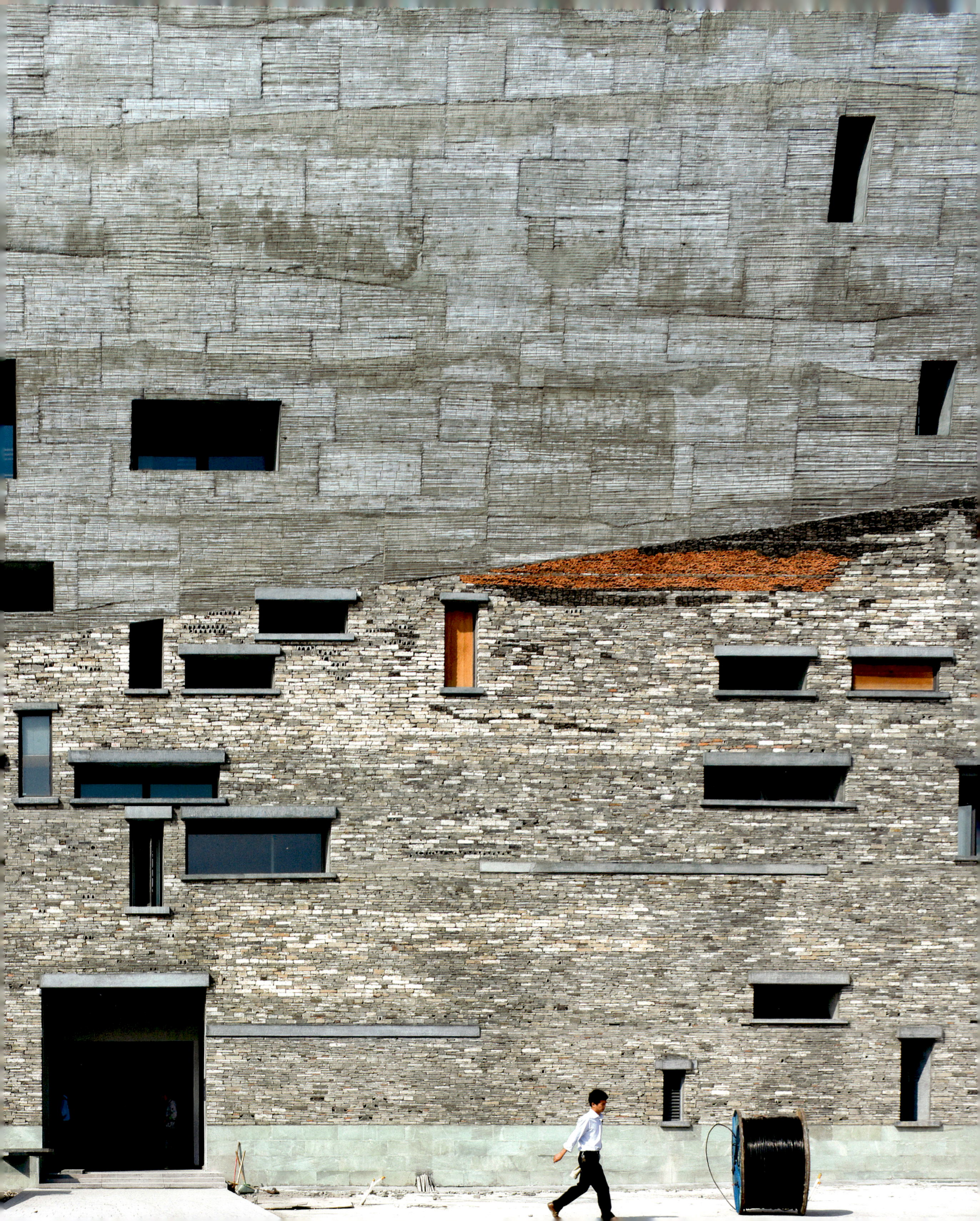

Zhang Lei
Two Brick Houses
Gaochun, Jiangsu (China)

Clients
Ye Hui & Wang Yongjun
Architects
Zhang Lei
Collaborators
Gaochun Architecture Design Institute
Photos
Iwan Baan

The houses are in a lakeside town and take from the traditional Chinese courtyard. The smaller one (for a poet) is private and simple, the larger building (for an official's family) opens on to views of the lake.

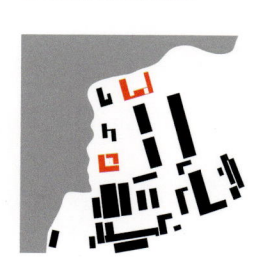

THESE TWO HOUSES are located in the outskirts of the town of Gaochun, in China's Jiangsu province. Since this is as much as an hour and a half away from the nearest city, the provincial capital of Nanjing, it was decided that the buildings should rely heavily on the bricks made in nearby fields and that abound in the buildings of the area. In this way, the construction workers could go about their tasks in ways that they were familiar with, and with the cost of materials and labor thus reduced, it was possible to stick to a modest budget of 80 euros per square meter.

The architect added sophistication to the brick facade by using three different brick textures. Where the skin is not flat, an interlocking pattern creates perforations, creating a sense of porosity. Elsewhere, protruding bricks produce shadows along the wall. From afar the textures, arranged in rectangular patches and punctuated by the occasional portal or window, present yet another geometry. The result is a surface of abstract shapes that the architect likens to a Mondrian painting.

The playful facades belie the houses' sober inspiration: the traditional inward-looking Chinese courtyard. That of the larger house, built for a government official's family, opens on one side to allow views of the neighboring lake from a double-height living room, but the other house, which was commissioned by a poet, has two L shapes closing in on a smaller, more private courtyard. A glassed-in room for parties and exhibitions looks on to the lake from the courtyard, where a small wooden tea house sits like a sculpture.

Sustainability and adaptability to climate were two main objectives, determining not only the double roof, but also the thick, heat-absorbing brick walls. The qualities of earth block were also capitalized on, this material being ideal for moderating the region's high temperatures.

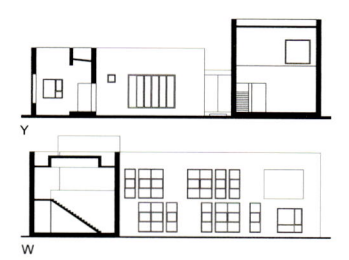

Because the place is remote, local materials and workers were used. The structure is of simple concrete beams on loadbearing brick walls: a double sheet that allows plays of texture in the facades. An interlocking pattern creates lattice-like perforations and bricks protruding from the surface produce shadows along the wall and a 'bristly canvas' effect. Each piece of facade is punctuated by a door, an opening, or a window.

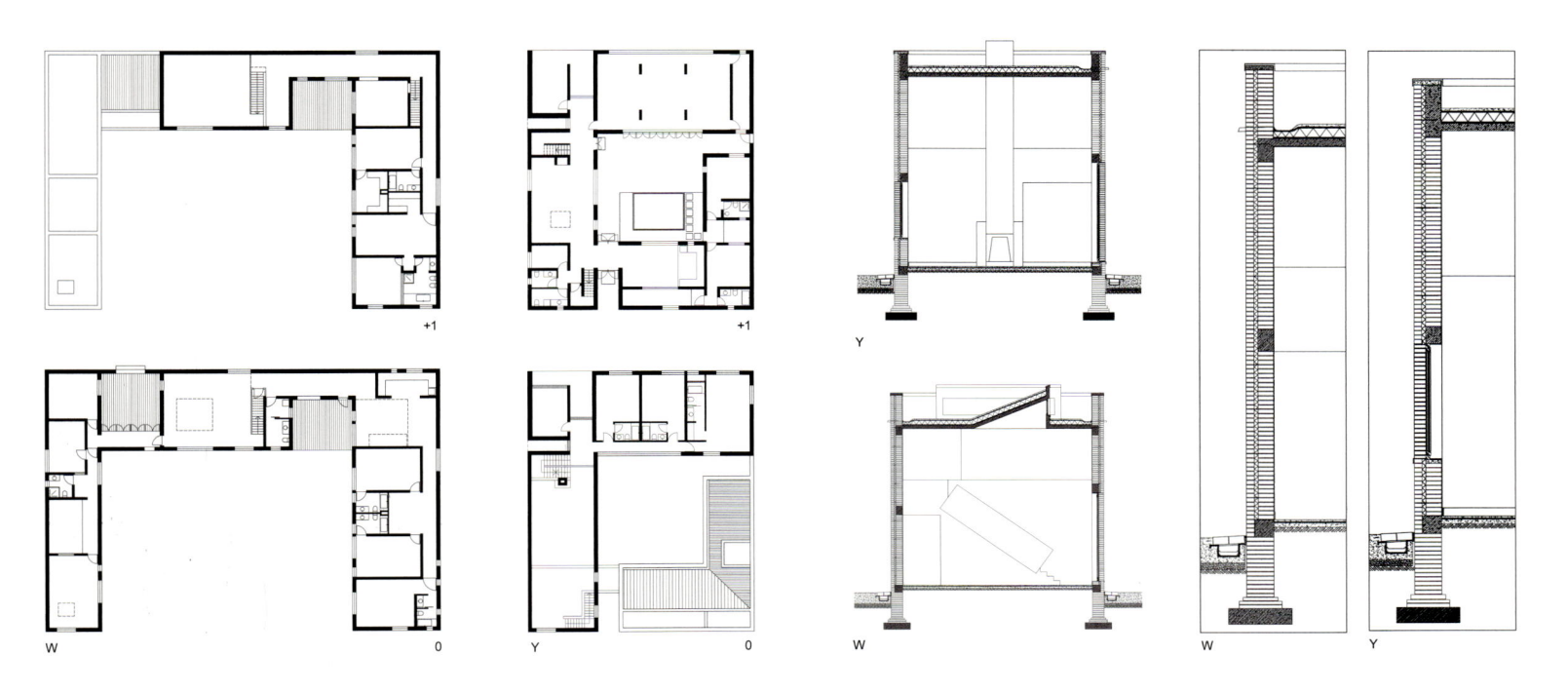

Atlas: Asia and Pacific

Zaha Hadid
Opera House
Guangzhou (China)

Client
Guangzhou Municipal Government
Architect
Zaha Hadid
Collaborators
Woody K.T. Yao, Patrik Schumacher (project director); Simon Yu (project architect); J. Guo, Y. Jingwen, L. Jiang, T. Hsu, Y. Liu, Z. Wang, C. Chow, C. Shing, F. Innocenti, L. Sanchez, H. Kwong; Competition: F. Innocenti, M. Musacchio, J. Huang, H. Chee, M. Planteu, P. Cattarin, T. Jacobs, F. Vera, Y. Brosilovski, V. Haremst, C. Ludwig, C. Beaumont, L. Grifantini, F. La Gioia, N. Safainia, M. Henn, A. Gergen, C. Shing, G. Modlen, I. Mahmood, Y. Hayano, A. De Gioannis, Y. Ma, B. Pfenningstorff
Consultants
Guangzhou Pearl River Foreign Investment Architectural Designing Institute (structure, building services & local design); SHTK (structure); Marshall Day (acoustics); KGE (facade); Beijing Light & View (lighting); Guangzhou Municipal Construction (project management); ENFI (theater); Jiancheng (costs).
Competition: Ove Arup (structure, services, acoustics); Davis Langdon & Everest (costs)
Contractor
China Construction Third Engineering
Photos
Christian Richters;
Virgile Simon Bertrand (pp. 147, 148)

AT THE HEART of a huge, major cultural sites development program is this complex, key to the southern Chinese city's efforts to improve its arts atmosphere and put an end to its reputation for mere money-orientedness. With its 46,000 square meters, it is the country's third largest performing center, after the National Grand Theater in Beijing and the Shanghai Grand Theater. Adopting the very latest technology in its design and construction, it is slated to resonate the high notes of Chinese opera in harmony with the tenor of its western brother, and in doing so, be a lasting monument to the New Millennium, confirming Guangzhou as one of Asia's cultural centers.

Two adjacent boulders of different shapes overlook the Pearl River. The larger one is the actual opera house with its grand theater seating 1,800. Besides the entrance hall, a lounge, and all attendant ancillary facilities, there is also an art exhibitions gallery. The smaller boulder is a multi-purpose hall for an audience of 400. This is a venue for anything from chamber music to fashion shows or news briefings. Here the stage, the scenery, and even the seats are moveable, making the hall ideal for experimental plays.

The giant twin 'pebbles' are set on undulating ground, with a grassy slope containing a five meter entrance. Under the grass to the south is a café, and on top of this is a ticket office. Inside the complex, the stone walls of the halls form an array of fabulous mountains. The transparent glass walls give people the illusion they are outdoors, amid natural scenery.

The building rises and falls at the foot of Zhujiang Boulevard. As an adjunct to the Haixinsha Tourist Park Island, it presents a contoured profile that gives visitors a wide riverside focus. Viewed from the center of the boulevard, it offers a visual prelude to the park island beyond. Seen from the Pearl, the towers of Zhujiang New Town are a dramatic backdrop for it, and help give a unified vision of civic and cultural buildings in a riverside setting.

An internal street which acts as an access promenade is cut into the landscape, beginning at a proposed museum site on the opposite side of the central boulevard and leading on to the Opera House. A café, a bar, a restaurant, and retail facilities, embedded like shells into these landforms, are located to one side of the promenade. Visitors coming by car or by bus are dropped off on the north of the site, on Huaniu Road. Service vehicles arrive at either end of this same street, whereas VIP access is from the western boundary facing Huaxia Road.

This cultural complex, due for completion in time for the Asian Games of 2010, consists of two giant pebbles propped on the bank of the Pearl River: an opera house with a seating capacity of 1,800 and a multi-purpose hall for an audience of 400. Viewed from the river, the soaring towers of the southern Chinese city's new business district will serve as a dramatic built backdrop for the sculptural volume of the opera house.

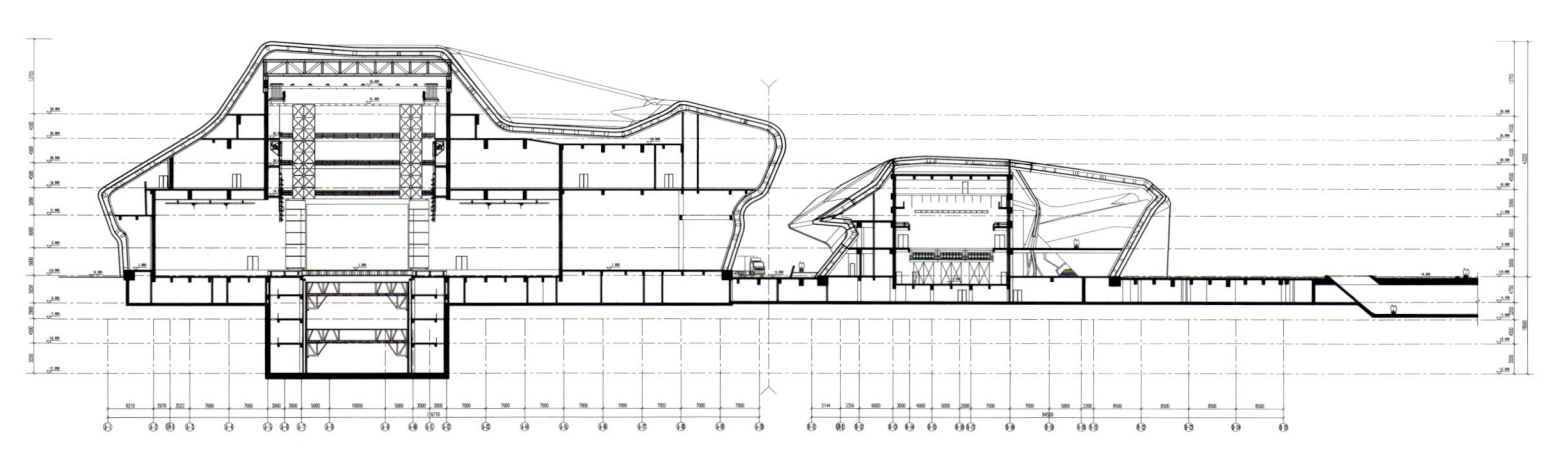

Building the 'skin' of the opera house was a huge challenge, structurally, owing to its irregularity and the inclination of its walls. These are rendered in accordance with a triangulated pattern of rectangular sections made of welded steel, and over forty 'nodes' of wrought steel, high-precision pieces whose cost would be exorbitant in the west. No less intricate, the main auditorium's geometry is built with stone-clad reinforced concrete.

148 Atlas: Asia and Pacific

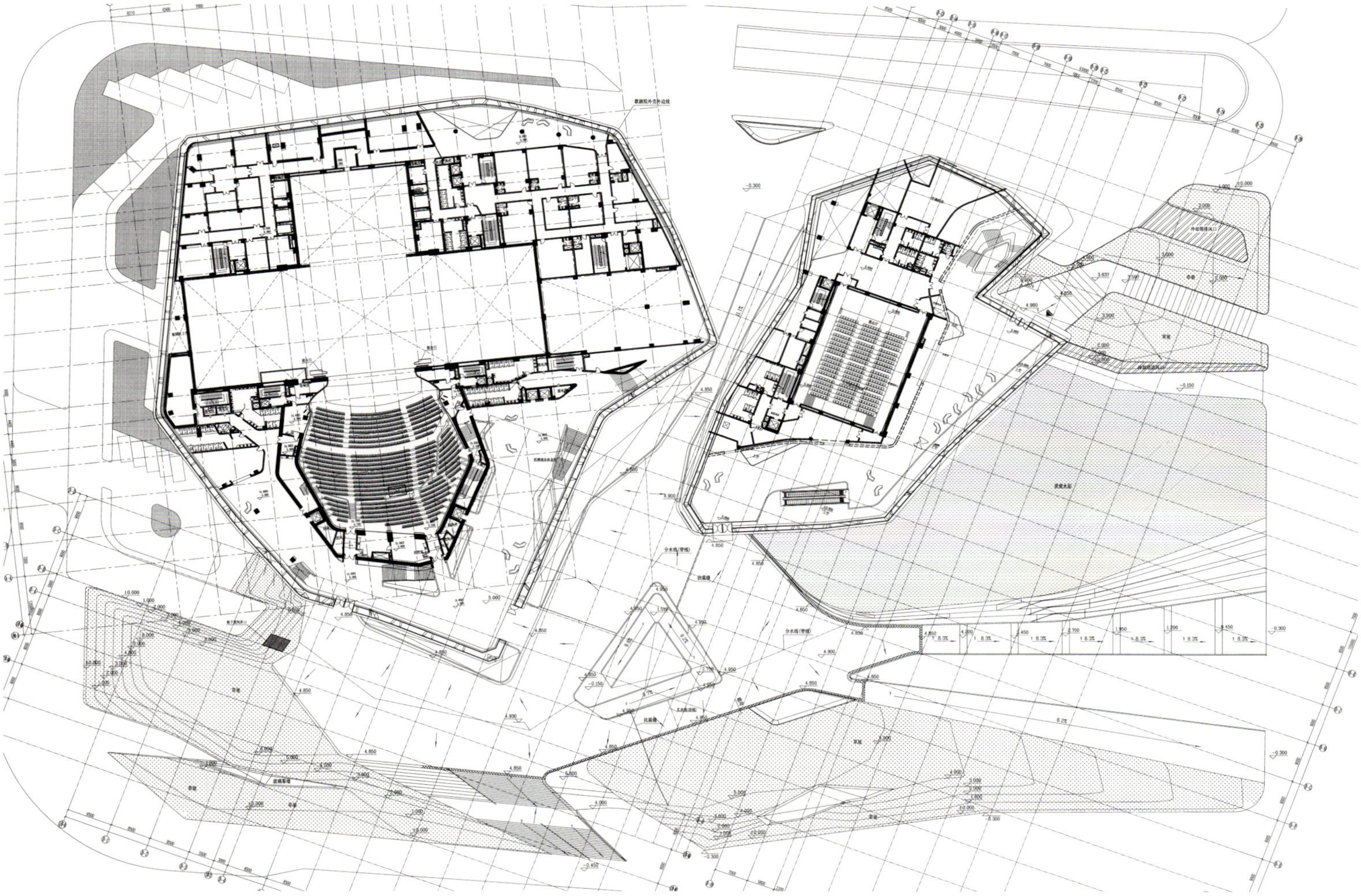

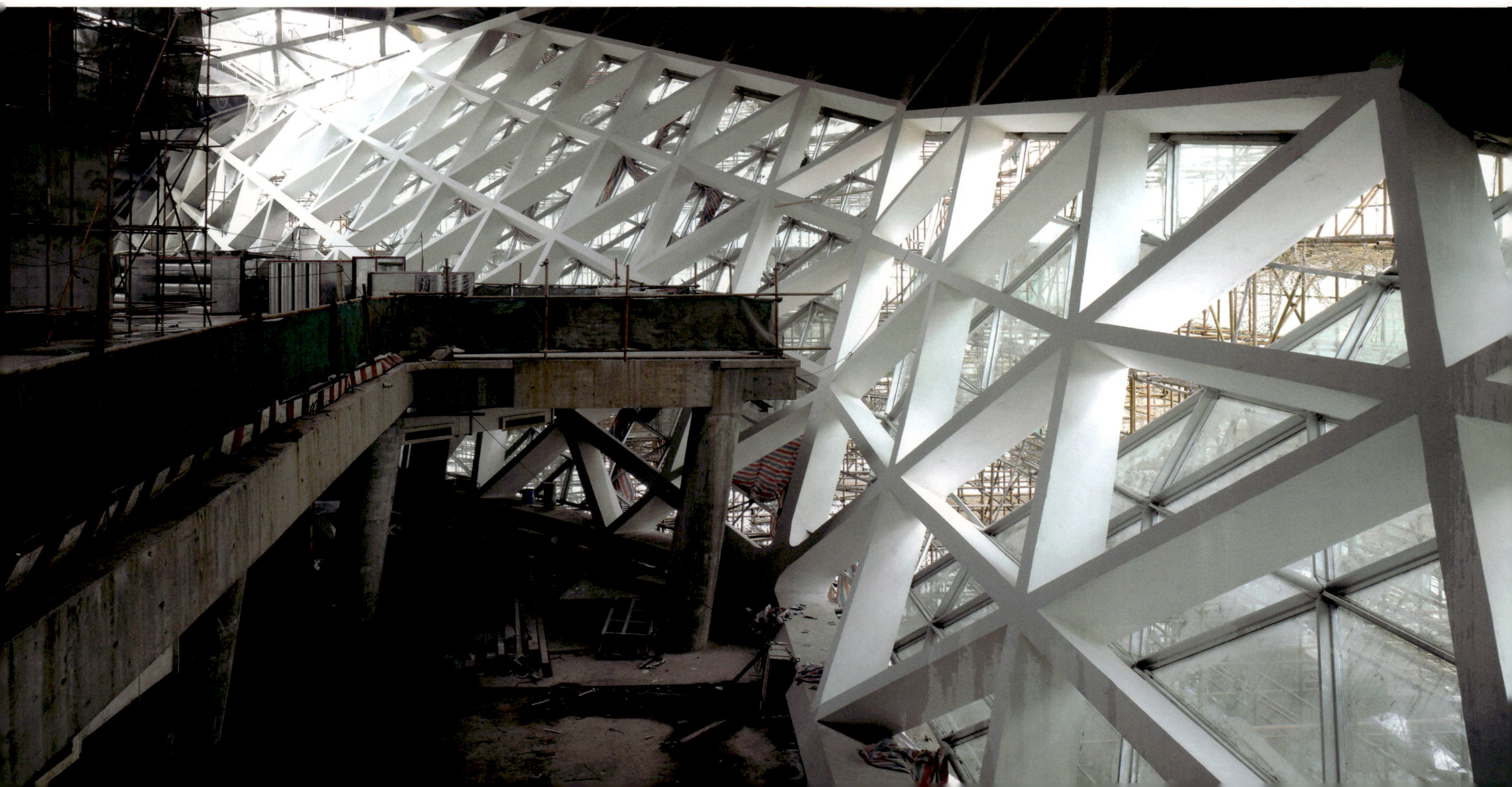

Studio Pei Zhu
Yue Minjun Museum
Qingcheng, Sichuan (China)

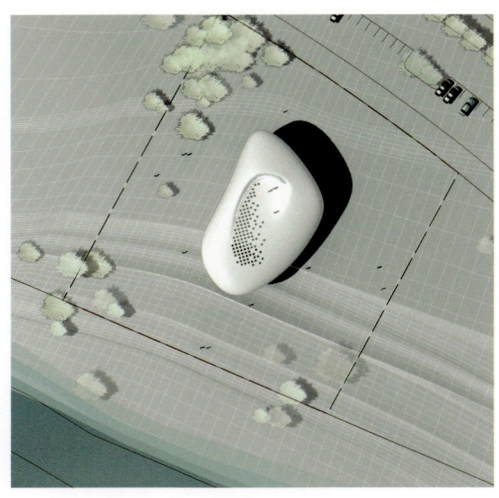

Client
Municipal Government of Dujiangyan
Architects
Studio Pei Zhu: Pei Zhu, Tong Wu
Collaborators
Zeng Xiaoming (associate in charge);
Design team: He Han, Jiao Chongxia,
Li Yongquan, Fan Xuelan
Consultants
Rory McGowan/Arup (structure);
Xu Minsheng/China High-Rise
Construction Investment Company:
Photos
Fang Zhenning

Set on the banks of the Shimeng, the museum is inspired by the gentle sinuous shapes of the boulders abounding along the riverbeds. Not far is the Dujiang reservoir, a place of great ecological and patrimonial value.

IN SICHUAN PROVINCE, in an extraordinary location on the banks of the Shimeng River, with the picturesque Qingcheng Mountains for a backdrop and not far from the ancient Dujiang Weir reservoir - a system of irrigation canals constructed in the 3rd century BC -, two sights which Unesco has declared Patrimony of Humanity, a large-scale project is being undertaken under the auspices of the government of Dujiangyan, which has ceded over seven hectares of land for the purpose. This is a complex of ten museums, each one dedicated to a particular iconic and influential Chinese artist. Zhang Xiaogang, Wang Guangyi, and Yue Minjun are among those selected.

The aim of the Dujiangyan authorities is to lure visitors to the area through a new sprout of attractions incorporating 21st-century elements into the landscape. A curved opaque building will showcase the work of Yue Minjun, a leader of the Cynical Realism movement that emerged in Beijing in the wake of the 1989 rallies in Tiananmen Square. Yue Minjun is a pioneering figure in Chinese contemporary art and is internationally famous for his signature images of repeated smiling and laughing faces, at once optimistic and thought-provoking self-portraits that he renders in sculptures, paintings, and drawings.

The location of this art museum is a marvellous landscape of brooks and creeks, wreaths of mist, and lovely mountains. The challenge was to defer to this timeless nature without necessarily succumbing to the use of local materials and traditional vocabularies, all the while addressing the artist's highly personal contemporary art attitudes. Inspired by a cobblestone he picked up one day along the riverbank, he conceived an oblong sphere to contain 1,000 square meters of private galleries and a small artist's studio. Then he gave its exterior surface, at once smooth and diverse like a cobble, a coating of highly polished zinc. Zinc is a soft light metal that blends nicely into the natural environment, mildly reflecting the surroundings and melting into them while giving the ancient organic form of a pebble a futuristic look, so that what looks like an irregular pebble that has just been tossed to the ground, still tottering, could also be a spaceship that is just landing on the spot.

The Yue Minjun Art Museum thus presents the artist's characteristic features, participates in nature, and engages in dialogue with eternity in a language of the future that surpasses realism and travels to the territory of the surreal. Despite delays caused by the earthquake that shook the area in May 2008, construction is underway.

Yue Minjun, among contemporary Chinese artists the most famous and sought after in the western market, will now have 1,000 square meters in which to display his works, along with a studio in the same place. The museum will be coated with sheets of zinc, a material that adapts to the geometry of the piece and reflects on its skin the surrounding natural environment, making the building perceivable as part of the landscape.

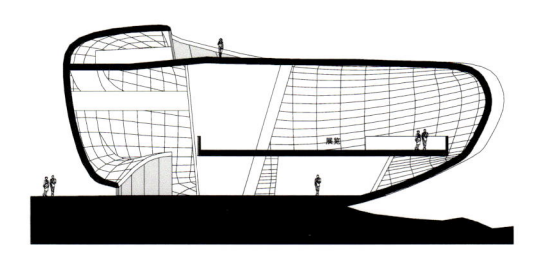

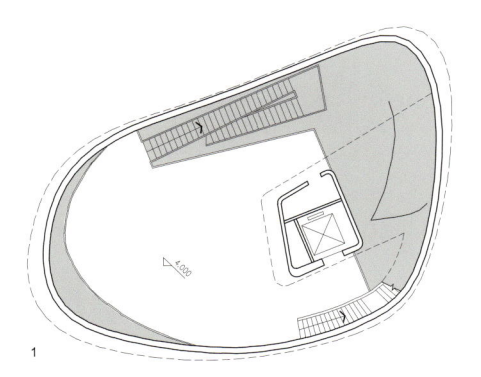

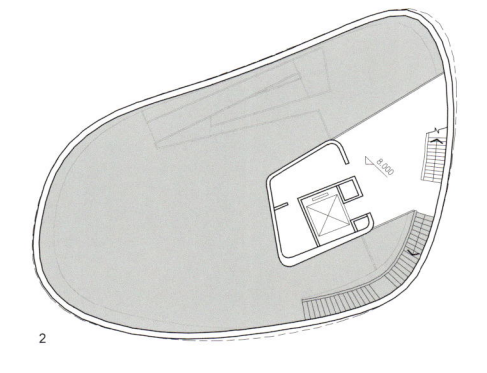

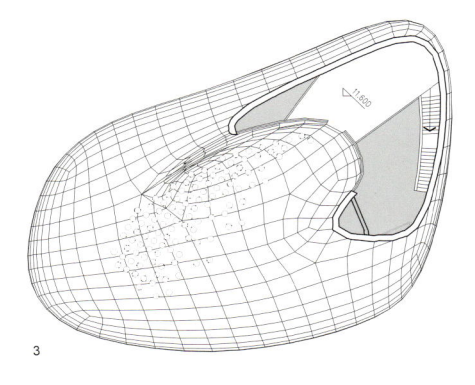

1

2

3

Atlas: Asia and Pacific **151**

Ai Weiwei
Ordos 100
Ordos, Inner Mongolia (China)

Client
Jiang Yuan Cultural & Creative Industrial Development, Jiang Yuan Water Engineering
Curator
Ai Weiwei & FAKE Design
Architect selection
Herzog & de Meuron;

On a 197 hectare land, the Ordos 100 project has invited a hundred architects from the world over to design a hundred mansions in a new growth area of Ordos, a city recently founded on the Mongolian steppes.

ORDOS IS A Chinese city in the autonomous region of Inner Mongolia, located 600 kilometers west of Beijing. It is in a territory of plateaus and mountains, with a continental climate of long, cold, dry winters, that in the past years has been subjected to a serious desertification process. Nevertheless, the reserves of oil, natural gas, and coal that abound in its subsoil have made it a candidate for rapid development. The city is a colonial settlement founded in 2001 along the Yellow River.

The aim of the Ordos 100 project is to catalyze the urban development of the city and the desert region surrounding it through the construction of a hundred villas, each of them a thousand square meters. The masterplan of the complex was drawn up by FAKE Design under the direction of Ai Weiwei. Herzog & de Meuron selected the 100 architectural firms to be summoned from all over the world to develop the individual projects. The final list names architects from 29 countries. Phase 1 of the operation involves the development of 28 parcels. Materialization of the remaining 72 projects will make up Phase 2.

The masterplan arranges the 100 parcels that will be settings for mansions of affluent families with a liking for contemporary art. The client has imposed certain conditions common to all the villas, such as number of bedrooms, installations of western standards, rooms for household staff, and covered swimming pools. Complying with these specifications, the architects have total freedom to experiment.

Given the area's harsh climate conditions and its tradition of nomadic architecture, with the Mongolian *yurtas* as the most significant building type, most of the projects resort to vernacular elements such as half-buried courtyards, thick walls with high thermal intertia, and concentrated arrangements of elements, which are then reinterpreted in a contemporary language.

In January 2008, the architects participating in the first phase of the project were summoned to present their proposals in a joint model (previous page) and sign the final contract. The projects put forward constitute a varied catalog of upscale contemporary residential architecture and were all developed in a matter of a few months, after a single visit by the architectural teams to the site (right), an area currently undergoing urbanization.

006. MOS

009. Barozzi Veiga

019. Coll & Leclerc

024. Multiplicities

026. R& Sie

035. Frente

046. Johnston Mark Lee

052. Tatiana Bilbao

070. Sou Fujimoto

074. JDS/ Julen de Smedt

092. SsD Architecture

098. HA:SKA

Atlas: Asia and Pacific

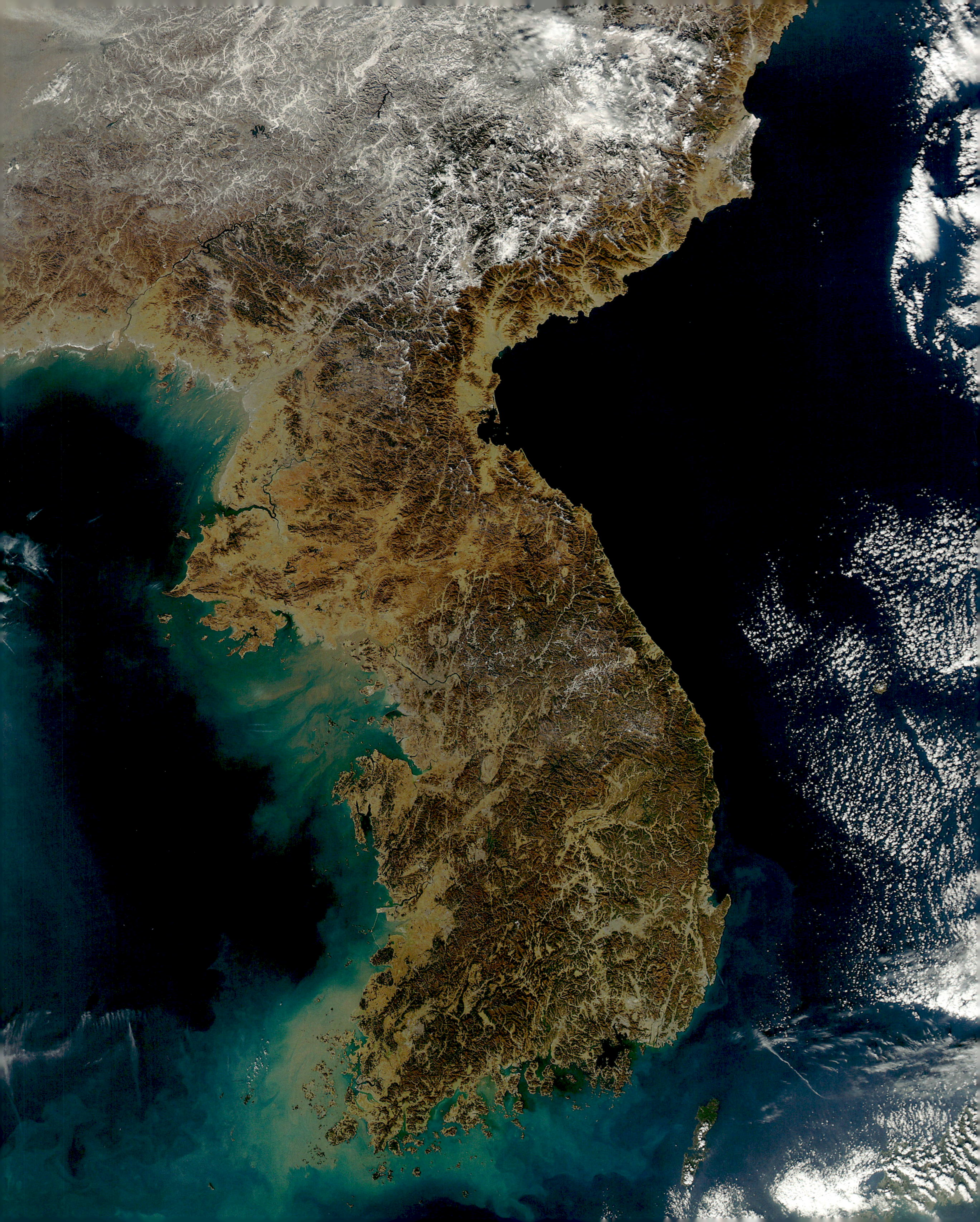

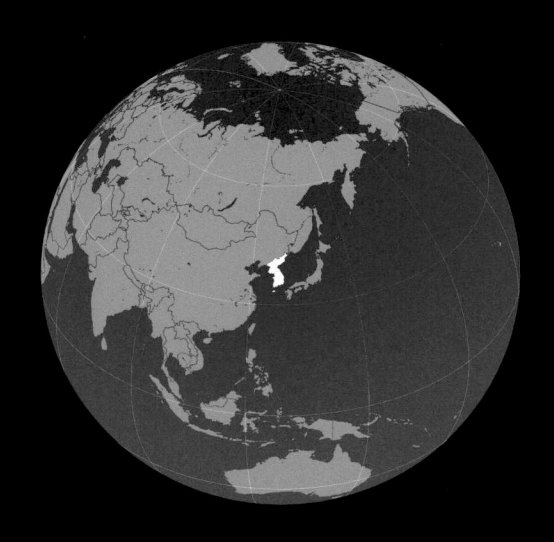

Korea

Divided by the 38th parallel, the Korean peninsula comprises two countries with completely opposite political systems. Our article deals with the democratic state, where a prosperous economy promotes an architecture whose great dilemmas are illustrated with the projects selected: the slender and sinuous Tower by Mass Studies and the bold concrete of the Gallery Yeh by UnSangDong, both in Seoul, represent the urban hyperdensity and the experimental vocation of the young local studios; for their part, both the suggestive Ewha Women's University by the French Perrault in Seoul, and the elegant pavilion by the Portuguese Siza in Anyang evidence the ubiquitous presence of foreign architects in the country, under the sign of a globalization process that is extended in the works by FOA, with the textured skin of their headquarters for a publishing house in Paju Book City, and by MVRDV, with the artificial hills of their Power Center in Gwang Gyo.

Mann-Young Chung
Experiment and Experience
South Korea, the Vertigo of Urban Hyperdensity

Heesoo Kwak, Tethys Building, Seoul (2006)

Four main issues – city and nature, professional scale, globalization and experimentation – synthesize the current architecture in Korea.

The hyperdense character of the Korean capital turns the visibility of buildings into one of the main pursuits, which the architects address in different manners. Some choose forms that imitate the dynamism of the city.

J. Ryu & C. Han, 7th Heaven (2007)

KOREAN ARCHITECTS, at the turn of the millennium, began distancing themselves from the legacies of Korean modern architecture of the last half century. It was due to external reasons rather than something internal to architecture. The 1997 Asian financial crisis was an unprecedented downfall for Koreans, who, since the 1960s, had only seen ceaseless growth. The trauma of the following International Monetary Fund intervention was deep. Global celebration of the new millennium was nowhere to be found in Korea. Aggressive experiments in architecture had no place confronted with the imminent demand for resilience. Young architects and students had to equip themselves with a different attitude and knowledge than their predecessors. They grew indifferent to nostalgic idealism or romanticism, and developed instead acute sensitivity toward capitalism and globalization. Many of today's emerging architects are trained outside of Korea, and care less about the legacies of Korean modern architecture. Meanwhile, the 2002 World Cup co-hosted by Korea and Japan triggered an unprecedented explosion of Korea's energy and reclaimed confidence. The IMF before 2000 and the World Cup after 2000 represent the opposite extremes of despair and hope, depression and passion for Koreans at the turn of the millennium.

In general, Koreans are reluctant to take the position of an extremist. Pessimism and optimism seem to coexist and mingle in the mind of a regular Korean. Rather than to remap, architects choose to operate within. The typical attitude is to negotiate and moderate. The value lies in realization despite the imposed restrictions. As such, attitudes in Korean contemporary architecture are often covert, making them difficult to articulate and grasp. My strategy, in response, is to suggest four sets of keyword opponents that function to frame the different attitudes, and to unfold the spectrum of Korean contemporary architecture.

Urbanity versus Rurality
Seoul is ranked 6th among world cities in population density. Its population exceeds 10 million, and it reaches 25 million when the city's vicinity is included. This means that 50% of the nation's population is concentrated in 10% of the nation's area. This condition of hyper-density has always been a challenge to architects practicing in Seoul and other cities in Korea.

Welcomm City (2000), by H-Sang Seung, has a horizontal concrete podium that evens the sloping site and four boxes cladded with corten plates. Between the boxes are gaps that contain partial views of the city, or the 'urban void' to use Seung's term, which are reminiscent of narrow alleyways in historic cities. Seung's earlier practice in the 1990s was based on what he called the "beauty of poverty". It represents the architecture that unfolds everyday lives in silence, rather than in an amplified manner. This attitude appeared as the "wall of silence", which was the key architectural element of his 1990s' work. At Welcomm City, however, the wall is replaced with the floor. The floor raises architecture off the site, and functions as the reference plane, with which the Cor-ten boxes, stairs, or corridors relate. This is not very different from the Miesian floor plane, described by Josep Quetglas in the essay 'The Fear of Glass': "Think of the coffee tray of a waiter or the surface of a table: there are no 'limits' to the virtual space that they construct, but that space becomes perfectly contained, cylindrical in one case and prismatic in the other, despite the absence of material closures that oppose its expansion. To be in that space means being on a cut plane." At Welcomm City, the cityscape does not project, but sits on the floor. On the contrary, at Seung's Museum of Locks (2003), the Cor-ten plates now clad the lower body, where the ascending glass

Among the strategies to capture the attention of the eye – which in a city context filled with information glides over the facades at a great speed – is the use of strong contrasts and bold forms, the exaggeration of gestures and of the narration. Only a few deliberately choose to let their projects take on a rather discreet presence, with silent and introverted projects that try to meld seamlessly into their urban environments.

H-Sang Seung, Welcomm City Office Building, Seoul (2000)

volume is encased. The separation is now vertical, rather than horizontal. The void is on the horizontal plane at Welcomm City, whereas it enters inside at the Museum of Locks, encased within vertical walls. The void opens outward at the former, whereas it closes inward at the latter.

Seventh Heaven (2007) by Jaeeun Ryu and Chulsoo Han demonstrates the young architects' keen sensitivity in dealing with the complexities of the site, in one of the busiest areas in Seoul. The street facade is a random accumulation of spatial units, and resembles Moshe Safdie's Habitat 67 or a Dutch structuralist work. The spatial units, however, are visual rather than structural. They are gestures that communicate the mixed voices of complex urban layers, hidden from the busy streets by large-scale office blocks. The units amplify difference, otherwise unnoticeable. The message of such architectural expression is clear and literal.

Heesoo Kwak's Tethys (2006), on the other hand, wrestles with an urban reality that we easily discard as banal parking. The building is located in Seoul's most high-end consumption space. Kwak resists the common situation of the area (valet-parked cars occupying pocket spaces around the entrance), by placing wide steps on street level. The parking is alternatively provided on half-floor below street level, suspended above the sunken space. Under the parking is a studio, and the ground floor, half-floor above street level, acquires a large deck as a result. The exposed concrete ceiling above the deck takes one's eyes into the inner space. The architect focuses on the urban reality itself. Once the surface is accepted as a condition of reality without any depth or foundation to mediate, we have no choice but to engage in a manipulative play. The rule of the play is to attract the eye. An image without attracting the eye has

UnSangDong Architects, Kring-Gumho Culture Complex, Seoul (2008)

Atlas: Asia and Pacific **157**

Namho Cho, Kyowon Training Institute (2000)

Evading the intense metropolitan experience, the attitude of Korean architects when designing in natural environments comes close to tradition, the main decision being how the building must be incorporated into the environment, and not so much its construction. This approach helps to deliver simple buildings made of materials like stone and wood, or adapted to the place by means of 'topographic' formal devices.

no place in a capitalist cityscape. Kwak obeys the rule with exaggerated gestures and narration, aiming to grasp the eye that can easily slide away. The strategy is to juxtapose: plane vs. volume, transparency vs. opacity, rustic vs. smooth, vertical vs. horizontal, and frontal vs. lateral. Tethys is a visual response-machine reacting to the ever-changing cityscape. Other examples of such a visual response-machine are the Kring Culture Center (2008), by UnSangDong Architects (Yoongyoo Jang and Chang-Hoon Shin); the Bati-2 building (2009), by Dong-Jin Kim; and the office tower Urbanhive (2009), by In-Cheurl Kim.

The Dukwon Gallery (2000), by Moon-Sung Kwon, or the Ssamzigil building (2004), by Moongyu Choi, on the other hand, focus on synchronizing architecture with the street's spaces. Both are located at Insadong, the most pedestrian-friendly neighborhood in the historic sector of Seoul. Both exist as part of their surrounding alleys. Ssamzigil incorporates an elongated courtyard paralleling the main alley, and provides various links with shops and displays that connect the courtyard and the alley. The large deck above connects the alley and the courtyard by creating framed views of the activities inside the courtyard. The Dukwon Gallery includes within its boundaries the alley that starts from the corner of the site, cuts across the building, and leads up to the fifth floor. The building cleverly combines the different textures. Horizontal layers of *kiwa* (Korean traditional black roof tile), joined with white plaster, appear in various colors and textures when seen from different angles. They resonate with the patterns of horizontal woodwork of the inner layer, and contrast with the vertical woodwork of the erected mass.

Metropolitan experience often triggers a nostalgic return to nature. Sunyudo Park (2002), a refurbishment of the once water-purifying plant on an island on Han River, has raised positive interest in sustainable design. The park is a collaborative work by the architect Sungyong Joh and Seoahn Landscape Architects. Rather than clearing the ruins, they chose to preserve the ruins, an icon of early Korean industrialization. The weathering rustic concrete walls from the past have become one with the surrounding greenery. They are now another nature. The park is an antithesis to inconsiderate urbanization. It crosses over between the histories and memories of past and present, nature and the man-made.

The architectural critic Kwang-Hyun Kim says that the most important decision in building a *hanok* (Korean traditional house) is not how it is built but how it is set in place. How architecture inhabits nature has been the core issue in Korean traditional architecture. The issue, in recent years, was revitalized with an imported architectural trend of topographic mapping or of 'landscape'. The Uijae Museum of Korean Art (2001), by Jongkyu Kim and Sung-Yong Joh, forms spatial layers parallel to the linear ramp that adapts itself to the contours of the mountainous site. At Park Sookeun Memorial Museum (2002), by Jongho Yi, the plan weaves through and along the natural contours, with transparent glass volumes rising from the rustic stonework. Namho Cho is renowned for his persistent search for adaptable wooden constructions in contemporary architecture. At the Kyowon Training Institute (2000), Cho shows a competitive execution of woodwork detailing and a superb coordination between architecture and natural sceneries. Cho integrates the western timber structure, which is relatively simpler in detail than the traditional way, with a poetic juxtaposition of architecture with nature. Guyon Chung is another architect, who has produced noticeable work focusing on sustainability using clay. The Pinx Museum of Wind, Museum of Stone, and Museum of Water (2005), by Jun Itami, a Korean-Japanese architect, and Genius Loci (2008), by Tadao Ando, are both based on motifs derived from natural elements of Jeju Island, the pleasant vacation place where they are located.

The winning entry of the Master Plan of the New Central Government Administration Town competition (2007), by Haeahn Architecture and Daina Balmori, is one of the most anticipated projects,

Jongkyu Kim and Sung-Yong Joh, Uijae Museum of Korean Art (2001)

In-Cheurl Kim, Woongjin Thinkbig Headquarters, Paju Book City (2007)

Due to the generalized trend in Korea of drawing up large-scale projects that require considerable financing, only big architectural firms have access to them, leaving a very narrow margin for small studios. An example of collaboration is that of the Book City in Paju which, at 30 kilometers from Seoul, is a new neighborhood dedicated to the publishing industry with buildings designed by both Korean and foreign architects.

as it truly converts the spatial structure of nature into urban structure. The 2.7 million square meter project suggests 30 meter high roof gardens that horizontally expand several kilometers as an alternative to vertically dense urban skyscrapers. The administrative offices do not inhabit individual buildings but an urban substructure, which assimilates with the entirety of the town. The open space and the mega-structure merge without distinction. The project, once realized, will become one of the most impressive achievements of 21st-century Korean architecture.

Corporate Firms versus Ateliers
As the turn-key, the build-transfer-lease, and project financing become common ways to initiate large-scale building projects, the traditional competition method for design selection seems less effective. Mid-size architecture firms can seldom compete with money and manpower from corporate firms, except the top design firms with daring and creative works such as iArch and Designcamp Moon-Park, winners of the Seoul City Hall competition (2008) and of the Seoul Performing Arts Center international competition (2009), respectively. The industry, in recent years, has reestablished itself with an extreme polarization of large corporate firms and atelier workshops. Corporate firms have adapted to the new demand with their know-how and competitiveness in high-rise skyscrapers and high-tech designs of amorphous forms, as well as in building information modeling and sustainable architecture. About 20 firms with 300-1,000 employees, such as Samwoo, Heerim, Junglim, Space Group, Gansam Partners, and Haeahn, monopolize the market using corporate capital and accumulated know-how. It has become harder for smaller firms and younger architects to survive in the market, let alone succeed. They are forced to turn to interior designs or smaller house designs abroad. This is unfortunate as the emerging talented architects are deprived of their fair opportunities. Corporate firms, in some cases, have engaged in the market to buy and sell designs by absorbing ideas from ateliers and conveying them into the market. This results in a plausible and creative design in some cases.

Individual ateliers have strived to survive in the industry by straining more into elaborative works that are smaller in scale, or by forming collaborations among ateliers. Paju Book City (2000) and Heyri Art Valley (2000) are significant achievements of such collaborations. H-Sang Seung and Hyun-Sik Min, the coordinators at Paju, along with many participating architects, have produced a new type of group architecture distinguishable from a typical urban neighborhood. What followed was Heyri, an artists' settlement not far away from the Book City. The Art Valley consists of nearly two hundred individual projects, coordinated by Jong-Gyu Kim and Junsung Kim. Paju and Heyri are now a huge exhibit of architectural design that display latest trends in Korean architecture. The architecture of Paju and Heyri is a significant measure in understanding Korean contemporary architecture.

The slices of cubic volumes typical of the Paju and Heyri derive from the design brief developed by the coordinators. The brief in detail determines to reserve space for airflow and view. The determined boundaries are very specific, and cannot be crossed by artifacts. Hun Kim's Hangilsa (2002) and Kyung-Kook Woo's Gallery MOA (2003) exemplified this tendency at an early stage. Cubic slices are easily convertible to modules, and modules in general are repeatable. They can also be multiplied or divided into smaller slices within systems of proportion. Such a system will likely create a form subordinate to a tight frame, where even the slightest deviation is easily recognized.

The brief, however, enforced a different guideline for buildings at the periphery of the town. One interesting type suggested by the brief was the 'rock-type'. The Woongjin Thinkbig building (2007) in Paju, by In-Cheurl Kim, demonstrates the most satisfying design solution among variations of this type. The curvilinear form is indeterminate as it is generated from differential calculus using digital

FOA, Dulnyouk Publishers Headquarters, Paju Book City (2005)

DMP Architects, Performing Arts Center, Seoul

The competitions for the construction of large urban pieces, and even new cities created from scratch, are a good opportunity for collaboration between local architects and professionals from other countries, which often receive a preferential treatment from the clients. In these collaborations the foreign architects generally offer the experimental factor and the local ones the knowledge of the place.

computation. In contrast to the logic of the module, Kim's form-making is indifferent to minute changes. Kim strives to overcome the rationalism of programming and detailing, and to reach transcendental minimalism by combining this indeterminate form-making and desire for emptiness. The new geometry is tamed within his established architectural language. Kim proves his ability to control and secure the otherwise explosive nature of indeterminacy inherent in the logic of differential calculus. The strategy will become prominent for the moderate group of architects as it is instructive for those who aim to cultivate the radical and experimental nature of digital form-making.

William Morris once said: "If I were asked to say what at once is the most important production of art and the thing most longed for, I should answer a beautiful house; and if I were further asked to name the production next in importance and the thing next to be longed for, I should answer a beautiful book." *The Works of Geoffrey Chaucer* (53-volumes), originally published in 1896 with William Morris's design, are exhibited at Junsung Kim's William Morris Museum (2007), which is another book house next to the Hangil one designed by the same architect. Inspired by the elaborate patterns that frame the pages of the Chaucer collection and the three-dimensional frames of Gustavo Torner's *La rectitud de las cosas XVI (The Rectitude of Things,* 1986), Kim projects the multiple layers of meanings into the deviated frames as if they were motives from the context of Morris, Heyri and Hangil Publishing Co. The fragmented interior spaces in between the layered planes are multi-faceted and dynamic.

Rapid industrialization in modern Korea has wrongly justified the exploitation of the weak. Ilhoon Lee's *Study along the Railroad* (1998) is an architectural attempt that resists such reality with considerate interest. Patronized by a well-known children's book writer, it is a space for educating children living in the slums of Incheon. Lee has translated the good deeds and the sound program into a formal and spatial language of the *chai* (a building unit of Korean traditional architecture). Lee summarizes his strategy as "division into the *chai*". His architecture is a group of slices of the *chai,* rearranged and set onto the site. The gaps between slices are filled with street experience, air, light, snow, and rain. The architecture, with its modest attitude, opens to children and the community, providing access from the street to the roof garden where children freely play.

Daekhan Joo's Cholam Project (2002-2004) is a radical statement against blind capitalism. Cholam, an abandoned town of closed mines, represents the distorted realities of radical transition from industrial society to post-industrial society. The movement, in collaboration with a group of architects, volunteer students, the community and non-government organizations, suggests an alternative solution to inconsiderate urban redevelopment. Based on careful observation of changes in spatial environment, it successfully built houses for the elderly who were left in the town. It proposed house types that can adapt to the unique conditions of the mountainous environment. The Cheolam Project reminds of the fact that architecture is not merely a matter of expression or a product of economy, but consists of social and programmatic issues that are deeply related to everyday lives.

Globalism versus Regionalism
The importation of designs by foreign architects is now fairly common in the Korean architectural scene. Collaboration between foreign and domestic architects is a typical form of competition entries. Skyscrapers designed by SOM, KPF,

X-TU Architecture, Anouk Legendre and Nicolas Desmazières, Jeongok Prehistory Museum

160 Atlas: Asia and Pacific

Zaha Hadid, Dongdaemun Plaza and Park, Seoul

DMJM, HOK, NBBJ, or The Jerde Partnership are now easy to find in Seoul and other cities. Internationally-renowned architects are generally favored by clients. Tadao Ando, Laurent Beaudouin, Florian Beigel, Terry Farrel, Norman Foster, Daniel Libeskind, Alvaro Siza, Rafael Viñoly, Jean-Michel Wilmotte, Riken Yamamoto, FOA, Morphosis, MVRDV, NL Architects, RAD, SANAA, UNStudio, and many others, have already built projects in Korea.

The Leeum Samsung Museum Complex (2004) consists of three wings designed by three world-class European architects. The Rem Koolhaas wing features a black box hovering seventeen meters above the interior, which resonates with the inclined exterior street and the acute angles of the access ramp, and creates an impressive vector of vision. The Mario Botta wing uses terracotta as its main material, reminiscent of Korean porcelain. The staircase also represents the content of the exhibition space figuratively. The Jean Nouvel wing is a random assembly of rusted stainless steel boxes that inhabit exhibition spaces. The three individual wings are linked by the underground lobby.

International design competitions frequently attract lesser-known yet talented emerging architects, as well as architects with established reputation. The winning competition entry titled Matrix (2003), by Kirsten Schmel for the Nam June Paik Art Center, was an impressive design solution that covered the valleys of the site with an expanded horizontal roof, with permeating landscapes beneath. This impressive concept of the original design, unfortunately, was modified radically when completed in 2008. The building was executed with a completely different scheme than the original, because of demands from the client, budget problems, and regulations.

Dominique Perrault's winning entry for the Ewha Campus Complex (2008), on the other hand, was completed without much

MVRDV, Gwang Gyo Power Center, Seoul

alteration from the original scheme. Perrault competed with Zaha Hadid and FOA in this invited competition, with a proposal that blends the earth with a mega-structure divided by a 250 meter long ramp that cuts across and into the site. The ramp is the main circulation, and transparent curtain walls run parallel to the ramp. Inside the walls are the linear corridors and vertical circulations that connect different levels and programs of classrooms, a library, conference rooms, a fitness center, a movie theater, and pocket spaces for reading and resting that cling to the corridors.

Other noticeable projects designed by foreign architects expected to be built in the coming years include the Dongdaemun Design Plaza and Park (2008) by Zaha Hadid, the Busan Cinema Complex (2005) by Coop Himmelb(l)au, the World Business Center in Busan (2007) by Asymptote, and the Jeongok Prehistory Museum (2006) by X-TU Architecture (Anouk Legendre and Nicolas Desmazières).

Young-Joon Kim has collaborated with many foreign architects such as NL Architects, Alejandro Zaera, and Vicente Guallart. Kim admits that the collaborations were his conscious effort to connect with the latest new thoughts of global architectural

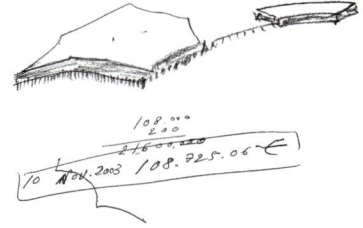

Alvaro Siza, Multipurpose Pavilion, Anyang (2006)

Jean Nouvel, Mario Botta and Rem Koolhaas, Leeum Samsung Museum Complex (2004)

practice. His struggle to ensure his identity, nonetheless, is still evident in his collaborative projects. The Heryoojae Hospital (2004), with its vast planes and spatial voids, resembles Villa VPro by MVRDV, and yet attempts to mediate regional identities with foreign influences. Jahajae (2005), a collective group of formal and spatial units, clearly shows his personal endeavor to redefine regional identities of Korean architecture.

Some architects choose to immerse into tradition, hoping to find a viable answer to new questions proposed by the current conditions. A large number of Korean architects since the 1960s had been preoccupied with the issues of modernity and tradition, but the question has never been clearly answered. This is perhaps because of modernist antipathy toward historical styles deeply-rooted in the Korean architectural scene, or because traditional architecture cannot avoid serious alterations when confronted with the program, the scale, or the material that derive from today's needs. Literal translation of tradition, which became fashionable with postmodernism, rarely succeeded in addressing the core issues of both architecture and society. However, the younger architects, who now distance themselves from the modernist discourses of architectural tradition, are now employing fresh ways to translate tradition. Jung-Goo Cho's Ragung Hotel (2007) accommodates a contemporary program without much deviation from the tectonic and the scales of traditional architecture. The building is a high-end hotel following the style of the *hanok,* combined with a touch of contemporary taste. The Ragung Hotel adopts the instruments of contemporary construction, yet succeeds in recreating the experience unique to the *hanok.*

If the Ragung Hotel is literal in conveying tradition, Doojin Hwang's Gahoeheon Building (2006) is transformative. It cleverly distorts the spatial characteristics of the traditional Korean dwelling. The unique spatial relationship of the *chai,* that between a *madang* (Korean traditional open space) and a chai, and the relationship between the street and the outer wall found in traditional architecture, are recreated with a contemporary program, language and technique. The building, which accommodates a bakery and an Italian restaurant, provides experience of an awkward yet pleasant juxtaposition of a contemporary program and form with a traditional configuration of space.

Expertise and Experimentation
The architectural critic Kil-Yong Park once questioned why the architects at Heyri were so reluctant to experimentation. "What led these architects to become so modest? What made them so reluctant in this age that values difference, freedom, and individualism?" The answer, according to Park, is that their architecture was overly theorized and conceptualized, and therefore, resulted in barren forms. My answer to this question is rather different. I would argue that it is due to their passive attitude toward the given constraints. Architects tend to securely position their work within limitation, rather than try to aggressively remap the limitation. Such passiveness is evident when we find that the sections of the Heyri buildings rarely defy orthogonal geometry. The creative expression on the exterior rarely carries into the interior to

162 Atlas: Asia and Pacific

Young Joon Kim, Heryoojae Hospital, Seoul (2004)

The commissioning of highly representative buildings to prestigious international architects is a typical phenomenon of globalization. The result comes in the form of 'signature' works, with the recognizable mark of their authors, but without a trace of the forms, techniques or materials of local tradition. In those cases in which the design team does include Korean professionals, these act as mediators between the local and the foreign.

affect its inherent spatial configuration. I do not intend to deny the merits of orthogonal geometry, known to be conventional, practical, and adaptable to unexpected situations. Nonetheless, I am disappointed when architects imprison themselves within their already established capabilities rather than suggest new possibilities. Korean architects, in general, seem to value proficient expertise over radical experimentation. Expertise trapped by conventions, however, cannot produce the new.

The Gallery SOSO (2007) at Heyri, by Sam-Young Choi, seems almost flawless. The geometry is simple and refined. The contrast between solid and void, spatial layering, and sectional changes is done with good taste. Placement is considerate of topographic contours, and spatial partitioning is precise. Materials are treated with control and care. Glass, wood, and concrete are used with appropriate logic. However, although the gallery is satisfying and pleasing, it lacks tension. It does not provoke.

Compared to this moderate attitude, the Dalki Theme Park (2000) by Minsuk Cho, Moongyu Choi, and Slade Architecture is surprisingly provocative and full of imagination. Its indeterminacy resists the suppressive mechanism that imprisons the Gallery SOSO. Minsuk Cho's Boutique Monaco (2008), at the heart of Gangnam, the most expensive area of the city, targets to reveal the latent desires of the high society, the desires suppressed by conservative values. The high-rise apartment cleverly utilizes the regulations of square-per-footage by scooping out fifteen missing voids, and stacks the 172 residential units that vary in 49 different types. Despite their very high price, the units of this megastructure were quickly sold out. Its gesture against the monotone streets of Gangnam and the nearby Samsung Tower by KPF is indeed provocative.

Kerl Yoo is the winner of the Seoul City Hall competition and a leading magnate in the Korean architectural circle, equipped with sensitivity for the new. His words that explain his own space are seemingly simple: "I like open spaces with fulfilling light." However, the open space he creates is filled

Dominique Perrault, Ewha Women's University, Seoul (2008)

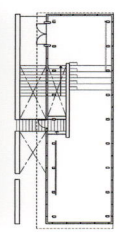

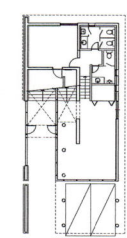

S.Y. Choi, Gallery SOSO, Seoul

While the average Korean generally wishes to avoid conflict, the latest generations of architects prefer to exploit them and bring them to the foreground, choosing a pragmatic way of addressing critical issues such as the relationship with the dense urban context, the capitalist system or globalization. Radical experimentation characterizes the most recent works of Mass Studies, Hoon Moon or Hun Kim.

with conflicting vectors that are ceaselessly in play, and underlying tensions appear at moments without notice. If we were to play music in his space, cacophony would be more appropriate than harmony. The Bethel Church (2007) contains an auditorium on the 8th floor that accommodates 3,000 worshippers. The 6th-floor lobby is accessible with an open ramp that extends from the street. The atrium is vertically open to all floors, in which various layers and slices of forms and spaces like ramps, bridges, rooms, and pocket spaces crash to echo the effects of architectural cacophony.

A similar kind of effect is found in Hyoman Kim's work. Kim pursues the idea of the 'distracted eye' in his smaller residential projects. The architect had spent his earlier career working inside the iconic Korean modernist building, Sookeun Kim's Space Group Building, and since has strived to recreate the personal spatial experience that he had in the place. The top-floor loft space at Jorin-Hun (2003) disturbs familiarity and comfort, which we typically accept as features of home. The building falls slightly short from being perfect, and that shortage, that seemingly little crack, explodes into possibilities that rub our sensibility. One sees inside the building the hovering volume within the volume, and surrounding the volume are various composite scenes that press against the central space. The various materials that create the scenes each express their identity, and continuously resist subordination. The radicality of the space comes from the intersecting point of architect's ability to control and passion to disturb.

If Kerl Yoo and Hyoman Kim appeal to the distracted senses, Hun Kim appeals to acute senses that react to even the smallest stimulus. If architectural criticism thinks of architecture as a machine that feeds stimuli to our bodies, the criterion for such criticism would be how intense the stimuli are. Kim's Chasm (2007), a complex of galleries and residences, amplifies the intensities of tension between the different programs squeezed into the larger rectangular framework. The pressure is intense, causing tension that is set to explode in any minute. As such, the tension acquires keen attention. One cannot retreat to comfort, once the tension is recognized. Thus, one cannot stop resisting comfort. The angular stairs and the fragmented gaps that penetrate between the walls and the openings play variations inside the interior. The lines, the volumes, and the chasm quiver in silence but with disturbing potential, conspiring to explode onto our senses.

Hoon Moon's architectural imagination comes from strange fantasies, fetishes, eroticism, and kitsch. His Sangsang Museum (2004) is located in perhaps the trendiest neighborhood in Seoul. His imagination resists any form of rationalization or systematization. The

Minsuk Cho (Mass Studies), Boutique Monaco in Gangnam, Seoul (2008)

Hun Kim, Chasm residential and commercial complex, Seoul (2007)

architect, for example, conspires with the client the plan to hide in the building a secret maze. The desire to penetrate inside the building without being noticed is in discord with the overflowing desires of the street that penetrate the building from outside. The discord between the two upper masses that accommodate the client's bedroom and the studio, or between the access to the 1st floor and the access to the 2nd and basement floors, appears radically different when viewed from different angles. The museum is a field of provocative imagination that intentionally lacks the desire for articulation or coherency.

Jaeyong Lim is at the opposite of Moon. Lim is obsessed with logic. His logic is merciless rather than exquisite, and his senses are distracted rather than elaborate. The Young-Jong-Do Residence (2005), according to the architect, is a "logical diagram in the form of a house". The walls rise awkwardly and the openings are clumsy without any aesthetic concern. How should we interpret this seemingly impulsive gesture that violates stability? As the boundaries that secure the forms of individual elements explode, the elements themselves simultaneously implode. Within this state of explosion and implosion, the irregular slopes of the wall or the wrinkles on the floor rarely matter. What dominates the architecture is the sense of distraction rather than concentration. The openings are cut as they are cut; and the materials join as they join. Such distraction is achieved by struggling against imposed constraints and what is familiar.

New Symptoms
The new generation of Korean contemporary architects is not used to their predecessors' persistent and enduring attitude. They carry none of the burdens that haunted the past generation of architects in the last half of the 20th century. The new generation instead quickly adapts to the changes by readily accepting the apparent values that currently operate here and now. As we scan the apparent symptoms of the current architectural practice focusing on the aforementioned four sets of keywords, one thing, at least, seems clear. The projects deal with the issues at hand, the realities of urbanity: capitalism and globalization. These are issues of reality, the issues that set the terrain. Can we then break the terrain? If so, how? The last group of projects introduced under the category of experimentation may provide us with the hint for an answer.

If persistent observation is impossible when understanding the vast spectrum of the current in Korean architecture, we have no choice than to scan only the apparent symptoms. If you ask, "is there any worth in looking after Korean contemporary architecture?", I can only answer, "it is up to the one who looks after".

Hoon Moon, Sangsang Museum, Seoul (2004)

Mass Studies
S-Trenue Tower
Seoul (South Korea)

Client
SK Networks
Architects
Mass Studies: Minsuk Cho
Collaborators
Kisu Park, Zongxoo U, Younkyoung Shin, Sangkyu Jeon, Jingyoung Ha, Geunmi Ryu, Jieun Lee, Joonhee Lee, Daeun Jeong, Bumhyun Chun, Kiwoong Ko, Hartmut Flothmann, Dongchul Yang, Seongbeom Mo, Byungkyun Kim, Jisoo Kim, Songmin Lee, Vin Kim, Young Kim, Ranhee Kim, Kwangjin Woo, Minho Hwang, Jiyoung Yoon, Chungwhan Park
Consultants
Junwoo (structure); HANA (installations); CG E&C (civil engineering); Alban Mannisi & Soltos (landscaping)
Contractor
SK E&C
Photos
Iwan Baan

Located along Seoul's Superior Treasure Avenue, from which it takes its name, S-Trenue Tower rises 36 floors (154 meters) and contains 122 'officetels', 100 square meter units for both office and residential use.

Yeouido, Seoul's main financial district, began its expansion in the eighties and saw how its city blocks quickly filled with towers that were much alike in geometry, the result of applying principles of minimizing costs and maximing available space. In the midst of this anonymous landscape rises the crooked profile of the new S-Trenue Tower, conceived as an alternative to traditional residential and office blocks. The design reinvents the skyscraper with a commercial plinth by shifting the shaft, which is usually centered, to the sidewalk edge, in the process tracing an L in the side elevation.

In this way it sets itself apart from the neighboring constructions while enhancing its visibility from the street. The building then splits into three vertical parts: a central concrete core and two slender steel towers flanking it and leaning on it, forming different angles. In the space that arises between the three elements are a total of thirty-two bridges that, besides serving to bind them together functionally and structurally, make it possible for all floor levels to have direct contact with the exterior, in contrast to the hermetic spaces that are habitual in skyscrapers. Each of these terraces is given green zones that act as pleasant gardens suspended in mid-air. The gaps in between stretch down to the lower commercial levels through an atrium-garden and other transit and rest areas, thereby doing away with the separation of base from shaft that has characterized a whole design generation.

The building follows a typology common in Korea: the 'officetel', from the words 'office' and 'hotel'. It mixes apartments, shops, and offices in such a way that practically all of one's everyday needs can be met without stepping out of it. In S-Trenue, the basements contain the car park; levels -1 to 4 offer offices, restaurants, shops, and other communal facilities; finally, on levels 5 to 36 are the studio-type apartments, rental units measuring about 100 square meters apiece that include a small service unit with bath, kitchen, storage, and a diaphanous room that can be divided into two with the help of sliding panels.

Amid the anonymous buildings of Yeouido, Seoul's main financial district, a new skyscraper rises in serpentine manner, reinventing the classic tower with a plinth by splitting its shaft into three slender pieces: a central concrete core containing the systems of vertical communication, and two steel towers flanking and leaning on it, creating gaps in between that are spanned by thirty-two bridges with gardens serving the apartments.

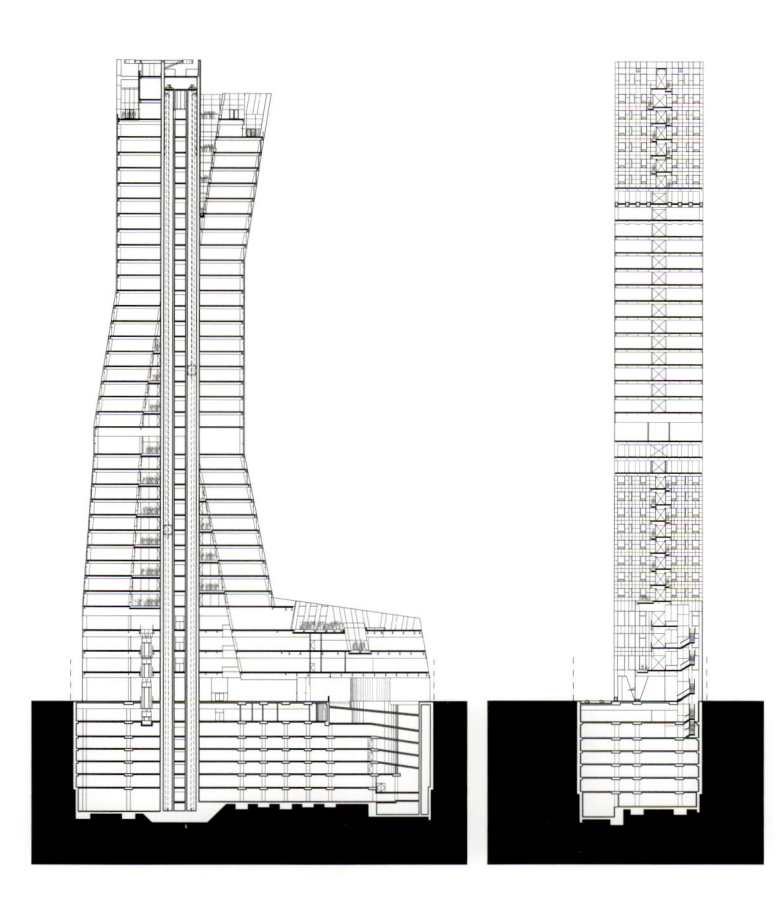

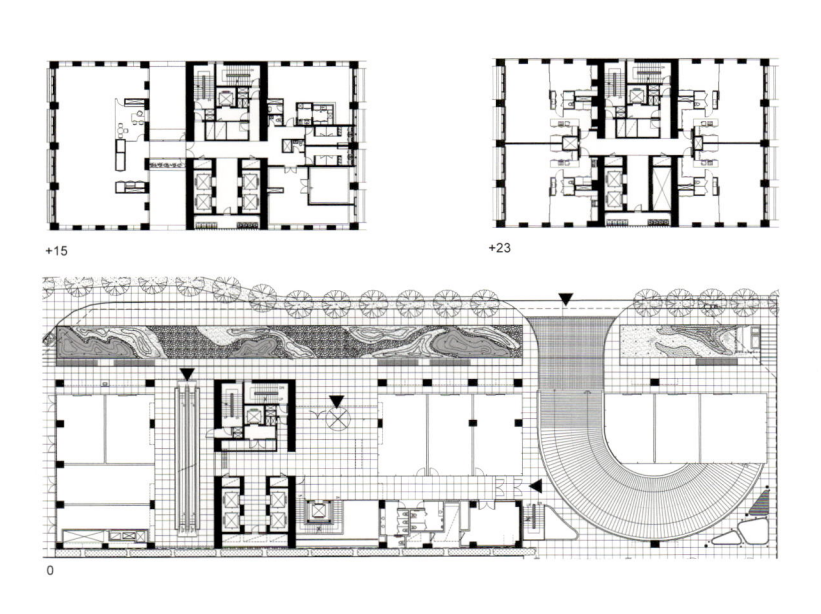

Atlas: Asia and Pacific 167

UnSangDong
Gallery Yeh
Seoul (South Korea)

Client
Lee Sook Young
Architect
Jang Yoon Gyoo
Collaborators
Shin Chang Hoon
Consultants
R.C (structure)
Contractor
GuJin Industrial Development
Photos
Kim Yong Kwan; Song Jae Young

The facade of the Gallery Yeh tower, conceived as a sculptural landmark in the horizontal fabric of Seoul's Sinsa-dong neighborhood, sends a clear visual message to passers-by about its commitment to art.

Founded in the late seventies, the Gallery Yeh is considered one of South Korea's leading galleries of contemporary art. This private institution is host, each year, to eight or nine shows presenting paintings, sculptures, engravings, and installations by local and foreign artists.

The clients' need for additional exhibition space led them to commission a new building altogether. The location is Garosu-gil, in Sinsa-dong, a trendy and artsy neighborhood of southern Seoul. The gallery stands on a 568 square meter lot and its gross floor area of 1,995 square meters is distributed in seven stories above ground level and two below. But surely the project's most significant element is the facade, which in itself is conceived as a work of art: an enormous experimental, sculptural urban canvas that heralds the institution's innovative contents. If a canvas is typically thought of as a two-dimensional medium, this particular one is a 'spatial skin' that has been developed from a new code arising between the floor plan and the three-dimensional medium. In effect, the two-dimensionality of the wall has become an opportunity for it to deform into a three-dimensional space.

Five strips of unfaced reinforced concrete rising the building's entire height are planted at a certain distance from the building's vertical communication core, and proceed to fold, bend, bulge, and buckle here and there, in the process forming narrow openings on their sides that are glazed to let daylight into the exhibition halls. The regulation of natural light through these gaps, combined with the use of exposed concrete and of panels coated with epoxy resin for the interior claddings, helps produce a minimalist atmosphere that is ideal for displaying a private collection of cutting-edge conceptual sculpture. When the envelope is manipulated to create gaps, the space within becomes a rich experience of discovering a whole world of hidden layers of logic and irony.

The canvas facade is a 'skinscape' that announces the gallery's contemporary program by providing visible firsthand information about its exhibits and events to onlookers in the city. A powerful statement in a dislocated urban milieu, the dramatic facade of the tower is both a memorable urban sculpture and a counterpoint to the predominantly horizontal banding of the constructions that surround it.

That a private gallery in Seoul should make such an energetic declaration of intentions is an unmistakable sign of South Korea's economic prosperity and rapid intake of contemporary global culture.

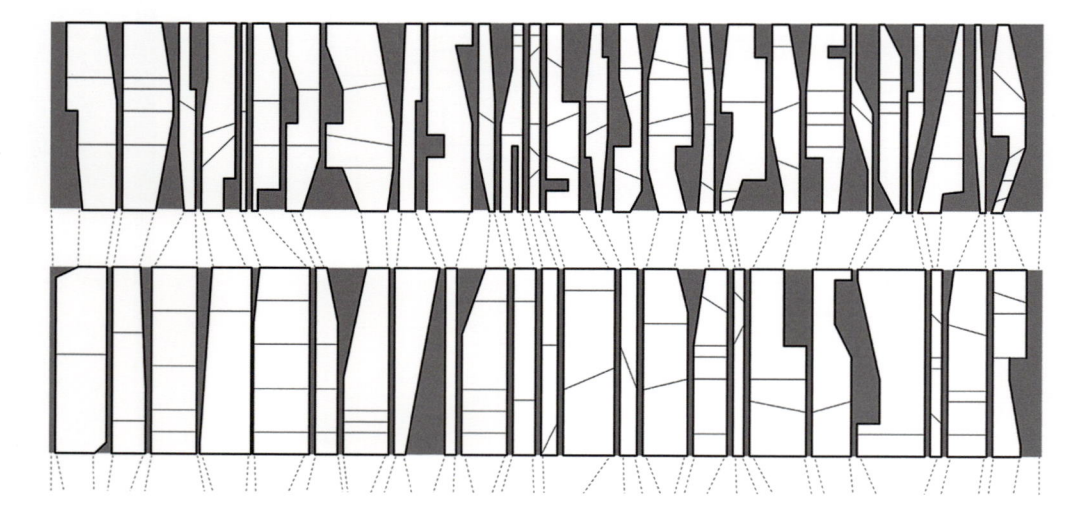

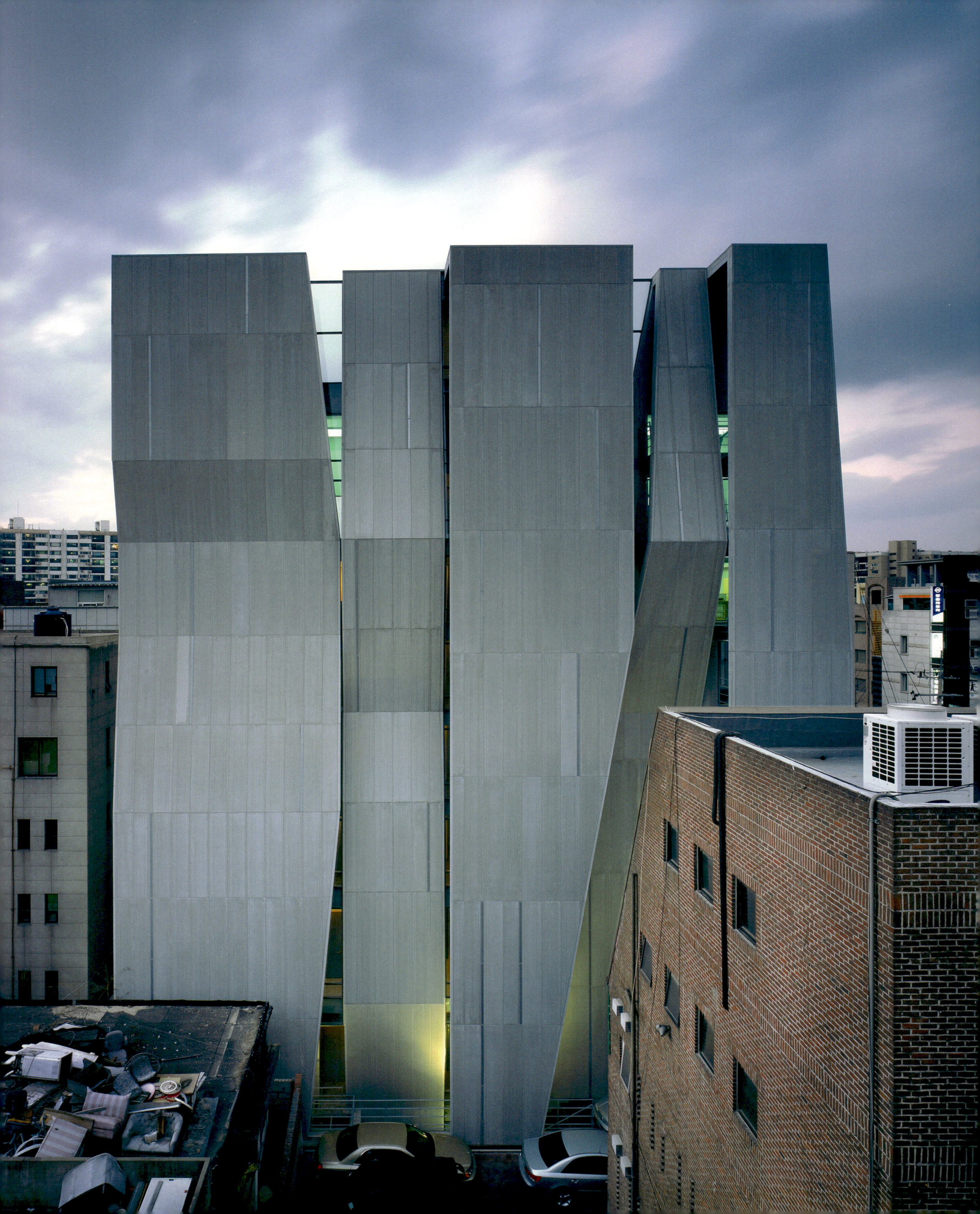

Set at a certain distance from the building's vertical core, five tall strips of reinforced concrete fold, bend, and bulge to create narrow side openings that are glazed to bring daylight into the exhibition galleries. Regulating natural light through the gaps, combined with using exposed concrete and panels coated with epoxy resin for the interiors, helps produce an ideal atmosphere for the displays inside.

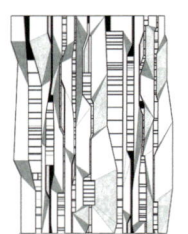

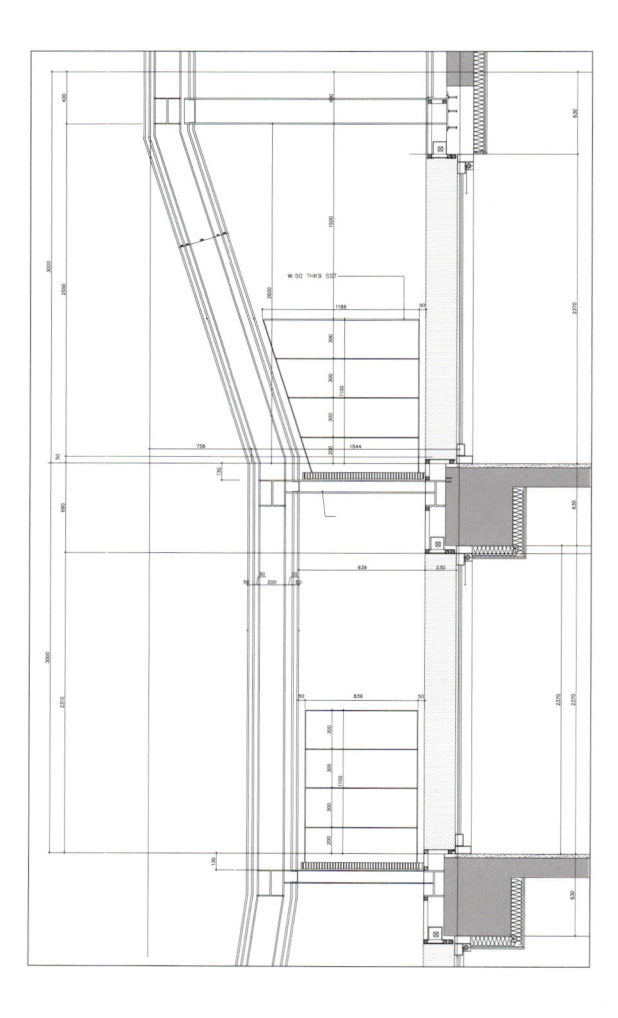

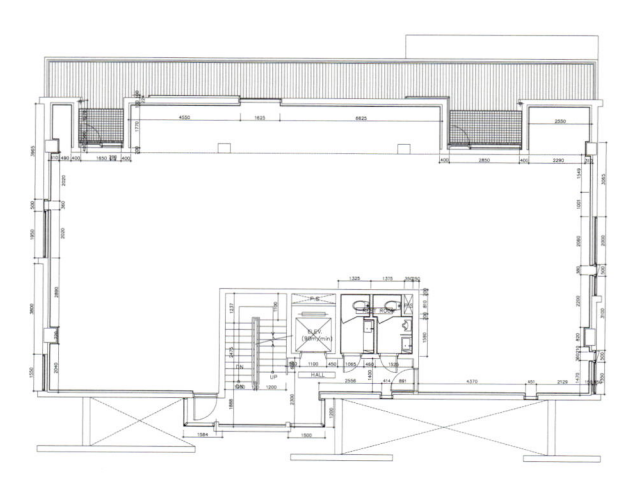

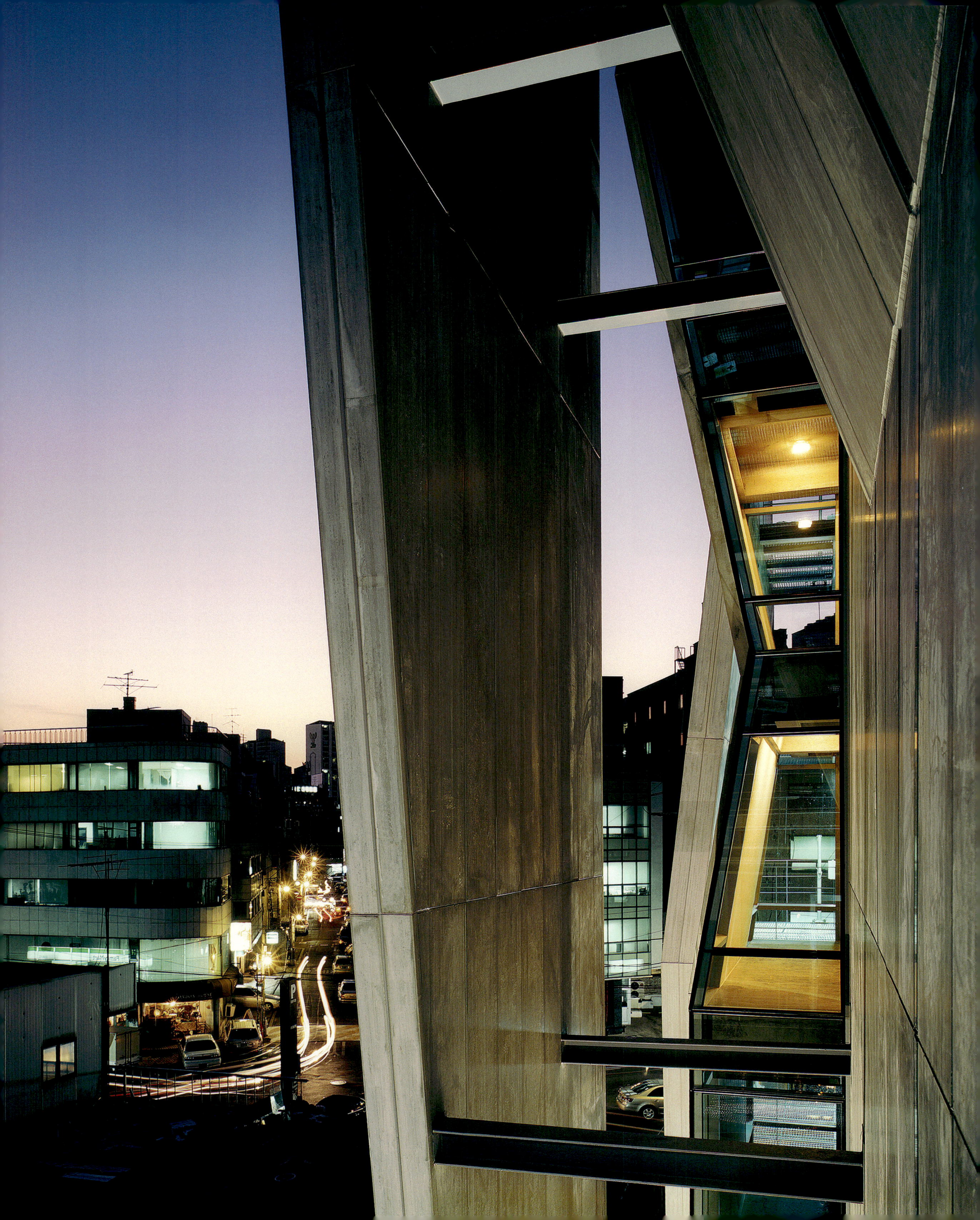

Dominique Perrault
Ewha Women's University
Seoul (South Korea)

Client
Ewha Women's University
Architect
Dominique Perrault
Collaborators
Baum (local architects)
Consultants
VP & Green (structural); HL-PP Consult (mechanical), Jean-Paul Lamoureux (acoustics); Rache-Willms (facade); local consultants: Jeon and Lee Partners (structural), HIMEC (mechanical), CG E & C (engineering), CnK (landscaping)
Contractor
Samsung
Photos
Christian Richters; André Morin (p. 172)

The new facilities address an essentially recreational and cultural program and are situated right at the center of the university campus, which now has a monumental entrance defined by a 'valley' of steel and glass.

THE WORLD'S LARGEST private women's university needed a new building to accommodate a miscellany of academic, sport, administrative, and recreational spaces. More a landscape than an architectural work, the so-called 'Campus Valley' is engraved into the ground, marking the university entrance like a huge furrow. It begins with a long descending esplanade, to rise at the far end through benches and steps that can double as tiers of an outdoor amphitheater. The contour of this 'valley' marks the axis of the campus, organizes the collective functions to be served, and distributes the buildings in the manner of an Anglo-Saxon campus.

This unique building transforms the topography of the place and altogether modifies the urban geography by physically and visually connecting the site's elements in a new landscape. The new entrance into the campus leads to a platform for sport training and other occasional events. This space creates a bond between the university and the city beyond. Inside the 'valley', the two facades erected face to face are like two glass cliffs that bring natural light into the buried spaces, where administrative offices and study areas mix with cultural and commercial premises like moviehouses, theaters, restaurants, and shops.

The three buildings that together address the program are buried in order to free up space at ground level. A contemporary metropolis like Seoul is in dire need of new open spaces to balance out the fast-paced densification imposed by the speculation of real-estate developers. Thanks to the simple and pure geometry of the building's contours both inside and out, a high degree of abstraction is achieved.

The 'valley' curtain wall, in particular the vertical mirror-finish steel slats, is a new technology that required an experimental process in collaboration with Samsung engineers. Designed and built to withstand high wind stress, the slats, bolts, brackets, and canopies disappear in the immense scale of the complex.

Finally, the building itself disappears beneath the rooftop garden. This is a very natural-looking place with rough stone paths, evergreen bushes, and flower trees planted at random. Designed in conjunction with the university's own landscaping department, the garden is really an extension of the existing park. The idea was to give this park space back to the student body and faculty, not only by making circulation free-flowing again, but also by generating a range of new campus activities and encouraging students and staff to make the place their own.

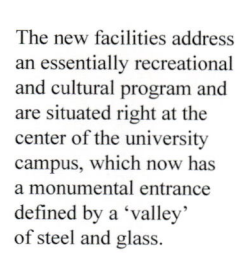

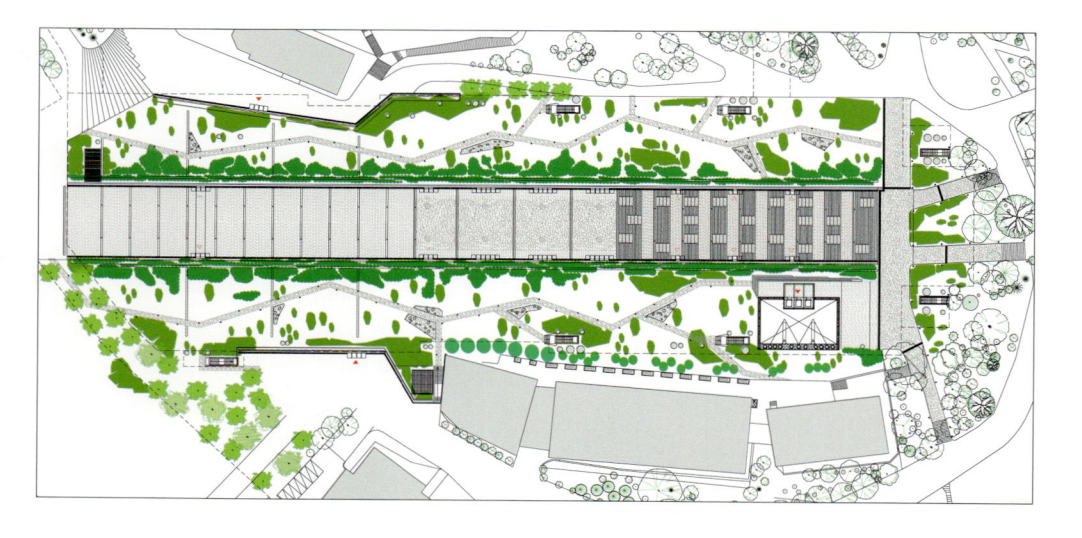

Despite its immense size, the new building manages to conceal its volume and practically disappear through a sweeping topographical gesture that involves the creation of a large rooftop garden. The geometry of the 'valley' that is carved out at its center, which descends gradually to then rise abruptly at the far end of the stretch, is finished off with steps and outdoor tiers, offering an informal space for students to leisurely get together in.

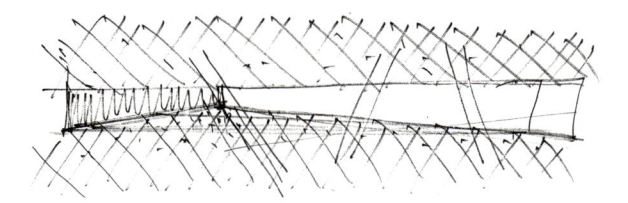

Floor -1

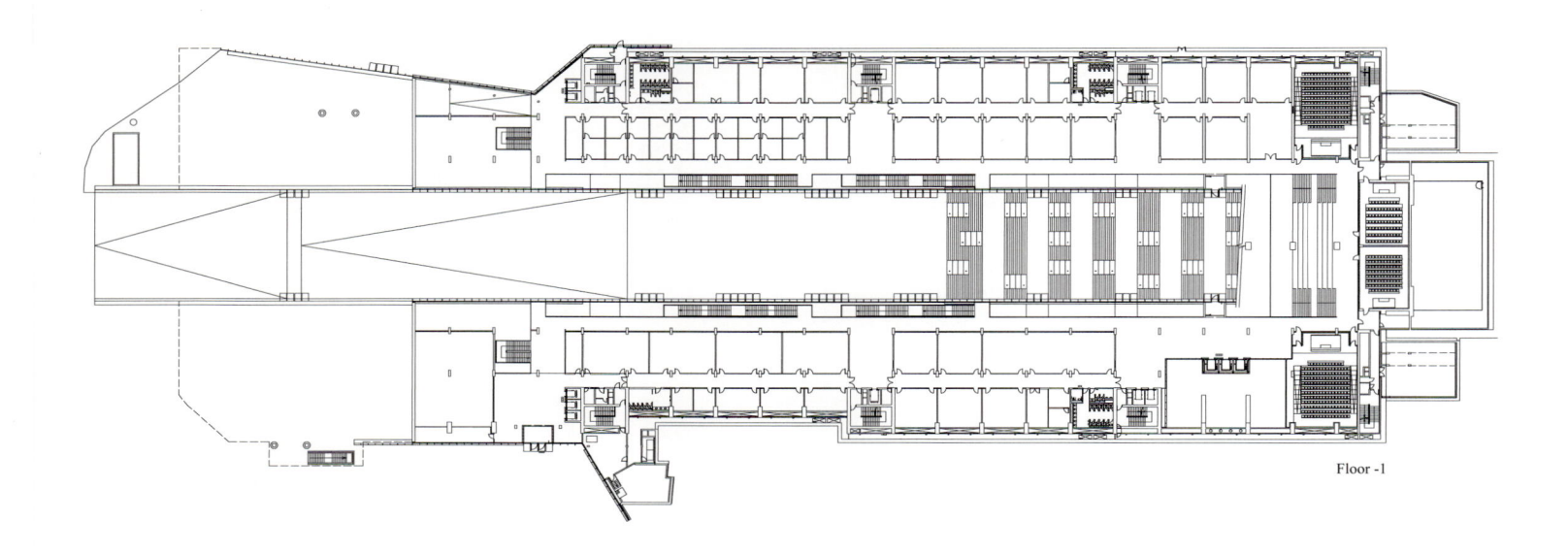

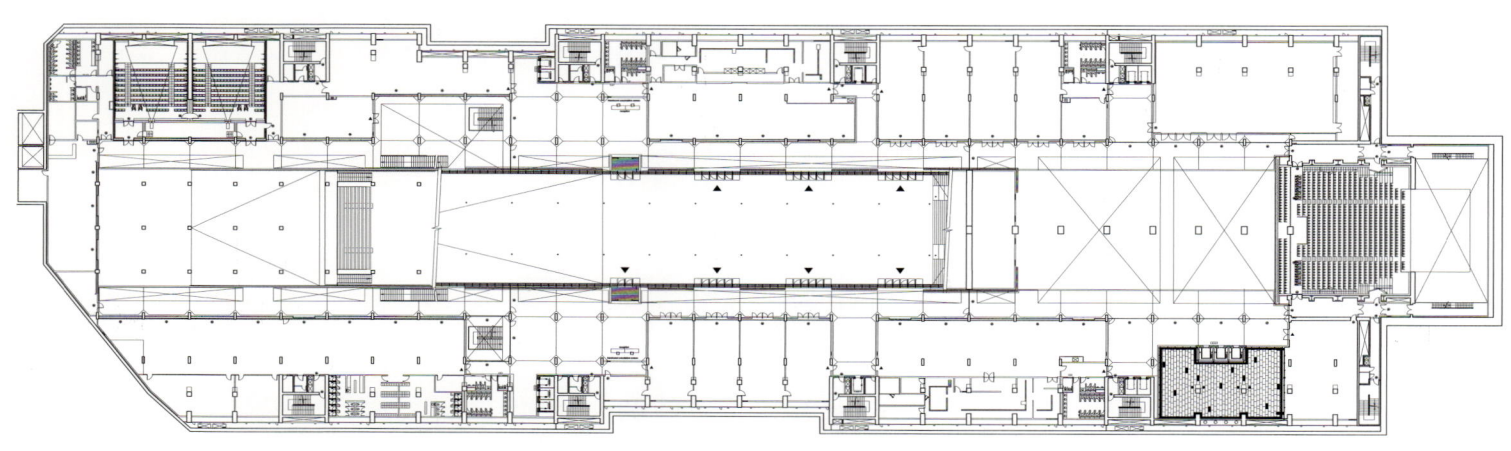

Floor -4

174 Atlas: Asia and Pacific

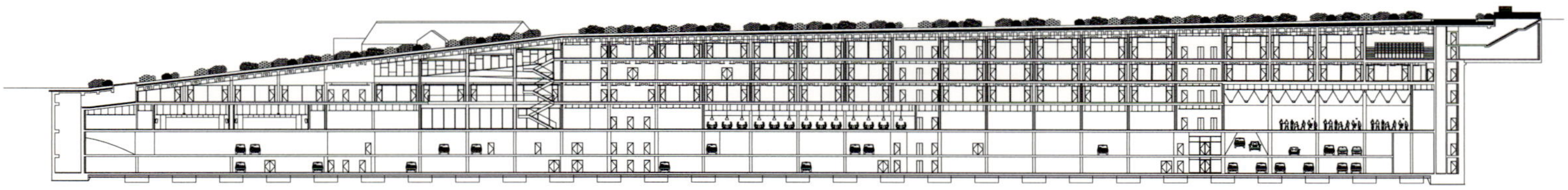

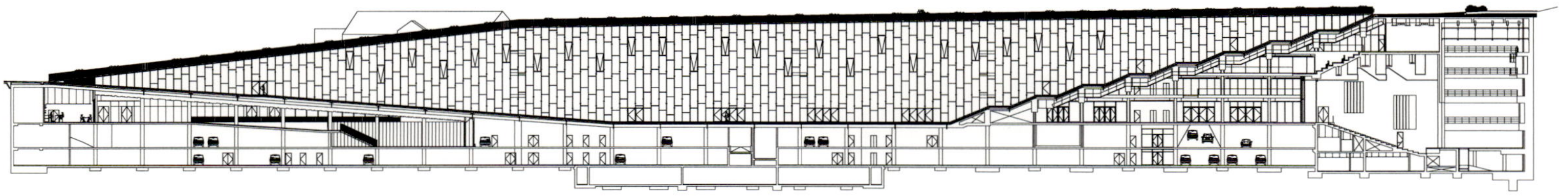

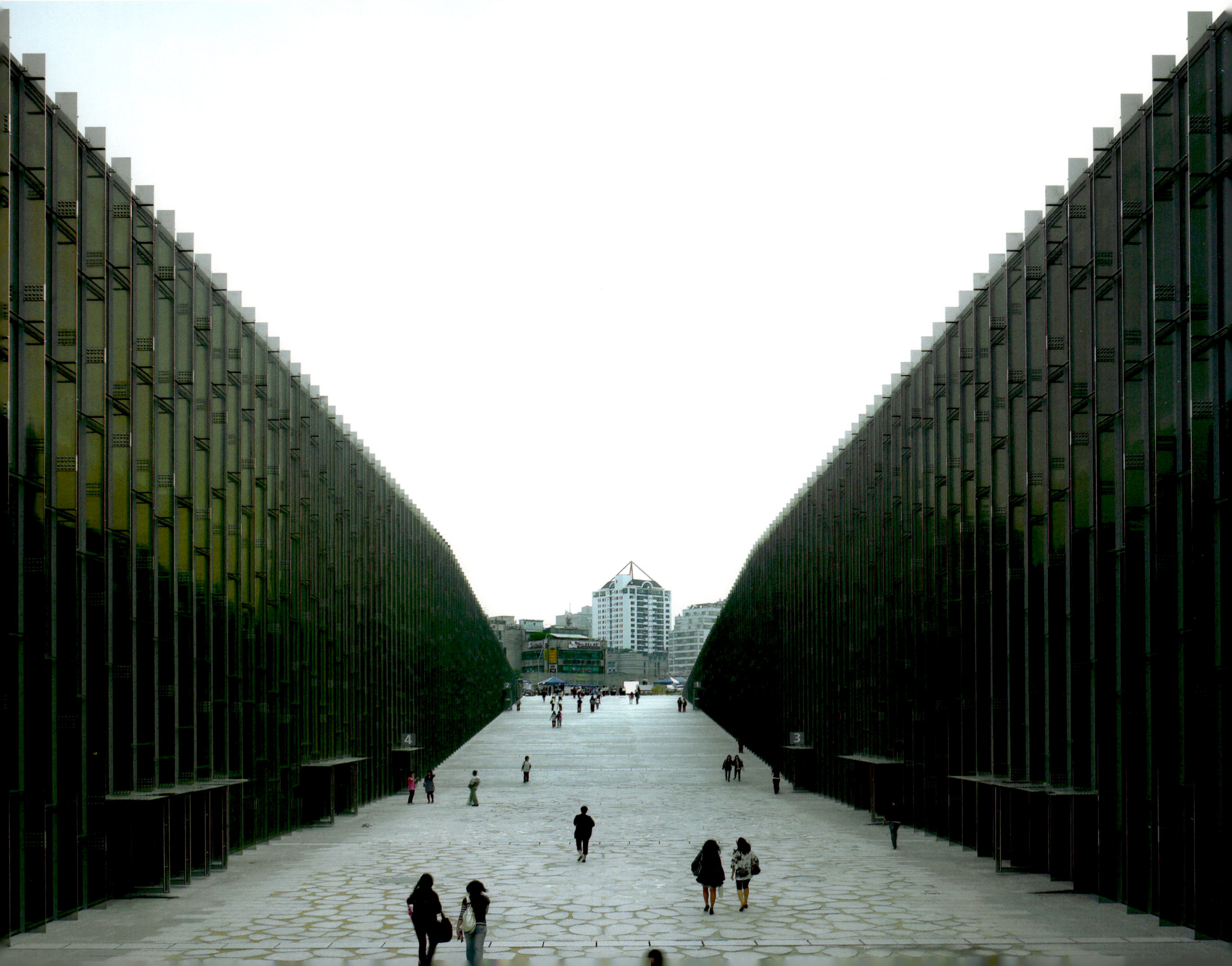
4
3

The envelope of the valley is a curtain wall of transparent glass and mirror-effect stainless steel that constitutes one of the project's most advanced technological pieces, having required an experimental process in collaboration with engineers of Samsung. The slender slats that serve to hold up the facade are braced to each other by the rectangular frames of the glass surfaces, and were calculated to withstand high wind stress. Through their mirror finish, they contribute to bringing abundant daylight into the half-buried building. Inserted in the space between the facade and the floor slabs are the staircases and corridors.

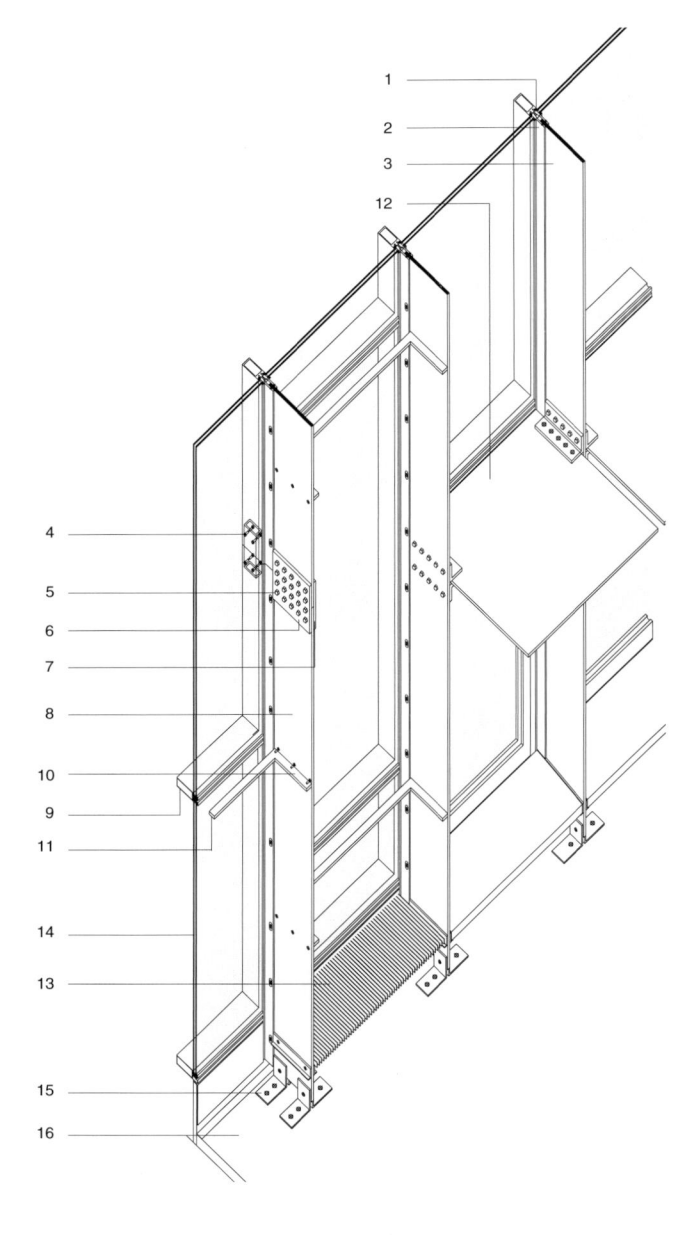

1. structural glazing sealant
2. aluminum profile
3. polished stainless steel fin
4. aluminum profile screwed on to inner steel reinforcement
5. polished stainless steel rod and cap nut
6. polished stainless steel plate
7. splice in fin length not to exceed 5400 mm
8. slotted hole for vertical movement between aluminum and stainless steel
9. horizontal aluminum profile
10. flish threaded stainless steel bolt every 400 mm
11. stainless steel horizontal bracket
12. polished stainless steel plate
13. galvanized steel grill
14. insulation
15. galvanized steel angle
16. concrete slab

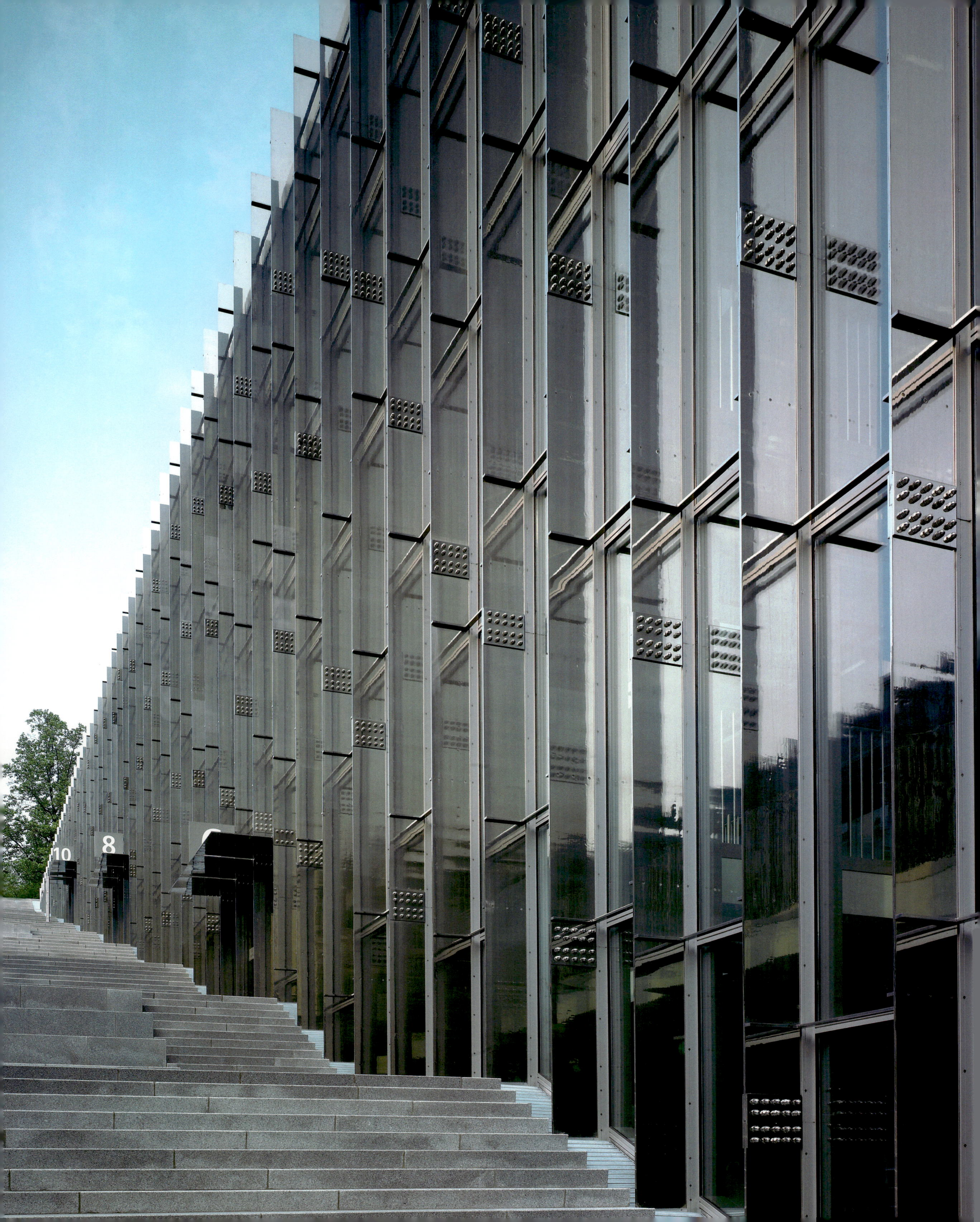
10
8

FOA
Dulnyouk Publishers
Paju Book City (South Korea)

THIS PROJECT WAS a commission from Dulnyouk Publishing Company to design a single headquarters for the firm's management, administrative, and editorial sections, heretofore dispersed in the South Korean capital. The building is located in Paju Book City, a satellite town of Seoul that was explicitly conceived to centralize the country's book industry and bring together its planning, production, and distribution aspects. The Paju area is conveniently close to the Jayu highway.

The site is a 1,953 square meter lot on the western edge of a hill overlooking the valley where Paju Book City is situated. To enforce the masterplan for the book city, the built mass occupying 3,906 square meters on the site had to be positioned in an east-west direction. This would avoid blockage of airflow between the hill and the riverside west of the site. The masterplan also imposed a three-story height limit.

Besides executive and administrative offices and facilities for overall editorial operations, the program includes space to hold events in, as well as an apartment to accommodate guests in, for a gross floor area of 1,637 square meters.

The complex was designed to capitalize on the advantages of its suburban location.

Client
Dulnyouk Publishers
Architects
FOA: Farshid Moussavi, Alejandro Zaera-Polo
Collaborators
Jorge Arribas, Natalia Rodriguez, Nuria Vallespin, Lluis Viu Rebes, Xavier Ortiz, Marco Guarnieri, Pablo Ros; yo2 Architects (local architects)
Consultants
Structural Design Group (structure); BDSP Partnership (services); Davis Langdon & Everest (cost consultant); Ninian Logan, Radlett (traffic engineer) Construction Phase: ALT Structural Engineering Group (structure); Hana High Tech (electricity); SeAH (machinery)
Photos
Kim Jae Kyeong (pp. 178-179, 180 top); Kim Jong Oh (p. 180 bottom, 35)

The new publishing house headquarters, situated in a satellite town of Seoul known as Paju Book City, where the country's book industry is concentrated, has been conceived as a huge split screen set between gardens.

Besides office space for management and the administrative staff as well as general publishing and editorial operations, the program includes venues for events and an apartment to house possible guests in, all this in a total floor area of 1,638 square meters. The lavatories and corridors line the longitudinal facades, thereby reinforcing the linear character of the organizational scheme that governs the proposal.

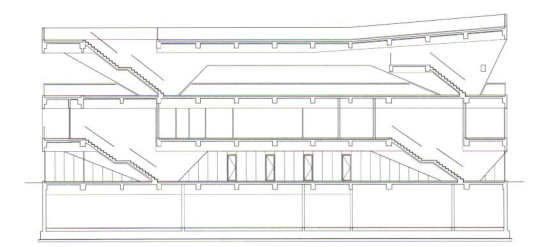

The workspaces are thought out as if they were extensions of the surrounding gardens. Intensifying the qualities of its assertive east-west orientation, the building is designed as a folding screen between a green garden on the south and a mineral garden on the north. Both virtually encroach on the screen's two faces, one clad with long wooden strips and the other cast in concrete.

The geometrical arrangement of the screen, which makes up the structure of the building, is such that each of the floors is oriented towards one of the two gardens, in turns. The result of this organization is that there is a constant alternation of landscapes and finishes as the observer moves across the building's section.

The exterior of the building reflects the split personality of the diagram through the opposition of the timber-coated side facing the green garden and the concrete facade looking towards the car park. The main construction materials used are *merbau* wood - in strips placed in varying directions to accentuate the facade's texture -, unfaced concrete, and pair glass.

The project's success lies not only in the clear diagram that brings the landscape into the building, but also in the clarity with which spaces and structure are organized.

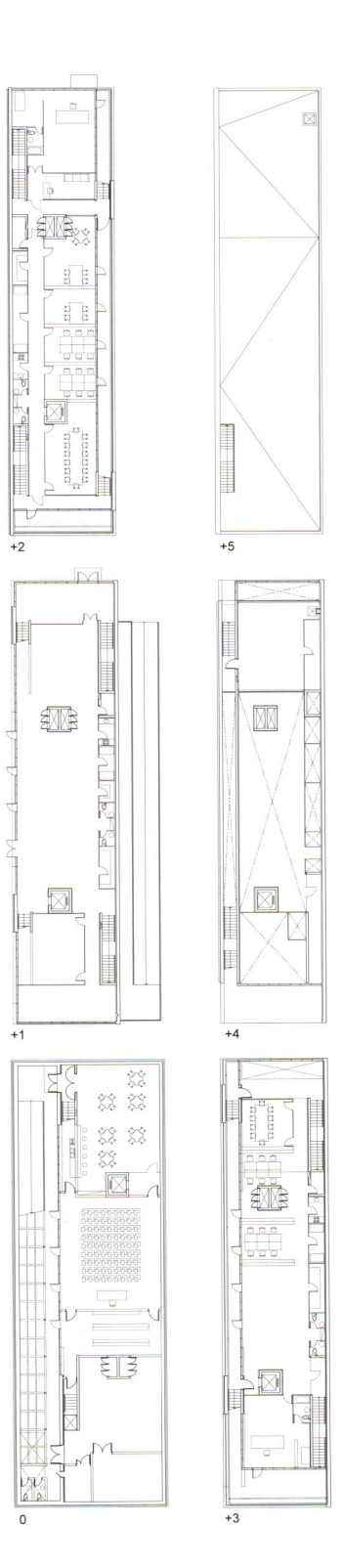

Atlas: Asia and Pacific **179**

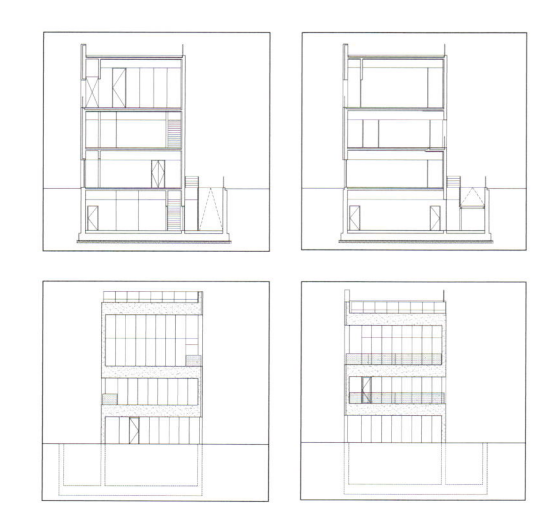

The complex reflects the split personality of the project diagram through the facades - clad with strips of merbau wood toward the green garden, and with concrete cast on site toward the car park -, which have windows only on one side or the other, floor by floor, thereby bringing in an alternation of the two opposite exterior landscapes and enriching the spatial experience of the users as they go through the building's section.

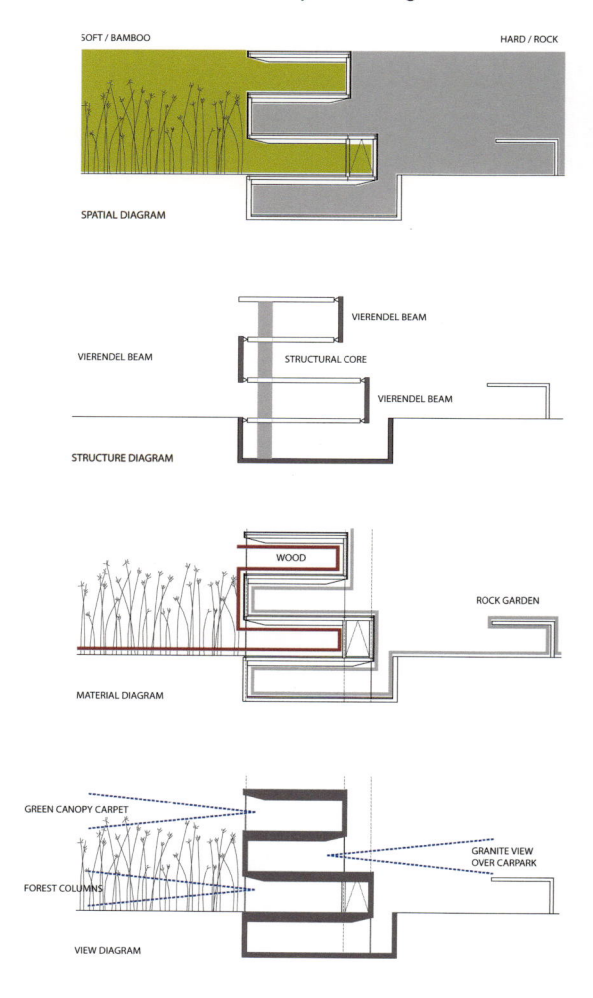

SOFT / BAMBOO   HARD / ROCK

SPATIAL DIAGRAM

VIERENDEL BEAM   STRUCTURAL CORE   VIERENDEL BEAM

STRUCTURE DIAGRAM

WOOD   ROCK GARDEN

MATERIAL DIAGRAM

GREEN CANOPY CARPET   GRANITE VIEW OVER CARPARK

FOREST COLUMNS

VIEW DIAGRAM

180 Atlas: Asia and Pacific

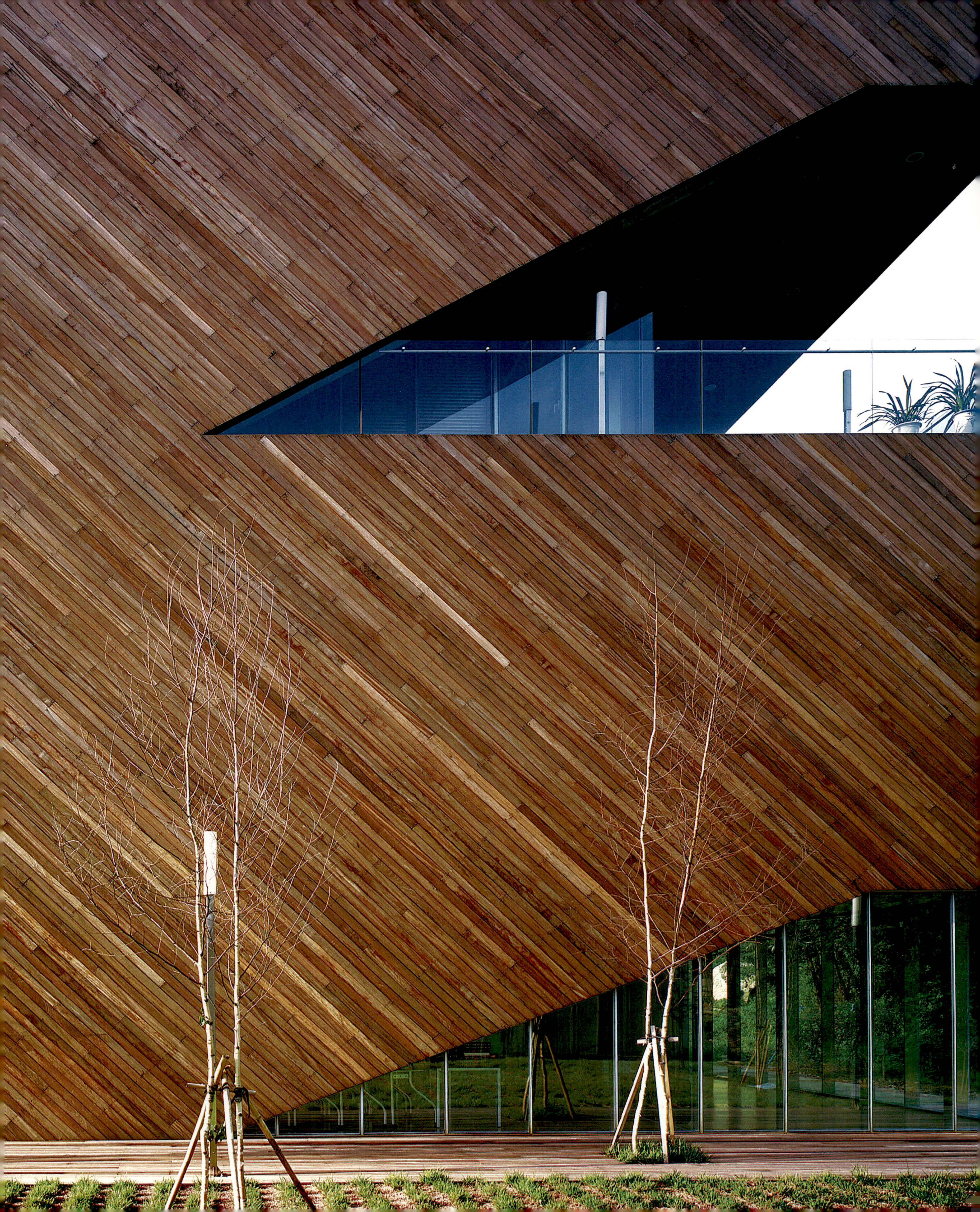

Álvaro Siza
Multifunctional Hall
Young-il Park (South Korea)

Client
Anyang Public Art Project
Architects
Álvaro Siza, Carlos Castanheira (associate architect); Jun Saung Kim
Collaborators
Carlos Castanheira & Clara Bastai: Orlando Sousa, Demis Lopes, Bruno André, João Figuereido; Sun Saung Kim: Young-il Park (project architect), Seungwook Kim, Dusuk Jang
Consultants
TNI (structural); Jung-Mioung (electrical); Sun-Woo (mechanical)
Contractor
Sambu
Photos
Fernando Guerra/FG+SG

Executed in eighteen months, the project resulted from an invitation of the curators of the Anyang Public Art Project, an international exhibition held in 2005 that gathered artists, architects, and designers.

IN THE YEAR 2005, in preparation for the Anyang Public Art Project, a major international event involving temporary and permanent art and architecture projects, a small town in the outskirts of Seoul began the construction of an ambitious cultural complex. The chosen site, located in the heart of a natural space amidst mountains, was a preexisting theme park of the city: a chaotic mix of Buddhist temples, shops, street vendor stands, and hotels. Contrary to previous attempts geared at forcefully eliminating the complexity and originality of the area, the Public Art operation aimed to create a regenerative framework that respected the particular character of the place, and it sought to do so through an interdisciplinary meeting of artists, architects, and designers.

Among numerous constructions carried out for the exhibition was a small, centrally located multifunctional pavilion. Launched immediately in the wake of initial contacts with the curators in charge of the event, because of tight deadlines the project was carried out in a very short period of time, no more than eighteen months therefore elapsing between the moment the design process began to opening day.

At ground level are the entrance, a double-height exhibition space, restrooms, and a small police station. Upstairs are offices, a meeting room, and technical areas. To one side of the building is the river that is the park's vertebra, and on the other side is the start of a forest. This determined a volumetric composition that nevertheless flows freely in between, giving rise to a dynamic space of curved lines.

Through bold gestures on plan, the strategically positioned openings are oriented towards one direction or another, depending on the program. The police station, an arm of the building, faces the river to the west. The entrance, sunken into the building's mass, looks northeast. The gallery protected by a large canopy, faces the woods to the south.

The proposal's monolithic character highlights its sculptural forms, giving the limelight to the reinforced concrete of a light gray tone. The curved inner walls are all white, stressing the importance of natural light in the pavilion's conception.

The pavilion's location between the river that crosses the exhibition park and the start of a lush forest determined a curved volumetric composition that flows freely within the limits imposed by the natural framework of the place. The project's monolithic character stresses its sculptural qualities, giving the limelight to the exterior's unfaced reinforced concrete of a light gray tone and the interior's white walls.

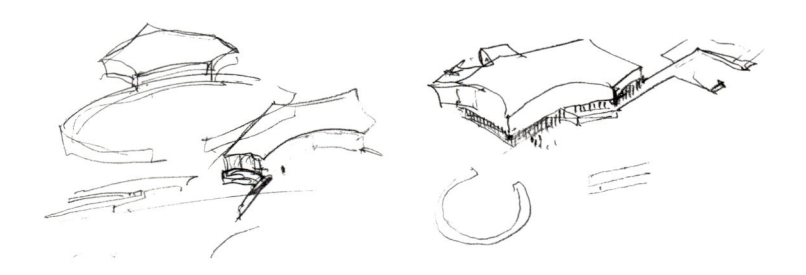

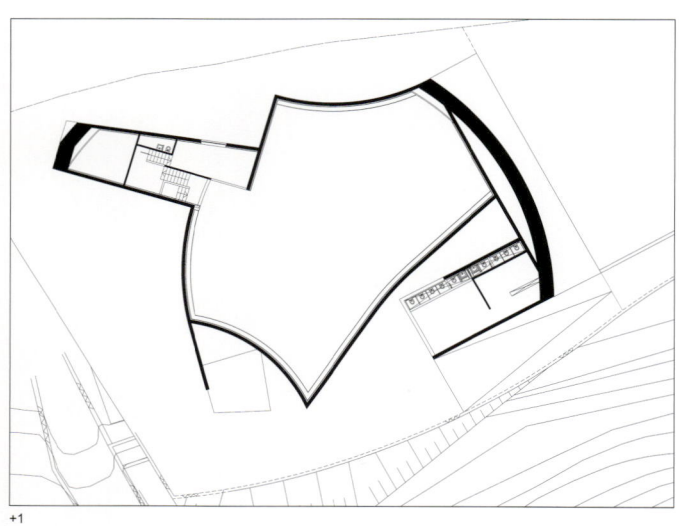

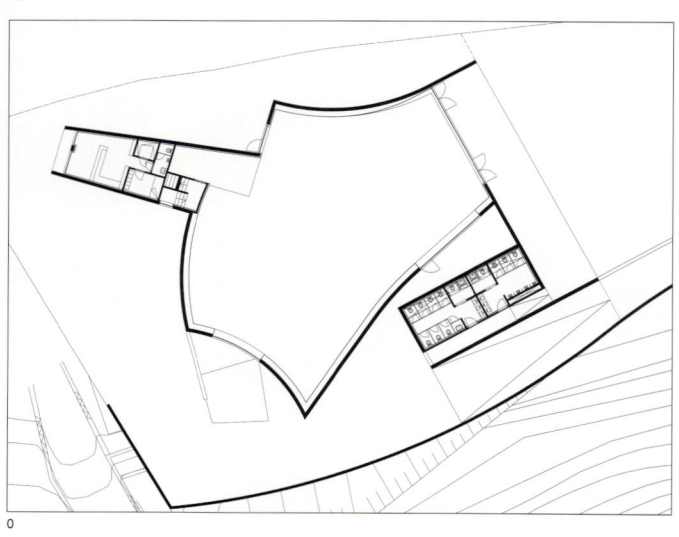

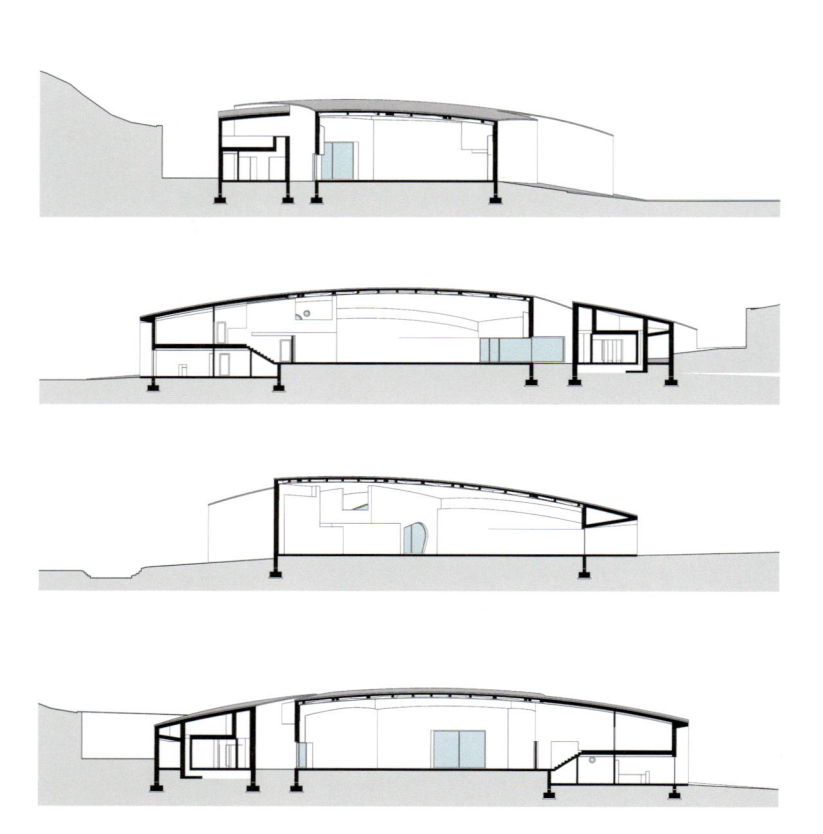

Apart from a large central hall for exhibitions, the building accommodates programs having to do with the management and running of the park, including a small police station shaped like an appendix oriented towards the river on the west, and a pavilion with restrooms on the east. The art gallery, a large double-height volume delimited above by a very tightly stretched vaulted ceiling, has an entrance porch that stretches the entire width of the building, thereby bringing plenty of natural light into the interior. The organic geometry of the roof also inspired the curving lines of the interior walls, creating a dynamic space where light plays a leading role.

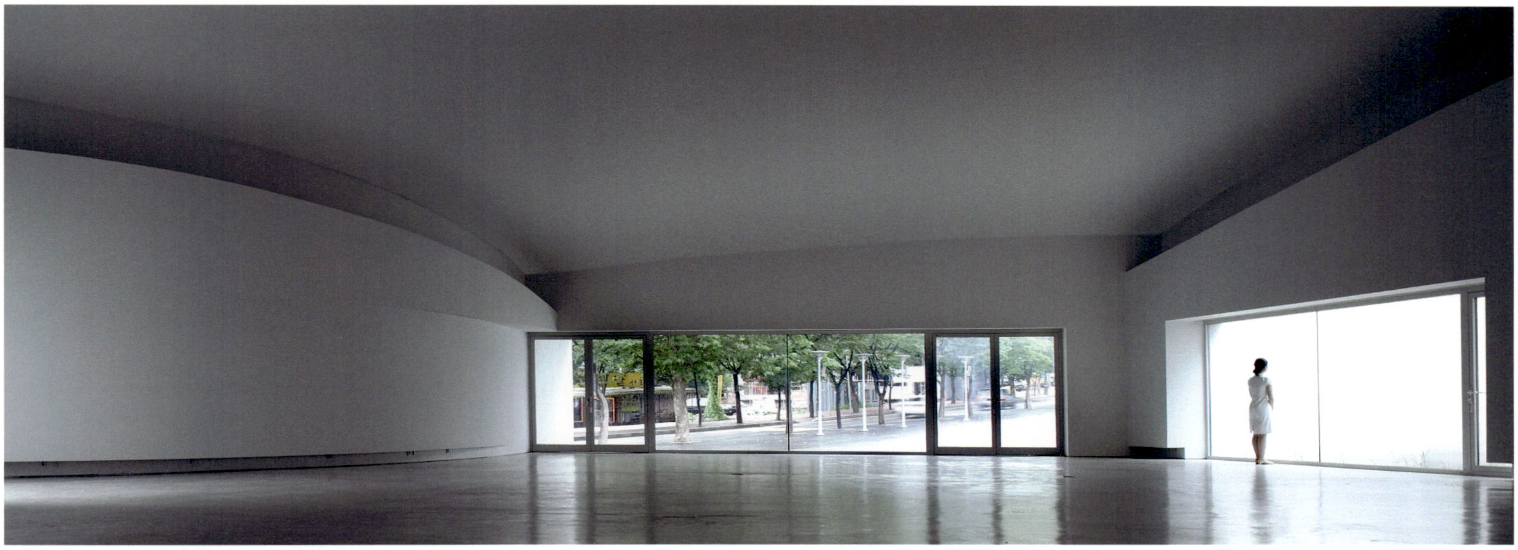

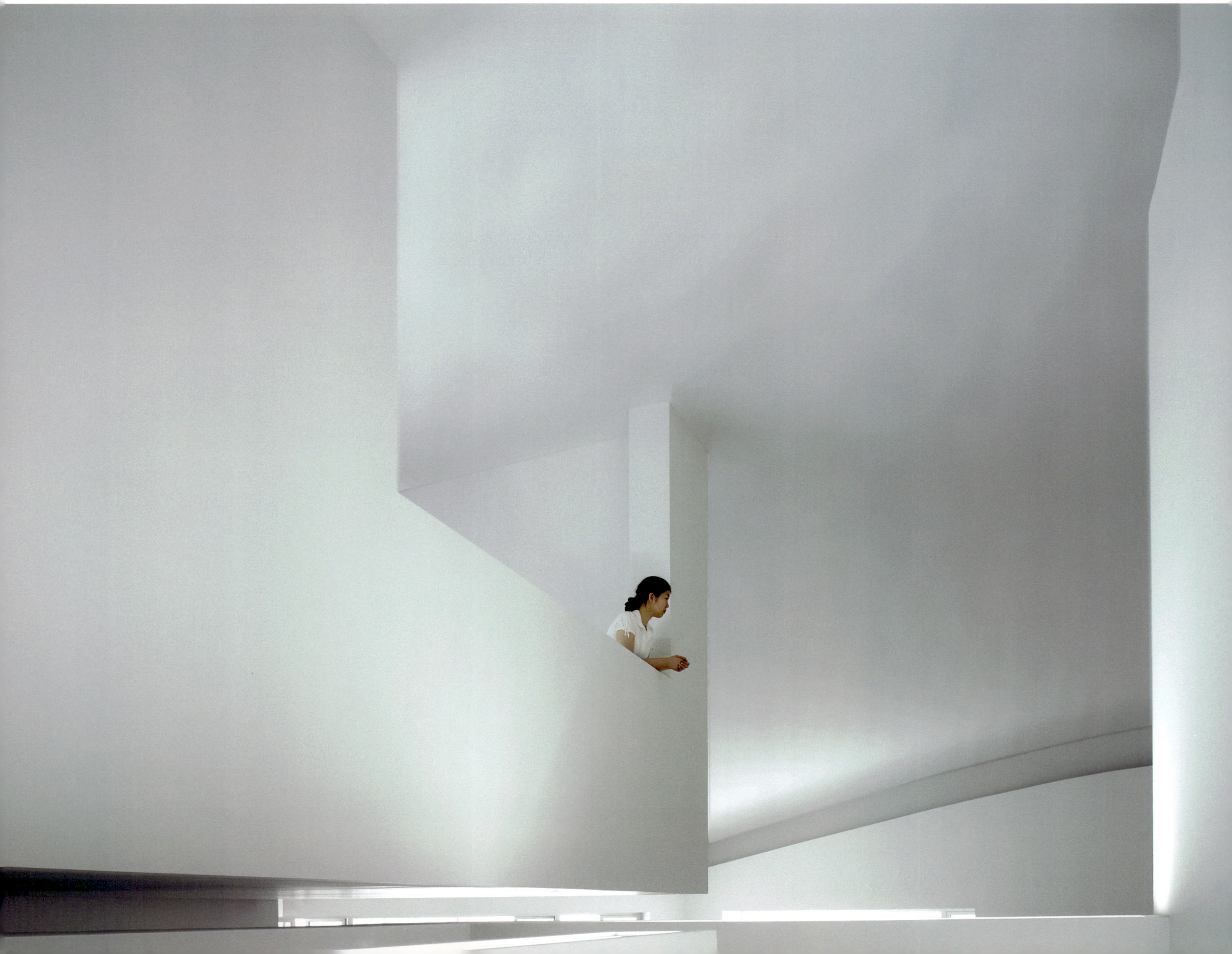

MVRDV
Power Center
Gwang Gyo, Gyeonggi (South Korea)

Clients
Daewoon Consortium and DA Group
Architects
MVRDV: Winy Maas, Jacob van Rijs, Nathalie de Vries
Local architects: DA Group
Collaborators
Youngwook Joung, Wenchian Shi, Raymond van den Broek, Paul Kroese, Naiara Arregi, Wenhua Deng, Doris Strauch, Bas Kalmeijer
Consultant
Arup (engineering)

The so-called 'power centers' are high-density high-rise complexes that endeavor to intensify activity in the newly created metropolitan areas of South Korea, stimulating urban growth around them.

THE TOWN PLANNING strategy of creating 'power centers' with a high concentration of mixed programs (public services, retail, culture, housing, offices, leisure) to inject life into new metropolitan areas while encouraging further development around them has been in use in Korea since the start of the millennium.

Alas, those that have sprung up in the past years all consist of towers on a shopping center plinth, each with its design gimmick. The challenge here is to innovate this typology by adding a green agenda and showing how the adoption of more site-specific, less generic designs can help accentuate differences between places, thereby exalting local identities and ultimately generating more remarkable communities, fostering diversity, and attracting more people.

Moreover, most Korean urban programs have tended to encroach upon and crowd the valleys, which are easier to access and build on. This pollutes them and blocks natural ventilation and cooling within them, hence increasing energy demands besides destroying greenery. It also closes up the valleys and eliminates them altogether, saving only the hilltops which are far less accessible and only usable for leisure.

This project is one of two major development nodes to go up as part of a large-scale operation for a new city. The other one is for the Gwang Gyo Central Business District. This, the Gwang Gyo Power Center, is located on the southern edge of the development, exactly 35 kilometers south of the city of Seoul, surrounded by a lake and wooded hills. The idea here is not to kill yet another valley, but to actually create a valley park that will, among other things, filter the lake water for internal needs and use it to create an energy-saving microclimate.

A new hilly landscape comes alive because all program elements are designed as rings pushing outward the lower they are. Each part of the program has a terrace planted with box hedges, creating open-air life and plantations with water falling from floor to floor. Connected by ramps, the terraces contain outdoor facilities.

The shifting of the floors has the effect of producing hollow cores that open at the bottom and become apartment and office lobbies, commercial plazas, or museum foyers. These communal spaces are connected by streets, forming a series of ground-level promenades. The main street leads to the lake. A whole park comes alive.

This 'power center' adopts the form of an artificial topography: a technological 'valley' that concentrates multiple uses and that is to serve as a catalyst for the future city of Gwang Gyo, located south of Seoul, on the banks of a lake and surrounded by wooded hills. Each of the rings making up the project has its own terrace with plants along the edge, giving rise to open-air spaces that are connected by ramps with undulating profiles.

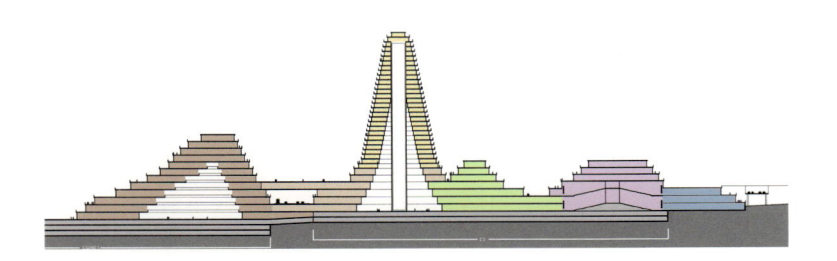

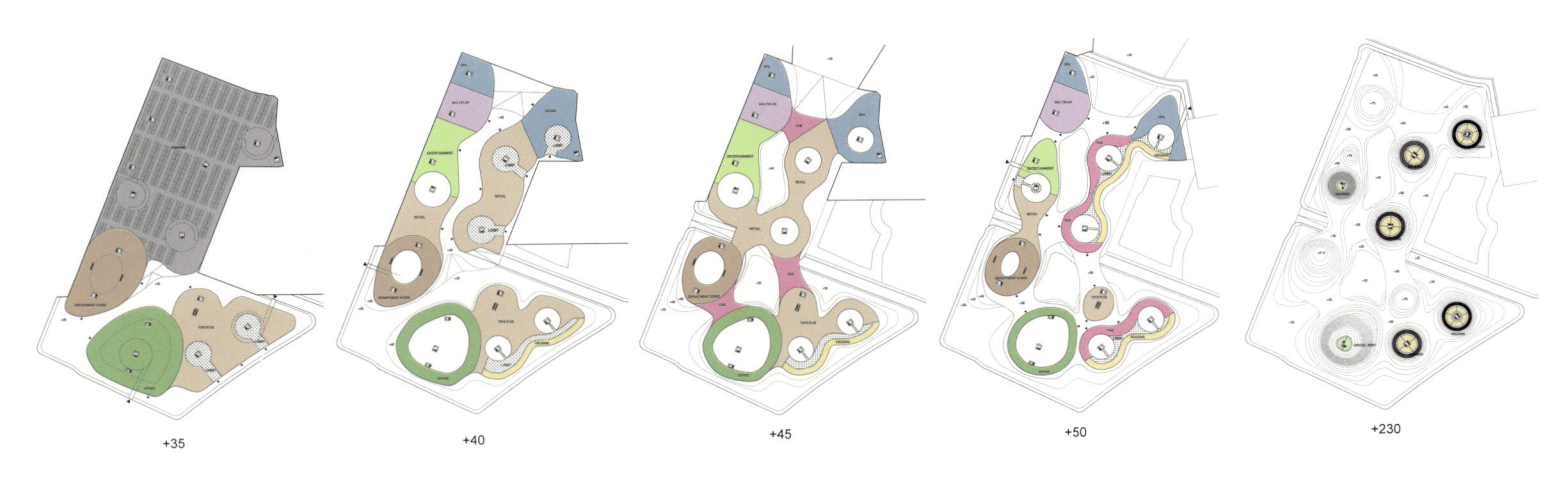

+35   +40   +45   +50   +230

Atlas: Asia and Pacific

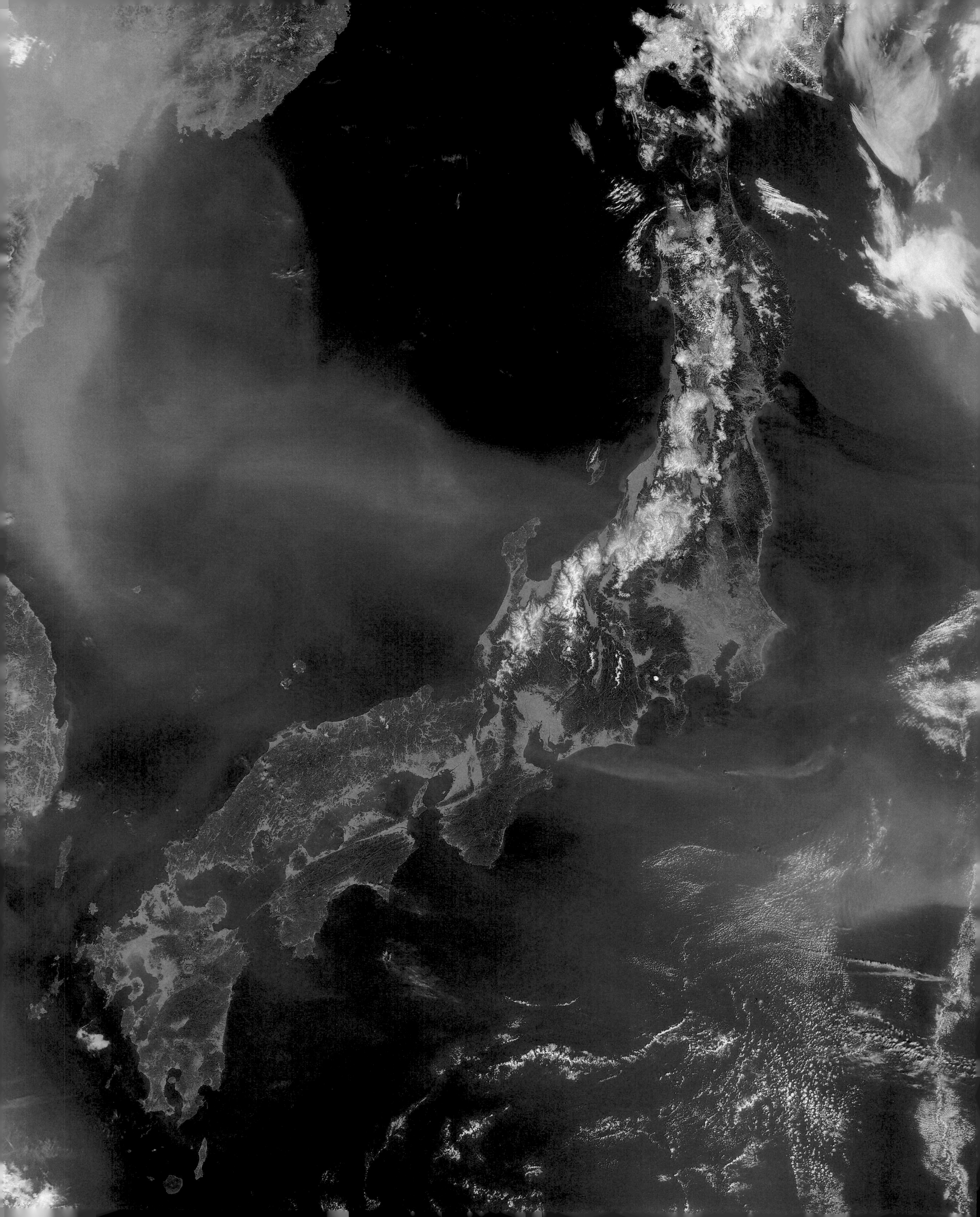

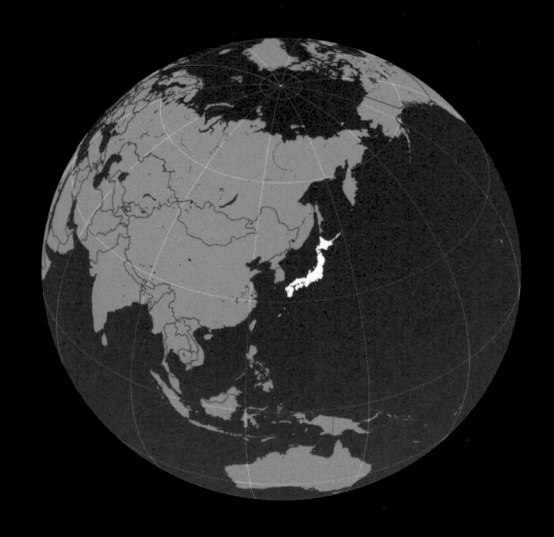

Japan

After three decades of unprecedented economic growth, in the nineties decade the country experienced a financial crisis from which it is still recovering. Recession and stagnation have shaped Japanese architecture, which exported prominent figures while inwardly shifting towards simpler designs. The Kobe earthquake also had an architectural dimension: it marked the end of deconstructivism and the return to a conceptual and small-scale modernism, as can be seen in the works of Toyo Ito, Jun Aoki , Ryue Nishizawa, Kazuyo Sejima, Takaharu & Yui Tezuka and Kengo Kuma. With relatively short generational periods, the latest crop of architects in Japan reflects sensitivity and sophistication, and their projects strike a contrast with the architectural icons of globalization: they make the most of the newest computer applications to create clear volumes, like those of the workshop by Junya Ishigami, or Borgesian projects such as the endless library of Sou Fujimoto.

Taro Igarashi
After the Earthquake and the Bubble
Japan, a Refined and Technological Mannerism

Makoto Sei Watanabe, Iidabashi subway station, Tokyo (2000)

Characterized by the hard coexistence of digital work and craftsmanship, and of luxury and fragility, the latest works in Japan are examples of sophistication.

IN DECEMBER of 2000, the Iidabashi subway station on the Oedo line, designed by an architect – a rare occurrence in Japan –, opened in Tokyo. Makoto Sei Watanabe, known for his innovative computer-generated architecture, designed the station. An image of a plant is carried out throughout the entire station. The entrance of the station is covered with mammoth-size metallic flowers, and its underground space, a green metal web-frame, follows the escalator corridor, similar to a root of a plant. A computer program automatically generated the design for this section, as it was not traditionally designed and drafted by the architect. In its process, the parameters determining which branching of the web should increase and which areas should not be invaded are specified by the architect beforehand, similarly to a plant that selects its sun gain and nourishment as its initial condition for growth.

A century ago, when the subway was once a symbol of a modern city, Hector Guimard glamorously designed the entrance of the Paris metro. This project was a critical reaction to the 19th-century architecture that did not look into newly available materials like iron and glass, but instead continued to cut and paste past styles picked up from a catalogue. As such, Art Nouveau aims at new art that does not refer to historical elements. In the 19th century it was not an architect but an engineer like Eiffel, who designed the Eiffel Tower, who presented new possibilities. As such, Art Nouveau architecture took advantage of the flexible properties of metal and produced magnificent works. Its free-flowing curvilinear forms and bold glass roofs became symbols of a city culture unbound by tradition.

Computerization and Organic Design
Though separated by a century, similarities are found between the two subway stations.

A century after the arrival of Art Nouveau to Paris with the organic motifs of the Metro entrances designed by Guimard, a computer has generated in Tokyo the form of a station with the parameters of a living creature.

M. S. Watanabe, Iidabashi subway station

FOA, Yokohama International Port Terminal (2002)

As several examples of recent Japanese architecture show, the use of computer programs in the architectural design process can take on different forms, from the use of glass skins on the facades as multimedia space to the resort to algorithms as form generators. These programs also make it possible to materialize radical ideas, as in the cases of the Yokohama Port Terminal or the Sendai Mediatheque.

Q-Front commercial complex in Shibuya, Tokyo (1999)

During the bubble economy of the 1980s, when postmodernism was a trend and the country was being flooded with quotations of a past style, Watanabe focused his attention on a plant-derived design for Iidabashi station. He was like Guimard, who escaped the style-driven architectures of the past and referenced to free-form plant-derived designs. Art Nouveau was born out of crisis in architecture. Later 19th-century architecture was in the midst of being left behind from the advancing technologies of mechanization and new materials such as iron and concrete. When architecture loses style and everything is measured by science and technology, it is no longer art. Art Nouveau brought in a new technology to architecture in an attempt to revive its status as art. As the philosopher Walter Benjamin points out, Art Nouveau represents "that last sortie of an art besieged in its tower by technology". This situation applies well to the end of the 20th century.

A wave of information technology surged architecture during the 1990s. There were quiet discussions at times about design becoming obsolete if every architecture became an information terminal. Indeed, in December of 1999, the Q-Front commercial complex appeared in front of the Shibuya station. Having an enormous screen, it lacked designed architectural space. Indeed the surface architecture that sends information resembles a scene from a future city in the science fiction film *Blade Runner* (1982). Reacting to such trend, Watanabe introduced computers into design and groped for the possibility of cyber-architecture. The fluid design led by simulation inevitably overlaps with the unconscious growth of a plant.

Opened in the New Year of 2001, the Sendai Mediatheque by Toyo Ito is also the architecture of the information age. Its biggest feature is its multiple twisting tubes that penetrate the floors instead of conventional columns. As his first sketch reveals, Ito imagined seaweeds in a water tank. The image of a plant is also present here. The exterior concrete structure in Tod's Omotesando Building (2004), also by Ito, incorporates overlapped tree patterns of Japanese zelkova trees grown on the building roadside. In between the structures, glass is in-filled, wrapping the whole building. Here, structure integrates with decoration, and the dichotomy between bone and skin or abstraction and concreteness is shaken.

Compared to the design method using physical models and drawings, computers make it easier to create complex forms. The Yokohama Port Terminal (2002) by FOA has continuous sections resembling a CT scan of a living organ. As a result, a landscape-like architecture with a heavily undulating surface was achieved. Nature and geographical features came to be

Toyo Ito, Sendai Mediatheque (2001)

An upshot of the social and cultural shock caused by the Japanese economic collapse of the nineties decade and the Kobe earthquake (1995) was the emergence of a transparent and simple modernity, with a fragile image and a minimalist inspiration. Among its practitioners are Kengo Kuma, Atelier Bow-Wow or the Mikan collective, all members of the Unit School, centered on the small scale and on the local, everyday aspects.

Atelier Bow-Wow, Crane House in Karuizawa, Nagano (2007)

mimicked by computers. In the past, structure dictated the framing of the whole, and ornamentation was added afterward, but with the advancement of computation, designs of those with structures that also contain ornamental effects are the focus of attention.

The introduction of computers not only affected design. Nobuaki Furuya's competition idea for the Sendai Mediatheque (1995) presented new spatial possibilities in programming. This stops library books from being put on a dedicated location according to the classification number, and promotes book distribution by its original bias within the library. The user uses the information device to locate the book positioned anywhere and can retrieve it. This might be a proposal that we should take notice of as the next spatial model.

Kobe and the Unit School
The Great Hanshin (Kobe) earthquake in January of 1995 had a huge impact on the movement of modern architecture in Japan. Synched with the bubble economy, the rise of postmodernism cooled with the economic stall, and the tragic scenery after the earthquake pierced the end to deconstructivism. With architectures in the city of rubbles collapsing or in complete destruction, a design of which the metaphor for deconstructivism brandishes with its abstruse theory seemed imprudent. Though at times its criticism lacked intrinsic value, the common notion of its time was that the collapse of the bubble economy and the earthquake were used to remove such flamboyant architectures. Since then, definite recurrence to a more transparent and simple modernism overtook flamboyant and complex design.

It might well be Kengo Kuma who most lucidly presented this change in his design after 1995 in Japan. He in the past has debuted as an American-type postmodern architect with his bold use of classical styles, but then dramatically shifted to minimalistic design expressing Japanese space using materials like trees and bamboo.

The Nakagawa-machi Bato Hiroshige Museum of Art (2000) is covered entirely with thin and delicate cedar louvers. Although not a traditional wood construction, it is a digitally-processed wooden architecture, like a bar code. The methodology of texture mapping local materials is widely applicable. Actually, similar techniques are used in his projects in various parts of the world away from Japan.

When architects born in the 1960s were out of school, the bubble economy collapsed, and work was lost. As a result, teams like Atelier Bow-Wow and Mikan, when setting up their firms, preferred the style of having two or more members collaborate instead of pursuing that heroic architect image that personal name portrays. This type of organization is called the Unit School. They despise postmodern architecture with their dramatically worked-over concepts, and have instead focused on observing the city in its true form, with designs that come as an extension of their daily life. Mikan advocated the design of usualness, and its non-author character. Moreover, Atelier Bow-Wow's research 'Made in Tokyo', devoted to neglected building types (multiuse facilities like supermarkets with driving schools on their roofs, for example), has caught worldwide attention.

The architectural critic Yoichi Iijima has criticized these Unit Schools for their abandonment of their will to be constructive and expressive due to being traumatized by the Great Hanshin earthquake. He adds that the Unit Schools lack strength in their ideas

Kengo Kuma, Nakagawa-machi Bato Hiroshige Museum of Art, Tochigi (2000)

Ryue Nishizawa, Moriyama House in Tokyo (2006)

and simply fiddle with small differences in daily life. However, the author cannot sympathize with such an opinion. Architects born in the 1960s have an extremely positive attitude toward the city. Albeit being small, they find constructive design to be possible. A monument alone is not architecture.

The mega-firms and famous architects from abroad are monopolizing large-scale urban development. Unlike the previous generation, the Unit School does not have large public projects or commercial buildings to work on, and had to settle with the growing demand for extremely small houses in the recent social trend of peoples' recurrence to the urban city. Ryue Nishizawa of SANAA designed, with the Moriyama House (2006), a multi-unit house of partitioned volumes that created an alley-like a scenic space. The Unit School generation moreover focused its attention on the stock of the city and used it to renovate, instead of the usual scrap-and-build method. Katsuhiro Miyamoto took his home in Takarazuka, whose complete destruction had been determined by officials after the Great Hanshin earthquake, and refurbished and regenerated it as Zenkai House (1997). The additional steel frame was inserted like a surgical cast to reinforce the existing structure while sustaining the atmosphere of an old house where he spent his early life. In 1996, he brought the rubbles from the Great Hanshin earthquake to the Japanese pavilion for the Venice Biennale and won The Golden Lion. Mikan, through the renovation plan for a housing complex and other projects, did not excessively deny the city space of postwar days but instead presented methods of rediscovering its charm. The new generation actively engages in art-related events and activities, expanding its active front beyond architecture. Such variegated activity was the strategy for the architect to survive after the burst of the economic bubble.

Facing Globalization
Since the Metabolist movement there have only been a few architectural philosophies which have gained fame overseas. However, in the 1990s, not just those mega-firms but Japanese architects also have an increasing number of overseas projects. In the first half of the 20th century, with Japan's expansionism into the Asian continent, they have handled modern architecture and city planning in various parts of Asia like China, South Korea, and Taiwan. After the 1970s, Kenzo Tange held projects in many parts of the world such as Europe, Africa, and Latin America along with the Middle East. Overseas presence of Japanese architects is reflective of globalism. Of course, in its background the presence of several unique original designs, supported by cooperative high engineering and construction accuracy, is to be mentioned, obtaining worldwide recognition from both domestic and foreign media.

Tadao Ando started with houses and commercial projects and shifted to public projects in the 1980s. In addition, responding to his international recognition, he began to handle overseas projects in the 1990s. Starting with completed projects like the Vitra Conference Pavilion (1993) in Germany and the Modern Art Museum of Fort Worth (2002) in the United States, he is expanding his simple modernism style using reinforced concrete. Toyo Ito is enthusiastically pursuing new possibilities for space and structures in projects in Belgium, Great Britain, Singapore, and Taiwan.

In 1997, Yoshio Taniguchi won the competition to redesign the Museum of Modern Art against architects like Rem

SANAA, Naoshima Ferry Terminal, Kagawa (2006)

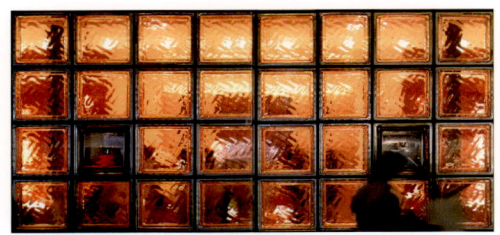

Renzo Piano, Maison Hermès, Tokyo (2001)

The massive consumption of items manufactured by western luxury brands has prompted the flourishing of a new building type: the flagship store. These landmark buildings line up along some of the most commercial streets of Tokyo, like Ginza or Omotesando, which have become showcases to display the latest architectural innovations, a role similar to that played by the pavilions of World Expos.

Kumiko Inui, Dior Building, Tokyo (2004)

Toyo Ito, Tod's Building, Tokyo (2004)

Herzog & de Meuron, Prada Building, Tokyo (2003)

Koolhaas and Dominique Perrault. The completed new building (2004) represents the ability of a Japanese architect who can achieve a modernism better refined than the original. In 2003, Shigeru Ban won the international competition for the construction of the new Centre Pompidou in Metz. With projects like the refugee shelter in Rwanda using paper tube and the Nomadic Museum (2005) using shipping containers, he is known for his effective use of recyclable materials. He currently places his focus on project activity overseas.

After completing the 21st Century Museum of Contemporary Art, Kanazawa (2004), SANAA was selected in the 2005 international competition as the architects for the new Louvre-Lens Museum. The former contains a plan of several exhibition volumes wrapped around a large round glass ring. In the latter, the glass ring is removed and takes on a more diffused format. They have won several international competitions and have now gained more overseas projects than domestic ones. They continue to challenge with experimental architecture with projects like the Glass Pavilion for the Toledo Museum of Art (2006), that extensively uses glass for both interior and exterior walls, and the Zollverein School (2006) in Germany.

Beyond architecture, the following activities are worth noting. In an attempt to revive the CIAM conference, Arata Isozaki and critic Akira Asada held ten international conferences, the ANY series, that crossed architecture and philosophy in the 1990s over several countries. In addition, in 2007 Hitoshi Abe, for the first time as an active young Japanese architect, earned the position of departmental chair for the University of California Los Angeles (UCLA). He has done projects like the Miyagi Stadium (2000), that was the venue of the 2002 World Cup, and the Kanno Museum (2006), taking an active part based in the local urban city of Sendai.

Luxury Adventures
Nearing its maturity, all necessary facilities are approaching completion in Japan, and so currently, chances for architects to actively build projects in public and national sectors are decreasing. Hence, the building type that has been under the spotlight in Japan during the first decade of the 21st century is the luxury brand retail shop, with architects working on the design of several stores. Luxury brand shops are deployed all over the world, but in Japan they have taken on an unusual development with respect to others. According to the investigation done in 2003, the ownership rate of Louis Vuitton handbags by Japanese females (ages 15 through 59) was 44%. For this company, the Japanese branch was responsible for 1/3 of its worldwide sales. In spite of the recession, sales of luxury brands were at their best. With an almost religious brand loyalty, such items have turned into everyone's uniform and not something to differentiate from others. In Japan, even high school girls carry luxury brand bags, but they simultaneously carry small items purchased from super discounted 100-yen shops, and yet this odd sensibility is permissible here.

The tendency of such super-brands to appoint architects is also seen overseas, but the numbers are by far more accentuated in Japan. The honeymoon relationship between architecture and fashion started with the success of Jun Aoki's Louis Vuitton Building in Nagoya (1999). When one reflects on the history of the brand, this was to be their first freestanding store in Japan. Aoki made use of not being able to fiddle with the interior, and instead presented a facade where the double-layered, checkered pattern printed on the glass side cause displacement by incorporating an op art type expression that creates special visual effects. Similar methodology is used in other Louis Vuitton stores all over the world. Louis Vuitton also requested female architects coming from Aoki's office like

Tadao Ando, Omotesando Hills, Tokyo (2006)

Kumiko Inui and Yuko Nagayama to design the brand's Kochi, Osaka, and Kyoto stores.

Omotesando and Ginza in Tokyo have become Japan's prominent streets for contemporary architects. Reaching the 21st century, in Omotesando, commercial buildings like Jun Aoki's Louis Vuitton Omotesando Building (2002); Kengo Kuma's One Omotesando (2003); SANAA's Dior Omotesando (2003), with its undulating acrylic drapes; Ito's Tod's Omotesando Building (2004); Kisho Kurokawa's Japanese Nursing Association Building (2004); Tadao Ando's Omotesando Hills (2006); and MVRDV's Gyre (1998) appeared one after another. In Ginza, Kazuyo Sejima's Opaque Ginza (1998), Aoki's Louis Vuitton Ginza (2000), Ricardo Bofill's Tokyo Ginza Shiseido Building, Renzo Piano's Maison Hermès (2001), Aoki's Louis Vuitton Ginza Namiki (2004), Inui's Dior Ginza (2004), Takuji Nakamura's Lanvin Boutique Ginza (2004), and Ito's Mikimoto Ginza 2 (2005) have emerged.

Although it is the same capitalist space, while the redevelopment projects of Tokyo often create mediocre business site buildings, the luxury brand buildings attempt to be experimental in their design. For example, the exterior of the Prada boutique in Aoyama (2003), by Herzog & de Meuron, has a futuristic form resembling cut crystal. It is able to achieve such bold facade thanks to its diamond pattern structure. In these projects, each architect's sensibility to material and surface treatment is effectively demonstrated. First of all, architecture and clothes are common in that they both wrap the body. Thus, the shops designed by architects with themes of surface treatment and ornamentation is abundant.

Are luxury brand architectures not similar to pavilions of the Expo? They both have the common feature of being actively adventurous with their designs instead of not having to think about the lifespan of their architectures to remain for eternity. The Expos of the past have created revolutionary architectures such as the Crystal Palace and the Eiffel Tower. However, in the 2005 Aichi Expo that was held in Japan, the pavilions were conservative. In its place, the luxury brand comes in to take its position. Now, fashion streets like Omotesando and Ginza are functioning as showcases for avant-garde architecture. Kenzo Tange built projects that were to be the face of the nation, Kunio Maekawa did local government offices, and Arata Isozaki mainly did museums, but they all considered commercial projects to be of lower class. The Disney Company appointed postmodern architects like Robert Venturi and Michael Graves around the 1990s. However, as we enter the 21st century, we are faced with an unprecedented situation where the experimental designs for luxury brands are at the forefront of architecture.

The design by architects is enhancing the image of the brands. Behind the connective relationship between architecture and fashion is the unprecedented architectural popularity in Japanese general magazines. Especially in 2000, the shift of *Casa Brutus* to a monthly publication was huge. In their issues, for themes based on travel, they

Jun Aoki, Louis Vuitton Namiki Building, Tokyo (2004)

Atelier Tezuka, Roof House in Tokyo (2001)

introduce designer hotels, and the latest works of 'starchitects' are presented as if they were famous star chefs. There are abundant photos that combine beautiful fashion models with contemporary architecture, and they frequently have special issues that unite fashion and architecture.

A New Generation
In 2001 the Gallery Ma held the exhibition 'From Space to Situation – 10 City Profiles from 10 Young Architects', devoted to the Unit School generation and which I helped to organize. The intent behind this exhibition was to present how Atelier Bow-Wow and Mikan observe the city and assemble their design logic based on the outside conditions of the site and the environment. They do not directly express the lucidity of the concept and even dare to consider further difficulty. However, for the new generation that follows, instead of attempting a roundabout explanation, they have come to go straight into the principles of architecture, or shall I say, "principle from situation" this time? It clearly takes on a different position from the Unit School. Among those in the new generation, that includes architects born in the 1970s, are Sousuke Fujimoto, Kumiko Inui, Yasutaka Yoshimura, Jun Igarashi, Takuji Nakamura, Junya Ishigami, Akihisa Hirata, Yuko Nagayama, Go Hasegawa, and Ryuji Fujimura.

As the number of once trendy and pop Unit School decreases, the number of individual architects with cool sensibility is growing. Except, as expected, they have distaste for powerful spaces. Let me introduce the works of Sou Fujimoto, Akihisa Hirata, and Junya Ishigami here. Where the Unit School un-emphasizes individuality, the members of the new generation all hold a genius character.

Fujimoto has been building several

Junya Ishigami, KAIT Workshop, Kanagawa (2008)

196 Atlas: Asia and Pacific

The youngest generation of emerging architects in Japan (Sou Fujimoto, Junya Ishigami, Akihisa Hirata, to name a few) are characterized by a desire to assert their authorship, and by an extreme delicacy, learned from predecessors like Toyo Ito or SANAA, whom they sometimes exceed in their search for maximum lightness, achieved thanks to a large amount of manual and technical means in a paradoxical case of refined mannerism.

Akihisa Hirata, Ienoie House, Yokohama Triennale (2008)

medical facilities in his hometown in Hokkaido, developing a commune-like world. The Treatment Center for Mentally Handicapped Children (2006) has a plan resembling 24 dice randomly rolled. At a glance, it may seem as if the squares queue up without order, but a pack of six to seven white boxes sensibly holds a settlement with a communal space in its center. One of the rooms facing many other boxes is the administration office, where the staff's eyes are subtle and faint instead of being blatantly observed. With this project, Fujimoto has invented a new geometrical form that generates diverse place. Or should I say architecture with innumerable centers? Each individual box, instead of being planned from the whole, or its perimeter decided by one center, holds a connective relationship with the others by carefully measuring their position, similar to the way a flock of bird flies over the sky.

Out of Toyo Ito's office, Hirata created Ienoie (2008), a full-scale housing model for the Yokohama Triennale. He focuses his attention on the architectural form and actual spatial experience. Ienoie carries a roof that is divided into several roofs instead of one. With large roof valleys digging in between the space, it gradually subdivides the space into rooms on the second floor while maintaining their spatial continuity. Therefore, one can hear others but cannot directly see their faces. In addition, a unique phenomenon to experience is being able to look into the next room of the same house through the roof window. Hirata pursues fundamental spaces of such twisting topology with other projects.

Out of SANAA's office, Ishigami is a new type of architect who is highly appraised even from the context of contemporary art. For the Kirin Art Project (2005) he presented a table with careful structural calculation that was able to achieve a tabletop with an unbelievable proportion of 9.5 meters long and only 3 millimeters thick. Like a soft paper unexpectedly cutting your finger, this work jolts your common sense for materials. In addition, the *Square Balloon* (2007) that was exhibited at the Museum of Contemporary Art in Tokyo is a balloon that weighs one ton, and with a height of 14 meters, its enormous architectural size hovers in space. These extreme designs are his traits. For the KAIT Workshop (2008) 305 columns of various sizes and directions are placed randomly. Its plan is unusual. It resembles more like a star map than a conventional architectural plan. Once inside, the visitor loses the sense of distance, and an unprecedented spatial experience is also invented here. And as for the Japanese pavilion for the Venice Biennale International Architecture Exhibition of 2008 – for which the author took on a commissioners position – Ishigami designed a group of small green houses and a garden that blurred the boundary between inside and out, receiving high appraisal worldwide. The world of Ishigami is realized with his highly delicate design, unlike those icon architectures in Dubai and China under the name of globalism. Perhaps this may well be Japanese refined mannerism.

Sou Fujimoto, H House in Tokyo (2009)

Toyo Ito
Tama Art University Library
Tokyo (Japan)

THIS IS A LIBRARY for an art university in the suburbs of Tokyo, on a parcel of land close to the campus's main entrance, which is covered with trees and has a slight slope. The quality of the landscape of the site pointed to an architecture that was uninvasive. In fact, the initial proposals assigned the entire volume of the library underground. For some reason, this solution turned out to be unfeasible. Nevertheless, it did not rule out the idea of a 'subterranean space above the ground' through the idea of a sequence of arches and domes. The floor slab of the ground floor, which brings the terrain's natural decline into the building, also contributed to the place being perceived as an extension of the garden itself.

Within the actual program, the cafeteria was the only place on the premises that students and staff alike, and whatever their specialization, could share, so the initial impetus of the designers was to ask how a space as functionally specific as a library could provide the welcoming communality desired. The architects hit upon the notion of a wide open gallery at ground level that would serve as a thoroughfare for people crossing the campus, even when not intending to use the library.

To allow all these people to both move

Client
Tama Art University
Architects
Toyo Ito & Associates
Collaborators
Takeo Higashi, Hideyuki Nakayama, Yoshitaka Ihara; Kajima Design (associate architect)
Consultants
Sasaki (structure); Workshop for Architecture and Urbanism (interaction design); Fujie Kazuko (furniture design); Nuno (curtains); Kyokujitsu, Kandenko, Toko (electrical installations); Techno Ryowa, Tonets, Sanken Setsubi Kogyo (air conditioning, plumbing and mechanical services)
Contractor
Kajima
Photos
Ishiguro Photographic Institute (pp. 198-199; Iwan Baan (pp. 200-201)

The library was designed as a prolongation of the garden at the entrance to the campus, so the natural slope of the terrain was maintained on the ground floor and the spaces under the large arches are made diaphanous.

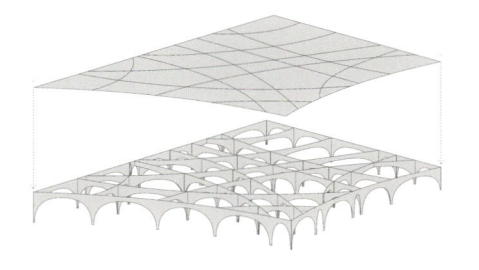

The project's prominent arches, constructed with concrete-clad steel plates, are arranged, on plan, in accordance with curved lines that criss-cross at several points, creating nodes that serve to structurally brace the ensemble and helping to form subtly separated zones within the library's one single large space, which are differentiated, including functionally, through a mix of furniture elements and light and spatial conditions.

through and see through the building freely, without obstructions, the design team began to work out a structure of randomly placed arches. The characteristic arches are made of steel plates and covered with concrete. On plan they are arranged along curved lines that criss-cross at several points. Thanks to these intersections, the arches are kept extremely slender at the bottom and yet are strong enough to support the heavy loads of the floor above. The spans of the arches vary between 1.8 and 16 meters but their widths are uniformly kept at 20 centimeters. The intersections of the rows of arches help to form subtly separated zones within the one large single space of the library. Elements like bookshelves, desks of various shapes, and glass partitions doubling as bulletin boards together contribute to giving these zones the functional as well as visual individuality they require.

A movie-browser that is like a bar counter and a large glass table for magazines invite students to spend bus-waiting time inside the library. Upstairs they can find large art books on low bookshelves crossing under arches. Distributed between the shelves are study desks of different sizes. A large table with state-of-the-art copy machines allows users to do professional editing work.

Because the arches present a constant variance of span, height, direction, and angle of intersection, the spatial diversity the observer experiences in the process of traversing the hall is a seamless journey from square-planned to triangle-planned, and from cloister-like and bathed with natural light to tunnel-like and visually impenetrable. The library is a new place of arcade-like spaces where a person makes connections simply by passing through, where everyone can discover and develop their own individual style of interacting with books while walking through a forest of pillars or a cave of concrete.

Atlas: Asia and Pacific **199**

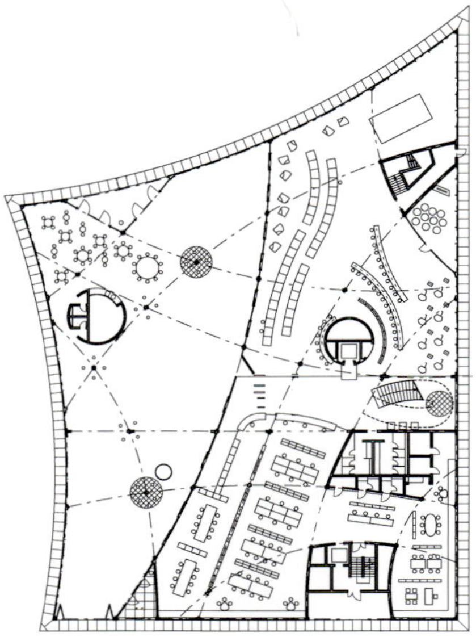

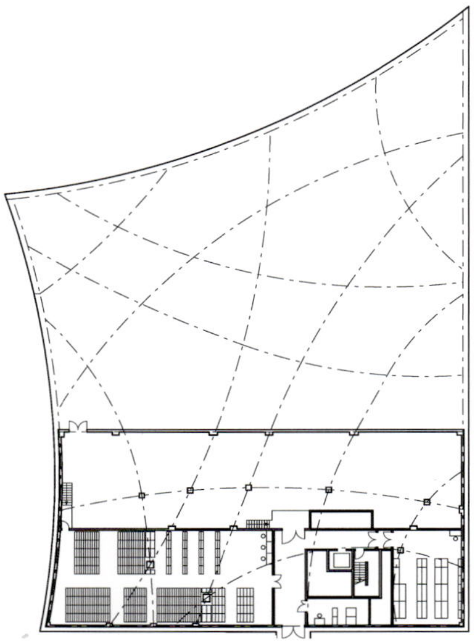

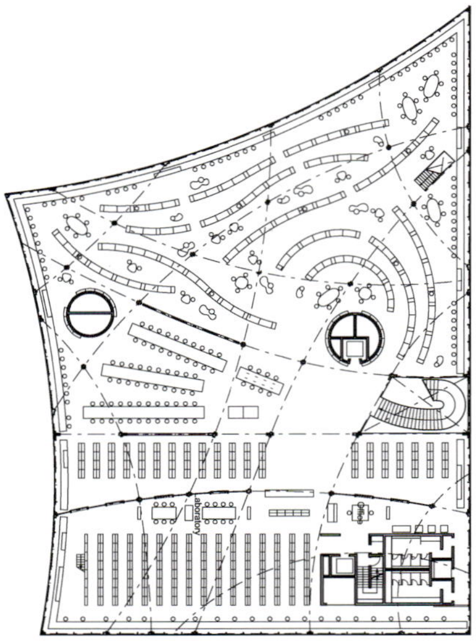

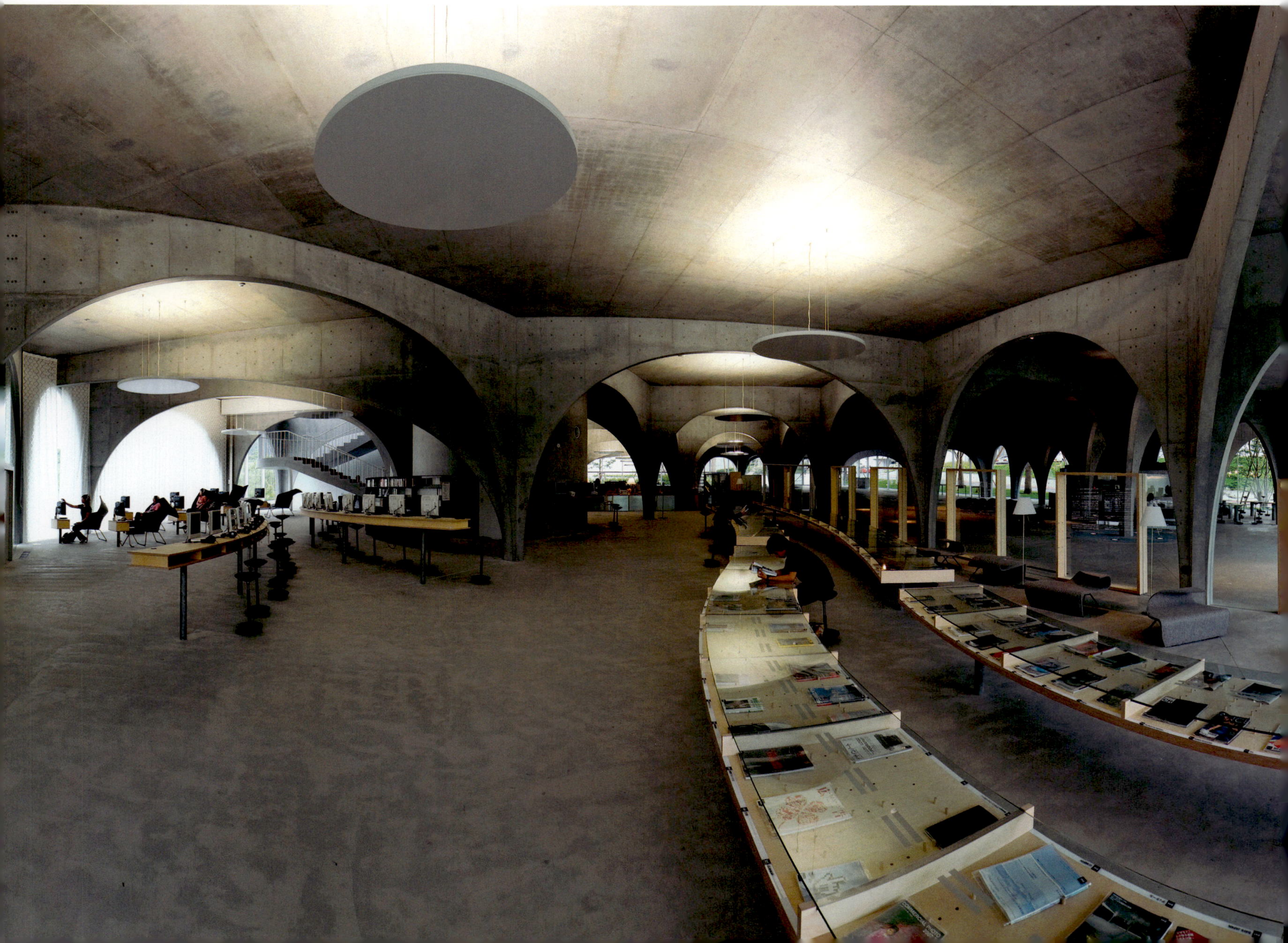

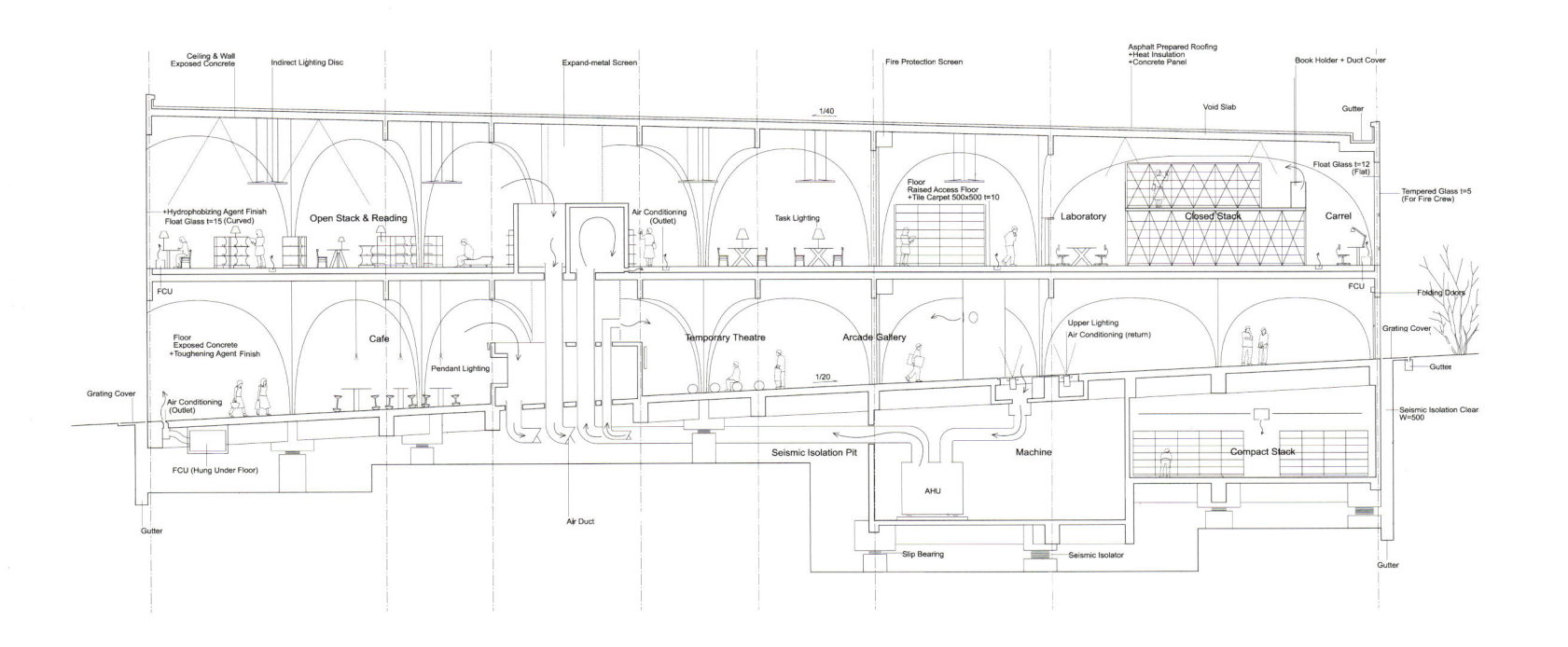

Section labels (top drawing, left to right, upper level):
- Ceiling & Wall Exposed Concrete
- Indirect Lighting Disc
- Expand-metal Screen
- Fire Protection Screen
- Asphalt Prepared Roofing + Heat Insulation + Concrete Panel
- Book Holder + Duct Cover
- Void Slab
- Gutter
- Float Glass t=12 (Flat)
- Tempered Glass t=5 (For Fire Crew)
- Hydrophobizing Agent Finish Float Glass t=15 (Curved)
- Open Stack & Reading
- Air Conditioning (Outlet)
- Task Lighting
- Floor Raised Access Floor + Tile Carpet 500x500 t=10
- Laboratory
- Closed Stack
- Carrel
- FCU
- FCU
- Folding Doors

Lower level labels:
- Floor Exposed Concrete + Toughening Agent Finish
- Cafe
- Pendant Lighting
- Temporary Theatre
- Arcade Gallery
- Upper Lighting
- Air Conditioning (return)
- Grating Cover
- Grating Cover
- Air Conditioning (Outlet)
- Seismic Isolation Pit
- Machine
- Compact Stack
- Seismic Isolation Clear W=500
- Gutter
- FCU (Hung Under Floor)
- Air Duct
- AHU
- Slip Bearing
- Seismic Isolator
- Gutter

Jun Aoki
SIA Aoyama Building
Tokyo (Japan)

Client
Simplex Investment Advisors
Architects
Jun Aoki & Associates
Consultants
Kanebako, Kajima (structural design);
P.T. Morimura & Associates, Kajima
(facility design)
Contractor
Kajima
Photos
Daici Ano

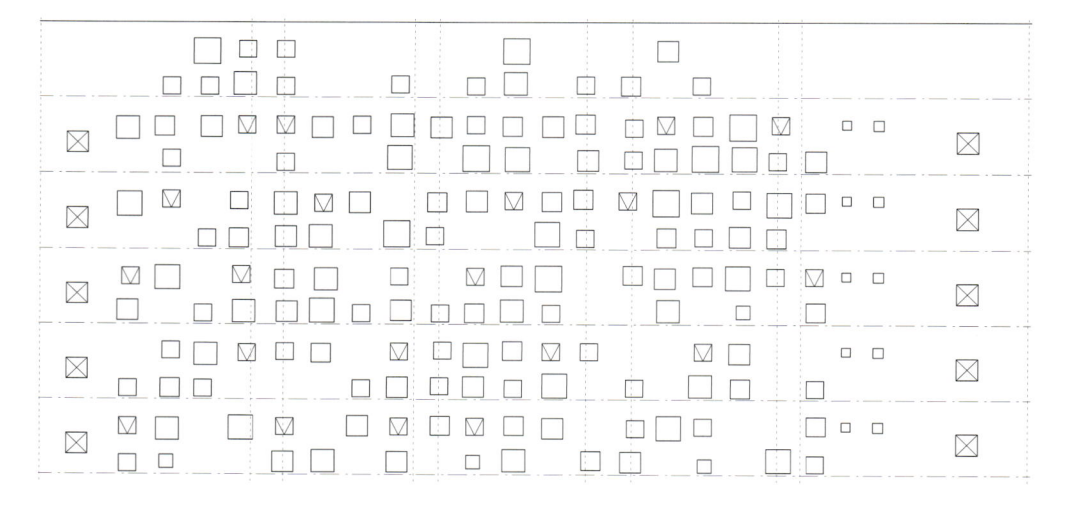

The building rises as a monolith dotted with square openings arranged in a seemingly random way. The varying sizes of the windows and the lack of alignments make it hard to distinguish the floor levels from outside.

NOT FAR AWAY from the fashionable Shibuya area and its railway station, this tower providing office spaces for rent stands in the middle of Omotesando, another swanky district with its growing number of international brand-name boutiques. In an area with a mix of residential and office blocks, the SIA Aoyama looks like neither, its proportions falling "somewhere between" those of an apartment and an office building. It also endeavors to make a very clear architectural statement by deviating from the usual notion of what a high-rise office building should look like.

The SIA Aoyama Tower comes across as a monolith with a smooth white surface dotted with square-shaped windows that vary substantially in dimensions and are arranged in seeming random disarray, purposely out of line. The impression the observer gets is that of a freehand drawing intended to be as accurate as possible. Since alignments do not necessarily coincide, it is difficult to determine from outside where exactly each story level begins and ends. The building rises to a height of 64 meters and could easily have been made to contain eighteen levels of rentable office space, but because of ceilings soaring almost five meters, there are in truth only nine floors. There was a deliberate search, from the very beginning of the project, for the effect of discrepancy between appearance and reality.

It is because of the high ceilings and high windows that even with the building's minimized total window area, as against the conventional wraparound fenestration of office towers, there is a sufficient inflow of daylight that then spreads evenly to the innermost areas. The interiors break away from the typical office also in the sense that the walls are curved and asymmetrical.

In what is a neighborhood of generally low-slung constructions, the monolith had to somehow blend in, not stand out. It is said that the SIA Aoyama manages to go unnoticed in the everyday urban life of the area. This is partly thanks to the rounded corners, but also to the decision to coat the facade of earthquake-resistant reinforced concrete with a white paint that had a splash of purple and gray mixed in so that it would not cast a harsh glare in sunlight.

The tower is inspired by ordinary objects and common materials but seeks a sense of contrast. Hence the quality of the materials, combined with mechanisms of repetition and pattern, yields a sense of the ornamental that is unstable and visually less distinct. This office capped one of the Good Design Gold awards given by the Japan Industrial Design Promotion Organization in 2008.

202 Atlas: Asia and Pacific

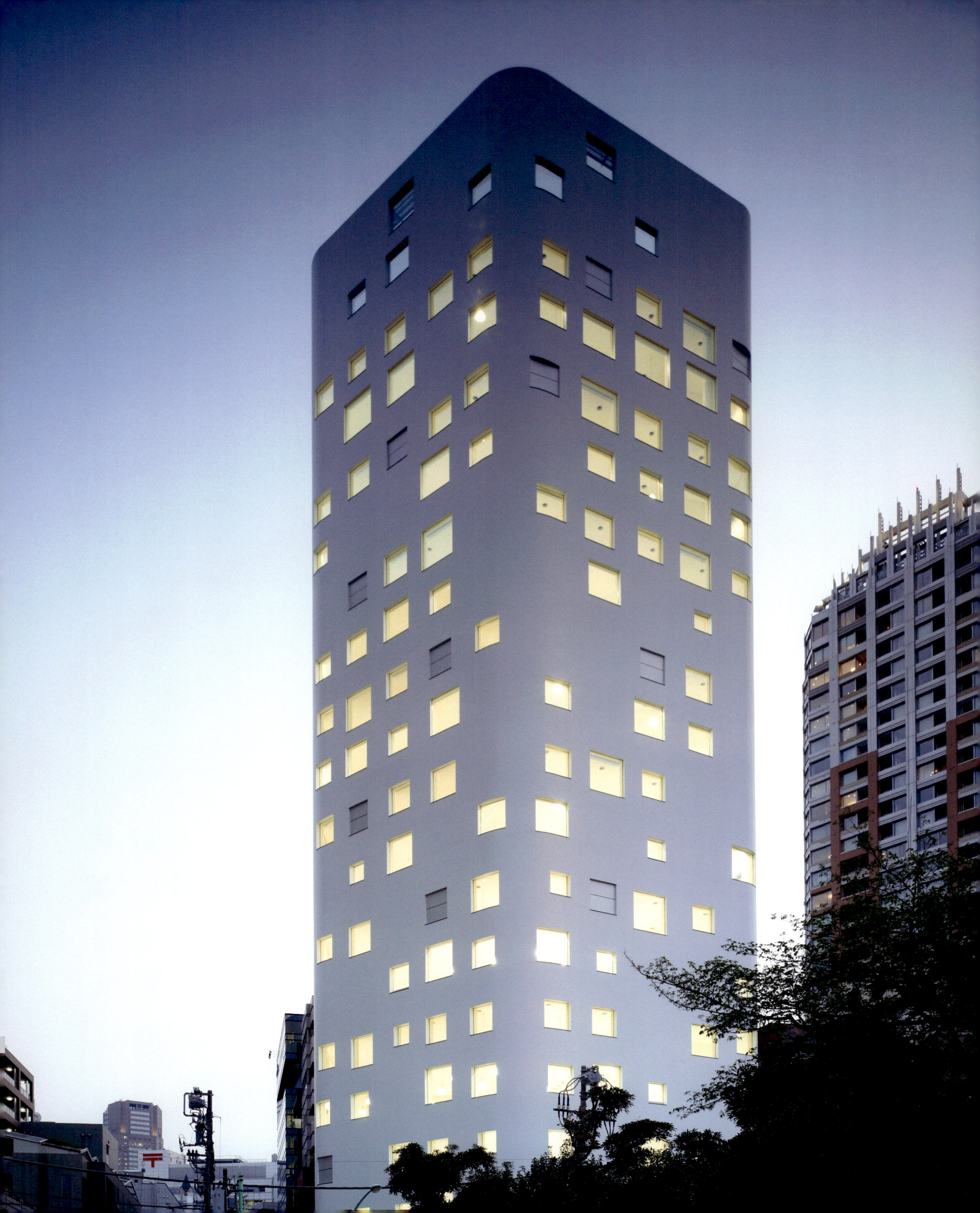

Despite the building's minimized total window area, as against the wraparound glass curtain walls of conventional office towers, there is a sufficient inflow of natural light that then spreads evenly through the offices, reaching the innermost areas. The concrete facade that forms the skin of the monolith is given a coat of white paint that has a splash of purple and gray mixed in so that it does not cast a harsh glare in sunlight.

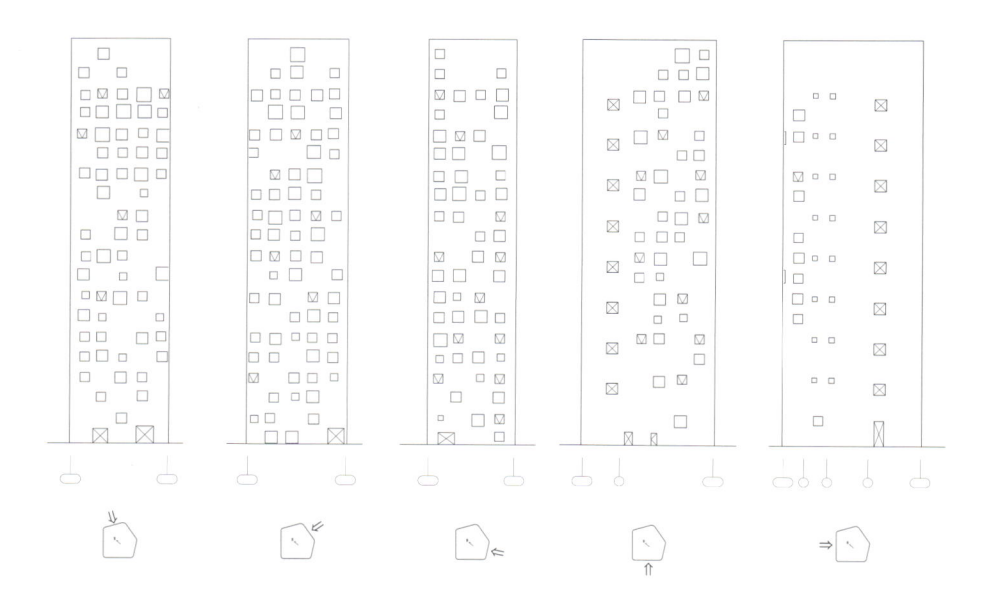

204 Atlas: Asia and Pacific

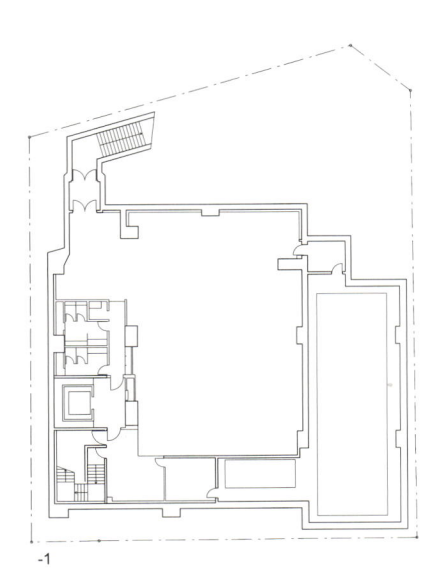

-1

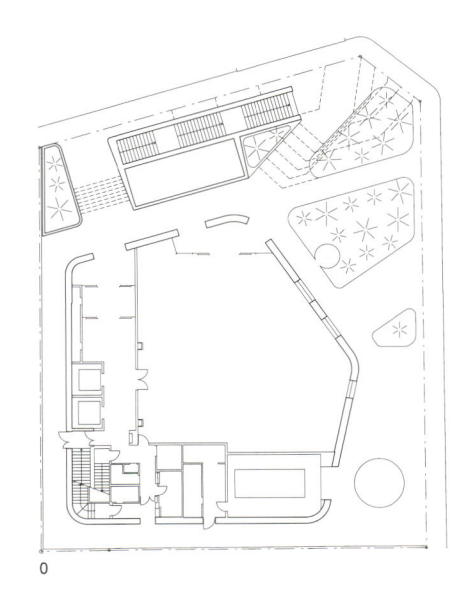

0

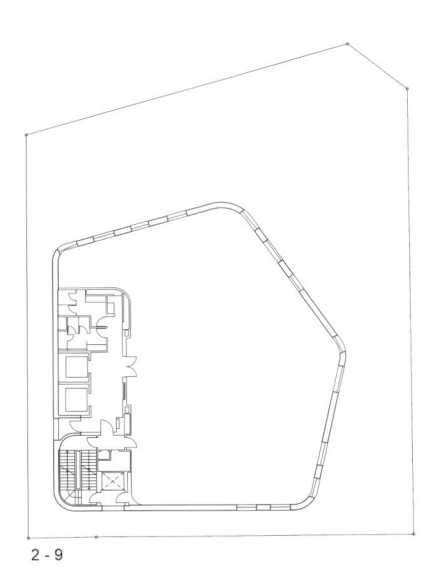

2 - 9

Atlas: Asia and Pacific

Ryue Nishizawa
House in Moriyama
Tokyo (Japan)

Architects
Office of Ryue Nishizawa
Collaborators
Ippei Takahashi, Kimihiko Okada, Yusuke Ohi
Consultants
Structured Environment: Alan Burden, Taizen Nieda, Hirohi de Tao (structure); Kankyo: Masakazu Gokita, Tsugihisa Narita (installations)
Photos
Shinkenchiku-sha

The fragmented fabric of low wooden houses and narrow streets of Ohta-ku, one of few remaining Tokyo neighborhoods still characterized by traditional architecture, inspired the project's de-composed structure.

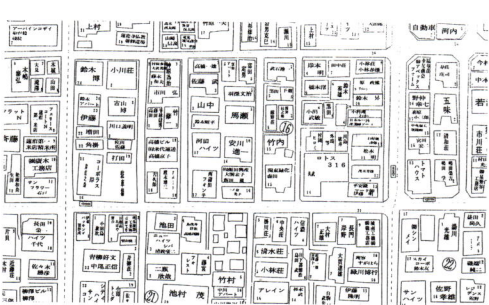

THE MORIYAMA HOUSE is located in Ohta-ku, a traditional neighborhood in the center of Tokyo that is characterized by its dense scheme of low wooden houses and narrow streets. Inspired by this fragmented fabric so typical of the Japanese city, the design of this complex avoids the idea of a monolithic block, which would not be appropriate to the place, choosing instead to reinvent the typology of the traditional Japanese dwelling by de-composing it to an extreme, accommodating each part of the program in a separate box-like volume. In the course of positioning the different volumes within the lot, a series of courtyards and small gardens is formed. These serve as points of transition between the parts and help enrich the interplay of spaces and enhance the variety of routes and views. There is no fence, nor a main gate, so the spaces between the box edges and the street take on both a private and a public character. The result is a microcosm of a city, complete with streets, squares, parks, and even towers.

Ten different module types are planted here and there on the 290 square meter parcel. Five are one-level, five are two- or three-level, and three have an underground basement. Organized around six connected courtyards, the complex is able to service a single one-family home that in terms usually attached to a conventional residential program would have five kitchen-dining rooms, seven living rooms, two studios, and four bedrooms. And yet, far from being assigned specific uses, the pieces are containers with qualities of their own, able to address different programs, in such a way that each tenant can build his own story. There is no strict way to live, one can choose from a whole range of spaces and lifestyles. The proprietor is free to decide which modules to make part of his residence, and which units to rent out.

Even with large openings on the facades and the proximity between openings, the privacy of each unit is safeguarded. This is because a lot of thought went into deciding where exactly on the parcel to place the boxes, how far apart they should be from one another, and where to put the windows, preferably never face to face.

The boxes are built with thin plates of galvanized steel, which are welded and coated with dirt-resistant paint. This solution was previously used in the cherry orchard house, although in that commission the exterior walls were only 50 millimeters thick, whereas here the fine skin is lined with insulation and plaques of plasterboard, resulting in an 85 millimeter thick wall. The floor slabs are built with composite boards and flagstones of reinforced concrete for the foundations. The pavements are either of walnut or cherry wood.

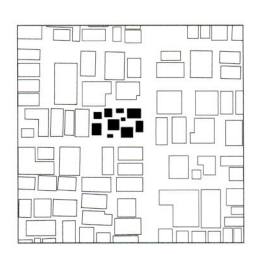

The Moriyama House is designed as a microcosm of a city on a 290 square meter rectangular parcel, complete with streets, squares, parks, and buildings: an ensemble of white boxes built with galvanized steel plates that were welded and coated with dirt-resistant white paint. The thin metal skin of the facade is lined inside with insulation material and plaques of plasterboard, resulting in an 85 millimeter thick wall.

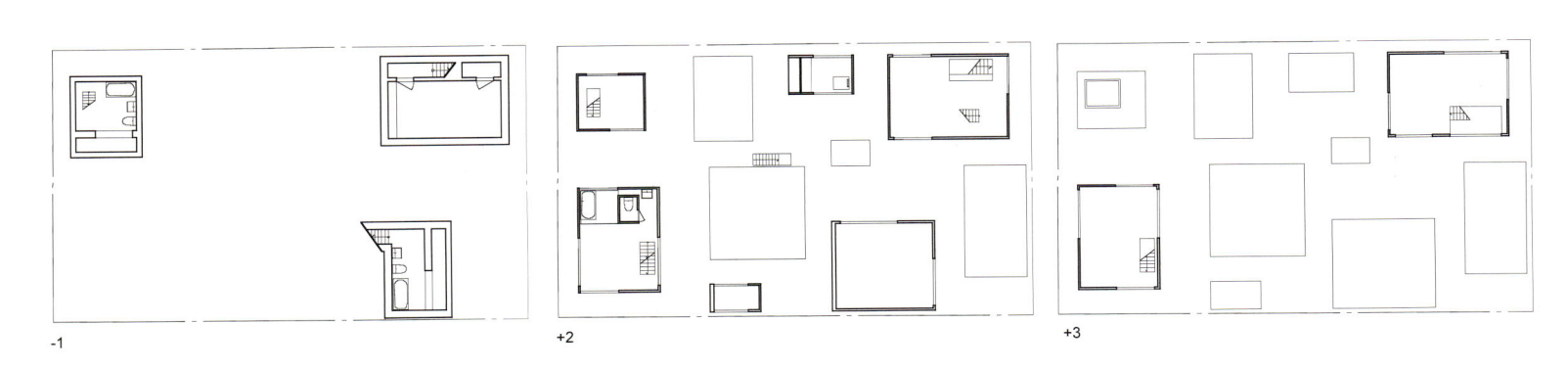

-1   +2   +3

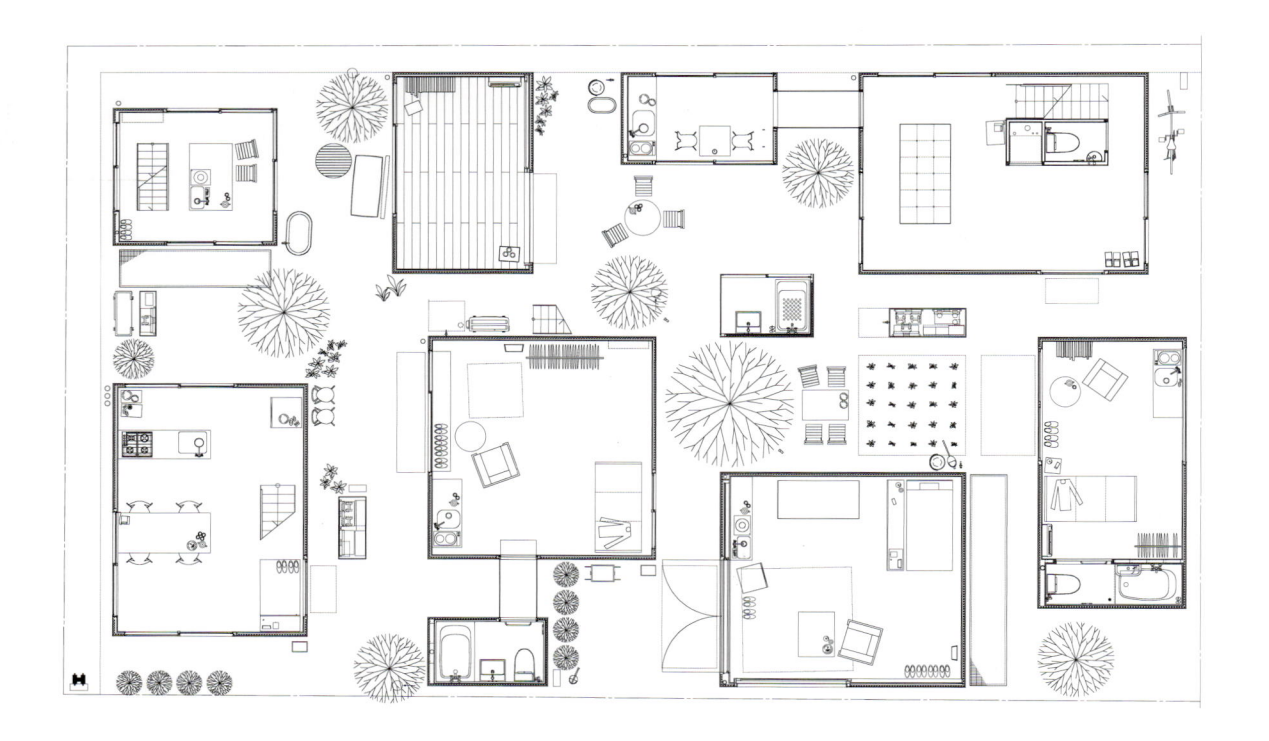

The boxes have been distributed on the parcel in such a way that all of them have an exterior space. The large windows that open on to these outdoor zones are never positioned face to face, so that everyone is guaranteed a certain degree of privacy. The gaps between volumes take on the character of semi-public, multi-functional areas that serve at once as internal passageways, recreational courtyards, and reception foyers. The boxes are conceived as containers where tenants can build their own worlds, and the owner is free to choose which of the modules to reserve for personal use and which of the units to rent out as apartments.

208 Atlas: Asia and Pacific

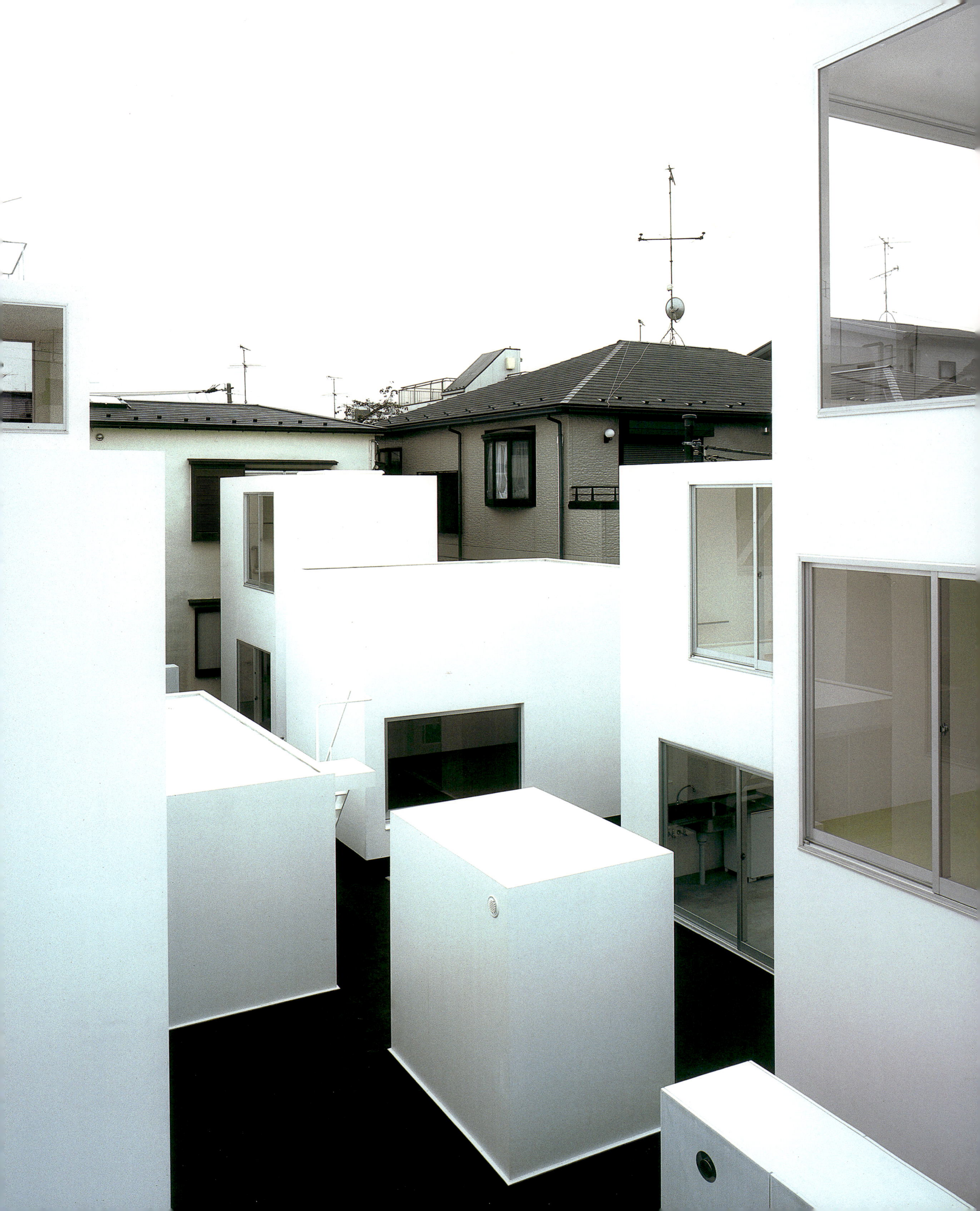

Kazuyo Sejima
Apartments in Okurayama
Yokohama, Kanagawa (Japan)

Architects
Kazuyo Sejima & Associates
Collaborators
Riyika Yamamoto, Erika Hidaka, Isao Shinohara, Mizuko Kaji
Consultants
Sasaki (structural engineering); Heisei (construction management)
Photos
Iwan Baan

The complex adjusts to the urban fabric by prioritizing spatial quality. It opens up inside like a sponge, creating some courtyards here and there that foster contact wih the exterior without sacrificing privacy.

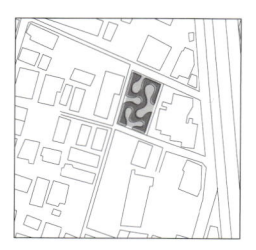

THE DESIGN FOR this apartment building is a true exercise in complexity. Through complexity, it refutes the very widespread Japanese practice of packing residences within inches of one another and yet cutting them off from each other, as well as from the surroundings, through windowless interiors. The word 'surroundings', moreover, takes on a new dimension as it no longer refers only to what there is around or beyond the site, but also to what there happens to be in clearings made within the reinforced concrete mass of the construction.

The location is Yokohama's Okurayama neighborhood, a ten-minute walk from the like-named station on the railway line that connects with Tokyo. The surrounding constructions are on the whole orthogonal in shape and in arrangement with one another, and this three-story building at the outstart similarly traces a prismatic volume and a rectangular perimeter, which practically reaches all four corners of the 458 square meter lot. But it does not max out the available space just to have as many units as possible; the program, consisting of only nine apartment units, each about 50 square meters, sought to produce spaces and an atmosphere that residents, ideally singles or couples, would enjoy spending time in. And neither does it create voids in the usual rectilinear scheme of the zone. Instead, different parts and levels snake fluidly, forming S shapes that interact like yin and yang figures, and leaving sinuous voids that are then made to accommodate private courtyards, gardens, terraces, and channels of natural light. In this way, each room opens toward an outdoor environment while maintaining privacy, and indoor and outdoor spaces intermingle comfortably.

Internally, the curved walls give each unit a unique profile. The irregular shapes work because the apartments have not been partitioned into rooms, and because each resident is happy to be free to turn the non-linearity into an advantage. Nevertheless, to make it easier to furnish, every unit is given two straight walls.

Neither are two units exactly alike in their relation to their exteriors. One dwelling might have a large room surrounded by a garden on the first floor and a small bedroom on the upper floor, another might have a three-pronged room and a terrace on the second floor, and so on and so forth. In this way, different living spaces can espouse different lifestyles by spreading gardens, bathrooms, bedrooms, and living rooms throughout the site three-dimensionally. The design manages to grant the users both privacy and a sense of community.

The curved outlines of the voids and actual living spaces create very special dynamic atmospheres that compensate for the small dimensions of the lot, and make each apartment unit a unique place by connecting it to the exterior in a different way. The voids, besides filling the dwellings with daylight, accommodate private courtyards, gardens, and terraces. The interior spaces unfold fluidly because they are unpartitioned.

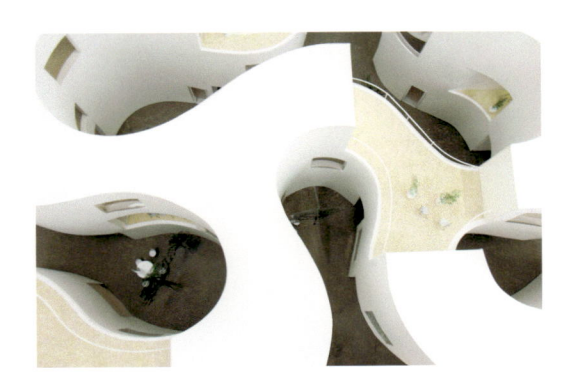

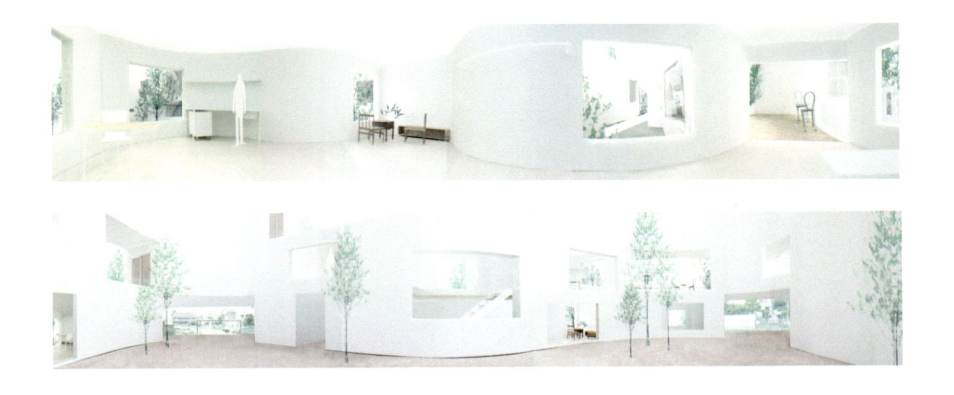

Atlas: Asia and Pacific 211

0 +1 +2

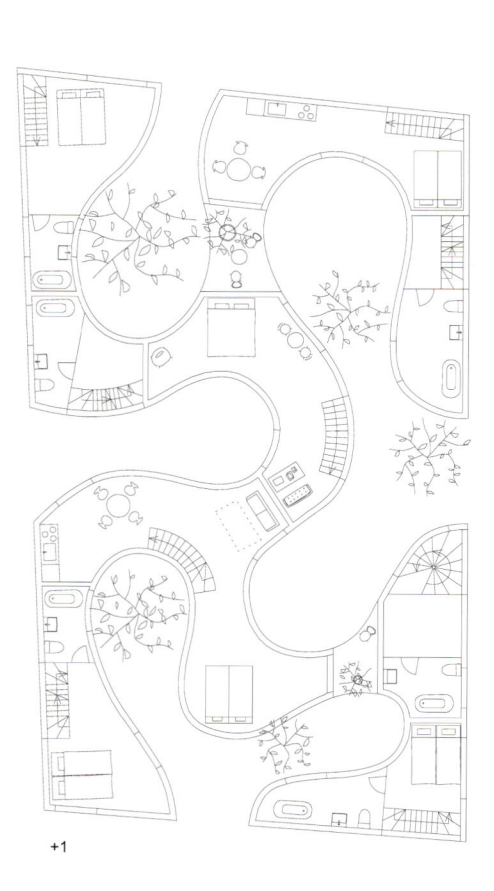

212 Atlas: Asia and Pacific

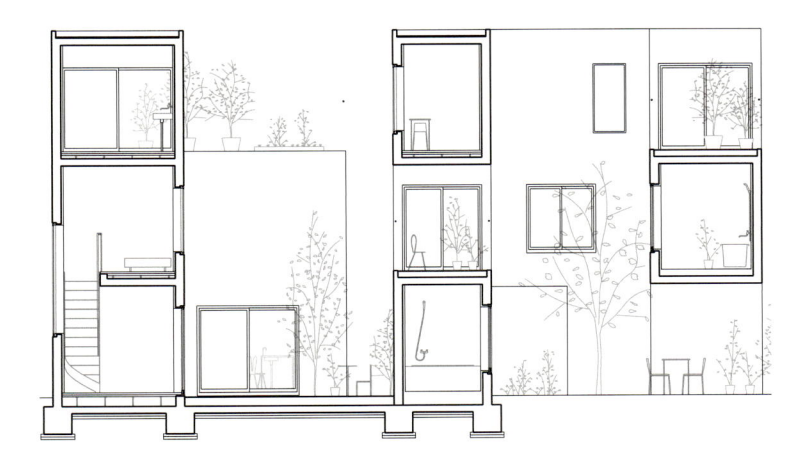

The building's three levels are occupied in very different ways, in accordance with orientations and the formal particularities of the curvilinear arms of reinforced concrete. In this way, while some of the dwellings have two differentiated levels and their own private outdoor courtyards, others concentrate the entire program in a single story, shifting the terrace to the roof. The complexity that these compositional mechanisms generate allows for greater variety of spatial experience and a better blending of exteriors and interiors, thereby also increasing the user's feeling of belonging to a small community of neighbors.

Junya Ishigami
KAIT Workshop
Atsuki, Kanagawa (Japan)

THE KANAGAWA INSTITUTE of Technology in Atsuki, located 30 kilometers from Tokyo, now has a place where students can work on self-initiated extra-curricular creative and research projects. To expand its everyday use, the client also thought of making it accommodate activities for the public, including local children.

With its total area of 1,930 square meters, the workshop building is modest in scale, and yet it is the center of the campus, whose original structures, erected back in the sixties, are progressively being replaced. When the overall renovation is finished, it will be visible from the KAIT's main entrance, which over 5,000 students pass through daily.

The floor plan's parallelogram shape defies the orthogonal scheme of the campus streets, adapting to existing paths around it. The volume opens on all four sides, the main door marked by a metal canopy on the side that is closest to the school entry. Looking like a pavilion with its single level and flat roof, it comes across as an ethereal structure surrounded by transparent glass. Inside, 305 slender metal columns, white-lacquered and arranged in a seemingly random fashion, work to create a wide diversity of spaces.

Client
Kanagawa Institute of Technology (KAIT)
Architect
Junya Ishigami
Collaborators
Motosuke Mandai
Consultants
Yasutaka Konishi (structure);
Tomonaga Tokuyama (CAD program);
Izumi Okayasu (lighting);
Asahi (curtain wall); Lonseal (roof);
Kansai (painting); ITL (environmental lighting); Kodama Tec (furniture)
Contractor
Kajima
Photos
Iwan Baan

The KAIT workshop building is a pavilion that seems diluted in the environment of the campus it is part of. During the day it reflects the surroundings, and at night it becomes a forest of slender pillars.

The project comes across to the observer as a structure of transparent glass and steel, inside of which a total of 305 slender columns, white-lacquered and arranged in a seemingly random fashion, go about creating a wide diversity of spaces. Bands of skylights furrow the roof, bringing in additional natural light, contributing to the overall picture of a thick forest where 'clearings' have been made to serve specific functions.

Bands of skylights furrowing the roof let natural light into the continuous interior space, both directly and reflected. The daylight shining in reinforces one's feeling of being in the midst of a thick forest of topless trees. This forest contains as many as fourteen clearings of varying dimensions: the foyer with its circular counter, different workshops (for ceramics or carpentry, a foundry, spaces for computer design, etc.), as well as four multi-purpose zones, a supplies store, and staff areas.

To modularize the interior space the architects used the actual pillars, as well as free-standing objects like furniture, air conditioning units, and potted plants, as part and parcel of the design. At first they tried to organize the inner space around a structural grid with four meter sides. In the end, the pillars were maintained, but their positions, dimensions, and orientations were modified to define the 'clearings'.

The whole design process took as many as three years and up to a thousand models of different scales and also numerous hand-made sketches, besides a CAD program custom-designed for this project that made it possible to visualize how any slight change in the composition or arrangement of the pillars would affect the entire ensemble.

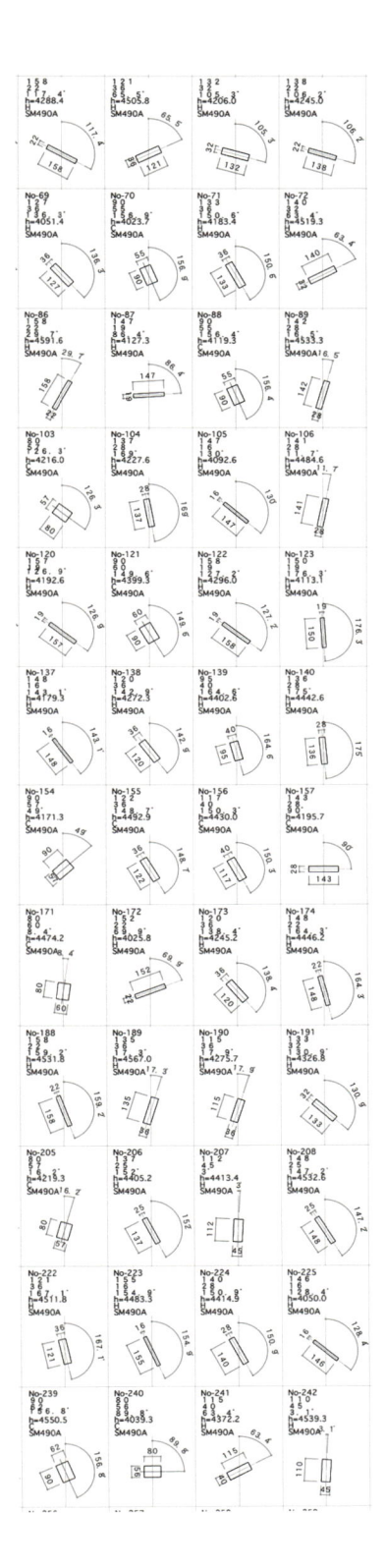

Atlas: Asia and Pacific 215

1. waterproof seal; heat insulating board t=30mm; deck plate t=1.2mm; indoor side urethane painting
2. wired sheet glass t=6.8mm; aluminum sash (baking painting)
3. beam H 200x80x4.5x7 mm with urethane painting
4. reinforced beam H 200x80x9x12mm
5. late t=6mm
6. horizontal bearing with urethane painting
7. vertical bearing with fireproof painting, putty, urethane painting
8. upper frame: outside aluminum t=2 mm, inside steel t=6mm
9. float glass t=10mm; rib glass/safety glass 15+15 mm
10. concrete slab; insulating material t=50mm; concrete sub-slab t=50mm; macadam t=60mm

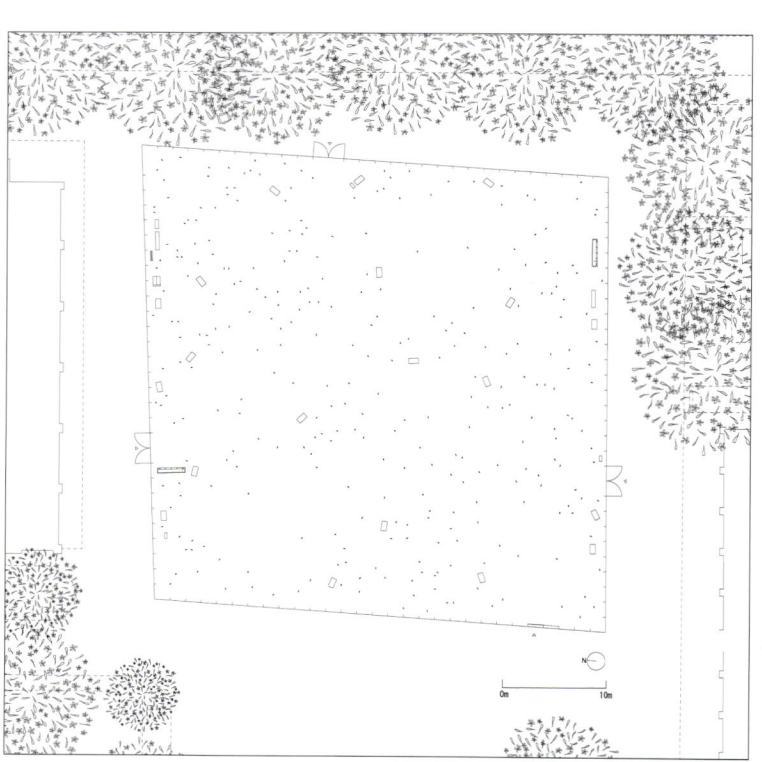

216 Atlas: Asia and Pacific

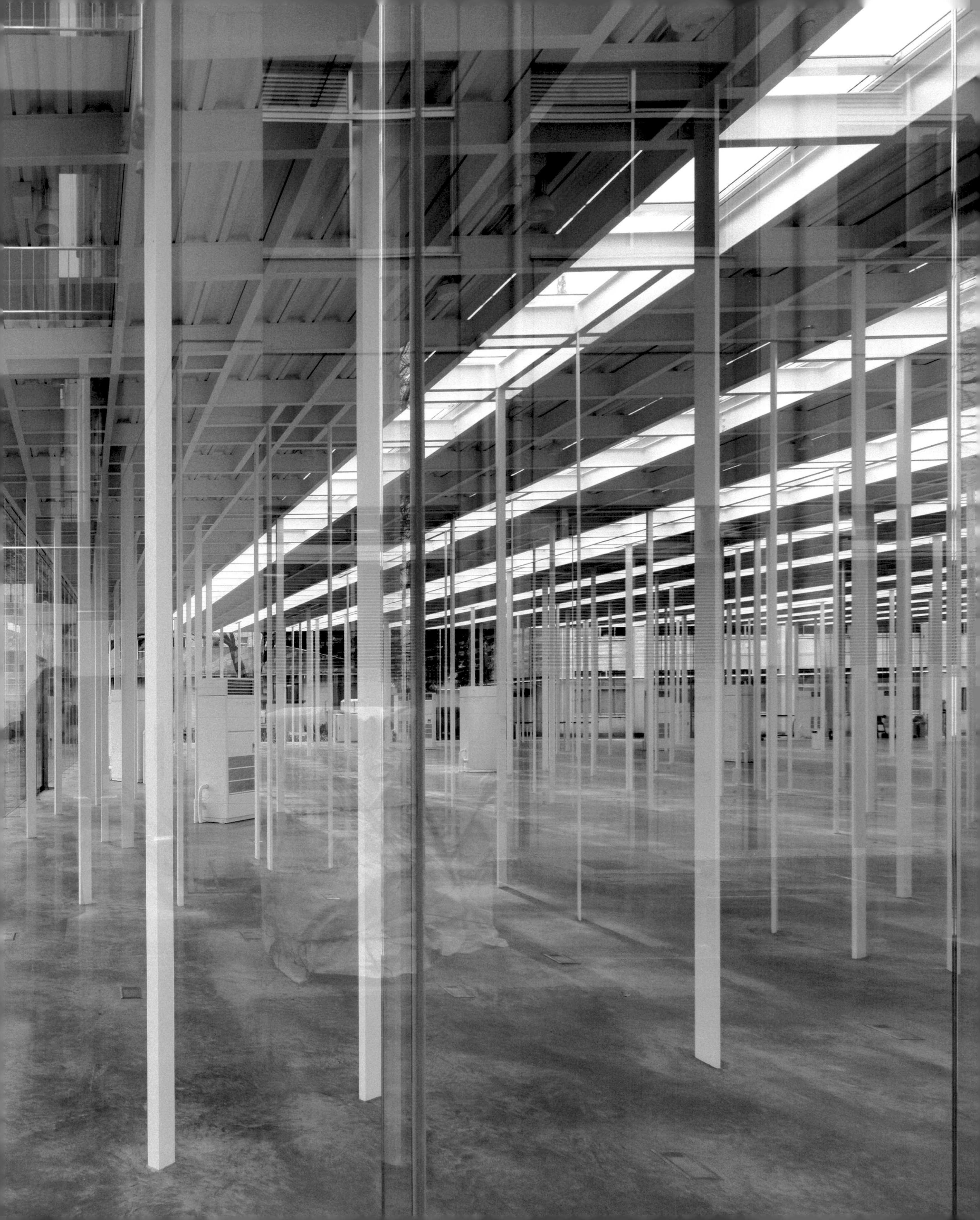

The small 'clearings' in the forest of pillars, varying in size and characteristics, make up the foyer, a range of specific work areas, four multi-purpose spaces, and a supplies store. Each one of the 305 pillars is different from the others in terms of both size and orientation; to determine their final layout, over one thousand hand-drawn sketches and models were done, aside from using specific computer programs.

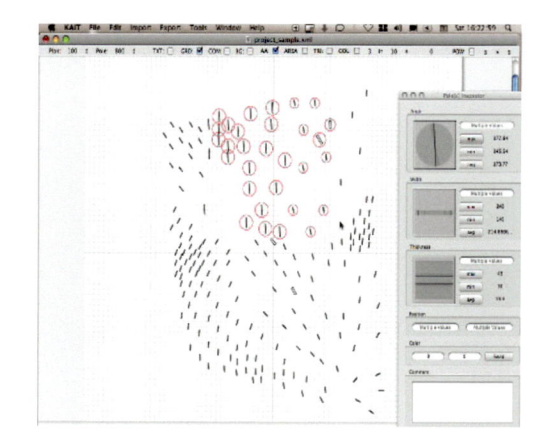

Atlas: Asia and Pacific 219

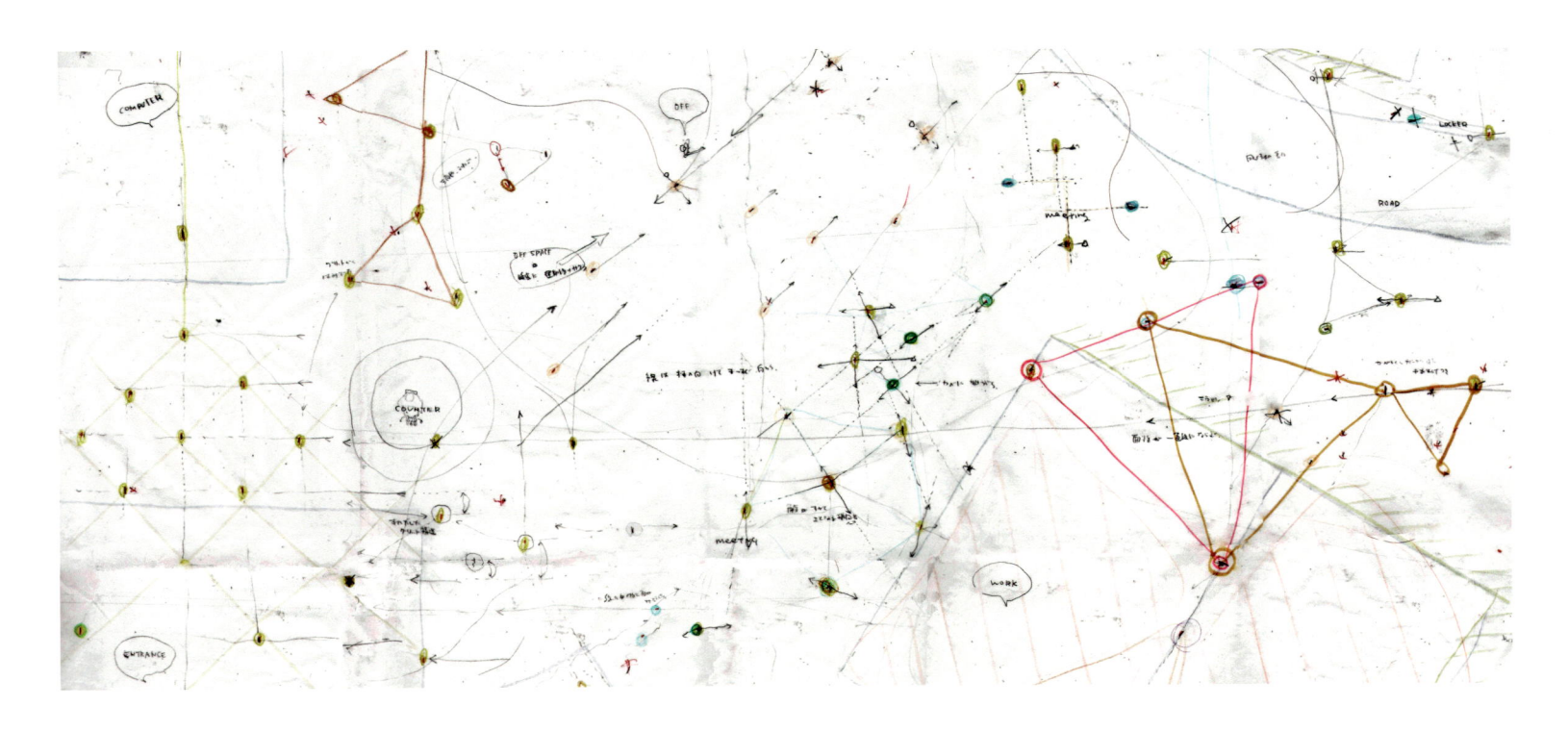

Takaharu & Yui Tezuka
Fuji Kindergarten
Tachikawa, Tokyo (Japan)

Client
Montessori School Fuji Kindergarten
Architects
Takaharu & Yui Tezuka Architects
Collaborators
Kashiwa Sato (director); C. Nabeshima, R. Maio, A. Kompal, K. Suzuki, N. Murakaji, S. Araki, S. Sakuma
Consultants
Masahiro Ikeda (structure); Masahide Kakudate (lighting); Hiroshi Kanemaru (mechanical)
Contractor
Takenaka
Photos
Katsuhisa Kida (p. 220, 221 below, 222); Edmund Sumner/View/Album (p. 223 top)

Inspired by a Tezuka house where much domestic life would take place on the roof, this school sought to maintain a relaxed mood and the *zelkova* tree specimens on the site, preserving these inside the building.

THE SEED OF THIS kindergarten is the Roof House, a single-family home previously built by Tezuka's studio where much domestic life takes place on the roof (see *Arquitectura Viva* **102**). A "Roof House for five hundred kindergarten pupils" is what the school directors asked of the architects. Certain aspects of the original schoolhouse would be maintained, such as its spontaneous mood and the trees, magnificent *zelkovas* which hindered the center's enlargement and were ultimately preserved inside the building. The school's irregular oval form came about in response to the desire for a continuous space adapted to the shape of the grounds. This desire for continuity led to the partitions between classrooms being determined exclusively by the need for washrooms. These aside, there are no walls; both classrooms and teachers' rooms are diaphanous. Marking out areas within these spaces are modules of *paulownia* wood that serve as furniture and shelves, with edges rounded for safety purposes. Furniture is not organized in rows. Instead, children sit facing different directions, turning toward the teacher when necessary.

Because the oval was distorted, its curves devoid of constant radiuses, defining the roof geometrically and constructively was complicated. Between the outer edge and the patio, the building's width varies, but the roof's inner and outer edges are horizontal. The rooftop therefore looks smooth, but is actually the three-dimensional curved surface of a changing hyperbolic shell. If the roof deck is a playground, some protection is in order. In place of the usual balustrade is a metal rail and thin balusters placed eleven centimeters apart: too small for a head to stick through, but not for legs, so children can sit along the roof's perimeter with their feet dangling and swinging.

The eaves have been lowered toward the ground to the legally permitted limit (2.1 meters), in such a way that from the courtyard, teachers can see all that is happening on the roof. Nets have been used to close the gaps between the roof and the tree trunks, preventing the children from climbing onto the branches. Lighting consists of naked bulbs activated by strings. The usual walled washbasins give way to cubic waterspout faucets. Free-standing like wells, the children can chat while using them. Another plumbing element, the faucets in the central garden, are designed to keep drain pans out of sight; round slices of tree trunks are set on the ground, and water enters their crevices from below the ground.

The building's shape addresses a desire to build a continuous space adapted to the shape of the grounds. Because the oval was distorted, its curves devoid of constant radiuses, defining the roof geometrically was a complex matter. The rooftop is in reality the three-dimensional curved surface of a changing hyperbolic shell, whose finish of wooden strips and protective vertical bars equip it for use as a playground.

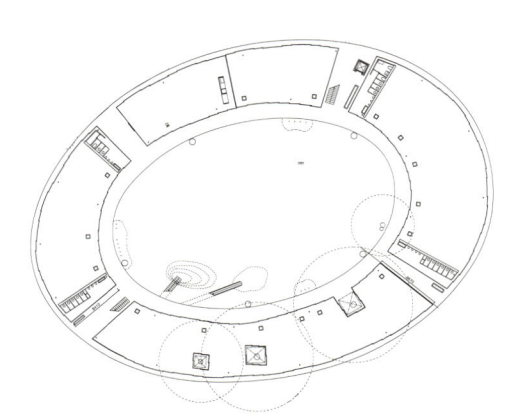

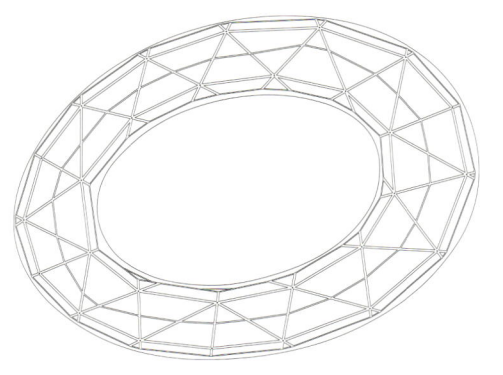

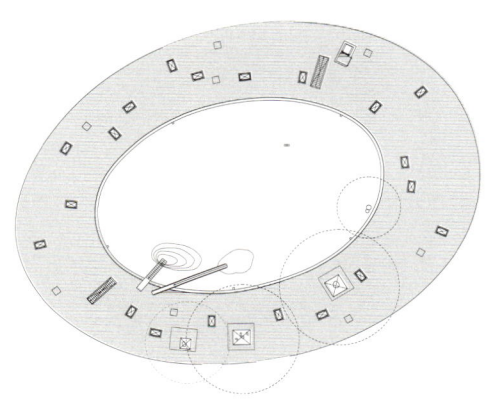

Atlas: Asia and Pacific 221

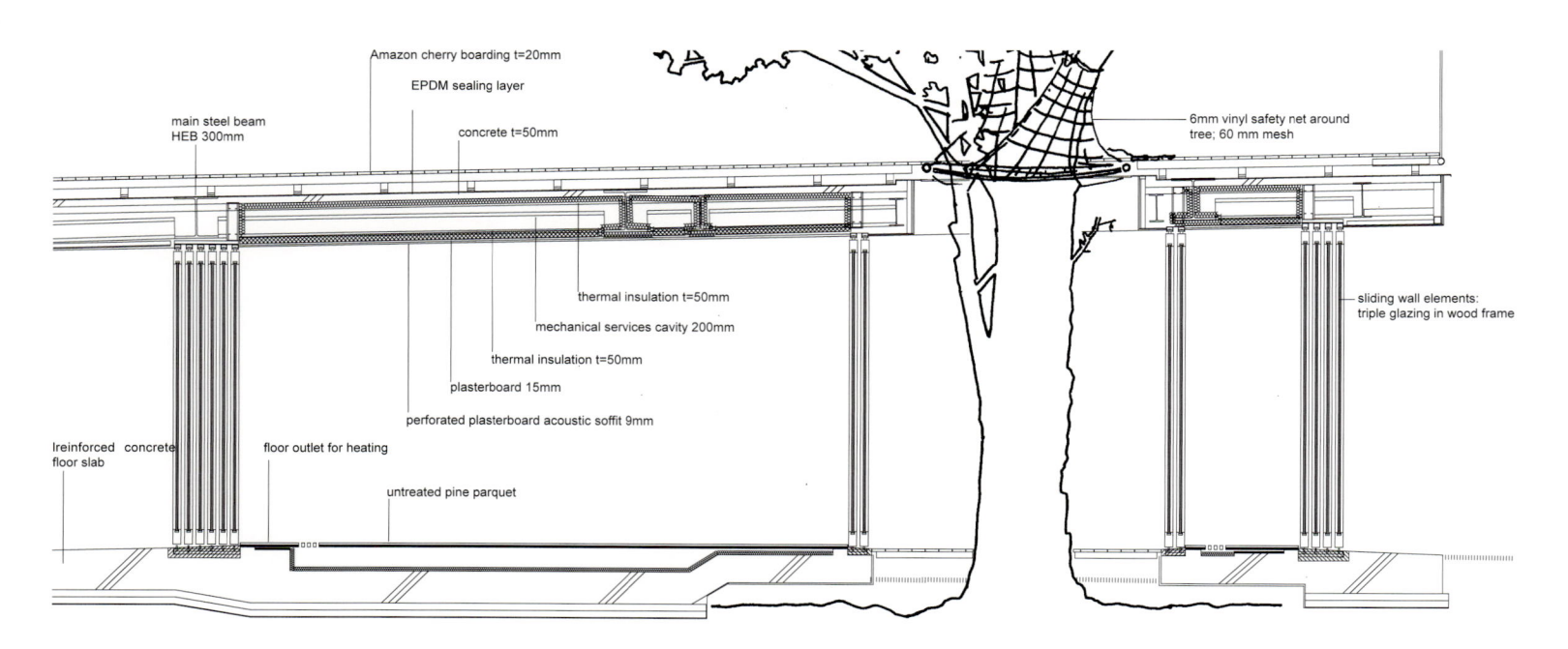

| main steel beam HEB 300mm | Amazon cherry boarding t=20mm |
| EPDM sealing layer |
| concrete t=50mm |
| 6mm vinyl safety net around tree; 60 mm mesh |
| thermal insulation t=50mm |
| mechanical services cavity 200mm |
| thermal insulation t=50mm |
| plasterboard 15mm |
| perforated plasterboard acoustic soffit 9mm |
| sliding wall elements: triple glazing in wood frame |
| lreinforced concrete floor slab | floor outlet for heating |
| untreated pine parquet |

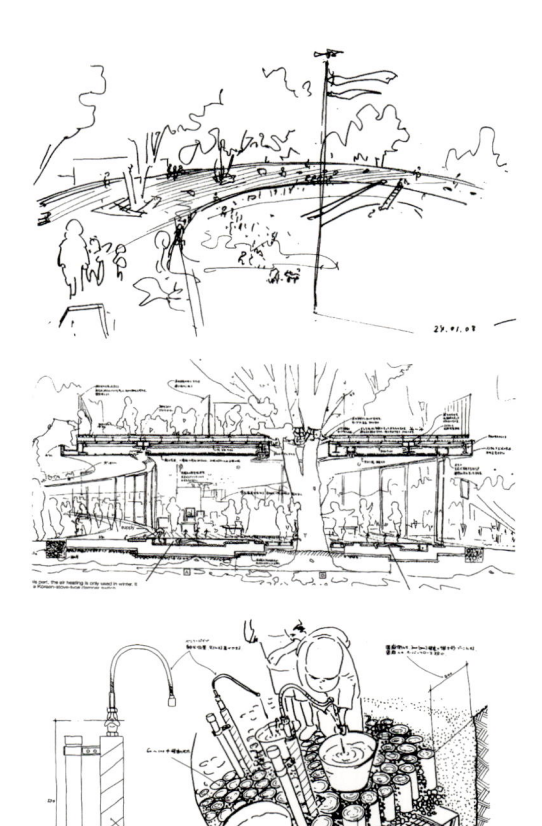

The desire for diaphanous interior spaces translates into open classrooms that are separated exclusively by washrooms and modules of *paolownia* wood. The latter serve as furniture and shelves, their edges rounded to make them safer for children. Outside, the spontaneous mood of the kindergarten extends to the design of the faucets in the central garden, where water is drained by means of crevices in the paving of wooden blocks.

Kengo Kuma
Town Hall
Yusuhara, Kochi (Japan)

Client
Yusuhara Town Hall
Architects
Kengo Kuma & Associates
Collaborator
Design Department of Keio University's School of Science and Technology
Consultants
K. Nakata (structure);
Nikken Sekkei (installations)
Photos
Mitsumasa Fujitsuka

The Yusuhara Town Hall was conceived as a reference for building with wood, and this is evident in the atrium, a multi-purpose space that offers services to the citizenry and is a venue for traditional festivals.

YUSUHARA IS A TOWN in southeastern Japan with a population of barely 5,000. Situated in mountainous Kochi Prefecture, it is known for its urban development using wood from *sugi*, Japanese cedar, which is the country's national tree. Its new Town Hall has been expressly designed to highlight the properties of this material.

The volume integrates itself into the city fabric, adjusting to the boundaries of the parcel and leaving a square in front that gives the building the degree of representativity appropriate to it. Its 2,970 square meters are distributed on two levels and a basement, with the more public functions appearing on the ground floor. In view of the region's climate, with temperatures averaging 13°C and rain in abundance that in winter tends to be snow, a large atrium was inserted and made to contain the facilities necessary for the everyday life of the town's residents, such as a bank, the Agricultural Cooperative Society, and the Chamber of Commerce.

This atrium also functions as a venue for traditional performances and festivals, and it is designed to spill out towards the street through huge sliding doors that make it possible to turn the indoor and outdoor plazas into one single public space.

Conceived to be a showcase for the excellence of *sugi* wood, the building uses it for both cladding and structure. To design the skeleton without losing out on a light and transparent image, the architect created a double lattice girder frame that, in the manner of a construction of toothpicks, has four 'layers' of 70 meter thick and 20 meter wide beams placed in two directions, thereby managing to span 18 meter distances. This complex design avoids the enormous sections that tend to be necessary when building with soft wood like *sugi*.

In the facade, wooden panels are interspersed with glass surfaces, forming a mosaic that serves to diffuse sunlight while warming up the interior spaces.

224 Atlas: Asia and Pacific

Sugi, also known as Japanese cedar, is the country's national tree. To use its soft wood to build the structure without having to make enormous sections, thereby keeping the town hall's image light and transparent, the architect worked out a complex assemblage of slender elements that recalls games of building with toothpicks. The facade of wooden and glass panels is a pixelled composition that serves to diffuse sunlight.

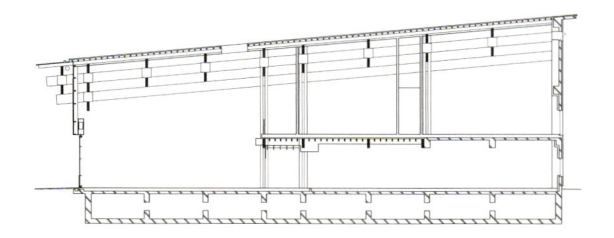

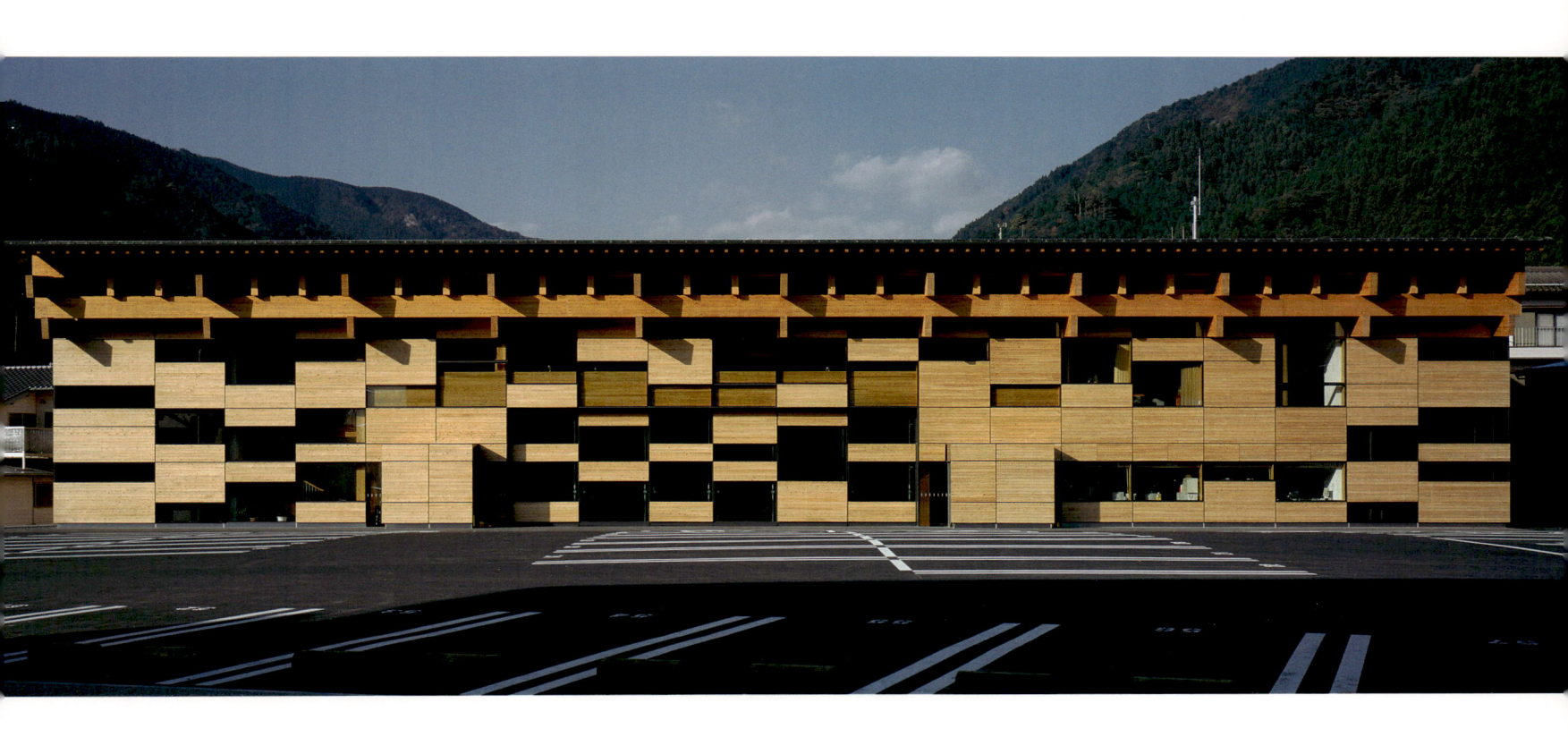

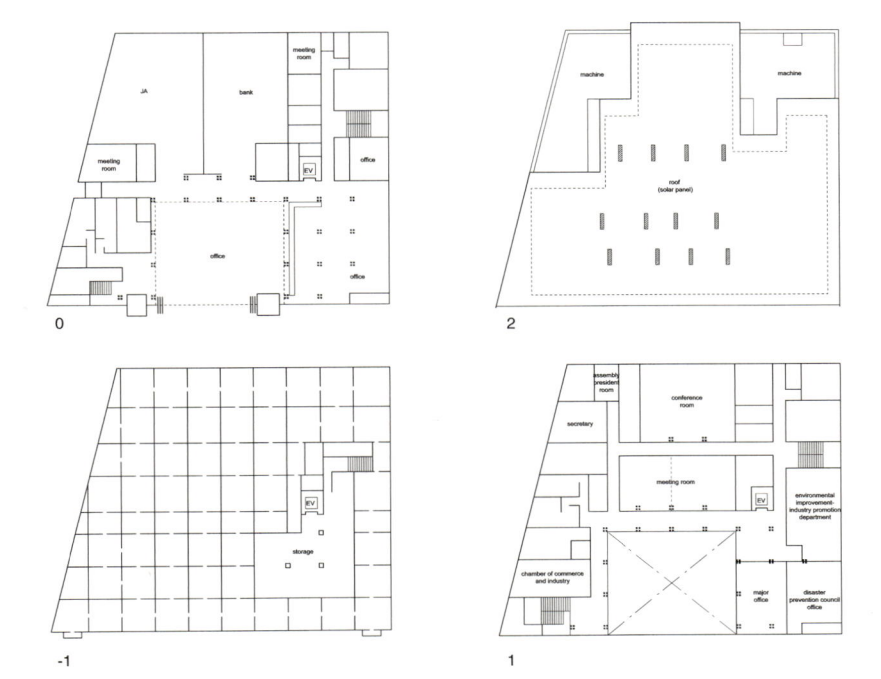

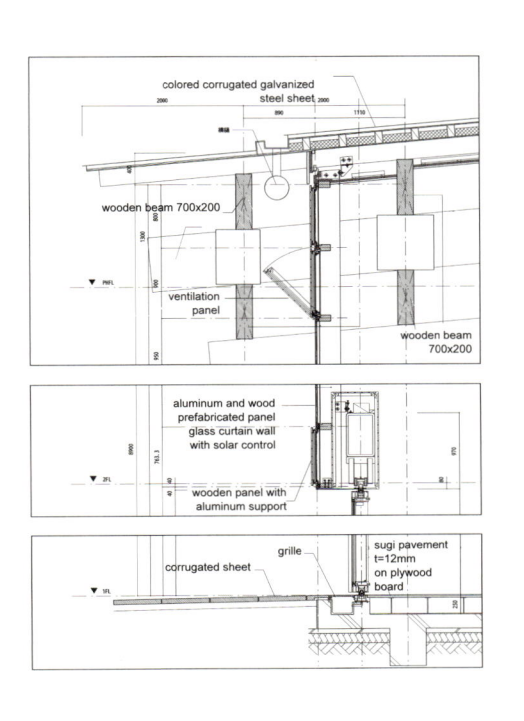

Atlas: Asia and Pacific 225

Sou Fujimoto
Musashino Art University Library
Kodaira, Tokyo (Japan)

Client
Musashino Art University
Architects
Sou Fujimoto Architects
Consultants
Jun Sato Engineers (structure); Kankyo (MEP); Sirius (lighting); Eishi Katsura, Studio Node (library planning)
Contractor
Taisei

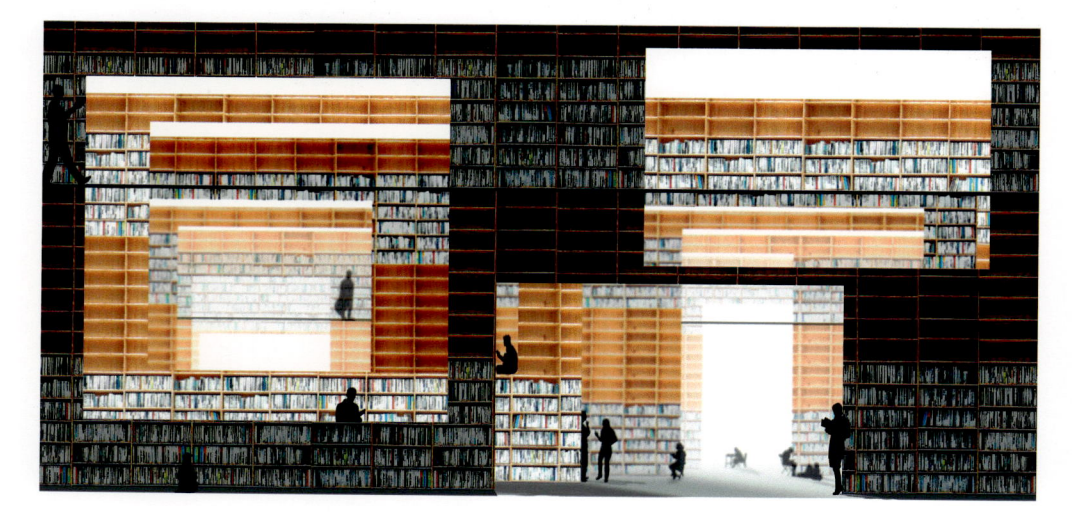

Located in the city of Kodaira, close to Tokyo, the university library adopts the bookcase module as the basic unit of the project, which takes on this archetypal form as much for the facades as for the interiors.

KODAIRA IS A CITY in the western part of Tokyo Region and is home to the multinational rubber conglomerate and tire manufacturer Bridgestone as well as to several institutions of higher learning, including Waseda University, Japan's oldest, and Musashino Art University. An offshoot of an imperial art school dating back to 1929, what is among the country's leading art and design universities offered degrees in fine arts and industrial design from the beginning and eventually added architecture and fashion to its academic program. Having thus outgrown its old library, MAU decided to turn it into an exhibition gallery and build a new library building.

The project concept can be described as a single bookcase that stretches on and on, bending a few times here and there to form an angular coil and a maze-like space. This is materialized through a succession of bookcases amounting to 200,000 shelf units. Half of these will be open to view, the other 100,000 will be closed deposits and archives. An infinite forest of books is created by layering 10 meter high walls that are punctuated by large apertures.

In its outward spiral movement, the bookcase eventually reaches the periphery of the site and becomes an outer wall, so the bookshelf-as-library composition of the building is discernible in its external appearance as well. To anyone coming across the colossally long bookcase within the university campus, it registers instantly as a library, and does not fail to astonish the onlooker for its dreamlike simplicity. It is a library in the most literal sense.

The building addresses the concepts of investigation and exploration, which are apparent contradictions. By definition, investigation calls for a spatial arrangement conceived for the purpose of making it possible to find specific books. Even in the age of Google, the experience of looking for titles in a library is marked by the physical order and organization of titles.

Exploration, on the other hand, addresses the library experience as something that includes the concept of exploration. The library experience includes discovery of the actual library space, which here is particularly labyrinthian. Here, users perceive the space in constant renewal and transformation, stumbling upon undefined relationships and gaining inspiration from unfamiliar fields. At any point in the interior, they have a faint awareness of the entirety of the library, but can imagine that there are unknown spaces rendered imperceptible. The concepts of investigation, exploration, and wonder are made to coexist.

A giant continuous furniture piece for storing books forms the angled spiral that defines the labyrinthian spaces, designed on the basis of two contradictory essential experiences. Investigation calls for a sequence of linear elements that makes it possible to locate titles easily, whereas the concept of exploration involves discovery and casual encounters between the geometric folds of the building.

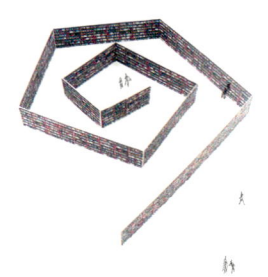

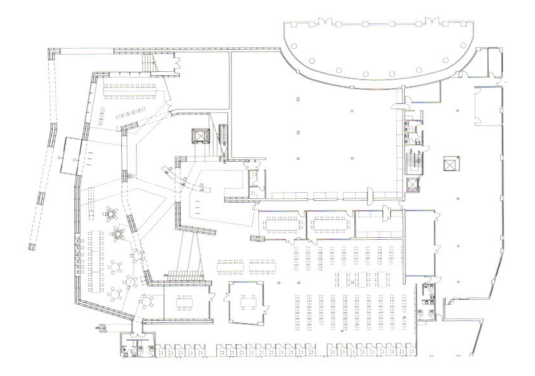

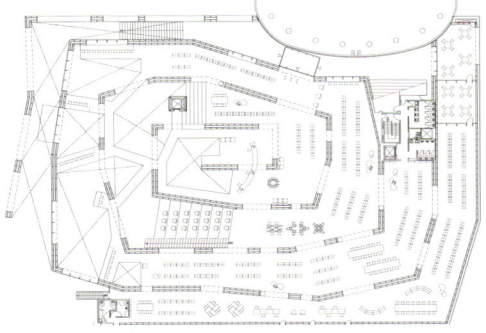

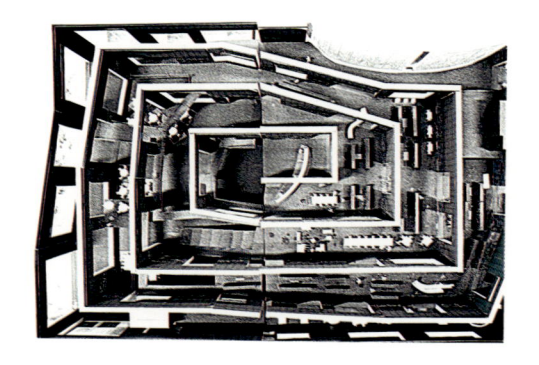

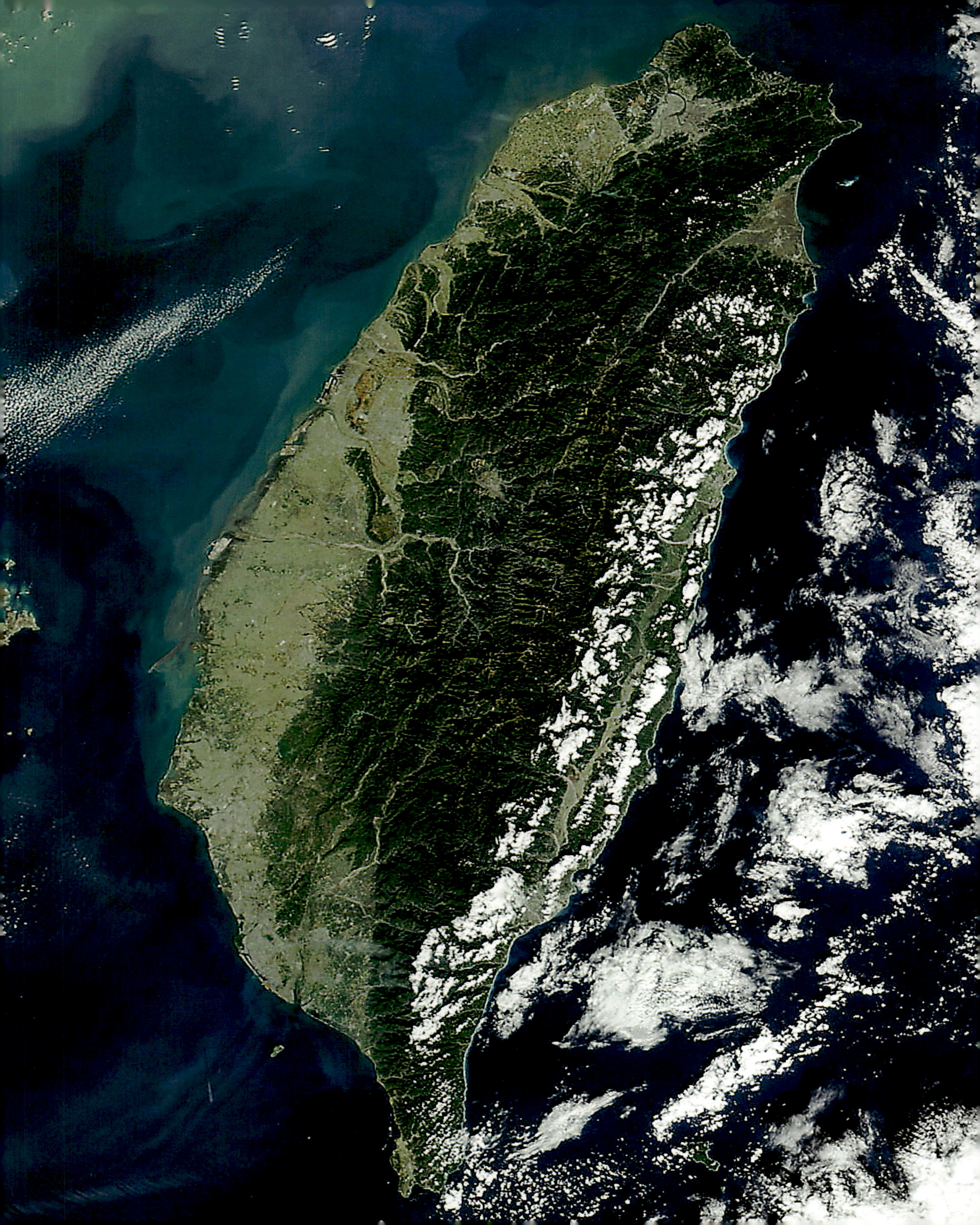

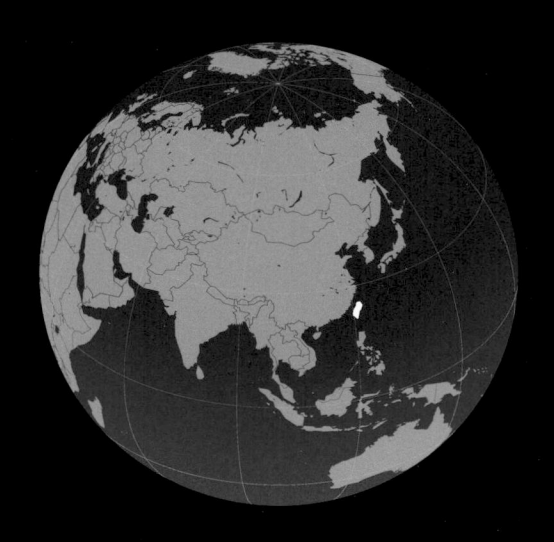

Taiwan

One of the most vigorous Asian 'tigers', Taiwan suffered the bursting of the financial bubble in the nineties decade, the effects of which are still felt today. Taiwanese architects addressed this difficult situation from two very different stances: the generous social commitment of the veterans and the skepticism of the young members of the 'post-bubble' generation, which are more interested in restricted interventions, like the extension of the Wood Sculpture Museum by Linli Su. Despite the recession, in large urban centers like Kaohsiung – a city under the administration of the government and that is the second of the island –, a large number of projects are still being carried out by foreign architects, like the Stadium by the Japanese Toyo Ito for the World Games of 2009, or the Shopping Center by the Dutch office UNStudio; meanwhile, in Taichung – the third city of the island –, the young team MAD, based in Beijing, has designed an organic Convention Center.

Ching-Yueh Roan
The Weary Tiger
Taiwan, the Search for a Post-Industrial Identity

UNStudio, Star Place Shopping Center, Kaohsiung (2008)

Two moods define today's architecture in Taiwan, the reformist optimism of the older generation and the skepticism of the post-bubble one.

The recent arrival in Taiwan of prominent international architects, Asian or from the West, is the result of the pressure to adjust the country's production to the new standards established by the globalization process.

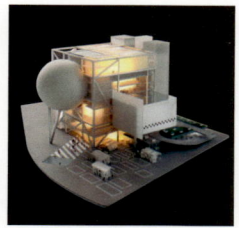

OMA, Arts Center, Taipei

THE HISTORY of modern architecture started only about one hundred years ago. It was driven by the Industrial Revolution and the French Revolution, which not only changed the direction of architecture, but also significantly overturned the social classes and the power structure. With rationalism and empiricism, technological development had facilitated the formation of modern architecture and cities in which individualism was encouraged. Almost no place in the world evaded the trend.

The enormous impacts resulting from the Industrial Revolution and the French Revolution in the West finally reached Far East Asia in the late 19th century. Throughout the entire 20th century, Far East Asia difficultly but gradually caught up with the West by learning and copying it. In the 21st century, the rising Far East Asia started to be heard with its own voice in many aspects. In the field of architecture, architects from the region have categorically placed their position in their own history and culture, searching for their own styles. Their professional perspective and ideology shall thoroughly change the development of the region and our understanding of human environment.

Due to their discrepancies in the process of modernization as well as the regional wars and confrontations, in the 20th century the East Asia nations had been respectively having either a dialogue with the West or a monologue with themselves. There were very few dialogues in-between each other. After the long century, as they are becoming more alike in terms of modernization and as confrontations in the region are relaxed, there seems to emerge a possibility for them to have a dialogue with each other and at the same time to vocalize together; the time seems to have been ripe for them. This is exactly where Taiwan architecture stands at this moment.

But to find the starting point of modern Taiwanese architecture is not easy, as it involves the complexity of recent Taiwanese history. The first crucial year to mark about this is 1945, when Japan returned Taiwan to the Kuomintang (from now on, KMT), the then ruling party of China, after 50 years of colonization. Before then, Japan had transferred its idea of modern architecture to Taiwan gradually and implicitly. But as the architects of major buildings mainly came from Japan during that period of time, they had left local architects with little opportunities. Soon after the Japanese left, the KMT lost its control of China in the late 1940s and retreated to Taiwan. A group of young architects, mainly from the Shanghai area, followed the KMT and started to practice and spread their ideology of modern architecture in Taiwan. The main direction of this period was to merge architecture with modern technology while integrating traditional styles such as temples and palaces, which are usually with monumental signatures. This direction went well with the ruling party's governing mentality for nearly 30 years.

In a simplified way, we can also say that modern Taiwanese architecture has evolved interchangeably between 'action' and 'recovery' periods. 'Action' refers to the way in which Taiwanese architecture imitates and learns from the West in the process of modernization. 'Recovery' refers to the way it examines and explores itself while trying to figure out where it is positioned. Evolving interchangeably between these two forces, I believe the development of Taiwanese architecture can be divided into the following five periods from 1945 till the recent moment.

There are three 'recovery' periods: one is between the end of World War II and the late 1960s, which was the period when newcomers from China expressed their architectural thoughts; the second one is the postmodernism period in the 1980s, which was influenced strongly by American commercialism; the third one is the

Since the mid-20th century, Taiwanese architecture has looked alternately towards the West and Japan in search of its forms, and towards the country's ancient traditions to rediscover its identity. Currently the world has its eyes on Taiwan, and the foreigners building on the island reflect local customs in their proposals: commercial night lighting, the cult of theater, or the imitation and embracing of nature.

MAD Architects, Convention Center, Taichung (2009)

social awakening period after the 1999 earthquake, mainly to engage themselves in self-examination and confirmation of identity, as well the beginning of local social movements. There are two 'action' periods: the first one is the group of the first Taiwan-trained generation of architects in the 1970s, who picked up the model directly from Japan, Europe and the United States; the second one is the multicultural development as well as its active interaction with the rest of the world following the end of Martial Law in 1988, seeking ways to build a connection with contemporary trends. The two forces that emerged after World War II have interchangeably defined modern architecture in Taiwan.

Both 'action' and 'recovery' can easily be found in the evolutionary process of human civilization, but the division between the two, whether in architecture or other fields, has never been clear. Very often, recovery can be seen in action, and action in recovery. They are, essentially, inseparable.

The Nineties, Turning Point
The crucial point in recent Taiwanese architecture definitely appeared at the end of the 1980s, when the government made several pivotal decisions: lifting Martial Law in the summer of 1987; eliminating the press censorship on New Year's Day in 1988; allowing the establishment of political parties in 1989 and of fifteen new banks in 1991. This relaxed political and economic environment stimulated a succession of lively cultural and artistic innovations in Taiwan, including a dazzling display of architectural aesthetics from the beginning of the 1990s. So as to introduce current Taiwanese architecture, this essay will deal with two groups of architects that emerged after the 1990s, and which represented one last 'recovery' period and one up-coming new 'action' period. The architects in the first group are about 50, and had largely risen to fame in the 1990s as representatives of the third 'recovery' period. They witnessed the dramatic political and economic change of the 1990s and in a way followed the tide to become optimistic toward the future. This means that their engagement is deeper and dreams are flying high. Hence, they had also shown strong aspirations and concern for social responsibility of architecture.

Architects from the second group are about ten years younger. They became known at the beginning of this decade, after Taiwan was hit hard by the 1997 Asian Financial Crisis, from which it has not been able to fully recover yet. Hence, this group of architects, compared with the previous one, has shown different interests and attitudes when it comes to the purpose and role of architecture. Especially with the descent of the bubble economy, they learnt to be independent early, not relying on big public projects or employment from big architecture offices. This phenomenon is pretty similar to that of Japan in the early 1990s, as written by Yoshiharu Tsukamoto and Momoyo Kaijima in the book *Bow-Wow from Post City Bubble*. This generation of architects shows a different yet interesting attitude towards architecture, which might deviate the direction of architecture in the future and that is definitely worth more attention.

Toyo Ito, World Games Stadium, Kaohsiung (2009)

Atlas: Asia and Pacific **231**

Wei-Li Liao, Wang-Gong Footbridge, Changhua County (2008)

The abolition of Martial Law in 1987 meant a stimulus for art and culture in Taiwan. During the first nineties, practicing architects were optimistic spectactors of the political changes of their time, and their works reflect a social and cultural commitment towards the environment. The reconstruction of villages in Sichuan, the footbridge in Changhua, and the Earthquake Museum and the Cultural Center of Luo-Dong are reflections of this trend.

The Commitment of Hsieh and Liao
Among all of them, Ying-chun Hsieh surely is the most unique one from the latest 'recovery' group. He has worked, for years, both as a contractor and architect and has been helping people rebuild their homes ever since the devastating 1999 earthquake which happened in central Taiwan. These cooperative construction projects of the Thao Tribe (a minority with less than 300 people officially on record) earned him international recognition. Within six months after the earthquake, Hsieh built the whole village together with the Thao people, with a limited budget and almost no government help. In recent years, Hsieh continues to help people in similar conditions, whether villagers in remote China or victims of the South East Asian Tsunami, to build their own houses.

When Hsieh embarks on architectural projects, he is very sensitive to the following issues: that the building material is environmentally friendly; that the material is collected from local communities; that the construction method is simple; that the cost is sensible; or that the structure is able to satisfy human needs (i.e., well-lit, well-ventilated and resistant to heat). He is also concerned about the housing supply problems of the minorities – the aboriginals, the disabled, and the low-income families – and the monopolization of the architectural technology by the elites, which make things more difficult or even impossible to buy or build.

Hsieh's ideas reveal the consequences of globalization, especially the difficulties that minorities face when confronted by capital and technology whilst in peril of being superannuated by the human ecosphere. Hsieh's cooperative construction projects, seemingly a simple idea, are in fact a thoughtful contemplation on the situation all humans are facing: a dire circumstance which challenges us to think about the many issues surrounding ecology and environment, corporate and commercial capital management, the very meaning of life as well the direction of modernism in architecture.

Hsieh is also one of the most active architects in the aftermath of Sichuan earthquake in China, on 12 May 2008, which killed over 70,000 people and left 20,000,000 people homeless. Hsieh not only tries to rebuild the housing, but helps locals with community solidarity, environmental protection and conservation of cultural heritage. He encourages locals to participate in the building process, so they can be equipped with construction knowledge and eventually have a skill of their own.

Wei-Li Liao gained attention for his bridge series – especially the Wang-Gong Footbridge. As modernism has been an easy target for criticism because of its inherent disassociation with everyday life and cultural environment, Liao accepts the mantle of modernism and writes: "Taiwan lies within the Asian tropical latitude and its thriving trees are truly diverse! Hence we see individual organization within varied cultures, which strive to coexist but resist reconciliation, showing a unique vibrant Taiwanese spirit in the environment. This spirit is full of change and never at peace with itself, like a wilderness full of uncertainty." In Liao's work, a comparison between the sub-tropical, tropical forestry in Taiwan, which contains a variety of trees, and the temperate forestry in most of the West and in Japan, which usually has fewer types of trees, serves as a metaphor to discuss the differences between Taiwan's architecture aesthetic and that of the West and Japan.

Furthermore, Liao believes that architecture is similar to a ritual. Just like human civilization, nature and cultural environment, architecture never stops evolving and is always examining itself. In this respect, architecture tears down barriers, merges oppositional forces, and eventually unites everything into an organic and coexisting body.

Liao's views on architectural aesthetics, though rooted in the foundational precepts of modernism, help him continually to search for possible ways to sprout forth new branches. Though his choice of construction materials assumes the leading and most visible role, he often begins with the form, which does not make reference to the specialized nature of the materials or the structure. His construction's *position* and *resonance* are antecedent to architectural language.

Ying-Chun Hsieh, reconstruction of basic services after the Sichuan earthquake, China (2008)

Jay W. Chiu, 921 Earthquake Museum, Wufong, Taichung (2007)

In his search for *position* and *resonance,* Liao avoids the defined and predictable solution; instead, he chooses to approach an archetype of indefinable character while searching for potentially new aesthetics. This approach is his most visible characteristic, and it cracks the key to designing comparatively monolithic physical aesthetics within environmental relationships. His recent project of Jiu-En Chapel is one good example to watch.

Local Modernity: Chiu and Huang

Jay W. Chiu is renowned for his 'History and Memory' series, such as East Gate Plaza in Hsinchu. Among them, 921 Earthquake Museum might be the best example to view his ideology, as it shows a humble yet confident mentality in dealing with the earthquake-shaken landscape and the collective memory of the public. Besides that, Chiu is also famous for his way of applying common local materials and construction methods in modern architecture in a simple and clear way. In a way, he is trying to answer modernism in a very local way. His recent project, the C-Pavilion, is a very good proof of this. The C-Pavilion, indeed, is Chiu's most important project to notice currently, as it suggests that he is parting from his early 'History and Memory' series. The new direction, for him, is to get closer to the origin of modernism and practice its ideology locally. This direction is also an important phenomenon to watch for in future Taiwanese architecture.

Chiu's persistent idealism produced designs that continually experiment, by utilizing modern materials and engineering methods that modernize Taiwan's architecture without internationalizing it. His rigorous sense of personal responsibility also allowed his designs to display a neat, fine and delicately sophisticated quality rarely seen amidst Taiwan's mediocre and crude building environment.

Sheng-yuan Huang settled in remote Yilan County 15 years ago and has practiced architecture there ever since. Huang successfully applies modern architecture in ordinary communities and daily life there. He reconstructed open spaces and alleys as a human-scale urban-system within small cities. At the same time, he changed public buildings from isolated monuments into open and friendly ones. Huang focuses his practice in a community-based concept, the scale of which is generally within 30-minute of driving distance, using simple materials and local laborers with a reasonable budget. He has successfully proven that it's possible to have good and modern architecture from the grass roots.

The other character of Huang's works is that he overthrows his idiosyncrasies through his disposition for 'perpetual transformation', which means that his designs are never the predictable models that might result from his personality and meditations – and this ever-changing variation consequently becomes his 'constancy'. This character of 'perpetual transformation' and 'constancy' has defined Huang's architectural objects, his forms of organic structure, his flair for the unfinished, the unobstructed structural framework; it is almost as if he disdains the straight and upright facades of monolithic unity. Challenging the perpetual, memorial nature to architecture, he confounds the engraved directives of interior and exterior designs, and the set boundaries of domains.

In his series of architectural designs such as the Jiaosi Life Learning Center, Huang has displayed several levels of skills: a spirit of craftsmanship, quietude, optimism, public correctness, an intellectual's grass roots appeal, a respect for time, a willingness to be open, and a commitment to self-sacrificing goodwill. He built his architecture in the remote Yilan County with respect and devotion, but more importantly, he showed us his love for a real place.

Sheng-yuan Huang, Luo-Dong Cultural Center, Yi-Lan County (2001)

Grace Cheung/Xrange, Ant House, Taipei (2006)

Skepticism after the Bubble
The following 'action' group of architects, in a way, is quite different from the previous ones as they have to face very different realities. In his aforementioned book, the Japanese architect Yoshiharu Tsukamoto said that he was from this so-called 'post-bubble generation', a generation that watches the economy collapse while growing up; it's the same growing up experience for this group of young architects in Taiwan, who are about the same age or a bit younger than Tsukamoto. The same author also believes that, with this experience, the younger architects have formed a professional attitude different from that of the older ones. They are more practical, independent, and they are happily doing 'small architecture' rather than 'big architecture', as the former is more reliable, trustful and controllable. This description is proper for the younger generation in Taiwan when it comes to the real situation of the society here. Hence, I would think they are the new third 'action' period ones.

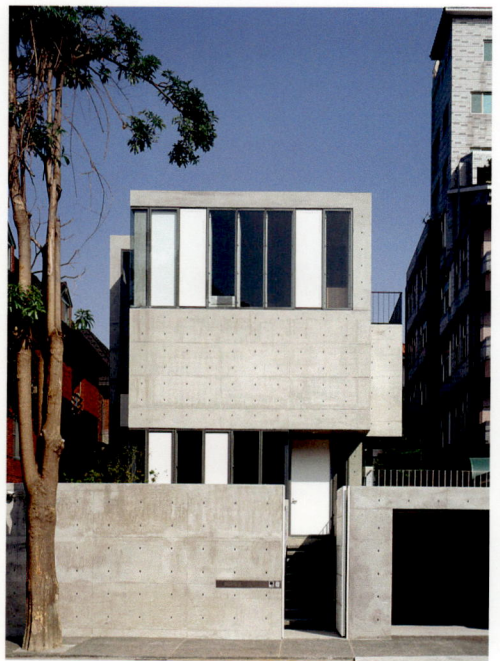

Yu Han Michael Lin, Peng House, Taichung (2005)

These architects might be restrained by a harsh reality or weak economy, but this new generation does show the strength of fighting against the reality. In general, they are less interested in issues such as social engagement or having dialogues with the cultural or political realm. They seem to focus more on the essence of architecture and basic realities such as weather, budget, function and surrounding environment. This difference has divided the two groups of architects in a rather clear way.

This 'post-bubble generation' described by Tsukamoto has its own way of dealing with reality. To them, reality is more about current situations such as budget, users, urban reality, and space functions rather than about social or historical issues, which are usually big and far away. They don't intend to burden themselves with such big issues, as they have watched the disillusionment of big dreams and ideologies.

I would like to introduce four architects as the examples to represent this 'post-bubble generation' in Taiwan. They are Grace Cheung/Xrange, Yu Han Michael Lin, Linli Su and Ming-Wei Huang, who are all around 40 years old and are expected to form the next wave in Taiwan Architecture with their peers together in the near future. The main features of their projects are lightness, good sense of humor and precision, which present a free spirit and pleasant atmosphere in architecture.

Grace Cheung's Ant Farm House is a double-shelter building, in which a new construction layer wraps up an existing stone structure. The space in-between two layers is only 80-170 centimeters wide, which is similar to small tunnels of ant farms, and connects all different rooms inside the house. The openings in two layers interrupt each other visually to form interesting framed views both inside-out or outside-in.

Yu Han Michael Lin practices architecture both in Taiwan and Germany. The single house series in central Taiwan has drawn him lots of attention at home. Michael's designs emphasize a pure, clean, and commanding subjective nature while displaying a peaceful quality. In responding to the obvious chaotic and offensive environment in big cities of Taiwan, his designs reveal a beautiful and anti-authoritarian spirit that would ennoble the visual aesthetics of the entire environment. He proves that even if a work clashes with its surrounding environment, they can still survive and flourish together.

The Extension Building of the Wood Sculpture Museum is the project that distinguishes Linli Su from his peers. In this project, Su carefully casts wood texture on cold concrete surface, which creates a subtle yet elegant feeling, and he emphasizes this quality with the skylight above throughout the inner spaces. The Organic Farm, another project by Su, is a building with an educational purpose, encouraging people to eat organic rice and live in harmony with nature. This building sits quietly in the middle of an organic rice field, and is constructed with concrete, brick and glass boxes which are at once separate and unitary.

The Humanities Building in Tunghai University is by far the most talked about project by Ming-Wei Huang. Huang creates an enclosure inner space at the center of this building while having dialogues with other traditional buildings on campus. A multi-level open space provides a friendly and interactive learning atmosphere. Besides this, his newly finished Wen-Der Police Station challenges the stereotype of boring, serious and unfriendly public buildings; the big whale also extends a cute and humorous welcome to the public.

By briefly reviewing the projects of these eight architects, you are expected to have a basic idea of what the 'action' and 'recovery' periods are like in current Taiwanese architecture. In a way, we can see that the 'action' periods mainly follow the trend of the West and Japan. We have to say that this

Unlike those of the previous generation, the architects at work after the real estate crash of the late nineties, from which Taiwan is still recovering, show interests that are more strictly related to the discipline proper, with small-size pieces like the houses of Xrange or Michael Lin, or the organic farm of Linli Su. Ming-wei Huan, from Studiobase, also belongs to this group, whose proposals reflect a greater concern for social issues.

Linli Su, Organic Farm in Miaoli (2004)

learning process is necessary to modernize and to catch up with the rest of the world. But when it comes to self-identity, the 'recovery' periods try to respond to Taiwan's own conditions and background, which is also very important. These two forces are expected to define, together in the future, and separately in the meantime, what architecture will be in Taiwan.

The Integration of Opposites

The confrontation and combination of these two trends sparks a debate about how to look for a balance between unity and diversity, as well as singularity and complexity. The two sides are competing to be heard all the time. Which linguistic form does architecture belong to? Which one is more reliable? All these are surely very interesting and deserve further attention.

Having said that, let's have a piece of literature as an example. Mikhail Bakhtin once quoted the Russian writer Vasily Grossman (1905-1964) in describing Dostoyevsky's novels: "The fundamental principle regarding the structure of his novels is like this: making opposing elements of description complied with unified philosophical conception and hurricane-like incidents… The conventional aesthetic tradition always requires the consistency between materials and writing style. It requires a unifying of all structural elements inside a novel, at least of the same kind or similarity. Dostoyevsky broke all the conventional rules and integrated all opposing interfaces… His mission is to resolve one of the greatest challenges for an artist: to create a solid and unified artwork with materials of huge contrast, different nature and values."

Hence, whether it is unity or diversity, singular or complex, they may not necessarily contradict each other. Rather, this can be the distinction of modern Taiwanese architecture. We may also say that it's a labyrinth, which is puzzling but does not need to be solved. Architecture has a duplicate-tone nature and possesses a mysterious blink zone, to which one can return to from time to time and always receive different messages. This is also the relation between the *flâneur* and the wanderer exclusively depicted and practiced by Walter Benjamin (1892-1940).

After appearing in the 21st century, globalization is developing at a rapid and furious pace, and the new generation of architectural professionals in Taiwan, unavoidably, will have to redefine the identity of Taiwanese architecture and cities. Taiwan, right now, is at the post-industrial period of time that is transforming the world. Yet in terms of capital, technology and interaction, it is still playing an outmoded, supporting role because of its position in the world division of labor. But from the examples above, we can see that Taiwan's architecture is showing its own strength and diversity, and is, in its own way, answering both the need at home and the calling abroad. Although this direction is complicated and difficult, it has given Taiwan's modern architecture a unique and important position to move forward from.

Ming-Wei Huang, Humanities Building, Tunghai University (2004)

Linli Su
Wood Sculpture Museum
Sanyi (Taiwan)

Client
Cultural Affairs Bureau of the Miaoli County Government
Architect
Su Lin-Lie Architect Studio
Consultants
Chang Hai Hui (electrical and mechanical); DaYan, Raya Yeh (structural)
Contractor
Hsin Hsiang Construction: Hsu Chung Pei
Photos
Gmonde Space/Liu Chun Chieh

TAIWAN'S TRADITION of wood carving, one of the most original art forms on the island, dates back to China's Ming and Ching dynasties, in the 14th century of our era. The Wood Sculpture Museum, which opened in 1995, is the only public museum in the region that focuses on this activity. Its location in the city of Sanyi reflects the craft's special importance in Miaoli County, which abounds in the camphor tree species that are much used for the purpose.

The recent enlargement of the museum tries to set these handcrafted works in a unique atmosphere, one dominated by the material presence of concrete and wood. The new building is placed flush with one of the sides of the hexagon that forms the floor plan of the preexisting structure, from which it is set apart through a transition piece that helps to give it greater autonomy of form. The ground level accommodates the entrance and information areas and the preparation, photography, and heritage collection rooms. The first, second, and third stories offer more exhibition halls besides a library, a small audio-visual room, and office spaces, leaving the fourth and the top floors as venues for temporary exhibitions of wood carvings. At the center of each level is a large rectangular void, forming a foyer of several heights that serves to light up the building's vertical circulation elements.

Exteriorly, the proposal comes across as a sculptural chunk of concrete where fissures of different shapes and sizes have been made to bring light into the interior in a controlled way. Small wood-lined pieces balance out this composition, visually compensating for the presence of the voids. The materials show substantial variations of texture, all in accordance with their position on the facade, fluctuating between the sleek satiny surfaces of the ground floor and the rich wrinkly texture of the higher levels.

Inside, the tactile presence of the materials is further reinforced through the scenographic use of light coming both from above and from the rectangular openings on the facades. Here, once again, the marks on the formwork of wooden planks on concrete take on a leading role, giving a high degree of poetry to these spaces that are intended to contain and display the patient result of generations of Taiwanese wood carvers.

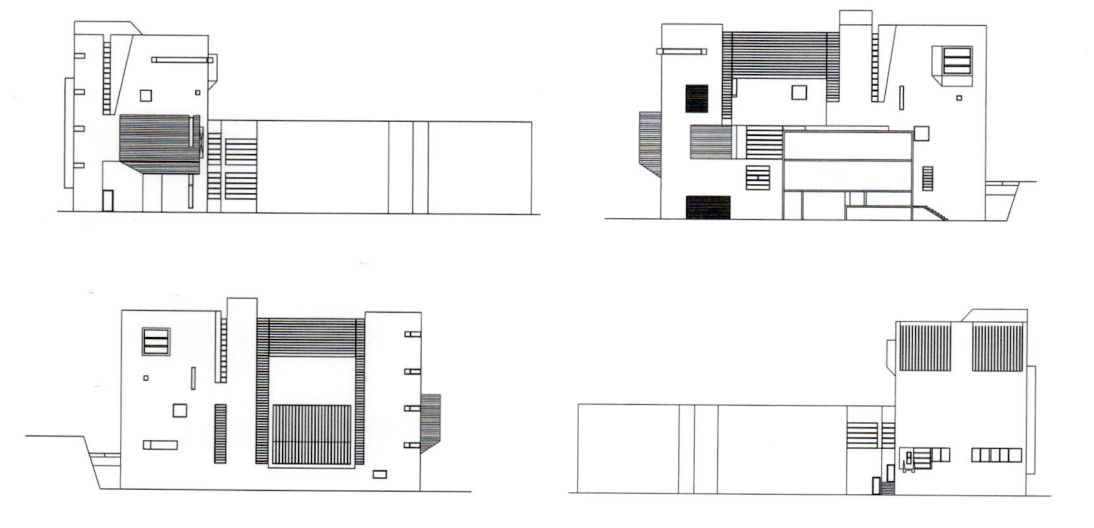

The abundant production of wood carvings in the city of Sanyi, situated in camphor tree-rich Miaoli County, gave rise to an important craft industry of which the museum and its new extension are clear testimonies.

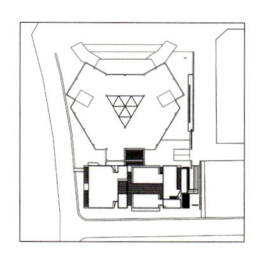

Placed flush with one side of the existing museum, the building takes on a sculptural form that is accentuated by the sharp contrast between textures - satiny versus wrinkly - and between materials - concrete versus wood -. The facade openings vary in geometry and size and bring light into the exhibition halls in a controlled way, creating on the elevations a play of solids and voids that evoke the organic quality of the works displayed.

238 Atlas: Asia and Pacific

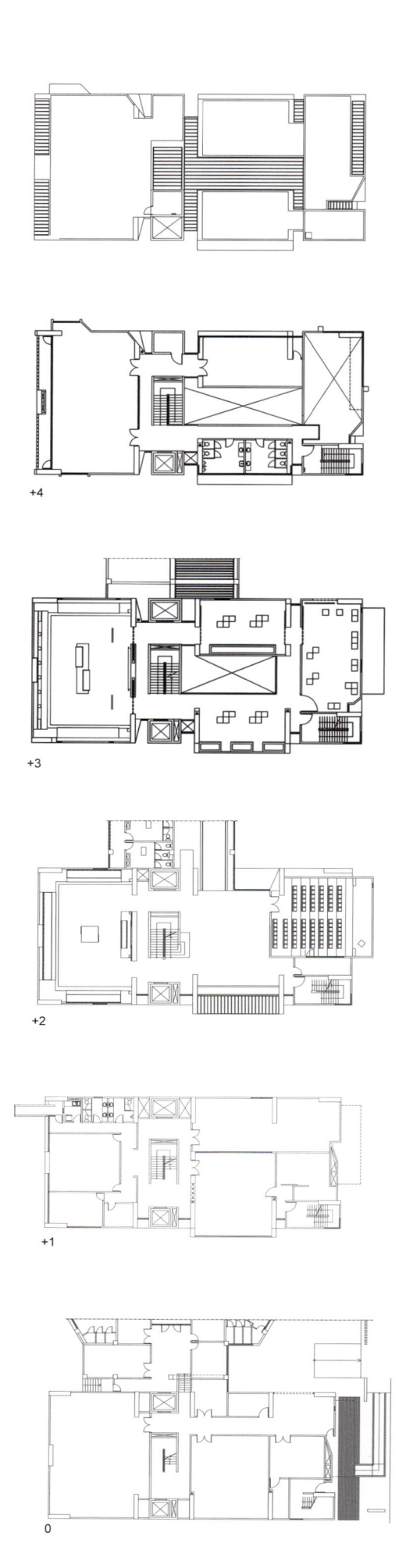

+4

+3

+2

+1

0

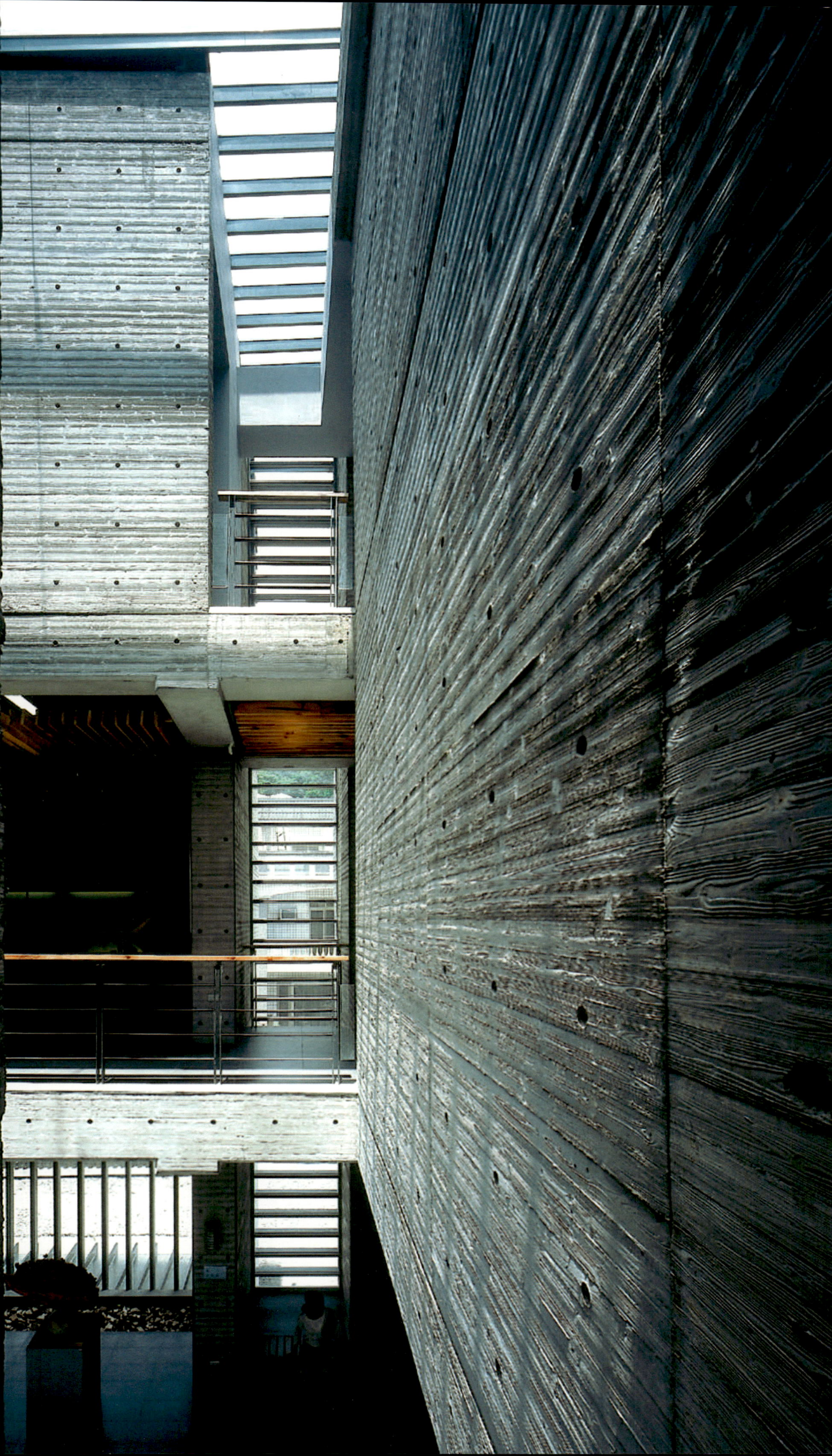

Toyo Ito
Stadium for World Games
Kaohsiung (Taiwan)

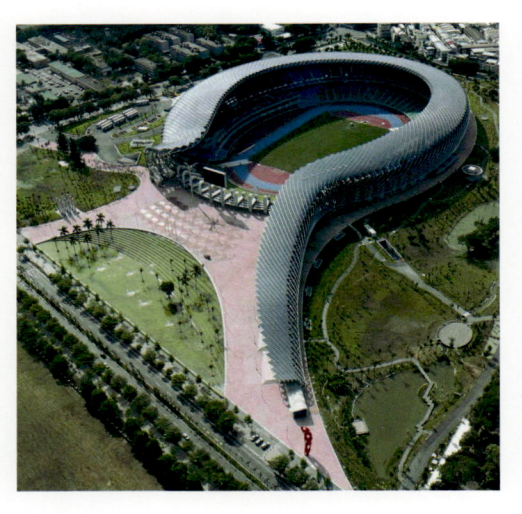

THE WORLD GAMES is one of the largest of international multiple-sport events, including, as it does, sports that are not part of the Olympic Games. It is held every four years, each time taking place a year after an Olympics. The host this time around is Kaohsiung, Taiwan's second largest city, a place endowed with nature, a pleasant climate, and lively citizens.

Designed as the main venue for the event, this sport arena takes in 40,000 people, as many as 55,000 if we count temporary seating that can be added when needed, and it is the first stadium in Taiwan to meet official world rulings, specifically the standards of the IAAF (International Association of Athletics Federations) and the FIFA (Fédération Internationale de Football Association).

In their entry to the competition that was held in 2005, the architects developed three key concepts: 'Open Stadium', 'Urban Park' and 'Spiral Continuum'. Open Stadium meant opening up the grandstand to the city. Unlike in the usual closed bowl, here the seats are made to look out toward the main gate to the south. This naturally attracts visitors from the newly constructed MRT (Mass Rapid Transit) station situated southeast of the stadium site.

Clients
National Council on Physical Fitness and Sports, Kaohsiung Bureau of Public Works
Architects
Toyo Ito & Associates
Collaborators
Takenaka, RLA
Consultants
Takenaka, Hsin-Yeh Engineering (structural engineers); Takenaka, Teddy & Assoc., C.C.Lee & Assoc. (mechanical engineers); Lancaster (lighting); Takenaka, Laboratory for Environment & Form (landscaping); Takenaka, Ricky Liu (interior design); Takenaka, Taiwan Fire Safety (disaster prevention); Lead Dao Technology (3D model creation)
Contractor
Fu Tsu Construction
Photos
Chi Po-Lin (p. 240 above);
Fu Tsu Construction (pp. 240-241, 242);
Christian Richters/ Album/ View (p. 243)

The design of the stadium that was the venue of the 2009 World Games in July revolves around three concepts: opening the grandstand to the exterior, including an urban park, and creating a tense and vibrant spiral continuum.

240 Atlas: Asia and Pacific

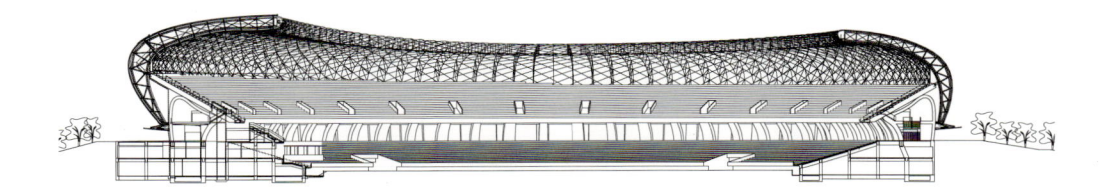

The Urban Park concept is intended to attract the public through a new urban park typology. In fact, because of Open Stadium, the front square and the sport field can be joined and used together on days when no events are slated.

The third concept, Spiral Continuum, has to do with the roof, a three-dimensional curve comprising three layers: trusses, hoops, and solar panel units. The 159 trusses of gradually changing sizes are the main structural elements, designed as they are to support the long-term load of the 22,000 square meter roof. The 32 helical-shaped steel pipes, the 'oscillating hoops', ascend along the whole roof as a second structure knitting together the trusses and handling short-term loads such as seismic forces and wind pressure. The two-dimensional solar panels of gradually changing widths, with their electricity-generating capacity of 1,100,000 kiloWatts per year, are hung between adjacent hoops. The resultant spiral continuum, which has a diameter of 318.5 millimeters, has the effect of heightening the spectators' excitement.

Built on these design concepts, the stadium embodies fluid movement like a vibrant athletic body and is sure to draw the city's attention as a hub of activity.

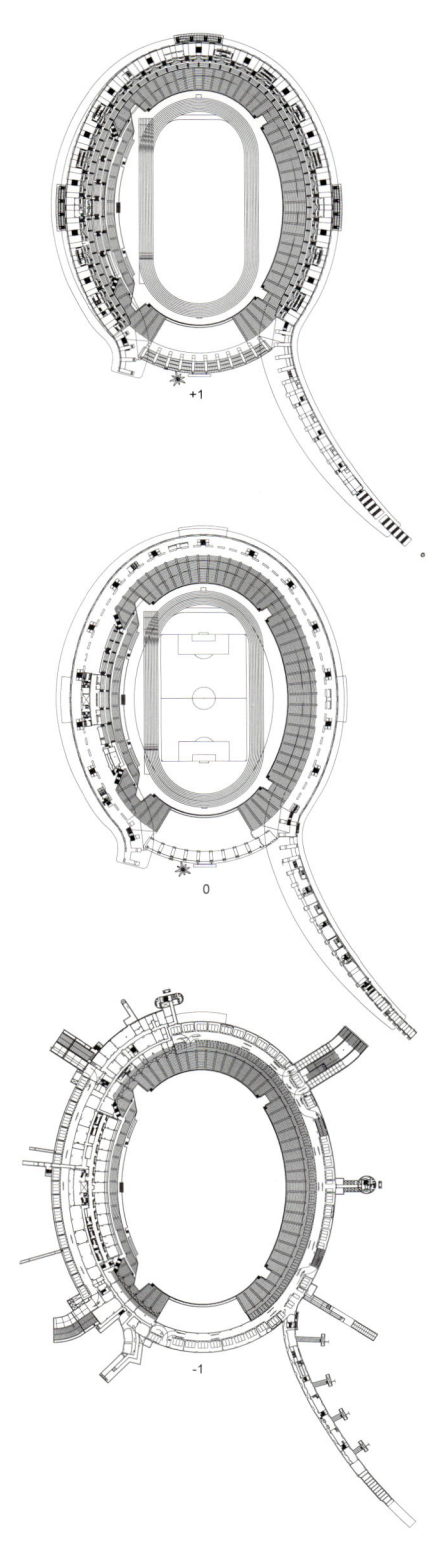

Atlas: Asia and Pacific 241

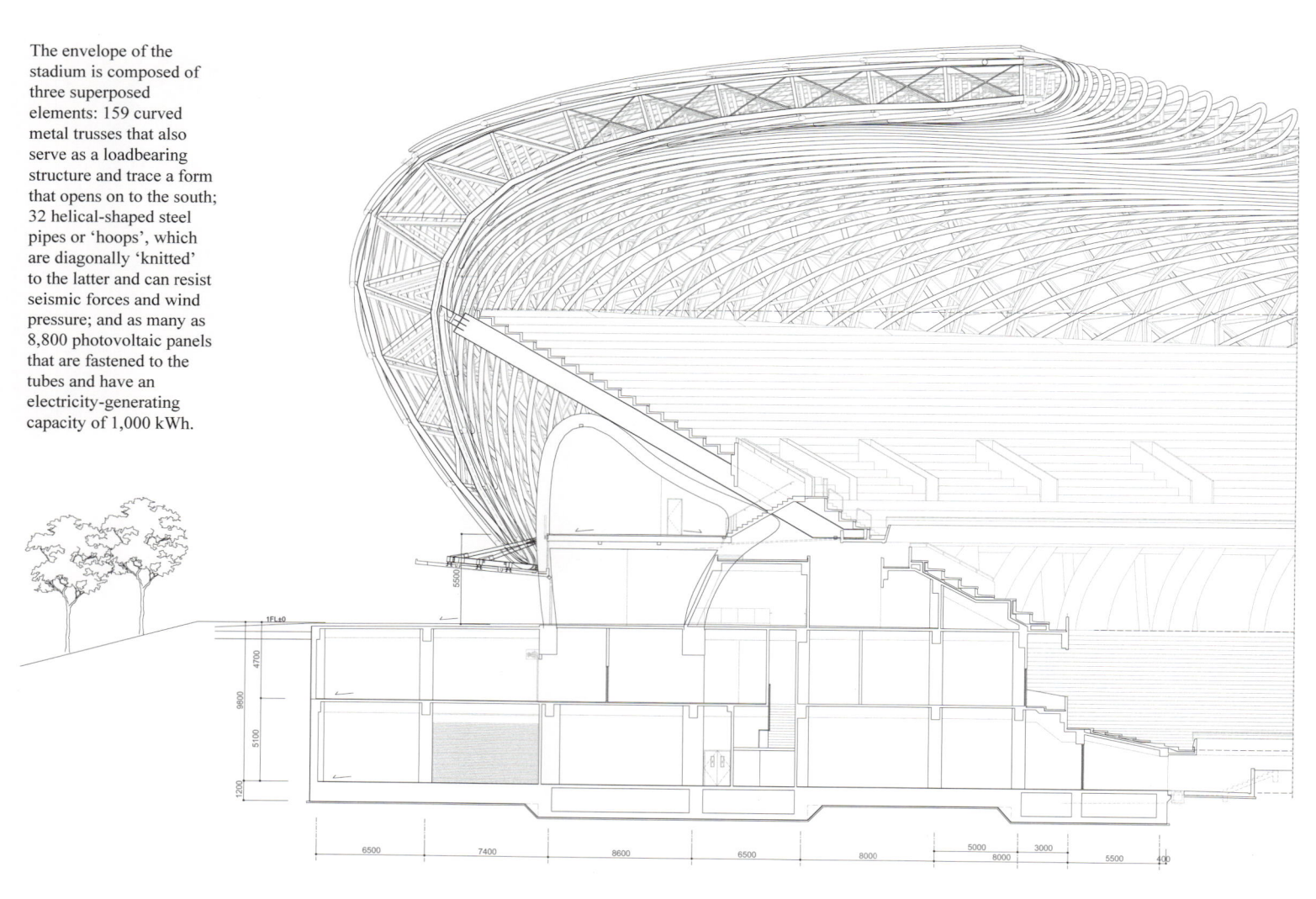

The envelope of the stadium is composed of three superposed elements: 159 curved metal trusses that also serve as a loadbearing structure and trace a form that opens on to the south; 32 helical-shaped steel pipes or 'hoops', which are diagonally 'knitted' to the latter and can resist seismic forces and wind pressure; and as many as 8,800 photovoltaic panels that are fastened to the tubes and have an electricity-generating capacity of 1,000 kWh.

242　Atlas: Asia and Pacific

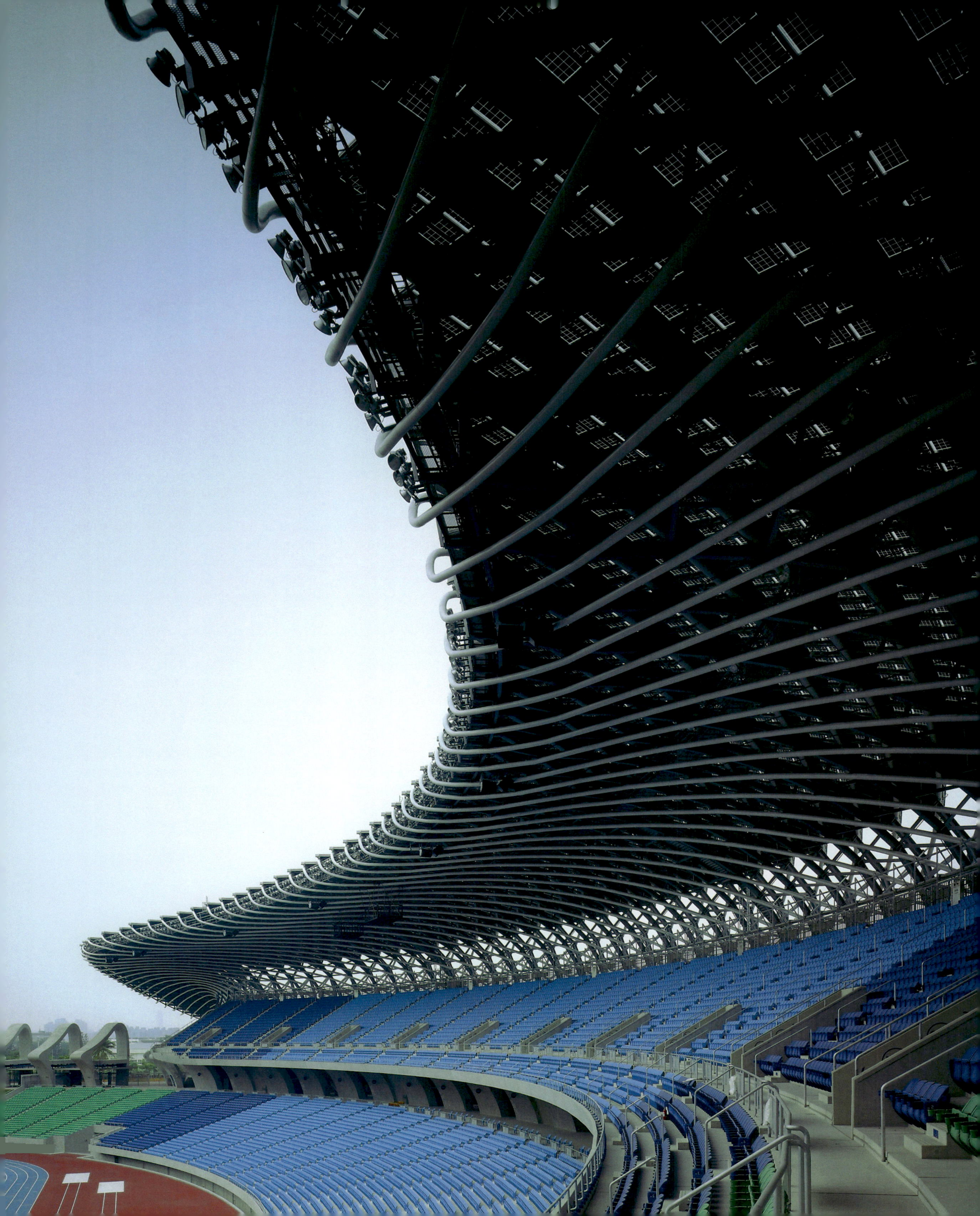

UNStudio
Star Place Shopping Center
Kaohsiung (Taiwan)

Client
President Group
Architects
UNStudio: Ben van Berkel, Astrid Piber
Collaborators
G. Gijzen, C. Veddeler, M. Bergmann, A. Gnodde, S. Schott, F. Koelemeijer, K. Groeger, J. Bars, A. Brink, S. Yan Chan; S. Kortemeier, HCF Architects, Dynasty Design (local architects)
Consultants
Arup & CHU (structure); Arup (lighting); Lightlife & Alliance Optotek (facade animation); H&K (facade engineering); Mulberry (design coordination); Bureau Mijksenaar (way finding concept phase)
Photos
Christian Richters

Situated on a triangular lot that had to be occupied in its entirety, the shopping center makes its high atrium the principal element vertically connecting the twelve floor levels of luxury stores.

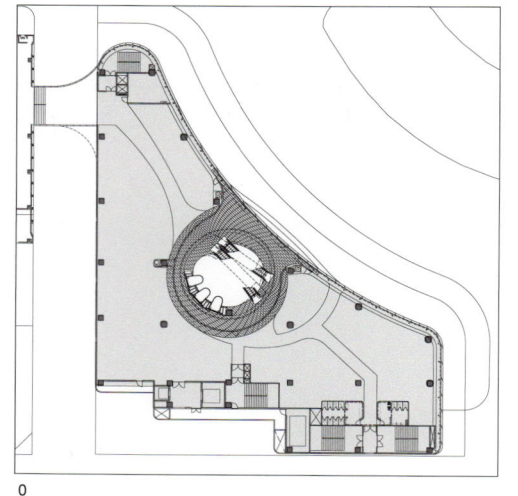

WHEN THE PROJECT was taken on by UNStudio, a proposal for the location had previously been drawn up by the firms Dynasty Design and HCF Architects. The outlines and structure of this proposal were preserved. Consequently, the main frame and volume of the current building were predetermined. Within this original scheme, UNStudio's characteristic integration of program and construction, that which yields its usual column-free spaces, was not possible. To achieve the visual and spatial effects of free-flowing, unobstructed spaces, a public void was introduced. Thought out in the manner of an atrium, it would serve to bring daylight into the interiors while establishing visual connections between the different floor levels.

Positioned on an urban plaza graced by a roundabout, the building occupies a triangular lot. It embraces this position by curving in such a way that its wide frontage opens itself fully to the city. The idea of the facade as an urban manifestation in all its splendor was at the outset toyed with, but the chosen solution of a three-dimensional front elevation, one with a prominent pattern of protruding elements, was soon reconnected to practical matters such as the arrangement of spaces around the atrium or the question of movement through this void.

The 12-floor atrium is placed flush with the facade, not deep within the building. It is the building's main connecting element, with three panoramic elevators and two sets of escalators. The void is a cylinder that appears to twist and slant, an optical illusion caused by the 10-degree rotation of the escalators at each floor level in the atrium space. From ground up to roof, the rotation amounts to 110 degrees.

On the facade, projecting horizontal lamellas and vertical fins together form a swirling pattern that has the effect of breaking up the scale of the building, which to the onlooker outside has no legible floor heights, thanks to the one-meter spacing between aluminum-faced lamellas. The fins are made of laminated, low-iron glass, and for transparency effects are fewer and shallower towards the top of the building where the restaurant is located. Varying in size, they were facilitated by parametric design and production techniques.

A dot pattern is printed on both sides of the glass so that the fins appeear white by day. At night, the dots pick up the colors distributed by LED-lights attached to the bases of the fins. The nighttime appearance of the building is important in a place like Taiwan, which has a tradition of late-night shopping and all-night markets.

0

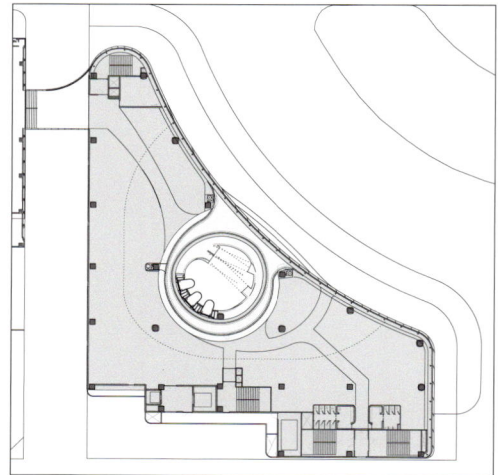

+3

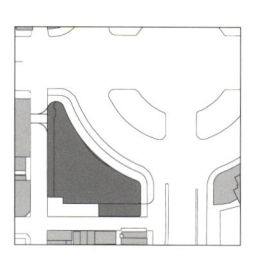

Instead of being put deep within the built volume, the atrium is placed flush with the main facade, giving it extra visibility from the street. The *moiré* effect is achieved through horizontal lamellas that protrude a meter from the surface of the facade, and vertical glass panels printed with a pattern of dots that make them look white during the day. At night, lit with LED-lights, they change color and transform the building's image altogether.

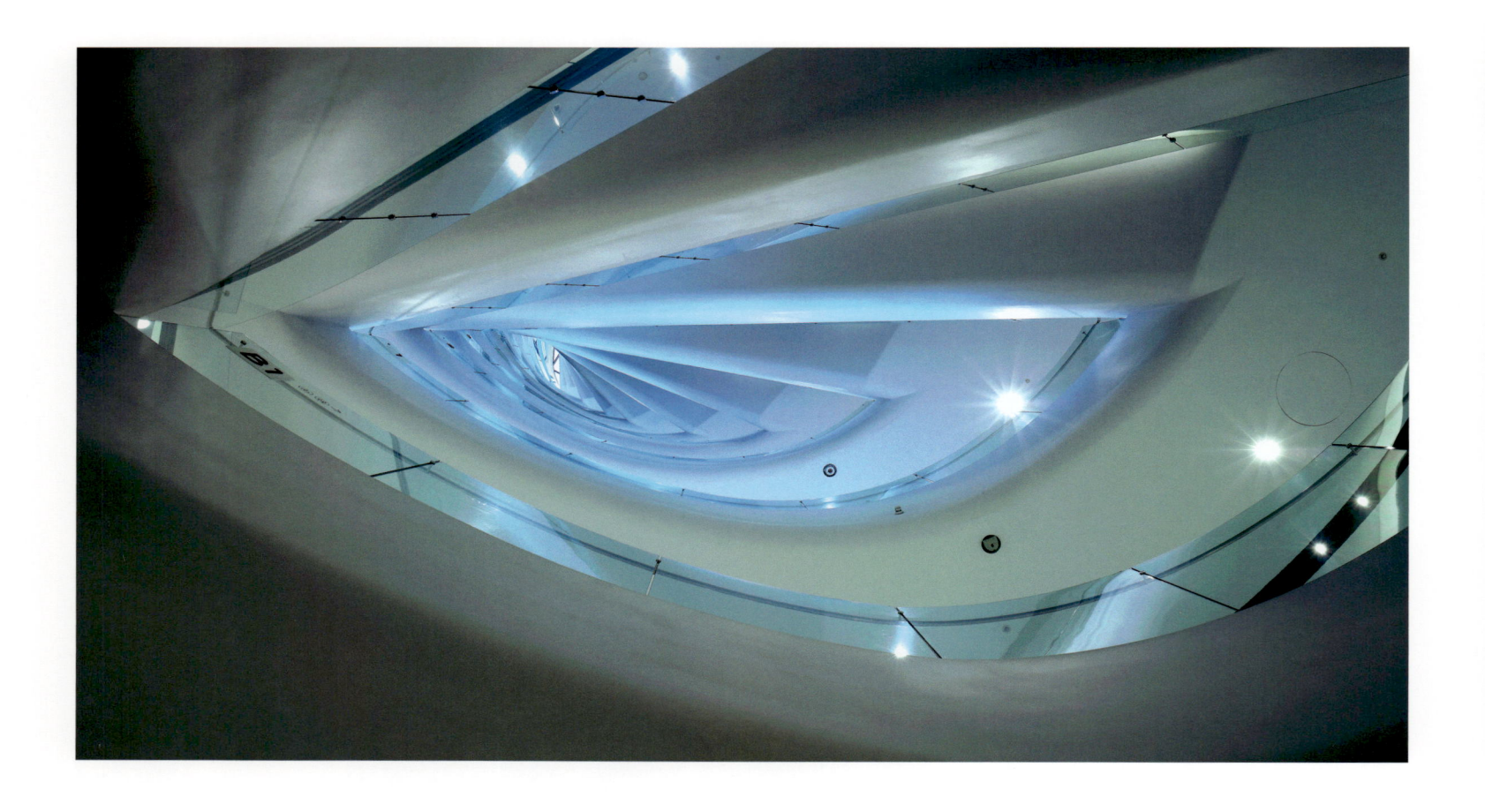

Three panoramic elevators combine with flights of escalators to form the vertical communication system. The staircases are equipped with continuous balustrades that curve gently and turn ten degrees at every floor level, making it seem as if the atrium itself were turning or twisting in a spiral. Of the six underground stories, which are down to the very bottom naturally lit by the skylight that crowns the atrium space, two are for commercial use and the remaining four make the car park. From outside, the swirling glass fins reflect the colorful lights of the interior and form the star from which the shopping center gets its name.

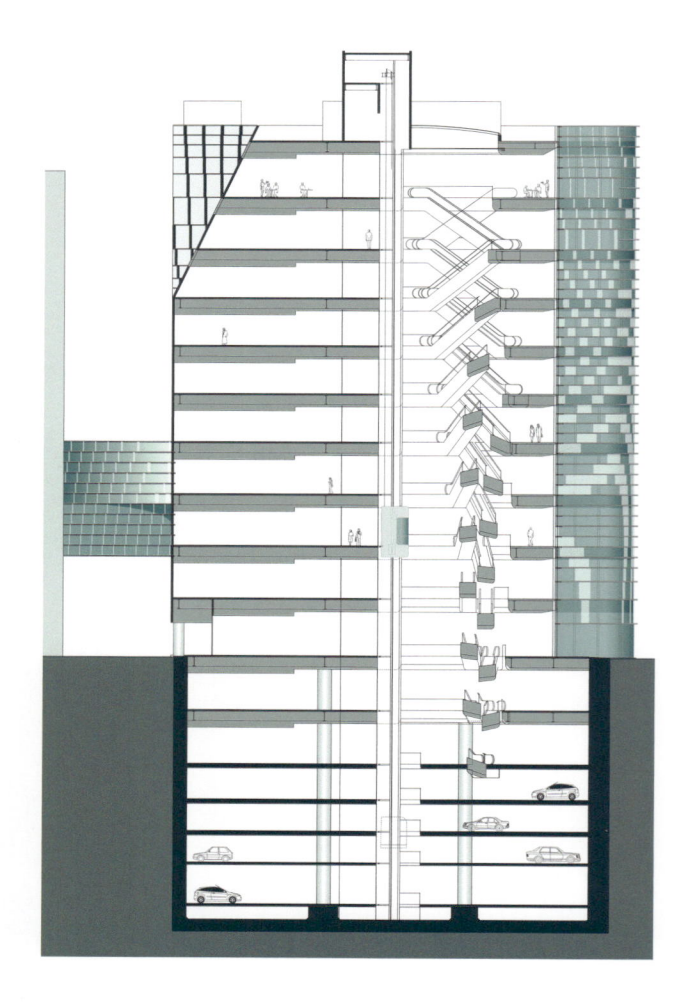

大立精品
Salvatore Ferragamo
Salvatore Ferragamo
Salvatore Ferragamo

MAD
Convention Center
Taichung (Taiwan)

Client
Taichung City Government
Architects
MAD: Ma Yansong, Dang Qun
Collaborators
Jordan Kanter, Jtravis Russett, Irmi Reiter, Diego Pérez,
Dai Pu, Rasmus Palmquist, Art Terry, Chie Fuyuki (design team)

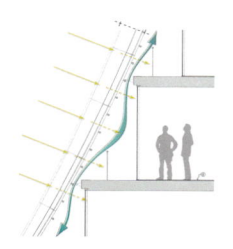

Situated in the subtropical climate of Taichung, the complex will have a technological skin that is equipped to bring fresh air into all the buildings, besides generating energy through the action of photovoltaic panels.

TAIWAN'S THIRD CITY after Taipei and Kaohsiung, Taichung is to be given a boost in its urban and economic life through a 216,000 square meter landmark complex that will provide new spaces for conventions, exhibitions, retail, offices, and a hotel. In line with the idea that landmark architectures should no longer be characterized by considerations of height and visual impact, but must foster public recreation and inspire communication and imagination, the volumes addressing the different parts of the program are not the usual clearly distinct individual blocks of large complexes, but are unified as a collective form.

The form adopted is a cluster of mounds of varying height (between 39 and 85 meters) on a land area of 70,000 square meters. As a continuous weave of construction and landscape where the boundaries between architecture and nature are blurred, it was taken from the landscape, under whose calm surface topological potentials await to be discovered and expressed as urban landmarks. The architecture's crater-shaped formations and resulting rotundas are the outcome of actual site conditions. They may also have been inspired by the nearby Central Mountain Range and the lower rolling hills stretching north. In the final analysis, the project takes from naturalist philosophies of the East, in particular holistic attitudes involving integration and harmony between humanity and nature.

The open courtyards that connect the 'mountains' of the complex are integrated into a natural sequence of outdoor spaces. As in the quest for a harmonious coexistence of people and nature exemplified by ancient Chinese gardens, the project seeks meaning in its non-material qualities or in the naturalistic spirit of the exteriors, where a single tree, a patch of bamboo, or a pond becomes central; all this in an approach to sustainable development that is based not on technology, but on traditional thought and aesthetics. The surface of the 'mountains', albeit a high-tech, smocking-like pleated skin, is eco-friendly, equipped as it is with a system that brings air into the building, as is fitting in a warm humid subtropical climate, while trapping solar energy through double panels of photovoltaic glass.

The proposal endeavors to recreate the continuity of a natural mountainous landscape through a sequence of 'mounds' with striated surfaces, in between which are courtyards with trees or ponds inspired by Eastern tradition. Inside the mounds are rotundas that receive daylight through the 'crater' openings above, and these address a wide range of programs, including spaces for conventions, exhibitions, cafés, and a hotel.

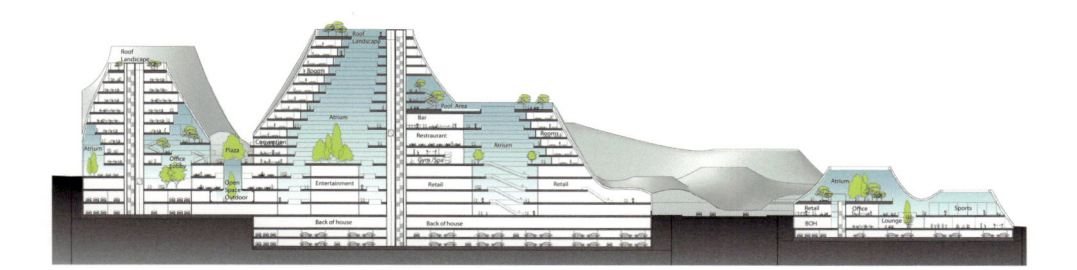

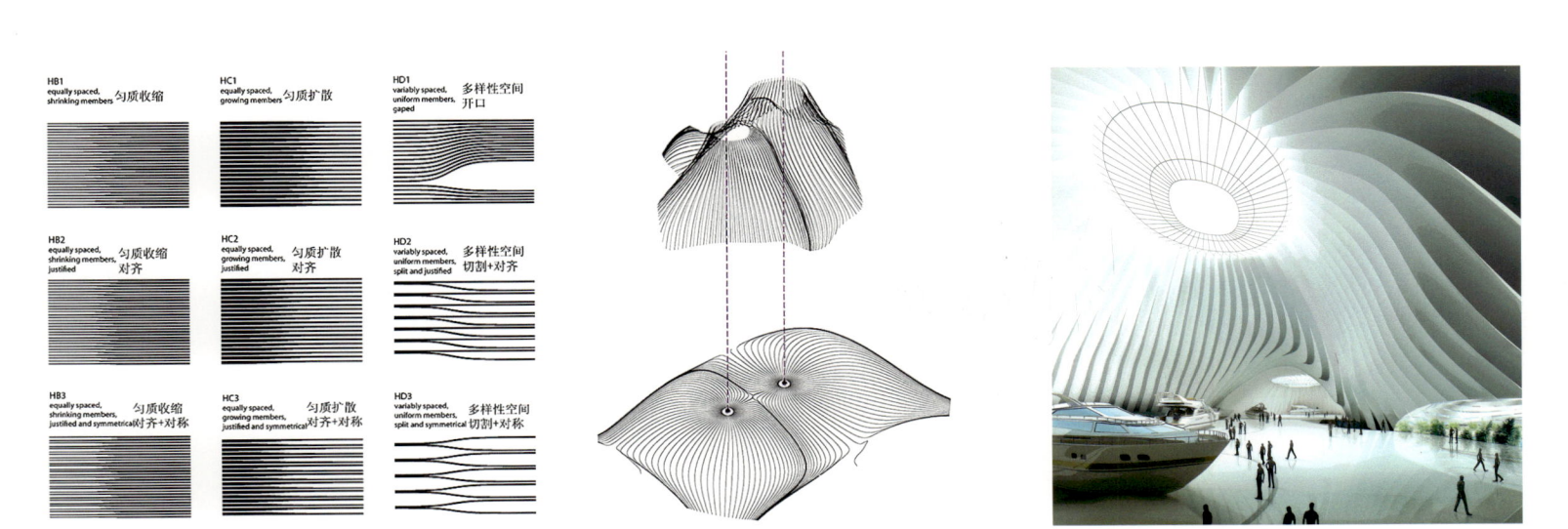

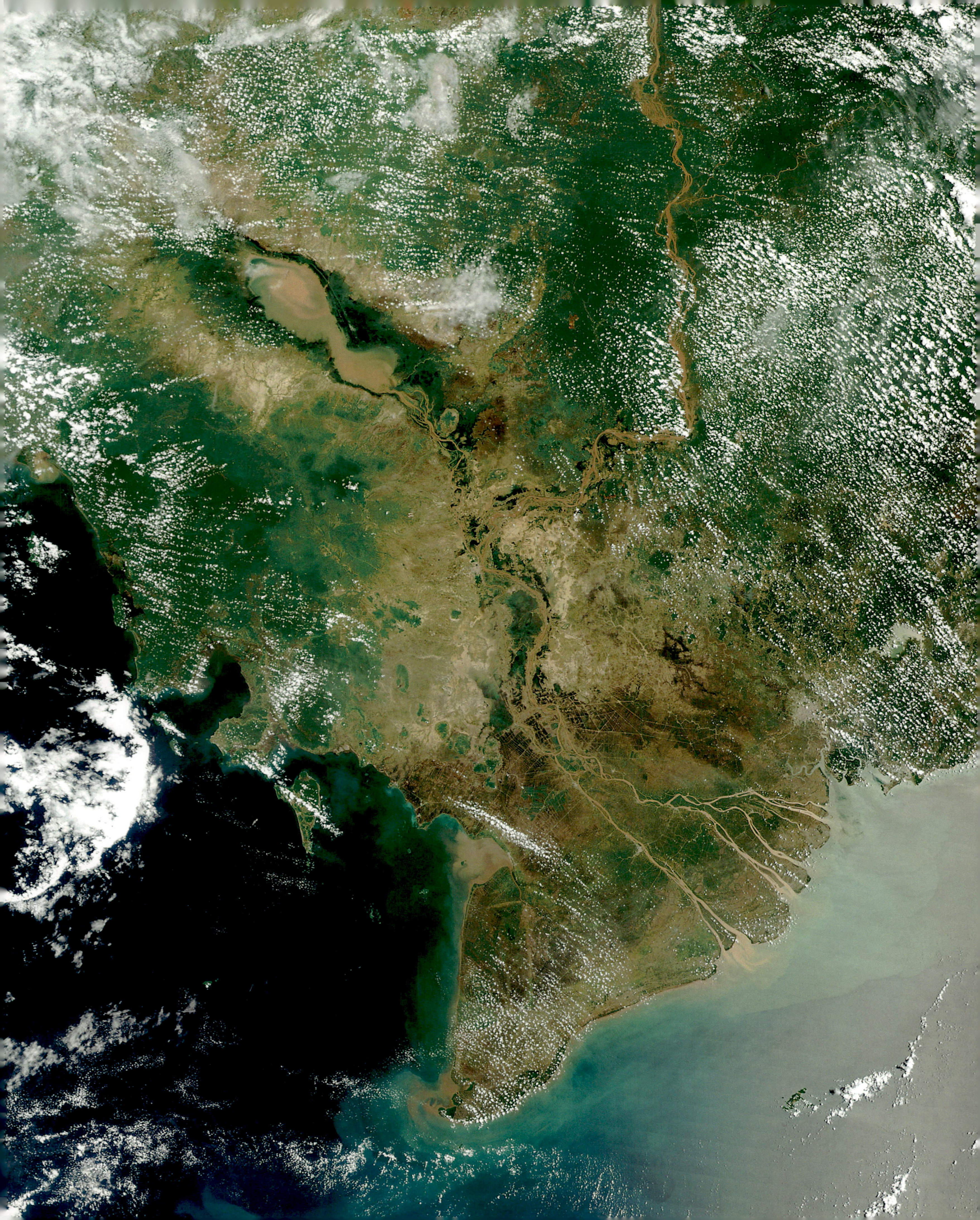

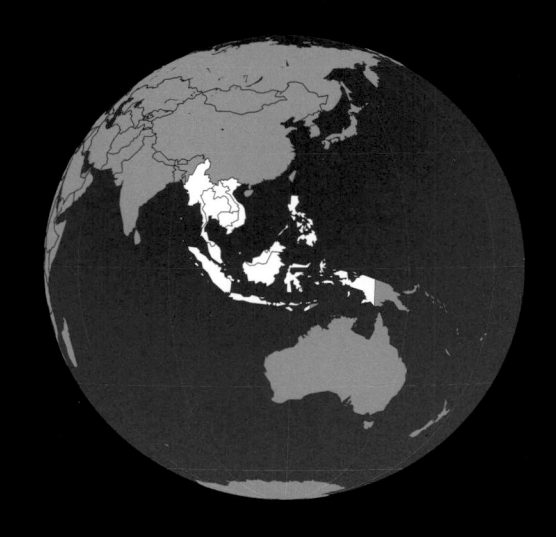

Southeast Asia

The processes of decolonization and the co-existence of different cultures and religions – Buddhism, Islamism and Catholicism – have shaped the idiosyncrasy of the countries of Southeast Asia, which try today to transform their economies with different degrees of success. In the field of architecture, as much the influence of climate as the cultural identity features have been determining factors. The projects selected here reflect these concerns in different countries: while the Petronas University in Malaysia endeavors to reduce its environmental impact, the reconversion of the British consulate into a hotel in Thailand and the Wind and Water Café in Vietnam use local materials as symbolic devices for national affirmation. Two projects in the capitals of these last countries express other intentions: the tallest tower in Bangkok rises as a gleaming totem, and the HUA University Campus in Ho Chi Minh City asserts its presence as an integrating element.

Evan J.S. Lin & C.J. Anderson-Wu
Cultures at the Crossroads
Southeast Asia, an Inorganic Urbanization

Shanty dwellings by the financial district in Manila, Philippines

After a long process of modernization that turned the area into the factory of the world, this amalgam of countries steps hopeful into the 21st century.

The geographic location and the fast-paced urban growth are the main features that characterize all the countries gathered under the name 'Southeast Asia'; among them and also within them there are strong contrasts.

SOUTHEAST ASIA includes Vietnam, Laos, Myanmar, Cambodia, Thailand, Malaysia, Singapore, Indonesia and the Philippines. It is an almost impossible task to discuss this area as a whole since Southeast Asia not only comprises different ethnic peoples and different languages but also clashing religions and cultural identities. Furthermore, political and cultural conflicts exist not only between nations but also within nations. No wonder this area is called 'the crossroads of cultures'.

Compared to Far East Asian countries such as China, Korea, Japan and Taiwan, that are still greatly under the influence of Confucianism, Southeast Asian countries are highly religious in respect to their political decisions, economic policies as well as their attitude toward modernization. The dominant religion in Vietnam, Cambodia, Myanmar, Laos and Thailand is Buddhism; in Malaysia and Indonesia it is Islam; and in the Philippines it is Catholicism.

Religions and the tropical climate decided the forms and styles of traditional architecture. And the most crucial fact that affected and still affects the recent development of architecture and urban spaces in Southeast Asian cities is, except Thailand, that all these countries had been colonized by Portugal, Spain, the Netherlands, Great Britain, France, the United States, and Japan. Not until the end of World War II were these countries liberated from their colonial rulers. Thus, the modernization of Southeast Asia has involved a manifold course of decolonization.

The renaissance of local culture in Malaysia, Singapore, Indonesia and the Philippines coincides with the overwhelming tides of globalization, making their decolonization in architecture and urban planning an even more challenging mission. Vietnam, Laos, Cambodia and Myanmar had belonged to the communist bloc during the Cold War, and for decades they were in extreme poverty. Up until today, this former annexed territory of communist China and the Soviet Union still suffers from social and political turmoil as it strives to turn around its stumbling economy.

Southeast Asian architecture is greatly enriched because, due to the torrid climate, natural ventilation is needed for all buildings. Sunshades, long eaves, trelliswork, patios, verandas, atriums, arcades, multi-layered roofs, pavilions, water scenes and vegetation are indispensable elements throughout history. Before the 1980s, Southeast Asian architecture carried the mission of restoring national identity, and many public constructions were their manifesto of independence. Indigenous elements were lavishly applied in architecture. However, the eagerness to explore or reestablish a local architectural language inevitably resulted in a pastiche or collage of architectural elements, and eclecticism in mixed styles.

Thai architect Sumer Jumsai criticized the mistake that the Thai government had made decades ago by giving out a set of formulae for architecture, such as certain styles of traditional roofs, with the purpose of rebuilding the national identity of Thailand. Sumer Jumsai pointed out that bringing political force into architecture not only results in social disquiet but also kills real traditional Thai architecture. In Java, the bureaucratic intervention and the champion of a group of nationalist architects did not bring traditional Indonesian architecture back to life from oblivion until another group of architects advocated to look ahead instead of indulging in the past.

In the 1960s and the 1970s, reinforced concrete was commonly used in Southeast Asia, even for sunshades and other additive structures. After the 1980s, metal structures, glass screens and membranes that symbolized high-tech were applied as propaganda of modernization. During this

The area is characterized by the sometimes conflictive coexistence between the different religions (Buddhism, Islamism, Catholicism) and the political and economic regimes (Laos, Vietnam, Cambodia and Myanmar belonged to the Soviet bloc, whereas Thailand, Malaysia, Indonesia and Philippines have been under a market economy for a long time), as well as by a colonial past that has not always been adequately solved.

View of the Phnom Penh Central Market, Cambodia

time, urbanization and the population in cities grew fast, and issues about urban sprawl also emerged in fast thriving metropolises including Bangkok, Kuala Lumpur, Jakarta and Manila.

Recently, wood, bamboo and bricks, among other traditional materials, are staged again as green architecture is supported by more and more people. And also because vernacular architecture, once taken as a way to resist colonialism or globalization, became better integrated into modern architecture thanks to the efforts of many architects over the course of past two decades.

In *Tropical Response: Contemporary Regional Architecture of Southeast Asia,* Chinese researcher Xie Jien-Hwa pointed out that, due to the practical need of traditional building elements in tropical areas, the fundamental logic in architecture has been accidentally preserved. Malaysian architect Ken Yeang also contends that climate is the most constant factor for architecture, thus: "While socio-economic and political conditions may change almost unrecognizably over a period of, say, one hundred years, as may visual taste and aesthetic sensibility, climate remains more or less unchanged in its cyclical course.

History shows us that, with accumulated human experience and imagination, the architecture of the shelter evolved into diverse solutions to meet the challenges of widely varying climates, indicating that the ancients recognized regional climatic adaptation as an essential principle of architecture. In this regard, the climatically responsive building can be seen as having a closer fit with its geographical context." Because of the tropical climate, architectural traditions in Southeast Asia have survived imperialism. The question therefore is: Can they outlive globalization in urban growth regarding spatial logic?

Mosque surrounded by skyscrapers in Jakarta, Indonesia

Atlas: Asia and Pacific

Nicoletti Associati & H. Kasturi, Sustainable Towers in Putrajaya, Malaysia

The debate about the cultural identity of the countries in the area has become more intense due to the inrush of globalization. As a consequence, local practitioners strive to maintain – and sometimes even to recover – vernacular materials and techniques, and to adapt their buildings to the social circumstances and the climate conditions. Some large studios, like A49 from Thailand, have also entered on the stage.

An Inorganic Urbanization

Most of the Southeast Asian countries are categorized as developing countries and one of the common things among these countries are the Export Processing Zones established since the 1960s. The 682-acre Cavite EPZ near Manila, for example, provides more than 50,000 jobs. Most of the jobs in EPZs are labors for assembly lines and most of them are young female workers from agricultural communities. In Malaysia, 85% of the workers in electronic factories are women. Better wages in EPZs lured girls to leave their hometowns in rural areas and settle down around the outskirts of metropolises, resulting in altered family structures and skewed urbanization. EPZs have helped generate significant foreign currencies for Southeast Asia over the past decades, and to repeat the successful experience, many industrial parks and special economic zones have been constructed to attract more international investment with incentives including favored taxation. These spaces separate working from other living functions such as leisure activities or social life for people working in the zones or parks. Furthermore, EPZs or industrial parks often accommodate highly polluting industries, so the environment is undermined and the living quality of their workers is worsened.

Lately, many high-tech industrial parks are planned for the purpose of upgrading research and development. For instance, a high-tech industrial park 30 kilometers from the city of Honai is combined with the new campus of Vietnam National University in order to stimulate cooperation between academy and enterprises. The Vietnam government has also promised to provide comprehensive infrastructure around this park to attract more international tenants.

Japanese scholar Kuwatsuka Kentaro has observed that, since the later half of the 1980s, a certain pattern of urbanization formed in Southeast Asia due to the global deployment of multinational corporations. Many multinational corporations set up their regional headquarters in city centers and their manufacturing bodies in the industrial parks nearby. Kuwatsuka calls such a phenomenon 'urbanization of direct foreign investment'.

It is not difficult to predict what will be happening in the following years if one looks into the experience of Silicon Valley in California and other industrial parks throughout the United States under overly aggressive policies for economic growth: despite excessive elevated expressways blocking the cityscape and dividing the urban spaces into fragments, surging prices of real estate around the parks expelled salary earners from the neighborhoods. They have no choice but to move out of the thriving towns and commute daily to where they work.

Indonesian architect Rivai Gaos thinks that Jakarta has suffered too much for excessive modernization. Following the footsteps of European and American cities, the urban forms of Jakarta are developing toward a converged, singular model for global economy, inevitably repeating the mistakes of European and American cities, including urban decay when economy hits downturns.

Environmental Problems

The overpowering postmodern phenomena all over the world and the prodigious use of symbolism since the 1980s have further provoked issues in regard to self-identity, regionalism and aesthetics that are required to contain the value of tradition as well as a contemporary lifestyle that is acceptable to the public.

The 'information economy' or 'knowledge economy' in the 1990s has reconfigured cities since they need sophisticated infrastructure to contain communication technology, the Multimedia Super Corridor in Kuala Lumpur is one example. Political or historical territories, once enhanced by the governments for stronger national identity, are blurred by the new pattern of economy. The ideas about cities have been reconceptualized – the states injected more resources in urban spaces so they will be able to play the game globally. Globalization has become a shared ideology in all Southeast Asian countries, and the imbalance between urban and rural areas has aggravated.

Architects of younger generations are convinced that globalization is unavoidable, and good architecture is obliged to characterize or reflect local culture through modern technology, concepts and styles.

Duangrit Bunnag, Costa Lanta resort, Krabi, Thailand (2005)

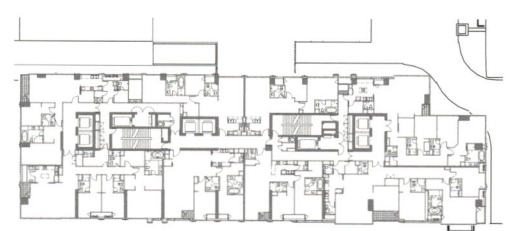

Architects49, Athénée Residence & Tower, Bangkok, Thailand (2007)

They have seen the consequences of overly westernized cities, the depressing homogeneity of the International Style and the impossibility of the dream plotted by Le Corbusier.

Contextualism, spatially and historically, has been emphasized both in practice and in architectural education. It helps rebuild the sense of place through reconnecting the present to the past, and nourishes diversity by juxtaposing contesting meanings. Younger architects turn that innate cultural relationship with the environment and that connection to the urban context into their ultimate goals in practice. In works of small scale, the brutalism of traditional architecture usually will be better carried out or transformed, but in high-rise buildings, the application of natural ventilation is still a challenge, and a uniform building technology still dominates the skylines.

On the other hand, the effort to remedy urban sprawl is to construct vertical cities, and sustainability of high-rise buildings is drawn out. For example, the Zero Energy Building sponsored by a Malaysian governmental agency is a more ambitious project following the successful Low Energy Office. In Indonesia, more techniques and materials for sustainable buildings have been developed after the devastating tsunami in 2004. In the Philippines, the Green Building Council promotes a green governmental policy together with architects and planners. Since 2003, the Association of Southeast Asian Nations (ASEAN) stages a series of conferences and workshops entitled 'Environmentally Sustainable Cities in ASEAN'. This event involves introducing advanced technology with the assistance of the United States Agency of International Development (USAID), to achieve the goals of 'clean air, clean water and clean land'.

The endeavors of building sustainably in Southeast Asian cities are remarkable. Currently, there are more than 235 million square feet of LEED-registered green

Vo Trong Nghia, Bar wNw, Binh Duong, Vietnam (2007)

building spaces in Southeast Asia. The Sustainable Towers located 30 kilometers south of Kuala Lumpur, designed by the Italian studio Nicoletti Associati and the local Malaysian architect Hijjas Kasturi, is highly credited for using alternative energy and reducing the emission of carbon dioxide into half compared to projects of the same scale.

Western architects and local architects trained in the West working together have brought tremendous influence to Southeast Asian architecture. Ken Yeang, a Malaysia-born architect, received his doctoral degree in the United Kingdom and pioneered the bioclimatic design for skyscrapers. Yeang also played a leading role in linking architecture to national identity in the early 1980s. Jimmy C.S. Lim, who studied architecture in Australia and practiced there before returning to Malaysia, is actively devoted to heritage preservation. The studio Architects 49 (A49) was founded in 1983 by Nithi Sthapitanonda, who is deemed as the guru of architecture in Thailand. Most of the works of Architects 49 are in Bangkok, and many of them are modernist high-rise buildings such as the Athénée Residence & Tower. A49 has ten affiliated firms and more than three hundred people

Atlas: Asia and Pacific 255

CPG Consultants, International Airport, Phu Quoc, Vietnam

Prominent western offices working in the area have specialized in two building types: the luxury resorts in beach areas, of which there are many due to the favorable climate conditions and to the vast extension of the coastline, and airports, large-scale infrastructures for transport whose form and image in some occasions pay tribute to the culture and the landscape of the countries where they are located.

teamed up with local or international clients. Quite a few eminent Thai architects had worked for Architects 49 before they established their own firms.

Younger architects have built up their visibility locally and internationally, too. Lisa Ros, a daughter of a Cambodian architect and his French wife, inherited her father's business and works on renovation projects in Siem Reap, where new developments are threatening the built heritage. Zenin Adrian from Indonesia and Duangrit Bunnag from Thailand commit themselves to reinterpreting living and housing in modern Southeast Asian cities without turning their back to the traditional legacy. Instead of studying what tropical architecture really is, Duangrit Bunnag's principles in design are based on "truth, context, ecological values and living through time". He has designed buildings that magically remained intact during the attacks of the tsunami, or steel structures with glass screens that do not need air conditioning at all.

Vo Trong Nighia, a Vietnamese architect who studied in Tokyo, has experimented building with local materials and with high technology to an extreme. The Ellipse Café in Ho Chi Minh City (old Saigon), exclusively built with bamboo, presents a unique poetry of wind and water (Feng Shui). The largest span of bamboo is 15 meters, constituting a light but stable structure. Vo Trong Nighia is the co-designer of the award-winning low-impact Greenfield University in Ho Chi Minh City. This building is well blended into the context of light, wind and water; furthermore, it allows teachers and students to interact on different occasions through free-flowing circulations.

Rooted in Southeast Asia, these architects understand the social, historical and cultural issues of local architecture by heart and have the perspective of 'world class' professionalism to aid them in fulfilling their purposes.

Surviving Globalization
Given the long coastline, sunny weather and the fast growth in urban centers of Southeast Asia, many western firms have seen the great potential for the development along the shores or in increasingly expensive downtowns. Large luxury resorts with exotic flavor and high-end villas are constructed with western capital as well as western design. The luxuriant YTL Residence, designed by Jouin Manku from Paris, was initiated by the Malaysian developer YTL Group in 2003 and completed in 2008. This 3,000 square meter house has nine bedrooms, a family library, a family chapel and twenty-one bathrooms. An outdoor pool accentuates the extravagance of this property. But western architectural firms set their eye not just on the advantages of waterfront resorts or high-profile housing: as they change the landscape, they are changed by the landscape as well. The Suvarnabhumi International Airport in Bangkok, by Murphy Jahn Architects, and the Soekarno-Hatta International Airport in Jakarta, by Paul Andreu, demonstrate the homage these noted architects have paid to the grandeur landscape and great culture. Australian architect Kerry Hill, who has practiced throughout Southeast Asia for more than thirty years, is no longer deemed as a foreign architect.

Nevertheless, harms done by globalization shouldn't be neglected. The damages to urban spaces resulting from capital speculation are devastating. During the 1980s, hot money from the West grasped the advantages of Southeast Asia, and as accumulation of wealth has always been taken as an achievement of modernization, Southeast Asian cities started large constructions in order to attract as much foreign investment as possible. Larger securities trading floors, higher office towers

Paul Andreu, Soekarno-Hatta International Airport, Jakarta, Indonesia (1985)

K. Kurokawa, Kuala Lumpur International Airport, Malaysia (1998)

and fancier shopping malls were erected at the price of demolished old streets and disappeared historical sites. Furthermore, as the illusion of wealth widened, the discrepancy between rich and poor grew, and social inequality was worsened.

In 1984, the first Asian Congress of Architects was held in Manila, focusing issues on Asian identity and cultural heritage. In the congress, Asian architects criticized the projects of foreign archtiects insensitive to local cultural and social value, and have brought negative impacts to Southeast Asian cities. Architect Leandro Locsin, from the hosting city, urged that the effort of modernization should be complemented by reaching back to the present in order to rediscover one's history and reaffirm the value of tradition.

In the late 1990s, the financial crisis sucked out a considerable portion of western capital, and the consequences were slums in marginalized urban areas, or cheaper labor exporting to neighboring countries. According to a statistic obtained in Balikpapan, Indonesia, in 2001, only 8% of poor households in urban areas maintained the job they had before the financial crisis.

The rapid growth in the 1980s and the early 1990s had sped up urban sprawl, leading to tough urban ailment since the beginning of the financial crisis in 1997. It was estimated that, in Southeast Asia, two years after the crisis, 35% of the urban population was living in poorly serviced communities on the outskirts of cities, where no drinkable water was available. Modernization with a capitalist perspective once again alienated people from their inherent assets, and Southeast Asia was at the crossroads again.

Broadened Sustainability
Globalization has facilitated spatial shift in Southeast Asian cities. Urban spaces have expanded and reshaped in a very short period of time to make room for 'investment friendly infrastructures'. Ports for international trade and logistics, tax free zones for exportation or intermediary trade, and Central Business Districts (CBDs) for financial services in Bangkok, Jakarta, Singapore or Manila were set up with national and international capital.

In the eye of transnational corporations, cities are the supplying nexuses of human resources, new technologies and systematic service. More and more people settled there to participate in the global race. Overgrown populations burdened urban spaces. Urban planners in Jakarta, a megacity of more than 10 million people, are facing day-to-day challenges in addressing the inadequate housing and insufficient infrastructure for people pouring in from rural areas.

In 1976, the Perumas Housing Project was initiated in Depok, southern Jakarta. Perumas was to provide 20,000 affordable housing units by transforming farm fields into residential lands. In the following decades, expressways connecting Depok and Jakarta were broadened and railways were constructed. The University of Indonesia was moved there from the overly cramped central Jakarta. Five hotels, four large shopping centers and more than sixty financial organizations stationed there. Depok has been reconfigured from a farm village into a satellite city of Jakarta; its density of population tripled, but living quality in this city has become polarized. Some people live in high-end communities, and others have stayed in the cheap units the government built thirty years ago.

In Malaysia, the thriving high-tech industries are mostly located around Kuala Lumpur, extending in all directions. New towns around the capital city such as Shah Alam and Bandar Baru Bangi rose and grew at an amazing speed. Kelang Valley in the southwest of the Kuala Lumpur is a heartland of industry and commerce. In 2004, the population of Kelang Valley was

Murphy Jahn Architects, Suvarnabhumi International Airport, Bangkok, Thailand (2005)

General view of downtown Jakarta, Indonesia

four million inhabitants; two years later, the number surged to 6.7 million. The successful development of industries lured a large number of migrants from other provinces within Malaysia and foreign workers largely from Indonesia, India, Bangladesh and Nepal. Many of the foreigners are inhabiting here illegally, in squatter slums.

In Vietnam, 300,000 people have moved to urban areas each year during the past decades, according to Ngo Trung Hai, deputy director of the Vienam Institute of Urban and Rural Planning. Ngo estimated that, in the next twenty years, 30% to 40% of the total 85 million Vietnamese people will be living in cities. Certainly, with such a huge urban population, more then one megacity will take shape. Currently the Vietnamese government is trying to transform the 700 ancient townships throughout Vietnam into satellite cities of major metropolises in order to address their inflating populations.

The reconfigurations of Jakarta, Kuala Lumpur and Vietnam were triggered, more or less, by the irresistible force of globalization. They enjoyed success in many aspects, but at considerable prices. Having gone through difficult times in history, Southeast Asian countries began to realize that sustainability does not merely mean low energy consumption or less emission of carbon dioxide. A city must face and deal with all the historical, cultural, economic and social issues so that it can sustain itself.

In recent years, issues regarding sustainable cities include housing, sanitation, public health, public transportation, crime prevention, employment, abolishment of social segregation, historical heritage preservation and greeneries among many others. The construction of a city is not to satisfy the needs or conditions of global competition, but of the people living within. To Asia, modernity doesn't mean a destination led by a small group of elites, but the commonly accepted self-definition.

The Creative Industry of Heritage
The 21st century turned a new page for Southeast Asia, which stood up with a deeper self-awareness. Breaking away from the vanity of wealth or progress that had been ushered in by capitalism, these countries have begun to strive for their own democracy, their own definition of well-being, their own styles of architecture and their own geographic balance between urban and rural development.

After a bitter lesson, the development of Southeast Asia is toward more self-fulfilling goals. The failure of the world financial system and the consequential social malady drove Southeast Asian cities to look into the assets they have inherited. And as the 'creative industry' became a passage toward a more humanistic urban renewal and a stimulus for struggling economies throughout the world, cultural tourism along with various creative products are expected to help cities recuperate from recession.

In April 2009, Jakarta governor Fauzi Bowo launched a master plan for the Kota Tua Jakarta (Jakarta Old Town), after eight failed redevelopment proposals since 1991. Fauzi Bowo himself is an urban planner and has participated in the restoration of historical buildings in Kota Tua in 1971. But all the efforts before were partially successful at best. Urban renewal rarely can be achieved through the unilateral ideas of the government. In order to not repeat the earlier mistakes, the new master plan is an outcome of broadened public participation. In addition to fixing all the current problems in Kuta Tua, including the crazy traffic load, governor Fauzi Bowo intends to introduce creative industry to the old town. He has

View of the Petronas Towers from Meanara Tower, Kuala Lumpur, Malaysia

258 Atlas: Asia and Pacific

After being able to weigh up the pros and cons of having left their territories in the hands of foreign companies in order to establish the location of intensive industrial use areas, the countries of Southeast Asia face the 21st century with more fulfilling goals of their own. The social inequality in the cities is counteracted with urban renewal projects that also aim to stimulate cultural tourism and to boost the economy.

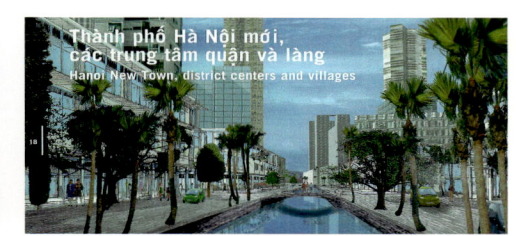

OMA, Master Plan for a new city, Hanoi, Vietnam (1997)

cinematography, fashion and publishing businesses in his mind.

In Malaysia, the Brickfields area in central Kuala Lumpur is also called Little India because of the significant population of Indian residents. It is one of the oldest settlements in Kuala Lumpur and has been the most popular spot for tourists, but it was notorious for its high crime rate. As early as 1997, a large scale makeover radiating from the Kuala Lumpur Central Station kicked off, based on the proposal of the Japanese architect Kisho Kurokawa. This ambitious project is to regenerate the old parts of the city, including the warehouses and locomotive maintaining yards by the station. The government also aims to integrate historical buildings such as the National Museum, Lake Gardens, the Planetarium, the National Mosque and the National Art Gallery into new developments that consist of hotels, retail centers, condominiums and auditoriums. This renewal project is expected to be accomplished by 2015.

In Myanmar, the ancient town of Mandalay was bombed during World War II and isolated during the Cold War. When the socialist regime broke down, the military government began constructing hotels, residential buildings and shopping centers with the investment of Chinese immigrants. Chinese festivities have been included in the local calendar now. The Mandalay Palace and an adjoining monastery of wood structure were destroyed during World War II. It is said that the government used hard labor to accomplish the renovation of the palace.

The above examples are merely combinations of historical heritage and cultural events or creative industry. There are also cities setting the goal to be creative cities. The fourth largest Indonesian city, Bandung, has demonstrated impressive achievements. The Bandung government set up a developing strategy titled 'Greater Bandung 2020: Friendly and Smart'. It aims

View of the Manila Bay skyline, Philippines

to build a safe, healthy, religious city with efficient, high-quality infrastructures. In order to accommodate cultural events and a cultural industry, the streets in Bandung have been remodeled to yield spaces for businesses. The Dago Area has been transformed from a residential area into a commercial area. But the city government does not wish to ruin the carefree ambiance by bringing businesses; every Saturday night, street musicians will attract many young people to enjoy their performances. In addition to accommodating more businesses, urban planners reflect upon how to encourage people in this city to be more imaginative and more productive. The boom of very affordable internet kiosks and cafés helps inspire thinking, especially among students. Art galleries, theaters or studios operated by artists themselves make Bandung a hot spot for artist gatherings. Art events usually are supported by communities, becoming a part of daily life of the public. The friendly and smart Bandung is not only a creative city, it is also the most livable city. The successful experience of Bandung has encouraged many rising cities in Asia to revitalize their cultural assets; Cebu in the Philippines is one of them. More and more rising cities in Southeast Asia have found their own pattern of development, and the common traits are the small scale, the creative, the environment-friendly and the autonomous.

A Path of One's Own
The Javanese medical doctor Raden Soetomo said in his autobiographic book that when he studied at a Dutch-language primary school in Bangil, he was always ashamed of being a Javanese. Until one day he realized he was not inferior to any one of his classmates because he was able to solve tough algebra questions. From that time on, he perceived his own capacity and stopped copying his classmates. Dr. Soetomo was a nationalist movement leader in the 1920s, and was deemed as the most influential figure in Indonesian history. Southeast Asian cities are not inferior to any other city in the world and should stop copying others. The transformation is still happening, and they should take their own path.

Kerry Hill
The Chedi Hotel
Chiang Mai (Thailand)

Client
Natural Park Company
Architect
Kerry Hill
Collaborators
Justin Hill, Marc Webb, Yvette Adams, Karen Lim, Patrick Kosky, Simon Cundy
Consultants
Page Kirkland (project management); Meinhardt (engineering); Page Kirkland (quantity surveyor); Tierra Design (landscape); Lighting Planners (lighting)
Contractor
Ritta
Photos
Richard Powers

THE HOTEL SITS on the banks of the Mae Ping River, in northern Thailand, and is the result of a rehabilitation and enlargement operation done on the former British Consulate in Chiang Mai. The design intent of the hotel, which features 84 rooms, a spa, and a restaurant, is to combine its urban location with the atmosphere of a vacation resort, all the while embracing and giving the old compound, which dates back to the 1920s, a pride of place.

Central to the scheme is the dialogue between the old consular building, where the hotel lobby is centered, and the new constructions, which are arranged around a central courtyard. Standing out among these new structures is the four-story volume containing the hotel rooms, an L-shape that turns its back on the city so that all the rooms look over the courtyard and on to the river beyond. Within the large courtyard are the spa and the swimming pool, both of which are designed to create a series of spaces that change in character as one moves through them to get to the riverside pier.

The block containing the hotel guestrooms is set apart from the edge of the lot by corridors that serve to buffer them from the road. These passageways are covered so that they are protected against rain, but their latticework facade made of wooden strips allows for natural cross ventilation in the rooms, entry into which is through a light-filled private court. Through large translucent glass surfaces, the light also filters into the bathrooms, which are presided by free-standing bathtubs and connect with the bedrooms through sliding screens.

All the guestroom balconies face the river and are lined with teakwood panels. Their being set inward with respect to the facade line protects the interior from excessive sunning, besides throwing an expressive shadow that prolongs in the window sills. The timber details are abstracted from traditional Thai houses, thereby connecting the project to national culture.

The use of local materials and ancestral techniques in the interiors, such as dark wooden floors, hand-made red wall tiles, terrazzo plinths, teak and rattan furniture, and items like paper and metal fittings evoking the parasols and lanterns typical of the place all help to root the building in the existing rich heritage. All these details extracted from tradition are nevertheless strongly contemporary, devoid of ornament. The effect is one of calm refuge.

Sitting on the banks of the Mae Ping River, the hotel addresses its urban location without losing out on its vacation atmosphere. At its center is a courtyard with a spa and a pool, on to which all the rooms look.

Central to the scheme is the establishment of a dialogue between the rehabilitated former consulate building and the pavilions containing the hotel guestrooms. For this to happen, the new constructions adopt materials and details extracted from local architectural tradition, such as the teakwood balconies that adjoin the rooms, which are shielded from excessive sunning by being set inward from the facade's surface.

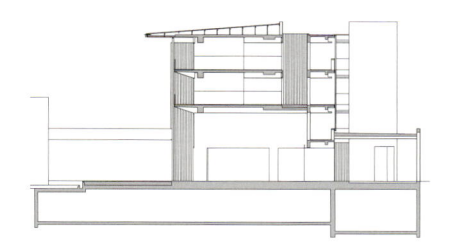

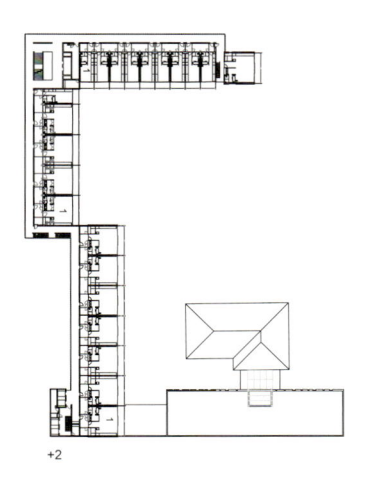

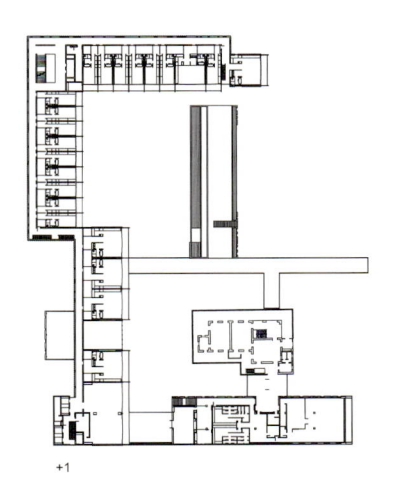

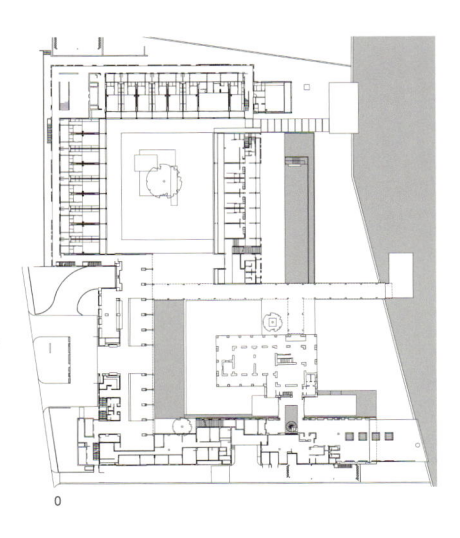

Atlas: Asia and Pacific

Vo Trong Nghia
Wind and Water Café
Ho Chi Minh City (Vietnam)

Client
VNLL Corporation
Architect
Vo Trong Nghia
Collaborators
Nguyen Hoa Hiep, Ohara Hisanori
Photos
Hoai Trang

ADAPTED TO THE tropical climate of Southeast Asia, this café in Ho Chi Minh City, formerly Saigon, is a pergola of bamboo trunks that has techniques of cooling through evaporation, as well as principles of aerodynamics, built into it. A comprehensive strategy for passive ventilation makes the building itself a natural air conditioning system based on three elements: the roof, a sheet of water with a depth of only 15 centimeters, and the space in between.

Besides providing shade, an essential shield against the Vietnamese sun, the huge roof is designed in V shapes to draw in winds from outside. The trapped air moves over the pool of water, is cooled by it, and spreads through the rest of the covered premises, refreshing the café space.

The frame of the pergola is basically set up with bamboo stalks, although the structural limitations of this light material made it necessary to reinforce the construction with metal elements, whether cross-shaped profiles concealed inside four bamboo trunks or braces exposed to view. With the exception of the plates of the finishes, all the materials that were utilized to construct the roof are natural: strips of rattan, fibers of *nipa* (an Asiatic palm tree), and of course stalks of bamboo. The furniture and the light fixtures are likewise made of this flexible material.

Bamboo is low-cost, abundant, and fast-growing. Since it disintegrates, it is an ecological construction material. Moreover, it lends itself to the building of contemporary architectural spaces that are close to nature, to tradition, as well as to local color. Here bamboo was also made to be energy-saving, as much in the course of construction as in the subsequent operation and maintenance of the café, by eliminating the need to invest on artificial air conditioning. This and its own low price helped make for a total building cost of only 58.430 euros.

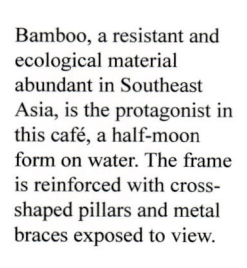

Bamboo, a resistant and ecological material abundant in Southeast Asia, is the protagonist in this café, a half-moon form on water. The frame is reinforced with cross-shaped pillars and metal braces exposed to view.

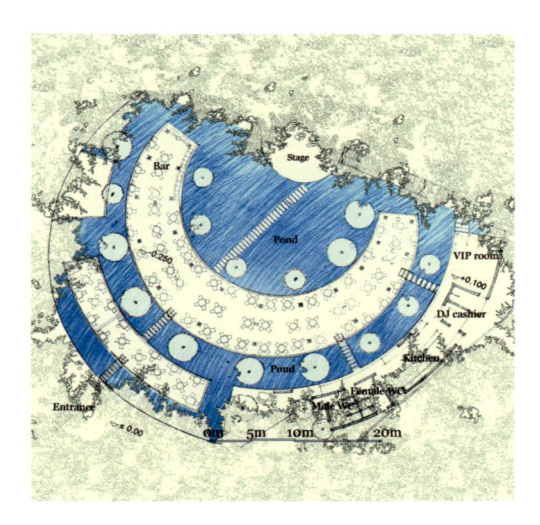

The project pays special attention to the matter of energy saving. Artificial air conditioning methods were hence done away with in favor of cooling systems based on the evaporation process and aerodynamics. Besides providing efficient protection against excessive solar exposure, the bamboo roof works to trap air currents, which cool up the interior space of the café when they come in contact with the pool of water.

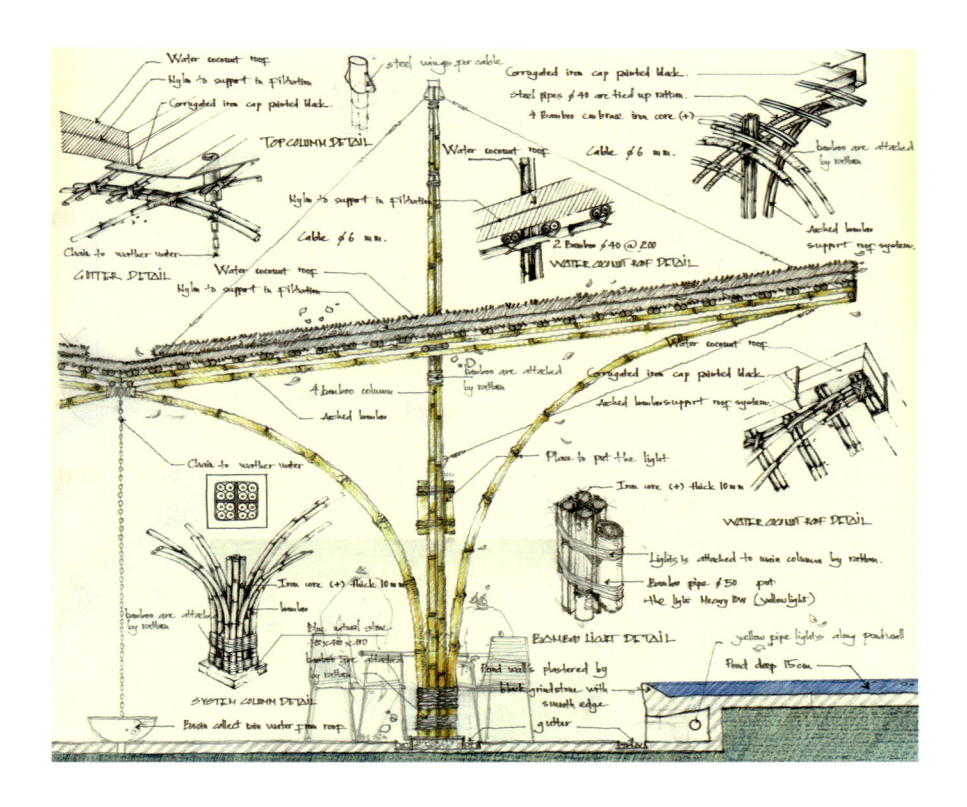

Atlas: Asia and Pacific 263

Norman Foster
Petronas University
Bandar Seri Iskandar (Malaysia)

Client
Universiti Teknologi Petronas
Architects
Foster & Partners;
GDP Architects (collaborating architects)
Collaborators
Norman Foster, David Nelson, Andy Miller, Jonathan Parr, Tom Politowicz, Brian Timmoney, Jake Atcheson, Toby Blunt, Marc Buchmann, Alan Chan, Tina Che, Ben Dobbin, Brynley Dyer, Michael Greville, Fleur Hutchings, Hannah Lehmann, Tony Miki, Clive Powell, Richard Scott-Wilson, Michael Sehmsdorf, Danny Shaw, Jonathan Shaw, Marilu Sicoli, Robin Snowden, Daniel Statham, Peter Stuck, Michael Wurzel, Edson Yabiku
Consultants
Ranhill Bersekutu, Wimsa HSS Integrated, Majid & Associates (structural engineering); Roger Preston & Partners, Majutek Perunding (mechanical and electrical), Research Facilities Design (laboratory consultants); Sandy Brown Associates, Marshall Day Acoustics (acoustics); BDG McColl (signage); Jurukur Bahan Malaysia/KPK (quantity surveyors); KLCC Projeks (project managers); Shah P K & Associates (landscape); Vision Design Studio, Lightsource (lighting)
Photos
Nigel Young; K L Ng (p. 265); Hamed Saiedi (p. 266)

FOUNDED AT THE instigation of the Malaysian government and funded by the oil company Petronas, the Universiti Teknologi Petronas (UTP) is the region's largest center for the study of civil, mechanical, chemical, and electrical engineering. Located in the new town of Bander Seri Iskandar, 300 kilometers north of Kuala Lumpur, the 450 hectare campus with room for 6,600 students responds to the site's naturally heterogeneous landscape of hills, woods, dunes, and man-made lakes formed by flooding disused tin mines.

To minimize interference with the natural, varied topography, particularly the jungle park situated at the center, the main academic buildings containing classrooms and research facilities, rising four stories, are organized around the base of the site's hills in groups of four or five rectangles that are not set parallelly, but in a way that their short sides trace curves. The curves closest to the park are then given a huge continuous canopy made of insulated metal decking and supported by slender tubular steel columns. The result is a five-pointed star formed by five semi-circles.

In response to the climate patterns of this part of the Malay Peninsula, where the monsoon season brings a merciless alternation of seething sun and torrential rain, the five canopies provide protection against glare, heat, and downpour for students and professors rushing from class to class along the pedestrian routes, as well as for the buildings themselves, the tips of which are tucked beneath their outer edges. They are pierced with rooflights and louvers that let daylight filter through the interiors of the buildings.

Four of the canopy intersections mark the entrances to student housing and 'pockets' of communal premises like cafés and shops as well as lecture theaters and a range of student support facilities. At the fifth node, by the campus's main entrance, is the drum-like chancellor complex, the university's principal social hub. Rising 21 meters and around 150 meters in diameter, it comprises two crescent-shaped halves connected by a public plaza. One half of it houses the university library and resource center. The other half contains a 3,000-seat multi-purpose auditorium.

The construction technology took account of the capabilities of local contractors. The chancellor complex is built with reinforced concrete slabs supported on steel columns. The academic buildings are predominantly flat-slab pre-stressed concrete and modularized bays sustained by reinforced concrete columns.

The environmental richness of the place where the university campus is situated suggested a layout that was disperse, not dense, so that the natural flora of the region would colonize the spaces between academic buildings. To help students and professors move around, a huge protective metal canopy was conceived. Its iconic shape, a five-pointed star, created a central void occupied by a forest park.

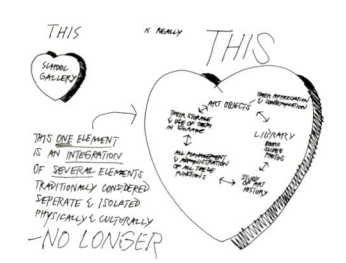

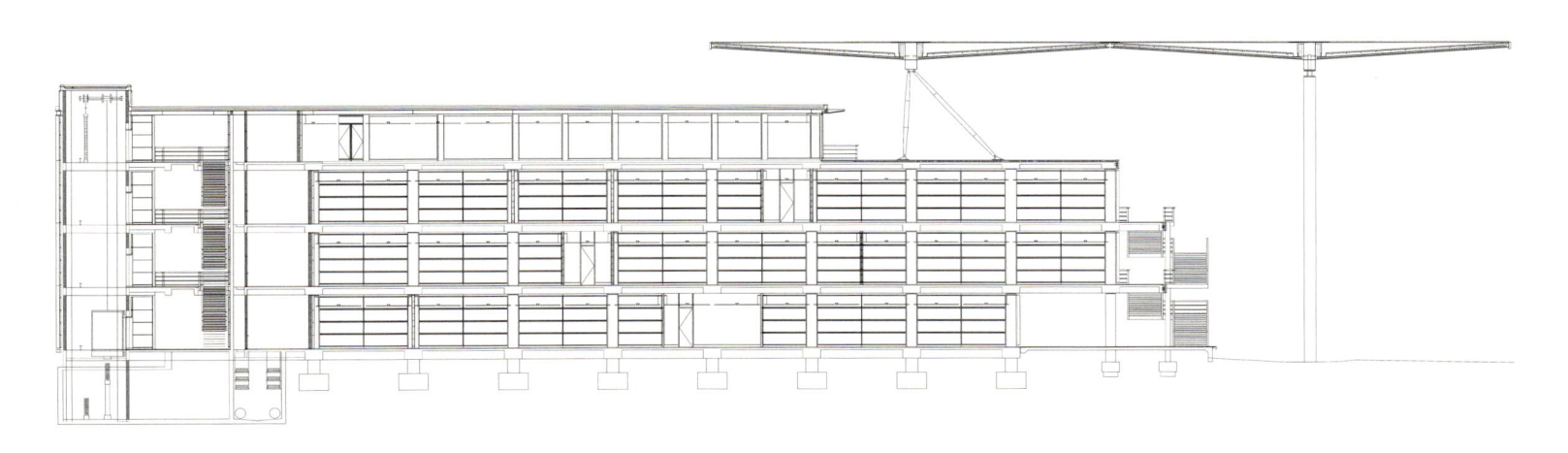

Atlas: Asia and Pacific 265

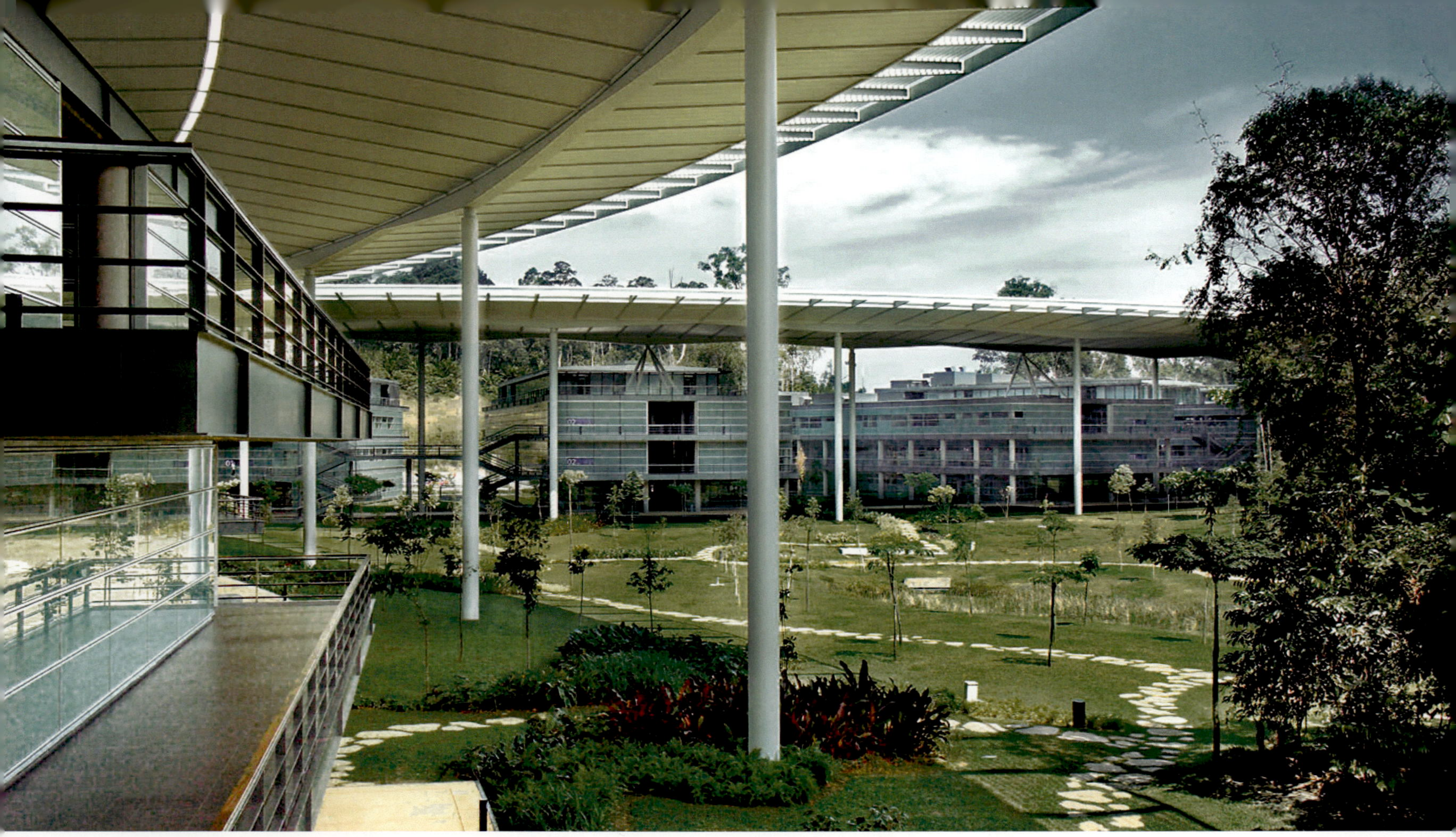

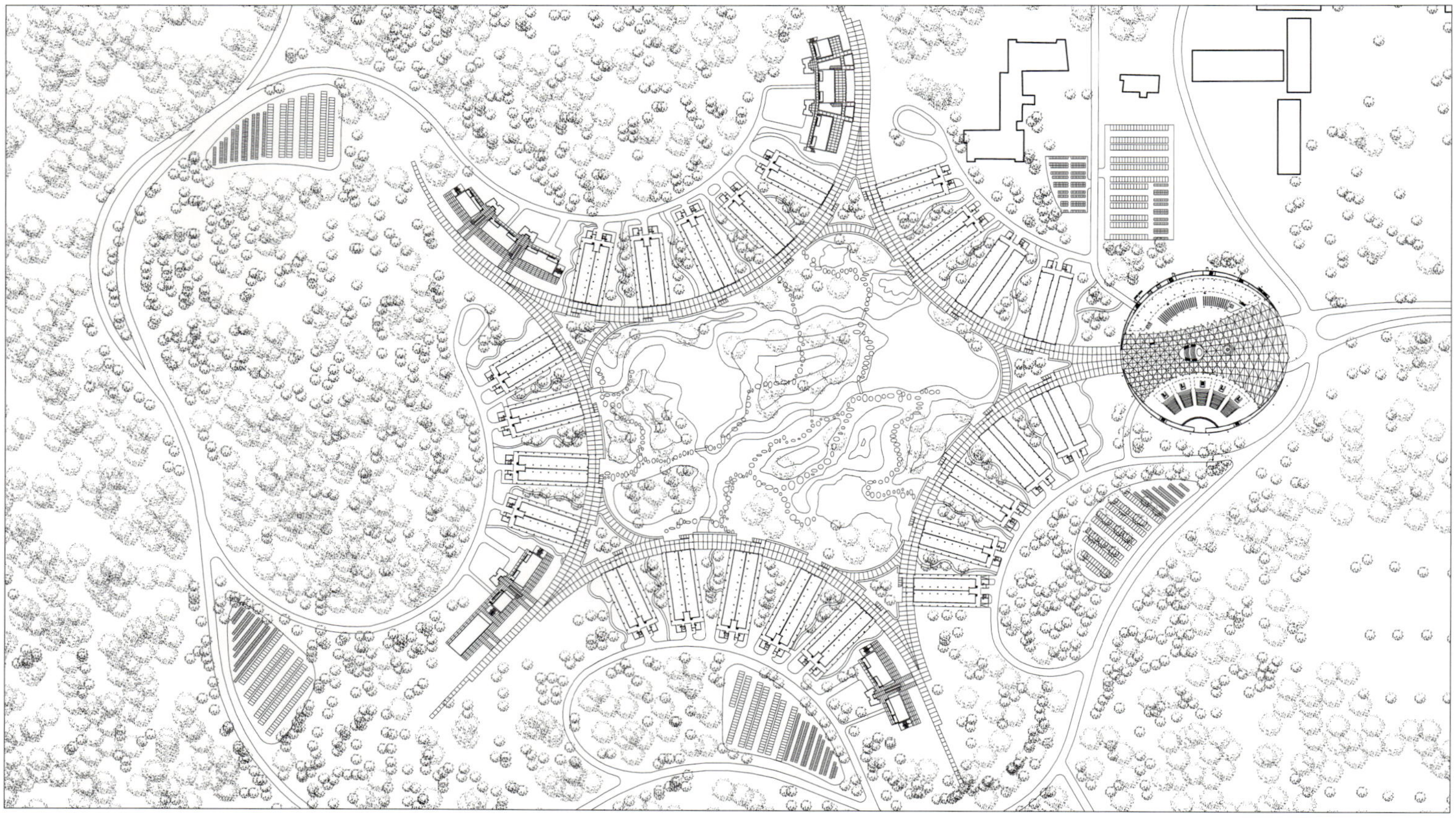

Four of the canopy's intersections mark the entrances to the student residences and to the communal services of the campus. The chancellor complex at the fifth corner, close to the main access to the premises, is a drum-like volume with a 150-meter diameter that contains the university library and an auditorium for 3,000 spectators. In between these two programs is a large covered square that serves as a social hub.

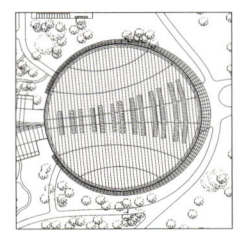

OMA/Rem Koolhaas & Ole Scheeren
Mahanakhon Tower
Bangkok (Thailand)

Client
PACE Development
Architect
OMA: Rem Koolhaas & Ole Scheeren
Collaborators
Eric Chang (associate), Tim Archambault (project manager), Giannantionio Bongiorno, Sirichai Bunchua, Sean Hoo Ch'ng, Darren Chang, Steven Y.N. Chen, Dan Cheong, Ryan Choe, Timothy Clark, Mitesh Dixit, Paola Mongiu, Joseph Tang, Shuo Wang, Xinyuan Wang (team); Chen Chen, Harvey Chung, Charles Curran, Jasmin Delic, Minqi Gu, Jerome Haferd, Zachary Heineman, Pengfei Liu, Anya Yan, Lichen Zhu (support)
Consultants
PACE (executive architect); Arup (structure, services and vertical transportation); Front (facade); Isometrix (lighting); Husband (retail consultant); PPS (project management); CPI (seismic/wind engineering testing); 2x4, JWT (brand development and graphic design); The Ritz-Carlton Residences (residences), Bangkok Edition Hotel by Marriott International in collaboration with Ian Schrager (hotel); OMA, Seventh Art, Crystal CG (computer renderings); Frans Parthesius (architectural model photography)

A VISIONARY NEW 77-story high-rise located on a 1.5 hectare site in the heart of Bangkok's Central Business District, this will be one of the most ambitious projects of contemporary architecture and urbanism to be carried out in Thailand, as well as Bangkok's tallest building. The over 150,000 square meter development will consist of Mahanakhon Square, a dramatic outdoor landscaped public plaza; Mahanakhon Terraces, a 10,000 square meter upscale retail center with lush gardens and decks spread over multiple levels for restaurants, cafés, and a 24-hour marketplace; The Ritz-Carlton Residences, with all 200 apartment units offering the atmosphere of a skybox penthouse; The Bangkok Edition, a signature hotel with 150 rooms; and a multi-level rooftop Sky Bar and restaurant.

With its sculptural appearance, Mahanakhon has been carved to introduce a three-dimensional ribbon of 'pixels' that circles the building's full height, as if excavating portions of the glass curtain wall to reveal the inner life of the building. The design dismantles the typical tower and podium typology, creating not a monolith in isolation, but a skyscraper that melds with the city by gradually 'dissolving' the architecture as it flows downward to meet the ground and upward to reach the sky. This is achieved through a series of generous cascading terraces at The Hill - the area of the building's base, housing the luxury retail center -, where the architecture is articulated to evoke the shifting protrusions of a mountain landscape.

The complex also features an adjacent free-standing seven-floor building known as The Cube, with multi-level terraces corresponding to those of Hill Terraces across the expanse of an outdoor atrium. Mahanakhon Square, located in front of the tower, is also intimately connected to the space between The Hill and the Cube. This dynamic public plaza will be a landscaped retreat for the city's inhabitants and a special venue for cultural and social interactivity, with direct connections to the Chongnonsi Skytrain station and a future rapid bus transit system; in sum, an urban oasis providing refuge from the intense daily clamor of greater Bangkok while offering constant easy access for reconnection to it.

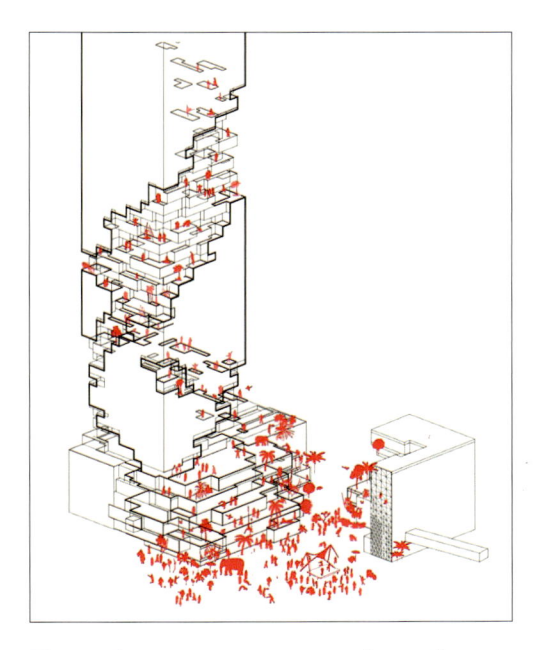

The new skyscraper, rising 77 floors, is circled by a spiral of excavated 'pixels' that make it possible to integrate the base of the structure into the fabric of the city. This 'dissolved' form has the effect of generating a system of terraced spaces that melt with the square situated at the entrance, forming a protected public zone across which stands a lower building known as the Cube, whose facade reproduces the voids of the tower.

Kazuhiro Kojima
New HUA Campus
Ho Chi Minh City (Vietnam)

Client
Ho Chi Minh University of Architecture
Architects
Kazuhiro Kojima
Collaborators
Daisuke Sanuki, Vo Trong Nghia
(associate architects)
Consultants
Oak Structural Design (structures)

The project breaks up the program into small blocks as a way of adapting to the topography of the place and including the numerous streams of the Mekong River Delta, which then help to cool up the complex.

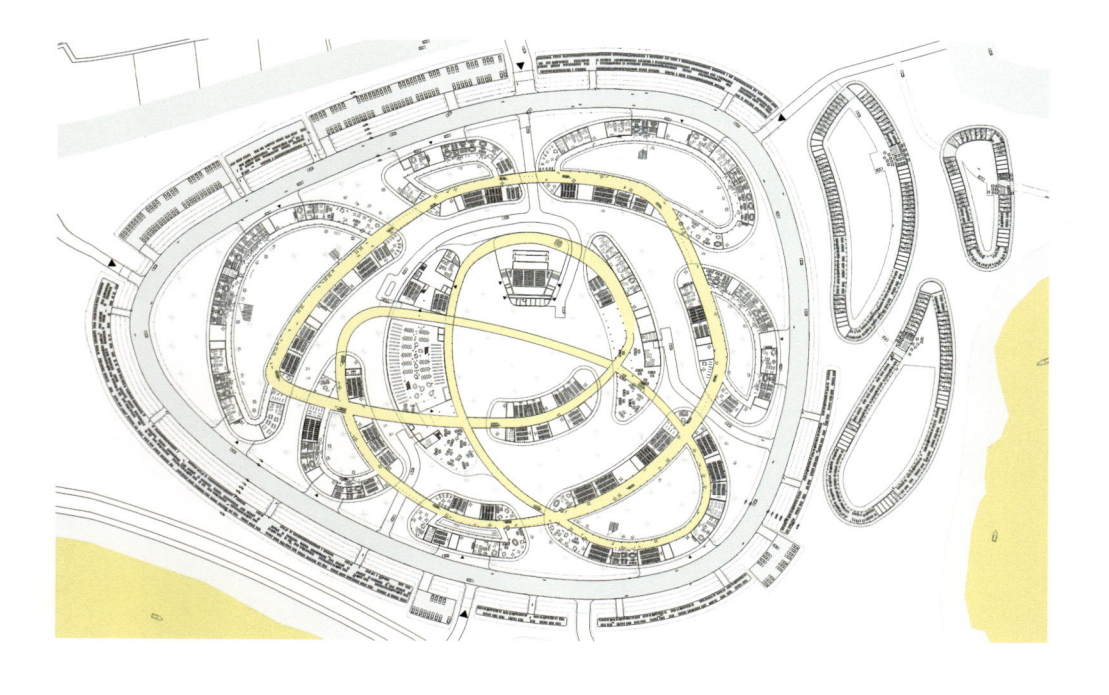

THE SEAT OF VIETNAM'S leading architecture university, HUA, located in the center of populous Ho Chi Minh City, has become too tight for its 6,000 and growing number of students. Hence this proposal for a new campus on the outskirts of what used to be Saigon, specifically on an island in the Mekong River Delta. The site abounds in tropical flora and fauna and in mangroves and streams that invariably overflow during the rainy season.

This project, winner of a competition, does not interfere with this primeval order of things. The campus just slips into it. In a clear low-impact and low-energy statement, the river's affluents go about coursing around and through the buildings. The natural cooling obtained in this way is reinforced by the shade provided by trees looming over the loops of the roofs connecting the university's different departments, facilities, and residences, and by the arrangement and orientation of the buildings, a result of simulations that were made with a Computational Fluid Dynamics program. To come up with a design addressing the needs and sensitivies of both nature and people, through CFD it was possible to analyze wind movements as well as the flow of student activity.

Within a ring road set high against seasonal floods, the university buildings lie low and sprawl out to minimize bulldozing where nature is unstable and biodiversity-rich. They will be constructed by local workers using a time-honored method: brick-filled concrete frames finished with a facade of porous, ventilation-enhancing, and daylight-welcoming organic materials like bamboo or mangrove timber. The facades have louvers on the outside and jalousie windows on the inside. The multi-use, changeable spaces like classrooms and study zones line the building peripheries, while laboratories and other specialized functions are pushed to the cores.

The buildings that make up the university campus are connected by a huge loop-shaped corridor, around which shade-providing trees emerge. The positions of the blocks were determined with the help of CFD (Computational Fluid Dynamics). This software program made it possible to analyze and optimize the flows of student activity, thereby addressing the needs of the surrounding nature and the complex's users.

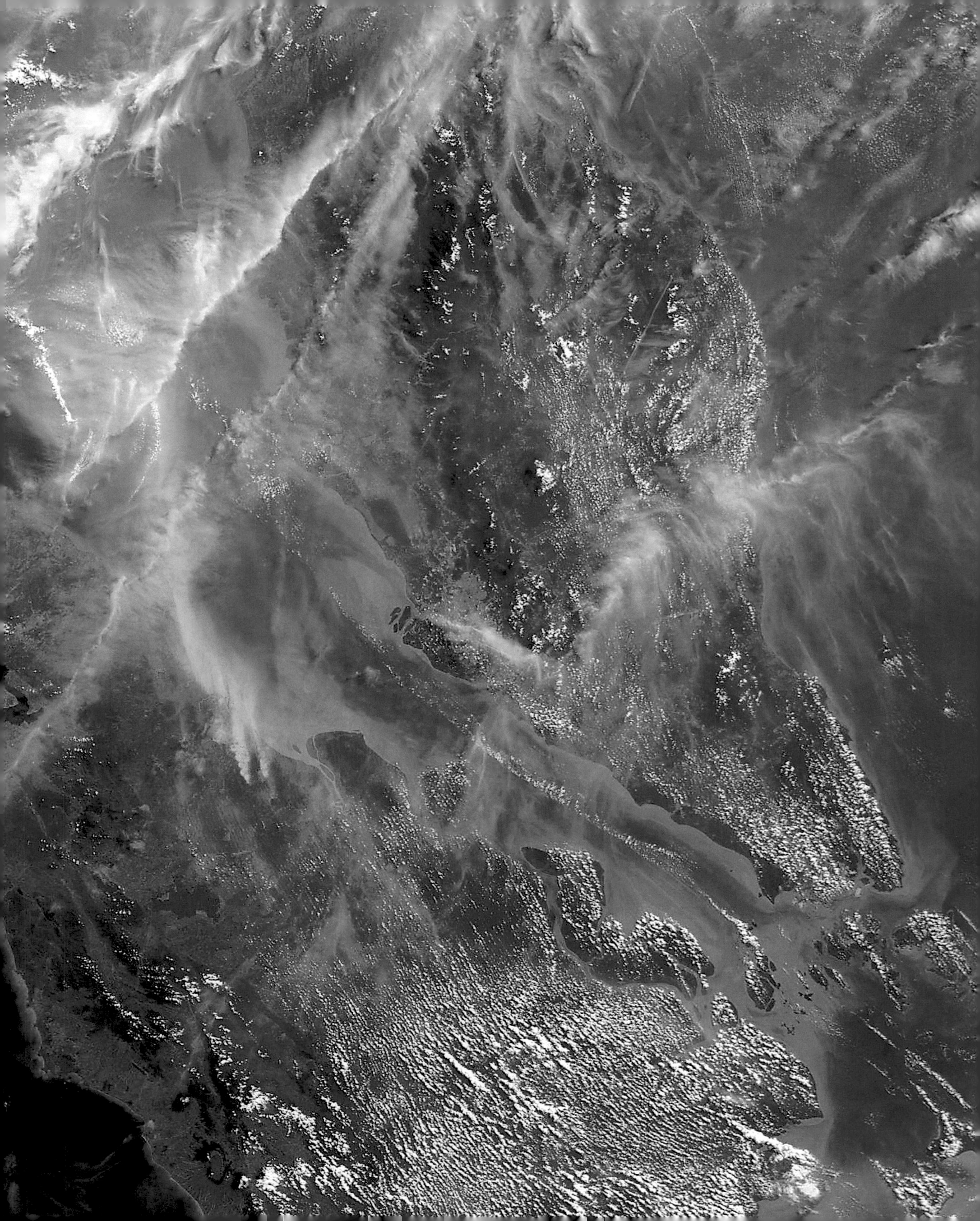

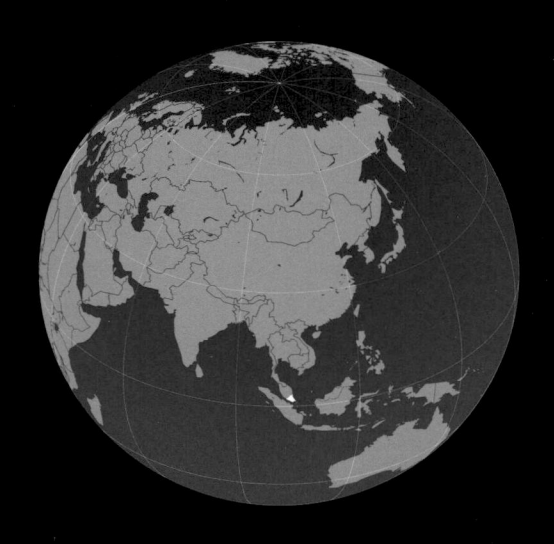

Singapore

The smallest country of Southeast Asia is an efflorescent city-state with one of the highest per capita income rates in the world, thanks to a service-based economy, to the highly-skilled labor force and to its advantageous location in the world's main sea lanes. The accelerated modernization of the country has been perhaps inevitably associated to an increasing environmental awareness, as can be seen in the projects selected here: the local studio WOHA recovers and updates the traditional ventilation systems in an upscale apartment tower; the British team Grant brings together the natural and the technological world in a master plan, proposing an exuberant landscape design as the background for a future business center; and the New York architect Daniel Libeskind is building in the historic port of Keppel a residential complex that combines waving skyscrapers and compact blocks of smaller size to adapt better to the demanding tropical climate.

Peter Rowe
Tropical Excellence
Singapore, towards a Vibrating and Livable City

Formula One Circuit and Singapore Flyer Ferris Wheel at Marina Bay

Based on a strict state planning, the growth of the booming city-state has meant the occupation of new territories while social control is reduced.

An old British colony and independent republic since 1965, Singapore has shifted from a manufacturing-based industry to an economy centered on financial services, logistics, commerce and tourism.

TODAY, THE Republic of Singapore finds itself well along a path of transition from being a 'development state', with a relatively narrowly yet well-orchestrated production orientation, to a 'competition state', capitalizing on a broader range of global transactions and supply-side investments to increase its advantage. Depending upon the dimensions under observation, this transition became perceptible around 1990, with the changing of the guard from the 'old' to the 'new' generation within the still very dominant founding political regime of the People's Action Party, and certainly at an accelerated rate since the turn into the new millennium. It has ushered in a more relaxed social and political climate, although remaining relatively restrictive in the latter regard, along with perceived needs for change to better accommodate rising affluence and concomitant demands of citizens, a necessary shift from manufacturing to knowledge-based industries, continued attraction of foreign investment and retention of a more highly-skilled labor force, expansion of leisure-time opportunities, and more concerted environmental conservation. Prior to this transition, the young independent state had pursued a path of industrial modernization, supported by collective consumption and the ever advantageous location of Singapore in the world's sea lanes. Having emerged reluctantly through rejection from the Malay Federation in 1965 – an outcome of Britain's dissolution of its colonial possessions – Singapore's new leadership, along with its majority, ethnically-Chinese citizenry, had to confront a nation building process against a background of declining trade, rising unemployment, massive immigration, appalling living conditions for many, and deteriorated infrastructure. Insisting upon the benefits of meritocracy, a clean bureaucracy, self reliance and a skilled and industrious labor force, the government then proceeded to play a very strong role in guiding and promoting economic development; providing public housing in support, among other things, of lower labor costs; and building infrastructure, notably to provide attractive, readily-occupiable facilities for foreign enterprises, as well as enhancing accessibility to employment for workers.

Supporting this heavily 'top-down' process was a master-planning exercise, that stretched back into the closing moments of the colonial period and with United Nation's assistance, resulting in the Ring Concept Plan of 1971. Beginning earnest development in 1965 under an ad-hoc government committee, this plan set forth a blue-print for future urbanization that proved to be enduring. Among other aspects, it can be characterized by designation of intensive development along the southern edge of the island with industrial locations especially to the west and concentration of business and government around the central city core. Transportation corridors inscribed a loop around environmental conservation areas in the center of the island, providing ready access to sites along its length for satellite urban communities, including housing – the Housing Development Board Estates – as well as for commercial and light industrial employment. The Urban Redevelopment Authority was established in 1974 under the Housing Development Board – one of two superboards alongside the Economic Development Board – to take a primary role in planning, guiding, and managing deployment of the plan. Later, in 1985, the economy went into recession for the first time since 1960, attributed to a loss of competitive edge under rising labor costs, as well as an over commitment of resources to aspects of collective consumption like housing. By 1991, with the further wake-up call of declining electoral popularity in the ruling party, as well as a population, now numbering around 4.5 million inhabitants, outstripping targets of the 1971 plan, a revision was made. Essentially, it broadened the aims of the island's master plan and

Night view of Marina Bay, with Singapore's downtown in the background

re-jiggered its priorities for future development. Among these aspects were opportunities for higher degrees of diversity in living environments, more intense use of marginal and newly-reclaimed lands, as well as a 'green-blue' overlay in the interests of further environmental conservation and protection. The master plan, approved in 2003, incorporated these revisions and further aimed to foster urbanization towards Singapore's current stance as a 'competition state'. The inevitable sloganeering that has accompanied this transition has variously included the combining of global and local ambitions into 'Glocal', labeling Singapore the 'City of Tropical Excellence' and, most recently, as a 'Vibrant and Livable City'.

In what follows, architectural projects, more or less since the mid-1990s, are bound up with 'territories' in the senses of tracts of land and/or as spheres of action. This compilation is by no means complete or exhaustive, but aims to highlight what is being built to make Singapore a more competitive, diverse, attractive and potentially-sustainable environment.

Road to Diversion and Consumption
One territory of note, in both senses of the term, is Orchard Road, a well-established route leading out from the center of the city, renowned in more recent times as an active site of retail and entertainment. Although not named as yet, the roadway appeared on maps of Singapore in the 1830s, running down the base of a valley, later becoming associated with the ill-fated production of *gambier* pepper responsible for clearing significant areas of the island's hinterlands. Over time this practice was replaced by nutmeg plantations and fruit orchards, giving the road its name. As part of ribbon developments associated with improved transportation and suburban expansion, housing began appearing along the road as early as 1846, multiplying in number by the 1860s in the form of private homes and bungalows on the adjacent hillsides looking down into the valley and the road passing through it. By the early 20th century Orchard Road appeared as a well-shaped avenue flanked by voluminous Angsana trees, among others, and played host to denser forms of development in adjacent areas, including Cairnhill and Emerald Hill, where affluent Chinese gathered in spacious row and court dwellings, along with the appearance of some shophouses and apartment buildings, like Amber mansions, closer in to town. Larger-scale retailing, now a hallmark of the area, first occurred in the 1950s, with Tangs, located on the corner of Orchard and Scotts Roads, among the first upmarket department stores in Singapore. By the time of the birth of the Republic, Orchard Road was a primary site of retail and associated commerce, with shopping malls, like the Yaohan Department Store, opening in the early 1970s. Underground Metro improvements, as part of the North-South Line of the Singapore Mass Rapid Transit System constructed in the relatively early development of the island state's Ring Concept Plan, significantly augmented earlier and often congested reliance on surface transportation. Running parallel to Orchard Road, on the south side, this line, with three station stops, further improved the area's

I. M. Pei, Tsao & McKown with the local office DP Architects, four towers of Suntec City in Marina North (1997)

Atlas: Asia and Pacific 275

Benoy with RSP, Ion Orchard Mall on Orchard Road (2009)

The old thoroughfare known as Orchard Road is today a primary site for shopping, leisure and entertainment, with malls, restaurants and hotels that transform this street, extending some two kilometers in length, into a global shopping paradise. As it stretches towards the sea it encounters Suntec City, with office blocks such as the Millennia Tower and facilities like the International Convention and Exhibition Center.

accessibility and sponsored additional commercial development. Also to relieve congestion, traffic flow along Orchard Road was made one-way, running in a south-easterly direction and compensated in the opposite direction by a loop system of parallel rights-of-way, like Somerset Road, on the southern side.

With improving economic circumstances during the 1980s and into the 1990s, construction of malls, hotels and related sites of entertainment burgeoned. Significant among them was the Ngee Ann City complex of 1993, by Raymond Woo & Associates. Straddling an elongated site with extensive frontage on Orchard Road, the complex comprises two 27-storey office towers on a multi-level podium of retail space, embracing a relatively small semi-circular public plaza, one of the very few in Singapore. In broader international terms, the external architectural expression of the complex is postmodern, with all the trappings of a symmetrical disposition of building volumes, trapezoidal roof lines, use of polished red granite panels and stainless steel cladding, all enveloped by a two-storey colonnade around the perimeter.

With a gross floor area of around 169,000 square meters it remains the largest complex along Orchard Road.

In 2007, the retail and entertainment core of Orchard Road, extending some 2 km in length, became the subject of multi-million dollar effort to rejuvenate its public pedestrian realm and to increase its retail venues. Although Orchard Road attracts more than seven million visitors each year, wear and tear over the years and the need to improve the pedestrian experience had become evident. Due to be completed in 2009, the planned landscape and infrastructure enhancement involves expansion of pedestrian walkways into one of the existing traffic lanes to create 'urban green rooms' to be used for performances and exhibitions in support of large and small public events. In addition, state-of-the-art lighting, co-ordinated street furnishings and multi-functional lamp posts will be installed, together with three floral themes – mainly in planters – along specific sections of the road. The initiative is being led by an inter-agency task force, including the Land Transport Authority, the Singapore Tourism Board and the Urban Redevelopment Authority. The Cox Group from Australia, in partnership with the local Architects 61, have been engaged to develop and elaborate design plans for the venture.

Prior to the announcement of this plan, Wisma Atria, the first major commercial development on the south side of Orchard Road, underwent extensive renovation to its five-storey podium of shopping, opened in 2005. The original complex, constructed in 1987, also consisted of an 18-storey tower block. While the tower block remains, the upgraded shopping center, designed by DP Architects, more directly engages with Orchard Road's bustling street life. Overall, this project took advantage of new guidelines from the Urban Redevelopment Authority aimed at increasing visual excitement, as well as providing for integration into pedestrian network links to the Mass Rapid Transit station and shopping venues like Ngee Ann City. Across from Orchard Turn, the massive Ion Orchard complex is due to open in 2009. Billed as yet another new retail experience, sitting above the Orchard Mass Transit Station and spread across 64,000 square meters of shopping comprised of some 300 stores, the eight-storey podium component of the complex is to be clad with a curvilinear, wave-like facade forming a 'media wall'. Rising behind is a 56-storey, 218 meter-high residential tower, also with a shapely curvilinear facade. Designed by Benoy and RSP Architects, Planners and Engineers, the complex is a joint venture between the local Capitaland Group and Hong Kong's Sun Hung Kai Properties, both very prominent real estate international companies.

Other building complexes now also contribute to the architectural exuberance of the Orchard Road area, like the Cineleisure Orchard complex by MGT Architects, completed in 1997. Clearly what has transpired, certainly in recent times under the watchful eye of the Urban Redevelopment Authority, is an increasing focus on up-to-the-minute venues for consumption and

I. M. Pei, Tsao & McKown with DP Architects, Singapore International Convention and Exhibition Center in Suntec City (1997)

The need to reclaim new territories to the sea around already built areas, like the city center at the mouth of the Singapore River, has meant a significant increase of the nation's land mass over the past thirty years, during which some 140 square kilometers have been added. The two main expansions are at the north and south of Marina Bay. The Esplanade Theaters complex is located at Marina North, facing the bay.

Michael Wilford & Partners, Esplanade Theaters (2002)

spectacle. This orientation along Orchard Road has no doubt been pushed, as alluded to earlier, by Singapore coming to grips with its perceptions of the local realities of being a competition state, including a rock-solid belief that the pitch and tone of urban-architectural environments do matter and that earlier conceptions of public space could be both more relaxed and yet directed with useful channeling. Whether, however, the almost hyper-active pursuit of this agenda will be fully successful in the emerging age of likely socio-environmental accountability, downplayed conspicuous consumption and even austerity, remains to be seen.

Reclamation, Events and Entertainment
A second territory, again in both senses of the term, is Singapore's seaward reclamations and its architecture of entertainment and events. Perhaps not surprisingly, given pressures for development balanced against needs for freshwater and related environmental conservancy, Singapore's land mass has been expanded significantly, especially during the past 30 years or so. Over this time, some 140 square kilometers have been added, amounting to around an additional 25 percent of the original land area. One such expansion occurred in the early 1980s and into the 1990s, adjacent to the city center around what became Marina Bay, at the mouth of the Singapore River, and the Kallang Basin at the mouth of the river of the same name. Three areas of reclaimed land have been made, including Marina North adjacent to Beach Road – the former sea frontage of colonial Singapore and the termination of the grid of streets in Coleman's 1837 plan – Marina East on the seaward side of Kallang Basin, and Marina South on the seaward side of Marina Bay. Of particular interest here are Marina North – the first area to be developed in the form of convention, hotel, entertainment and related commercial complexes – and Marina South, only now undergoing development. Also of note is Marina Bay itself, with a marine barrage across its mouth preventing saline intrusion and an active process of osmosis, creating it into a fresh-water body for future non-potable fresh-water use. Marina North is transected by a relatively sparse and curvilinear network of major roadways, freeing up broad sites for development. By contrast, Marina South is slated to have a tighter grid work of streets, leading seaward from existing adjacent

Atlas: Asia and Pacific 277

Once completed, the Marina North expansion will be linked to Marina South by a double-helix bridge. Several of the projects under way in the area, such as the 'Gardens by the Sea', devised by the landscape architects of Grant; the Marina Bay Sands resort – three towers joined by a sky park –; or the Universal Studios theme park in the nearby Sentosa Island, aim to become centers of attraction for tourists and visitors.

Cox Group with Arup, pedestrian footbridge in Marina Bay

development and around the edge of Marina Bay. Also within this 360 hectares of prime land are several undesignated reserve parcels, the spacious 'Gardens by the Sea' – a public park – and a cruise terminal along the seaboard side.

An enduring landmark in Marina North is Suntec City. Comprised of four 45-storey office towers, the 18-storey Suntec City Tower, some 55,000 square meters of retail space in a four-storey podium, as well as the Singapore International Convention and Exhibition Center. Completed in 1997, the concept design resulted from a collaboration between the firms I.M. Pei and Partners and Tsao & McKown, with the local firm of DP Architects joining Tsao & McKown in design development. The five towers are arranged around a spacious, tree-lined fountain plaza, with a further backdrop to this active public open space provided by the L-shaped podium wrapping around the north, or back side, of the project. Although not identical, the strong sculptural forms of the towers share a common architectural language, including well-proportioned, raised portico entries. Vaguely reminiscent of Rockefeller Center in New York in its formal devices, Suntec City has been successful in creating its own sense of a context in what was a flat, relatively featureless area. Integrated into the commercial complex, through lower-level links of retail space, stands the Convention and Exhibition Center. Adroitly organized around vertically-stacked halls, theaters and break-out rooms, the compact volume of the facility provides for straight-forward access to various conference venues. These qualities are further supported by an expansive glazed area for circulation, replete with multiple escalators and running full height along the street-side of the center, facilitating access to buses and para-transit. The multi-pyramidal roof, formed from a lattice of triangular truss sections, spans 170 meters by 69 meters, allowing for internal flexibility in arrangement of convention venues, and is one of the largest spans of its kind in the world. The adjacent Millennia Singapore project, of 1998, brought more instant context to the land reclamation site, with an additional gross floor area of some 293,000 square meters. Comprised of four towers, dominated by the pyramidally-capped Millennia Tower at 41 storeys, the complex is a mix of hotels, commercial space, and a retail galleria. Another joint venture, between the firms of Kevin Roche, John Burgee and Philip Johnson, again with DP Architects, the somewhat over-scaled architecture and postmodern expressive forms nowadays seem out of date. Podium-level pedestrian circulation through the complex also comes across, in places, as being overly contorted and theatrical.

Along the water's edge of Marina Bay, although tied in by location to the heart of the civic and cultural district of Singapore, stands the Esplanade Theaters on the Bay, by Michael Wilford & Partners. Completed in 2002, it ranks among the larger performing arts facilities in the world. Occupying a six-hectare site, at the corner of Esplanade Drive and Raffles Road, the complex consists of a 1,800-seat concert hall, a 1,900-seat lyric theater, a 200-seat black box theater, a 200-seat recital studio, outdoor performance spaces, and commercial augmentation via the three-storey Esplanade Mall. Most striking is the vast, curvilinear and organic-appearing form of its overarching glass shells, replete with a mesh of sun-shading devices of varying geometry – affectionately called locally, the 'durian', after the fruit. Beneath these layers, the two large theaters effectively appear as buildings inside the large covered volumes. The interplay of light and shadow, especially within the foyer areas, can vary from dazzling to dappled, giving one the sensation of being under a large tree and extending the sun-shading function well into the metaphorical realm emblematic of dwelling in the tropics. The roofscape of the

Michael Graves & Associates, Universal Studios Resort Singapore, Sentosa

complex is also handled as a respite from the bustle below and a vantage point from which to view the broader context of Marina Bay. Landscaped open spaces are arranged, deftly taking into account appropriate sight lines and offering, within them, moments of both community and privacy. A third large theater is also planned for the complex, to be further knitted in to the ground-level pedestrian experience of the water's edge. In effect the resulting Waterfront Promenade recovers a hallmark of the much earlier colonial termination of the city with the seashore along Beach Road, mentioned earlier.

Marina South is largely a work in progress. Prominent among the projects underway is the Marina Bay Sands complex, by Moshe Safdie. To be opened in 2010, the complex will feature three 50-storey hotel towers, housing some 2,600 luxury accommodations and forming upward swooping pedestals for a sky park spanning and cantilevering across the top. Close to one hectare in area, this sky park will host a variety of outdoor amenities, including jogging paths, swimming pools, gardens and spas, as well as offering a panoramic view towards both the central city and to the sea. The Waterfront Promenade, slated to be continuous around the Bay, will be integrated into the complex via a multi-level retail arcade made up of three shell-like structures, combining civic spaces, shopping and both indoor and outdoor public spaces. The sculptural form of an Arts and Sciences Museum is to be located on the promontory, where Marina Bay moves out towards the sea. All told, the integration of the Waterfront Promenade and the shopping arcade will incorporate some 100,000 square meters of space and almost an equal area in the form of a convention center and two 2,000-seat theaters. The further inclusion of a casino into what has otherwise been described as an 'integrated resort' with strong governmental backing, is something of a departure, programmatically, from Singapore's earlier straight-laced attitude, although not without considerable debate. Linking the promontory back across the mouth of Marina Bay towards the Esplanade Theater complex, is an unusual double-helix pedestrian bridge, designed by the Cox Group in conjunction with Arup engineers. Due to be completed in 2009, the 280 meter-long span is the first of its kind in the world, with an obvious reference to the structure of DNA and, by extension, to a symbol of 'life' and its continuity. Further fun and sport have also been overlaid on the Marina Bay district, with the Singapore Flyer – a giant ferris wheel – and the spectacle of night-time Formula One car racing, winding in a tortuous loop along city streets. This temporary venue, first made public to rapt audiences around the world in 2008, was also the site of technological innovation and prowess, in the form of special night-lighting installations.

The territory of seaward reclamations and an architecture of entertainment and events also extends to Sentosa Island and its adjacent mainland environs. Close to the Sentosa Mass Rapid Train Station and the bridge causeway to Sentosa Island is Vivo City – a large shopping mall, by Toyo Ito, opened in 2006. With a gross floor area around 140,000 square meters, this otherwise compact multi-storey structure houses some 350 entertainment, food-beverage, and retail outlets. Probably most distinguished by its large, curved and sculptural exterior cladding, the swirling lines of the interior's major circulation and gathering spaces, also marks a departure from standard mall design. In addition, this fluid sensibility extends to the broad expanse of the complex's roof structure and outdoor open-spaces – perhaps the most successful and publicly-spirited aspect of the scheme. There, a variety of spaces, incorporating water elements, public art and theatrical night lighting, cohere into a playful and delightfully whacky environment, inviting children to play, adults to wander or relax and for all to have an unusual vantage

Moshe Safdie, rendering of the Marina Bay Sands complex

Lee Soo Khoong & CPG Consultants, Tuas Checkpoint (1998)

Singapore's transit system is characterized by its effective coordination with land-use distribution, the result of a careful urban planning. The most widely used public mode of transportation is the train, with stations that have become urban landmarks. Other important pieces of the system are the airport of Changi, the checkpoint at the frontier with Malaysia, or the high-rise building connecting Marina Bay with the city center.

point to view Sentosa beyond. A 1,000 seat open-air amphitheatre, against a backdrop of the nearby hills, also provides a venue for fashion shows, international bazaars and local festivals. Across the strait of water, separating Vivo City from Sentosa Island, lies the site of the second 'integrated resort' promoted by the government, including a 15,000 square meter casino, six hotels, a theme park by Universal Studios, a convention center, a maritime museum and marine animal park, as well as extensive retail and related commercial space. Launched as a project in 2006 and due for completion in 2009 or 2010, the master planner and design architect for this massive complex is the firm of Michael Graves & Associates. To date, images of the project can only be described as formally exuberant and even phantasmagorical, portending a Las Vegas-like atmosphere, along with many of its material trappings. Again, the critical comments leveled at Orchard Road might also apply here, along with the as yet untested regressive social aspects of gambling.

Arrival and Linkage
A third territory, at least as a sphere of action, is infrastructure and an architecture of arrival and linkage. At present, Singapore is served by three Mass Rapid Transit lines – the East-West Line, running across the southern part of the island; the North-South Line, completing a broad loop to the north from the city center to Jurong in the west; and the North-East Line, moving in a north-easterly direction away from the city center. As mentioned earlier, from the inception and development of the post-colonial plan of Singapore, a strong spatial relationship between land-use and transit has been insisted upon to ensure reasonable and equitable access to employment sites and residential locations, as well as to guide urban expansion. A high modal share of transportation in favor of public transit has also been reinforced through cordon taxes and other disincentives to private automobile use into the city center and dense adjacent areas. Indeed, Singapore boasts one of the most efficient transportation systems in the world. Moreover, train stations have been sites of architectural celebration and imageability in the broader landscape. The recent Expo Mass Rapid Transit Station in Changi on the eastern side of the island is no exception. Designed by Foster & Partners and opened in 2000, this station provides a gateway to the Singapore Expo. As an exercise in providing clarity to user navigation, environmental comfort, and a distinctive architectural presence, two dramatic roof structures dominate the station design. The first, in the form of an elevated 40-meter diameter stainless steel disk, marks the station entrance and ticketing facilities. Close by, the second roof, in the form of a 130-meter long titanium-clad elongated shape defined by two radii, provides shelter and lighting to the platform and to the concourse below. Environmentally, the hovering roofs serve to funnel and agitate breezes, cooling waiting passengers. The highly-reflective cladding reflects sunlight and provides shading, as well as reducing the underside need for artificial lighting. Iconically, the elemental, futuristic overall shape – like something from a space comic – establishes a strong and memorable identity to the station stop, which is afterall a major entrance to another futuristic venue, the Expo.

Vehicular expressways also form another element of Singapore's broader transportation system, running in a roughly parallel though spatially complementary layout with the rail transit system. They also form the links

Foster & Partners, Expo Mass Rapid Transit Station, Changi (2000)

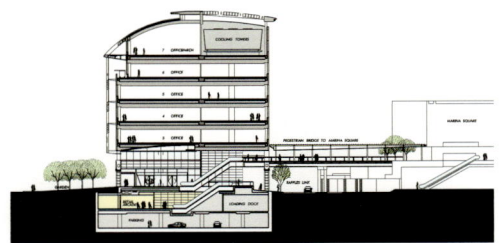

Kohn Pedersen Fox, One Raffles Link building (2000)

across the Straits of Johor with neighboring Malaysia, a major trading partner. Recently, in 1998, the Tuas Checkpoint was built serving the Second Link Bridge to Malaysia on the west of the island. Designed by the architect Lee Soo Khoong in collaboration with CPG Consultants – the prime contractor and engineer – the high security complex is bifurcated into a departure area and a larger arrival area, separated by an administrative building providing clear viewing of border operations. Roofed by elevated barrel-vaulted enclosures, supported on light-weight trusses, amelioration of the local climate was clearly a consideration. Overall, the complex, set in a 20-hectare reclaimed land site, designed by Peridian Asia as landscape architects, projects an image of being relatively utilitarian, yet contemporary and inviting.

Another aspect of linkage in Singapore is the abundance of underground and above-grade pedestrian connections. Climatically this makes sense, given the city's equatorial location, and provides for an extensive interior pedestrian environment, even if many are closed for security reasons at night. One strategy the Urban Redevelopment Authority adopted in 1999, when trying to knit the emerging Marina Bay complexes into the historical civic core of Singapore, as well as providing broader pedestrian access to the City Hall Station, was provision of an underground link across Beach Road and Nicoll Highway, two otherwise divisive major thoroughfares. Also involved was provision of a second-storey link to Marina Square. Resolution of this transition, as well as provision of an architecturally-sensitive backdrop for War Memorial Park and a sympathetic scale for the neighboring Suntec Convention Center, was accomplished by One Raffles Link. Designed by the firm of Kohn Pedersen Fox and completed in 2000, this seven-storey structure, with a curvilinear roof form, clear-glazed and spandrel-panel facades breaking out into a lattice of external sun-shading devices on the west, occupies a tapered elongated site. With some 5,000 meters of office space per floor and an underground mall, One Raffles Link is essentially a ground scraper and the largest of its kind in Singapore. Transition in the levels of pedestrian access is marked through a tall, light and airy, multi-height space.

A further aspect of arrival and linkage that has received recent attention is Terminal E at the Singapore International Airport in Changi. Now serving as a principal point of departure for major international routes, the terminal was designed by Skidmore Owings & Merrill. Fundamentally, it fits in with the modern architectural context of the airport, but also offers a contemporary interpretation of the terminal type. Under a tall and well-articulated roof structure, that seems to float over the main hall, the interior space which appears almost diaphanous with the outside arrival area, is layered, as one progresses inside, with extraordinary planting walls, and elongated light wells. The unfolding spatial experience is both inviting and calming, as well as expressive of its time and place.

Reconciling Old and New

A fourth territory, again more in the sense of a sphere of action, although also literally taking place in certain parts of the city, is historic conservation and architecture of modern juxtaposition. Unfortunately, as the new state of Singapore wrestled with the consequences of mass inmigration, dwindling trade and the need to stimulate employment during the 1960s and early 1970s, many parts of its historic urban fabric became egregiously overcrowded, dilapidated and fell into

SOM, Terminal E of Singapore International Airport in Changi (2007)

DP Architects, redevelopment of Far East Square (1999)

Burdened with other priorities, during the sixties and seventies the state paid less attention to the conservancy of the old quarters of the city, with a rich ethnic variety, like Chinatown or Indiatown. This has changed in recent years, when many of these areas have been recovered, valued as parts integral to Singapore's identity. One of the building types preserved is the shophouse, once ubiquitous throughout Southeast Asia.

disrepair. With recovery and better economic times, relatively short shrift was also paid to these older quarters and parts of them were demolished to make way for needed modern projects. These attitudes, however, changed in recent times both from sensed needs to preserve material of the past as integral to Singapore's identity, and in recognition of the value of this heritage to outside visitors and to tourist trade. Of course, Singapore is hardly alone in this progression of events. Today, parts of Chinatown, Indiatown, the Boat Quay, Clarke Quay, as well as historic buildings of colonial occupation, have been stringently preserved and many restored. An issue of both conservancy and architecture remains, however, around how to deal effectively with remnants of the past and new building, particularly in broader environments where the exigencies of both must clearly remain in play.

One area in which 'old' and 'new' have been combined is in the redevelopment and revitalization of China Square (the site of one of Singapore's earliest Chinese settlements), jam packed at one time with shophouses interspersed with occasional temples and civic buildings. The shophouse building type was once ubiquitous throughout Southeast Asia and in parts of China. As its name implies, it takes the form of a shop on the ground floor, facing a street and with storage space behind, atop of which is a residence, usually of the shopowner, and sometimes with additional rental accommodations. Arranged in rows with party walls between units, each shophouse occupied a proportionally elongated site with a narrow frontage, thus maximizing the number of commercial establishments along a given street. Alleys at the back frequently provided service access to ground-floor storage areas and in many places, including Singapore, protection from inclement weather was provided by a semi-open arcade along the street, colloquially referred to as 'five foot wides'. Typically rising in height to two and three storeys, capped with tiled pitched roofs, the front facades often manifested considerable architectural investment in bold cornice lines, decoration and shuttered windows. Having fallen into disrepair, and ravaged by later building, the area was ripe if not overdue for redevelopment in the latter part of the 1990s. Indeed, several projects were undertaken almost at once, including Capital Square and Far East Square.

Occupying an irregular 1.1 hectare site, forming a transition between Singapore's financial district and the China Square area, the Capital Square complex, by the local firm Architects 61, unabashedly brings together a 16-storey modern office tower with restoration of 19 three-storey traditional shophouses along both China and Pekin Streets. Opened in 1998, the significant footprint of the office structure, with a gross floor area of some 35,800 square meters on a relatively small site, is cleverly broken down into three components, punctuated by slender unfenestrated shafts, thus reducing its apparent scale. The highlight of the complex, however, is the variegated pedestrian experience that is provided, deftly integrating the shophouses with the office tower through a sequence of informal outdoor spatial parentheses. This pedestrian experience is

Redevelopment of Chinatown with the traditional shophouses and the Marina Bay skyscrapers as backdrop

During the post-colonial period, the country's effort pursued economic growth through industrialization, planning new high-density residential developments located close to the main centers of employment. Today, 85 percent of the population live in what was or remains public housing. The construction of up-scale, high-rise apartment buildings designed following local climate and environmental criteria is a relatively recent phenomenon.

P. Rudolph, The Colonnade (1981)   P. Rudolph, The Concourse (1994)

further augmented by a more formal urban plaza, created by setting back components of the office tower on the corner of Church and Telok Ayer Streets at the edge of the financial district. A fully-glazed, double-height entry to the tower's lobby eases the transition between external and internal space, perpetuating the continuity of the open pedestrian sequence. In addition, a podium-level parking structure adjacent to the urban plaza, usefully mitigates the otherwise inherent incongruity of the office tower and the nearby shophouses. By contrast the Far East Square development, across Pekin Street from Capital Square, by DP Architects, called for conservation of some 60 shophouses in its 1.4 hectare site and inclusion of a low-rise car park. Again, though, contemporary architecture was unabashedly combined with the historical fabric of the shophouses, in the form of steel and glass coverings to several pedestrianized existing streets, offering welcome climatic relief, as well as location of needed elevators and escalators outside of the shophouses to help maintain their authenticity. The glass-clad parking structure, with its inward sloping facade facing the forecourt of the complex on Gross Street, also makes no pretense of being literally contextual. Programmatically, Far East Square is home to a broad collection of creative agencies and media companies, along with restaurants, shops and cultural venues, like the conversion of Fuk Tak Chi – the first Chinese temple in Singapore – into a heritage museum. Also, nearby is a hyper-contemporary reinterpretation of a single shophouse at 31 Boon Tat Street by Forum Architects. Completed in 2003, the folded and overlapping elements of the facades and roof structure enclose a four-storey program of office space. Still, the provision of shelter along the footpath, the disposition of services and vertical circulation, as well as through-floor connections, maintain the integrity of the shophouse type. Also, the striking, multi-faceted external appearance of the building, *mutatis mutandis,* is not out of keeping with similar levels of architectural investment on traditional examples mentioned earlier.

High-Rise Living in the Tropics

A fifth territory is apartment towers and an architecture of high-rise living coupled with environmental response. Singapore is no stranger to either, both coming on by way of public provision in the wake of the Singapore Housing Trust in 1962 and then far more strongly with the creation of the post-colonial Housing Development Board. Today, some 85 percent of the island's population live in what was or remains public housing, the largest proportion in the industrialized world. Principally, this was in the form of substantial housing estates closely linked to new-town developments or other centers of employment. Relatively speaking, then, up-scale, private high-rise development is a comparatively recent phenomenon, as are approaches that deal more conspicuously with Singapore's tropical location. Built in 1993, the Abelia, by Tangguanbee Architects and located in an upmarket residential area, is a 12-storey arrangement of maisonettes with three different layouts. Double-height, well-landscaped terraces with lattice screens and shading pergolas enliven the architecture. In conjunction with voids among the units, they also enhance natural ventilation through facades subtly contrived to interplay with different aspects. Varying elevational treatments and climate relief can also be found at the more recent Thr3e Thre3 Robin condominium development by W. Architects, of 2005. Substantial louvered timber panels on lower levels temper heat gains and also provide for privacy, whereas upper floors, affording excellent views, are framed by open balconies with deep overhangs. Low-energy strategies for climate control are also an integral part of the 28-storey Moulmein Rise Residential Tower, situated close to the reserve zone of a national park and the President of the Republic's house. Designed by Wong Mun Summ and Richard Hassell of WOHA Architects, the very thin, rhythmically-composed tower accommodates 48 apartments and two penthouses, with recreational and parking facilities below. A number of devices drawn from vernacular housing work together to acclimatize the building, including a north-south orientation, operable monsoon windows, deep overhangs, sun screens, internal planning and ready cross ventilation, in addition to an environmentally-responsive glass curtain wall. Clever use is also made of a modular system to regulate architectural dimensioning and to provide for individuation of residential units.

WOHA, Moulmein Rise Residential Tower (2003)

Atlas: Asia and Pacific **283**

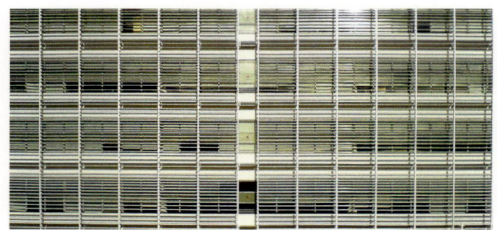

Maki & Associates with DP Architects, Republic Polytechnic (2007)

The government's strategy of steering Singapore's economy towards one based on knowledge and services demands raising the education level of the population, increasing the number of citizens with a higher education. This challenge called for the creation of new universities, such as the Republic Polytechnic, and of new cultural facilities, like the National Library. Institutional headquarters, like the Supreme Court, have also been renewed.

Institutional Re-Orientation
Finally, a sixth territory is institutions and an architecture of higher learning and of community services. Early in this millennium, the Singapore government held discussions around education and the need to further create a knowledge-based economy. An aim was to have 25 percent of each eligible cohort with a tertiary degree, up from about 10 percent. One upshot was the creation of new universities, in addition to the National University of Singapore, and to create polytechnical institutions providing for tertiary-level diplomas. One of several new campuses of this educational era is Republic Polytechnic, by Maki & Associates with DP Architects. Programmatically the pedagogy of this institution was to be based on interaction, high levels of access to digital dissemination and information processing, and project research as the fundamental basis of study in lieu of conventional lecture-based models of instruction. This decision then led to a master plan incorporating eleven 40 meter by 40 meter learning modules, with each rising to eight or nine storeys in height, and comprising multi-purpose areas. Also, close by, a faculty center was constructed and the entire complex became unified by two elliptically-shaped decks of common facilities and cross links, creating a continuous semi-public domain fostering student and faculty interaction, as well as cross-disciplinary learning. At some 240,000 square meters in gross floor area, the essential layout of accommodations remained compact though varied. Elegantly glazed and screened where appropriate, the building ensemble nestles into the contours of an existing park, with landscape carried into the complex via formal and informal open spaces. Public access and zones of activity also reinforce the openness of the otherwise institutional complex.

In 1998 the National Library of Singapore held a design competition for their central facility, which was won by T. R. Hamzah and Yeang from Malaysia. Located in the central Bras Basah Road area of the city, the building was completed in 2005, primarily consisting of two blocks, accommodating a total area of around 63,000 square meters and rising to a height of 16 stories. Linked by an enclosed though day-lit internal 'street' with bridge connections across at appropriate levels, the larger of the two blocks accommodates the library collection, whereas the smaller one houses administrative, curatorial and cataloguing functions. Below the larger block at street level is an open plaza providing venues for outdoor events, cafés and other publicly-oriented programs. Well known for his avocation of green architecture, over the past three decades, Ken Yeang paid considerable attention to lowering energy embodiment and operating costs, reducing them well below those usually incurred in similar buildings of comparable volume. The library exterior is striking for its curvilinear shape, sun-shading protrusions and overhangs as well as for the panoramic viewing capsule on top – yet another nod in the direction of public interaction and use.

Provision of local community services have also become the subject of architectural investigation and invigoration, exemplified in at least two recent projects. The Bishan Public Library was completed in 2006 with a modest gross floor area of around 4,200 square meters, rising on a tight site near the Bishan Mass Rapid Transit Station to five stories in height. Designed locally by Look Architects, the layout of the library stacks, with distinctive adjacent reading rooms registering on both the inside and outside of the structure, was alikened to a bookshelf in action. The light enveloping curtain wall provides both easy visual access to the interior and a crisp, sheer and unencumbered background for the well-composed protrusions of the reading rooms. The broad roof overhang floating above the top floor also helps to unify and reduce the overall scale of the structure. The Marine Parade Community Club of 2000, by contrast, presents an effusive and some might say jarring juxtaposition of elements. In the past 'community clubs' were called 'community centers', typically rendered in muted modernist tones seemingly aligned with the idea of ameliorating social distinctions and disseminating officially-shared political and social values at the local level. As Singapore has moved away from this stance towards social unity and control, at least symbolically portraying a more relaxed atmosphere, the architecture of several of its community facilities have followed suit. Indeed, at Marine Parade, the architect William Lim has operated in the opposite direction, creating a community center that rather clearly, if quirkily, signs in the direction of populism, pluralism and a certain excess. Replete with interlocking roof forms that spill over on to the facade, which also appears to have been patched together by enclosing elements, the social theme of diversity is on display. Openness of the center, especially at street

Foster & Partners with CPG Corporation, Supreme Court (2007)

284 Atlas: Asia and Pacific

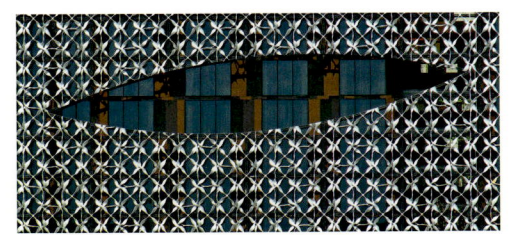

WOHA, Hotel Crowne Plaza at Changi Airport (2008)

Overall, the works built recently in the country seem to be headed in the 'right' direction: they are following sustainability and climate criteria, and the presence of foreign offices is being balanced out with the increasing presence of local teams, thus guaranteeing technical transfer and the adaptation to global standards. Nevertheless, building hyperactivity and massive material consumption may entail risks in the future.

level, also plays a part in overcoming any particular sense of attachment or entitlement.

Perfectability of the City
In this account, other territories of interest in either sense of the term might have been mentioned. For example, the fate of older industrial sites and a new architecture of mixed use might have been raised, as at Jurong – the manufacturing concentration that was so much a part of Singapore's period of production-oriented development. Nevertheless, little as yet has been reconstructed. To be sure, ever since its independence, Singapore has harbored a strong commitment to physical planning, urban design and architecture, in line with a deeply-held belief in the perfectability of the city. Of late this has manifested itself in a broadened public realm, a re-orientation to the sea, intensified and even novel environmental conservation strategies along with more emphasis on contact with natural circumstances, and a wide embrace of leisure-time activities and a recognition of pleasure. A strong role in this agenda remains in the hands of public authorities, under which an extensive and broad ranging number of architectural projects have been built or are being built. In comparison to other periods, new or more emphatic architectural features of this agenda, both large and small as well as somewhat at random, include: substantial roof terraces on display at places like the Esplanade Theaters and Vivo mall or in massive overhanging structures at the Marina Bay Sands and even in the publicly-sponsored housing competition for The Pinnacle at Duxton. Also in line with Singapore's tropical location, lower-energy approaches, including a broadened variety of sun-shading and other climatic tempering devices, have enlivened the city's architecture. The blurring of indoor and outdoor situations, via thick facades like the older 'five-foot wides', or in manners where the usual division is rendered diaphanous, have also been updated and brought into play. Prowess in engineering, with several 'firsts' or 'largests' have also emerged, with particular reference to the Suntec convention hall roof and the double-helix structure of the Marina Bay Promenade bridge. The presence of numerous high-profile foreign firms has also endured, if not been given broader leeway, although always partnered with local offices in the spirit of technical transfer and in order to fulfill architectural ambitions beyond the scope of local capacities.

During the current transition, however, there has also been a substantial drift towards both material and cultural consumption, with both inwardly and outwardly directed orientations. Singapore, after all, is a small nation. Sometimes one gets the impression that 'buzz' and 'excitement', to use two commonly-heard local terms, are being lead and manufactured by building and architectural means, even if at root they are social categories. As mentioned earlier, one risk that potentially excessive material consumption confronts, especially in the guise of even more glitzy shopping and entertainment, is a glut, let alone impingement on other and perhaps more noble endeavours and when the broader context, to which it is outwardly directed, maybe shifting in other directions. A risk cultural consumption runs, at least with respect to architecture when it becomes too closely aligned with particular and relatively momentary socio-political and related economic agendas, is one of redundancy and outmodedness. Laudable though good planning and strong architectural guidance may be in pushing supply-lead public objectives forward, it can also become over-bearing and awkward in this regard. At present, however, the general fate of the apparent emphases of Singapore's urgency in pursuing an urban-architectural transition, makeover and re-invented presence on the world stage, remains to be fully appreciated.

Look Architects, Public Library, Bishan (2006)

Atlas: Asia and Pacific 285

WOHA
Moulmein Rise Tower
Novena (Singapore)

Client
UOL Development
Architects
WOHA Architects: Wong Mun Summ, Richard Hassell
Consultants
KPK (quantity surveyors); Meinhardt (mechanical engineers); Dai-Dan (electrical engineers); Acacia (plumbing)
Contractors
Shining, Arzbergh, Fairways, Hitachi Asia, Sum Cheong Piling, Venus, Focchi, Magnificent Seven
Photos
Tim Griffith

The facade of this 28-story tower located in the city's central district takes inspiration from the works of the Dutch artist M.C. Escher, while the design of the building is organized on the basis of a 300 mm modular system.

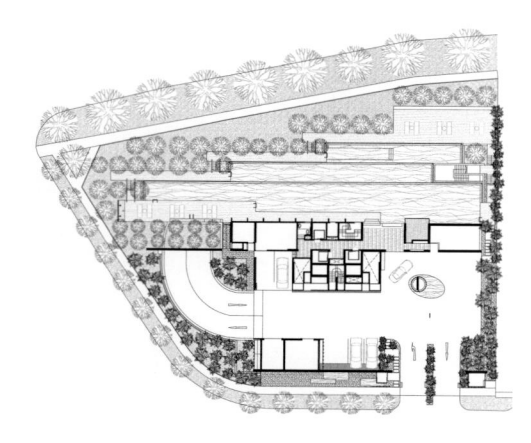

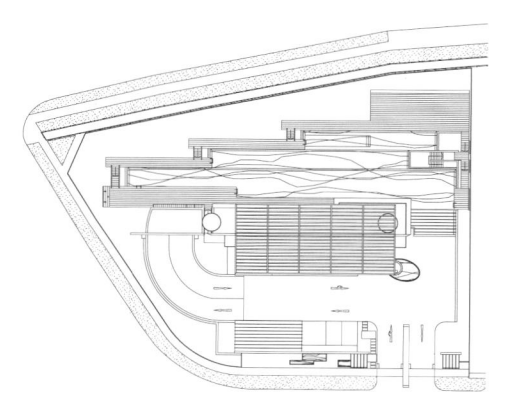

THE LOCATION of this tower is a residential neighborhood mixing high-rises, mid-rises, and one-family homes. Immediately south of the site is a conservation area where buildings are restricted to four stories. Further along south is a national park containing the president's residence. For security reasons, no building around may face it directly, but Moulmein Rise lies just outside the cordon. This works to the tower's advantage, allowing it unobstructed views and fresher, cooler air. Instead of entrusting climate control to expensive mechanical systems, the architects resorted to low-cost strategies used in vernacular architecture, updated with aluminum panels, such as the traditional monsoon window: a horizontal opening that lets in the breeze but not the rain, which can be unpredictable in the tropics. Orientation, internal planning, overhangs, cross-ventilation, shading, and perforation are also all studied and applied here to minimize the need for air conditioning.

The tower contains 48 apartments and two penthouses. At ground level are a gym and a swimming pool set in a tropical garden. A modular system based on multiples of 300 millimeters regulates all architectural dimensioning, from floor-to-floor heights down to the smallest details. In this way, instead of treating future occupants as identical consumers, the design allows for variation in both the plan and the facade. Individuality is expressed through recombinations and rearrangements of overhangs (1 meter on the north, 0.6 meters with sun screens on the south), screens, and windows. The visual complexity is based on M.C. Escher's tessellations, in turn inspired by mosaics in Granada's Alhambra.

The plan of the apartments is simple. The living room, dining room, and master bedroom are placed to one side of the circulation spine, and the kitchen, two smaller bedrooms, a washroom, and a utility room are put on the other. To accommodate changing user needs, the two smaller bedrooms can be joined into one and the living area can be adapted to different functions. Each unit has three open sides, giving uninterrupted views of the surroundings. This also creates the sense of a continuous flow of space, right from the entry to the far end of the apartment, which is usually the large window of the main bedroom. For easy cleaning, the windows are made to open inwards. The choice of materials was determined by issues of budget, durability, availability, and aesthetics, all to make the project as coherent and sustainable as possible.

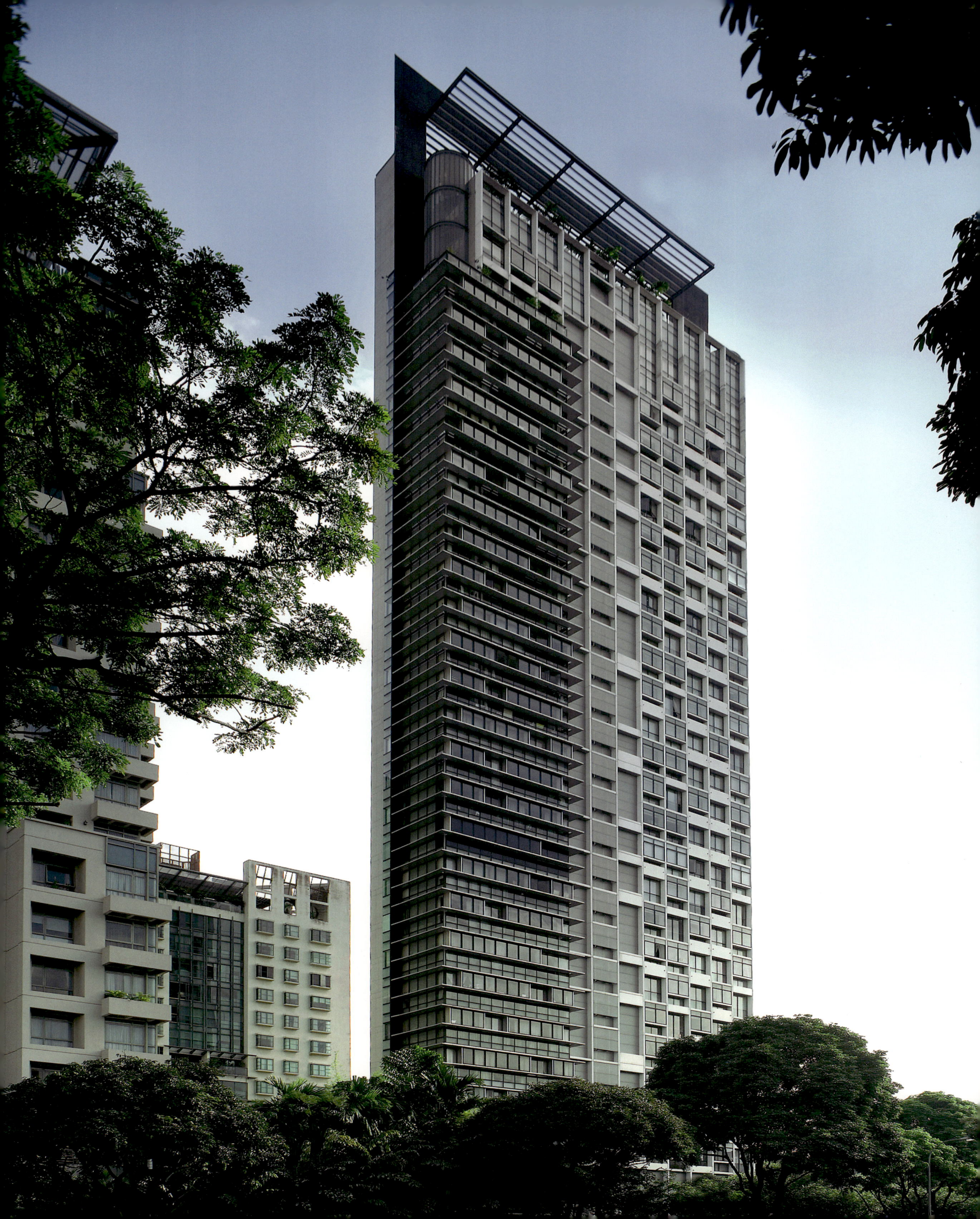

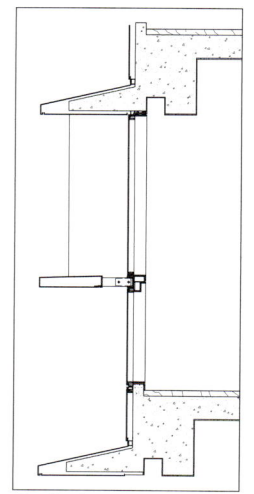

West facade 1 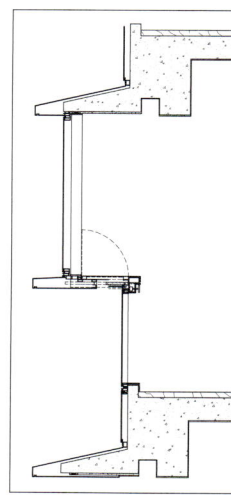   West facade 2

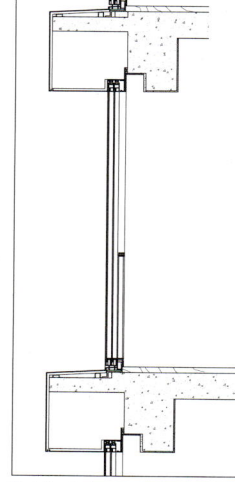

East facade 1 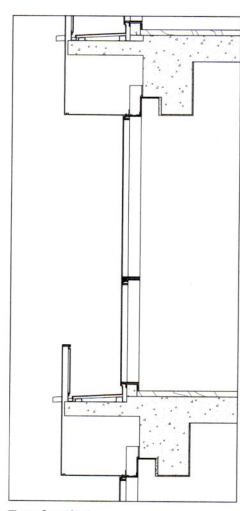   East facade 2

Taking into account the region's tropical climate, the builders considered using systems that would let in the breezes but not the rain, which can be unrelenting during the typhoon season, and reduce the need for electrical air conditioning. Traditional monsoon windows were installed, updated in aluminum. The tower also includes a covered swimming pool and a flexible floor plan layout that each client can manipulate as desired.

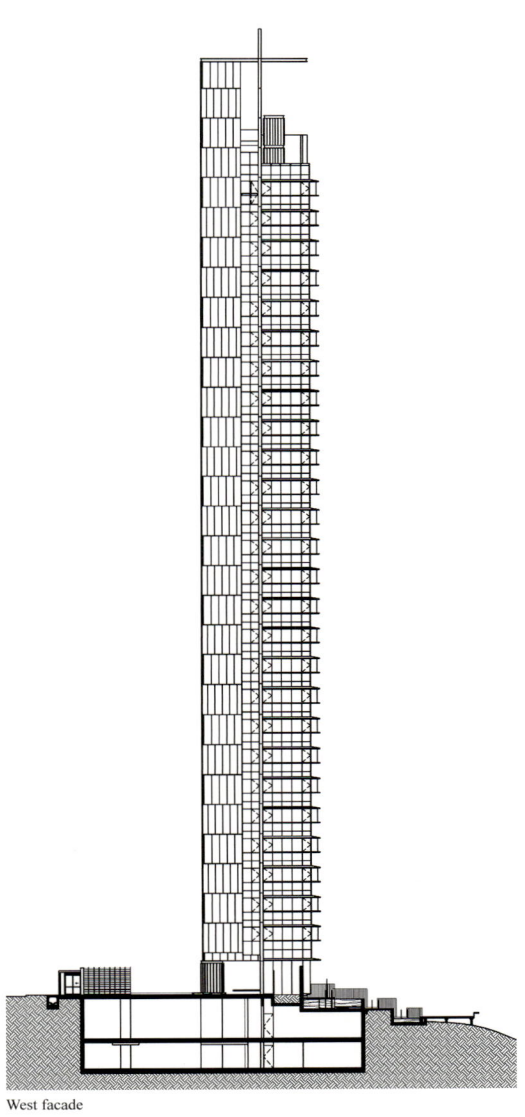

West facade

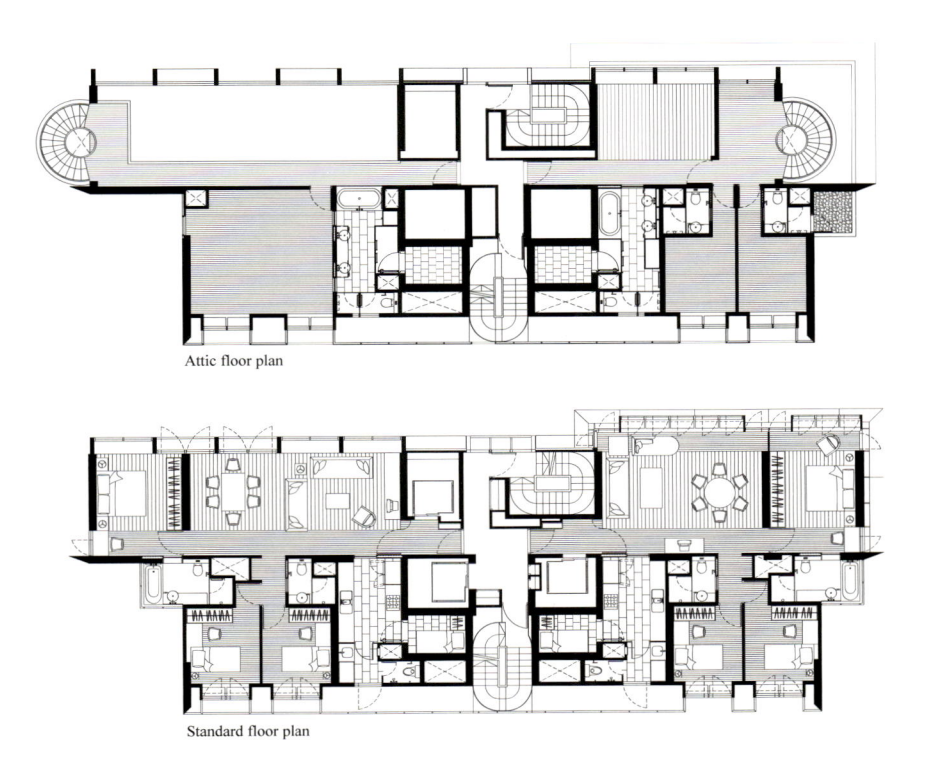

Attic floor plan

Standard floor plan

Atlas: Asia and Pacific **289**

Grant
Gardens by the Bay Park
Marina South (Singapore)

Client
National Parks Board of Singapore
Architects
Grant Associates (masterplan);
Wilkinson Eyre (conservatories)
Collaborators
Atelier One, Atelier Ten (engineers);
Davis Langdon & Seah (quantity surveyors)

SINGAPORE'S HIGH PROFILE as a major global hub of activity that is at the same time a leading garden city is being cemented by a colossal bayside operation being undertaken by the National Parks Board. The 101-hectare Gardens by the Bay project is divided and phased into three themed parks: Marina South, Marina East, and Marina Center. The 54-hectare Gardens at Marina South is first to be carried out and is due for completion in late 2010, following a masterplan drawn up by the team led by Grant Associates in the wake of an international design competition that was organized for the purpose.

Inspired by the orchid shape, the masterplan addresses two main themes: 'Plants and People' and 'Plants and Planet'. Both narratives encompass the length of the park and feature special attractions with the help of an intelligent infrastructure that even allows the cultivation of plants which would not otherwise grow in Singapore.

The Plant Edutainment Gardens will tackle the theme 'Plant Use by Man' through an interactive display of botanical products that have been economically important for Singapore and the rest of Southeast Asia. It will also look at ethnobotany through species that play a role in the daily lives of people in the tropics. The Horticultural Show Gardens will present the best of tropical flora, and be a spectacle of color and fragrance on the paths leading to the Gardens' two grand centerpieces: the Super Tree cluster and the Conservatory Complex.

Sure to be "wow"-eliciting icons for the Gardens and Singapore itself, the 'supertrees' are magical vertical gardens soaring between 25 and 50 meters, some to be connected by aerial walkways. Besides providing shade by day, lighting up at night, and housing a food-and-beverage outlet and exclusive bar, they will incorporate rainwater and photovoltaic collectors and serve as environment-friendly engines for the conservatories. The Conservatory Complex is a group of greenhouses along the edge of Marina Bay. The Cool Dry and Cool Moist conservatories showcase Mediterranean, tropical montane, and temperate annual plants, and provide a flexible flower-themed venue for events and exhibitions.

The Flower Market at the entrance, with underpass connections to the Marina Bayfront metropolitan railway, will offer visitor services facilities, retail outlets, and indoor events venues. The Main Events Space will stage performances and other activities for as many as 7,000 people.

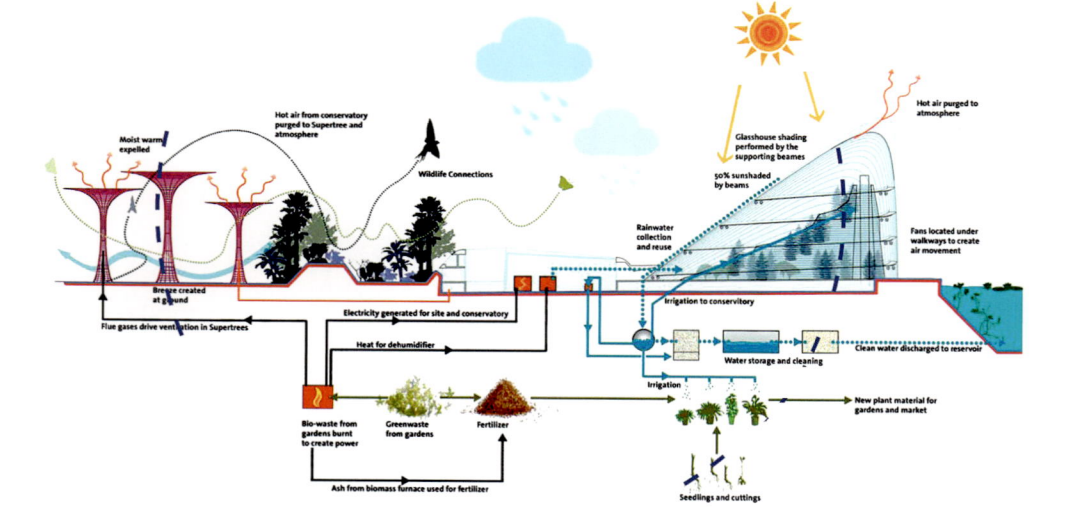

Designed as an ecosystem combining natural and man-made elements on land reclaimed from the sea, the Gardens by the Bay project is the largest landscaping development ever to be carried out in Singapore.

Inspired by the shape of an orchid, the Gardens by the Bay enclave includes among its features the so-called 'supertrees'. Discernible from a great distance, these are enormous, mushroom-like metal structures decked with vegetation and devices for collecting water and energy. The two conservatories contain specimens of plants from cold climates.

Atlas: Asia and Pacific 291

Daniel Libeskind
Reflections Residential Complex
Keppel Bay (Singapore)

Client
Keppel Land International
Architects
Daniel Libeskind;
DCA Architects (architects of record)
Collaborators
Yama Karim, Stefan Blach (project architects); Arnault Biou, Seungki Min, Patrick Head, Ilana Altman, Jennifer Milliron, Vicky Lam, Bora Temelkuran, Maxi Spina, Raul Correa-Smith, Casey Miller, Josh Draper
Consultants
Keppel Land (project management); T. Y. Lin International (structural and civil engineers); Beca Carter Hollings & Ferner (mechanical, electrical, plumbing engineers); Hargreaves, Sitetectonix (landscape architects); R. A. Heintges & Associates (curtain wall); LPA (lighting designer)
Contractor
Who Hup

The name of the complex has two meanings, referring on one hand to the interplay of reflections of the water and sky on the curved glass facades; and on the other hand to the project reflecting 21st-century living.

PROMINENTLY MARKING the entrance to the historic Keppel Harbour, in Singapore Bay, Reflections is an entirely new expression for high-rise living within a tropical climate. Enjoying a choice spot situated close to the city and to well-known natural and recreational enclaves like Vivo City and Senstosa Island, the complex is a unique blend of posh residential sky-suites and villa-styled low-rises along a 750 meter coastline. The focal point of the iconic proposal is a symphony of undulating towers. Six all in all and with alternating heights, half of them counting 41 floors and the rest 24, the towers are slender, with sleek facades of reflective glass that create curved surfaces and different crowns featuring plant-filled greenhouses closed with slanting glazed planes.

The buildings have interesting, graceful openings and gaps between them, and they connect with one another by means of nine bridges, set at different heights, that make for open zones in the exterior as well as platforms affording almost 360-degree views of the spectacular surroundings and more distant horizons. As for the eleven lower blocks, they rise six to eight levels and create a smaller-scale urban complex at the foot of the towers, repeating their dialogue of undulating facades but this time with aluminum panels for cladding.

The complex will include 100,000 square meters of swimming pools that will bring seawater right to the doorsteps of the various buildings. The resulting composition is an ensemble of urban scales that is livened up by a creative interplay of planes and reflections and equipped with all the infrastructures necessary for it to become a small city in itself, one that will contribute immensely to the richness of Singapore's skyline and to its vitality as a competitive and forward-thinking world-class city.

Construction work is already underway and in 2011, the year the complex is scheduled to be completed, it will boast 1,129 apartments ranging from 25 square meter studios to 450 square meter five-bedroom units, some of which are so far still available and up for sale at a maximum price of US$2,000 per square meter.

Situated close to the city of Singapore and to important recreational and natural enclaves, this new residential complex, Daniel Libesind's first project in Asia, unfolds along 750 meters of coastline and is equipped with the infrastructures necessary for it to become a small city in itself. When construction work finishes in 2011, Reflections will boast 1,129 apartment units ranging in size from 70 to 1,100 square meters.

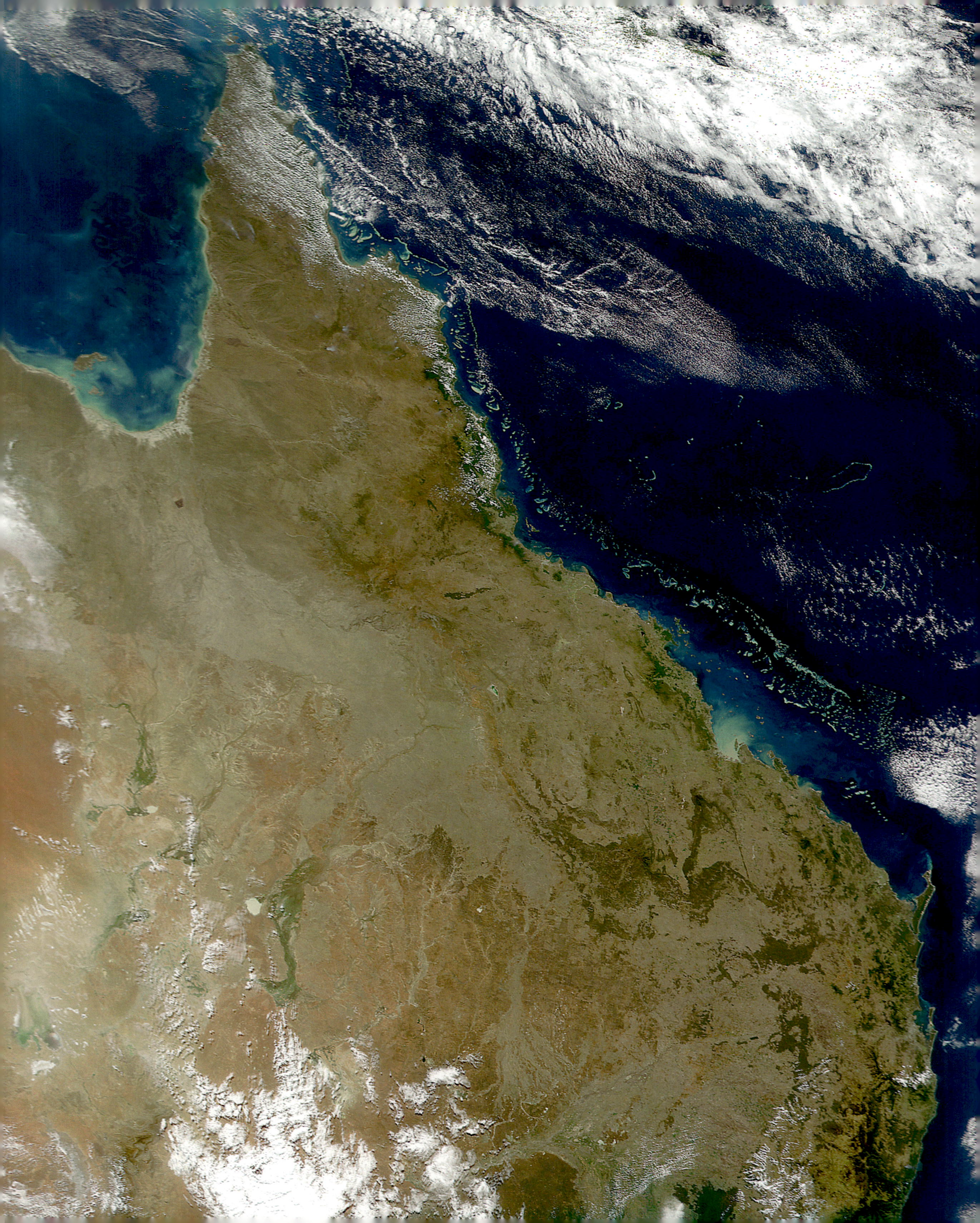

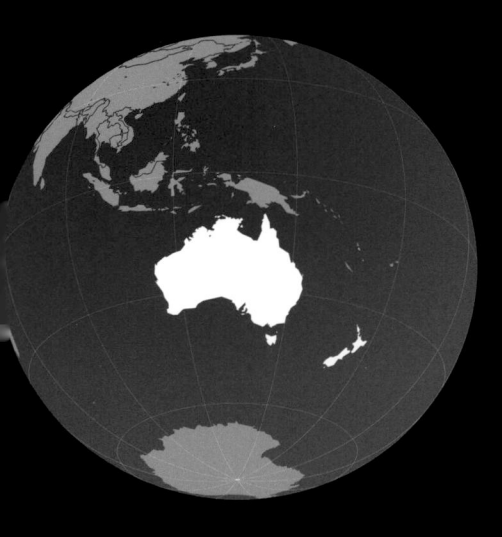

Australia and Pacific

Geographic isolation was not enough to prevent the arrival to Australia of international trends, whose influence was already very present in the 19th century. Despite the current cultural homogenization, the architecture of each province has managed to find its own expression, generating several schools whose common denominator is the concern for climate matters. The projects selected here represent the different regional traditions: in Melbourne the studio Phooey has built a Children's Center with recycled materials, and John Wardle a Grammar School which explores different textures; the Brisbane School is illustrated with a striking University Laboratory by m3architects; and that of Sydney with an angular University Building in the center of the city, by the Denton Corker Marshall team. Finally, Glenn Murcutt, the Sydney architect who is the most prominent of Australia, is featured with one of his very characteristic houses, in Kangaroo Valley.

Haig Beck & Jackie Cooper
An Insular Continent?
Australia and New Zealand, Propositive Regionalism

Aerial view of Queenstown, in South Island, New Zealand

The architecture of the fifth continent reflects the vitality of youth, and its adaptation to climate generates an identity without complexes.

INSULARITY IS A matter of degree. Both 'insular' and 'peninsular' derive from the Latin 'insula', meaning 'island'. Spain (a peninsula) is geographically isolated from Europe by the Pyrenees, and for many years the country was ideologically isolated from modern democratic Europe. Even so, modern architecture in Spain flourished throughout the 20th century, as it did in geographically (though not ideologically) isolated Australia. And during this period, as in Australia, Spanish architecture expressed distinctive regional characteristics. Local circumstances, different in Barcelona and Madrid, for example, have shaped the contemporary architecture of those two cities differently. In much the same way, circumstances local to Brisbane have made its contemporary architecture different from that of Sydney or Melbourne. The task of this essay is not only to identify representative examples of 'Australian' (or 'New Zealand') contemporary architecture but also to explain how these architectural manifestations of insularity and regionalism arise and thrive in an age of cultural globalisation.

Global Influences
The spires of the Anglican Cathedral of St John's in Brisbane, Australia, were finally completed only in 2009. The last Gothic-style cathedral in the world was finished. Begun 120 years previously, it had been one of numerous cathedrals the Anglican church began building around the world in the latter half of the 19th century. That was at the moment that globalisation began.

Cultural globalisation is now understood as a process of homogenisation. Driven by communications technology and the worldwide marketing of western cultural industries, the global domination of American culture has occurred at the expense of traditional, regional diversity.

The British roots of the architecture produced in Oceania have blended in with the local features, leading to the creation of the 'schools' of Sydney, Melbourne and Brisbane in Australia, and also to that of New Zealand.

Aerial view of Sydney, capital of the state of New South Wales, with the bridge and the Sydney Opera House in the background

296 Atlas: Asia and Pacific

Separated from one another by vast distances, the four main cities of Oceania have in common a remote location with respect to the central areas of cultural production, compatible with a close relationship with them since colonial times, at the end of the 19th century. The ideas and the people have travelled from the 'empires', and on the road the global trends have adapted to the local ways, weather and techniques.

Aerial view of Melbourne, capital of the state of Victoria and second city of Australia

However, in the late 19th century, it was not America but the British Empire that was at its apotheosis – its trade, ideals and culture were dominant – and the Gothic Revival designs of British architects were built (or copied) around the English-speaking world. Gothic cathedrals that might have been built by master masons in late-medieval England and France arrived, like a fleet of retro alien space ships, on all the pink bits of the globe: in the British colonial cities of Africa, India, North America, Australia and the Pacific islands.

But there were local anomalies. Instead of the austere white Caen limestone used in many of the Gothic cathedrals of northern France and in England, the abutments to the west front of St John's in Brisbane are built in local sandstone, generally deep mauve in colour but riotously interspersed with pastel pinks, blues, greens and yellows. In Wellington, New Zealand, the imperative of local circumstance was even more extreme. In 1865, the Reverend Frederick Thatcher built St Paul's, a 'Gothic' cathedral constructed entirely from New Zealand native timbers. Internally, the exposed stud framing and curving 'Gothic' trusses reveal the naturally finished interior face of the Kauri pine boards that clad the cathedral exterior. Externally, the spire is Gothic inspired, but the overall composition of the building – a conglomeration of small gable-roofed units – belongs formally to the tiny timber-clad vernacular cottages built by English colonists, to which they made many ad hoc additions.

Cultural globalisation arrived in Australia and the south Pacific in the late 19th century, and it persists to this day in an ever-increasingly aggressive form. As Paul Ricoeur noted more than 40 years ago: "Everywhere throughout the world, one finds the same bad movie, the same slot machines, the same plastic or aluminium atrocities, the same twisting of language by propaganda." But while our television programs and movies have been progressively stripped of local content and flavour, our architecture has largely resisted the homogenising pressures of universalisation, and it retains its local identity.

Why should this be? An answer lies in the 19th-century mauve-coloured sandstone and Kauri pine cathedrals. Unlike movies, where rolls of film can be transported from cinemas in one country to cinemas in another, buildings do not arrive from some other place complete. They arrive as ideas. And so it was in the 19th century when designs for Gothic Revival cathedrals were transported from England to its colonies.

When those ideas arrived codified in drawings, locally-trained craftsmen working with local materials necessarily adjusted them to suit local circumstances (resulting in the colourful and very un-Gothic mauve abutments of St John's in Brisbane). In the case of St Paul's in Wellington, the adjustments were far more extreme. The Reverend Thatcher (who was an architect as well as being an Anglican minister) responded to local circumstances by recasting the heavy masonry construction of Gothic cathedral architecture in lightweight timber.

Those involved in the commissioning, designing and building of Anglican cathedrals in the late 19th century were collectively engaged in promoting the globalisation of the Anglican Communion. They enlisted the emblematic power of Gothic Revival architecture to give authority to the 'Englishness' of their cause. But in choosing to do this, they soon encountered (and had to resolve) the tensions exposed by the practice of Gothic Revival architecture in distant, new world colonies. They found themselves

Aerial view of Brisbane, capital of the state of Queensland and third city of the country

Atlas: Asia and Pacific 297

The Sydney School, marked by the adaptation to the city's mild, almost Mediterranean climate, found in Leslie Wilkinson, in the 1930s, its first 'master'. Glenn Murcutt is the best representative of a characteristic way of building that 'lightly touches the ground', pays heed to details and to orientation, and uses frameworks of steel and large glass surfaces. Functionalism sensitive to context, better known as 'Sydney Minimalism'.

I. Moore, Kings Lane residential complex in Darlinghurst, Sydney (2003)

participating in what Michel Foucault identified in *The Archaeology of Knowledge* as a 'discourse'.

A Plural Discourse
In respect of Foucault's concept of discourse, Roy Landau noted: "We learn and inform through making statements in a discourse. To take part in a discourse there is no requirement for debate… architectural discourse has a scope which involves words and objects… and such objects may be projects as well as built artefacts… The scope of the architectural discourse is not bounded by words… Contributions to architectural discourse… take place through many sorts of exchanges which involve different sorts of actors far beyond the community of architectural designers… Patrons of architecture… professional, cultural, and educational institutions… journals and the media… the critic, historian, and writer… (even craftsmen)… all possess the… capacity for making and shaping architectural discourse."

Foucault's concept of discourse is important because it sidesteps the Eurocentricity of many architectural historians and the preoccupation with antecedents, precedents and influences. Some architects of the early 20th century – for example, Frank Lloyd Wright and Charles Rennie Mackintosh – were viewed by Pevsner and Giedion as precursors of modernism; while others – like the Greene brothers – went unnoticed until the 1950s and were then pigeonholed as craftsmen designers of Californian timber bungalows. And there are also architects – such as the Australian Robin Dods – who still remain largely unknown.

Yet these five architects – all born within two years of each other (1868-1870) – were simultaneously engaged not in some as yet to be defined Modern Movement but in what they would have understood to be the Arts and Crafts discourse. And while each worked locally for local clients with local needs – using local craftsmen working local materials, and in the local climate and landscape – there was nothing insular about their practice, and they did not work in isolation. All five were working within a well-defined tradition theorised by Ruskin, Morris, Thoreau, Lethaby and others. Dods, the geographically most isolated of this group, had trained in Edinburgh and corresponded with his life-long friend the Scottish Arts and Crafts architect, Robert Lorimer. Even in Australia Dods did not work alone: the local Arts and Crafts discourse included cultural societies, patrons, clients, artists, architects, furniture makers and other craftspeople – to the extent that it was recognisably an 'Australian' Arts and Crafts movement using Australian materials and Australian motifs.

Rather than British sources, Mackintosh and Lorimer turned to Scottish vernacular antecedents to guide their practice, and when Dods returned to Brisbane in 1896, he developed an Arts and Crafts practice that drew on the local Queensland vernacular. Robert Riddel, his biographer, notes that "his domestic work adopted many local techniques in wood, but had a sophisticated discipline and a common-sense response to climate which were radically new."

Residential Regionalism
There are parallels between the Australian Arts and Crafts discourse that Dods participated in 100 years ago and the various tendencies to be observed in contemporary Australian and New Zealand architecture. These tendencies are also framed as discourses that have both international and local constituents. Like the earlier Australian Arts and Crafts movement, they are discernibly Australian (or New Zealand) too; though with one important difference: they are much more regional. There is a Brisbane School, a Sydney School, a Melbourne School and a New Zealand School. In the smaller cities and in the less inhabited regions of Australia and New Zealand, there seem to be other, emerging, regional schools, but the density of building in those places is still too low for this to be verified. (As Harwell Hamilton Harris, one of the earliest commentators on regionalism observed more than 50 years ago, "To express regionalism architecturally it is necessary that there be building – preferably a lot of building at one time.")

Where regional schools can be discerned,

FJMT, School of Information Technology, Sydney (2009)

298 Atlas: Asia and Pacific

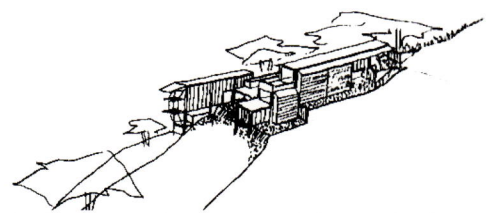

Stutchbury & Pape, Springwater House, Seaforth, New South Wales (2005)

in the local discourses that fuel them are present the exemplars of earlier architects as well as buildings just completed; the lessons of respected teachers; the memory of vernacular traditions; the imperatives of climate and local constructional practices and materials; the voice of the home-grown architectural media; and generational interactions. In these discourses, the force of the native contributions far outweighs the impact of foreign influences; and the past is always present, shaping the future.

Most Australians and New Zealanders live in freestanding houses located in sprawling suburbs that spread out from city centres. They have no tradition of urbanism in the European sense; social housing is largely non-existent; infrastructure tends to be utilitarian; and commercial buildings have historically followed North American models. So it should not be surprising that throughout the 20th century, it is the house that has been the locus of most architectural experimentation. With considerable economy, the house addresses most of the major questions of architecture, whether social, aesthetic, typological, technological, environmental or philosophical. And so it is in the design of houses, rather than larger commissions, that the emerging architectural tendencies of the region are best observed.

Sydney, the First City
Aesthetically (and geographically), the Sydney School falls between two extremes: Melbourne and Brisbane. It is a coastal city with a benign warm temperate, almost Mediterranean climate. During the 1920s and 1930s, Leslie Wilkinson, then Dean of the Faculty of Architecture at the University of Sydney, used his forceful personality and pedagogical position to push for a climatically appropriate architecture, one that merged the Neo-Classical details of Australia's colonial heritage with Mediterranean building forms. He built a few beautiful demonstrations; but his students were more excited by the abstracted forms of the Bauhaus. Nevertheless, they did heed his lessons on the importance of the climate in shaping architecture, incorporating climatic sensitivity into their functionalist credo. Climatically-responsive design still shapes the architecture of the Sydney School, as does the architecture of functionalism, which is now more readily recognised as Sydney Minimalism.

From the late 1940s, other young Australian architects began designing houses based on Frank Lloyd Wright's Usonian houses. For them, the appeal of these houses of Wright's lay not only in their low-cost construction using brick and timber (both readily available in Australia), but also in their 'natural' settings and climatic responsiveness. This interest in Wright's 'organic' philosophy and practice occurred at a moment when Australian artists and architects were becoming sensitised to the wild beauty of the Australian bush, previously denigrated. Architects working with small budgets discovered that their Usonian experiments were suited to the affordable building sites amongst the gums and sandstone outcrops on the steep sides of

Glenn Murcutt, Simpson Lee House, Mt. Wilson, Sydney (1994)

Peter McIntyre, sketch for an A-Frame House, Melbourne (1955)

The school of Melbourne, a city of changing weather located 1.000 km south of Sydney, is characterized by a plastic and formalist approach in which the building is treated as a sculpture, unrelated to the exterior. Two figures, the intellectual of experimentation Robin Boyd and the iconoclast and theater designer Peter Corrigan, have promoted an architecture of 'skin and bones' in which the surface captures all the attention.

Edmond & Corrigan, Lux House Extension, Caulfield, Victoria (2005)

the ravine-like chases that drain down into Sydney Harbour. In the early 1960s, the next generation of young architects (returning from the obligatory trip overseas and their stop-over to work in London), drew parallels between the New Brutalism they encountered in England and the now well-established Sydney Usonian tradition. From these two sources, they developed a hybrid Nuts and Berries aesthetic based on finely-detailed, exposed brickwork and timber framing. This interest in beautifully crafted timber construction (frequently combined with elegantly detailed steel structural members) continues to flourish in Sydney.

Of all the contemporary Sydney architects, one stands out: Glenn Murcutt. His work unifies into a single aesthetic Sydney's two contrasting tendencies: the machine-like, stripped precision of functionalism and the hand-crafted materiality of the Nuts and Berries School. Through the examples of his work and his teaching, this sole practitioner has made a significant contribution to the Sydney architectural discourse (and to other discourses around the world). Everywhere the environmental rationality of his designs, their formal clarity and their sensitive engagement with sites are recognised and admired. Significantly, the lyrical tectonics of the work depends on a very high standard of detailing that is now emulated (and even surpassed) by many other Sydney architects. The obvious pleasure they take in fine detailing has become a hallmark of the Sydney School.

The Sydney School, as an identifiable architectural aesthetic, is not solely restricted to the design of houses. Even so, most buildings in the public realm are only distinguished from similar buildings to be encountered anywhere else by the fineness of their detailing. There are exceptions. And these are buildings that, although frequently modest in scale, treat the interior ground plane as an extension of the public realm, dissolving the barriers between inside and out.

Melbourne, Forms and Surfaces
In Sydney's temperate climate, the wall plane opens up to the world outside: interior space becomes external, with only the slightest sense of threshold, and the architecture of the interior segues so seamlessly into the architecture of the exterior that they are one. Located nearly 1,000 kilometres further south, Melbourne has a climate that is more continental. Summers can be scorchingly hot and winters frosty and wet; and the weather on any day can be highly erratic (as Melburnians explain: 'four seasons in one day'). Traditionally, houses in Melbourne have a heavyweight shell of protective, insulating masonry. Although lightweight contemporary materials can now provide the necessary protection, the concept of the house as a sealed box remains. When inside and outside are experienced as separate realms, the architecture of the interior frequently becomes divorced from that of the exterior. The result is an architecture of skin and bones: of surface and concealed supporting structure. Architectural form-making becomes a plastic art: building-sized sculpture into which program and structure are inserted.

This interest in an architecture of the surface begins in the 1930s when modernism first arrived in Melbourne as streamlined moderne. It was not until the late 1940s when Robin Boyd (a member of a distinguished artistic dynasty in Australia) began writing weekly newspaper articles on modern domestic architecture that the more analytical approach of functionalism began to take hold. Boyd was highly influential. He attacked the ugliness of suburbia, publishing several books on the necessity of a modern Australian architecture; designed experimental houses; curated exhibitions on contemporary architecture; and lectured in the School of Architecture at the University of Melbourne. Boyd's architectural experiments extended to building type, structure, materials, and program. In the 1950s they inspired young architects like Peter McIntyre to undertake even riskier architectural experiments in formal and structural expressionism.

The quasi-intellectual environment of avant-garde experimentation that Boyd and his followers established still persists as a significant component of the Melbourne architectural discourse. In the 1960s it

300 Atlas: Asia and Pacific

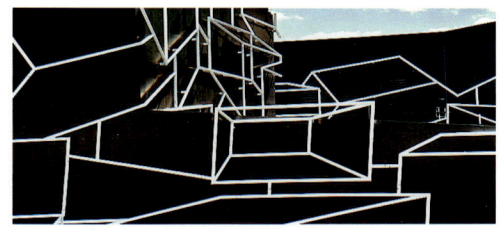

ARM, Melbourne Recital Centre (2008)

John Wardle, Vineyard House, Victoria (2004)

provided the context in which the young Peter Corrigan thrived. Corrigan, architect, theatre designer, charismatic teacher, theorist, and iconoclast, had gone to Yale in America in the late 1960s to test his ideas about complexity and contradiction in architecture and the ugly beauty of suburbia with its uncharted iconography. His architecture had a theatrical, dream-like quality. Colliding, distorted geometric fragments of plan and section were loosely sequenced along a circulation route; and the building surfaces festooned with vulgar motifs from the suburban domestic landscape inhabited by ordinary working people. The work was an attack on the modernist canon: on its well-mannered formalism and its abandonment of a social program (and on Boyd, who despised suburban taste).

Why didn't Sydney produce a Corrigan? From the time of Federation in 1901 until the 1970s, Melbourne was the commercial, cultural and intellectual centre of Australia. In the 1950s and 1960s it was home to the debate on the nation's social conscience. Melbourne architects were intimately engaged in this discourse; it supported the social agenda underlying Corrigan's interest in the ugly beauty of suburbia, his enquiry into its iconography, and his iconoclastic architectural populism that envisaged an architecture of the people.

Corrigan's followers revelled in his populist iconoclasm. However, lacking his ideological perspective and visual genius, they turned to football, religion and consumerism for their story lines and resorted to abusing photocopiers to disturb their plans and elevations, until CAD came along and opened the way to fractal geometry, warped planes, structural skins and other modes of digital dreaming. Theirs is an architecture of skin and bones, of digitally-derived plastic form, and of surface. Unusually, the conventional pattern of first testing ideas through the design of houses before moving onto larger projects was reversed. It is only in the last few years that there has been a proliferation of houses based on the sealed box, digitalised formalism that now characterises much of the Melbourne School.

And where is Melbourne's Murcutt? There isn't one: climate was never such a part of the Melbourne discourse as it was in Sydney. Thanks to Wilkinson and functionalism, Murcutt (and many other Sydney architects) continue to be engaged in a discourse that enables them to theorise the architectural dimensions of climate. In contrast, most Melbourne architects have accepted the inside/outside duality of their architecture without question, and – unconstrained by the need to express functionalist, climatic considerations – they have been free to develop an architecture of sculptural form and surface.

Brisbane, the Light Tradition
In Brisbane, 1,200 kilometres north of Sydney in south-east Queensland, the subtropical coastal climate is central to the way of life: people spend a lot of time outdoors. In summer, cool breezes off the ocean are a welcome respite to the humidity

McBride Charles Ryan, Klein Bottle House, Melbourne (2007)

The subtropical climate of Brisbane, 1,200 km north of Sydney, is central to the city's way of life. Relatively far from Melbourne and Sydney, this distance has helped to create a tightly-woven and active cultural community. Andresen & O'Gorman have introduced lightweight construction, inspired by local tradition and adapted to the climate, paying very special attention to the design of the exteriors.

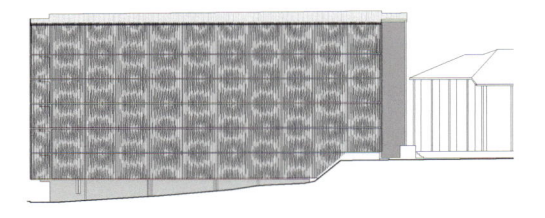

m3architecture, High School, Brisbane (2008)

Andresen & O'Gorman, Moreton Bay Houses, Brisbane (2000)

and heat. In winter, a warm place in the sun is a delight. Since the beginning of European settlement, the best buildings have been finely-tuned machines designed to ameliorate the climatic extremes. By the late 19th century, a vernacular architecture had evolved peculiar to the region: timber-framed, raised off the uneven ground on timber posts (called 'stumps'), surrounded by deep shaded verandahs, and crowned with an all-enveloping roof.

Until the recent advent of cheap air fares, Brisbane was geographically (and culturally) isolated from Sydney and Melbourne. Viewed from afar as an economic and artistic backwater, Brisbane allowed architects to be largely left to their own devices. This insularity excluded them from the architectural discourses of Sydney and Melbourne. However, it did not inhibit the development of a local discourse or its fertilisation with ideas from abroad, which happened in the late-1940s when European functionalism, Wright's Usonian organic architecture and the Californian Case Study houses arrived in Brisbane almost simultaneously.

Isolation can be an effective cultural condenser. Although below the radar of the Sydney/Melbourne axis, Brisbane's artists, architects, authors and academics were a culturally active and mutually supportive community. In the 1950s, a period of intense architectural experimentation began (and it continues). The climate was a given, lightweight timber construction a tradition, and bush blocks the only affordable sites. Architects soon discovered that flat roofs, though much admired (they were 'modern'), leaked in the heavy sub-monsoonal downpours, so in the 1960s architects, led by John Dalton, began incorporating into their designs the pitched roofs observed in the Queensland vernacular.

Architecture students also began looking at the vernacular. In the process they discovered the Arts and Crafts houses of Robin Dods. From Dods they learned that the vernacular could be adapted and abstracted. They took particular notice of the detailing of lightweight timber construction based on the use of Queensland hardwoods, and expressed all the framing members. Once in practice, they built a lot of houses. By the late-1980s a 'thin' timber-framed architecture was rapidly evolving. As in the vernacular, walls were frequently lined on one side only; very fine timber batten screens were used both as sun and rain shields; whole walls were detailed to slide away; interior space merged with exterior space, and in time 'outdoor' rooms became part of the vocabulary. Cross-ventilation, effective sun-shading and correct solar orientation were as fundamental to the design process as foundations were to the building.

At the University of Queensland, Brit Andresen and Peter O'Gorman were influential. They introduced the current generation of young architects to the theory and practice of a lightweight Queensland architecture. They taught the poetics of space, place and type and the detailing of Queensland hardwoods in the design studio and demonstrated their ideas in the field

Richard Kirk, Highgate House, Brisbane (2007)

with the houses they built. Many of the architects they mentored have made the transition from designing lightweight timber houses to major public buildings – changing materials, technologies and scale – without compromising the expressive open engagement with place and climate that characterises the architecture of the region.

New Zealand, a Double Heritage

If the emotional heartland of Australia is its sweeping plains of sunburnt bush, then for New Zealand it is its precipitous hillsides of cool misty rainforest. Climatically these are very different countries. Both were settled by British colonists (often fiercely resisted by the native people: the Maoris were Polynesians who arrived in New Zealand about 1,000 years ago; and the Australian Aborigines were a stone age people who arrived more than 60,000 years ago). In each country, 19th-century European settlers developed vernacular houses based on memories of 'home' adapted to the local climate and building materials.

In the cooler, wetter climate of New Zealand there was little need to shade external walls, so eaves – let alone verandahs – were not essential (however, steep roof pitches helped shed the rain). Houses were built with the local timber: beautiful softwoods used for framing, cladding, floors and furniture. With pioneer/settler economy, houses were initially built with few rooms (often quite small, as softwood construction limited spans). With the flexibility that timber framing permits and with no existing eaves to get in the way, additions could be made as required. The New Zealand vernacular house is an accretive assemblage of small-scale, gabled- and hipped-roofed units. This compositional tactic of accretive assemblage lingers in the collective architectural consciousness, as does lightweight timber framing.

Just as there are imagined cultural tensions and rivalries between Sydney and Melbourne architects, so there are in New Zealand between architects in Auckland and Wellington. The reality is more a matter of the regional differences that arise from the insularity of geographical separation (some 500 kilometres); from two distinct types of patronage (private in Auckland, the country's centre of commerce; public in Wellington, its centre of governance); and from Wellington's cooler, wetter climate. As in Australia, there is also a similarly forgotten third city, Christchurch,

Lindsay & Kerry Clare (Architectus), Gallery of Modern Art, Brisbane (2004)

Ian Athfield, Buck House, Te Mata Estate, New Zealand (1980)

on the South Island, with its own regional architectural identity.

While Auckland can claim the first full-time architecture school (1925), in 1946 Wellington established the earliest cultural organisation, the Architecture Centre, which in turn founded the first architecture school in Wellington and the first town planning school in New Zealand. The modernist debate appears to have taken hold in New Zealand by the mid-1930s. In Auckland in the 1940s and 1950s, Vernon Brown (a charismatic practitioner/teacher) built a series of houses using the local lightweight timber framing tradition. The stripped modernist forms were functionally planned for solar access and cross-ventilation. Their timber weatherboard cladding was treated with black creosote and offset by white painted industrial steel windows. Brown's 'black' houses are remembered in several contemporary 'black' houses.

In New Zealand, a relatively young country with a population of only 4 million and the tensions of a bi-cultural heritage, national identity is an issue. The existential longing to know their place in the world that New Zealanders experience usually finds expression through sport. However, there are many cultural manifestations of this condition as well, including some that are architectural. In even the most contemporary work there are echoes of the vernacular tradition, the references to the architectural pioneers of modernism, and to the 'bach'. The traditional bach (as in 'bachelor') is a holiday house, usually no more than a skillion-roofed shed improvised from found or abandoned materials. They were frequently squats built beside remote beaches and rivers or in the bush on land with no clear title. The poetics of the siting of these little buildings and their anarchical, make-do informality have given baches a special place in the New Zealand national identity.

Peripheral Culture Complex
A characteristic of provincial societies is cultural cringe, a sense of cultural insecurity that grows with distance from the perceived centre. It often leads to an uncritical eclecticism, as the latest fashions picked up from European magazines are regurgitated under the guise of avant-garde mystique. Under constant pressure from consumerism, the novelty of newness quickly wears off, and a new cycle of plunder and regurgitation begins.

The result is an architectural version of the cultural universalisation that Paul

Modern Architecture Partners, Breamtail House, Northland, New Zealand (2005)

Vernon Brown, Haigh House, Auckland, New Zealand (1942)

The national identity of New Zealand, a young country of four million inhabitants, is based on two cultures, the colonial and the native (the Maoris and the Australian Aborigines). The two main cities, Auckland and Wellington, have schools of architecture to which modernity arrived in the 1930s, with figures like Vernon Brown, whose wood houses, simple as the traditional *bach*, still influence the younger generations of architects.

Ricoeur referred to ("the same bad movie, the same slot machines, the same plastic or aluminium atrocities," and so on). There is an alienating placelessness about many buildings. Air-conditioned to seal them from the world outside, and with twisted, multi-faceted forms clad with cheap Chinese facade systems, they could be almost anywhere. There are, however, signs of resistance to these practices, which Kenneth Frampton has identified as Critical Regionalism. Critical Regionalism is a self-aware form of local practice that prospers when the architects of a region are sufficiently self-confident to participate in the global discourses that engage them from outside while remaining in tune with place: its climate, materials, technologies and traditions.

Frampton notes that no one has expressed this idea of Critical Regionalism more forcefully than Harwell Hamilton Harris, who in an address to the North West Regional Council of the AIA in Oregon in 1954 said: "Opposed to the Regionalism of Restriction is… the Regionalism of Liberation. This is the manifestation of a region that is especially in tune with the emerging thought of the time. We call such a manifestation 'regional' only because it has not yet emerged elsewhere. It is the genius of this region to be more than ordinarily aware and more than ordinarily free. Its virtue is that it has significance for the world outside itself. To express this regionalism architecturally it is necessary that there be building – preferably a lot of building at one time. Only so can the expression be sufficiently general, sufficiently varied, sufficiently forceful to capture people's imaginations and provide a friendly climate long enough for a new school of design to develop."

Peter Robb in his book *Midnight in Sicily* anecdotally touches on this 'Regionalism of Liberation'. Robb remembers Vincenzo, an architecture student in Palermo, "who would have given anything to work with Murcutt." Robb describes why. "Moving inland into the hills of Sicily, where the villas are bigger, more costly and solid, the new houses look more and more like dreadful fortified bunkers. As they are. There is no grimmer or more palpable expression of the social ethos in Sicily… [The houses] are the ultimate expression of fear and mistrust of your neighbours. Thinking this now… I saw the amazing appeal the Australian houses of Glenn Murcutt must have had for the student Vincenzo, sitting so airily and lightly and modestly on the earth, minimal, essential and open to the world around them. From Sicily such houses seem models or dreams of another world, another way of living, and seeing this, I realized as I hadn't earlier the politics of Vincenzo's enthusiasm."

When Robb speaks of Glenn Murcutt's houses as "sitting so airily and lightly and modestly on the earth, minimal, essential and open to the world around them…models or dreams of another world, another way of living", he might equally have been speaking of a multitude of houses by any number of architects in Australia and New Zealand. Many of these houses are constructed from materials Murcutt does not use, and most of them do not rise to the formal clarity he achieves, nor are they such finely tuned climatic machines. However, they all exhibit an airy openness, a tectonic lightness, and an engagement with the landscape that identify them as members of a new school of design that has become "sufficiently general, sufficiently varied, sufficiently forceful to capture people's imaginations" around the world.

Moller Architects, Orua Bay House, New Zealand (2007)

John Wardle
Nigel Peck Center
Melbourne, Victoria (Australia)

Client
Melbourne Grammar School
Architects
John Wardle Architects: John Wardle, Stefan Mee
Collaborators
Andy Wong, Diego Bekinschtein (associates); Barry Hayes, Nick Harding, Kirrilly Wilson, Stuart Mann, Toby Horrocks, Fiona Dunin, Paul Evans, Renee Weeden, James Juricevich, Oscar Paolone, Georgia Novak
Consultants
Connell Wagner (structure/facade); Lincolne Scott (services); Webb (lighting); Umow Lai (IT); GHD (hydraulics); Wilde & Woollard (quantity surveyor); AEC (ESD); Taylor Cullity Lethlean (landscaping); Treelogic (arborist); McKenzie (building surveyor); Watson Moss Growcott (acoustics); Blythe-Sanderson (disability consultant); Fulcrum (town planners); Bryce Raworth (heritage consultant); Emery Studio (graphic designer)
Contractor
Probuild
Photos
Trevor Mein (pp. 306 above, 307 below), Peter Hyatt (pp. 306 bottom, 307 top)

The Melbourne Grammar School is a prestigious and exclusive secondary institution, predominantly for boys, whose history goes back to 1858. The campus of South Yarra, an affluent suburb of Australia's second city, was built in accordance with age-old ideas of self-withdrawn educational sanctuaries. Twentieth-century additions, rising along the perimeter of the site, served to enhance this cloistral, 'ivory tower' notion of scholarship by creating an inscrutable wall between the school and the outside world, including neighbors like the Royal Botanic Gardens and the Shrine of Remembrance. Of primary importance in the brief for the MGS's Nigel Peck Center for Learning and Leadership, hence, was to dissolve such barriers, both visually and functionally, while remaining conscious of and giving due highlighting to the school's long history and tradition.

Putting the NPCLL along the campus's busy Domain Road boundary was a sure first step towards making the MGS more interactive with the urban and public realms. The facade of the new building is split to create what is the school's only clearly distinguishable entrance to the campus on this frontage. The entrance hall slices through the building to frame a live picture of the original bluestone quadrangle within the grounds, some venerable 19th-century structures that are on the Victorian Heritage Register. Attention is likewise drawn to an old elm, the view of which is then reflected by the equally magnificent trees of the park across the street.

Expressive of the school's desire for transparency, the NPCLL's elevation is a primarily glass facade with differentiated parts symbolically relating to the particular uses they house behind: offices, classrooms, meeting rooms, a theater, and the now consolidated school library/learning center. The patterning in the glazing is an allusion to the irregular ashlar stonework of the historical 'bluestones' inside the campus. Towards the street, the glass panes tilt in different directions, offering the insider varied views of the world beyond and the 'outsider' varied reflections of it. Jewel-like steel projections cradle the glass panels.

Two enormous glass surfaces weighing 700 kilograms apiece cover the area which is reserved for the graduating class, as if to prepare the older students for their imminent foray into the real world beyond. Where the library's book stacks are located, glazing gives way to specially fired brickwork that is articulated in what the architects call 'book bond', with vertically placed bricks resembling the volumes shelved within.

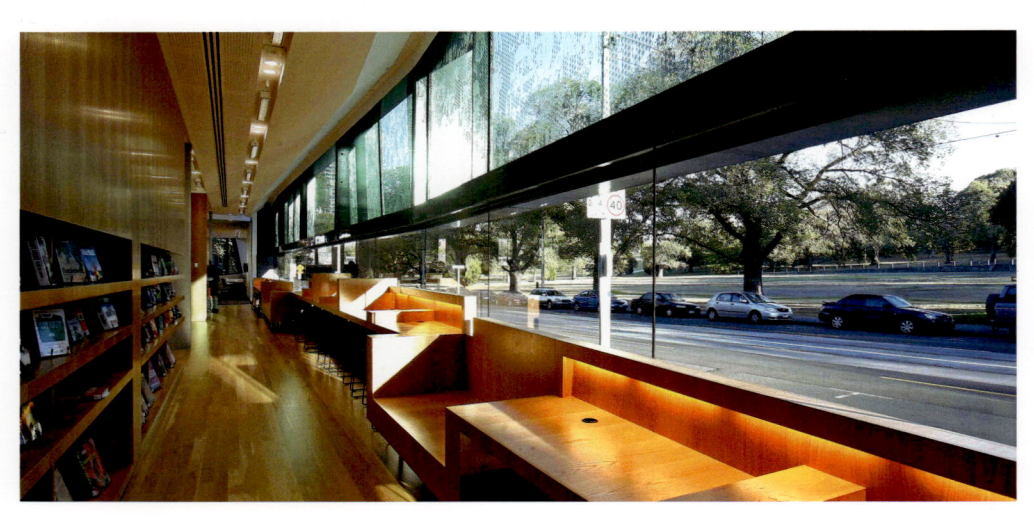

The main facade of the building is divided into rectangles of different sizes and has tilted glass panels that have the effect of providing varied views and reflections. The glazed surfaces have been treated with a serigraphed pattern that resembles the irregular texture of the stone walls inside the campus. The rear facade of the library is articulated in a special bond of vertically placed bricks evoking the volumes that are shelved within.

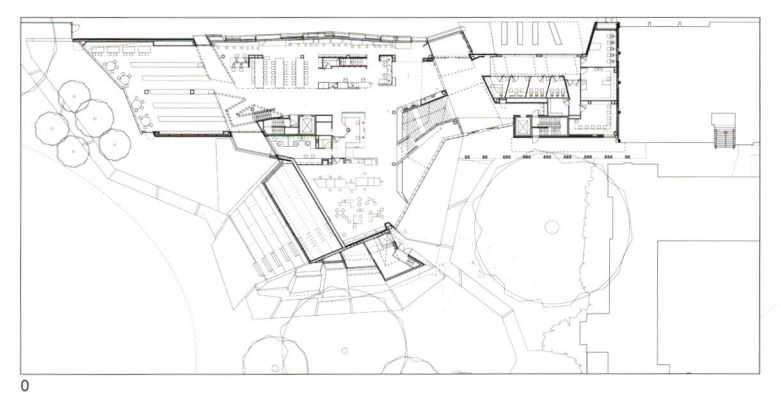

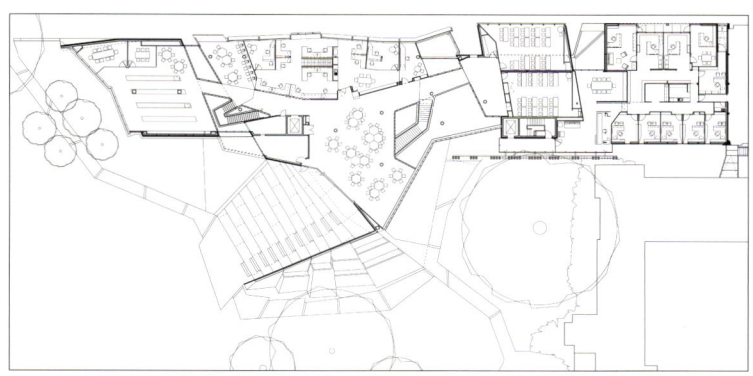

Atlas: Asia and Pacific

Phooey
Children's Activity Center
Port Phillip, Victoria (Australia)

Client
City of Port Phillip
Architect
Phooey Architects: Peter Ho, Emma Young
Collaborators
Peter Ho, Alan Ting, James Baradine
Consultants
Perrett Simpson Consulting Engineers (structure)
Contractor
Speller Constructions
Photos
Peter Bennetts

The project was based on stacking up four containers in disuse, perforating them here and there, and adding other elements salvaged from demolition to adapt them to their new use as a children's center.

SKINNERS PLAYGROUND, a park in a South Melbourne residential suburb, is the location of this children's activity center, a place where neighborhood children can spend time after school hours, tapping their creativity in a safe atmosphere.

One of the purposes of the project was to use the center as an opportunity to make the most of materials recycled or salvaged from demolition, whether for the decking, for the joinery, or for the windows. The basic components of the construction were four shipping containers in disuse, of the kind that abound in this port city of southern Australia. Two of them were clamped together with a slight shift at ground level, the sides of contact removed to create a single large space. The other two, shorter than the latter, were placed at a 45 degree angle on top of them at one end. This created projecting balconies and protected the entrance into the building from inclement weather. An exterior metal stair connects the two floor levels.

To make them usable, numerous cuttings were made in the containers, and scraps and leftovers were then reused as well. The cut-offs resulting from making openings in the containers were refashioned into balustrades, sun-shade awnings, and decorative elements, while rainwater spilling off the roofs was made to drain into a pond and reed bed. Unlike in other modular projects of a similar nature, here the outward appearance of the shipping containers has received no embellishing treatment. On the contrary, they are deliberately left as is, complete with commercial logos and graffiti.

The way the boxes are joined or piled up and staggered creates a mixture of communal and more private spaces to accommodate a variety of activities in, from doing homework or painting to dancing or simply playing around or lounging about. The interiors are rooms with bean bags and toys, and square-shaped carpet tiles go from the floor up the wall and across the ceiling, peeling out in triangles where the fluorescent tubes are installed. At one far end is a quiet computer-equipped room.

Thermal conditioning was tackled with the same spirit of environmental awareness that governs the center's other aspects. So in summer, a series of terraces, balconies, and shaded spaces cools up the place, while in winter, energy consumption is reduced through insulation and orientation. The openings are positioned in such a way that the children have a visual connection with the park as they go about their games and activities in an atmosphere adapted to their young needs and concerns.

The cut-offs resulting from making perforations in the containers were recycled as well, used to make balustrades for the terraces and the stairs, sun-shade awnings, and decorative elements. Unlike in other modular projects of a similar nature, here the exterior surfaces have hardly been treated. In this way, the quality of shipping containers is preserved, complete with their characteristic commercial logos and graffiti.

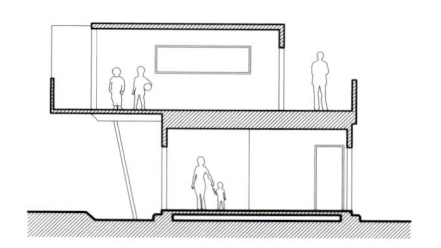

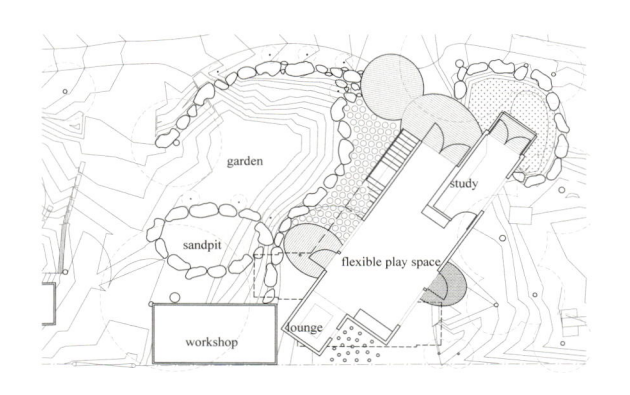

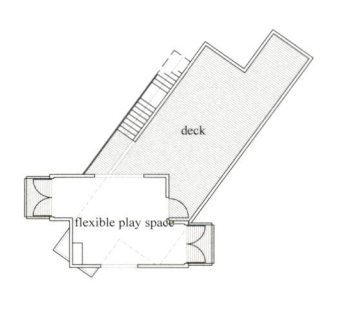

Glenn Murcutt
Walsh House
Kangaroo Valley, New South Wales (Australia)

Client
Walsh Family
Architect
Glenn Murcutt
Collaborator
Sue Barnsley (landscaping)
Contractor
Tony Lane
Photos
Anthony Browell,
Reiner Blunck (pp. 310 above, 312)

TWO HOURS SOUTHWEST of Sydney is Kangaroo Valley, a natural enclave of great beauty that is known to have been among the first tourist destinations in the world ever to launch a carbon neutral development program. On one of its green plains surrounded by mountains sits the Walsh House, a private dwelling with a single floor level measuring 43x4.7 meters and a mono-pitched roof. The main facade opens on the north towards the wooded sloopes. The roof of corrugated metal projects outward to protect the windows that are lined up right below the ceiling. This makes curtains unnecessary and the inhabitants have a year-round picture of the mountains inside the house.

The interior is not conceived as a continuous space, but as a series of adjoining rooms that are distinguishable from outside through small protrusions sealed with slanting glass panes. These glass surfaces are protected with slats that can be manipulated as needed to regulate the intensity of incoming daylight in summer. Each of these protruding volumes serves a particular purpose. The two that stick out of bedrooms serve as niches for a day bed and a small greenhouse, respectively, and the third one, belonging to the living room, accommodates a desk.

The house presents four different facades. Two sides beaten by southwest winds take on the character of a farmhouse of rustic materials and predominantly opaque surfaces, while the north and east open onto spectacular views of the area and are rendered with closer attention to detail and more refined materials.

The living room-kitchen is the only space that opens both to the north, through a large window, and to the south. Its south wall has two small windows framing carefully chosen fragments of the landscape beyond. This room is prolonged by a terrace, where a sheet of water casts vibrant reflections on the underside of the roof projection while tempering the summer air. Outside, a battery of tanks collects rainwater spilling from the roof and filters it for use in the house, which is equipped with a system for treating residual water.

The Walsh House, a single-level dwelling with a mono-pitched roof, is located in Kangaroo Valley, a beautiful enclave of rolling hills to the south of Sydney that was a pioneer in launching carbon neutral programs.

Protected against solar radiation by the roof projection and by manipulable slats, the house has a terrace that blurs the lines between interior and exterior. The dwelling, which at first had no water channeling setup, is equipped with large tanks and a scheme for collecting rainwater in the roof. It also has a system for treating residual waters, and solar panels reduce the building's impact on the environment.

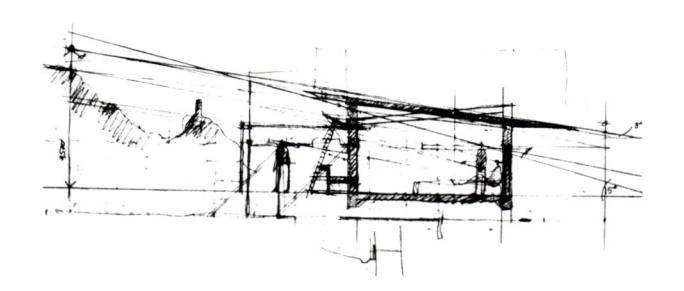

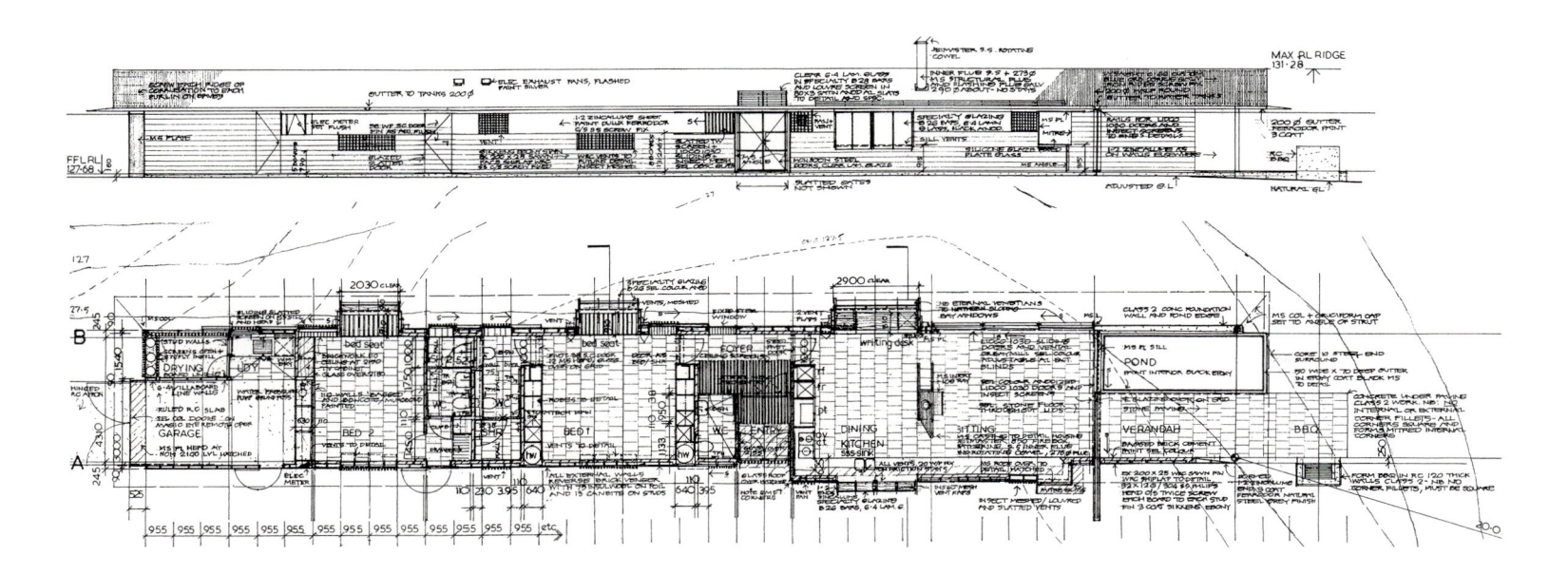

312 Atlas: Asia and Pacific

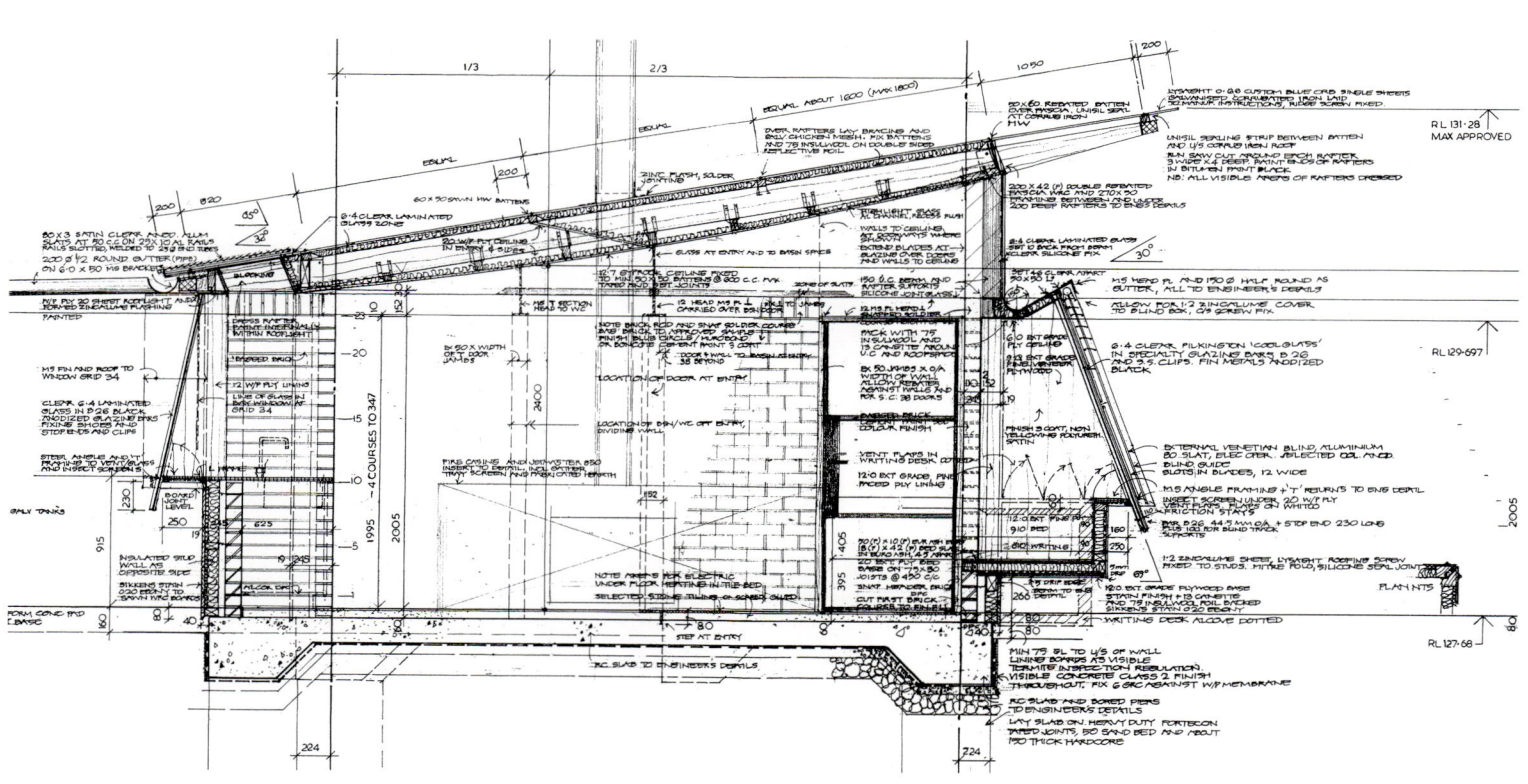

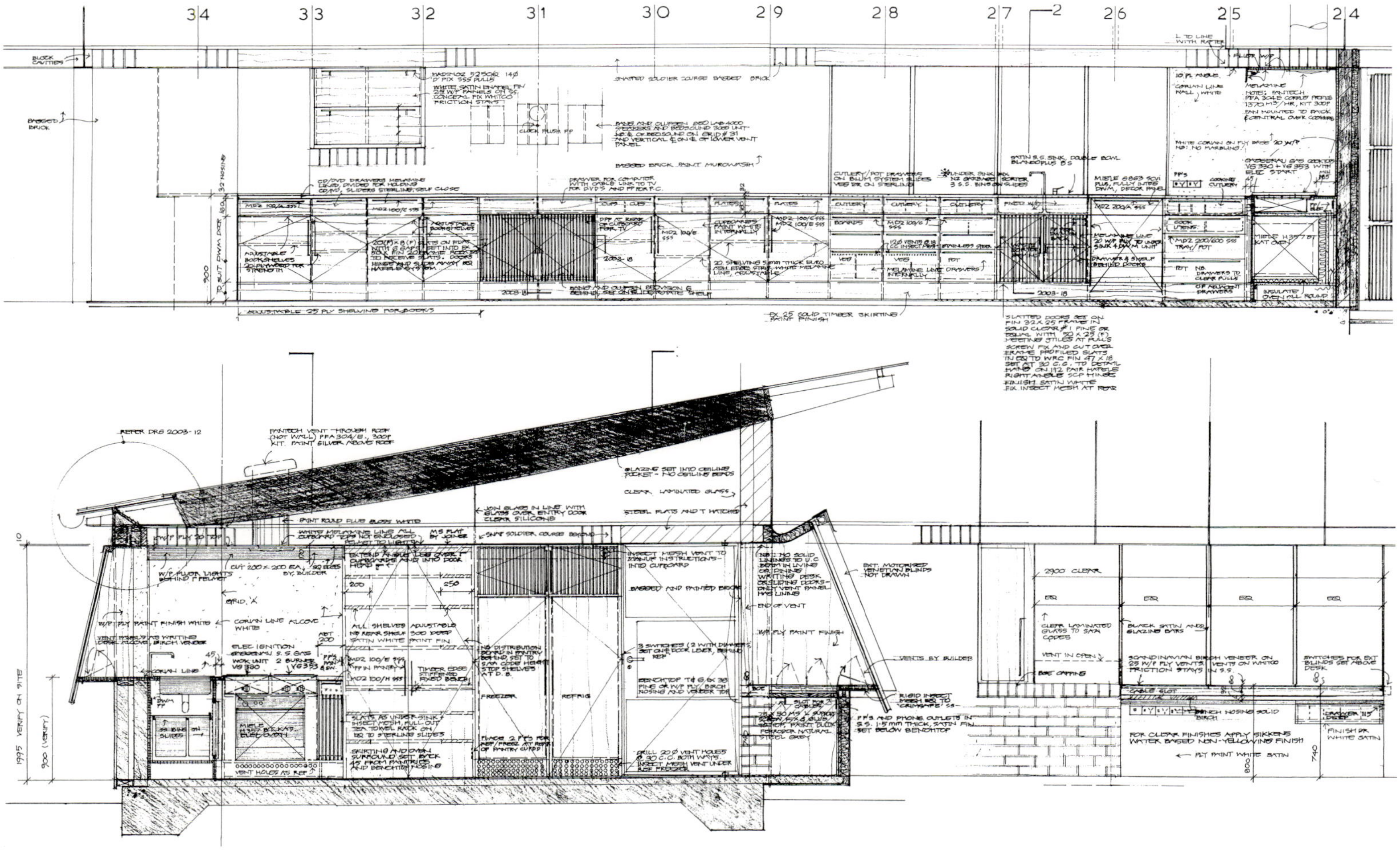
34
33
32
31
30
29
28
27
26
25
24

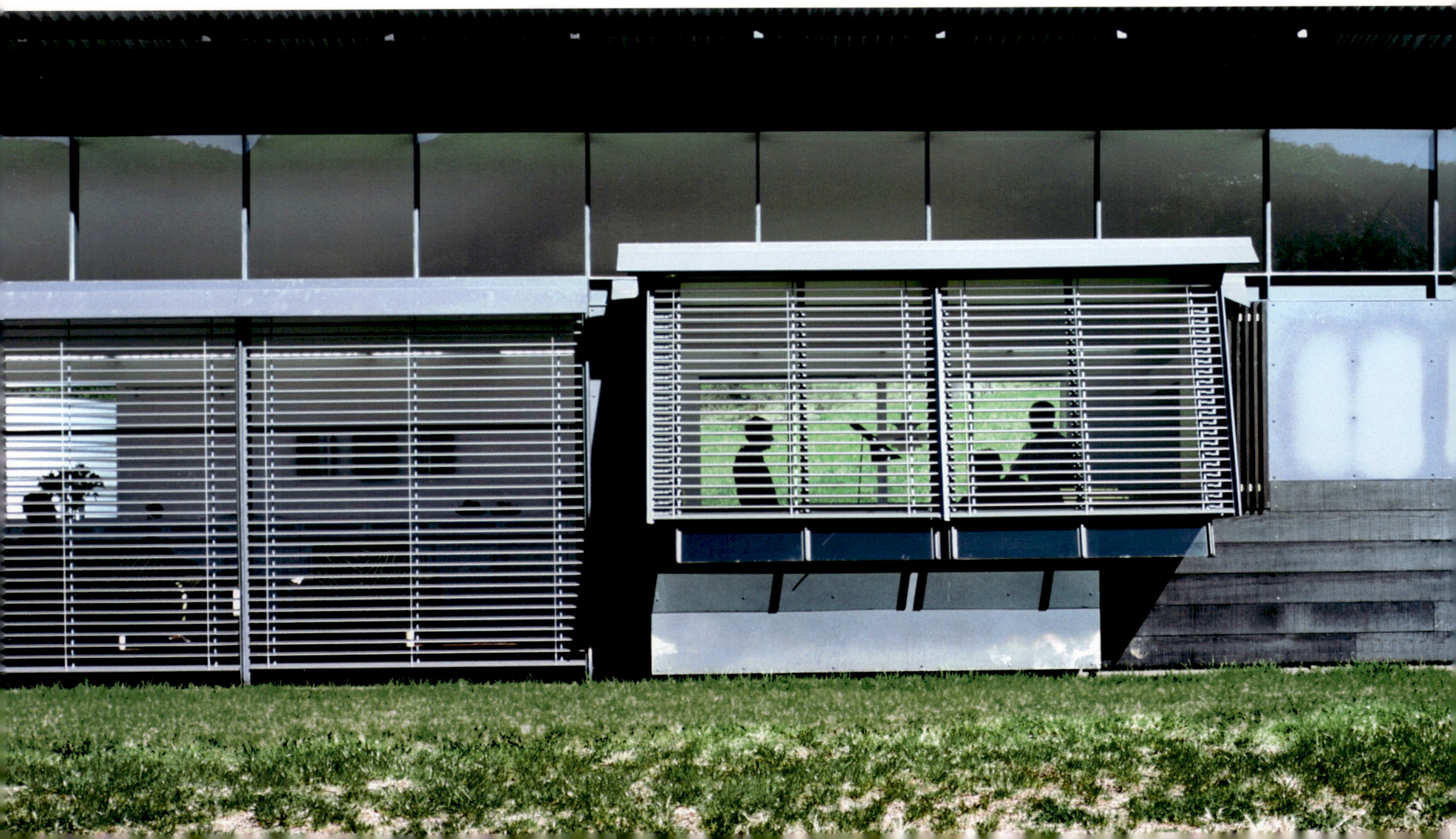

m3architecture
University Laboratory
Gatton, Queensland (Australia)

Client
University of Queensland
Architects
m3architecture: Michael Banney,
Michael Christensen,
Collaborators
Ben Vielle, Ashley Paine (artist)
Consultants
Mills Engineers (structure); Hawkins
Jenkins Ross (mechanical/eletrical);
Rocol (hydraulic); Philip Chun
& Associates (building surveyor)
Contractor
McNab Constructions
Photos
Jon Linkins

The new facility defies the codes governing the older buildings on the campus. For example, against the high-set openings and flat facade of nearby laboratories, here the windows are low and the skin textured.

THE NEW UNIVERSITY laboratory is the result of a masterplan that was drawn up to accommodate the upgrade and expansion of the School of Animal Studies at the Gatton campus of the University of Queensland. Gatton, near Brisbane, is located in the Lockyer Valley, an important farming district, so this campus is focused on agricultural and related curriculums. The periphery of the campus is rural, merging into the surrounding farms. Its core, however, is urban, with simple brick 1970s buildings planned around a ceremonial walkway. The complexes facing this campus axis feature sculptural forms, striking a contrast with the plain orthogonal structures in the background.

The masterplan called for the raising of new facilities behind the existing veterinary school. The back part of the complex had none of the variety visible along the main walkway, so the design for the annex aimed from the very start to break the monotony of the rear. The project expresses a duality of art and science in the facade/interior relationship, which holds creative and pragmatic needs as parallel but distinct aspects of architecture. There is a clear distinction made between the sealed and sterile quality of the laboratory interior, which is necessarily subject to strict codes, mathematical formulas, and safety regulations, and the freer, more impulse-driven, textured aesthetics of the outer brick skin, in itself an artwork exploring the points of contact between art and architecture. Red brick was chosen for cladding in order to connect with the buildings around, but the richly detailed and varied bonds is a counterpoint to their plainness.

The new facility challenges the adjacent 1970s laboratory models. Instead of being set high and curtained, the windows are placed at floor-to-head height for a "see and be seen" effect. The laboratory and preparation areas have openable windows so that these spaces where veterinary experiments take place can be ventilated naturally, with exhaust fans maintaining the negative pressure that a physical containment laboratory requires. The building has a north-south orientation and has deep reveals inset to provide protection from excessive sunning. The east wall where the entrance is situated is fully shaded and the west wall is partly protected by an adjacent construction. The north, rear facade uses existing trees and a covered walkway to further shield inset windows from solar glare and heat. Windows are insect-screened with a heavy woven stainless steel mesh that serves as an additional layer of solar control.

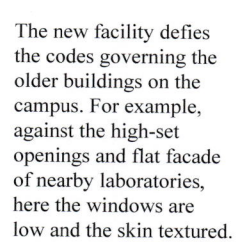

Rendered with red brick like the surrounding university buildings, the facade is designed in a way that brings together architectural and artistic aspects through the wealth of its details and the different bonds used. The idea is to present the duality that exists between art and science through a composition that clearly separates the sealed, sterile, controlled space of the interior from the freer, more impulse-driven skin of the exterior.

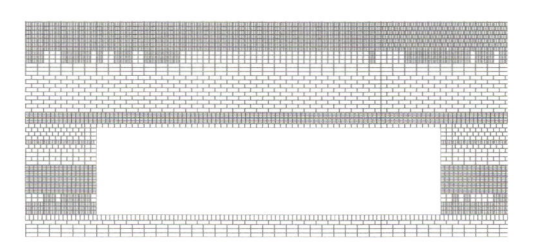

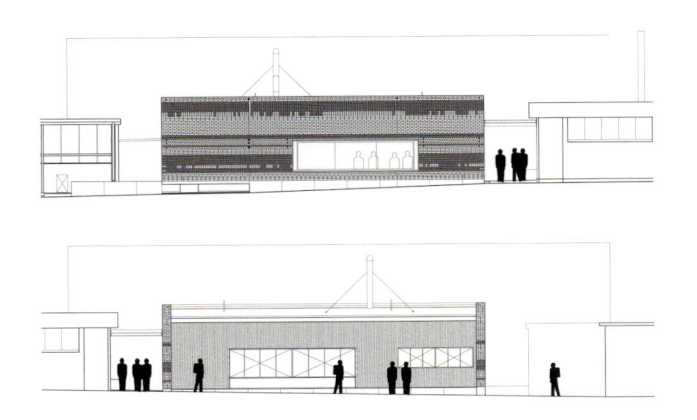

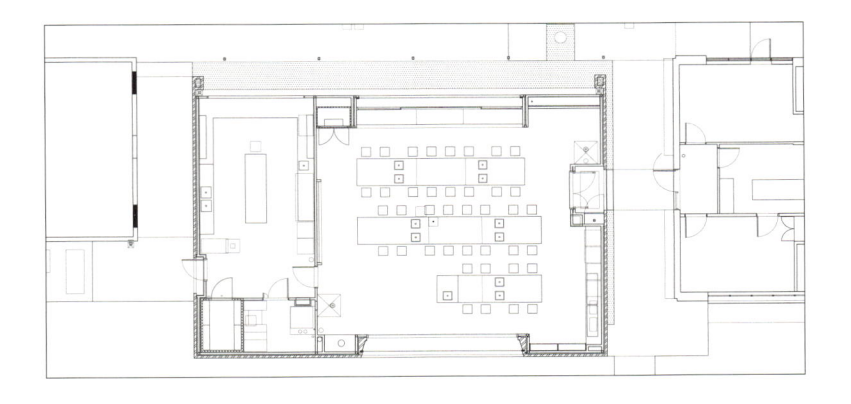

Denton Corker Marshall
Broadway Building
Sydney, New South Wales (Australia)

AN INTEGRAL COMPONENT of a campus masterplan for Sydney's University of Technology, the Broadway Building, selected from among over sixty entries in a 2009 competition, will house in its 27,000 square meters the new Faculty of Engineering and Information Technology. The parcel is located on the north side of Broadway, close to the Central Railway Station, on a prominent city corner that will make the school highly visible. Because of this choice spot, the building may stand out as a sculptural object, a translucent volume pierced by a zigzagging 'crevasse' giving pedestrian access to the building and connecting with the surrounding locality, creating a direct link between the central court of the campus and the intersection of Broadway and Wattle Street.

Containing the building's main vertical communication elements, the atrium is the void to which the internal circulation corridors of the upper floors lead. At ground level, its broken geometry adapts to the site's 4.6-meter grade difference, resulting in spaces of variable height along the way. The lower-ceilinged spaces, situated at the end closest to the campus, are taken up by a cafeteria, a bookshop, the foyer of the student association, and a battery of elevators. At the opposite corner, facing the road intersection, the high-ceilinged areas accommodate the conference rooms featuring screens giving the latest information about the building's impact on the environment. Upstairs are classrooms, research laboratories, and offices. The roof is crowned with a garden terrace and the atrium is protected by photovoltaic panels.

Outside, the building is covered with four tilted and skewed plates, one for each facade. The geometry they form leads to the creation of triangular openings at the corners which then extend to ground level, marking the entrance to the premises. The outer side of the plates presents gill-shaped perforations that reinforce their epithelial character. This skin is not a smooth, continuous surface, but is made permeable by a lattice composition inspired by binary language. Hence, the sequence of characters forming the name of the institution is translated into a series of 1's and 0's that in turn is constructionally expressed through aluminum sheet elements with square-shaped holes for the 0's and rectangular ones for the 1's. The 'binary screens' resulting from this process envelope the school with a fabric of changing opacity, giving it a dynamic image and a visible presence in Sydney's city center.

Client
University of Technology of Sydney
Architects
Denton Corker Marshall

Besides enhancing its importance within the urban context, the corner location of Broadway Building inspired the idea of an atrium penetrating the volume and serving to connect the city to the interior of the campus.

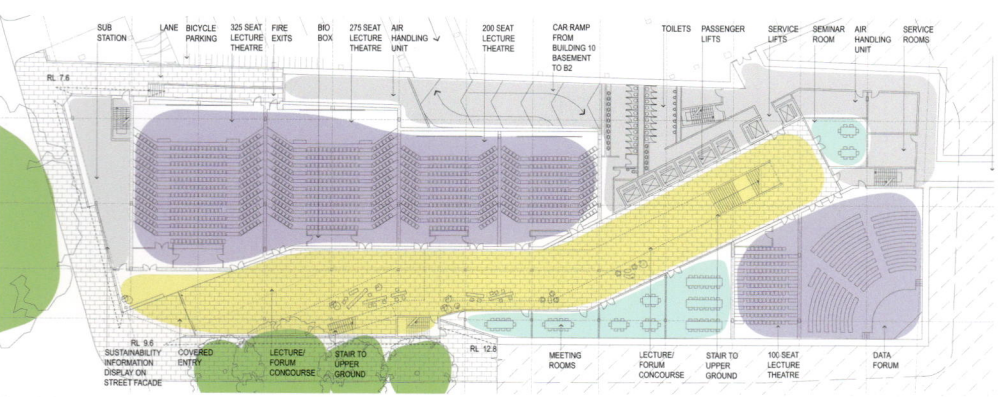

Planta baja

The volume of the faculty building is covered with four tilted and skewed plates perforated by gill-shaped gashes. The plates, made with steel sheets, in turn reveal square and rectangular openings that translate the alphabetical character string of the institution's name in a binary code of 1's and 0's. The lattice that this process generates creates a dynamic image, part transparant and part opaque, depending on the observer's viewpoint.

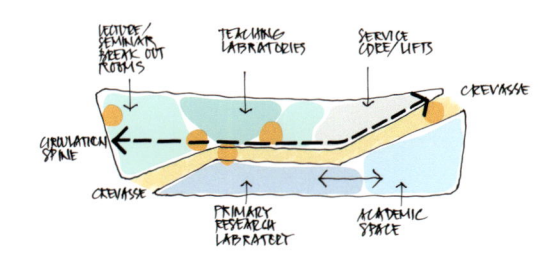

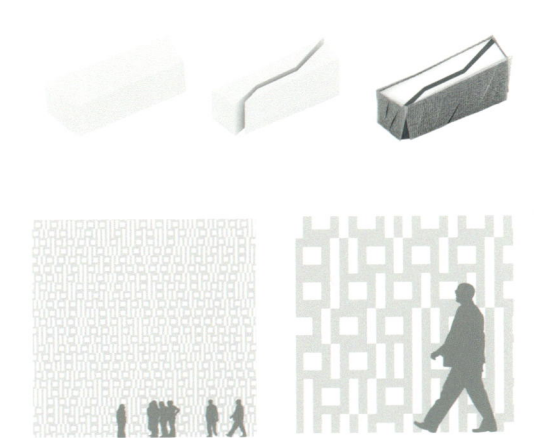

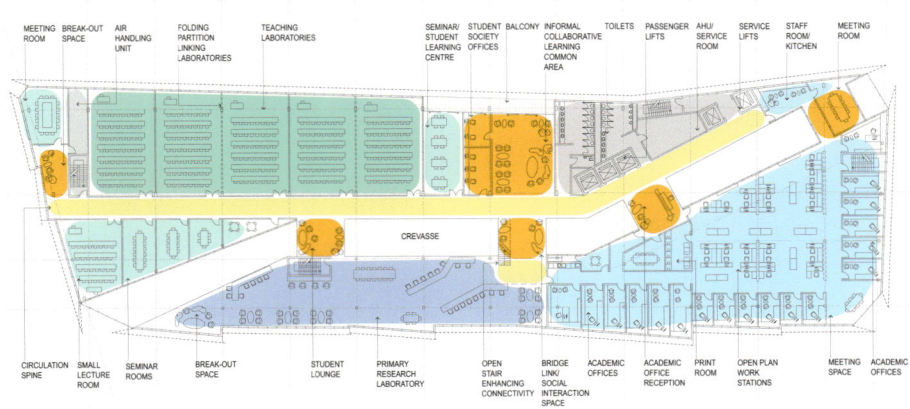

Planta tipo

Atlas: Asia and Pacific 317

Photographic Credits

Authors of images illustrating the works published in detail appear in the data list of the respective projects. The following list serves to credit photographs found in the articles or elsewhere in the publication. The numbers refer to the corresponding pages.

J. Amean/Aga Khan Award for Architecture : 39 (bottom). Satoshi Asakawa: 86 (bottom). Sergio Astrelin: 18 (top). Iwan Baan: 80, 83 (bottom), 91 (bottom), 196 (bottom), 197 (bottom). Peter Bialobrzeski: 9, 11 (below). Dan Bibb/Nader Tehrani: 86 (top). Mark Bibo: 231 (bottom). bildebk: 14 (above). Hélène Binet: 55 (bottom). Patrick Bingham-Hall: 302. Aaron Black/Getty Images: 258 (bottom). Torsten Blackwood/Getty Images: 296 (bottom). Anders Blomqvist/Getty Images: 253 (top). Anthony Browell: 299. Richard Bryant/Arcaid: 280 (bottom). Sam-Young Choi: 164 (top). Andrew Chung: 298 (bottom). Constantinos and Emma Doxiadis Foundation: 32 (bottom). Christopher Cronsoie: 276 (bottom). Crystal CG: 49 (bottom). Nayyar Ali Dada/Aga Khan Award for Architecture: 32 (above). Sallu Dada: 36 (bottom). Mark Dadswell/Getty Images: 297 (top). D. Domenicali/fabpics: 275 (bottom). Todd Eberle: 87 (bottom). Andre Fanthome: 50 (bottom). Gatozilla: 258 (top). Richard Glover/Album/View: 303 (bottom). John Gollings: 300, 301. Tim Griffith: 281 (bottom), 283 (bottom). Christine Hansen: 304 (bottom). Shu He: 85 (bottom). Arnulf Hettrich/Fnoxx: 277. Ross Honeysett: 298 (top). John Horner: 279 (bottom). Julia Jungfer/arturimages: 82 (bottom). Bi Kejian: 90 (bottom). Jae-Kyeong Kim: 159 (bottom). Jong-Oh Kim: 157 (bottom), 159 (top). Yong-Kwan Kim: 164 (bottom). Nick Koudis/Getty Images: 296 (above). Yasmeen Lari/Aga Khan Award for Architecture: 38. Mark Lewis/Getty Images: 253 (bottom). Jon Linkins: 303 (top). Gurjit Singh Matharoo: 51. Paul Maurer: 256 (bottom). METI/ERSDAC: 33 (bottom). Christopher Michel/Getty Images: 11 (top). André Morin: 163 (bottom). Azhar Munir: 35 (bottom). naoyafujii: 192 (bottom). NASA The Visible Earth: 8, 12, 30, 46, 78, 154, 188, 228, 250, 272, 294. Tomio Ohashi: 84 (bottom). Saurabh Pandey: 50 (top). Kyong Park: 14-15 (bottom), 16 (top). Winfield Parks/Getty Images: 297 (bottom). Cheryl Ravelo/Cordon Press: 252. Christian Richters: 57 (bottom), 83 (top), 85 (top), 230 (above), 234 (bottom). Hiro Sakaguchi: 191 (bottom). Shinkenchiku-Sha: 190 (bottom), 193 (bottom). tleerberg 195 (bottom). Keren Su/Getty Images: 259. Ken Usami/Getty Images: 10. Rainer Viertlböck: 257 (bottom). wobblyturkey: 56. worldisround: 282 (bottom). wswaqas: 34 (bottom). How Hwee Young/epa/Corbis: 276 (top). Nigel Young: 20 (bottom), 81, 82 (top), 284 (bottom). Jin Zhan: 91 (bottom).

Contributors

Haig Beck & Jackie Cooper (Brisbane, 1944; London, 1950) have been writing about architecture since the mid-1970s. Beck was editor of *Architectural Design* (1975-1979), after graduating from the Architectural Association School (1973), where Cooper worked throughout the 1970s in the AA Communications Unit. Together they edited and published *International Architect* in London (1979-1986), before returning to Australia. In 1996 they launched *UME*, now an online publication available as free downloads. Their magazines are notably devoid of advertising.

Ching-Yueh Roan (Taipei, 1957) received his master's degree from the University of Pennsylvania, and is a licensed architect both in the United States and in Taiwan. He directed his own architectural practice between 1992 and 2002, and is currently associate professor at Yuan-Ze University. Curator of the Taiwan Pavilion at the 6th International Architecture Exhibition of the Venice Biennale and of shows like *The Rumor of China Towns: Chinese Architecture 2004*, held at Taipei's MoCA, he is the author of over twenty books, among which the acclaimed novel *Lin Xiu-Tzi and Her Family*.

Hammad Husain (Rawalpindi, 1970) is an architect and writer based in Islamabad. Graduate of the Middle East Technical University (METU) of Ankara, in 1996 he established his own architectural practice, through which he has carried out residential works, office buildings and interior design projects. After the 2005 earthquake in Northern Pakistan, he designed low-cost shelters that have been later adopted by international aid agencies. Associate professor at the National College of Art of Rawalpindi, he writes a monthly column in *Archi Times*.

Taro Igarashi (Paris, 1967) studied architecture at the University of Tokyo, where he obtained his doctorate in engineering. Presently he is a professor at the graduate school of Tohoku University. Curator for Japan's Section at the Lisbon Architecture Triennale in 2007 and commissioner for the Japanese Pavilion at the 11th International Architecture Exhibition of the Venice Biennale, his list of articles includes, among others, those published in the books *Japan: Towards Total Scape* and *Kisho Kurokawa: Metabolism and Symbiosis*.

Evan J.S. Lin y C.J. Anderson-Wu (Yilan 1960; Chia Yi, 1967) are editor-in-chief and editor of *Taiwan Architect Magazine*, the oldest architectural journal among Chinese readership. Lin studied architecture at Tamkang University in Taipei, and obtained his master's degree at New York's Cornell University. Anderson-Wu studied mathematics, and was a freelance writer before joining *TAM* in 2002. She has published books like *Dance with Diseases, Public Art in Healthcare Institutions* and *The Second Generation of Taiwanese Architects after World War II*, and also translates novels.

Rahul Mehrotra (New Delhi, 1959) studied at the Ahmedabad School of Architecture and at Harvard University. In 1990 he established his own studio, RMA Architects, through which he has carried out residential works, institutional buildings and projects for the renovation of historics buildings and precincts. He is the author of monographs about Bombay as *Bombay: The Cities Within* (1995), with S. Dwivedi, and *Bombay to Mumbai: Changing Perspectives* (1997) with P. Godrej and P. Rohatgi. He has also directed the Urban Design Research Institute. Currently he teaches at MIT.

Peter G. Rowe (Wellington, 1945) is the Raymond Garbe Professor of Architecture and Urban Design at Harvard University, where he served as Dean of the Faculty of Design between 1992 and 2004. Previously he was director of the School of Architecture at Rice University. Honorary Professor at Tongji and Xi'an universities in China since 1999, he also serves as Education Programme Director of the Aga Khan Trust for Culture. Some of his recent books are *Shanghai: Architecture and Urbanism for Modern China* (2004); and *East Asia Modern: Shaping the Contemporary City* (2005).

Takashi Tsubokura (Kyoto, 1970) earned his master's degree from the Moscow Architectural Institute. He worked at Kisho Kurokawa's studio between 1999 and 2005, and participated in the development of the master plan of the new capital of the Republic of Kazakhstan and in the construction of the Astana International Airport. After leaving the studio he worked in the design of the Presidential Park in Astana City, one of the largest landscape projects in the territory of the former USSR. In 2006 he established the design company TG Architect, and now directs its Kazakhstan branch.

Mann-Young Chung (Seoul, 1959) is professor of architecture at the Seoul National University of Technology, where he served as Dean of the School of Architecture between 2007 and 2009. He has published various articles ranging from modern and contemporary architecture to architectural theory. His recent studies deal with Korean experimental architecture, focusing on the arbitrary genesis in architectural organization. He is also the director of the SAKIA (School of Architecture, Korean Institute of Architects), which is open twice a year in the form of a summer/winter workshop.

Jianfei Zhu (Shanghai, 1962) studied architecture at Tianjin University and University College London. He is associate professor at the University of Melbourne, and has lectured at schools worldwide. His research concerns the relationship between architecture, politics, social space and modernity, with a special reference to China and China-West comparisons. He is the author, among other essays, of 'Criticality in between China and the West' *(The Journal of Architecture*, 2005) and editor of *Sixty Years of Chinese Architecture 1949-2009: History, Theory and Criticism* (2009).